CHINA SAGA

CHINA SAGA

a novel by

C.Y. LEE

WEIDENFELD & NICOLSON *New York*

Published by Weidenfeld & Nicolson, New York
A Division of Wheatland Corporation
10 East 53rd Street
New York, NY 10022

Library of Congress Cataloging-in-Publication Data

Lee, C. Y., 1917-
   China saga.

   I. Title.
PS3523.E3158C4   1987   813'.54   86-24672
ISBN 1-55584-056-6

Manufactured in the United States of America
Designed by Helen Barrow
First Edition
10 9 8 7 6 5 4 3 2 1

F Lee

*

This book is dedicated to both the Chinese and Western heroes and heroines of this story. Some of them are composites of real characters. Their personal experiences, their struggles for a better China and their tremendous sacrifices will serve as a beacon for China's future freedom.

ACKNOWLEDGMENTS

The idea for writing *China Saga* was born in a Beijing hotel room while I was visiting China in 1981. The room was often full of visitors whose chitchat and excitement about China's new direction created in me an irresistible desire to write a family saga reflecting the tumultuous changes in modern China.

During my first year of research and subsequent trips to China, I discovered that this enormous task would not have begun without the encouragement of many relatives and friends, particularly my niece Lee Ming-yang, her husband, Eugene Fong, and their good friend, Xue Xiao-hung, whose wealth of information was most valuable.

I am also indebted to my agent, Robert Gottlieb, and my editor, John Herman, whose help and enthusiasm served as an invaluable driving force in the creation of this work.

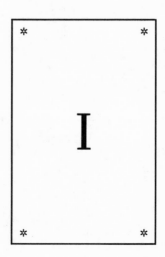

I

1

O n his way to Heavenly Bridge outside Peking's Chien Men Gate, Fong Tai stopped to watch the Imperial troops drilling in the nearby wheatfield. "Sha! Sha! Sha!" they shouted at the top of their lungs as they thrust their bayonets into imaginary enemies—undoubtedly the Red Turbans, the Long Beards and the Long Hairs, the major rebels fomenting a revolution in the south to overthrow the Great Ching Dynasty.

The battle cry of "Sha!"—*Kill!*—shattered the calm of suburban Peking. Too bad, Fong thought. Otherwise it was a nice day, a sunny late afternoon with a gentle breeze. Fong had just finished his last class at the Foreign School and was looking forward to a pleasant visit to the open-air coolie market.

Chien Men Street, wide and shabby, was almost deserted. He knew why. At the Foreign School he had heard rumors. Tsu Hsi, the Empress Dowager, had sent out detectives to watch suspicious-looking people. Her Majesty had a peculiar idea about who looked suspicious, all based on the theories of a blind soothsayer: those with thin lips were liars; those with heavy eyebrows were potential killers; those with triangular eyes were disloyal; those with sunken cheeks and buckteeth were cheaters. In her opinion, all those untrustworthy characters were Red Turbans and Long Beards.

As Fong Tai hurried along the street, he glanced around to see if anyone was watching him. His eyebrows were a bit on the heavy side. By Chinese standards, he was hairy. Growing up, he had felt that he was getting more hairy everywhere. At nineteen, he could even grow a beard. In the eyes of Tsu Hsi he would undoubtedly have been a suspicious-looking character.

Feeling a chill, he cast another glance backward to make sure he was not being followed. While glancing around, he caught a glimpse of the yellow glazed tile roofs of the Imperial Palaces that rose in the distance above the squalor of the outer city. He had often wondered what life was like under the gleaming roofs and massive red walls of the Forbidden City.

Next opportunity he intended to ask Li Hung-chang, his mentor, about the Manchu royal family. Li was one of the few trusted Hans, China's majority race, who could enter the Imperial Palaces freely. Fong Tai admired the old man, who held numerous positions from Viceroy of Chi

Li to Royal Grand Councilor in Charge of Foreign Affairs. He had founded the Foreign School and advocated an Open-Door Policy to learn from the West; he was one of the clever Hans who had risen high, even over the heads of many Manchu princes and ministers.

Yes, Fong Tai thought, one day he would work up enough courage to ask Li if all those rumors about the Empress Dowager were true. In the Foreign School they talked about Tsu Hsi's open love of birds and her secret staged orgies, her humble origins and her climb to the top through intrigue and manipulation, including murder and the lure of sex.

Within the confines of the Foreign School, a history professor, speaking in English, had compared Her Majesty to Catherine the Great of Russia. Fong Tai thought about that professor and shuddered. If his derogatory remarks had been made elsewhere and in Chinese, the professor would certainly have found his head dangling over Chien Men Gate. Or worse, "his body torn apart by five horses," as Tsu Hsi used to say about her enemies.

Fong Tai wondered what kind of people the Red Turbans really were. Were they true revolutionaries or just a horde of rebels trying to seize power? They claimed they were building a utopia called Heavenly Kingdom of Peace. Too high-sounding a name, he thought. He did not like it. Exaggerations were often a sign of falsehood. A man who shouted the loudest was usually a coward.

Whatever might befall China, he saw a dark future looming ahead. The only comfort he felt was that he had been one of the eleven in the graduating class of the Foreign School selected to study in America. As the departure date neared, his excitement about the trip mounted.

He was grateful to Li, his mentor. His late father, Fong Yuen-nan, had served Li well as a consultant. Li had not only taken a personal interest in him but had helped his family build a little nest egg—some income property in Peking. Fong Tai's father, a frugal man, had also invested his savings in a chien chuang, a sort of savings and loan that paid the family a handsome semiannual dividend. After his father's death, the family had lived comfortably on the combined income, which was well managed by Fong Tai's Third Uncle, his mother's third brother.

For these reasons Fong Tai felt grateful to Li and believed that Li's Open-Door Policy was a necessity. Ever since China's defeat in the Opium War in 1842, the British had been forcing China to buy opium from India, a British colony. Having shown such weakness and backwardness, China by 1880 had become a mulberry leaf, Li declared: foreign powers like England, France, Italy, Germany, Russia and Japan had been nibbling away China's territory like silkworms. Li had repeatedly said that China must open to the West, learn from the West and catch up with the West. The Foreign School was his first step in that direction.

Fong Tai found the prospect of going to America exciting. Everything in America seemed vague; it was so far and mysterious. He was often amused by the common saying "All foreigners look alike, they are all yellow-haired and blue-eyed barbarians. They drink cow's milk, eat raw meat with knives and prongs and smell like goats." Liu Mah, the family maid, was more specific. She claimed that the foreigners in China had only one purpose—to lure women and children to their churches, cut their eyes out, boil them in oil and eat them as elixir.

Although anxious to go, Fong Tai still needed time to settle unfinished business. His uncle had hinted that if a man went to an unknown land across a vast ocean, nobody knew if he would ever return, so a seed had to be planted before he could be allowed to leave. In other words, an arranged marriage had to be contracted so that he could fulfill his filial duty by planting such a seed. The family name had to be carried on in accordance with Confucius's teachings. The sage had said, "The greatest sin of all three great sins against filial piety is a life without an offspring."

"Too bad you are the only son of a widowed mother," his Third Uncle once sighed, clapping a hand on his shoulder. But the next moment he winked at him and assured him that marriage was not really an unpleasant duty; he might even enjoy it.

At nineteen, Fong Tai had reservations about a prearranged marriage, but the constant tickling in his groin kept telling him, "Why not?" Anyhow, he was not an innocent, having learned quite a bit by reading *Jin Ping Mei*, the famous novel about secret love and wife-stealing.

Chien Men Street was gradually coming alive. Perhaps people thought it was safer, now that night approached, to wander out and conduct business. He always enjoyed walking along the cobblestoned boulevard, unchanged for centuries. It was lined with tiny shops, flagged with stone blocks and ornamented with painted arches. Everything looked dusty and a bit sloppy, and yet it had the elegance of a bedraggled dowager who had seen better days.

As he approached Heavenly Bridge, the street became even livelier. Shopowners called out to him, inviting him to step in to inspect their wares —leather goods, cosmetics, cotton and silk, ready-made clothes, dog-eared books for lending. Passing a herb store, he stopped. The numerous jars displayed in the ceiling-high shelves looked intriguing.

Thinking about his wedding night, Fong Tai entered. From the novel

Jin Ping Mei he had learned there were miracle drugs that would enhance a man's sexual power. Perhaps he could find something that would enable him to plant the seed on the first try, so that he could fulfill his filial duty before sailing for America.

The wizened shopkeeper hurried out from behind the counter, an ingratiating smile on his gaunt, dark face, a gold tooth gleaming. His blue silk gown was almost threadbare. "Have you eaten, sir?"

"I have eaten," Fong Tai replied politely. It was a silly traditional greeting. What if he had not yet eaten? Would the shopkeeper ask him to stay for dinner? He wondered how this common greeting had originated. Perhaps during bad times people were so starved that they could think of nothing but food.

"I am interested in some tonic."

"Tonic! You have come to the right place, sir! We have tonic of all kinds. Tonic for the brain, for the liver and kidneys . . ."

"I . . . I am getting married."

"Ah! Getting married! Congratulations! Sit down, sit down, please! A cup of tea?"

"No, no," Fong said, glancing at the labels on the row of jars.

The shopkeeper hastened to the jars. He rattled off the names of the sex tonics on the shelf: "Great grass worm with chicken concentrate, Korean Ginseng with wildcat concentrate, Peking King Bee Concentrate, pills made of deer horn, sea horse and sea dragon pills, ancient turtle powder, Eight Immortals Rejuvenation Pills. . . . Ah, I have got just the right thing for a would-be bridegroom!"

He brought down a large jar and flashed it in front of Fong Tai's face. "The famous three-whip potion with ingredients extracted from the male sex organs of seals, deer and dogs."

Fong Tai pushed the large black ghoul-like jar out of his face and quickly settled for an ounce of Peking King Bee Concentrate.

He hurried away as the shopkeeper shouted after him, "Come again, come again! We also sell nourishing pills for heart and lung, paste for bone fractures and wounds, powder for scabs and sores. . . ."

Though Heavenly Bridge was crowded and dusty, Fong found it warm and friendly too. He was among the Hans; it made him feel at home and relaxed. The market was an enormous open-air bazaar where the poor congregated, shopped, ate, drank, gossiped and enjoyed themselves. Here he could breathe the pungent smell of peasant food, listen to the clatter of mule carts, watch peddlers hawk their wares with hands cupped behind their ears, and beggars limping past, their exposed sores covered with grease and chicken blood. He especially enjoyed ogling the red-cheeked peasant girls who always smiled with their mouths closed, a habit developed because of the Gobi winds that blew sand into every crevice in Peking. Heavenly Bridge was a happy gathering place for the deprived and the oppressed. The Manchus, a minority from the northeast, had conquered China and ruled the majority Hans for three hundred years. As a resentful Han, Fong often found comfort and comradery in this coolie market.

Refreshed, he wandered about, soaking in the sights and sounds, watching the traveling cooks and barbers, fortune tellers, calligraphers, storytellers, magicians, wrestlers and other entertainers. The place was teeming with old and young, the colorfully dressed minority races from the northwest provinces and Inner Mongolia. The richly stitched red and blue costumes, the different accents of ethnic dialects, the skills of the storytellers, the acrobats and the Flower Drum Song singers from the south all fascinated him. This was the real China.

He liked the coolie kitchens, often devouring food of unknown substance that had simmered in a large caldron for days. Entering one, he ate ravenously, making sucking noises like a coolie. It all tasted better than the delicacies served at home, prepared by an expensive chef.

At home, both his mother and grandmother ate their food daintily, sometimes with a slight frown as though they were taking medicine. Life at home had lost its flavor. Even marriage was arranged and served only one purpose—to carry on the family name. Only Third Uncle still knew something about living. He still ate and drank for pleasure.

While he was wiping his mouth with a handkerchief, Fong Tai was attracted by the sound of a gong beaten by a Flower Drum Song singer, a young woman gaudily dressed in a yellow silk gown embroidered with red flowers. He was torn between watching the Flower Drum Song show and the Mongolian wrestlers, his favorite performers. Three huge Mongolians were prancing around, warming up for a match.

He watched the three brothers wrestle for a while, applauding their skill and strength, wondering which of the three was the strongest. They wore padded jackets, which were tightly stretched over their muscles.

"I am the oldest," one of them said, pointing at himself jokingly. "See my weather-beaten face and the bulging blue veins on my legs? They are my credentials. Wei, my younger brother, come here!" The youngest brother obeyed. He was a handsome man, tall, broad-shouldered, with limbs like tree trunks. He still had bright eyes, a straight nose and even teeth, which he probably would soon lose, as his two older brothers had.

"This youngest piglet," the oldest brother went on, "is spoiled rotten. He was born a weakling. Our father calls him Little Ugly Piggy so evil spirits will leave him alone and give him a chance to grow up. Here he is, nineteen years old, fully grown. Now, kindhearted ladies and gentlemen, I want you to look at his spindly ugly legs."

He paused, waiting for laughter. The audience looked at the youth's legs and laughed. "Now, I have here a silver dollar," the oldest brother continued. He bit the coin, then waved it in the air as he pranced around, showing it to the audience. "A real silver dollar, minted by the government of the Great Ching Dynasty. Now, I want to make a bet and lose this dollar."

With a cry of horror, the second brother rushed over, bug-eyed. "What do you mean you are going to lose it? That is our only dollar!"

The oldest looked at him askance. "Second Younger Brother," he said despairingly, "don't show our shabbiness in front of all these ladies and gentlemen."

"But . . . but if we lose it, we will have nothing to eat!"

"Eating is all you think of day and night. Can you think of something more exciting?"

"Such as what?" the second youngest asked, striking a tragic expression.

"Such as losing a dollar. Kindhearted ladies and gentlemen. If any of you can move a leg of my youngest brother here as much as half an inch, you win this dollar."

"I will move it!" The second youngest rushed to the middle of the ring, ready to try.

The oldest shook his head. "Second Younger Brother," he said with a sigh, "what in the name of a turtle's egg are you doing?"

"I am going to win the dollar so we can have something to eat!"

"Expect the best, brother."

"Expect the best? What if we lose the dollar?"

"Then prepare for the worst," the oldest one said, turning back to the audience. "Any challenger? Anyone? If my Second Brother gets ahead of you, you have my permission to give him a kick in the behind!"

Again there was laughter.

Fong Tai did not care for this comedy routine or the silver dollar, but he wanted to have his own strength tested. As a student of martial arts, he always liked to accept physical challenges. When he was little he would often run a few steps up a wall and climb it, until his father gave him a whipping for having ruined some glazed yellow tiles on the wall. That ended his attempts to emulate the cat burglars described in action novels.

When three robust coolies from the audience had failed to win the coin, Fong Tai took off his silk gown, tossed it on the dusty ground with a flourish and stepped forward to tremendous applause. Although, at five feet ten, more than the equal of the wrestler in height, he was far from his equal in girth. A few people in the audience gaped in surprise. No Mandarin-gown-wearing nobility had ever accepted the challenge of a common wrestler, especially a member of a lowly minority race.

The young wrestler, a confident smile on his rugged dark face, planted himself in a squatting stance in the center of the human ring, arms akimbo, and invited Fong Tai to attack. Taking a deep breath, Fong grabbed the wrestler's right arm and yanked with all his strength. It was like trying to topple a large tree by pulling at a branch. Had it been a tree, he would have at least shaken a few leaves off, but this human specimen was like a granite statue; he stood there and chuckled without even shifting a hair out of place.

Amid laughter and shouts of encouragement, Fong tried again, tugging, pushing, climbing on the man's back and doing everything he could think of. But he could not unplant the garlic-smelling giant. Finally, in a desperate gamble, he walked away from the target a few yards, turned around and, running like a bull, rammed the wrestler's stomach with his right shoulder, throwing all his weight behind it. The impact jolted the young Mongolian and forced him to move one of his legs backward to keep balance. The audience roared and cheered. The Mongolian lifted him up like a child to congratulate him.

"Well, well," the oldest brother said, coming to him with a broad smile. "You have won our last dollar. You have won it by beating a descendant of the mighty warrior Genghis Khan! Congratulations!"

Fong Tai accepted the dollar, then tossed it back onto the appreciation plate on the ground. There was more applause, this time for his generosity. He took a bow like a performer. Almost immediately, others started throwing coins onto the plate. The brothers kept bowing and thanking everybody.

Fong Tai left Heavenly Bridge that evening feeling happy. Moving the leg of a lowly Mongolian wrestler was nothing to be especially proud of, but in the eyes of the street people it had been a great achievement. His uncle would probably feel his muscle, shake his head and say, "A marvel, can't be true, but I believe it."

On his way back home he whistled a merry tune. When he reached the Chien Men Gate, it was almost pitch dark. As he entered the gate, he stumbled over something and fell. He touched a cold wet body, its clothes soaked with blood. In the darkness he could vaguely see what it was—a headless corpse. Horrified, he leaped away from the gruesome remains only to fall over another body a few feet away. Then he saw four of them lying in a bloody pool.

Now he remembered: the newspaper had made an announcement that morning saying that four Long Hairs were scheduled for decapitation outside the Chien Men Gate and that their heads would be hoisted over the gate for public viewing. The secret-society Long Hairs, like the Red Turbans, were considered fair game because of their attempt to overthrow the Great Ching Dynasty.

With a shudder, Fong Tai hurried away from the execution ground. But hardly had he entered the gate, than he heard someone yell, "Halt!" Sensing trouble, he made a mad dash into a small lane off the wide boulevard.

"Stop running! Halt!" more angry voices shouted after him. He heard footsteps behind him. He gathered speed and ran as fast as he could, but soon the sound of horses' hooves overtook the footsteps.

The moon had come out from behind the dark clouds, shining over the flat tile roofs of the narrow alley. He cast a quick glance back and saw several figures nearing him. One of them was on horseback, waving a long sword. He was followed by others carrying long spears.

The galloping horse quickly caught up with him. He ducked the slashing sword and narrowly escaped having his head cut off. As he was running and dodging the horse, he felt a hand grab him from the back, then several men pounced on him, wrestling him to the ground. He blinked and saw three foot soldiers in the dark uniforms of the Imperial Bannermen Guards, which the Manchu General Jung Lu commanded. They hoisted him to his feet and threw a rope around his neck. One of them tightened the rope and started to pull him back to the Chien Men Gate.

An officer rode beside him, trying to rein in his frightened horse. He asked in the same rough voice Fong had heard before, "Trying to get away, eh? What are you? Long Hair or petty thief?"

"I am neither," Fong Tai answered, surprised that he was calm and unafraid. Once his uncle had told him that when extreme pain reached a certain point, it stopped; so did extreme fear. It was Heaven's way of being merciful.

"Only a thief would come here to rob the dead," the officer said, his voice more contemptuous now. "Or a Long Hair would come to steal the corpses. Which are you?"

"I am neither."

"No matter. You will die."

Fear was gradually gaining on him, making him feel nauseated. He knew the judicial system. Thieves and revolutionaries were often summarily executed without a trial, and the next day their heads were hoisted over Chien Men Gate for public viewing. "Kill a few chickens to warn the monkeys," Jung Lu liked to say publicly.

Fong Tai took several deep breaths to calm his nerves. He regretted that he had not joined a secret society; now he was going to die like a chicken thief who had not stolen any chickens. What a shame!

Fong took several more deep breaths. Now that he was being treated like a criminal, why not die like one? In the novels he had read, cowards died whimpering and shitting in their pants; heroes and criminals died heroically and defiantly. When he entered the gate of Heaven he should walk with his head high, proud and unashamed. Both his father and grandfather might be there to greet him. The only son, who had already committed the inexcusable sin of cutting off the family name without offspring, should at least die like a hero.

As he thought of death and Heaven, he suddenly found himself unafraid. He decided to do something heroic. He was familiar with the soldier's spear—something unwieldy and good only for a show of force. He grabbed it and delivered a vicious kick to the soldier's groin. As the man doubled up, Fong hit him on the head with the spear, knocking him down. The other two soldiers lunged at him. He ran, trying to escape to an alley. But the officer, who was riding a few yards ahead, turned around and galloped after him. Fong dashed toward Heavenly Bridge, zigzagging to avoid the officer's slashing sword.

Exhausted, breathing hard and feeling a pain in his chest, he stopped. His time was up—at least he had knocked a soldier down. Enough heroics. Perhaps time to die. He glared at the officer defiantly, waiting for the sword to fall. But the officer merely circled him, laughing and slashing at him with the sword, purposely missing his neck. Then he pretended to trample him. Every time he reared his horse, he laughed, then reined the animal away, letting its hooves strike beside Fong, narrowly missing his face.

Fong Tai stood his ground. His mind was blank, devoid of fear or emotion. Now the foot soldiers were watching, laughing and cursing his mother. The officer had become a circus performer, cutting the air with his sword to humiliate his victim, taunting, laughing and tearing Fong's clothing with his sword.

Suddenly Fong Tai saw three dark shadows leap out of nowhere. One of them grabbed the officer from behind and pulled him off his horse. The other two quickly disarmed the foot soldiers with wrestling holds. The struggle was brief, followed by the sounds of cracking bones and a few low moans.

"Run, run!" a cracked voice shouted at him. He immediately recognized the voice of the Mongolian brute who had lost the silver dollar in the contest. Without looking back, he ran for dear life.

2

Still shaken by the experience at the Chien Men Gate the night before, Fong Tai came out of the Foreign School feeling depressed. His mother had sent a note to the principal requesting that he be excused for the rest of the day. Old Liu, the servant who delivered the note, had told him what it was all about. The matchmaker had paid his mother a visit to complete a deal.

Complete a deal! His marriage sounded like buying a side of beef. Except that buying beef involved some sort of inspection. He did not object to prearranged marriages, but at least he might be consulted! At least he should have a chance to look at the girl's picture!

Old Liu said his mother wanted him home to make preparations for the wedding. She had probably invited all the relatives for dinner that night and a game of mahjong, and to listen to the matchmaker's description of the girl's family. Undoubtedly it was a noble family that lived in a home with a high door, with ancestors who had all passed the Imperial examination and earned the title of Senior Wrangler, the highest-ranking scholar. To the elders, the family of the betrothed was more important than the betrothed. The accomplishments of a father or grandfather were important criteria for husband- or wife-choosing. Love wasn't a consideration. "Love will grow," they said.

It was a windy afternoon in Peking. The sand blown over the Eastern City from the Gobi Desert hit Fong like tiny slingshot pellets. Suddenly the thought of marriage lost its allure. Only the anticipation of going to America was still pleasant.

"How does she look?" he asked Old Liu, who was walking behind him, trying to keep up with him. Old Liu was probably going on sixty, already stooped. He had inherited his position from his father, a slave bought into the Fong family during a famine some sixty years earlier.

Fong Tai realized that Old Liu was a bit deaf, too. He repeated the question, his voice loud and tinged with irritation. "How does she look, I said!"

"Who?"

"That woman I am supposed to marry. I am not supposed to know, but you can tell me."

"The matchmaker did not say," Old Liu said, breathing hard. "Don't worry, young master, the Fong family will not take an ugly bride. I am sure she is not pockmarked. If she is, the matchmaker would not have made the match. You know why? Because pockmarks bring bad luck. Madame Fong would not allow it!"

Realizing that Old Liu was also wordy and long-winded, Fong Tai interrupted irritably, "All right, Old Liu."

They turned into Smoke Pipe Lane, a narrow street lined with impressive houses. Most of them had glazed tile roofs and red-lacquered doors guarded by lion dogs. It was a street inhabited by rich Hans. Perhaps that was why it still had an ugly name. The Manchus had been ruling the Hans for three hundred years now, and they had never wanted the Hans to forget that they were still second-class citizens. In the early days of their conquest, they had ordered the Hans to grow pigtails so that soldiers could easily grab them if they rebelled. The Manchus also made the Han women bind their feet so that no Han woman could run fast enough to escape. Fong Tai hated his queue. He always wound it around his head and hid it under a cap.

Arriving at the vermilion door, Old Liu stepped forward to open it for him. A young maid was sweeping the courtyard. Old Liu broke into a smile and ogled her. A bachelor, Old Liu always ogled servant women, regardless of looks or age. Another maid was bending over a washtub scrubbing clothes, her behind moving back and forth. Fong Tai watched the moving round buttocks from the corner of his eye as he walked past her.

Entering the middle hall, he heard voices and mahjong tiles scraping the mahogany table in the gaming room. He knew that the game would last another four hours. But in the middle hall, several relatives were already waiting for him. They were sitting in the ancestral chairs, sipping tea, puffing on water pipes and cracking watermelon seeds. He was glad that his Third Uncle was there. So were three male cousins, all properly dressed in silk gowns with black satin jackets over them.

He greeted them with a bow and they all rose to their feet and congratulated him loudly, some still with watermelon-seed shells in their mouths.

Madame Fong, his mother, came out of the gaming room, a broad smile on her powdered face. She was followed by a fat, middle-aged man gaudily dressed in a purple silk gown and a black satin jacket which reached to his knees. "Tai, my son," his mother said happily. "You are home. Please greet Mr. Sing, the matchmaker."

Fong Tai bowed to the fat man, who returned the bow, his smiling little eyes studying him carefully from head to toe. "Ah, he is just as I had expected, madame. Handsome and intelligent, with bright eyes and a sensitive mouth. A perfect match!"

A maid brought tea and watermelon seeds as Madame Fong and Mr. Sing sat down on the remaining empty ancestral chairs. On the altar, against the wall facing the entrance, incense sticks had been lit and two large red candles were flickering in front of the ancestral tablets. Fong Tai stood in the middle of the hall, shifting his legs awkwardly and feeling like a fool. He knew it was an inspection, or some kind of engagement initiation. He would not be asked to sit down until the ritual was over.

"Mr. Sing," his mother said in her high-pitched voice, full of excitement and pride, a voice that embarrassed him, "please tell us how you know he is intelligent. You have never met him before."

"It is easy to tell, madame," Mr. Sing replied, chuckling pleasantly. "The high forehead always indicates intelligence, and the rather prominent nose is a sign of prosperity. Ah . . . it also foretells many children. The other family will be delighted. An excellent match, I say!"

"And tell us why this match is so excellent, Mr. Sing," Madame Fong said in her trilling voice. Obviously she had heard the answer before and now she wanted everybody to hear it again.

"Madame," Mr. Sing said after clearing his throat, "both families have unusual pedigrees and both doors are unusually prominent and high."

With a significant nod, Madame Fong cast her brother Third Uncle a glance and said, "And this betrothal already has Third Uncle's approval."

Third Uncle coughed with authority and said to Fong Tai, "Indeed! Since your father died, Tai, I have acted as the head of the Fong family. And I have made this decision, ah. . . ." He stopped to cast a quick glance at his sister as if to seek her approval. "I have, ah, made the decision with pleasure. You are going to be married on the fifteenth day of the fourth moon in the Year of the Ram."

"That is day after tomorrow," Madame Fong said happily. "A lucky day selected by Mr. Sing from the Almanac. Now you may thank Mr. Sing."

Fong gave Mr. Sing a hasty bow. His three cousins, all more than ten years older than he, smiled mischievously. They were probably enjoying the fact that he was now hooked like a fish.

"What does she look like?" Fong asked.

The question stunned his mother. Mr. Sing said quickly, "Tai, it is not customary to inquire about looks. If you want to know about your future wife's intelligence and family background, yes, but not her looks."

"But I am the one who is going to marry her!" Fong blurted out.

"Tai!" his mother said sharply. "Be civil! I am ashamed of you!"

"That is all right, madame," Mr. Sing said placatingly. "He is learning the Western ways. A sad sign, but the world is changing." He turned to Fong Tai and added with a reassuring smile, "She is as beautiful as a fresh lotus flower."

As expected, everyone was asked to stay for dinner. Fong Tai knew that the ordeal would not be over until the ladies had finished their mahjong game. His mother ordered him to the gaming room to greet the cousins' wives, who had been playing mahjong with Grandmother.

The greeting was formal and polite. It took a little while for his grandmother to recognize him. At eighty-nine, she was losing her eyesight and her hearing, but her mind was still as sharp as anybody's. Playing mahjong with Grandmother was always a chore. She was suspicious of cheating, and in answering questions, one had to shout politely and have a magnifying glass ready when she demanded an examination of documents or money. Fong Tai admired the three cousins' wives for keeping the little old lady company at the mahjong table for so long. He decided to treat his cousins a little better.

"So you are engaged to be married," his grandmother said, stopping the game momentarily to stare at him through a pair of thick glasses. "Too bad your father could not be here to witness the ceremony. But we will invite his spirit, and a seat at the banquet table will be reserved for it. You will behave like a gentleman and a filial son. Keep your mind clean and pure, so that Heaven will bless you with a son. I will not die until I can enjoy my dinner with four generations under one roof, remember that! Never forget your filial piety. Confucius has well said, 'When a minister is ordered by his Emperor to die, he is not loyal if he does not; if a son is ordered by his parents to beget an offspring, he is not filial if he does not.' "

"Grandmother," Madame Fong interrupted hastily, "it is not lucky to mention death so many times on such an occasion. You have a good hand, please resume your game." To spare Fong Tai a long lecture, she hustled him out of the gaming room and ordered him to her own room.

There, he sat on one of the uncomfortable, intricately carved redwood chairs with a straight back. She sat in a similar rocking chair and allowed Little Peach, her personal maid, to light her water pipe. While puffing on the brass pipe, with water bubbling noisily in the bowl, she lectured: "Tai, you are the only son . . ."

"Mother," he interrupted, "whenever people talk to me, the first thing they always say is, 'You are the only son.' "

His mother looked offended. At fifty she was still pretty, her smooth white skin still tight over her round face and slightly plump body, but when she was offended, her eyes hardened. Everybody said she was a strong woman, with a soft heart. He believed it and felt sorry that he had said anything to displease her. Just as he was about to make amends, she sighed.

"All right, Tai," she said, her eyes softening a little. "I am not a selfish woman, you know that. And I am not even old-fashioned. I let you go to the Foreign School. I hear that there are girl students in that school."

"There are only a few girl students in my school, Mother. What is wrong with that?"

"I have to lie to your grandmother about them. She would be horrified if she knew that women from noble families sit side by side with men in a schoolroom. I suppose they don't ride in sedan chairs to the school, either?"

"No, Mother."

"You see? Your grandmother must not know about that. When your father died, he left me with only one son . . ." She stopped and looked at him with an apologetic smile. Her eyes became soft and moist. "I am sorry, Tai."

"That's all right, Mother."

"It was a slip of the tongue; I can't help it. Too bad you don't have a brother to share the burden of filial piety. That is why you must also bear the burden of our attention. Still, I am not very strict with you. I let you do a lot of things that I must hide from the elders, especially your grand-mother. My brother is very old-fashioned. You know his sons, the three cousins you have met. They were engaged to be married when they were still sucking milk from wet nurses. When their wives were carried to them in sedan chairs, none of the girls was older than twelve, and all of them already had tiny bound feet. They were grinding their teeth at night from foot-binding pain. But all of them turned out to be good wives, even though their husbands don't seem to appreciate them."

She paused to take a sip of tea. After a long sigh, she went on, "I tell you all this for a reason, my son. Shao Mei will have bound feet. This is a tradition. Nobody can change it.

"Who is Shao Mei?"

"Your future wife. Three years at the Foreign School have influenced you, giving you many strange ideas, such as shaking hands with strangers and going to study in a foreign land, as though what you learn at home is no longer good enough. But you must also learn to live with your own traditions, such as Shao Mei's feet . . ."

"Mother," he interrupted, trying not to sound impatient. "I am not interested in discussing my future wife's feet. If they are bound, they are bound, and there is nothing I can do to correct the situation. May I go? I have an examination tomorrow. I must study."

His mother's eyes hardened briefly. But they softened when she spoke again. "All right, son," she said with a wave of her hand. There was even a flicker of a smile on her lips.

*

The wedding preparations were elaborate. Hundreds of lanterns had been installed. A stage was built in the courtyard for the performance of the Peking Opera, which would last all day. The wedding banquet was set for six o'clock. Five extra cooks had been hired to feed five-hundred-odd guests in various areas of the house, with ladies sitting inside the house and gentlemen in the courtyard. Fifty round tables complete with lucky red tablecloths had been rented from the Double Happiness Wedding Service Company. Fong Tai, confined to his room in the morning, heard all the activities—servants cleaning the house, sweeping the courtyard, carrying furniture, bringing in meat and groceries, all commanded by his mother's trilling voice. A professional interior decorator who doubled as an expert on *wind and water* was busy working in the wedding chamber, deciding where to put the canopied bed, where to place the dressing table and chairs, all in accordance with the best *wind and water position,* so that no evil spirits would be able to invade the privacy of the newlyweds.

The wedding looked so complicated that Fong Tai began to dread it. But he admired the Han efficiency—an enormous wedding had been prepared within two days.

A list had been handed to him by his mother, detailing what he must do before the ceremony, which was to start at two o'clock in the afternoon in the middle hall. When he heard a long string of firecrackers exploding outside the front door, he knew that the bride's luggage was arriving. He had learned that her dowry was fifty mus of prime land in Hunan Province in the south, her ancestral home. A tenant farming family had been raising vegetables on the land for generations. Now he was going to own it—or co-own it. His uncle had told him that the Wang family was enormously wealthy; they owned thousands of mus in Li Ling County, with the family mansion built in the center of its holdings. The bride's grandfather, Master Wang, was now residing there as the family patriarch. He was a famous philanthropist, generous with food and money. He gave elaborate banquets for friends and relatives on any occasion—even a pet parakeet's birthday was an excuse for a feast. The most important feasting was to celebrate a relative's passing of the Imperial examination. Old Master Wang liked to show off all his relatives' high achievements and scholarship. Since his landholdings were so vast, he believed that anyone who was feasted in his house was bound to leave something behind to fertilize his land.

Old Liu knocked on his door and reminded him that it was ten in the morning. Madame Fong wanted to know if he had dressed for the wedding ceremony. He had not, but he told Old Liu to say that he was ready and was resting.

He lay on his bed, wondering if his mother was more nervous than he was. He wanted to take a nap before the ceremony; only when he was sleeping could he be himself. When he went to the wedding, he would be obliged to wear a mask—pretend that he was content and happy, grateful to Heaven that he was born into such a noble family and that he was soon to be married to a noble lady. For all that, he had not lifted a finger.

Perhaps he should feel really lucky and happy. If he had had the chance to chase the popular Miss Woo at the Foreign School, he probably would have spent a lot of time and money and suffered many heartaches and pains. Besides, Miss Woo seemed to be interested only in Manchu students. He got up and examined himself in the mirror. He looked fine in the wedding costume. He decided he might as well enjoy the occasion. At nineteen he was going through the second greatest experience of his life —getting married. His first—birth—had happened without mishap. He imagined that his third—death—would come smoothly, too.

Fong Tai brought out the jar of Peking King Bee Concentrate that he had purchased a week earlier. He studied the label briefly. Good: no complicated ways to take the tonic. Just wash it down with a cup of tea.

A spoonful at a time, twice a day, after dinner and before bed. He took two spoonfuls.

Now his mood changed; the vague gloom was replaced by a surge of courage and expectation. His uncle had told him that getting married was like going off to war. He had to perform his duty with bravado. Only yesterday his uncle had asked him if he was still a virgin. After he had murmured a sheepish "Yes," his uncle had told him that there was more reason than ever for him to act like a brave man.

"Go to it like a soldier," he had said seriously. "Hit the target the first time out."

Fong Tai glanced around the small room where he had lived almost all of his nineteen years. He was glad he was moving out; the room was cold in winter and hot in summer. "Farewell, room," he said, believing that the wedding chamber could not possibly be worse. And even if it turned out to be less comfortable than he hoped, he was soon leaving for America.

The middle hall was now crowded with relatives and friends. The ladies were well dressed in bright costumes of silk and satin, their hair decorated with flowers and pearly combs. The Peking Opera, which had been playing since early afternoon, had stopped so that the audience could witness the ceremony.

As expected, the bride, dressed in a red silk wedding gown, her face covered with an embroidered silk veil, was ushered in by two lady relatives. Fong Tai was made to stand in front of the altar, waiting, accompanied by Third Uncle, who, for the first time, had trimmed his mustache, and the front part of his head was clean-shaven. Third Uncle was not near-sighted, but today he wore a pair of decorative eyeglasses to look more dignified.

The master of ceremonies, who also made a living as a funeral mourner for hire, called out the wedding rituals: three kowtows to Heaven and Earth and three kowtows to the elders. While Fong Tai knocked his head on the ground, he could not help wondering what his bride looked like. All he could see was a woman covered from top to toe by her colorful wedding costume.

After the bride and groom had kowtowed to each other, the master of ceremonies pronounced them husband and wife, and almost immediately someone set off a long string of firecrackers in the courtyard to announce the happy occasion, the turning of a new page in two young people's lives.

The wedding banquet started almost immediately. The opera resumed, the musicians playing with gusto, the actors singing their parts in squeaky voices. Men were playing women's roles and vice versa.

Fifty-two tables of food served in the middle hall and in the courtyard by a swarm of servants were consumed by the five hundred guests, who laughed and played finger-guessing games noisily while the bridegroom, accompanied by Third Uncle, circled among the male guests in the courtyard, thanking them for their presence.

The bride, guided by her new mother-in-law, was doing the same, toasting the female guests. For the moment she was unveiled, but her face would be covered again as soon as the banquet concluded. Grandmother firmly believed that it was bad luck for the groom to see the bride's face before the consummation of their marriage.

While toasting and being toasted, Fong Tai tried to alleviate his impatience by downing cup after cup of strong mao tai. The guests meanwhile all seemed to enjoy the eighteen-course banquet. They made the proper noises, smacking their lips, clicking their red-lacquered chopsticks and belching—all a necessary part of festivity and good cheer.

At Fong Tai's table, an empty seat was reserved for his father's spirit and another for His Excellency Li Hung-chang. Nobody expected Li to show up, for a man of position usually had no time for weddings or funerals, except those of high government officials.

By the time Fong Tai finished making his rounds, the floor seemed to rock under his feet and the walls to wave. On the way back to his table, he felt dizzy and high-spirited as he thought of his bride. Swaying from side to side, he sang a song he had learned at the Foreign School. "Time to take a look," he said, wobbling toward the middle hall.

His uncle grabbed him. "Where do you think you're going?"

"Well, well, Third Uncle," Fong said drunkenly, "time to take a look!"

"Take a look at what?"

"The bride, of course! Does she have pockmarks? I've got to know. . . ."

"Please go back to your table," Third Uncle begged, trying to steer him back to his seat.

Fong Tai never got there, for just then Li Hung-chang arrived in his sedan chair carried by eight uniformed coolies and followed by an aide with two armed guards. All the guests rose to their feet to greet him. An aide helped His Excellency out, holding his thin arm as the old man stepped over one of the tilted carrying poles.

Li was dressed in his official robe of Grand Councilor of the First Rank. A small man, he looked magnificent in his elaborately embroidered costume with the horseshoe sleeves and an official cap with a large red button on top. With his graying queue falling behind his slightly stooped back, he appeared older than his age. But at sixty-nine, he was still alert, working almost twelve hours a day.

Fong Tai was excited to see his mentor. His Excellency's appearance at the wedding gave the family a *great face*. Fong Tai tried to reach the sedan chair, but he staggered and fell to his knees. He tried to get up, but everything swam before his eyes and then went black.

✱

When he woke up, he was lying on his bed, attended by his mother and two maids, one of them feeding him a hot brew that smelled of ginger. His uncle was there, too, standing behind his mother, winking at him.

Seeing so many people in his room, he instantly became wide awake. "You are drunk!" his mother said, looking chagrined. "I have lost much face. Worse yet, you passed out just as His Excellency Li Hung-chang asked about you!"

Fong Tai grimaced, feeling slight nausea and a wild throbbing in his temples. "Did he say anything?" he asked anxiously.

"Don't worry," Third Uncle said with a little roguish smile. "He said that a boy does not become a man unless he gets drunk once, and nobody should get married unless he has become a man. So there—no harm done. Now get up and do your duty."

"The bride is waiting for you in the wedding chamber," his mother said, casting her brother a sidelong glance of disapproval. "And don't forget the good-luck nuts."

"All in my pocket," Third Uncle said, patting his bulging silk gown. "Follow me, nephew."

Fong Tai swallowed another mouthful of the ginger brew and struggled out of bed. He followed his waddling uncle across the courtyard toward the wedding chamber. It was dark, but the lanterns were still lit, giving the yard a festive glow. The air smelled of food, firecrackers and tuberoses, which Old Liu had grown in the flower beds.

Through the open latticed paper window of the wedding chamber, he could see many guests still chatting and laughing. His heart sank as he remembered the nuts-tossing ceremony, an obligatory ritual before the consummation of the marriage. The guests would tease and toss rice and nuts at the couple while they sat on the bed. The practical jokes included tying cowbells under the bed and hiding false hairy spiders in the canopy —the spiders would fall when the bed shook.

The bride, her face covered again, was sitting on the bed, stiff as a board. Amid a round of loud congratulations, the guests made Fong Tai sit beside her. His uncle dug out from his pockets handfuls of rice and nuts; he handed them to the guests, who immediately started tossing them at the newlyweds, shouting, "Do your duty right!" "Don't miss the target!" "Let the lucky red flow, but be gentle."

Presently, the ritual began to get out of hand and the shouting overly racy and improper. Third Uncle, although enjoying every moment of it, stepped out and raised both his hands. "Enough!" he said. "Time for bed."

Ignoring protests, he herded the guests toward the door and, after pushing the most reluctant ones out, stepped out of the room himself. With a wink, he closed the door behind him.

Fong Tai bent down and gently unveiled his bride. He saw a thin, heavily painted face with a small nose and small slitlike eyes. She looked at him anxiously, her broad smile exposing two gold teeth that gleamed like fangs under the bright oil lamps. She looked about twenty-five or older.

As they stared at each other, all Fong's desire disappeared.

He should have guessed that she would be skinny. Had she been round, Mr. Sing would have said that she was plump, for plumpness indicated fertility, a desired quality that any good matchmaker loved to emphasize.

"What should I call you?" he asked politely.

"Shao Mei," she said, lowering her head and no longer smiling. "If you prefer, you may call me Mei Mei, my milk name." After a timid glance at him, she asked, "What is your milk name?"

"I have no milk name. Call me Fong Tai."

"That's your school name."

"I have no milk names or nicknames. If you are tired, you may go to sleep."

She sensed the coldness in his voice. "What are you going to do?" she asked.

"I shall read for a while."

"Oh." Shao Mei turned her head away and stared at the floor. There was a moment of awkward silence. Suddenly she asked, her head still turned away, her voice low, almost timid, "Don't you want to disrobe me?"

"No," he said quickly and firmly.

She climbed into the bed, lay down and turned toward the wall. Fong felt sorry for her. He wanted to comfort her but could not bring himself to touch her or say anything sweet.

"It was a beautiful wedding, wasn't it?" she whispered, turning her head slightly toward him.

"Yes, it was."

"And the weather was good," she said after another long pause.

She made a few more attempts to chat, but he discouraged her by simply grunting. He knew that he was being rude, but he didn't care to discuss whether the sun rose from the east or if egg white was white and egg yolk was yellow. He felt terrible, hating himself.

After a few more uncomfortable moments, Shao Mei suddenly jerked her head back and said, her voice tinged with anger, "Don't flatter yourself and think I am anxious for a child. May you grow old and lonely without an offspring, and may your life be as barren as a monk's head!" With a little snort she turned back to the wall and went to sleep in her wedding gown.

3

For two nights Fong Tai slept in the wedding chamber without disrobing. When he bathed in his former room, he felt guilty, wondering if he should go back and fulfill his conjugal duty. At breakfast, his mother, smiling broadly, casually mentioned that she had already bought a crib.

His mother was an intense lady but a bad actor. On many occasions, when she was irritated, she pretended to be terribly angry. When she made a great show of casualness, she was actually deadly serious. He had learned to read his mother's true feelings from her eyes. Often when she had a burst of anger, her loud scolding and heavy scowl did not match the expression of her eyes. Sometimes they even showed a gleam of amusement as she shouted and banged things around. On the other hand, when she was quiet and overly polite, she could glare at a person in a way that was unnerving.

He wondered what kind of woman Shao Mei was. He sat on his single bed thinking about his bride, hating himself, wishing there were a spark of desire that would bridge the distance. He knew that if he forced himself to perform his duty, he would feel like a draftee conscripted to fight a war, perhaps resulting in the sexual malfunction known as *inhuman*.

Once he had heard a story in which a bride cried all the way to her mother after the wedding night, accusing her new husband of being *inhuman*. This showed how serious inhuman was; it could upset not only the bride but also her whole family, which could result in an annulment. He did not care about the risk of an annulment, but his reputation as a man would be ruined and all professional matchmakers in Peking would blacklist him.

Taking a deep breath, Fong Tai left his old room, dragging his feet toward the wedding chamber. Old Liu, sweeping the yard with a large broom, greeted him with a wink. He knew that the ill manners of his servant were associated with his conjugal duties. He had no doubt that when someone saw a bride or a groom, the first thing he thought of was the performance of that duty. "How many times will it be?" "Will the bride look tired in the morning?" These were the questions he had often asked himself when he attended somebody else's wedding.

As he walked past the two maids who were scrubbing clothes under the eaves, he noticed that one of them was stealing glances at him. Walking away, he heard both of them giggle. He wondered if they were asking each other the same question: "How many times last night?"

"Tai," he heard his mother calling from the east wing. He turned and saw her rushing toward him waving a piece of paper. "A message from your school," she said breathlessly. "Just arrived. What were you doing in your old room?"

"Taking a bath."

"Why take a bath in your old room? What is wrong with your wedding chamber?"

"Mother, let me read the message."

"It is written in that wormlike language," she said. "I want you to translate it."

Fong Tai read the message. It was written by the student dean in flowery capital letters: REPORT TRAIN STATION TOMORROW AT 9:00 A.M. REGARDING YOUR IMMEDIATE DEPARTURE FOR AMERICA. Signed, JOSEPH BENJAMIN TUNG, PH.D.

"Well, what does it say?"

Fong translated it faithfully. "Immediately?" his mother cried, her voice tinged with anger.

"Yes, Mother."

"Read it again!"

"Mother, I have studied English for six years . . ."

"You have studied Chinese more than ten years! Even in Chinese you often misread words."

"I must go, Mother," he said wearily. Pocketing the message, he hurried back to the wedding chamber.

Shao Mei was embroidering a handkerchief in front of the garden window. Through the open latticed window he could see the plum tree in full bloom, with bees humming and hovering over the brilliant pink flowers. With Shao Mei's back against it, the scene was picturesque, even romantic, like an illustration in one of the sensual novels he had read secretly.

For a brief moment he felt an urge to walk up behind her and hug her. But when she turned to look at him, the urge vanished. The anxious smile on her narrow face framed by an enormous shiny hairdo was like water poured over a small fire.

"Your mother was looking for you," she said in her high-pitched, overly pleasing voice. "Tai, where have you been?"

"I have been out," he said, stopping a few feet from her. Her strong metallic perfume, which he did not like, tickled his nose. He was relieved that he was going to America. When he spoke again, he sounded cheerful.

"Shao Mei, the dean wants me to leave for America immediately. I must pack . . . I shall write to you."

He opened one of the red-lacquered trunks and started packing. The trunks were their common property, given by his uncle as wedding gifts. "Do you mind if I take one of the small ones?"

"Take any you like, I don't care!" Her unhappy voice startled him. Without looking, he knew she had resumed her embroidery. Her stitching sounded unnecessarily rapid and loud.

*

That evening the wedding chamber was once again filled with relatives and friends who had come to bid him goodbye. Many had brought farewell gifts, mostly bottled Chinese herb medicine for various ailments. A few had brought Chinese food—preserved vegetables, dried sweetmeats and thousand-year eggs, all packed in jars or boxes and wrapped in lucky red paper.

His mother had given him a purple satin gown and a black satin jacket to match. He wondered if he should take them to America. He would look ridiculous in them in a foreign country. As he turned the gown over in his hands, unable to make up his mind, he felt an unusual weight in one pocket. It was money—his mother had put a red packet of fifty silver dollars in one of the pockets.

Shao Mei had been sitting quietly at her dressing table combing her long black hair, anxious to start a conversation. "Why are you so happy?" she asked.

The question first startled, then irritated him. He did not know how to answer. It was true that he was excited about leaving; but how could he tell her the truth?

"I know why you are so happy . . ."

He did not want to hear her reason. "Are you trying to pick a fight?"

"Pick a fight?" she said hotly. "I am waiting for you to say something nice. What do you do, you accuse me of trying to pick a fight."

"Shao Mei, please," he said quietly. "I know I am stupid. I am no good at saying nice things. Besides, I don't know what things a woman wants to hear. If you want me to say, 'I am sorry to be leaving for America,' I'll say it a hundred times."

"I don't want you to say it a hundred times. You have not even said it once."

"Shao Mei, I am sorry I am leaving."

She turned to look at him, her eyes glistening with tears. "Do you mean it?"

"What must I do, write it in blood?"

With a sob she got up from her dressing table and disappeared into the next room. He sighed, regretting his bluntness. He wished he were a better liar. Why was it so difficult for him to say things that he did not mean?

There was a knock on the door. Almost immediately the door opened and Third Uncle came in, waving a gold watch in his hand. "I want you to take this with you, Tai," he said cheerfully. "It was your grandfather's, probably a hundred years old, made in Switzerland. It keeps good time, only a few minutes slow every three days because of its old age. Adjust it once every week and you won't be late for your classes in America."

Fong Tai was glad that his uncle had dropped in. He did not know how to deal with his wife. His Third Uncle was always a welcome sight; he was easygoing and understanding. With that roguish glint in his eyes, he served as an antidote to his mother's pressure.

He quickly poured a cup of tea for Third Uncle. The teapot was kept warm in a padded warmer on the tea stand next to the bed. Lotus, the maid who came as part of the dowry, had proven her loyalty by constantly filling the vessel. At sixteen she was no beauty but had the freshness of an innocent, naive girl, and her chest, even though tightly strapped, was bulging. She had a peasant woman's big feet, which Fong found interesting, even attractive. Too bad Shao Mei didn't resemble her!

Third Uncle sipped the tea and accepted the guest water pipe from Lotus. "So you are leaving for America," he said after blowing out smoke heavily.

"By order of the dean," Fong said, trying to sound a bit sad for the benefit of his wife, who was undoubtedly within hearing range in the next room.

"Tai," Third Uncle said after a noisy sip of tea, "I have another parting gift, which is only an old saying: 'Do your best in whatever you do, but leave the results to Heaven.' Since I started following this wisdom myself, I have discovered that my hair has stopped falling out and my whiskers have become less gray. I give this old wisdom all the credit for my youthful look at fifty-eight."

"You look much younger than your age, Third Uncle."

"If that is true, nephew, embrace this saying. Follow it all your life. Believe me, you will wipe out all those little devils that age a man quickly: anxiety, regret, remorse and worst of all, anger. 'Do your best, but leave the results to Heaven.' Repeat that every day. If things do not turn out right, why be angry? It is the will of Heaven. When you return from America, I want you to look as you look today, not a day older."

For the first time Third Uncle looked serious and sounded serious—no roguish glint in the eyes, no winking. He went on: "And the watch is your reminder. Wind it every night and let it tick under your pillow."

Fong put the watch in his pocket. "Thank you, Third Uncle. I'll do just that. As a matter of fact, I feel better already."

He heard footsteps. Through the open door he saw his mother marching toward the wedding chamber, unsmiling. His heart sank.

To Madame Fong, the message from school had brought Heaven crashing down. She imagined herself storming into the dean's office, demanding a retraction of the order. She even imagined herself pleading, "Please give him three more days to fulfill his filial piety."

She burst into the wedding chamber and impatiently gestured for Old Liu to hurry. Old Liu, carrying a brand-new crib, staggered in breathlessly.

"Hello, Mother," Fong greeted her at the door.

Madame Fong ignored the greeting and ordered Old Liu to put the crib beside the bed. Fong stared at the crib, which was elaborately decorated with flowers and birds and carved Foo Dogs. He was flabbergasted. He glanced at Third Uncle, who shrugged helplessly with a grin. "Tai," he said, "your mother wants the crib to be occupied not too long after you leave for America."

"It will be occupied," Madame Fong said. "The Iron Rooster said the position beside the bed is most favorable."

Fong knew who Iron Rooster was, the local fortune teller, who had made himself rich by analyzing *wind and water* for those who believed that everything had to be placed in the right position to avoid evil spirits. Fong Tai hated such nonsense. To avoid taking sides, Third Uncle rose.

"Well, Tai, you still have a chance to make a last effort. As I said, 'Do your best and leave the result to Heaven.' " As he left, he gave his nephew a secret encouraging wink.

Without a word, his mother fished out a handkerchief. Dabbing her eyes and blowing her nose, she muffled a sob and left the room hurriedly.

　　　　*

That night Fong Tai and Shao Mei had little to say to each other. He finished packing, changed his clothes and went to bed. Shao Mei lay on her side, facing the wall. As he adjusted his pillow, he found a jade Foo Dog under it. "Is this yours, Shao Mei?" he asked, showing her the jade piece.

She did not respond. Instead she started to snore. "Also a bad actor," he thought, a bit amused. "Just like Mother."

Next morning he got up early. Shao Mei stirred and yawned, pretending that she had just awakened. "Don't forget your good-luck Foo Dog," she said.

"Mine?"

"Yes. My parting gift to you. It is my family treasure."

"No. I can't take your family treasure."

"It is for good luck. Your good luck is the family's good luck."

Fong was touched. "All right, I'll carry it always." He took her hand and held it briefly. She looked at him softly, her eyes full of tears.

"May good luck be with you," she said.

4

When Fong Tai arrived at the train station at nine the next morning, Father Andrew Barrington, Li Hung-chang's personal emissary and escort for the eleven students—eight Manchus and three Hans—was already there, standing on the platform, gesturing and lecturing the early arrivals.

"You are going to a city in God's country," he was saying. "Boston is also a city of beans and cod and clam chowder—a city of traditions, of pigeons and morning fog. It is situated on a peninsula, connected by a narrow neck like a Chinese gourd. I shall elaborate on Boston's history and geography in due course, but right now I would like to emphasize America, the country you are going to visit, and the era you are in, a great era of industrialization.

"Today, the streets in America have begun to twinkle with gas lights, steamships are swarming in and out of modern harbors. Tall buildings, factories with billowing funnels, and freight depots are now mushrooming in large American cities. I want you to prepare yourselves for a shocking change, a totally different civilization. In America you will see steam locomotives racing across the land; one day you will hear telephones ring in people's homes. Many new sounds will greet your ears and new sights will dazzle your eyes. Be prepared, boys.

"But America will welcome you with open arms. The Lord has spoken, and His words always ring true, especially in America. He said, 'But the stranger that dwelleth with you shall be unto you as one born among you, and thou shalt love him as thyself.' "

As Barrington lectured, gesticulating wildly, idle bystanders began to gather around him. Some stared, some looked fascinated, none understood much of what he said. It was not until three blasts of the train's whistle drowned out his voice that he finished his lecture with a roar. "That's all, boys, that's all. Hop in! Take your seats. And watch your luggage. God will watch your soul but not your personal property."

*

The *Flying Cloud*, a six-thousand-ton ship seventy feet long, was freshly painted white, with several sails gleaming in the morning sun. A trail of smoke rose from its slender funnel as it rested at anchor in Shanghai's crowded harbor. But inside the ship, it looked a little shabby; the dilapidated second-class cabins on the boat deck had four bunks each. Fong Tai, his Han friend Ling and two Manchus were assigned to the last cabin on the starboard side toward the stern. Fong counted himself lucky that he did not share a cabin with some of the Manchus he disliked the most.

Father Barrington had warned them that the journey would be long and tedious; it would probably take three months to cross the Pacific, then sail south and reach Boston by way of Cape Horn. Fong Tai had decided to settle down and enjoy the trip; he also wanted to take the opportunity to mingle with other passengers and get to know some members of the crew. He could use the three months' time to practice English and learn American ways. He had already spotted several friendly-looking Americans who shouted greetings at him, waving and smiling, when he was coming aboard.

He had changed into a Western suit which he had bought in Shanghai for ten dollars. Some of the Manchu students had arrived in their Manchu gowns, probably trying to show the foreigners on the ship that they were not ordinary Chinese, but Mandarins. Fong Tai was sure that the foreigners were not impressed. He had noticed that two seamen even pointed at them and chortled.

Father Barrington had instructed them to look cheerful, wave and greet their fellow passengers. Only he and Ling had followed instructions. Although far from handsome—his eyes were too close together and his Adam's apple was too prominent—Ling was warm and helpful. Fong was sorry that the other Han, Kao Sung, was stiff and shy.

Before the ship sailed, Father Barrington called a meeting on the deck and made everybody sit in a semicircle. The seamen were busy working nearby, casting curious glances at them. The Whampoo River was crowded with steamers and sailing ships, making the waterfront a forest of masts. In the distance, the yellow water from the river was pouring into the bay, creating a giant yellow palm leaf fan at the Yangtze estuary.

Fong Tai had prepared a notebook. He was ready to supply notes to those who had difficulty following Barrington's lectures. With these notes he could repay favors, make demands; he might even wield a little power over the Manchus. Barrington would make reports to the school. He might secretly grade everybody according to his progress and behavior. Fong Tai hoped that his notes would be a valuable, sought-after commodity, especially to the Manchus, who often stared blankly like deaf-mutes during the Barrington lectures.

"Well, boys," Barrington was saying, his voice cheerful and strong, "within an hour we shall be on our way. To many of you this will be your maiden voyage. It will have more meaning if you understand the great events and changes around you.

"Look at the bay!" He flung a finger at a Manchu and asked, "Kong, what do you see? Look around you. What do see that is different?"

Kong was a stuffed shirt, arrogant and aloof. He looked around and said hesitantly, "Water?"

With a sweeping hand, Barrington asked another student. "Chang, you tell me what you see over there around us."

Chang, another Manchu, said triumphantly, "Sea gulls!"

"There are things bigger and more beautiful than sea gulls . . . things beneficial to mankind."

A hand shot up. Yao piped up, "Ships!"

"Aha!" Barrington said with a broad smile. "Now we have a man who is not blind! Ships! Years ago we saw only sampans, fishing junks and clumsy barges. Now we see . . . what?" He looked around significantly, inviting an answer.

Chang's hand went up. "Foreign devils . . . uh, foreign ships!"

"Yes, foreign ships! Brigs, schooners, sloops, square-riggers and graceful clippers. Boys, these ships represent progress. These are the kinds of ships you will see in Boston Harbor. Before the revolution, America was nothing. After the War of Independence, England recognized a new nation in 1783. In 1789, George Washington became the first President of the USA. Now Boston . . . anybody know anything about Boston? Anyone?"

Fong Tai raised his hand. "Boston was the birthplace of America's independence."

"Good!" Father Barrington's voice boomed. "Why?"

"Because of the Boston Tea Party."

"Excellent!" Barrington shouted enthusiastically. "So you see? You are not going just anywhere. You are going to a city with great historical significance. Boston and China have had close ties for almost a hundred years, and I'll tell you why."

For the next fifteen minutes, Father Barrington talked about China and Boston, their friendship and trade. As fast as he could, Fong Tai took down notes:

  · The first merchandise sold to China was a weed that grew wild in the woods of New England; it was a root shaped like the human body, called ginseng.
  · The merchandise, used as a medicine, was carried by the clipper Empress of China, year 1784, during the reign of Emperor Chien Lung. Major Samuel Shaw of Boston was on board to act as honorary American consul. He laid the foundation for friendly relations between the two countries.
  · Boston merchants soon found that the Chinese would also pay high prices for sea-otter pelts. The Americans made a deal with the Indians, who supplied the pelts in exchange for blankets, mirrors, beads and chisels—especially chisels.
  · In 1788 the clipper Columbia sailed from New York carrying a full load of pelts. Sailors on board made chisels during the voyage for extra pay. The Boston merchants before the next voyage exchanged the chisels for pelts, one chisel per pelt. Chisels cost about a dime apiece, but pelts could bring $50 apiece in China. A gold mine for the Bostonians. Boston and China became very friendly.

· On the return trip Columbia carried China tea and porcelain. In 1790 the ship was anchored in Boston Harbor and the city was flooded with China tea and porcelain; it was the beginning of a glorious period of trade and cultural exchange between China and Boston.

· The Chinese students could expect to be treated with decency and cordiality in Boston, for half of Boston's fortune was made through dime chisels and animal pelts. In turn, the profits were instrumental in introducing Chinese culture to America.

When Father Barrington ended his lecture on a note of enthusiasm and optimism, Fong Tai closed his notebook. He whispered to Ling, "Look at the Manchus; they are still staring blankly into space. I'll sell my notes to them for a good price."

Ling nodded. "Get as much as you can. The dirty rats are all filthy rich."

The *Flying Cloud* soon sailed out of the Yangtze estuary and headed for the open sea. Most of the students returned to their cabins, lay on their bunks and felt sick.

The next morning Fong Tai went up on deck. There were quite a few sailors working there. Anxious to practice his English, Fong went around greeting everyone he met on the deck. Most of them only grunted or said in pidgin English, "No sabe, Charlie. No sabe."

The sea was rough but Fong Tai liked it. The rocking motion forced him to do a little balancing act, and the wind cleared his mind as well as his nose. He saw a young seaman mopping the deck and greeted him cheerfully. To his surprise, the seaman touched his cap in a smart salute and said, "Good morning, Charlie." He was a muscular young man wearing a dark windbreaker and boots, his blond hair fluttering in the wind. There was a short beard stubble growing on his deeply tanned square face.

Fong Tai extended his hand and introduced himself.

"Fong Tai, eh?" the seaman said, shaking his hand. Fong almost grimaced from the strong grip. "Tough to remember that. My name's Max."

Max was a talkative man. He would stop mopping once in a while to concentrate on the conversation. Fong did not understand everything Max said. After a few minutes of nonstop talking, Max paused long enough to ask Fong if he was Chinese or Japanese.

"Aha, a Chinaman!" Max said enthusiastically. "I should know. I'm from California. My old man knows a lot of Chinamen there. He joined the gold rush, you know. He dug gold for thirty years. Ever heard of the Mother Lode?"

"Someone's mother?"

"Nobody's mother. Just the name of a place in California. They found gold there—gold nuggets as big as goose eggs. My old man should have staked his own claim, but he didn't. He dug gold for others and wound up with nothing but a bunch of kids in rags. I was one of them." He laughed boisterously.

"Hey, let me call you Charlie," Max went on. "Every Chinaman in California is called Charlie. You know why? Because Chinese names can break a fellow's jaw. My old man knows a lot of Charlies. Nice chaps. Always mind their own business. Never ogle a white woman."

"Ogle? What is ogle?"

"Don't you know what ogle is?" Max was surprised.

"No."

"Well, it's about time you learned. You're heading for America, aren't you? Well, they don't like Oriental men to ogle white women. I personally don't care. You can do anything to a white woman, as long as she isn't my wife." He laughed again, then went on. "Listen, Charlie, it's time you knew all this so you won't get strung up on the nearest oak tree. There are quite a few narrow-minded geezers in America. So don't ever ogle a white lady."

"I still don't understand what you mean," Fong said, feeling frustrated.

"Well, how shall I explain it? Hell, I'll show you." He put down his mop and took a few mincing steps, turned his head coquettishly, then walked away with a toss of his head, fluttering his eyelashes. "This is an American lady passing by, see? Suppose you like her and you do this."

He took a few quick steps trying to follow an imaginary lady. He caught up with her, and putting on a big smile demonstrated ogling by rolling his eyes seductively. "Got the idea, Charlie?"

Fong tried not to laugh. Max was funny, like one of those clownish storytellers in Heavenly Bridge. "I think I understand," he said. "You mean flirt."

"Good, good! You married?"

"Yes, I guess."

"You guess! Either you're married or you aren't. What do you mean, 'guess'? What kind of marriage is that?"

"Yes, I am married."

"That's better. That's good!"

"Why good?"

"Because you need a wife in America. No Chinawomen there, see? Hardly any. At least, I never saw one. I saw millions of you China boys, but not one woman, except in pictures carried by some of you Charlies."

Then he lowered his voice and asked confidentially, "Say, is it true that a China woman's sex organ grows sideways?"

Fong was dumbfounded for a moment. Nobody had ever asked him about such a forbidden subject before. Luckily, Max had had the decency to lower his voice.

"I–I don't know," Fong stammered, deeply embarrassed.

Max looked at him askance. "Did you say you're married?"

"Y–yes."

"Married and you don't know anything about that?" Max clucked his tongue, shaking his head. "I don't know much about you fellows."

The sea was getting rougher. Fong decided he had had enough of learning about the West for that morning. Making the excuse of going to the head, he left the deck.

"Nice knowing you, Charlie!" Max shouted after him. "Let's talk about it some more after you've relieved yourself."

＊

The next day the sea was calm. The Chinese students had recovered and were partaking of their breakfast on time. They ate quietly, observing Western table manners, cutting their food carefully and holding their knives and forks at the right angle, just as Dr. Tung, the dean of the Foreign School, had shown them. When they took a sip of coffee, they remembered to hold their cups with their small fingers extended like the petals of an orchid. Dr. Tung had said that the way a man holds his coffee cup usually revealed his upbringing. "And remember, never never make any noise!" he emphasized repeatedly.

Not making noise was the hard part. Fong Tai had tried and scalded his lips every time. In China people were accustomed to sipping hot tea. Unless you made noise, you got your lips scalded. But this morning everybody was sipping coffee without any sucking noise and trying not to grimace.

Father Barrington took a seat at the head of the dining table and gestured for the cups and dishes to be cleared away. Then he spread his elbows on the table and asked, "Enjoy your breakfast?"

"Yes!" the students said in unison, with the Manchus' voices the loudest.

"Good! Very good!" the priest said happily in his booming voice. He had just had an excellent breakfast in the first-class section and felt spirited and refreshed.

"Today we will discuss the similarities and differences between China and Boston. Boston will be your second home for four years, so you'd better familiarize yourselves with that fair city. First, let us discuss symbols. China's symbol is the dragon, a nonexistent mythical animal; Boston's symbol is the eagle. There are eagle emblems everywhere in Boston; over doorways, in hallways, embroidered on shirts and hankerchiefs. You'll find almost everything in Boston is ornamented with an eagle. Even our money has eagles on it. That's why we have a saying, 'New Englanders are so frugal that they hold on to a quarter until the eagle squeals.' "

He paused for his listeners to laugh, but none did. He went on, "Anyway, the eagle is a down-to-earth kind of bird. There is no mystery about it. When an eagle circles in the sky, you know it has spotted its dinner. That's Boston; that's America; easy to understand, nothing to hide.

"But China is shrouded in mystery. Having spent half of my life in China, I still don't understand the country and the people. You don't laugh at jokes, but you cry your eyes out at funerals and weddings. In China, death is not a sad occasion; you celebrate it with elaborate banquets, believing that the dead have entered another world. But you hire professional mourners to wail in funeral processions. When a young bride is carried in a sedan chair to her new home, she is supposed to cry as though she is being exiled to the Gobi Desert. The waterworks of her mother are equally impressive; she cries as if her daughter were being kidnapped. All this is beyond the Westerners' comprehension. I don't try to find answers. There are your characteristics; that's your tradition.

"In America, you may be looked upon as mysterious creatures, treated politely but with suspicion. Don't let that bother you. When you deal with an American, think of an eagle—a bird that's straightforward and down-to-earth. There is nothing to hide.

"In the State of Massachusetts, we have another emblem—a sacred cod. There is a five-foot-long fish hung in our State House, a sacred cod carved out of a solid block of pine. Why worship a fish? Because codfishing is the welfare of the people in that fair state. Codfish have put food on the table and clothes on people's backs. We New Englanders are not ingrates. You do us a good deed and we'll never forget, even if the benefactors are codfish. But we eat them."

He paused again for laughter, but again none came. Fong wrote as fast as he could, knowing that his fellow students had not understood even half of what Father Barrington had been saying. He was happy that the value of his notebook was increasing as he scribbled away.

Father Barrington looked at the students on one side, then the other, and asked, "I see a lot of Chinese wear gold and jade fish around their necks; does anybody know why fish are worshiped in China?"

Most of the students stared blankly. Fong quickly translated the question and instantly all the Manchus shot up their arms and answered simultaneously.

Father Barrington quieted them and pointed to one. "Chang, you tell me."

Chang's English was so hard to understand that Fong had to translate for Father Barrington. "The word fish in Chinese has the same sound as abundance. Therefore, fish also means good luck."

"Aha! So we are both fish worshipers." Father Barrington laughed. "Another similarity. Tell that to the Bostonians. Let fish strengthen our ties! Let fish further our friendship and understanding!"

The morning session again ended on a happy note. The students were getting more enthusiastic about the trip. They could hardly wait to arrive in their host city of Codfish.

5

The first Sunday at sea, Father Barrington arrived in the second-class dining room to deliver a sermon. He sat down at the head of one of the dining tables, smelling of shaving lotion. Fong, sitting close to him, analyzed his face and his full beard. He came to the conclusion that if Father Barrington had not shaved, his whole face would have been covered with stubble.

After he had acknowledged the students' greetings, the priest leaned back in his chair and started his sermon without further ado: "The Greeks said the world was a disk around which flowed a great ocean. The Bible says the formation of the seas was one part of the Lord's works, on the third day of creation. The Chinese say the world was created by Shun Lung, with China as the center and the rest of the world her subordinates.

"But time has proven that China is not the center of the world, but a delicacy surrounded by world powers ready to pounce on her as on a piece of meat.

"But we must not let that happen. China has a culture and history more than five thousand years old. In ancient times ships were often lost in the seven seas until Chinese invented the compass. The Western Powers, which have colonized many other countries, are now threatening China with the very thing that China invented—gunpowder. China rendered world civilization a great service by introducing paper and the printing press. As you can see, the world owes China a great debt."

He paused for a moment to make sure nobody was doodling or dozing. Then he went on: "Now, how does the West repay this enormous debt? As a Westerner, I am ashamed to discuss it, but discuss it I must, because you will one day be the masters of China. One day you will correct the wrong and save China from further degradation.

"But the Lord will only help those who help themselves. That's why you are here, crossing the great Pacific Ocean to get an education, to learn from the West first-hand.

"With this in mind, I want you to take your education seriously, devote your every waking hour to your studies and to God. Before this ship reaches San Francisco, I want to give each of you a test to see what you have learned on this journey."

He paused again to let the information sink in. Some students stared, a few looked worried. Fong was doubly pleased that he was keeping his notes. Suddenly Father Barrington launched into a great peroration.

"God has uplifted America to be a guardian of the weak, guaranteeing progress and restoring prosperity all over the world," he said. "Mark my words, gentlemen, America will be the champion of the oppressed and the unfortunate. We will send pioneers to help others, to sacrifice for others. Have you ever heard of an American by the name of General Frederick Townsend Ward?"

He paused to wait for an answer, looking from face to face. There was no response.

"Frederick Townsend Ward was an American," he went on. "He led Chinese armies to quell the southern rebels who were destroying the country. His ten thousand men were called the Forever Victorious Army, because he never suffered a defeat—as if the Lord were watching over him. He won one hundred and one battles before he was killed. Two Chinese temples were built for him. He was the only white man thus worshiped in a pagan country. But the Lord does not mind a hero thus worshiped and admired. The Lord was proud to see hundreds of natives kowtowing to this man, offering him incense sticks, bowls of steaming rice and red-cooked ham hocks.

"Mark my words, gentlemen, there will be more Wards in this world, marching into battle for the downtrodden. It is the Lord who will be sending such fine men to save the world. Amen."

He rose and conducted a prayer. Most of the students said the prayer after him. They had memorized many prayers without understanding them.

When Father Barrington was leaving, he stopped at the door, turned around and said with a benevolent smile, "And don't forget the test."

*

The next morning, when Fong left the breakfast table for his daily walk on deck, Chang, the leader of the Manchu students, followed him quietly. When they were out of the others' hearing, Chang tugged at his sleeve and whispered, "Fong Tai, may I speak to you about something?"

"What is it?"

"Let's discuss it somewhere else. Too many people passing by here."

They walked toward the bow. The sea was calm, the morning sun warm and the breeze soothing. There were a few sea gulls hovering over the ship, and a distant speck of land was in sight, half hidden by the haze. Leaning against the rail, Fong Tai folded his arms, waiting for Chang to speak. He had sensed what Chang was going to say. None of the Manchus were studious types; they were being sent abroad because of their families' political connections.

After a furtive glance around, Chang cleared his throat. "You have taken notes, have you not?"

"What notes?" Fong said, preparing himself to bargain hard. He wanted to appear casual and nonchalant; he was dealing with a shrewd Manchu.

"Those notes you took during Barrington's long-winded lectures. They put me to sleep. Dry as last year's weeds. That's why my mind always wanders off and I do not hear everything. But the foreign devil is going to give us a test. I would like to borrow your notes for a few hours. One day I will do you a favor in return."

"That's cheating, you understand."

"Who is going to know, if you keep your mouth shut? I can do a lot for you; you know that."

"I never ask for favors. I am a practical man."

Chang's smile vanished. "Do you mean you want money?"

"I am just being practical."

"Name your price. For two hours, no more."

"I'll tell you what," Fong said. "You may have my notes for twenty-four hours, but I want you to sell them to everybody and charge each fifteen dollars. I'll pay you ten percent commission, plus bonus, which means you may read my notes free of charge."

Chang closed his eyes for a brief moment, his lips moving, calculating his commission. "Done!" he said, trying not to sound excited. After another furtive glance around, he put out his hand for the notebook.

"I want something in advance," Fong said, his face expressionless, his arms still folded.

"Advance?" Chang frowned. "How much?"

"Ten dollars per person."

"How do you know they will buy?"

"They will buy. Nine people, excluding you and me."

"I am not sure I can collect, but I'll try." Chang looked at him like a downcast dog just fished out of the water.

"I want the advance right now, from you," Fong said, jabbing a finger at his chest.

"From me? Impossible!"

"All right. Good luck with your test." He turned to look at the ocean and waved at some sea birds.

There was a moment of silence. "I'll go get the money," Chang said, his voice bitter. "Let me have your notebook."

"The advance first," Fong said without looking at him. He could visualize the crestfallen face.

With an oath, Chang left the deck. When he returned with ninety dollars, Fong gave him the notebook, demanding that he return it within twenty-four hours along with the balance of the money, minus the commission.

✻

Fong did not know if Chang had sold the notes to everybody, but in the next twenty-four hours he noticed that his notebook was being circulated secretly. Some were reading it, trying to memorize it; others were copying it, scribbling away frantically in their bunks.

The next day, at the same time and the same place, Chang returned the notebook along with the balance of the money, minus his commission. As Fong pocketed the money, he could not help admiring Chang's efficiency. Chang looked sad, as though he had gotten the short end of the stick. As he left the deck, Fong even felt a bit sorry for him.

That night Fong ran into Yao in the smoking room. Yao picked up a magazine and sank beside him on a sofa. "You are a greedy man, Fong Tai," he said unhappily.

"What do you mean?" Fong asked, surprised.

"How can you charge everybody twenty dollars for reading your smelly notes for two hours? Are you not ashamed of yourself?"

"Did you pay twenty dollars?"

"Everybody paid twenty dollars. Like a cruel tax levied on a bunch of helpless peasants."

Fong Tai kept quiet, feeling anger rising in him. He was sorry that he had been outsmarted; sorry, too, that the Great Ching Dynasty was going to have another crooked official in service within four years.

6

When the *Flying Cloud* anchored in San Francisco Bay for a night to unload passengers and cargo, the students were not permitted to go ashore. Most of them had become pale and thin, except the fat Manchu, Wei Kung, who seemed to be rosier and fatter than ever. In the morning, they all crowded onto the deck to watch, enjoying the view of the famous Land of the Golden Mountain, its busy waterfront and hills dotted with wooden buildings.

The dock was piled high with cargo and teamed with workmen, horse carriages, and pushcarts. There were black people, something the students had never seen before. They chatted and pointed excitedly, like children who had discovered an exotic land inhabited by strange people. They argued about why blacks were black. Chang was the loudest, insisting that they were painted, like the Vietnamese who paint their teeth black to be fashionable.

Everybody was searching for the golden mountain, but everything seemed to be gray—gray wooden shacks built on gray hills. In the bay, sailing ships and steamers came and went, churning up gray water.

When the fog lifted, they saw another kind of strange people who wore large woklike hats and blankets around their shoulders. Chang, always the smart one, said they were red-skinned men without scalps. "That is why they wear such large hats," he said.

Wu, another knowledgeable Manchu, said that Indians lived in high mountains; they were not allowed in big cities because they were naked. Soon most of the students were participating in the argument.

Then the students caught a glimpse of an American lady walking on the dock in high-heeled boots and a long trailing gown. Some wondered why she had such a small waist and enormous hips. Fong Tai, disgusted by their ignorance, said that they should have studied Victorian styles in any of the American magazines. "We like small bound feet," Fong said. "Why can't the Americans like big fat hips?"

Some made faces, still unable to believe or understand such bizarre fashions.

*

The *Flying Cloud* was scheduled to reach New England on June 16, 1880. It reached Boston Harbor a day ahead of schedule. On that morning all of the students, well dressed in their new Western clothes, their leather shoes polished, lined up on the deck to watch the city silhouetted against the cloudless but hazy morning sky. They had spent eighty-nine days at sea.

Ling, standing beside Fong Tai, his elbows resting on the railing, looked at the city dreamily. He kept making little throaty noises to show his excitement. The Manchus were talking among themselves, arguing and agreeing alternately with each other, pointing at buildings which gradually became clear in the vanishing haze.

They argued about whether Boston was really a peninsula. They asked about the narrow neck of land called Roxbury and wondered about the three mountains. Chang again showed his superior knowledge by shouting the names of the three peaks: Copp's Hill, Frog Hill and Trimountain. Then he looked around as if expecting applause. Wu said he was all wrong. Those hills had been leveled. The remaining ones were Cotton Hill, Beacon Hill and Mount Vernon. He shouted the names even louder, counting the hills on his fingers.

Obviously the Manchus had read quite a bit about their host city during the journey, to prepare for Father Barrington's test. But the test never took place. Fong Tai guessed it was the priest's trick to make the students study harder. He was glad. He had made money out of it. It was honest money. When he sent gifts home, his mother would undoubtedly show them around, announcing with pride and exaggeration that her son had already become a success, buying expensive gifts for her family with money of his own. It was a good feeling. He gave the notebook in his pocket an affectionate pat.

When the ship entered the harbor, the waterfront came into clear view. Behind it were tall red brick buildings, spires and belfries of distant white churches. Sea gulls were crying and hovering, dipping and soaring as if they were extending a rousing welcome to the newcomers.

The students all seemed to be moved by the sight. Boston, the oldest and most cultured city in America, the earliest trading partner of China, the birthplace of a hero who was worshiped in two Chinese temples; Boston, where mansions had been built by great Bostonian names whose families had made fortunes in the China trade. Fong Tai stared at the skyline and felt his throat tighten and his eyes moisten. He already felt a strong kinship with the city.

The waterfront was buzzing with activity—pushcarts loaded with vegetables, pedestrians dodging traffic, working women carrying heavy bags, fashionable ladies holding parasols, men in dark suits hurrying along with briefcases. . . .

*

When the ship docked, a swarm of dockhands came aboard. Father Barrington was an efficient manager. He hired three carriages and ordered the students to take the first two, then had all the luggage loaded into the third.

As the carriages drove off the dock, the Chinese soaked in the sights and sounds hungrily. Craning their necks and chattering noisily, they watched the distant land, the cobblestoned streets lined with frame houses, the passing horses and wagons. In the center of the city, they entered tree-shaded streets of handsome brick houses. Strolling on both sides were ladies in trailing gowns or in high-waisted, straight-skirted dresses; stylish men in long straight trousers and long black coats tipped their hats as they walked by the ladies. Some houses were ornamented with gilded eagles, their wings spread over the front doors. These were mansions with iron balconies and protruding porches with large windows. Some were framed with recessed arches.

Fong Tai, having read several books on Boston, knew they were climbing fashionable Beacon Hill. He even recognized one of the churches with red brick and white wooden pilasters on the façade, a clock tower with an eastern dome.

He admired these beautiful homes, built before the War of 1812. The brick sidewalks were wide and clean, lined with shady elms. He especially liked the three-storied houses with slate roofs and wished he could one day build one like them in China.

For a change, nobody talked in the carriage. Obviously, every student was savoring his own private thoughts and dreams. Father Barrington had said that the college had no available dormitory for the Chinese students, but had contracted with two boardinghouses to accommodate them within walking distance of their classes.

The carriage stopped in front of a large house with a long iron balcony. It had stone steps leading to an impressive double door inside an enclosed entrance porch. There were recessed arches framing the first-floor windows and pilasters on the façade above.

Father Barrington, who had been riding in the other carriage, appeared at the window. "Here we are, boys," he said. "Let me take you in and introduce you to the landlady. Bring your own luggage, please."

Fong and the four Manchus unloaded their luggage from the third carriage. Three students from the other carriage leaped out to help them. Ling took Fong's trunk and staggered toward the entrance in a show of warm friendship. Fong was sorry that Ling had been assigned to the other boardinghouse, but on the other hand, he was glad; he did not want to see him every day. For one thing, Ling would probably suggest that they cook Chinese food together every night. Ling was one of those who would faint in front of a rare American steak.

Father Barrington gave the doorbell three pulls. In a few moments the door opened. Framed in it was an ample lady in her fifties, a friendly smile on her rouged plump face. A whiff of strong perfume hit Fong Tai's face and he had to wriggle his nose to keep from sneezing.

"Mrs. Harrison?" Father Barrington asked, tipping his hat.

"Yes. You are Father Barrington, no doubt. I've been expecting you, Father. Ah, here are your charges, I suppose." She gave the students a sweeping glance.

Father Barrington introduced everyone, and they shook hands with Mrs. Harrison. "Mrs. Harrison is your landlady," Father Barrington said cheerfully. "You are in good hands, boys. Some of you have starved on the *Flying Cloud;* let Mrs. Harrison fatten you up a little." He turned to the landlady and added quickly, "Don't be shocked, Mrs. Harrison. You only have to feed five. These other three will go to another house. If you have any heavy chores, these boys will be happy to help—fetching water, carrying out garbage, anything."

"Thank you, Father," Mrs. Harrison said with a laugh. "I have someone to do the heavy work, but I won't mind some help in the kitchen. Help with the dishes, for instance. My daughters will dry them. Come, I'll show you your rooms, gentlemen."

They followed the landlady into the front parlor. The interior was old and dilapidated, smelling of mildew, but it was tidy and clean. Opposite it, on the left, was the dining room, with the kitchen in the rear. In between was a spacious hall, with a straight flight of stairs leading to the second floor. Mrs. Harrison was a frugal person; she and her two daughters slept in the servants' quarters in the back.

Fong was given the single small bedroom downstairs. The four Manchus shared two large rooms upstairs. He liked the arrangement. He had not met the daughters yet, but he had learned that Mrs. Harrison was a widow who depended on the two girls to run the boardinghouse.

After stowing their luggage, Fong and the Manchus walked the priest back to his carriage. Father Barrington had promised to come back the next day to take them to the college to register.

As soon as the carriage had disappeared around the corner, Chang said, "I don't like the landlady. She has already made us her dishwashers. How presumptuous!"

"We'd better let her know who we are," Wu suggested.

Fong Tai kept quiet. He did not mind washing dishes, especially if the landlady's daughters would help. He proposed to the Manchus that he would wash all the dishes for ten dollars a month.

"Ten dollars a month!" Chang cried in shock. "What greed! You ought to be ashamed of yourself!"

"Wash your own dishes then," Fong said, entering his little bedroom with a grin.

*

Father Barrington came the next morning promptly at eight o'clock. The students followed him to the college, a short distance away. None seemed very happy. Fong knew what was bothering them—the American food.

The night before, Mrs. Harrison had served them an enormous dinner, which the Manchus had eaten with a frown. Luckily, Mrs. Harrison was not sensitive, or perhaps not very observant. She praised her own cooking and urged everybody to eat. Fong ate the Boston baked beans and pie without much appetite. Everything smelled a bit fishy. Knowing that Bostonians ate a lot of cod, he tried to get used to the smell.

This morning Mrs. Harrison's big breakfast of potatoes and fried eggs sunny-side-up had again spoiled their appetites. Potatoes were poor men's food in China. The Manchus simply refused to touch them. Eggs were good, but they had to be properly fried or scrambled—well done, seasoned with soy sauce and green onions, or steamed with lime and Chinese sausages.

St. Mary's College was exactly as Barrington had described it, set in a neighborhood of red brick buildings and cobblestoned streets, near a church with a bell tower. On the tree-lined main street, the shops were neat, carrying mostly antique and modern objects of art, books and stationery. Obviously it was a genteel neighborhood, not rich but cultured, leisurely and relaxed. Strolling on the sidewalks were Caucasian ladies, mostly young and pretty, wearing colorful dresses and holding parasols. They stared at the Chinese curiously, as though they could not make out who they were. Fong Tai overheard one of them say to another, "Some peculiar-looking Indians."

According to Father Barrington, St. Mary's College was a progressive school, one of the earliest to admit both women and aliens.

Caucasian students, both men and women, were hurrying from building to building, carrying books and folders. A few were studying on park benches. They all seemed friendly. A few smiled at the new arrivals, waving and saying, "Hello." Fong noticed that two women pretended they were not curious. After they had walked past the Chinese, they turned and stared. Fong remembered that he had read somewhere that in 1849 two Chinese were displayed as novelties in a circus sideshow in New York City with a sign saying: COME AND SEE STRANGE HUMANS FROM FARAWAY LAND WHO EAT WITH BAMBOO STICKS AND TALK GIBBERISH.

"Why are you chuckling?" Ling asked, walking beside him.

"I wonder what these American girls are thinking of us," Fong said.

"I don't know what they are thinking," Ling said, "but they sure look peculiar!"

*

The classes started almost immediately, that afternoon. The classrooms were spacious, decorated with maps and pictures of dignified men in dark suits and stiff white collars.

The Chinese were assigned seats among the other freshman students. Fong Tai sat in the back row beside Yao, who looked self-conscious and uncomfortable. On Fong's other side sat a bespectacled American girl.

The courses were similar to those at the Foreign School in Peking, with emphasis on English, philosophy and political science. There were history and science courses as well, all taught by dull middle-aged professors whose lectures were hard to follow.

Thereafter Yao often dozed in his seat. Sometimes he even started to snore. Fong had to poke him to wake him up before he attracted the professor's attention. Every time this happened, the bespectacled girl glanced at Fong with a mischievous smile.

Father Barrington was seldom seen. Two weeks after classes started, he called a meeting and told them that he was returning to China and would come back each year to check on their progress.

After he had left, the students felt a little frightened and lonely; they often congregated to chat in Chinese. They also got together once a week for a game of mahjong and sometimes to have an evening of Chinese opera, singing and playing the two-stringed violin, the fu chin.

Fong Tai ate at his own boardinghouse regularly and helped with the dishes. The Manchus grudgingly paid him ten dollars a month for their share of the chore. Fong did it gladly, for he enjoyed chatting with Mrs. Harrison's two daughters, Mary and Jane, seventeen and fifteen. Both were plump and pretty, their growing breasts padded with lace under their blouses.

The girls seemed to enjoy his company. When they got to know him better, they became inquisitive and started asking him personal questions. Every evening, after dinner, Mary and Jane could hardly wait for their mother to leave the kitchen so they could talk to Fong freely. Many times Mrs. Harrison interrupted the girls' questions with a resounding "No!," saying that ladies simply did not ask gentlemen such things.

"Do you have a sister, Fong?" Mary asked as soon as her mother had left.

"No," he said politely. The girls were washing the dishes leisurely and he was drying them, then stacking them in a cupboard.

"I wish you had a sister. She could come and live with us."

"What does a Chinese woman look like, Fong?" Jane asked.

"She looks just like you—two eyes, two ears and one nose."

"In school our history teacher said that the Chinese think we are monsters with green eyes and that we're covered with yellow hair. We thought Chinese looked different, too—their eyes were little slits like cuts in a melon. Fong, your eyes don't look like little cuts in a melon."

"You don't look like a green-eyed monster covered with yellow hair, either."

"Jane," Mary said, "don't keep saying foolish things."

"As a matter of fact," Fong said with a laugh, "you're pretty."

"Really?" Mary asked anxiously. "Do you mean it?"

"Yes—you are very pretty."

"Do you think people would stare if you took me out walking?"

Fong thought for a moment. He would have liked to take Mary out, but he was sure that people *would* stare. But if he took both of them out, they might not. He changed the subject. "Your mother is a very good cook."

"In China do you eat with your hands?" Jane asked.

"No, we eat with chopsticks."

"What are chopsticks? Do you have some?"

"No, I didn't bring any."

"What do they look like?"

"Like drumsticks."

"Chicken or turkey?"

"Stop asking silly questions, Jane," Mary said. "In China you eat a lot of rice, don't you?"

"We eat a lot of bread, too. The Northerners eat nothing but bread."

"Really? Just like we do?" Jane stared at him, looking disappointed. "I thought you Chinese were so different, but you aren't."

7

Weeks and months passed slowly. After four months, the Chinese students began to feel restless and uneasy. But Fong Tai kept busy and active associating with the Americans. He even started going out with Cathy Dubois, from New Orleans, the bespectacled girl who sat beside him in the classroom.

Without her glasses, Cathy was pretty, with thick black hair, a sensuous mouth and sparkling dark eyes. Their mutual physical attraction made them glance at each other once in a while in the classroom. When they did, Fong Tai would look away quickly, embarrassed, but Cathy's eyes would linger. Sometimes when he looked at her again he found her smiling at him.

One afternoon after class he suggested they take a walk on the campus. She readily accepted, and even went a step further by offering to show him around Boston. After that they often strolled on the campus together or sat on the well-cultivated lawn or on the park bench in the rose garden reviewing lectures and comparing notes. Their association often invited disapproving stares, but most of the students were friendly, waving and smiling. Some pretended they had not noticed them; they passed by them looking straight ahead or busy in conversation.

Cathy volunteered to help Fong with his English. Sometimes they had coffee and cake at a Greek restaurant in the alley behind the campus. He had developed a taste for a kind of coffee called half and half (half coffee and half milk). Cake he always liked, Greek and American. He had become Mrs. Harrison's favorite boarder because he always asked for a second helping of her cake or pie.

Lately the Manchus had stopped eating at the boardinghouse altogether. They had organized their own kitchen in the back of a laundry owned by a Cantonese. They didn't much care for Cantonese food, but after their introduction to American food, they ate it with gratitude. The laundryman cooked, and washed all the dishes, and the students footed the bills. So far the arrangement had been satisfactory.

Chang had become more cocky, telling Fong Tai that he could go take his notebook to the devil. From now on there would be no more extortionate fees, either for dishwashing or for note-borrowing. Fong noticed that Chang's English had been improving. He had even learned a few swearwords. "Go to hell, Fong Tai!" he often said with a wide grin.

Fong was happy that the Manchus were now independent. He liked to avoid them, so that he could stop speaking Chinese altogether. In four years he hoped to be able to shed his Chinese accent. Right now he still spoke English with a few marbles in his mouth, as Cathy had told him.

Cathy was always happy to see him and eager to help. A week after they had met, she came to class one day with her thick black hair piled high on her head. The changed hairdo made her appear taller and more elegant. Fong Tai liked it. Her lightly dimpled face with the heavy eyebrows had had a habitually pensive look before; now the slightly gloomy look had disappeared. Before, when she talked to people, she had been in the habit of staring at the floor. Now she began to look people in the eye. When she talked to Fong Tai, she gazed at him boldly, with a flickering smile on her lips, her nostrils flaring. It intrigued Fong and made him wonder what went on in her mind.

Cathy had a part-time job in the library. Every evening, after closing, she put the books back on the shelves, wiped the two dozen reading tables and emptied the wastebaskets. She sometimes read the crumpled papers, discarded letters, doodlings and secret messages that had been tossed into them. She knew who was carrying on a love affair with whom.

Fong Tai found her knowledgeable, well read—and quite opinionated. Sometimes when she studied late in the library, he helped her dust and clean. Under her Victorian clothing, she appeared to have a voluptuous body, with a large bust, full hips and a small waist. She also had smooth skin, except for her dimpled face. He had read somewhere that dimples and heavy eyebrows were signs of strong sexual desire.

One beautiful Sunday, while sitting in the rose garden, Cathy suddenly said, "Let's have a picnic on the Common."

"Picnic? What is it?"

She looked at him incredulously. Instead of explaining, she took his hand and pulled him away from the garden bench. "Come on, I'll show you!"

She first took him to her boardinghouse. Like his own, it was an old mansion with iron balconies extending across the second story; it had an arched entranceway decorated with an eagle. Inside, in the entrance hall, there was a large glittering chandelier and a staircase that curved around an oval well. The house was decorated with luxurious but faded satin draperies.

"What a house!" Fong couldn't help marveling.

In the kitchen, Cathy put a long loaf of bread on the table and handed Fong a knife. "Please slice the bread. We are going to have Southern fried chicken and French bread for our picnic." She brought out chunks of fried chicken from a storage bin and packed them in a picnic basket along with a stone jug and napkins.

"Is this your house now?" Fong Tai asked as he carefully sliced the bread.

"How in the world could I own a house like this?" she said with a laugh. "Even though my grandfather was some kind of duke from Southern France, our house in New Orleans is a chicken coop compared to this. No, this is a boardinghouse."

"Where is everybody?"

"The landlady and her six students have gone to church. They're all Catholics, and Sunday services are as important as their weekly bath."

"Are you Catholic?"

"I am a Catholic by birth, a black sheep by choice. I have an excuse for not going to church with them. I have a bad knee injury and I can't kneel. A lie, of course. So the landlady makes me promise to pray at home. Voilà!"

She packed the bread into a basket and covered it with a towel. "Let's go!"

She took him to the Common, where people were strolling, napping, walking dogs and feeding ducks on the pond. "John Hancock milked everybody's cows here when his own went dry," she said. "He was almost arrested for stealing. That's why the Common is so famous."

As she spread the food on a blanket, a flock of birds flew over their heads, dropping a few souvenirs and barely missing the Southern fried chicken. With a little oath, she quickly repacked the food into the blanket.

"Let's go to the Public Garden across the road. Here we have too many bird feeders. In the Public Garden people are so poor that they steal from the birds instead of feeding them."

"Did John Hancock really steal somebody else's milk here?" Fong asked, helping with the packing. He was keenly interested in famous Americans.

"The historians are supposed to be accurate. They also have said that many people were hanged on the Common, including three women." She shuddered. Fong was interested, but Cathy was reluctant to elaborate. "They were Quakers and witches," she said, handing him an egg. "Here, have a hard-boiled egg to tide you over."

"Is it raw?"

"If it were raw, I wouldn't call it a *hard-boiled* egg, would I?" She laughed. "By the way, I chatted with one of your fellow Chinese the other day. He said that in China people are afraid of two things—evil spirits and raw eggs. With so many hangings on the Common, the place may have a lot of evil spirits!"

They walked across the cobblestoned road and entered another park, which was less formal and where the people were more casually dressed. They again selected a spot away from the crowd and spread the blanket. Fong Tai took a look at the blue clear sky and, sure enough, there was not a single bird in sight.

Cathy was in a talkative mood. "You know," she said, "a hundred years ago we could have been arrested in Boston. Do you know why?"

Eating a chicken leg, Fong shook his head.

"Because we have not gone to church. We've done a lot of things to violate the Sabbath."

When she finished her chicken, she poured a cup of coffee for him.

"I'm told that you and Chang are not the same. He is a Manchu and you are a minority."

"It's the other way around," Fong said. "I'm a Han and he is a minority. The Manchus conquered China. The Han Emperor of the Ming Dynasty hanged himself on the Hill of Longevity in Peking."

"You two are so different," Cathy said. "You Hans laugh. I haven't heard a Manchu laugh yet. By the way, are the Manchus good rulers?"

"We had two good Manchu Emperors, Kang Hsi and Chien Lung. Under their rule China produced the best porcelain."

"Have you Hans ever thought of rising up? I mean, overthrowing the Manchu Dynasty?"

"Aiyoo!" Fong said, grimacing facetiously. He felt his neck with a hand.

"What's the matter?"

"I could be hanged for answering your question."

"You mean the Manchus are cruel, like the rulers we had in Boston two hundred years ago?"

"How cruel were the Boston rulers?"

"Well, just to give you an example: they disliked the Quakers. If a Quaker came to town, he was punished by public flogging. If he came again, his ears were cut off and his tongue bored with a hot iron. If he came a third time, he was hanged."

"The Manchus invented a punishment called *a thousand cuts*. It is for you to judge who was more lenient."

"Do you have trials in China?"

"Yes. We have a judge and a bottom-beater. The bottom-beater beats a suspect's bare bottom until he or she confesses. Then the judge hammers his desk with a piece of wood called a *hall-shocking wood* and calls out the sentence."

"That's very lenient," she said with a laugh. "At least more so than the judicial system in Boston two hundred years ago. One time we caught a woman who grabbed a bonnet from another woman on the street; she was hanged as a highway robber without the courtesy of a trial—not even the services of a bottom-beater." Both laughed. "Besides Quakers and highway robbers," she went on, "we also hanged many witches. Do you have witches in China?"

Fong told her that every doctor in China would probably be regarded as a witch in America, for no Chinese doctor had a diploma and all of them had secret formulas that had been handed down from their ancestors.

"Margaret Jones, the witch hanged on the Common," Cathy said, "had a secret formula—a mixture of aniseed, vegetable oil and a touch of 'Jersey Lightning,' which was a popular liquor in those days."

"We Chinese eat aniseed all the time," Fong informed her. "We cook beef gristle with it. Delicious. Add some wine—we'll have American witch medicine."

Both laughed. Cathy was enjoying the conversation so much that her voice had become high-pitched and her laughter loud and frequent. She suggested that Fong cook some beef gristle with aniseed for her and she would prepare some famous Boston clam chowder for him in return.

*

Thereafter Fong and Cathy visited the Common and the Public Garden often, boating on the frog pond, picnicking on the grass, joking and discussing serious subjects. Fong especially enjoyed the weeping willows and the noble trees, the giant poplars that flourished at the pond's edge. Sometimes they sat beside the pond for hours, watching ducks preen their plumage and other birds take to the sky. He recognized a Chinese ginkgo tree with its fanlike leaves and pointed it out to Cathy. The tree seemed to him a long-lost friend, and he felt a special kinship with it.

By going out with Cathy Dubois, he learned a great deal about her and America. He cooked beef gristle with aniseed for her, and she made Boston baked beans for him. While the food simmered over a small fire for hours, their conversation would move from subject to subject. He found her thinking a bit too radical and tried to avoid serious arguments.

She was fighting for women's rights and had memorized a number of satirical poems written by women who considered themselves second-class citizens.

She said that in Boston, if a woman was denied her rights, she did not whine or put her neck out and say, "Chop it off!" She fought.

*

Cathy could be dead serious when she discussed industrialization and women's rights. Her voice became charged with indignation and her eyes flashed angrily. This startled Fong a little, but he could not help admiring the woman. If she had been born in China, she would have been a perfect candidate for the thousand-cuts punishment.

One fine Sunday morning, she seemed electric with energy. After an hour's discussion of social problems, she stood up, faced a crowd in the Public Garden and began to talk like a fervent evangelist preaching the Gospel. "Brethren," she shouted, "new ideas must triumph, progress must march on! I assure you! Electric lights will shine on our asphalt boulevards, Americans' way of life will change, old ideas will disappear! Arise, you thinkers! Arise and challenge the old ways! Be brave enough to question the Holy Bible. Man controls his own destiny, not God! Charles Darwin is the modern hero! The survival of the fittest is the new Gospel."

A few onlookers walked away in disgust. Some waved their fists and shouted insults at her. One man spat at her feet and called her a witch. He said she ought to be hanged.

8

As the term progressed, Fong Tai and Cathy Dubois went out more and more often. They discovered that Boston had a number of Chinese plants besides magnolias and ginkgo trees. There were cherry trees, azaleas and rhododendrons blooming in private gardens. Fong had also discovered that there were many other Chinese-American links in culture and trade. A great many stores sold Chinese merchandise—ivory-handled parasols and canes, porcelain, silk, black-lacquered ware, cashmere wool shawls and stoles, all made in China according to American specifications and taste. They reminded Fong of the Mandarin gown and jacket which his mother had given him. He immediately gave them to Cathy as souvenirs.

One day Cathy appeared at the college wearing the Mandarin gown and jacket and carrying books about China. She sat beside Fong and said unabashedly, "Don't look so worried—I'm not going to ask you to teach me Chinese!" She attracted a great deal of attention. The Manchus kept casting glances at her and giggling. Fong was uncomfortable, but Cathy acted as though nothing had happened.

After that the Manchus whispered constantly among themselves. Fong suspected that some kind of rumor was going around. He decided to ignore it. "Let them gossip," he thought. Let them think that he and Cathy had started an illicit relationship; he didn't care.

As he drifted further away from his fellow Chinese, he saw Cathy even more frequently. Christmas was approaching; most of the students were leaving Boston for the holiday. Cathy extended Fong an invitation to spend Christmas Eve at her boardinghouse. The landlady was giving a party and had asked the boarders to invite their friends for an evening of food, wine and singing. Cathy had promised to contribute a Chinese dessert, *eight treasured rice,* and asked Fong to help her decorate it.

By then the frog pond on the Common was frozen and the streets were covered with snow, which men shoveled every morning to clear their doorways. Fong enjoyed walking in the ankle-deep powder on his way to school, listening to the rhythmic squeaking of his knee-high boots.

A large pine tree was set up in the rose garden in front of the administration building, decorated with snow. His landlady, Mrs. Harrison, was disappointed that he could not attend her annual Christmas party. The Manchus were invited, but they would come only for her pumpkin dessert, since they had planned their own Christmas dinner at the Chinese laundry. Yao told Fong Tai that the turkeys were so enormous that the Manchus didn't have the stomach to face them. Besides, they had received delicacies from home: birds' nests, sharks' fins, dried bears' paws and sea slugs.

Finally school was out and gifts were exchanged. Under Mrs. Harrison's Christmas tree, colorful packages were piling up. Fong found three of them bearing his name—one from Mrs. Harrison and one each from her daughters. He had purchased some Chinese trinkets from one of the stores that carried Chinese merchandise. He wrapped them in fine rice paper. Since he did not know any standard Christmas greetings in Chinese, he wrote the usual New Year greeting on them: *Hope you make a lot of money*.

On Christmas Eve, Fong found himself the only Chinese at the party Cathy had invited him to; the others were Mrs. Cross's boarders and their friends. It was Fong Tai's first turkey dinner. To his surprise, it tasted like chicken. The American ham was not as tasty as Chinese ham, but it was sweet and tender. The side dishes were copious, and all had difficult names. Since it was a holiday, he decided not to tax his brains by learning these tongue-twisters. However, he reminded himself to observe all the American customs. He valiantly drank eggnog laced with brandy, even knowing that it had raw eggs in it.

When Mrs. Cross played Christmas carols on her grand piano, he joined in the singing with gusto. He had never learned any of the songs, but he found them easy to follow and soon his tenor voice was heard above the others, with an occasional off-key note. But the Christmas spirit was high and nobody seemed to mind.

During the evening somebody hung a branch over a door. When a woman passed under it, a man would grab her and kiss her on the mouth. Fong realized it was mistletoe. When Cathy Dubois passed under it, he wondered if he should kiss her. As he hesitated, somebody else stepped ahead of him and gave her a lingering kiss. Quite a few men also got kissed by the women while passing under it. He again wondered if he should try to see if any woman would kiss him. He hesitated. What if nobody wanted to? It would be quite embarrassing. After some debate he decided to play safe and wait for Cathy to step under it again.

He watched the door, his heart pounding. Luckily, everybody was chatting and nobody noticed his nervousness. When Cathy rose from a sofa where she had been engaged in deep conversation with another woman, Fong leaped up. As soon as she reached the door, he grabbed her and planted a kiss on her lips.

To his surprise she held him and kissed him back, gently and lingeringly. He felt the tip of her tongue entering his mouth. He had never experienced anything like it before—it overwhelmed him. He felt dizzy, floating, with a shooting pleasure throughout his body.

It was not until she let him go that he felt embarrassed. His face hot and his heart pounding, he quickly returned to his own seat. With a smile, Cathy picked up her drink and returned to the sofa to resume her conversation with the other woman.

That night he slept restlessly. He could not get rid of the memory of that lengthy kiss. It had excited and aroused him, making him hungry for more.

Cathy left town to visit a relative the next day, and he did not see her again until school resumed a week later. In the classroom he could hardly concentrate, glancing at her frequently. He began to stammer when he talked and found himself absentminded, mislaying fountain pens and books. It was like a fever he had caught—a fever with annoying symptoms such as anxiety, nervousness and distraction.

They met at the library in the evening. At closing, he leaped up to help her tidy up and put the books away. Conversation no longer came easily. He found his mind occupied with only one thing—more kisses.

Cathy was also unusually quiet and did her chores leisurely with a faint smile on her lips. His heart thumping and his hands wet, Fong wondered if he should simply walk up to her and kiss her or wait for the right moment and ask for her permission first. He wished he knew the right procedure.

At closing, Cathy quickly dumped the contents of the wastebaskets into the trash can in the back room. When she was finished, she locked the doors, fished out a package of peanuts from her bag and invited him to share it at a long reading table.

"Now you can relax," she said with that flicker of a smile, making herself comfortable in her chair. "Did you enjoy the Christmas party?"

"Yes, very much," Fong stammered, popping a few peanuts into his mouth and chewing them nervously.

"What was your most enjoyable moment?" she inquired, her eyes lingering on his face, her voice low and husky.

Fong found himself no longer embarrassed, but breathless. "The moment we were under the mistletoe," he said.

"I thought you would never say that." Cathy reached out and held his head with both hands, then kissed him hard on the mouth, making little throaty sounds.

Without stopping the kiss, she moved over to sit on his lap, wrapped her arms around him and this time kissed him passionately, her tongue darting and searching, her hands clutching him tightly.

Suddenly she stopped. She moved back to her own chair and took a deep breath, her face flushed. "Take your clothes off."

Hands shaking, he obeyed impatiently. She started unbuttoning her own blouse. Both naked, they got up on the reading table.

As they lay next to each other, she kissed his ear and neck. "You didn't attract me at first, you know," she whispered. "You were only a curiosity."

"I know." He swallowed, enjoying the little kisses and the warmth of her body.

"But when I found the connection of our minds, the juice began to flow."

"Juice?"

"Yes." She climbed on him, riding him astride, rubbing herself against him. She responded to the entry with a low moan, and he began to synchronize his movements with her thrusts. Automatically, she moved her body up and down, her hands clutching his sides, her head thrown back, her breath short and her humming louder as she increased her rhythm. Suddenly she uttered a cry as if of agony and he too felt a shuddering pleasure that shook his entire body.

After that night they met twice a week in the library. They made love on the same table after closing. Cathy suggested a number of variations, saying that they were French and that the French were the best lovers in the world. He followed her lead, remembering what Father Barrington had said: "In Rome, do as the Romans do. Never stop learning."

*

One night in his boardinghouse Fong Tai found Professor Hu waiting for him. The professor, a friend of Cathy's and a recent acquaintance, was a Chinese expatriate who taught history at Harvard. The landlady's daughters were admiring a Chinese coin which the professor was showing them.

"What a pleasant surprise!" Fong said, greeting the professor.

"Fong," Mary said, "in one hour we have learned more about China than we learned from you in six months."

"They have just completed my course in Chinese history," Professor Hu said with a laugh. He was a small man and middle-aged, but leonine. "Now we have started on Chinese economics and finance, studying the beauty of Chinese coins."

"How beautiful!" Mary said excitedly, holding the coin gingerly and lovingly. "It would make a wonderful pendant, don't you think, professor?"

"Very creative thinking," Professor Hu said. He folded Mary's fingers over the coin and gave her fist a pat. "Allow me to present the first Chinese coin pendant." He fished out another coin and gave it to Jane, who shrieked with delight and hurried to a wall mirror to see how it looked on her.

After the girls were gone, Hu settled down comfortably in Fong Tai's little room and revealed the purpose of his visit. "Do you know what the curse of modern China is?" he began.

Fong thought for a moment. "As one Han to another," he said, "I should say the Empress Dowager."

Professor Hu cast a quick glance around. "Good Lord!" he said in English. "I hope no other Chinese heard you."

"We have four Manchus here. But they are never home."

The professor heaved a long sigh of relief. "Let me tell you the curse. It's the eight-legged essay."

Fong had learned about the eight-legged essay in school. It was the literary form prescribed in the system of civil-service examinations under China's feudal dynasties. Anyone who mastered it could pass the Imperial examination and become a high government official. "The eight-legged essay is like the Western limerick," the professor said. "It is a game of words. Just imagine the American Cabinet members selected from those who can write the best limericks. What kind of America would that be? And yet for generations China has been ruled by the idiots who could write the best essays!"

"What can we do?" Fong asked, agreeing with him.

"We must get rid of it!",

"How?"

"You have heard of Kang Yu-wei, the reform leader?"

"Yes."

"Here is a letter from him. I just received it." The professor fished a letter out of his pocket and read: " 'For fifty years China has been invaded by foreign powers, along with Vietnam, Burma and Sikkim. Britain has launched a new aggression to take China's Tibet. Russia is eyeing our territory north of the Heiling River. Japan, too, is increasing pressure on Northeast China. All the past humiliations have been brought about by gross misrule by the country's feudal bureaucrats, whose only expertise is to write eight-legged essays. Their main occupation is to practice word games; they never tire of reading their own meaningless compositions, humming and shaking their heads and wagging their pigtails in self-admiration. It is imperative that we, progressive citizens of a bereaved nation, petition the Emperor that these civil-service examinations for government officials be abolished immediately. Any support from overseas Chinese will be deeply appreciated.' "

When he finished reading the letter, Professor Hu, looking grave and sad, stared at Fong Tai, waiting for Fong's response.

Fong knew that Kang Yu-wei had been working on China's reform programs with the young Emperor's approval, but behind the back of Tsu Hsi, the powerful Empress Dowager. He also knew that one of the program's priorities was to get rid of eight-legged essays and the civil-service examinations. This would enhance those who had studied modern subjects.

"What do you want me to do, professor?"

"Talk to your fellow students. Write to Kang Yu-wei and support his effort. When he petitions the Emperor, he will bring all the letters of support from the four corners of the world."

Fong Tai thought of his mentor.

"Wouldn't it be better if Li Hung-chang supported him?"

"Li Hung-chang is a clever man. He will not stick his neck out while the opposition swords are poised to fall."

"What opposition swords?"

"The feudal bureaucrats' swords. They will fight for their survival."

Fong thought for a moment. "You know the Manchus will not write such a letter," he said with a bitter smile. "They are from the feudal class."

"Then tell them their families are facing serious and imminent danger. Secret societies are rising everywhere, trying to overthrow the Great Ching Dynasty. The White Lotus, Yellow Turbans, Red Turbans will break out again unless there is a drastic change in government policy."

Fong was uneasy. He felt helpless, knowing that the Manchus would consider it outrageous for an unknown scholar like Kang Yu-wei to offer advice to the throne. "I'll do what I can. Perhaps we, the Hans, can add our names to your letter."

*

Three months later lightning struck. Fong Tai received a terse letter from the Foreign School ordering him to return to Peking immediately. He still had more than three years to go before graduating from St. Mary's.

For several days he couldn't sleep; he lost his appetite and felt he was hovering on the edge of a nervous breakdown. But he kept the bad news secret. It was not until Ling asked, "What is the matter? Why do you look as if you just returned from the Gobi Desert?" Fong Tai, knowing that he could not keep his secret for long, told Ling what had happened.

"Who introduced you to that crazy professor?" Ling asked sympathetically. "He has brought you nothing but disaster. Didn't I tell you to cut all your ties with Kang and his crazy ideas? You should have spent all your time visiting the American bordello with me."

"It's too late to tell me how to save the boat," Fong protested. "It has already sunk." They were talking in Fong's room. While Fong agonized on his bed, Ling rocked in an antique rocking chair, looking as though the bordello had changed him into a man of the world, sophisticated and wise. Fong couldn't bear to look at him. Ling was no longer the old Ling. Instead of always asking for advice, he was now giving it.

"Don't worry too much, Fong," Ling said. "You are Li Hung-chang's favorite boy. If your head is supposed to be cut off for what you have done, he will save it. Three or four years in jail is all you are going to get, I imagine. If there is anything I can do . . ."

"All right, Ling. You can do something. You can stop talking about what is going to happen to me, please!"

"Fine, fine," Ling exclaimed, rising to his feet and hitching up his trousers manfully. "You have my sympathy, Fong. I'll pray for you."

To Fong's surprise, all the students expressed their sympathy. They cooked a dinner for him as a farewell gesture and they ate it quietly in the back of the Cantonese laundry. Even the Manchus were quiet and gloomy, as though this were their last supper together. Fong was touched by the sympathy of his fellow Chinese. But they made him feel that he was being sent back to die and that his head would dangle over the Chien Men Gate with the Red Turbans.

That night, Fong Tai lay on his bed, trying to block out his problems and bitterness, replacing them with fond memories of Cathy, thinking of her kisses, her lovemaking, her body, her beliefs; but his depression was so overwhelming that he only saw her shrugging despairingly with an apologetic grin.

Tossing, unable to sleep, he thought of disappearing into America. He wondered what would happen if he lost himself in a big city. Would the American government help China hunt him down as a traitor? The thought depressed him even more. He thought of his mother, his wife, Third Uncle, even Old Liu. He had seldom thought of them since his arrival in Boston, but now he missed them all. He thought of Third Uncle's advice, "Do your best, but leave the result to Heaven."

The door opened and Ling came in quietly. Fong quickly turned to the wall. "Go away," he said. "I don't want to see you. I don't want to see anybody. Leave me alone!"

"Yao, you tell him," he heard Ling's unhappy voice say. "Tell him."

There was a moment of silence, then Fong heard Yao say after a long heavy sigh, "Fong Tai, cheer up. You are not going to die."

Fong Tai turned in his bed to face his visitors. "What are you talking about?"

"Fong Tai," Yao said, "Chang wants me to tell you that he is sorry for what he has done and asks your forgiveness."

"What has he done?"

"He reported to the Foreign School that you had damaged everybody's reputation by carrying on an illicit romance with a foreign woman in a foreign country. That's why you are being called back."

"Nothing to worry about, Tai," Ling's high-pitched voice piped up. "They will never cut a man's head off because he has slept with a foreign woman, you know that. A year or two in jail to cool you off may do you some good."

9

Peking was gray and cold, a typical autumn day, when Fong Tai arrived by train from Shanghai. He had been away more than a year, including travel time. At twenty-one, he regarded himself as wiser and hardened, ready to face the world with a new outlook.

While he was riding home from the train station in a horse carriage provided by the Foreign School, he felt a vague fear. He was not disappointed that he had been met only by the carriage driver. It could have been worse. With the Manchus accusing him of damaging the country's reputation, a harsh punishment was possible. But since no soldiers had grabbed him by his pigtail at the station, he decided not to think about it.

The memory of Cathy Dubois soothed him. Before his departure, they had spent a night in the library. He had not told her she was the real reason for his recall, only saying that there was a death in the family; in a way it was true, for his grandmother had died not too long ago.

They had spent the night talking and making love on their table. She had almost played the man's part, kissing him aggressively, first his mouth and then his body, humming and groaning, reluctant to stop. She said she was hungry, wanting to make up for all the months when he would be away. . . . Before parting, they promised to write to each other. He hoped he could invite her to China someday. While he thought of Cathy, he also remembered his wife. Suddenly his heart sank. Seeing her again was one of the things he dreaded most.

He found the house a bit older and grayer, the courtyard dirtier, littered as usual with dead date leaves. Old Liu was happy to see him; he chatted away about things of little interest. Fong Tai was not in a talkative mood. To discourage the old servant, he said little and grunted a lot.

Nothing had materially changed, except that his grandmother was gone. Carrying his luggage, Old Liu asked him whether to put it in his old room or the young Madame Fong's room.

"My old room," Fong said quickly.

His mother and his wife were waiting for him in the middle hall, sipping tea and smoking water pipes. A maid was poking some burning wood into a potbellied stove, over which a kettle was humming. The room was warm, smelling of incense. On the altar, below the ancestral tablets, two red candles and a few sticks of incense had been lit. There were a number of bowls of offering food—the rice, red-cooked pork and a whole chicken were still steaming. He bowed to his mother and greeted her uneasily, waiting for a scolding.

"My son, my son," Madame Fong said softly, her eyes moist. "You look well. I am happy that you have returned."

"So am I, Mother."

"Tai," his wife said with a smile, "welcome home." She looked different, a little heavier and healthier, with natural good color in her cheeks. When he bowed to her, she rose and returned the bow with her hands clasped together.

For a moment he did not know what to say. Just as he was searching for appropriate words, his mother ordered him to thank the ancestors for his safe return.

He had kowtowed to his ancestors' tablets before, but now he felt silly, wondering if the spirits of his ancestors were really there. If they were, he suspected they were not pleased. Or were they too busy eating the red-cooked pork to pay any attention to him? The fragrance of this dish made him hungry for home-cooked food again.

When Fong Tai finished paying obeisance to his ancestors, his mother stepped forward and prostrated herself on the cushion. With her forehead touching the floor, she murmured a prayer. He was glad her voice was so low that he did not hear it, for it always embarrassed him to hear what his mother had to say to people, dead or alive. Even the name she had given him still embarrassed him. In Boston, Cathy had asked him what his name meant. He had had a hard time translating it. Finally he had settled for "Fong the Big Duke." It had given Cathy a good laugh.

To his surprise nobody at home asked about his misbehavior in America. In a way it was a relief, but it was like a little bone sticking in his throat. Knowing that Shao Mei would mention it when they were alone at night, he wondered if he should tell the truth without going into detail. Since he would have to face the school authorities anyway, he might as well prepare his statement—or confession. He decided that it should be simple and straightforward, spoken in a firm voice. He would try it out in front of his wife, a statement in which he would not admit guilt or plead innocence. He would remain calm. God forbid he should stammer.

His mother had invited a few close relatives to dinner that night. Third Uncle was the first to arrive. He looked a little older, but his voice was still cheerful and warm. After the greetings, he fell silent. When the other relatives arrived, they all exchanged small talk. Some of them asked about the weather in America. This indifference to his life in America bothered him; a few even avoided looking at him.

Third Uncle, sitting opposite him, finally gave him a secretive wink. It was a great relief. His uncle seemed to say everything with that roguish wink: "Don't worry about it. If I were your age, I would have done the same!"

During dinner the relatives talked mostly about mahjong. As soon as they put down their chopsticks, they quickly disappeared into the next room. Obviously, his wife had also become a mahjong addict. She followed them and presently the tiles began to clatter loudly on the mahogany gaming table.

He slept in his wife's room that night. When she returned from the mahjong game, she was quiet. He felt a great urge to scream, "All right, out with it! Ask me what happened!" But, thinking of Third Uncle's philosophy, "Leave everything to Heaven," he was able to control himself.

For the first time he touched his wife and disrobed her. Fantasizing about Cathy Dubois, he performed his conjugal duty. To his surprise, the experience was more pleasant than he had expected. His wife lay on her back, passive and silent, like a hen trying to lay an egg. He suspected that it was exactly what she had in mind: sex was only a necessity prior to egg-laying.

"What is America like?" she asked when he was about to turn away and sleep.

"Very good country. I like it." He tried to fake a yawn but stopped. Was he so mean that he wouldn't even bother to answer a simple question? Feeling guilty, Fong Tai turned back to her and smiled. "What do you want to know about? The country or the people?"

"Everything. What do Americans look like?"

"They look like the Americans in this country."

"I never saw an American in this country. Is the world really round like a ball?"

He wondered who had told her that—a sheltered woman who had never seen a foreigner.

"Yes."

"Where is America on this big ball?"

"The other side of the ball."

"Really? When you were in America, did you feel you were walking upside down?"

Fong Tai did not know how to answer the question. He had never thought about why he hadn't felt as though he were walking upside down, or why he did not fall off.

"Go to sleep," he said. He quickly blew out the red candle beside the bed and pulled the silk quilt over his head.

The next morning the carriage appeared again. But instead of taking him to the Foreign School, it took him to Li Hung-chang's yamen in the Eastern City. The palatial building, with green glazed tile roofs, carved eaves and red-lacquered double doors, was magnificent in the bright sunlight. The guards saluted him; Fong tipped his bowler hat.

Li Hung-chang always treated his protégé like a son, but somehow a vague fear persisted in Fong as he was ushered to Li's office by one of the door guards. Sitting in a thickly cushioned chair and reading a Chinese book, Li lifted his eyes with a slight frown. Fong Tai bowed deeply.

"How are you, Your Excellency?"

"Sit down," Li said in his soft, high-pitched voice, waving a hand. He looked a little frail, but his eyes were still bright, and at seventy-one he still did not wear glasses.

"Do you remember Mr. Anson Burlingame?" he asked.

Fong Tai paused. He vaguely remembered that he had read about Burlingame in one of the Foreign School's newsletters. He wondered why Li Hung-chang was asking him about this foreigner who had held a peculiar position in the Great Ching Dynasty with a title he never learned how to pronounce correctly.

"Yes, Your Excellency. I remember him."

"Mr. Burlingame was a very good High Minister Plenipotentiary and one of the best friends of China. We lost a great man when he died. That was eleven years ago. Now I have recommended Father Barrington to occupy the same position. What do you think?"

"It will be a loss to the Foreign School, sir, but a gain for China's foreign policy."

Li Hung-chang stared at him for a moment, his face expressionless. "Good. He likes you. Perhaps you can serve as his assistant. Do you think you are qualified?"

Fong was dumbfounded for a moment. Could this really be happening or was he dreaming?"

"Are you qualified or not?"

"It is not for me to say, sir," Fong said, finally finding his voice. He was glad that he was not stammering.

"I shall see. But Father Barrington seems to like you. Go see him at his church. By the way, how are the other students doing in America?"

"They study hard and behave well, sir." The extraordinary news had finally sunk in. Surprises usually knocked people down, but this was a surprise that was about to lift him off the ground. "They study hard and behave well, sir," he said again, feeling happiness and goodwill surging in him. "They are a credit to the Chinese."

"Are you sure?" Li asked, his face still expressionless.

"Just one fault. They keep to themselves too much, depriving themselves of the opportunity to learn from Americans."

Li put his fingertips together and watched him with a faint smile, as if amused. "Do you mean to say that they should follow your example, consorting with a foreign woman?"

Fong Tai's heart leaped. He knew that the hatchet was about to fall. He had heard many people call Li a smiling tiger. Was that faint smile an omen? He knew he must answer him quickly and properly. "No, Your

Excellency. But consorting with a foreign woman makes learning a little easier and faster."

Li's smile broadened. The smile seemed almost as dangerous as a tiger's growl. Fong waited for the claws to slash and teeth to sink in.

"So you admit your unsavory behavior in America."

"I am not trying to justify my behavior, sir," he said, determined not to be intimidated. "But in one year I learned more about America than I would otherwise have learned in four."

He was surprised that his voice was firm and forceful. He stared into Li's sharp eyes, waiting for the worst.

Li's smile disappeared. He opened a drawer, took out a piece of paper and handed it to Fong. "I want you to be Father Barrington's assistant. This is your official appointment. Serve him well."

✳

When Fong Tai left Li Hung-chang's office, he went directly to see Father Barrington at his Catholic church in the Western City.

The little white church with the spire and stained glass windows was neatly kept. The well-cultivated lawn—perhaps the only lawn in Peking— was protected by a white picket fence. A gardener was hand-sprinkling the grass from a bucket. He put down the bucket and bowed to Fong, probably a habit formed through years of serving a foreigner. Fong had noticed that bowing had made many Chinese stooped. It was easy to tell a man's station in life by simply looking at the degree of his stoopedness. The more stooped he was, the lower his status. He wished that one day someone would have the nerve to petition the Emperor to outlaw bowing in China—like Kang Yu-wei's movement to eliminate the eight-legged essay.

Father Barrington was working in his small office at the back of the church. He was packing his papers and books into a red-lacquered trunk, discarding certain documents and crumpling them into paper balls. He was doing the job with amazing speed, filing away the papers he wanted to save and tossing the paper balls into an enormous wastebasket.

Fong coughed to attract his attention. Barrington looked up and broke into a broad smile as he saw Fong standing in the doorway. "Come in, come in," he said, extending a hand and inviting him to sit down on one of the chairs in front of his desk.

Fong handed him the appointment paper from Li Hung-chang. "Thank you for this, sir," he said politely. "I did not expect such a great honor."

"Not at all," Barrington said. "I had made up my mind quite a while ago, ever since His Excellency told to me about the new position. Your English seems to be better than the others', you don't drink or smoke or play mahjong, and you can walk among foreigners as an equal. You may have vices, but those other qualities I have just mentioned will serve both of us well for the moment. My new job is more or less in an advisory capacity. I need an assistant who will not come to work in the morning with bloodshot eyes from all-night mahjong playing. So I recommended you. Having observed you for a while, I think you will do. Can you report to work tomorrow?"

"I certainly can, sir."

"Very good. I am taking over the late Mr. Burlingame's position. You can see that I am packing. The church has already assigned somebody to move in here. From now on my life will be totally involved with foreign affairs. So will yours. You will do a lot of reading and provide me with all the necessary information on events and movements that might affect China's foreign policy. I demand accuracy. I don't care about your spelling or grammar, but the messages you hand me must be accurate. This is rule number one."

"Yes, sir."

"That's all."

"What is rule number two, sir?"

"There is no rule number two," Barrington said with a smile. "I might have some advice about consorting with ladies, but since you are now living at home, that will be your wife's territory. She is probably a better watchdog than I am." He rose to his feet and extended a hand. "All right, Tai, see you tomorrow morning."

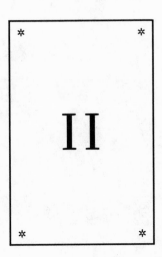

II

10

Fong Tai often brooded and fidgeted, lamenting the fate of both the Great Ching Dynasty and himself. His mother was often irritated by his indifference to family matters and his absentmindedness.

By the early 1890s Li Hung-chang was getting old and rusty, forgetting important dates and events. High Minister Barrington had been touring America and Europe, campaigning for the cause of China. He had not been very successful. Now Barrington was back. He was growing old and had lost much of his energy. Even his booming voice sounded weak and hoarse because of his heart condition and emphysema. The silkworms kept nibbling away; China, the mulberry leaf, was getting steadily smaller during those years Fong Tai was in Barrington's employment.

Fong followed the news of the rebel bands that were coming out into the open all over China. The Long Hairs, the Red Lance Society, the Boxers and other secret societies had begun to attack regular armies and government yamens. Some were patriots, many were bandits and oppositionists; all were anxious to overthrow the rotten Ching Dynasty. They posted antiforeign and antigovernment slogans on walls, recruited new members and robbed villagers to finance their activities.

Attracted by the reform movement, Fong had tried to contact Kang Yu-wei, whom Professor Hu had told him about in Boston. Kang seemed to head a well-organized and powerful group. The Foreign School's New Movement had become a dog without bite compared to Kang's organization, which had become a genuine force among the intellectuals.

Fong heard a number of rumors through the grapevine. One was that the Emperor had approved all of Kang Yu-wei's reform programs. But few believed it, because inside the Forbidden City the Empress Dowager, Tsu Hsi, still had iron control of the government. Many even suspected that the Chief Eunuch, Li Lien-ying, had been manipulating Tsu Hsi for power, sneaking actors into the palace for her pleasure. No reform could coexist with that.

Fong felt sorry for Emperor Kwang Shu. His Majesty had had a very unfortunate life. He had been placed on the throne at the age of five; at sixteen he had been forced to marry a woman he had never loved; at eighteen he had been obliged to govern a declining dynasty riddled with problems, and was himself governed by a cruel aunt, the Empress Dowager. Now that His Majesty had determined to have his own way, Fong's heart went out to him.

To get rid of his frustrations, Fong began to practice martial arts every morning, kicking and yelling in the courtyard. As a boy, he had learned Twelve Ways of Kicking, the Monkey Fist and the Fighting Arts of Shao Ling from a Peking master who could pierce a two-inch-thick wooden board with his fingers. Now in his early thirties, Fong discovered that he was more agile than ever, his body and soul fired up by suppressed anger and restlessness.

One murky morning while he was taking a walk outside his house, he came upon a Han boy being chased by several Manchu teenagers. They caught him by his pigtail, threw him down and urinated on him one by one, laughing and shouting insults. Fong rushed up to the Manchu who was holding the Han boy and gave him a vicious kick in the behind, sending him tumbling. Then he shielded the Han boy with his body and dared anyone to come near them. The Manchus thought better of the situation and decided to abandon their entertainment. Laughing and screaming insults, they backed away and disappeared around a corner.

"You need a change of clothes, I suppose," Fong said to the Han boy. "What is your name?"

"Tang San, sir," the boy said, giving him a low bow. "Thank you, sir."

"Don't mention it." He gestured toward the house. "Come in and wash up."

In his wet trousers, Tang San waddled behind Fong into the courtyard. Fong called Old Liu, who was tending the roses in a flower bed.

"Let him wash up and give him a change of clothes. Burn his trousers; they are soaked with Manchu urine."

Old Liu stopped about ten feet away from Tang San and scowled. "Boy, come with me," he said. Tang San gave Fong another bow and waddled through a side door with Old Liu, leaving behind him only the unpleasant smell.

Early next morning Old Liu announced to Fong Tai that the Han boy would like to see him. Fong hesitated for a moment. He was in the middle of reading several books written by Kang Yu-wei, a Han who had probably suffered the same fate as Tang San. "All right, send him in."

Tang San came in carrying a bamboo basket covered with a piece of old newspaper. He bowed low, then offered the basket to Fong with both his hands and thanked him for rescuing him from his tormentors. Fong accepted the gift and half a dozen small eggs in the basket. "Thank you, Tang San. You shouldn't have brought me anything."

"Please look under the eggs."

Under the eggs was a pair of trousers, washed and ironed. Fong asked the boy to sit down.

"My family is here to thank you personally, sir."

The family—parents, sisters and brothers, six in all, shabbily dressed—trooped into the room. The father, a pale fat man wearing a frayed silk gown, stepped up and bowed. "Master," he announced in a cracked voice, "yesterday you protected my dog-son from harm. We are grateful. But more harm has befallen us because of it. Our family has been persecuted and driven out of our humble house. Homeless and without food, we have no recourse but to come to you for help."

The man made it sound as though Fong had been responsible for their misfortune. Fong wondered why the man was so fat; he couldn't possibly be starving. He had a good mind to give him a kick on his fat behind and send him packing. Controlling his anger, he thought about finding the man a job, but as he watched the man's shifty eyes, he changed his mind. He dug out a handful of silver dollars from his pocket. "Take this money and move away," he said, "but send your son here tomorrow."

The father counted the money, making throaty noises as if he were making love. He chuckled and seemed satisfied.

After the whole brood had left, Fong went to the courtyard and hit the date tree hard with his fist, drawing blood on his knuckles. He hated himself for always meddling in other people's misfortunes. His own fate was a lot worse than theirs. With an oath, he withdrew to his old room, wondering who those Manchu youths had been. Probably the brats of some minor officials, influential enough to evict ordinary Hans from their homes and yet not powerful enough to cause trouble in higher society.

And now the evicted family had become his burden.

Two days later, Tang San showed up with his meager belongings tied on his back. He was washed and his hair braided into a shiny pigtail. He greeted everybody with a low bow, including the servants.

Fong took him to his study, where he asked him to unfasten the bundle and sit down. Tang San obeyed and sat on the edge of a rattan chair, his hands clasped and a big grin on his dark thin face. He said he was sixteen years old.

Fong studied him. The boy looked nineteen, if not older. Fong disliked his perpetual grin, which showed too many uneven teeth and a lot of gums. But on the whole he was not a bad-looking fellow, a bit underweight, but with good features and straight posture. Restraining a desire to tell him to stop grinning, Fong asked him about his schooling.

"Well, sir," Tang said, "I finished four years of private school, taught by Mr. Leong, who received two pigs and ten catties of rice a year, donated by fifteen families in our village. On festival days, an extra chicken and some eggs . . ."

"What did you study?" Fong interrupted.

"Well, sir, Confucius and Mencius mostly. Mr. Leong does not know anything else."

"So you have never studied modern subjects, such as history, geography and arithmetic."

"No, sir!" Tang San exclaimed, thinking that Fong Tai objected to such subjects.

Fong took a sheet of paper from his drawer, scribbled something on it and handed it to Tang San. "I want you to enroll at Hung Miao Grammar School. Take this to the schoolmaster. In the meantime you will stay here in the servants' quarters and study full time. If your grades are good, you will go to a Christian middle school; if not, you will become a servant. Is this arrangement agreeable?"

"Yes, sir!"

"And don't grin so much. Smile only when it is necessary. Now you may go."

"Thank you, sir." Tang San rose to his feet and pocketed the piece of paper, unsmiling. "A good actor," Fong thought.

Tang San marched to the door, tipped an imaginary hat and left. Fong wondered where the boy had learned to tip a cap like a foreigner. He had a feeling that he was not going to get along very well with his new responsibility.

Tang San proved to be a good student. In one year he finished grammar school; the next, he entered the Christian middle school in the neighborhood. In six months he was at the head of his class and planned to finish the entire middle school in two years. Because he was doing so well, nobody ridiculed him about his age. He was twenty, but claimed to be seventeen.

But Fong was still not sure he should keep him. The young man was funny, entertaining his classmates like a clown, twisting his eyes and mouth when he told childish stories about ghosts and fox spirits. He learned the modern subjects fast, especially English. To impress people he often rattled off foreign names and places and swearwords like a monk reciting Buddhist scriptures. Fong was often irritated by these shenanigans; sometimes he questioned his own sense of humor and forced himself to be more tolerant.

In the servants' quarters, Tang San was not a welcome guest. The cook and gardener hated him, for he found fault with the food and refused to do any work. He was regarded as an aching tooth—a pain that it was difficult to get rid of.

Fong Tai was not usually superstitious but he thought Tang San had brought him luck. Not too long ago, when Li Hung-chang learned that he had taken in a poor boy, he sent Fong a note praising his charitable act. Two days later, Li sent him another note offering him a job with a solid title—adviser. Fong preferred a longer title, such as Adviser to the Governor of Chi-li Province, for instance, but he was in no position to bargain.

He was surprised that Li wanted him to start the job immediately. Soon he was disappointed to find that his work was mostly secretarial—writing letters, classifying incoming mail and filing documents. He hardly saw Li. But Li had become almost senile, and Fong hoped to influence the old man.

He and Father Barrington also continued their friendship. Semiretired by then, Barrington enjoyed his rocking chair in the backyard of his Western bungalow where he watched swallows making nests under the eaves. Because of his worsening arthritis, he seldom went to his office and he welcomed Fong Tai's frequent visits.

"Dr. White told me one day," he said to Fong during a lunch served by Barrington's young maid, "either you save the Great Ching Dynasty or you save your own life. I've decided to save my own life."

Every time Barrington entertained, he jammed a chef's cap onto his head and cooked a dish or two himself. His specialty was Boston baked beans or underdone New York steaks. Fong had no trouble eating the former—it reminded him of Boston, bringing back fond memories of Cathy Dubois. But New York steak was something else.

"It's the only way to eat steak," Father Barrington said. "Bloody. Gives you the energy you need for whatever you do, especially the heavy work ahead."

"You are retired, Father. What heavy work do you mean?" Fong asked, cutting his rare steak with a shudder.

"With my arthritis and heart condition, nobody expects me to live to eighty," Barrington said. "But you can bet your last Chinese dollar that I will celebrate my eightieth birthday. Why am I so sure? Raw steaks: protein! Lots of it. All kept in here like money in the bank." He patted his ample stomach with a hearty laugh.

Then he filled their glasses with whiskey and continued, "By the way, since I became the High Minister, I've developed a liking for whiskey. Dr. White says it's good for the heart. It makes your blood run faster, cleanses your system and brain. He says if I had taken up the bottle a decade or two ago, I wouldn't have this damned heart condition. Irregular beating. Debris clogging up the arteries. Hard to get rid of, but a shot or two of this stuff always helps. So nothing is too late." He laughed.

Fong was surprised to find to what degree liquor could change a person. Barrington was no longer the preacher of God or the High Minister of Foreign Affairs, full of nervous energy and high ideals. He seldom talked religion or politics now. He seemed to have converted from a moralist Confucian to a casual, fatalistic Taoist. He often downed his drink in one gulp. When he had too much, he became uninhibited in conversation, which sometimes embarrassed Fong.

"Listen," Barrington said after several glasses of whiskey, "something else is supposed to be good for your health. A good session with a passionate woman. I missed it. As a priest, I had very little chance; as the High Minister, I had a lot of chances, but I had to watch my step. Now that there are no steps to watch, what happens? No chance at all!" With another laugh, he finished his drink. "However, liquor will do the same for your health. Of course, it's only man's second choice. How is your sex life?"

Fong shrugged, also feeling the effects of the whiskey. "It doesn't cleanse my heart or my brain, I'm afraid."

"Then find a woman who can!" Laughing, Barrington fished out another bottle from under his bed.

11

Tang San finished the Christian middle school at the age of twenty, having passed all the modern courses with high grades. He had become thoroughly Westernized, to Fong Tai's embarrassment, copying all the Western habits that Father Barrington had once promoted as part of China's modernization program.

Fong had finally developed a fondness for the young man, despite Tang San's irritating mannerisms. Like Fong, Tang San often sprinkled English words in his Chinese conversations, like a man shaking salt on his food. As advocated by Barrington, both men liked to eat with a knife and fork, claiming that it was more civilized and more sanitary. The new method of eating, however, horrified Madame Fong, who regarded it as barbaric.

Fong had tried to smoke a cigar but he hated it. Tang San adopted the habit readily. He even imitated the cigar-smoking foreigners he had seen in Peking, going through all their rituals like a veteran smoker, smelling the cigar, biting off its tip, wetting it with his tongue, puffing on it while talking or tapping its ashes unnecessarily; sometimes he added a final stroke of his own, wriggling his eyebrows while exhaling. When there was a shortage of cigars, he chewed on one for days, shifting it from one side of his mouth to the other.

One bright Sunday morning, Fong Tai was in his study working on a book he was trying to write, *The Goal of New China*. Tang San sauntered in and announced the arrival in Peking of a new prostitute who was so beautiful that all the government officials were trying to get her.

"Why do you tell me this?" Fong asked irritably. "I don't like you to barge in like that. And for God's sake, don't wriggle your damned eyebrows like a clown!" Just as the offended Tang San was about to back out of the room, Fong added quickly, "By the way, where did you learn all this? Why can't the high government officials get her?"

"It is rumored all over town. Anyway, you aren't interested."

"Why is she so difficult to get?"

Tang San started to wriggle his eyebrows but thought better of it. "Why? Because none of them can beat her in a sword fight."

Fong stared at him with a heavy scowl. "Are you drunk?"

"It's the truth, Mr. Fong," Tang San said, sinking into a rattan chair and crossing his legs. He knew that he had caught Fong's attention. He produced a cigar and struck a match. Between puffs, he went on. "The woman will receive a gentleman only if he can beat her in a sword fight. That's her house rule."

"Nonsense!" Fong said. "No prostitute is stupid enough to have such a rule." He turned back to his work, waiting for Tang San to say more on the subject, but Tang San took his time.

"How beautiful is she?" Fong asked, unable to control his curiosity.

"As beautiful as a fresh lotus flower. The best in the Eight Great Lanes."

Fong again returned to his work. He decided not to waste any more time on the subject. He didn't know why he tolerated the young man's audacity and ill manners. Perhaps he had sensed some sort of fascinating evil in him, yet could not pinpoint what it was. Besides, Tang had not done anything terribly bad. When the room was almost suffocating with cigar smoke, Fong had a good mind to kick him out, but he held his temper. He wanted to know more about the so-called Sword Prostitute. Unable to concentrate on his work, he tossed his pen away and looked up.

"All right," he said bluntly. "What do you want?"

"If you intend to pay Rose a visit," Tang San announced after a few more puffs on the cigar, "I don't mind going with you."

"Rose? What Rose?"

"She is the courtesan I just mentioned. Her professional name is Rose the Sword Courtesan."

"How dare you! I am a family man. I have a wife!"

"Same bed, different dreams," Tang San said, broadening his grin.

"What do you mean by that?"

"That is your relationship with your wife. You told me . . ."

"I don't need a prostitute to solve my problems!" Fong Tai said hotly.

"She is not a common prostitute. She has rented a nice house in Eight Great Lanes. And she does not accept just anybody."

Fong Tai glared at him, controlling a strong desire to box his ears. "If you want to visit a prostitute, go ahead," he said, picking up his pen and returning to his work.

"I can't," Tang San said. "I can't fight. But you can. If she accepts you, I wouldn't mind going with you and . . ."

"Get out! Get out!" Fong exploded, rising to his feet threateningly.

With a deep sigh, Tang San got up from his chair. "Don't be upset, Mr. Fong," he said, still grinning. "The desire for food and sex is human nature. Confucius said that . . ."

"Confucius be damned!" Fong shouted. "I said get out of my sight!"

With another sigh, Tang San left the room, puffing on his cigar and shaking his head sadly.

Fong Tai was fuming, unable to concentrate on his work anymore. He wondered if he should throw the rascal out of his house. He opened all the windows to let the cigar smoke out and cursed himself for tolerating such bad manners.

For several days he could not sleep well, nor could he concentrate on what he was doing. Nobody had told him how this new prostitute looked, but he could not help seeing her in his mind's eye—vivacious and lean, soft-skinned, feminine yet strong. When he thought about this imaginary woman, especially at night lying beside Shao Mei, he felt guilty.

He had not enjoyed a woman since Cathy Dubois.

Fong Tai's wife had become apathetic. No matter what he did or did not do, she did not seem to care one way or another. Indeed, their relationship had become what Tang San had described: same bed, different dreams.

One fine afternoon on a warm spring day, he felt restless and decided to take a walk. While sauntering along the cobblestoned street, he fought a strong desire to see Rose the Sword Courtesan. While trying not to think about her, he found himself approaching the famous red-light district, Eight Great Lanes.

During the long walk he tried to convince himself that the visit was only to satisfy his curiosity. He had heard a great deal about the famous lanes where the singsong girls, old and young, had settled by the hundreds for more than half a century, selling their services to rich merchants, high government officials and commoners, or even coolies. He had heard that there were peasant girls and highly skilled, well-educated young ladies working in three classes of houses in the lanes. The lower the number of the lane, the higher the class.

Arriving in the district, he found it depressing. The narrow wet alleys had a deserted look. Most of the low brick buildings had flat roofs with lucky sayings pasted on them and peeled red paint on the doors. A scabby dog hunting for food snarled at him.

As he entered the lower numbered lanes, the houses looked neater. When he reached No. 1 Lane, he found the place almost a different world. It was a short street, wide enough for two sedan chairs to pass each other. The brick buildings all had blue glazed tile roofs. The lucky sayings pasted on the freshly painted red double doors were the same: BRING IN WEALTH AND TREASURES, RISE IN NOBILITY AND RANK, and other unabashed blessings and good luck, written on couplet scrolls of expensive red paper.

He stopped a prosperous-looking middle-aged passerby in a silk gown and asked him about the Sword Courtesan. The man looked him up and down as if surprised to find such fools in the world. Then he smiled and pointed to a door that was standing ajar. "In there. Anyone can walk in. But most of them crawl out."

Fong Tai thanked him, went to the door and peeked in. The courtyard inside was paved, with pots of chrysanthemums and geraniums placed at the entrance of each building. A solitary date tree, lush and tall, served as an umbrella in the middle of the courtyard. Most of the latticed, papered windows, with colors that matched the carved eaves, were open. This indicated that business was slow.

He pushed at the door and it squealed loudly. The squeal promptly brought out a servant from a side building. He was a middle-aged man wearing a blue tunic and carrying a bird cage in which two parakeets chattered merrily. Bowing with a broad smile, he invited Fong to the main building.

Inside, several rosewood ancestral chairs were placed against one wall; on the opposite side was a weapon stand with traditional Chinese weapons leaning against it. Near the wall facing the entrance was an altar to Kwanti, the red-faced god of war. Fong felt as if he had walked into a miniature Kwanti temple. The three-foot statue of the war god, glistening in gilded armor and carrying his famous long-handled sword, stared out at the world almost contemptuously.

"Please sit down," the servant said. "I'll call Madame Rose."

Presently a young woman in her twenties entered the room from a side door. She was dressed in a red silk blouse and pair of matching pantaloons. She looked rather frail, with a watermelon-seed-shaped face that was framed by a well-oiled coiffure. He stared at her, dumbfounded for a moment. He had never seen any woman so beautiful without makeup. He had visualized an athletic woman in a glittering costume, like a woman warrior in an opera. This young courtesan was much more than he had expected.

He rose quickly to greet her. Unsmiling, she picked up a spear from the weapon stand and tossed it at him. The action was so abrupt and unceremonious that he almost missed catching it.

"You have passed the first test," she said with a smile. "Many cannot even catch the spear. Now choose your weapon. I am going to use a long sword."

"Tang San did not lie," Fong Tai said, almost smiling but too surprised by this unusual reception to do so. "I'll take this." He replaced the long spear and picked up a three-pronged fork with a long handle. It was a weapon he had trained with when attending the martial arts class at the Foreign School.

He followed her to the courtyard, cautioning himself not to hurt the lady. The fork was a dangerous weapon; the three sharp spikes could easily catch a sword and disarm its user. He had selected it mainly for comic effect.

Reaching the center of the courtyard, she attacked without warning. Her sword whizzed in the air, narrowly missing his head. She was so fast that for a moment he saw only a blur of blade, like a fast windmill; he could even feel the wind it created.

After dodging the sword a few times, he abandoned his planned comedy act and took her seriously. He fought back with all his skill but found that he could not even touch her sword, let alone catch it. The sword had become a phantom weapon, slashing the air around him, avoiding the fork and yet dangerously close to cutting him.

After she had intimidated him with her speed and skill, he began to feel awkward and clumsy. He knew he looked like a clown. He regretted having selected such an unwieldy weapon. Every time he staggered, Rose waited like an adult playing with a child in a rough game. When he regained his balance and was ready to fight again, she resumed her fighting stance, her lips tightly pursed—probably trying not to laugh, he thought. When she attacked again, she used new tactics, feinting, slashing, thrusting, hacking and poking with her magic sword. She was taunting and yet graceful, like a dancer.

Knowing that she would probably not hurt him, he continued to fight, hating to admit defeat. He managed to ward off her blows by blocking, leaping and dodging, using all the skills he had acquired during years of martial arts training. But she was so good that he never found an opening for a counterattack. He was too busy keeping himself from looking stupid and funny.

Soon he felt sweat creeping down his back. As the sword narrowly missed his nose and ears, he wondered if Rose was trying to humiliate him. She showed no sign of fatigue; she was not even breathing hard.

Suddenly, with a backhand swing and a forward thrust, Rose penetrated his defense. She let out a sharp battle cry and the battle was over. He found himself staggering and falling to his haunches. The sword followed him to the ground, stopping just short of his throat. Lying on his back and staring up at her, he felt like laughing. He should have known better; the joke was on him. He was glad that nobody was watching the fight.

"Now get up and leave," Rose said, withdrawing the sword.

He got up and dusted off his clothes, trying to act casual and relaxed. "I have not come to fight. Can't we talk?"

"Not until you can beat me," Rose said with a faint smile. Without another word, she tossed her weapon on the ground and disappeared into the main building, leaving behind a whiff of rose-scented perfume.

The servant, smiling sympathetically, quickly picked up both weapons and started for the main building. At the door, he bowed. "Try again next time, sir," he said. "You may win someday."

Fong Tai flipped a coin at him. The servant caught it and shook his head. It was a silver dollar and the man was fighting his own battle over whether to accept it or not. Finally, greed triumphed over house rules. He slipped the coin into his pocket.

"How can she make a living this way?" Fong asked.

"Oh, sometimes she loses, too," the servant said, winking. He entered the building and closed the door.

Feeling foolish, Fong sighed. He wondered how many men in Peking could beat Rose in a sword fight. If she lost to anyone, she probably did it on purpose. As he turned to leave, he not only felt humiliated but jealous as well. The contest had made the damned woman more hard to reach and more desirable. He envied those who had succeeded.

*

After the sword fight Fong Tai could not get Rose out of his mind. Who was she? Where had she come from? Why had she become a prostitute? Why was she not married—or was she? Curiosity gnawed at him day and night. He decided to pay her another visit.

The reception he received this time was almost a repetition of the first. Rose insisted on the house rule. She was all business. He accepted the fight, hoping that she would lose on purpose this time. Soon he found out that it was only wishful thinking. The contest was a repetition of the first one. He quickly acknowledged defeat and saved himself more humiliation.

As if apologizing for his mistress, the servant came over and dusted Fong's clothes while Fong got up from the ground. When the servant invited him to come back and try again, Fong decided not to leave this time. The whole thing angered him. If she could lose to others, why couldn't she lose to him? Was he that unattractive? Falling on his behind was not painful; his pride was hurting more. He felt like a louse rejected by a lady who said to him, "Take a look at yourself in the mirror; don't be a scabby frog who wishes to eat the flesh of a flying swan." His injured pride made him angry.

He marched to her door and knocked, much to the servant's surprise. Rose opened the door and stared at him, amazed. "Why are you still here?"

"I want to see you," he said bluntly.

"Ah Lai," she said to the servant, "show him the front gate."

The servant trotted over and swallowed hard a couple of times. "M–miss," he stammered, "he cannot beat you, but he can beat me."

"Did he bribe you?"

"No, I did not bribe him," Fong said. "He knows how to treat guests with courtesy. You have humiliated me twice. The least you can do is to ask me in for a cup of tea."

Rose stared at him. She had never encountered anyone like this before, so outspoken and persistent. "All right," she said with a toss of her head. "Come in. Ah Lai, serve tea."

To Fong's surprise, the spacious reception room was luxuriously furnished with rosewood chairs and tea stands, all exquisitely carved and inlaid with mother-of-pearl birds and flowers. The walls were decorated with couplet scrolls in watercolors and calligraphy. This was not a sing-song house, but the living room of a Mandarin scholar of great means. Rose invited him to sit down on one of the straightbacked and cushioned chairs, and she herself took a seat on the other side of the tea stand. The servant smilingly served cups of tea and a plate of roasted watermelon seeds. Feeling at home in such surroundings, Fong relaxed, picked up a few watermelon seeds and started cracking them expertly between his teeth.

"You are a brave man, sir," Rose said. "Are such visits worth risking your life?"

"You are good enough to kill me or spare me," he replied with a smile. "Since we are not enemies, I see no danger."

"Why are you so persistent?"

"Determination is my bad habit. Perhaps my curse, but I can't help it."

"You know I never do business with anyone who cannot beat me."

"Business is not the only thing on my mind. I shall be quite content if I can have a cup of tea with you, like this."

Rose picked up her tea and took a sip of it, studying him with a faint smile. "What is your name, sir?"

He told her his name and his title. "I am not trying to impress you, but I want you to know me better, just in case you decide to choose me as a friend."

"A man of your position is always discreet," she said, her voice softening and her stiffness gone. "I am surprised that you are not."

"I intend to be your friend. There is no need to be discreet. I shall be proud to associate with you openly, anytime, anywhere."

Rose took another sip of tea. She was visibly touched. In her world men treated her like an expensive plaything, a treasure to be purchased and then disposed of. She smiled.

"Don't you think your valuable time can be better spent elsewhere? There are many other houses in the neighborhood you can visit, you know."

"I have no interest in other houses. I am not buying what is being sold in this neighborhood."

She raised her eyebrows. "Oh? Then why are your here, Mr. Fong?"

"To see you," he said seriously, looking straight into her eyes.

"Why?" she inquired, eyeing him over the brim of her teacup.

"First, out of curiosity. After I fought you, I felt an uncontrollable urge to see you again. Your beauty, your skill at sword fighting and your . . ."

"No, no," she interrupted him with a little chuckle. "None of that. It is your determination—your bad habit—remember? Don't blame me for your desires."

He laughed and took a sip of the fragrant jasmine tea. "Tell me, Miss Rose, you are not an ordinary lady. Why do you take up such a . . ."

He stopped and she finished the sentence for him: "Why do I take up such a lowly profession?"

"Yes. If you prefer not to discuss it, just pretend that I have not asked."

She looked away. Fong waited, thinking that he had asked a foolish question too abruptly and too soon. Just as he was about to change the subject, she poured out her story without emotion, her face expressionless. It was apparent that she did not want sympathy. Fong had heard many sob stories, and he knew that this was not one of them.

She was from a rich Han family in Tung Chow, she told him, a small town outside the Eastern City of Peking. As a young girl she had studied the classics, the Yuan drama and Tang poetry under a Senior Wrangler, a scholar with the highest degree. She had also studied martial arts, especially sword fighting, a sport popular among young women of high society. Her tutor was the famous Phantom Swordsman, Master Hai, who was said to be able to fend off a bucket of water without getting his clothes wet.

Because of her accomplishments she was sought by men in the best social circles. One day a Manchu official saw her in a food store selecting fish with a maid. She ignored him when he approached her. Offended, he demanded her name and address from the storekeeper. A few days later the official arrived at her house and asked if she would be interested in being a candidate for a palace maid for Prince Kung. If selected, she would have the privilege of living in the Forbidden City. If she did well, she might even be lucky enough to become one of the Prince's concubines.

Being a Han and having a personal maid herself, she considered the invitation an insult. She rejected the offer, to the surprise of the official as well as her own father.

The next day half a dozen armed guards from the Peking garrison stormed into their house, arrested her father, banished the family from

Tung Chow and confiscated their house and noodle factory. Homeless, she and her mother and two younger brothers had drifted to Peking and settled in a shack in the Outer City. Unable to find a job, she secretly took up residence in Eight Great Lanes, sponsored by the property owner. In order to be selective, she devised the sword-fight rule so that she would not have to receive every Chang San or Li Su, like a common harlot.

As she finished her story, she stared at her hands as if she wanted to wring someone's neck.

"Where is your father now?"

"Still in prison."

Fong Tai was quiet. He wondered what he could do to help her. Feeling her hate and pain, he left without comment or promises.

✳

Late one night, Fong Tai was reading in his study when Tang San sauntered in, puffing a cigar. He sank into a chair and crossed his legs, a grin on his thin tanned face. He was getting more familiar and casual, and Fong did not like it.

"Tai," the young man said, "a rumor is spreading. Even your mother knows about it."

Fong resented the way Tang San addressed him. Nobody called him Tai except his immediate family or close friends. The young man's casualness and lack of respect irritated him more every day. "What are you talking about?" he demanded gruffly.

"Your frequent visits to Eight Great Lanes, of course. Your mother is unhappy about it."

"How did she find out?"

"Rumors have a way of traveling to unwelcome ears. But I think I can help."

Fong was not sure that he wanted Tang San's help, but he worried about his mother's health. "How?"

Tang San leaned forward and said confidentially, "Just leave it to me. But on one condition: I would like to pay Rose a visit. You can open the door for me."

"Go open your own door!" Fong shouted. Such a suggestion was like a needle poking in his ear.

"But I can't go through that silly sword-fighting routine. I am no fighter. If you help me, I will help you."

Controlling his anger, Fong said with a shrug, "How can I help you? It's her house rule."

Tang San leaned back confidently and puffed on his cigar. "All right. I will help you anyway. I will talk to your mother. Don't worry."

Fong looked up from his book sharply. Tang's words sounded like a threat. He had to know what was on Tang San's mind. "What are you going to tell her?"

"I will tell her that you visit Eight Great Lanes—not to enjoy yourself but to fight prostitution." Then, with a wink, he added, "It is not a lie. You did fight the Sword Courtesan twice, didn't you?"

"Have you been spying on me?" Fong demanded, his voice ominous.

Tang San looked at him as if amused. He tapped some cigar ashes into a cuspidor and rose. "Rumor, Tai, has a way of traveling fast—to both friendly and unfriendly ears. Why should I spy on you?" Then, puffing on his cigar, he left the room.

Fong resisted the urge to throw his ink stand after him.

12

Madame Fong's condition had been worsening. The doctor had prescribed the kind of herbs that were usually required for serious cases, such as terminal cancer. Fong visited her briefly every day.

But this afternoon he entered her incense-filled room with apprehension. In constant pain, she groaned as she talked, her thin voice barely audible. To his surprise she had not yet mentioned the feared subject, Eight Great Lanes. Her main concern was that he had passed thirty without having a son. She kept quoting Confucius: "Of all the three offenses to filial piety, the worst is to grow old without posterity."

Worried and tired of Confucius, he said, "Mother, I am not too old. Shao Mei and I are working on it."

"That is not good enough. You two should visit Sun Tse, the baby goddess, who is responsible for sending babies to this world."

Fong took a deep breath, trying not to grimace. If anyone else had suggested going to a baby goddess for help, he would have laughed. "We will, Mother. Don't worry about it."

"And you had better hurry," she mumbled. "I want you to go to the Temple of Sun Tse with your wife immediately. Make food offerings and pray. Do that right now . . . before I die."

As Fong watched his mother, he agonized over her suffering. The pain and anxiety were so acute that she twisted her head and moaned, tears unwillingly creeping down from her sunken eyes.

"Mother," he said, holding one of her bony hands, "please don't talk about death. You will not die; not for a long time."

"Who are you to tell me that?" she shot back impatiently. "You are not Heaven. I will die! I want to die! But I shall not have a happy trip to the other world if the Fong family is not continued."

"It will be continued, I promise you, Mother," Fong said, feeling a lump in his throat.

As he left his mother's room, he threw all the windows open. If the old woman did not die of cancer, she would certainly be choked to death by incense smoke. Knowing that she would not last long, he was determined to make her trip to the other world a happy one. But visiting the temple of the baby goddess was not what he had in mind.

That night he tossed in bed, unable to sleep. It had been proven in his mind beyond any doubt that he and Shao Mei were incapable of producing a child. He had no idea who was at fault. Even if they could, it would be too late; his mother simply could not wait another nine months. He wished there were really such a thing as a baby goddess who could pick up her magic wand, point it at Shao Mei's stomach and, presto, out would come a fat little boy. If any goddess could do that, he would be willing to give her a thousand kowtows.

Distressed, he climbed out of his bed without disturbing Shao Mei and got dressed. He had to talk to someone. He thought of waking Tang San, but changed his mind. Then he wondered if he should visit Third Uncle. As he came out of his house, he automatically turned in the direction of the Eight Great Lanes.

Rose was happy to see him. She asked him to stay for an evening meal. She would personally cook four Soochow dishes—chicken, pork, beef and fish, all delicately minced, lightly spiced and sautéed with various fresh vegetables. Her mother was from Soochow.

"She is talented in cooking and producing children, and I have inherited one of the talents," Rose said with a laugh as he followed her to the kitchen.

He was amazed by her skill with the wok, which she handled like her sword. Instead of using a spatula, she shook and bounced the wok in such a way that the food turned and flipped and wound up being stir-fried to perfection. Although he preferred the heavily seasoned Szechuan dishes, he enjoyed Soochow cuisine, which always brought out the natural flavors of the food.

After the elaborate evening meal, they shared several cups of shao hsing, a yellow wine that she warmed in a bucket of hot water. She filled tiny Kwangsi cups as though she were a trained singsong girl, holding the wine jar with a flowery hand, her small finger extended like the petal of an orchid. After several cups of the warm wine, he felt his depression gradually melting away. But there was a vague uneasiness that kept returning. It seemed there was no solution to his problem. He had found love, but his loveless marriage was hanging between him and his happiness.

Somehow Rose detected his mood. "What is the matter?" she asked, filling his cup.

He told her. "My mother is dying and she wants to see a grandson."

"Oh," she said. Without prying into the subject, she warmed another jar of shao hsing. She filled both their tiny cups again and proposed a toast. "To your health—and a happy future!"

When he emptied his cup, he felt a sudden sadness. The more he wanted Rose, the more depressed he became. "My health is good, but my future is bleak and unpredictable," he said.

To his surprise, Rose did not share his concern. "How about a game of chess?" she suggested cheerfully. "And I promise not to win all the time."

"Win or lose, it is always a diversion," he said, trying to sound pleased. "But I would rather do something else tonight."

Rose looked at him with a close-mouthed smile, her eyes soft and unblinking. "Do what?"

"I would rather listen to you read."

"I have a copy of *Red Chamber Dream.*"

"No, I want to listen to your poems."

"Oh," she said, flattered. "But I can do something better."

"Better? You are full of surprises, Rose. You have so many talents, you make me feel inferior."

"I have no talents. I only have likes and dislikes."

"What can you do that is better than your poems? Show me."

Rose brought out a pi-pah from under the daybed in the living room. It was a four-string Chinese guitar with a long handle, one of Fong's favorite ancient musical instruments. She sat on the daybed and started to play a melody with her long fingernails. After a lovely overture, she began to sing in a fine soft voice. It was a haunting song about a young woman who tried to support her family during a famine by selling herself to a rich man.

It was a familiar tale, but her rendition made it deeply moving. He swallowed a lump in his throat and applauded enthusiastically. In lieu of a bow, Rose played a short flurry of pi-pah music, her fingers flying, her eyes closed in concentration. When she finished, she opened her eyes slowly as if gradually waking up from a deep sleep. "It is my own composition," she said.

"I love it," Fong said, impressed. "It is such a sad song, it does not match your mood."

"Sadness is either man-made or nature-made. No matter what makes it, you can always isolate it. You can almost frame it like a picture and hang it in a cheerful room."

"I am glad you are so optimistic."

"More shao hsing?"

"Yes, please." He felt ashamed. Her fate was so much worse than his, and yet she managed to counter it with philosophy and emerge from it a cheerful woman.

They finished another jar of wine. As they chatted and laughed, he almost forgot his problems. It was after midnight when he got up to leave. Rose went to the door, then blocked it.

This sudden move surprised him. They looked at each other quietly. She did not have to say anything, for her eyes conveyed an invitation that could not be better expressed in words.

Silently he followed her to her bedroom. Everything was so spontaneous that the experience overwhelmed him; it brought back the memory of Cathy Dubois and more. With Cathy it had been only passion and pleasure; with Rose the feeling reached far beyond. If there was a perfect state of physical, mental and spiritual well-being, he had finally experienced it. It was ironic that he should achieve such a miracle in Eight Great Lanes, of all places.

Fong went home and slept soundly. Rising at noon, he felt refreshed and energized, ready for any challenge.

*

Li Hung-chang, ill and senile, seldom came to the office. The next day Fong went directly to Li's office, sat behind his desk and imagined himself as the Governor of Chi-li. He remembered the old saying, "Disasters come in pairs—and so do blessings." Perhaps one miracle would follow another. It was impossible to beat Rose in a sword fight, but a miracle had happened. For a Han to attain the goal of high office and put the country in order was also perhaps not impossible.

Sitting in the Governor's chair, he fantasized about his double blessings:

power in office and love at home. Other pleasant thoughts ran through his mind—Father Barrington, the American Constitution, Boston baked beans, Christmas and Cathy Dubois.

He almost jumped up, badly startled, when the door opened and Li Hung-chang walked in, helped by an aide.

"Good morning!" Fong said, leaping up. "I did not expect you so early, Your Excellency."

"I did not expect to find you sitting behind my desk," Li replied, looking at him suspiciously.

"I was just trying to put my feet in your shoes, sir," Fong said with a little laugh. "It may help me see your viewpoint, sir."

"With all the problems this country is facing," Li said gruffly, "I wish I were in *your* shoes." He dismissed the aide. Thumping his cane on the floor, he moved toward his desk. Fong quickly held his chair for him.

Li sank down with a sigh. He sat quietly for a moment as if to regain his breath. Fong stood in front of him waiting for disaster or blessing to strike.

Li dug out his snuff bottle from a deep pocket of his satin Mandarin gown, almost as a ritual, and passed it under his nose a few times. After a loud sneeze, he blew his nose into a silk handkerchief and asked, "Do you know why I am here this morning?"

"To find out who is lazy," Fong said with a little laugh. He was still cheerful enough to risk a joke.

"No," Li said sternly. "To investigate your office irregularities."

Stunned, Fong at first could not believe his ears. During Li's absence he had indeed done a few things that would have displeased any superior. For one thing, he had spent a number of afternoons with Rose when he should have been in his office working.

"I am sorry, Your Excellency," he said humbly. "I can do just as much work at home . . ."

Li interrupted him impatiently. "I don't care where you work as long as the work is done! But using another man's name to write official letters is a crime punishable by a long prison term. Don't you know that? What other letters did you write in my name besides the one to Prince Kung?"

Fong was puzzled for a moment. Suddenly he remembered that he had written a letter to the Prince complaining about the illegal imprisonment of Rose's father. "It is another case of injustice suffered by a Han family at the hands of Manchus, sir," he said. "I thought Prince Kung should know about it."

"Why did you write the letter in my name?"

"Because you are seldom in the office, sir; besides, your name bears more weight. It might bring the man's freedom."

"First of all, you wrote to the wrong person," Li said. "Prince Kung is a turtle's egg who will do anything to protect a Manchu, not a Han. Secondly, forging somebody's name is like stealing his wife. When you are caught you must face the consequences. Don't you know that?"

"I know that, sir. I will not do it again."

Li stared at him as if disappointed. "Don't say a thing like that!" Li's raised voice became cracked and high-pitched. "Don't look like an urchin caught stealing candy! Where is your courage?"

"What courage?" Fong asked, surprised by the question.

Li pointed a long, yellowish fingernail at him. "Years ago you were foolish enough to sign your name to a letter written by Kang Yu-wei. I believe you were encouraged to do so by a professor at Harvard." He smiled ever so slightly. "That was courage. Have you lost that?"

"Honestly, yes," Fong said, disarmed. They stared silently at each other for a moment.

Finally Li shook his head. "Tai," he said, "that foolish adventure did you a great deal of good. It made me sit up and pay you some notice. I even risked my head to defend you . . ." He stopped. With a sigh, he kept shaking his head as if he were terribly disillusioned.

"What do you want me to do, Your Excellency?" Fong asked, getting more confused now.

"Write that letter in your own name, damn it!" Li's cracked voice exploded. "Let the Manchus take notice! Be a fighter on your own. Don't ever hide behind somebody else. I can't live forever." He leaned back to take a breath; the brief explosion had already exhausted him. After he had regained some strength, he leaned forward and asked quietly, "Do you know why I gave you this job? Because you had more gall than all the other turtle's eggs working for me in this office combined. Don't you understand that?"

Fong did not know what to say. He was touched. Li never praised anyone lightly. If he did, it meant a great deal, even though the praise came in the form of a scolding.

Li went on. "Now I want you to write the same letter to Prince Ying, the head of the Bureau of Royal Affairs. Use your own name this time. If that does not work, I will call on the Prince personally. He is a pigheaded Manchu without a sense of humor, but he is a rather decent turtle's egg. By the way, who is this man you claim was illegally imprisoned?"

Fong thought for a brief moment then decided not to lie. "He is the father of my mistress, sir."

"Oh?" Li said, looking at him askance. "I should have guessed."

*

Back in his own office, Fong finished the letter to Prince Ying. He reread it several times and made some minor changes, keeping his words polite but firm, hinting that the country was suffering from the misbehavior of a few members of the royal family and that this might be detrimental to the reputation of the whole family. It was a bold letter, but he could not disappoint Li Hung-chang. He had to put his head on the line to prove that he indeed had gall. Feeling a bit apprehensive, he ordered Mr. Meng, the chief clerk, a meek middle-aged man, to deliver the letter immediately to the Bureau of Royal Affairs.

The next day he went to see Rose. Ah Lai, the servant, was delighted to see him, offering him tea and watermelon seeds. It was not until he had finished two cups of tea that he was surprised by belated information: Rose was not in and would not be back for several days.

"Why didn't you tell me sooner?" Fong said irritably. "You know I have no time for tea or watermelon seeds."

The servant looked hurt. Fong realized that he had become too Westernized. Time was not money in China, and politeness was the first social priority. With a quick smile, he gently asked where Miss Rose had gone.

"She has gone home, sir," Ah Lai said.

"Where is her home?"

The servant shook his head repeatedly and declared emphatically that he did not know. This overacting indicated that he was lying; he must have been instructed by Rose not to reveal her home address. Frustrated and worried, Fong returned home. Would he see her again? Why had she gone home so suddenly? Had it anything to do with his letter to Prince Ying? He could have paid Ah Lai for more information, but he had an aversion to bribery.

Shao Mei was embroidering in front of the window when he entered. He wondered if he owed her an explanation for his frequent absences during the past several months. Lately she had been unusually quiet, always embroidering in front of the window like a ghost. She looked older, with a streak of gray showing faintly in her coiffure.

Fong coughed gently, waiting for her to turn and greet him, but she kept stitching without saying anything. He walked behind her, about to touch her shoulders, but changed his mind. "A lovely lotus flower you are embroidering," he said, breaking the uncomfortable silence. "Is it your favorite subject?"

"Somebody told me that you have been visiting that infamous Eight Great Lanes," his wife announced without emotion and without looking up from her embroidery.

"Yes. I have come to tell you why I have not been home very much. I have been working hard at the office; occasionally I visit a friend . . ."

"I don't mind your taking a concubine," she interrupted, "but I shall not tolerate your living under the same roof with a prostitute."

"Who says I am going to take a concubine? The thought never entered my mind."

"Then why do you visit her so often?" she snapped, turning to look at him abruptly. "Her home has become your home. You eat there and sleep there."

"Who told you all this?"

"I have ears and eyes."

"I go there to play a few games of chess once in a while; I read her poems and . . ."

"I don't want to hear it!" With a snort, she returned to her embroidery, stitching angrily.

"Do you want a divorce?"

"I don't know what you are talking about."

"Divorce is a Western custom." While he explained it, Shao Mei did not respond. "All right," Fong said, starting for the door. "If you want one, I will arrange it."

When he reached the door, she blurted out, "If you want a concubine, go ahead! I don't care!"

Fong stopped, turned and stared at her. Her voice was full of pain and sorrow; it hurt him deeply to realize how much the woman was suffering. He would rather have had her throw something at him or claw at him. "Why?" he asked, his heart aching for her. "Why do you say that?"

"So you will not visit Eight Great Lanes all the time to satisfy your animal desires."

Withdrawing quickly from the room, he strode across the courtyard to Tang San's room. Without knocking, he pushed the door open and burst in. Tang San was in bed, eating watermelon and spitting the seeds onto the floor. He had moved out of the servants' quarters and for several months now had been treated like a member of the family.

"Hello," he greeted Fong in English.

"Did you tell my wife about Rose?"

Tang San wiped his mouth with the back of his hand. "What is there to tell?" he said with a grin. "Everybody knows about it."

"I want you to keep your mouth shut."

"Go ask your wife. Go ask your mother. See if I told them anything. Your mother has other things to worry about."

"Such as?"

"Any woman her age is hungry for the pleasure of tickling a plump little grandson. You have deprived the old lady of such a pleasure."

"My problems are none of your business. From now on I forbid you to talk about my affairs."

"Of course, of course," Tang San said. He struck a match and lit a cigar. "Tell you what . . . I can make your mother happy. When the time comes, I assure you she will die with a happy smile on her face. But one condition: introduce me to Rose. I want an arrangement with the understanding that I'll spend the night with her without going through that silly sword fight. She is worth the money, is she not?"

Fong slapped him hard, knocking the cigar out of his mouth. Tang San looked stunned. Fong left the room quickly, slamming the door.

13

I t was almost midnight when Rose returned, looking contented. She had brought back a bamboo basket full of little packages. She was surprised to see Fong.

"How long have you been waiting?" she asked, sitting beside him.

He reached for her hand and held it tightly. "Three days."

"What?"

"I came every evening. It has been three days. Where have you been?"

"Home. Didn't Ah Lai tell you?"

"Should I believe him?"

Rose laughed. "Let me tell you what happened," she said cheerfully, opening some of the packages. "A man visited my family the other day. He had a beard; his clothes were wrinkled and dirty. He walked in without ceremony, made himself comfortable and ordered food." She stopped and put the contents of a package on a plate. "Here—have some tidbits my mother made."

"Who was he?" Fong asked, thinking of the bearded man.

"My father," Rose said with a laugh. "He came home and nobody recognized him. My mother nearly fainted."

"Congratulations!" Fong said, picking up a sesame bun from the plate. "I am so happy for you, Rose. So your father has finally been released from jail."

"Yes—a miracle! We never expected that he would be released so soon. Somebody must have felt sorry for him. It calls for a cup of shao hsing."

As she poured two cups of the yellow wine, he wondered if he should tell her about his letter to Prince Ying, but he decided to keep quiet. He did not believe that his letter could have worked such a miracle. Li Hung-chang could have put some pressure on Prince Kung at the same time. "What are you going to do?" he asked.

"First we are trying to get our business back. Without the noodle factory, we have no means of support. It is our livelihood."

They finished two jars of shao hsing and then made love on the daybed in the living room. It signaled the beginning of a new life. On her bed she was a prostitute; on the daybed she was the daughter of a good family, pure and innocent. She had never allowed anyone to touch her on the daybed until now.

*

Fong's happy mood was interrupted the next day when Old Liu arrived at his office and announced breathlessly that Madame Fong was dying.

Dropping his work, Fong rushed home. He prayed he was not too late. He knew that his mother was a brave woman, unafraid of death. To her, it was only a trip to another world, a reunion with her dead ancestors. But she refused to die without seeing a grandson who would carry on the family name. Now that she was dying, he hated himself for having denied her the fulfillment of perhaps the greatest desire of her life.

Her room was crowded with half a dozen relatives who had gathered around her canopied bed and were sobbing and wringing their hands. The room smelled of strong incense and herb medicine. Fong brushed aside a cousin, rushed to his mother's bedside and examined her. He found her more heartbroken than sick. Twisting her head, she kept mumbling and quoting Confucius.

Fong had heard the famous quotation about lack of posterity all his life and he hated it. When he was fourteen, his parents had already wanted him to marry someone old enough to bear a child. They had chosen a wife for him, a plump woman six years his senior. He had taken one look at her picture and fled his home for six days. Later, he learned that his mother had chosen her because she believed that plumpness was a sign of fertility.

At nineteen he had succumbed to more pressure and married Shao Mei, a skinny woman. He wondered if his mother had been right in the first place. Had he married a plump one, he might have had several sons by now.

Aunt Loo, his mother's youngest sister and a widowed busybody who did not have any children, was trying to feed his mother some juice. She was another strong force in the son-demanding faction. Only Third Uncle took the whole thing casually, often expressing his opinion with a shrug. Of all the relatives who were sobbing without tears, only a few seemed to be genuinely saddened, Third Uncle among them. His eyes were moist and he kept swallowing, refusing to wipe his eyes or blow his nose.

"Call her, Tai," Aunt Loo said. "When she hears your voice, she will eat."

Fong called his mother. Madame Fong stopped twisting her head and opened her eyes. "Why are you here?" she demanded. "I have not seen you for so long."

Fong had a hard time convincing his mother that he had not been back to Eight Great Lanes.

"What crime did you commit this time?" she demanded.

"She is delirious," Aunt Loo said, sneaking a spoonful of food into her mouth. The old lady choked. "Do something!" Aunt Loo cried. "Do something! She is dying!"

Now all the relatives became alarmed. Two cousins pulled her to a sitting position, another started beating her shoulders to ease her cough. Fong backed out of the room quickly, remembering what Tang San had told him.

Tang was reading in bed. "My mother is dying," Fong said. "How can I make her die happy?"

Tang San leaped out of bed and threw on his clothes. "Follow me," he ordered, hurrying out of the room. Fong followed him, feeling foolish. "My sister will solve this," Tang explained as he rushed into the street. He hailed a donkey cart. Thrusting coins into the hand of the driver, he leaped on the cart and yelled at Fong, "Climb up!"

Fong climbed onto the cart and sat precariously atop its cargo of animal feed and bales of hay. "Where are we going?" he asked Tang San, who was sitting beside the driver, urging the emaciated donkey to hurry.

"We are going to borrow a concubine."

Totally bewildered now, Fong resigned himself to Tang's shenanigans.

All he wanted was to make his mother die happy, and since there was not much time, he had little choice.

Luckily, it was a short ride. As they arrived in front of a mud house in the slums, Tang San ordered the driver to wait. He leaped down and rapped on the door of a shack. A dirty-faced child of about six opened the door and Tang San disappeared inside. Fong sat on top of the hay, waiting uneasily and feeling stupid.

Presently Tan San came out with a young woman carrying a baby and a little bundle. She looked like a peasant woman, her silk tunic faded with age. Her face seemed familiar. The sleeping baby, bundled in rags, looked healthy. It was about a year old, had pink cheeks and a large head.

"My sister," Tang San announced as he helped the woman up onto the cart. "You've met before." He climbed onto the cart and ordered the driver to get going.

While they drove back to Fong's house, the woman opened a little bundle and brought out some baby clothes—a red jacket, a red cap and a pair of red shoes, all with tiger heads embroidered on them to ward off evil spirits.

"We have forgotten his pants!" the woman shouted at Tang San.

"Never mind," Tang San said, taking off his blue silk jacket and tossing it to his sister. "Wrap him in this—but not before he relieves himself."

The woman put the new jacket on the boy, then, carrying him in a sitting position, she hissed to urge him to relieve himself. All this fuss had finally awakened the child, who obediently urinated into the hay. When he had finished, the woman wrapped the lower part of his body with Tang San's jacket.

"My sister and her baby son; remember her?" Tang San asked Fong.

"Yes," Fong said thoughtfully, remembering that fateful day when Tang San's father had brought the entire brood to his home, demanding compensation. The sister had been about fifteen then. Fong recalled her pretty face.

"My sister is a widow," Tang San went on. "Now you have a concubine and a baby son. When your mother sees them, she will die happy."

Fong did not know what to think about the fraud, but he decided to go along with it.

"I know what you are thinking," Tang San said. "Your mother will wonder why you have been hiding her all these years. Just tell her that you kept your concubine a secret because she is a peasant woman. You were ashamed. . . ."

Fong found himself drifting helplessly. He had no choice but to listen to this shady character, whom he had rescued, helped and educated. If this ridiculous conspiracy to fool his dying mother failed, he would give himself the immense pleasure of throwing Tang San out of his house and washing his hands of him forever.

When they returned to the house, Aunt Loo was frantic. "Where have you been?" she cried. "Your mother is dying and you disappear! Where is your filial piety?"

"Is she still alive?" Fong asked anxiously.

"Don't worry. She won't go until she has given you a last tongue-lashing. Who are these people?"

He started to stammer an explanation, but Tang San spoke for him instead. He introduced his sister and the baby to Aunt Loo, who shook her head despairingly but went along with the scheme.

They hurried to Madame Fong's room as the old lady was about to slip into a coma. When she heard the cry of a baby, she jerked her head and opened her eyes. Fong took the baby to her and made a hurried confession about his secret concubine. While bouncing the baby in front of his mother's eyes, he introduced the baby's mother.

"Surprise, surprise!" Aunt Loo cried with a hollow laugh. "The boy's name is Little Fei. Call your grandmother, Little Fei."

Frightened by all the hullabaloo, Little Fei let out an ear-splitting howl that wakened Madame Fong sufficiently to realize what was going on. She put out a trembling hand to touch the baby.

"Strong boy," she mumbled weakly. "He has a powerful cry. . . ."

"His mother is a strong peasant woman, Mother . . ." Fong began. But he never finished what he had intended to say. Madame Fong closed her eyes and died with a smile on her face—just as Tang San had promised.

14

One day while he was working at his office, Fong had an unexpected visitor. The man walked in like an old friend, extended a large hand over his desk and greeted him in English with a heavy accent. Both his broad dark face and his voice were familiar. Fong stared at him, unable to place him.

"So you don't recognize me, eh?" the man said with a laugh. "All men of noble birth are forgetful, as the old saying goes."

Fong regarded him for another moment, then laughed. "Of course!" he cried with delight. "My old Manchu friend. How are you, Yao? You look entirely different."

"Fifty pounds' difference—all in the wrong places," Yao chuckled. "Nobody can fight the onslaught of age. But you still look as young and handsome as ever."

"Thank you. Flattery is good for the ego. Let's go to a teahouse so we can talk."

They went to a small teahouse behind the yamen and took a corner table. They could not stop talking; both were hungry for information about each other and about their friends of Boston days. Yao had been in contact with most of the eleven students. All the Manchus were back in Peking, highly placed in government service. "I don't know about you Hans," Yao said. "Remember Ling?"

"Of course," Fong said. "Where is he?"

"He came back with a venereal disease. Exiled back to his own province, Hunan. Last I heard, he was selling eggs on the street. Did you take him to visit any Boston prostitutes?"

The news shocked Fong. He had been very fond of Ling, a little fellow who was annoying and pleasing at the same time. He and Ling had been close.

"Selling eggs! Couldn't he do better than that? He could at least teach."

"How can he teach? Everybody knows he has an incurable, immoral disease."

"What happened to Kao Sung?"

"He died of gallstones. Ate too much good food. I hate to call a dead man a glutton, but he was, and died for it. I don't know about you Hans. Hope you continue to have your luck."

"Well, I am not so sure," Fong said. Saddened, he wiped a tear from his eye, pretending that some dust had gotten into it.

"We Manchus don't have your bad habits—women and food," Yao said, shaking his head.

"How about you? You seem to have had the best of luck; you look prosperous."

Yao was modest about his good luck, but he confessed that all he had learned in Boston was dishwashing. Fortunately, he hadn't needed much ability in his job. In the past several years he had been leading an easy life at the Bureau of Royal Affairs—smoking, sipping tea, leafing through government documents without actually reading them. Sometimes he dozed with his eyes open so that he could claim he was always working, always reading something. "But one day not too long ago," he said, "I came across a document from Li Hung-chang's yamen. It made me sit up. It was a letter from you, my daring, woman-chasing friend from the good old Boston days. You were complaining about a Han being ill-treated by some Manchus. Nothing of great significance . . ."

"Yao," Fong said, interrupting him, "a Han and his family were banished from their home and his properties confiscated—all because his daughter refused to become a maid for Prince Kung. Do you call that nothing?"

"Quite a girl!" Yao said with a sigh. "All the others are dying to become royal maids so that one day they might become royal concubines. Anyway, when I saw your signature and seal on that letter, I almost leaped out of my chair and cheered. I wanted to visit you immediately, but I told myself to wait. I had to bring my old friend a gift. So I went to see Prince Ying, the pinheaded administrator of the bureau, and begged him to release the prisoner. I was lucky. Prince Ying had just finished a pipe of opium and was in a good mood. Was the gift delivered?"

"Thank you, Yao. The father's return made the whole family very happy and grateful. For a while I almost believed it was my letter that did it. Without you, it would probably have landed in a wastebasket."

"Who is he, a relative?"

"No, just the father of a lady I have befriended."

Yao looked at him with a mischievous smile. "Of course. Is the romance serious?"

"Quite."

"Of course, of course," Yao said with a loud laugh, pointing a nicotined finger at Fong's nose. "You—always a ladies' man. You would risk your life for a woman. Tell me about her."

"You'll learn everything in time."

"I wonder what happened to your American girlfriend. Remember her?"

"You haven't changed," Fong said, laughing with him. "By the way—I have another request. Count it as a gift, too."

"What is it?"

"It's about the same man. The government confiscated his noodle factory. Can you get it back for him? The family is destitute. The factory is their livelihood."

"When is your birthday?"

"Two months from now."

Yao scratched his chin pensively for a moment. Then he took a sip of tea and said, "Tai, to tell you the truth, we Manchus don't mind releasing a Han from prison, but returning his property is another matter. It's like pulling a good tooth. If I can do it, count it as my birthday gift to you. Let's talk about your lady friend."

"Let's talk about you. I have known you for years, but I know little about you and nothing about your family."

"A Manchu's family is the least exciting part of his life. A Manchu marries at seventeen, by order of his father. He has a baby the next year, by order of his father, and from then on a baby every two years until he becomes impotent. At forty-seven, he is old. If he lives to be fifty, he will have the biggest birthday party of his life. Everyone follows this pattern, duller than the life of a mountain ant."

"How many children do you have now?"

"Three more to go before I fulfill my quota of five. I'm already tired."

"Tired, but with no complications. I envy you."

Yao studied him. "You know," he said with a little amused smile, "if there were magic that could make people exchange lives, I wouldn't mind exchanging with you. Not your entire life, mind you, but a few of your dull years, which would be terribly exciting to me." He took a sip of tea, leaned back and rubbed his hands eagerly. "Now, let me hear about your new complications."

✻

Fong Tai had kept his complications to himself. So far, probably only his wife and Tang San knew about them. He rarely saw Yao, but visited Rose every day. He expected his wife to protest—to make a scene—but she did not. Silence was her weapon, which bothered him more than yelling or whining. In her silence, he imagined all sorts of agony—jealousy, anger, hate—pent up in her heart, ready to explode.

"Listen, Shao Mei," Fong urged her one night after dinner, "let your troubled thoughts out. Speak up. Your silence is worse than screaming."

"Where is your filial piety?" she answered quietly.

Fong threw up his hands and groaned. "Not again! I am tired of Confucius and his gibberish about fertility, posterity and filial piety! It takes two to produce a son. I am not too sure who is at fault."

"I am not talking about a son," Shao Mei said, casting him a quick sharp glance. "Everybody is still in mourning, and yet you keep visiting that prostitute. What will your mother think?"

"My mother is dead; she does not think."

"Her spirit is with us, like all the other ancestors."

There was a knock on the door. Fong jumped to open it. Tang San stepped in. Fong was ready to welcome anybody, even Tang San. "Come in and have a cup of tea," he said.

Tang San sat on one of the rattan chairs, picked up an orange from a plate and started peeling it. "Tai, your mother died with a happy smile on her face, did she not?"

"Yes, she did, thanks to you," Fong said, pouring a cup of tea for him from a pot in a tea warmer.

"Please don't thank me; thank my sister."

"She has been well paid for the service."

"Now, remember this: nobody is sure you can fool a spirit."

"What do you mean?"

"Just in case your mother's spirit cannot be fooled . . . nobody is sure that she is happy about it. That's what I mean."

"Don't beat around the bush! What are you talking about?"

"Assume we can't fool a spirit," Tang San said, chewing the orange and swallowing its juice noisily. "It is not too late to correct the situation. My sister says she does not mind moving in here with the baby. We can make the whole thing real. She is a widow, you know. Then you two can become a couple in the eyes of your mother's spirit. Your wife has already given her consent."

Fong turned to Shao Mei. "Did you discuss this with him?" he asked sharply.

"Yes," she said without looking at him. "It is better than having you visit a prostitute every night."

"Mr. Fong," Tang San said, "be reasonable. Save your reputation, save your marriage, make your mother's spirit happy. The rumors about you and the Sword Courtesan are traveling fast. Paper cannot wrap fire. All your relatives have been whispering behind your back. . . ."

Fong looked at his wife, who was fighting tears. "Shao Mei," he said. He felt like flooring Tan San with a flying kick. "Shao Mei, I want you to ask me for a divorce."

"I don't know what you are talking about."

"Get rid of me. I am no good for you. I am cruel to a wife. I don't deserve you."

"Now, listen," Tang San chimed in. "My sister only asks to be your concubine, not your wife."

"You shut up!" Fong shouted, his fists clenched.

Tang San merely shrugged and picked up another orange.

Pretending to blow her nose, Shao Mei covered her face with her handkerchief. She was trembling. Unable to endure the sight of her suffering, Fong rose and started for the door. At the door he turned, pointing a warning finger at Tang San.

"Tang San," he said ominously, "I am not going to say this again: from now on you mind your own business—understand?"

"Sure, Mr. Fong," Tang San said cheerfully. "I'll do anything to help, believe me."

15

I t was still early in the evening. Since Rose had dismissed her servant to save money, she cooked an early dinner—a few unusual dishes garnished with spices and a herb called dong quei, Fong Tai's favorite. After the meal and several jars of warm shao hsing, they started a game of chess. But the dong quei and shao hsing together made both of them impatient and anxious, unable to concentrate on the game. Without a word, gripping each other's hands, they moved into the bedroom like fish plunging back into water.

They made love naturally and spontaneously. The silent communication between them intensified the pleasure. They drifted happily together, enjoying every move and every part of their bodies, then coming to climax and a wonderful afterglow.

Rose nestled against him in the canopied bed, her naked body warm and soft. Sighing with pleasure, she clung to him as though she never wanted to let go.

This feeling of mutual closeness made him oblivious to his troubled marriage. Most of his troubles had been caused by his association with Rose, yet the sight of her had become the only soothing medicine for all his discomforts and pain. He was grateful. She was worth more than all the problems she had created.

"You are so quiet," she whispered. "What are you thinking about?"

"At the moment I am only thinking about how lucky I am," he whispered, feeling the soft black hair that she had just brushed away from her face.

"I have something to tell you," she said. "But you may be afraid to hear it."

"Afraid?" he said with a chuckle. "What is it? A ghost story?"

"I am pregnant."

Fong was stunned. Had he not wanted a child? Wasn't that his mother's greatest wish? He felt a sudden surge of emotion. Giving her a passionate kiss, he said, "Rose, this will be the greatest birthday gift I'll ever have in my life. Thank you!"

Rose buried her face in his chest and sobbed. He held her tightly until she had recovered. "I am so happy, so happy," she said, drying her tears. "I was so afraid at first. From now on I am all yours. What are we going to name him?"

"Who?"

"The baby."

"We don't know if it is a boy or a girl."

"Suppose it is a boy. What will you name him?"

Fong thought for a moment. With a sigh, he said a bit humorously, "We shall call him Fong Pu-chi—Fong Never Too Late. Wait until I tell Father Barrington; it will give him a good laugh."

They lay quietly for a long while, enjoying the new bond. "Tai," she said, "I don't want you to worry about anything. I'll do anything to support the child—sweep floors, wash rice bowls, anything. . . ."

"Nonsense! You will devote all your time to the three of us: yourself, me and Fong Pu-chi. From now on we shall have the best of everything." He stopped. How were they going to have the best of everything? He was suddenly hit by reality and his dreams crashed to earth. He quickly changed the subject.

"Let's finish the game of chess." Pretending to be cheerful and chatty, he climbed out of bed and got dressed.

*

During one of Li Hung-chang's rare appearances, he called Fong to his office. After the ritual of snuff-bottle sniffing and sneezing, he said in his birdlike voice, "From now on I am going to put more responsibility on your shoulders. Here are your new titles." He pushed an impressive document toward him.

Fong read the appointments: "Administrative Assistant to the Governor of Chi-li and Adviser to the Grand Councilor of Foreign Affairs." Fong stared at the titles and swallowed several times. Never in his wildest dreams had he expected such a quick promotion. The appointment made him dizzy. Li Hung-chang went on, "I have also petitioned the Emperor to consider you as a possible successor to the Governor of Chi-li. You are rather young, but the Emperor is in favor of Western-educated young men to replace all the withered old mummies in the government. His Majesty is studying the history of foreign powers. Your chance of succeeding me is very good. But two factions are fighting within the government: the Emperor's reform supporters versus the Empress Dowager's conservatives. A man must have his beliefs, but he must also know how to survive political struggle."

*

Rose's pregnancy was kept secret until one day when a messenger brought Fong a note saying that she was in labor. He dropped his work and rushed home with mixed emotions. In his troubled mind, excitement was struggling against his problem with Shao Mei, who had refused to grant him a divorce. Since her return from her own home, she had been waging a war. She was silently angry without demonstrating her feelings. Fong felt her pain and it in turn ruined his own happiness, spoiled all the recent good tidings—his promotion and now the birth of his child.

A baby girl had already been delivered when he arrived. He marked the date, June 16, 1893; he was thirty-two years old. Rose's family—parents and two brothers—were all there, fussing over her, feeding her dong quei and other nourishing herbal foods. He almost lost his temper when he saw that two New York steaks which Barrington had bought for him were lying on the floor being devoured by the family dog.

The family greeted him coldly, but Rose was happy to see him. "It's a girl," she said. "Too bad we cannot use the name Fong Pu-chi." She was still in pain, but managed a smile and pointed to a darkish baby being rocked and cooed at by her grandmother.

"We will reserve that name for our next one," Fong said, sitting on her bed. He took her hand and held it tightly.

Rose, oblivious to her discomfort, looked at him tenderly, her eyes full of tears. Rose's mother handed the baby to Fong. Rocking it gently, Fong hummed a little tune, his heart aglow with love.

"Don't worry, Mrs. Liang," he said to Rose's mother. "She will be raised with a proper name and proper support."

*

For several weeks Fong's main interest was the baby. He had named her Fong Yun, or Beautiful Face. He visited her every day, bringing her baby food which Father Barrington had bought at the Foreign Legation Store.

He also brought her Western clothes, but Rose's family insisted that Fong Yun wear the traditional Chinese jacket, tiger-head cap and tiger-head shoes, which were supposed to repel evil spirits.

16

Fong Tai was truly a happy man. His career was on the rise. Any day now Li Hung-chang might die or retire, and Fong might step into one or several of Li's awesome positions. The only grain of sand in his eye was his wife's refusal to grant him a divorce.

When he returned home one evening, Fong was walking on a cloud. He carried an unfinished cheesecake which the legation ladies had baked for Father Barrington. At a crossroads, he wondered if he should go see Rose or continue home. He had never brought anything to his wife. Perhaps he should go home, serve her tea and cake and say something nice.

The front gate of his house was wide open. The moment he walked in, he discovered a crowd of relatives waiting for him in the middle hall. They all looked gloomy and miserable.

"Tai, Tai!" Aunt Loo said tearfully. "Your mother would turn in her grave if she heard this. Shame, shame!"

"My mother is dead. She certainly will not turn in her grave, no matter what I do!"

"Tai," Third Uncle said, grimacing, "be civil. When did this happen?"

"When did what happen? Will someone please tell me? Did I commit a crime?"

"Worse than that!" a cousin shouted, pointing an accusing finger at him.

"Tai," Aunt Loo said, wiping her red eyes, "how could you? Make a prostitute bear your child! You have ruined our family name. You have insulted our ancestors!"

Without waiting for her to finish, Fong walked out. He marched across the yard and burst into Tang San's room. Tang San, as usual, was lying in bed cracking watermelon seeds and reading. Fong grabbed him by his shirtfront and slapped him repeatedly. Tang San, too stunned to resist or say anything, dropped back onto the pillow and stared at Fong with an injured expression.

"I warned you!" Fong snarled. "You should have kept your damned mouth shut!"

Tang San wiped a trickle of blood from his mouth. "You should not have done this, Fong Tai," he said quietly. "I haven't done anything. I don't know why you struck me."

"Why did you tell my family about Rose and the baby?"

"Your wife told them. She even showed everybody your letter. I never said anything."

Fong remembered that he had written to Shao Mei about Rose's pregnancy. Relenting, he apologized. "Where is my wife?"

"She went to see her mother again. Do you blame her?"

✳

Fong withdrew from Tang San's room, angry with himself. To seek consolation, he started out to see Yao, but before reaching Yao's house, he changed his mind. He decided to see Rose first and ask her to prepare for unpleasant news. He did not know what was going to happen, but he had to make sure that nothing would shock her.

Rose was breast-feeding the baby when he walked in. Fong Yun looked different, growing fast on Western baby food and Rose's milk. Her complexion had changed from darkish to pink. She had gained several pounds.

Fong sat on the bed and stroked the baby. "Fong Yun, my little heart and liver, you had better grow up to be a beautiful woman, like your mother. Now give me a little smile . . ." He tickled her and the baby started to howl.

Rose bared her breast quickly. Fong Yun sought the nipple and started sucking hungrily.

"God, she is a glutton!" he said with a laugh. "Rose, you had better eat more New York steaks."

"Tai," Rose said, "Western food is too expensive! Some good red-cooked pork is just as nourishing."

"Don't worry about money; it is not your responsibility. By the way, I may have some good news for you soon. I talked to a Manchu friend who works for Prince Ying, the head of the Bureau of Royal Affairs. He told me that the government might return your father's noodle factory."

"If that happens," she said happily, "it will be the greatest blessing to our family. No, the second-greatest blessing. The greatest is that I met you." She took his hand and looked at him tenderly.

After a light dinner, they put the baby to bed and started a game of chess. But Rose sensed that something was wrong.

"What can be wrong?" he said in response to her question.

"The frown on your brow. What is it?"

"A frown can be caused by many things," he said, trying to sound casual. "A little itch in the back can make a man scowl."

"Do you have an itch? I have a back-scratcher."

"All right," Fong admitted, "there *is* something that bothers me. Everyone knows we have a baby, and my wife still refuses to divorce me."

Rose was quiet.

"Are you disappointed?" Fong asked.

"I can wait."

Fong knew she was deeply disappointed but that she refused to show it. He decided not to stay. It was too hard to hide his troubled mind.

After he left, Fong paid Yao a visit. Yao lived in a pleasant house with a large courtyard and an impressive entrance that was guarded by two stone lion-dogs. This was almost like a sign saying, "Mandarin's residence, keep off!" The doorman took his calling card inside and soon Yao came out to greet him. They went to Yao's tidy, book-lined study, where a maid served tea and tidbits.

"What brings you here at this hour?" Yao asked. "Did you have dinner?"

"Yes. Any good news about the noodle factory?"

Yao waited until the maid had finished serving. As soon as she had left the room, he shook his head. "I bought some mao tai this morning to celebrate, but things changed this afternoon. If you want a jar of it anyway, we still can drink it, celebration or no celebration."

"All right, Yao. I can take it. Tell me what happened."

"When I heard about it, I argued with myself as to whether I should tell you."

Fong suspected that the news about Rose's baby had ruined everything, including the possible return of her father's noodle factory. "So you heard about it, too?"

"Hasn't everybody?" Yao said. "You are a famous man. Anyway, we'll have some mao tai."

Fong began to feel angry. "Yes, I slept with a prostitute!" he cried, his voice wavering between rage and despair. "And she bore my child. I damaged the good reputation of the government. I gave the Great Ching Dynasty a bad name. But it was my responsibility, wasn't it? Why should her family be deprived of a livelihood? Why doesn't the government decapitate me and hoist my head over Chien Men Gate?" He sank into a chair and buried his face in his hands.

Yao brought him the mao tai. "Let's have a drink," he said quietly. "Not to celebrate, but to kill the memories of a bad day."

Fong gulped down the drink. "Yao," he said, his anger spent, "I'm sorry I lost control. You know it's not like me."

"I know," Yao said with a smile. "If I hadn't known you before, I would personally have thrown you out and given you a kick in the behind."

"Can I stay here for a few days? Do you have a spare bed?"

"I have room for twelve children; I have produced only two so far. Stay as long as you wish. If the children are too noisy, I'll be happy to supply some cotton for your ears."

"It can't be any worse than the chatter of my relatives," Fong said, forcing a smile.

17

When Fong Tai arrived at his office the next morning he found a note on his desk. Li Hung-chang wanted to see him at once. The yamen was full of gloom; everybody was talking about Li's impending death. On his way to Li's house, Fong wondered if it was already too late. It would be another blow if Li had already passed away. A dying man's last words were his will, and it would be disastrous if he had missed the chance to hear them.

An armed guard at the front gate saluted him as he mounted the marble steps. The two lion-dogs guarding the red-lacquered double doors looked a little older and dirtier. The large, almost bare courtyard inside the gate was neat and clean, and the freshly painted palatial buildings with glazed tiles and carved eaves were still bright and cheerful; but the numerous servants and maids doing chores inside looked gloomy.

Fong hurried to Li's bedroom. Li, propped up with several pillows, was lying in a large carved bed. Sitting beside him in an ancestral chair was a bearded doctor who was holding Li's wrist, his eyes closed in concentration, trying to feel the old man's pulse. A maid was busy dusting the antique art objects that decorated the dark, incense-filled room. The first urge Fong felt was to throw all the windows open and toss out the incense bowls along with the herb doctor. But at least Li was still alive.

With a sigh of relief, Fong approached the bed. "I came as soon as I read your note, Your Excellency," he said with a bow.

Li was alert. Waving a hand, he told the doctor and the maid to leave. After the two had withdrawn, Fong took the doctor's chair and waited for Li to assign all his duties to him.

"Tai," Li said, his voice so weak that Fong had to lean closer to hear him, "I am disappointed and chagrined."

"Don't be, Your Excellency," Fong said encouragingly. "The affairs of state are not that bad, and you'll get well. I will do my best to perform whatever duries you entrust . . ."

"No, no!" Li said irritably. "I'm talking about you."

Fong felt a sudden chill. Li did not have to say anything more. It was the same curse—his affair with a prostitute.

"Your incorrigible way of life is ruining your career," Li went on. "I am giving you a choice: either abandon your sinful ways or resign your job."

"Do I have to decide now?"

"I give you a week. I need time to find another man to take your place."

"You mean I am dismissed whether I think it over or not."

"Knowing you, I can predict your answer," Li said, his voice squeaking like a bird's. "I want you to think it over carefully. You are a good man. You can do a great deal. It would be a shame to ruin your life . . . all because of your one great weakness—women. I am very disappointed."

"Anything else, Your Excellency?" Fong asked, rising quickly.

"No," Li said with a wave of the hand. "Tell the doctor to come in."

"Yes, Your Excellency."

Fong left Li's house in a daze. For a while he wandered in the neighborhood, not knowing where he was going. His mind was a blank; he walked aimlessly until he reached Heavenly Bridge, the poor men's playground which he had frequented as a boy. Old memories came back vividly—the decapitated bodies over which he had stumbled and fallen, the Mongolian wrestlers who had rescued him when he was being chased by Manchu guards at Chien Men Gate. . . .

He went to the spot where the wrestling team had performed. Occupying the spot was a professional letter-writer, a withered old man in a faded and patched silk gown who sat behind a small unpainted desk, writing letters for illiterate coolies.

Fong tossed a silver coin onto the man's desk and hurried away, horrified at the thought that he himself might one day end up sitting behind such a crude desk writing letters. He had often visualized himself sitting behind Li Hung-chang's desk. Now the hope seemed dashed.

Fong walked until he was exhausted. Unwilling to face his family or his colleagues, he dropped into a small inn and slept restlessly for a few hours. Next morning he rose early and had a breakfast of soy milk and sesame cake at an open-air coolie restaurant outside Chien Men Gate. The hub-bub of the market annoyed him. Feeling increasingly depressed and lonely, he decided to pay Rose a visit. Rose and the baby were his only consolation now, even though they were the cause of his troubles.

Rose was in the courtyard, kneeling on the ground, washing clothes in a small tub when he arrived. She scrubbed energetically, a tuft of loose hair bobbing on her forehead. There was perspiration on her flushed face. The drudgery and her haggard look wrung his heart, bringing tears to his eyes.

Her face lit up momentarily when she saw him. She got up quickly and they greeted each other with a warm embrace, then she broke away, trying to hide her face. He grabbed her by the arm and turned her around.

"I am sorry about what happened," he said, "but everything will work out. Let's go inside. I want to see the baby."

Inside her bedroom, Fong Yun was sound asleep on the large bed. She looked beautiful, innocent and helpless. What was going to happen to her? What would her future be? He glanced at Rose, who also looked troubled.

"Are you hungry?" Rose asked. "Shall I warm some food?"

"No. But I don't mind having a cup of tea."

They went to the middle hall and sat on the daybed. Rose poured two cups of hot tea from a pot in a tea warmer. Sipping the fragrant jasmine tea, Fong said, "I'm sorry I have not come to see you for a few days."

"I know you have been busy," she said, serving him a dish of water-melon seeds.

They sipped tea and cracked melon seeds quietly for a few moments.

"Are you all right?" Rose asked.

"Yes, yes," he said without conviction.

"Your Aunt Loo visited me yesterday," she said after a pause. "She asked me to move away."

"She did, eh?" Fong said with a forced laugh. "I'm surprised she didn't visit you sooner. Did my uncle come, too?"

"No, she came alone."

"To tell you the truth, I expected her to come with the whole noisy brood of the Fong family, cousins and all, three generations strong. What else did my Aunt Loo say? Don't answer. 'If you don't move away,' she said, 'I'll report you to the Peking Garrison and they'll throw you in jail.'"

"Tai"—Rose interrupted him quickly—"she did not say any such thing!

She was polite. She loves you. She does not want to see you ruined. She says if I too love you, I must help you by not seeing you again."

"How easy, how simple! How convenient! What did you say?"

"I told her I would think about it."

"Are you serious?"

"No."

Fong held her and kissed her. "You've made the right decision, Rose. In fact, I saw Li Hung-chang yesterday. He gave me a choice. He said, 'Fong Tai, either your sinful life or your job.' I chose my sinful life, except that I don't call it sinful. I call it love."

Rose smiled. He took her hand. "Rose, as long as we love each other, nothing else matters. This morning I've come to tell you of my choice. I'll abandon everything for you—my family, my job, my comfort, my work, my future, everything! Look at me, Rose. There is one thing that nobody can take away from us—our happiness. I value that above anything you can name—glory, fame, fortune . . ."

He got up and began to pace. "I'm happy, can't you see? For the first time in my life I'm free! Free of all the shackles, free from bureaucracy, Confucius, filial piety, patriotism, loyalty. Everything! I'm free from all the traditional nonsense, free from everything except your love!"

He returned to the daybed and held both her hands again. "Rose, there is only one thing that could ruin me now . . . four words from your mouth: 'I don't love you.' Only those four words from you could ruin me, crush me and bury me."

Tears began to stream down Rose's cheeks. She kissed both his hands. "I love you, Tai. I love you! I'll never stop loving you!"

18

Fong made three stops that afternoon. First he went to the Governor's yamen, wrote a letter of resignation on a plain piece of paper, collected his private papers and left without saying goodbye to his colleagues. He was reluctant to see them, for fear they might be embarrassed. He decided that he might as well save everybody the painful awkwardness of expressing sympathy that they did not really feel.

As he sneaked out of the yamen, he hoped that someone would discover his letter of resignation soon enough to prevent a rumor that he had been dismissed. Tang San, by then his assistant, would probably hear about it first. Fong still felt uncomfortable about slapping him. Even though he resented the man, he still felt some affection for the rascal.

His next stop was Father Barrington's house. Barrington was not in. The young maid opened the door and allowed Fong to write a letter in the living room. Using a quill pen, he scribbled a long letter on Barrington's cluttered desk. He told Barrington of his resignation and asked him to buy more Western food at the Foreign Legation Store for his new family. He even extended an invitation to a family dinner. "Let's give Eight Great Lanes a good name," he concluded. "If you, the High Minister, dine there, nobody will feel ashamed to visit me. I've traded my sinful life for a decent one, right in the middle of Peking's red-light district. Who knows, I might raise my daughter there as a Catholic. With the Lord's help, we might even convert all the girls." He signed the letter with a flourish and put Barrington's magnifying glass on top of it.

He left the priest's residence in a better mood. Now he was beginning to see humor in everything. With the Lord's help, he might become a preacher. He might even have a new calling card printed with his new address under his name and his self-designated title. That would shock his friends and relatives.

He stopped at Yao's house to collect his belongings. Yao was home nursing a cold in his head. When he told Yao of his plans, the Manchu reacted to the news with a sneezing spell. After it had subsided, he threw his head back and laughed so hard he shook the bed.

"Tai," he said, "I'm a pretty good musician; I'll come to conduct your choir of prostitutes. To keep my government job, I'll disguise myself as a foreigner. Are you going to have a confession box?"

"We'll have an extra-large one," Fong said with a smile. "When the girls come to confess, you may eavesdrop and collect some interesting names."

"What a list!" Yao said, chuckling. "It will make Prince Ying return that noodle factory to its rightful owner without a second thought."

After many good laughs, Fong left Yao and went to see Rose. He wanted to move to his new home in style, a move that would symbolize the beginning of a new life.

But when he arrived, he found the small courtyard full of people, mostly curious bystanders from the neighborhood. A woman's wailing inside the house surprised him and gave him a sudden sick feeling. He pushed through the crowd and hurried into the main house. In Rose's bedroom, a middle-aged woman was crying over something that was covered with a blanket.

Fong rushed to the bed and tore the blanket away. Rose lay pale and lifeless, her eyes still open.

"What happened?" he demanded, ignoring the rising pain in his chest.

"She hanged herself," one of her brothers said. Fong immediately recognized the crying woman as Rose's mother. Standing behind them was Chin, Rose's other brother, glaring at Fong. He even made a threatening move but was quickly restrained by his older brother.

"Keep away from her," Chin said. "We don't need you here!"

Fong felt a numbness for a brief moment, then chill and nausea began to rise. He stared at Rose's body, dry-eyed, while her mother moaned and called her daughter's name, knocking her head against the bed in agony.

More relatives flocked in. Some threw themselves on the floor and wailed.

Fong heard the cry of a baby. He turned and found Fong Yun lying in a crib in the corner, frightened by all the noise. He picked her up and rocked her in his arms, talking to her softly. He carried her and her bottle to a chair, where he sat down and fed her, his torn heart soothed by the little girl.

As she sucked on the bottle, he adjusted her tiger-head cap and smoothed her red clothes. Then he saw a piece of paper sticking out of her pocket. The note was from Rose, shakily written on rice paper with a brush:

> My darling, this is my only wish—to save you from complete ruin. Fong Yun will take my place. I shall go in peace, as I know you will raise her with all your love. Yours forever, Rose.

Fong pocketed the note and walked quietly out of the crowded room, holding Fong Yun close to his heart. Using meditation, he shut everything out of his mind. He remained undisturbed until he reached the front gate. Suddenly a hand grabbed him from behind. "Where are you taking her?" a voice demanded.

Fong stopped, recognizing the voice of Rose's younger brother, Chin.

"Let me go," he said. "She is my daughter."

Chin pointed a knife at his throat, glaring at him with murderous eyes. Ting, the other brother, rushed over and restrained Chin, grabbing his arm.

"Let him take the damned brat," he said. "We don't want his flesh and blood in our family."

"Get out!" the younger brother shouted, spitting in Fong's face. "We don't want to see you again; you are bad luck, you despicable dog!"

Suppressing his anger, Fong left the courtyard. As he walked away from Eight Great Lanes, he felt the warmth of his daughter in his arms. Wriggling, she even managed a little smile. He looked at her and smiled himself. And suddenly his hatred and anger disappeared, filling his heart were love and tenderness.

Where would he go? He was free, yet all doors were closed to him. He could probably impose on Yao or Father Barrington. It was ironic, he thought, that he, a successful Han, had only two friends, one Manchu and one foreigner.

He turned in the direction of Smoke Pipe Lane, his own home. It was the only logical place to go.

Old Liu looked surprised but was happy to see his master. He was the only servant who was always loyal and obedient.

"Yes, Mrs. Fong is in," he said. "She is in her room."

Fong squared his shoulders and walked into his wife's room with the sleeping baby in his arms.

Shao Mei looked up from her embroidery as he greeted her gruffly. She looked much older than her age. Life had not been kind to her, and Fong felt partly responsible. Her graying hair and premature wrinkles hurt him, softening his hostility. His belligerence gone, he approached her with a slight smile. "I haven't seen you for quite a while, Shao Mei. You look well."

"Thank you," she replied coldly, returning to her embroidery after a quick glance at him.

"I have brought Fong Yun. She is going to live here with us."

He waited for his wife to protest, but Shao Mei was silent. For a while there was no sound but her stitching, her busy needle punching up and down through the tautly framed silk. "She lost her mother, you know," Fong went on, his voice rising slightly. "She killed herself. So I'm asking you to accept this little girl."

Again there was no response. "Please, Shao Mei," he said with a tinge of anger in his voice now, "I want you to understand. Her mother killed herself to protect me. It was stupid. She should have lived to protect the little girl. Now Fong Yun needs a home. She won't be a burden to you. I will take care of her."

His wife was still silent.

"If you object, say so!"

When she ignored him again, he lost his temper. "It doesn't matter," he said. "Whether you object or not, she is going to stay here! After all, this is my house, too, and there is nothing you can do . . ."

Before he had finished, a horde of relatives, headed by Aunt Loo, marched in, talking and arguing. Third Uncle was among them, looking distressed. When Aunt Loo saw the baby, she shot out a finger at it and demanded, "What is that?"

"That's my daughter, Fong Yun," Fong replied defiantly. "She is going to live here."

"So this is the illegitimate baby from your prostitute friend," a cousin said with a raised eyebrow. Several others began to leer, making throaty noises.

"Shao Mei," another cousin said, "how dare he bring that thing home?"

"Tai," Aunt Loo said, "Shao Mei may have something to say about this. We shall all lose face if you allow that thing to live here."

"She is not 'that thing'!" Fong shouted. "She is my daughter! Her name is Fong Yun!"

"She was born out of wedlock," Aunt Loo argued. "How are you going to face your ancestors?"

"My ancestors be damned! Even dead, they are probably more sympathetic and humane than all of you!"

"Shao Mei," Aunt Loo said, her face flushed, "don't you have anything to say about this? This is your house, you know. . . ."

Shao Mei stopped stitching. She glared at Aunt Loo. "Yes, this is my house! It is not your concern who can live here and who cannot!"

Aunt Loo gasped. She turned to Third Uncle for help. Third Uncle studied the ceiling, feigning indifference.

"Third Uncle," she implored, "did you hear that? You are the head of this family; do you allow someone to talk like that to your face?"

Third Uncle spread his arms with a shrug. "Why can't she talk like that? I am the head—but she owns the house."

A few of the cousins also gaped.

"Tai owns it, too," Shao Mei said, her voice sharp and forceful. "Don't you forget that! Now I want you to leave us alone—all of you!"

The relatives looked stunned, except for Third Uncle. With a snort, Aunt Loo walked out, followed by the others. Third Uncle sighed. "Remember, I'm only a barking dog without teeth. Now I'm even too old to bark." With a wink, he left the room.

Fong looked at his wife, still too surprised to say anything. He had never cried in his life, always considering crying to be a woman's privilege. Now he could not stop tears from welling in his eyes. He put Fong Yun on the bed, took his wife's hands and said, his voice choking, "Shao Mei, now that I'm alone and desperate, you are the only one who . . ." He could not continue. He buried his face against her shoulder and wept.

✳

When the baby cried, Shao Mei picked her up and patted her gently, singing and cooing. She rocked her until Fong Yun fell asleep again. Every time the baby whined or twisted in discomfort, Shao Mei dropped whatever she was doing and rushed to see what was wrong. She cradled her in her arms, cooing to her, her voice full of tenderness and love.

When Fong Tai watched them, he realized that Shao Mei was a woman who had longed for a child; to his great relief, his daughter had found a loving mother.

Within a month the baby had brought many changes into the house. Aunt Loo and the cousins were seldom seen. The only relative who still came was Third Uncle, bringing food and toys. Shao Mei's room was redecorated, cluttered with colorful baby clothes, stuffed dogs, cats and panda bears. The ancestors' pictures, incense bowls and candleholders had been replaced with animal pictures, milk bottles, cans and stacks of diapers. Gone was Shao Mei's embroidery. She had not stitched once since Fong brought back the baby three months previously. All her time was devoted to Fong Yun, who had changed Shao Mei into a different person. Fong marveled at the change. She spoke with a chuckle, color had returned to her skin, and her sunken cheeks were fuller. Now she walked briskly with a little bounce, like a young woman.

Fong Yun was not demanding. Her smile, the little gurgling sounds she made, or her kick of ecstasy were great entertainments. Fong, Shao Mei, sometimes Third Uncle and the maids, would crowd around her, talking, teasing and cooing at the little girl.

19

E ventually Fong began to recover from his grief over Rose's death. Ironically, his letter of resignation had not been accepted. After Rose's suicide the incident was hushed up, and Fong's life at the office continued as if nothing had happened. Indeed, if anything his standing was enhanced.

Now, with a baby daughter to bring up, Fong had financial worries. Despite Fong's rise in the bureaucracy, the family finances were strained, and he often bought things on credit. As Fong's debts mounted, Third Uncle, who handled the family's investments, would visit the family with a stack of account books and try to straighten out their finances.

One day, as the family gathered in the living room, Fong feared what was coming. He realized now that he was no good at handling money. He had prepared a little speech.

Third Uncle was serious for the first time. "Tai, the debts you have incurred are eating away the interest you are earning. The family income is reduced to half since your mother passed away. There has been famine in the south, and the tenant farmer on the three hundred acres of rice land cannot meet the rent with this crop. The two houses in the Western City are occupied by destitute families, and again it is hard to collect rent. And I am getting old; I'm a poor debt-collector. I have brought all the books. My advice is, sell everything you own and toss the account books into that potbellied stove. Let a good fire wipe out all your headaches and your financial problems."

Fong thought for a moment. "Can the sale bring enough to pay my debts?"

"More than enough. You might have enough left to buy the baby a few more toys after you put the bulk of it in a savings bank. The interest will give the family a modest living if you cut down your mao tai and shao hsing consumption."

Before Third Uncle had finished, Fong went to the table, gathered the account books and started tossing them into the stove. "Wait a minute," Third Uncle said, trying to stop him. "There are important figures you should know."

"Such as what?"

"Such as how much those tenants still owe you."

"If the sale of these properties can wipe out my debts, there is no reason why it can't wipe out theirs, too."

Third Uncle shook his head in mock despair. Fong said, "We have done our best. We'll just leave the rest to Heaven."

Laughing, both watched the books burn.

✳

After death of Rose, Fong Tai gave much of his spare time to Kang Yu-wei's reform movement, which was increasingly coming out into the open. Many intellectuals had joined it, and several national publications had begun to publicize its activities. The first time Fong Tai met Kang Yu-wei was in a little office in the Western City. The place was hot and crowded with volunteer workers. Papers and books were piled on tables and floors. Kang, a few years older than Fong, was a tense man with a lot of nervous energy. He was tall and slim, wore a faded blue cotton gown and spoke Mandarin with a heavy Cantonese accent. Having read all of Kang's books, Fong felt that he knew the man well and found him easy to talk to.

Kang was a collector of idealists, mostly young and frustrated. He had had an immediate rapport with Fong and both could talk for hours in Kang's little private room in the back. Kang had been corresponding with Professor Hu at Harvard and had learned a great deal about overseas Chinese and Chinese students in America. He had thanked Fong for his signature on one of their petitions a decade earlier and told him that he appreciated his courage in supporting him.

"After many years of difficulty, we have finally reached the Emperor," Kang said. "But we still face strong opposition from the Empress Dowager's inner circle. Fortunately, we have His Excellency Weng Tung-ho, the Imperial Tutor, on our side. We have organized the Learn-to-Be-Strong Society, and the membership is growing rapidly. Even Li Hung-chang has offered to donate two thousand taels of silver, but we have turned it down."

"Why?" Fong asked, surprised.

"Li is known to be quite treacherous. We think he is trying to worm his way into our society for information."

Fong still felt loyalty toward Li, his old mentor and sponsor. "He is always interested in reform," he said rather heatedly.

Kang chuckled. It was a friendly chuckle but he disagreed. "His Excellency Li is like a weed on a muddy wall; it sways with the wind. His New

Movement has only one purpose: to learn from the West. It does not offend the Empress Dowager, and yet at the same time pleases the foreigners. But it is time to eat. Stay and have a bowl of wonton with me. I can hear the food peddler's yell."

He sent an old hunchbacked servant out to buy the food from the peddler. "After some hot food," he went on, "we are going to have a meeting. You are welcome to participate. By the way, we have recruited many foreign friends. Since you are fluent in English, we would like you to join our staff. We have little money, but I guarantee that you will enjoy Cripple Mah's hot wonton. You can eat as many bowls as you wish."

He laughed abruptly and became serious again, as though he had no time for laughter or frivolous talk. "Mr. Timothy Richard," he said in a lowered voice, almost confidentially, "is our most trusted friend. He is a British missionary, a true friend of our reform program. We advocate change; this is the difference between our movement and Li Hung-chang's New Movement. We have petitioned for drastic changes in the government."

"What other changes do you advocate besides trying to get rid of the eight-legged essays?" Fong asked.

"We are trying to get rid of everything old. We have a slogan: the new is strong, the old is rotten; the new is bright, the old dark; the new is pure, the old decadent."

Fong thought the statement was too sweeping and vague, but he kept quiet. "Sounds a bit childish, eh?" Kang asked. "Well, we want the common people to embrace it. Can't use big words or high-sounding slogans. We simply want the country to refute the die-hards' idea of sticking to the ancestors' established ways. The people are restless; a band of rebels called Boxers is rising. We must do something quickly to quiet these rascals down before they tear the country apart. A weakened nation becomes easier prey for foreign powers, as witness the recent struggle with Japan. Kiaochow was forcibly occupied by Germany, Lushun and Talien soon after by Czarist Russia, Kwangchow Bay by France, and Weihaiwei and Kowloon by Britain. At this critical juncture China faces total partition. The meeting tonight is going to deal with how we'll petition the Emperor for drastic action."

After they finished the tea, they repaired to the front room, where more than twenty members of the Learn-to-Be-Strong Society had gathered. The introductions were warm and friendly.

The purpose of the meeting was to draft the petition to the Emperor.

The wording was forceful and daring. It described China's grave situation, stating with alarm that the Japanese Diet had been meeting every day to discuss a plan to carve up China. It quoted foreign-language papers in which various other countries reportedly were clamoring for the same action. The foreign powers were like mines, it said. "It is as if mines were laid all around with their fuses connected. If one fuse is lighted, all the mines will explode. If the government does not hasten to start reform, it will be impossible to rule even half a country, and the Emperor and ministers will be reduced to commoners or worse. . . ."

The fact that the writers dared to use such strong language impressed Fong deeply. He secretly wiped his sweating hands under the table as they voted for the final draft.

When they finished, they proposed a toast to their expected victory. Besides the Imperial Tutor, another important man had also joined them—General Yuan Shih-kai, the commander of the seven-thousand-man modern army. With these two powerful men supporting the reforms, the members felt confident that the petition would reach the Emperor himself despite obstruction from the opposition.

After the meeting, Fong had agreed to work with the group. His main job was to compile an annotated list of books for publication. Kang had done most of the research. Fong was deeply impressed by the material and Kang's analysis of it. He also suggested his own ideas on how to organize the material to help the Emperor understand the steps and measures of the reform. The most daring book was about the French Revolution. It emphasized that Louis XVI was a good sovereign, but because he shelved the reform programs, the people finally sent him to the guillotine. When Fong Tai wrote the final draft of this analysis, not only did his hands begin to sweat, but his entire body felt chilled.

*

Increasingly Fong Tai divided his spare time between Barrington's bungalow and Kang Yu-wei's cottage at the back of his reform movement headquarters. During the Learn-to-Be-Strong Society meetings, he quickly tired of listening to redundant speeches in which the members always lamented government corruption and analyzed the symptoms of a dying dynasty. These dull dissertations often put Fong to sleep.

It was not until Liang Chi-chao, the most articulate of them all, started dealing with a new area for reform that Fong perked up. Liang specifically pointed to Tsu Hsi's indulgence in pleasure and her weakness for trusting eunuchs, especially the Chief Eunuch Li Lien-ying. She had recently used defense funds to build a stationary stone boat in the Summer Palace, which had caused a horrible scandal. Liang said that all these mistakes had provoked the silent anger of the nation.

20

One day when Fong arrived at his office he found that Li Hung-chang had already arrived and was holding a meeting with counselors and senior advisers. Fong took a seat quietly in the back of the conference room. Li saw him but did not interrupt his preliminary talk. He was repeating what China had been facing, and he wanted new ideas about how to deal with the hungry foreign powers.

From the meetings at Kang Yu-wei's headquarters, Fong had learned all about what the foreign powers had done to China during the past fifty years, cutting China up like a melon. It had started with the French wresting Vietnam away. Following that, Japan had swallowed Taiwan, Germany had seized Tsingtao, Russia had taken Li Shun and Ta Lian, the northeastern ports. Having barely digested Vietnam, France had again invaded Wei Hai in Shantung Province. England, seeing herself left behind, had quickly grabbed the Gulf of Canton. Li Hung-chang was repeating all these losses.

Finally, Li finished his dissertation. "Now," he said, eyeing the dozen men in the conference room, "a little country also wants to steal a bite of the melon. Have you heard of a place called Italy?"

Fong was jerked out of his slumber by this question. He had been doing research on Italy for one of Kang Yu-wei's books. He watched the elderly Mandarins in the room. From their blank expressions, he suspected that most of them had never heard of Italy.

Li continued, his voice getting more high-pitched, sounding like the little squeaks of a mouse. "On the map, Italy looks like a smelly little boot. This country has just given China an ultimatum, demanding a seaport in Chekiang Province. It has threatened to send battleships if we refuse."

He stopped and stared at the audience, moving his cloudy eyes from one face to another. "Tai, you were late," he said, pointing a long fingernail at Fong. "And you look sleepy. If your mind is not elsewhere, I want your opinion."

But Fong was wide awake now. Luckily his research had informed him of Italy's latest demand. The report in *The Foreign Legation Weekly* had said that England, Germany and France had already announced their willingness to support Italy's aggression.

Clearing his throat, he stood up and spoke loudly so that Li, who was hard of hearing, could understand him. "The foreign powers always say, 'Barking dogs do not bite.' China has always been regarded as a sleeping dragon or a barking dog. To deal with Italy, we must stop protesting and show a strong fist." His loud voice wakened several old-timers who had been dozing.

"What strong fist?" Li Hung-chang asked. "I don't see any strong fist, only fleeing feet."

"I can think of one, sir," Fong said. "General Liu Shu-tung, the Garrison Commander of Chekiang Province."

Li scowled as if he did not believe his ears.

"Your Excellency," Fong continued, "even a sick old dog will snarl if cornered and threatened. As long as General Liu is stationed in Chekiang Province, you will not see the back of his fleeing feet. He is like a cornered dog, sir."

There was laughter from the audience. Li rapped on the table with a letter opener for silence. "Are you serious? Or are you trying to be humorous?" He stared at Fong, unsmiling.

"I am dead serious, sir. I compare General Liu to a fist. It may not have the strength to strike, but at least it will wave."

"Wave a fist?"

"Yes, sir. It is better than barking."

"What do you mean, wave a fist?"

"Order him to send a few of his old gunboats to sea and fire a few rounds."

"Is that all?"

"No. In the meantime, tell the Japanese what will happen if Italy is allowed to occupy a Chekiang seaport. It will become the greatest threat to Japan's trade in China. This way we can use one foreign devil to fend off another."

A few old men grunted loudly and nodded their approval. "Hm," Li mumbled. "Not a bad idea. . . . Using one foreign devil to fend off another. Not a bad idea at all!"

As soon as the meeting was over, most of the elderly Mandarins gathered around Fong, congratulating him and embarrassing him with florid praise. It was, nevertheless, an honor to have so many withered Mandarins paying him so much attention.

*

Arriving home early one afternoon a few days hence, Fong smelled sulfur in the air, which usually lingered after a long explosion of firecrackers. He found debris from firecrackers in the courtyard. Rushing to greet him were Third Uncle and Aunt Loo, who excitedly reported that some of his colleagues from the Governor's yamen had just left. They had brought him gifts and a scroll. They had also hired lion dancers, who had danced amid the explosions of ten thousand firecrackers.

"Congratulations, Tai," Third Uncle exclaimed happily, slapping him on the shoulder. "You have brought honor to the Fong family. The ancestors ought to be proud."

Fong was puzzled. "Why? What have I done?"

"You should see the gifts," Aunt Loo said, leading the way toward the middle hall.

There was a black-lacquered chest in the middle of the hall. Aunt Loo and Third Uncle opened a large scroll and laid it on the incense table near the ancestral tablets. The message, written in classical language, praised Fong's wisdom and patriotism in flattering terms; it lauded his good counsel that had effectively deterred a foreign invasion.

"Isn't that wonderful!" Aunt Loo said with tears in her eyes. She had read the scroll many times. "I am putting it here so that the ancestors' spirits can all read it, especially your mother. She will be so proud!"

"What did you do to repel a foreign invasion?" Third Uncle asked.

Fong shrugged. He was utterly baffled. He had written so many memos and attended so many meetings in Li Hung-chang's yamen that he honestly did not know what he had done to deserve all this.

"Ah, such modesty!" Aunt Loo said. "An excellent virtue—all inherited from your mother's side." She opened the chest to show him the gifts inside. The two-by-four footchest, inlaid with mother of pearl, was packed with food—smoked hams, birds' nests, sharks' fins, dried fungus, mushrooms, octopus, bears' paws and other expensive delicacies.

"Tai," Third Uncle said with a laugh, "if you find me always arriving at dinnertime, you will know why."

"You had better write a thank-you letter to your colleagues," Aunt Loo said, closing the chest carefully.

*

That evening Fong paid a visit to Father Barrington. Barrington was tending his Chinese miniature garden in his antique-filled living room when Fong arrived. The European-type bungalow, warmer and cozier than the massive Chinese houses, always brought back pleasant memories of America to Fong. He thought it was one of the reasons he enjoyed visiting Barrington so much.

He and Barrington were close enough to be informal. Barrington did not bother to ask him to sit down. "I was about to send for you," he said, fishing out the latest issue of *The Foreign Legation Weekly* from a drawer. "Here's something that might interest you." He took it to his oversized sofa, sank into it and waved the magazine at Fong. "Interested in what it says?"

"I am always interested in the English-language papers' lies about China," Fong commented wryly, sitting down carefully on one of the shaky antique chairs.

Father Barrington opened the paper and cleared his throat. He read the headline in his still-sonorous but cracked voice: "China Has a New Policy." Glancing at his guest significantly, he read the story aloud:

"This new policy, 'To use one foreign devil to fend off another,' was devised by Fong Tai, Li Hung-chang's right-hand man. According to reliable reports, the policy is working. A recent example is that when Italy declared her intention of occupying a Chekiang seaport, the Manchu government was not frightened. Instead it not only rattled a saber loudly but also set the Japanese against the Italians, claiming that an Italian invasion would pose a serious threat to Japan's China trade. Italy retracted her threat immediately and recalled her battleships from the China Sea.' "

Barrington finished the article and looked up with a smile. "Use one foreign devil to fend off another, eh?" he said admiringly. "Wish I had thought of that years ago. Congratulations!"

"It was just an accident, really," Fong said modestly with a shrug.

"Accident? I never heard of any accident that could drive away battleships."

"Well, during a meeting Li Hung-chang thought I was dozing," Fong explained with a chuckle. "He asked me a question, trying to find out if I was listening to his monologue. I wasn't. His question was about the Italian invasion. I fished an answer out of thin air and it became this new foreign policy." With a shrug and a short laugh, he added, "It just shows you how China's foreign policy is usually formed. By the way, I brought you some smoked ham—compliments of the Italians."

"What do you mean?" Raising an eyebrow, Barrington accepted the large side of meat wrapped in brown Chinese oil-paper.

"Because the Italians changed their minds about invading China, my colleagues brought me a trunkful of gifts. Without the Italian threat, who would have thought of giving me anything? Now my daughter is spoiled with delicacies!"

*

One busy day at the office, Fong felt particularly restless. He could hardly wait to see Fong Yun and rock her in his arms. Just as he was about to leave, a messenger arrived to say that Father Barrington wanted to see him.

When he arrived at Barrington's residence, drinks had already been poured, newspapers spread on the dining table and a beef stew was simmering on the stove. Taking off his white apron, Barrington sat down at the dining table and pushed *The Foreign Legation Weekly* toward him. "Read that." Fong read the headline: OPEN-DOOR POLICY FOR CHINA.

Fong read the report avidly. It urged both the U.S. Congress and the British Parliament to propose an Open-Door Policy to keep China from being cut up by foreign powers. It also urged the study of a new policy to encourage international trade in China without violating China's authority to impose tariffs. Furthermore, China, as a trading partner, should be treated as an equal.

"Do you know the significance of all this?" Barrington asked as soon as Fong had finished reading the report.

"Yes," Fong said with a nod. "It means that every foreign power has an equal trade interest in China. The sight of any foreign battleships in Chinese waters will be regarded as a threat to everyone else."

"Exactly!" Barrington said, banging the table with the palm of his hand. "A damned good deterrent! I must take my hat off to Joseph Chamberlain, but the laurels actually should go to you first, my boy."

"To me? What do you mean?"

"It's based on the same principle as using one foreign devil to fend off another. Can't you see? They have stolen your idea. You may have permanently saved China from being cut up, my boy. It calls for another round of drinks."

Knowing that Barrington would find every excuse to have another round of drinks, anyway, Fong poured two more. Laughing, both proposed a toast to the Open-Door Policy.

21

O ne evening Fong was called to a meeting of the Learn-to-Be-Strong Society. Since China's brush with partition by the foreign powers earlier that year, he had become more deeply involved with the reform movement than ever.

When he arrived, the meeting had already started, with Liang Chi-chao standing at the end of the conference table, making a report. Kang Yu-wei sat beside him taking notes. Liang, Kang's right-hand man, often did the talking. He was an eloquent young man, as intense as Kang.

Liang said that the influence of the Czar was growing within the Empress Dowager's faction, while the British and the USA had shown interest and concern in the Emperor's faction, represented by the Learn-to-Be-Strong Society. The British and Americans had announced that they would contribute books to the society. They had contacted Weng Tung-ho, the Emperor's Tutor, seeking an audience with the Emperor to offer some new reform ideas.

"But not all is good news," Liang said. "Censor Young Chung-yi has submitted a memorandum to both the throne and Empress Dowager Tsu Hsi, condemning our society, saying that we are peddling China's interests to foreign powers. He suggests that our society be abolished and our publications banned."

"Censor Young is a dog without teeth," one member said with a snort. "His bark is loud, that is all."

"But his noise was heard by the Empress Dowager," another member countered. "She is sensitive to every noise and is easily alarmed."

Liang asked, "Fong Tai, you are a quick thinker. How are we going to deal with this situation? We certainly don't want a turtle's egg like Censor Young to pull the rug out from under us. Do you know anyone in the government who can talk to him . . . perhaps use a little friendly persuasion?"

Fong thought for a moment. Clearing his throat, he stood up and said, his voice grave, "I am afraid friendly persuasion does not work on everybody. To certain people, fear works better—especially fear that threatens their security. I understand that Censor Young is a little pebble in the gutter. No, a rotten apple; it spoils other apples. Let us spread some fear

and shake people up. We should publish an article in our magazine emphasizing the increase of secret societies. Make people believe that these
developments will bring down the government. Unless the government
reforms, we cannot control the masses. We must warn the country that
gangsters and secret societies have overrun the country. They are biding
their time, waiting for a chance to rise up. Anybody working against reform
is siding with these gangsters.

"I have another idea," Fong continued. "Learn-to-Be-Strong is such a
clumsy name. Perhaps we should change the society's name to something
with a more positive attitude, something even suggesting violence. That
will make people sit up and pay attention. I suggest that we change the
society's name from Learn-to-Be-Strong to Protect-Our-Country. When
we announce the change of name, we can also mention our new added
power, such as new membership and influence."

"What kind of fear do we want to inject?" Liang asked.

"Make them fear the secret societies, of course," Fong explained. "That
fear will sway them to our side."

"Very complicated, but I like it," Kang Yu-wei said. "Let's take a vote
and see if we should change our name."

They voted and approved the new name: the Protect-Our-Country
Society.

By giving the organization a new name, Fong had become closer to it.
He attended its meetings more frequently, working harder for its goals.

At the same time, Fong Yun was growing fast. She was a delight,
crawling and toddling all over the house. Shao Mei and Fong never tired
of watching her; even when she was asleep, they sneaked into her room
and peeked under the mosquito netting.

＊

On June 11, 1898, the young Emperor issued a stern Imperial decree of
reform bearing his vermilion seal, enlisting the services of many new
intellectuals and brushing aside the objections of all the high-ranking
Mandarins. This move alerted Tsu Hsi, who felt threatened.

The next day, to everybody's surprise, the Emperor issued several new
decrees, reversing his previous stand. He first dismissed Weng Tung-ho,
the Imperial Tutor, and banished him to his own Kiangsu Province. The
second decree directed all officers and officials above second rank who had
received new appointments to send their thanks directly to Tsu Hsi. The
third ordered Jung Lu, the Commander of the Bannermen, Tsu Hsi's
personal guard, to take command of all the northern troops.

An urgent meeting was called at the Protect-Our-Country Society headquarters. Liang Chi-chao declared that the new edicts meant serious trouble, a prelude to the Empress Dowager's design to resume the regency. The new power of Jung Lu was the most disturbing of all. In his new capacity, he automatically became commander of three army corps, the Kansu Corps, the Wuyi Corps and the modern corps of Yuan Shih-kai.

"Yuan Shih-kai is our own man," Fong said. "We should contact him for more information."

"I agree. He is a loyal member of the reform movement," Kang said. "If the Empress Dowager plans to seize power, Yuan Shih-kai is the only one who can stop her. To save the movement, a drastic step is necessary." He looked around, studying the other members' responses.

After a furtive glance around, one member whispered, "You mean assassinate the Empress Dowager?"

There was immediate silence. Many faces whitened. A few wiped their brows. "No," Kang said quietly, his sharp eyes glistening in the dim light of kerosene lamps. "We shall assassinate Jung Lu."

"Who can do that?" another member asked, still wiping sweat from his forehead.

"No one but Yuan Shih-kai," Kang said.

"Will he do it?"

"We'll never know until we ask. Who will ask him?" Kang said, looking from face to face. "We need a volunteer."

Nobody raised a hand.

Kang looked disappointed. "Well, I'll go myself," he said.

Several voices raised objections simultaneously. "You are the head of the movement," Fong said. "To see Yuan Shih-kai is a job for a courier. Anybody can go, but I think we should send someone who not only knows Yuan personally but is also a friend. If we cannot find such a person, the mission will be too risky."

The members all nodded agreement. But nobody among the membership knew Yuan well enough to discuss with him Jung Lu's assassination. The meeting was adjourned that evening without a solution having been reached.

✳

When Fong returned home, he played with Fong Yun, forgetting about the plot. He had never liked violence; now he decided not to get involved. It was Fong Yun's bedtime. Shao Mei had just bathed her and the child wriggled in her arms, refusing to go to bed.

That evening, there was a rap on the door. Fong opened it and was surprised to find Kang standing in the doorway, looking tense and worried.

"Tai, read this," he said, handing him a piece of paper. "A messenger just delivered it."

Fong glanced at the message. It was from the young Emperor asking for immediate help: "The throne is in danger. You—Kang Yu-wei, Liang Chi-chao, Yang Jui, Lin Shu, Tan Su-tung and Liu Kwang-ti—should take secret measures posthaste to save me!"

"What are we going to do?" Fong asked.

"I am going to see Yuan Shih-kai right away. In case I don't return, you will know what has happened."

"No," Fong said. "You cannot take this risk. I'll go. Tell me where to find General Yuan."

"You have never met Yuan. At least I am his acquaintance. I'll go."

"I am not trying to be heroic. Nobody will recognize me, but everybody knows you. Let me go."

*

Tucking the Emperor's secret message into his Mandarin gown, Fong left the house without telling Shao Mei where he was going. Yuan's headquarters was in Hsiao-chan, thirty-five kilometers from Peking. Riding a fast horse that had been hired by Old Liu, he arrived at Yuan Shih-kai's headquarters at dawn. Guards, armed with modern rifles and wearing Western uniforms, stopped him at the vermilion gate of a massive building surrounded by ten-foot walls. It was not until Fong told the guards that he had an urgent message for General Yuan that he was allowed to approach the second gate, where the captain of the guards kept him waiting for almost an hour before admitting him to the inner courtyard.

When Fong was finally called into the middle hall, the General was not there. His aide, a young lieutenant wearing several ribbons on his chest, wanted to know the purpose of the visit. Fong insisted that he must see the General in person. The officer suggested that he forward the message. Fong refused. Irritated by the red tape, Fong shouted, "His Majesty the Emperor is in danger! I must see the General!" His voice was loud enough to be heard several rooms away. Outside, soldiers could be heard drilling behind the buildings, shouting, "Sha, sha, sha!"

The aide hesitated for a moment. "You wait," he said and disappeared through a side door. The latticed paper windows were all open, and the sun shone into the spacious hall. As Fong glanced around, he was surprised to see that the place looked like a miniature throne room. Fong shivered. He wondered if General Yuan was preparing for a war to take over the dynasty. Had he come to the wrong place for the Emperor's rescue?

The officer reappeared and gestured for Fong to follow him. Obeying, he stepped through the side door into an anteroom where several officers were working at desks. Entering an inner room, Fong smelled coffee. Sitting behind a large desk was General Yuan, fully dressed in a Western uniform, his chest covered with decorations and ribbons. He was a rotund man with a Western-style mustache. Yuan was busily scribbling something with a quill pen.

"Yes?" he asked without raising his head.

"Your Excellency," Fong said after a bow, "I have brought you an urgent message from Kang Yu-wei."

Yuan looked up. "I am a member of his society," he said. "It does not mean that I entirely approve of his programs, you understand."

"The message is not about his reform programs, Your Excellency." Fong stepped forward and handed the long envelope to Yuan, who slit it with a letter opener and read it casually. Suddenly he sat up and reread it, his eyebrows knitted and his mouth gaping in surprise.

"Does anybody else know about this?"

"No. Only Your Excellency, Mr. Kang Yu-wei and I."

"Go tell Mr. Kang I shall try my best."

"Only you can save the Emperor. If Your Excellency is successful, you will win great merit."

Yuan glared at him. "Winning merit is the last thing on my mind. It is the duty of a military man to serve."

"Mr. Kang also says that if you don't want to save His Majesty, if instead you inform the Empress Dowager of the plot, she will have many of our heads. Either way, you will be highly rewarded."

Yuan interrupted him with a blow on his desk. "What sort of person do you take me for? The Emperor is the divine lord of us all! I, as well as you, am duty-bound to ensure his safety. Should His Majesty be in danger, I can kill Jung Lu as easily as killing a dog!" He turned to his aide. "Make preparations for my trip to Tientsin immediately."

"Yes, Your Excellency." The aide saluted and withdrew.

✳

For two days after his return to Peking, Fong felt his eyelids trembling. He had once been told by Third Uncle that a jumping eyelid is a prelude to happy events. But it could also mean impending disaster, depending on which eyelid jumped.

Not really superstitious, Fong jokingly told Shao Mei that he was expecting both good news and bad.

"Good news or bad, we are going to have an outing tomorrow," Shao Mei said. "And don't try to find excuses to get out of your promise, or . . ."

Before she had finished speaking, there was an urgent rapping on the front door. Through the open window, Fong saw Old Liu hurrying to open it. Presently the servant brought Yao directly to the study. It was almost ten at night. Fong hurried to his study, wondering what had happened. He hoped that the jumping eyelid had not been a premonition.

"What wind blows you here at this hour of the night, Yao?" he said after greeting him.

Yao settled into a chair, looking gloomy. "You remember Chang?" he asked.

"How could anyone forget Chang? The most arrogant Manchu I have ever known. You are wearing a funereal look on your face. Don't tell me he has passed away."

"No. He loathes you," Yao said.

"The feeling is mutual. But if he has passed away, I shall contribute something to buy him a paper house or a paper boat for his pleasure in the other world."

"Even though he loathes you," Yao continued, "he called on me this evening and told me to bring you a warning. This is very urgent. That's why I came to see you at this ungodly hour."

"What's the warning? My eyelids jumped all morning. I am prepared for any news."

"Keep away from Kang Yu-wei's headquarters. Tomorrow Jung Lu's Bannermen will raid the place. A hundred sixty-five members of the Protect-Our-Country Society will be arrested. Many heads will roll. Chang, who works for the Bureau of Punishment, has secretly withdrawn your name from the file. You will be safe, but you must not set foot near Kang's headquarters again."

"When will they raid the place?" Fong asked, his heart sinking.

"Tomorrow at dawn."

"What happened? Why this raid?"

"Yuan Shih-kai has told Jung Lu of Kang Yu-wei's plot to kill the Empress Dowager."

"Nobody is plotting to kill the Empress Dowager!"

Yao looked at him askance. "How do you know that?"

Fong stared at him, tongue-tied for a moment. It was too late to hide his involvement now.

"Kang Yu-wei told me. He only planned to have Jung Lu killed to save the Emperor."

"Well, Jung Lu changed the story a little, obviously."

"What did Yuan tell Jung Lu, exactly?"

"Does it matter? The reform movement is over. By tomorrow many heads will dangle on Chien Men Gate, and that will be the end of the Protect-Our-Country Society. You are lucky that you will be spared because of a Manchu classmate who loathes you but respects you. We Manchus are not all rotten blackguards, you know."

"What is going to happen to the Emperor?"

"Nobody knows. But the Empress Dowager is very angry. Through inside information in Manchu circles, I learned this. Yesterday afternoon —September 21, 1898: remember the date, it is history—the Empress Dowager hastily left the Summer Palace and proceeded to the Forbidden City. Rushing into the Emperor's apartments, she shouted at him, 'I've kept you on the throne for all these twenty years and more, but you still listen to artful minions and want to murder me! You silly ass! Without me you would never have become an emperor!'

"With that, she snatched away all the important documents and had the Emperor conveyed to an island called Ocean Terrace, in Central South Lake, where he has been placed under house arrest. From now on, the Empress Dowager will be the sole ruler of China. It is a coup."

After Yao left, Fong went to bed without mentioning anything to Shao Mei. But, unable to sleep, he got up at midnight and got dressed.

"Where are you going?" Shao Mei asked sleepily.

"I can't sleep. I am going to take a walk."

"At this hour?"

"I often walk at night; I have even made the acquaintance of the neighborhood time-beater."

As he mentioned the time-beater, he got an idea. The official time-beater hired by each neighborhood went around beating a wooden drum to report the time of night and to drive away ghosts and demons. As a night watchman, he could come and go without arousing anybody's suspicion.

Galvanized, he woke Old Liu and asked him to lend him a suit of coolie clothes. Fong changed into the blouse, took a wooden bowl from the kitchen and sneaked out of the house. Beating the bowl with a wooden spoon, he began to yell, "Midnight, midnight. . . ."

He hurried to Kang's headquarters. Kang Yu-wei and another devoted member, Tan Su-tung, were still in the office working. Fong, out of breath, managed to tell them what had happened. He urged both of them to escape as soon as possible.

Kang immediately packed some important papers, deciding to seek help from Timothy Richard, the British missionary. He asked Tan Su-tung to go with him.

To Fong's surprise, Tan declined. "If none escapes with his life," he said, "there will be none left to plan the future. But if no one is ready to lay down his life, how can the sacred mission be carried out?"

Both Fong and Kang tried to argue with him, but Tan cut them short. "Go! Don't waste valuable time. Man's fate is predestined by Heaven. If I am to be arrested and sentenced to die, I cannot escape it."

He pushed both of them out and locked the door.

After a quick handshake, Kang disappeared into the darkness and Fong returned to his house, beating the wooden bowl and yelling, "Midnight, midnight."

Inside his house, Fong began to be afraid. Panting and leaning against the gate, he tried to calm his nerves, reminding himself that a man's life is predestined by Heaven. "Do your best," he murmured. "Leave the result to Heaven."

*

The next day Fong got up early to wait for news, his heart racing. He avoided talking to his family and isolated himself in his study. He determined not to leave the house until things cooled down. He had ordered Old Liu to the street to watch for wall papers and listen to gossip. By noon Old Liu returned. Jung Lu had mustered three thousand soldiers at dawn. They had blocked the city gates and halted traffic in an effort to hunt down the reformists and the Emperor's followers. Almost a hundred had been arrested and thrown into prison.

Fong learned from Yao that Tan Su-tung had been arrested at the society's headquarters. When the soldiers grabbed him by the queue, he had laughed defiantly and recited a death-defying poem, shouting, "Hold my sword, I smile up at the sky!"

A week later, on September 28, his head was found dangling on Chien Men Gate with those of five other martyrs of the reform movement. From the Emperor's first edict ordering the whole country to reform, to the death of the six men, the reforms had only lasted some one hundred days.

Fong knew that one of his eyelids had jumped for the one hundred days of reform, a total disaster, and the other had jumped for his good luck in miraculously having escaped death.

22

After the failure of the reform movement in 1898, Fong Tai decided to abandon his writing, but he still kept a log of China's losses to foreign powers. He did this like a family account book, keeping track of creditors and debtors, and the amount China gave and borrowed.

He discovered that his country was so heavily in debt that it reminded him of a beggar in rags with red eyes and sunken cheeks covered with sores and ugly cuts.

It perplexed him why the foreigners were interested in such a beggar. Since China had lost the last war with Japan and signed the Treaty of Shimonoseki in 1895, Russia, France, England and Germany had all clamored to lend money to the vanquished nation to help pay her war indemnity to Japan. At first glance the Europeans seemed to be either kind or stupid, but as Fong studied the loan documents, he discovered that every tael of silver lent to China had a string attached. The Anglo-German loan of three hundred million taels, for instance, provided a clause in the agreement that assured China's hiring of an Englishman as head of customs. As a result of that war, China had not only lost the Liaotung Peninsula and Taiwan to Japan, she had also borrowed money to pay Japan's war indemnity. And because of the loan, China had hired a foreigner to collect her customs duties. It was almost like a man hiring a wolf to guard his chickens.

As Fong compiled the account, he wrote his comments at the bottom: "Thus, in less than four years, 1894–1898, most of China's vast territory has been marked out into spheres of foreign influence: the areas north of the Great Wall for Russia; the Yangtze River Valley for Britain; Shantung for Germany; Fukien for Japan; Yunan, Kwangtung and Kwangsi for France."

Under the comments he also drew a grave and a flower with the bitter remark: "In remembrance of the reform movement, a flower that bloomed for a day and died."

*

By 1899 Father Barrington was deeply worried. When Fong Tai came to visit, he spread several newspapers on the kitchen table without explanation. He looked gloomy.

"Father, why all the old newspapers?" Fong asked cheerfully. "For wrapping things? Ready to open a fish market?"

"Look at the news," Barrington said. "Secret societies are springing up everywhere to fight the foreigners. It's frightening!"

Fong glanced at the closest English-language paper, in which an article sounded an alarm about the uprising of the Heaven and Earth Society in Kwangsi Province, calling on the people to expel the foreign aggressors.

"Look at this," Barrington said, pointing to another article. "This uprising is in Shantung Province, practically next door."

Fong first saw a patriotic song printed under a photograph of a group of people practicing martial arts in front of an altar:

> Yi Ho-chuan, Yi Ho-chuan,
> Stand up in Shantung.
> Heroes we are!
> Protect our nation;
> Jade Emperor in Heaven,
> Bring us magic power!
> Kill the foreign devils,
> Burn their houses.
> We have magic fire,
> Burn, burn, burn!
> Kill, kill, kill!

The article went on to say that Yi Ho-chuan was the so-called Society of Boxers, organized by a Shantung bandit who was supposed to possess magic powers. Destitute and superstitious peasants had been easily recruited. As the province had been devastated by floods and famine, the peasants' uprising had spread rapidly to other affected provinces. Through their songs and slogans, the foreign missionaries were their first targets, then they searched for Christian converts and those who bought foreign goods, branding them as *secondary devils*.

In some areas the Boxers had already started manufacturing magic swords and spears. They had burned churches, felled electricity poles and thrown kerosene lamps out into the streets. Thousands of urban and rural working people had been attracted to their ranks. They paraded in the streets and shouted, "Foreigners, foreigners! They do us harm! They build railways and carry away our wealth!"

Fong read a few more articles. He was not alarmed until one of them said, "Some Boxer leaders have started antiforeign propaganda by spreading stories about missionaries poisoning wells and maiming children." He had always regarded such stories as harmless jokes; now he was not sure.

Father Barrington sat in an armchair, drumming his fingers as he waited for Fong's comment. "Well? Well?"

"It looks like the foreign powers have created the Boxer uprising themselves."

"No moral judgments, please," Barrington said, drumming more rapidly. "You are a government official; can't you do something about it? If this is allowed to go on, it will touch off a crisis that will bring the curtain down on China."

"What can I do?" Fong asked defensively.

"Alert Li Hung-chang. Warn your influential Manchu friends. Do anything you can to stop this foolishness."

"Father, your words are weightier than mine."

"Fiddlesticks! You know I am only a decoration. Anything I say will be misconstrued as siding with the foreigners."

"What did Dr. White tell you? Save your own health before you save China. The way you drum that chair arm begins to worry me."

"Oh, oh, I'm sorry," Barrington said with a short laugh. "A sign of high blood pressure, I suppose. You're right, Fong. By the time the Boxers burn my church, I probably won't be here to see it. A drink?"

"I don't think so," Fong said. "Your whiskey is not good for your blood pressure. How about a cup of tea?"

Barrington threw up his hands. "Oh, well, tea it is, then. I brought this on myself."

And both men laughed.

*

The Boxer uprising spread faster than Fong had expected. The members started shadow-boxing and sword drilling in every province; they had set up altars everywhere to worship the Jade Emperor in Heaven. By offering food and incense in front of the altars, they were supposed to gain magic power that would make them invulnerable to firearms.

There were also female Boxers. Those under twenty-seven years old were classified as Red Lanterns; over twenty-seven they were Blue Lanterns. The members carried red or blue lanterns and fans, and formed shock units to aid their male counterparts with more magic power, which Fong suspected was sex used to boost the male Boxers' morale.

The Boxers' first slogan was *Topple the Ching Dynasty, exterminate the foreign devils!* This was later changed to *Uphold the Great Ching Dynasty, exterminate the foreign devils!* The clever change won the Empress Dowager Tsu Hsi's praise and approval.

When the Boxers reached Peking in 1900, thousands paraded in colorful uniforms—red turbans on their heads, red belts around their waists, their shoes and socks decorated with red borders. They were armed with broadswords and long spears, and carried bright-colored banners. In a few days shrines were set up on the main thoroughfares.

Soon Peking was dominated by the Boxers; their warriors were stationed everywhere—in Imperial palaces, government buildings, residences of royal families. The roaring of their slogans could be heard day and night. They warned people not to buy foreign goods. To show their determination, they set fire to stores that sold foreign goods and medicine.

Soon the Boxers burned down every British church in the south section of the city; the French bishop Guillou was killed.

One tense evening, Li Hung-chang sent for Fong Tai.

Dazed by all the killing and burning, Fong arrived at Li's mansion in a carriage. Li had been recuperating from a long illness. Lying in his canopied bed, he waved an emaciated hand to indicate a chair. Fong sat down. After a spasm of coughing, Li said, "I have tendered my resignation to the Empress Dowager, but she refuses to accept it. Instead, she has given me another assignment—Viceroy of Kwangtung and Kwangsi provinces. General Jung Lu will succeed me as the Governor of Chi-li. Prince Kung will replace me as the Grand Councilor in Charge of Foreign Affairs. Now, I want you to know that I have recommended you as Jung Lu's assistant."

Fong remembered Jung Lu, the Commander of the Bannermen, Tsu Hsi's bodyguard. He was also the new Commander of the Northern Army, defender of the Forbidden City. He was the man who had staged the coup against the Emperor.

Fong was not pleased by the recommendation. He remained silent.

"I know what you are thinking," Li said. "Jung Lu is an ignorant man. But he is not stupid. And he has power—a sword that cuts both ways."

"Why do you recommend me, sir?"

"You are an informed man," Li said, his voice getting stronger; there was urgency in it. "The Empress Dowager's die-hard inner circle is uninformed. If they believe in the Boxers' slogan, the country will be ruined. The only man who can control the Boxers is Jung Lu. Your mission is to influence him. You are a clever man. I hope you know how best to deal with him when the time comes."

"I'll do my best, sir," Fong said, already feeling the heavy burden of the mission.

He left Li's mansion with mixed feelings. It was flattering to have Li still think highly of him, and he hoped he could live up to Li's expectations. He had not yet met Jung Lu, a notorious butcher who had seized the young Emperor, arrested the 160 reformers and had six of them decapitated. Thinking of the man, Fong saw a storm gathering on the horizon. He wished his eyelids would jump again and foretell the future, luck or disaster.

*

There were two persons with whom he could discuss his problem: Yao and Father Barrington. He chose Yao, who usually knew what was going on in the Forbidden City.

He paid Yao a visit after dark, telling the carriage driver to avoid the main thoroughfares. In the distance he could hear the Boxers drilling and shouting slogans, crying, "Sha, sha, sha!"

The word *sha* made him shudder. When would they stop killing? Human life seemed cheap these days. . . .

He was ushered into Yao's study. His friend, as usual, was happy to see him. "You don't look so good," Yao said after greeting him.

"Li Hung-chang has appointed me Jung Lu's assistant. Is that good news or bad?"

"It calls for a drink," Yao said. He fished a jar of liquor out from under his bed and poured two cups. "Mao tai. I also have shao hsing, but your appointment deserves the best and the strongest."

"You mean this is good news?" Fong asked after the toast.

"You are a lucky dog, Fong Tai," Yao said. "Who wouldn't want to work for the most powerful man in Peking? He is the ears and eyes and . . ." He stopped, then lowering his voice, he added, "and the pleasure of the Old Buddha."

Fong knew that Old Buddha was Tsu Hsi's favorite nickname, and the word *pleasure* was self-explanatory. He asked, "What is the Old Buddha's policy regarding the Boxers?"

"Tsu Hsi has changed her mind several times about those mountebanks. Recently she saw a demonstration of their magic power and was impressed. So you should know how to conduct yourself. Do you know why Li Hung-chang wanted to change his job?"

"He wants to retire but the Old Buddha won't let him."

Yao laughed. "Li Hung-chang wants to retire? That's a likely story! It's like a cat swearing off fish. Listen, Li Hung-chang is a clever, slippery little fellow. He wants to get out of a house when there is a fire, but he will not get out until there is another house waiting for him. He requested the job of Viceroy of Kwangtung and Kwangsi so that he could get away from Peking until the fire is put out."

"So there is going to be a fire. Do you really expect it?"

Yao closed his eyes and rubbed his face with both hands as though he too were troubled. "Fong," he said, "you know Tsu Hsi is surrounded by a few powerful men, Manchus and Hans. These men are so ignorant and superstitious that it is appalling. Yesterday one of them said, 'I never believed that there were many foreign powers in this world. England, France and Germany may be real, but most of the other countries are pure inventions created by foreigners to intimidate us. Let the Boxers kill some of the foreign devils. Let's show them that we cannot be intimidated!' "

"Who said that?"

"A prince. The less you know about him, the better, so you won't get yourself into trouble by repeating the story."

"How about Jung Lu? Is he just as ignorant?"

"Equally ignorant but not equally stupid."

"That's what Li Hung-chang said. Thanks. This is what I wanted to know."

*

Fong left Yao's house hurriedly. He decided that he would have to make some preparations for the *fire,* which seemed to him unavoidable. He went to see Father Barrington, hoping that his friend had not gone to bed. He would have to wake him, if necessary, he decided; this was urgent.

Barrington was ready for bed when Fong arrived. Wearing longjohns and a cap, the priest received him warmly. Fong apologized for arriving at such an hour.

"Don't worry about it. Your presence beats counting sheep. That's what I've been doing every night since I threw away my bottles."

Fong was not in the mood for chitchat. He told Barrington about his new appointment and what Yao had told him. Barrington did not mince words. "Get your family out of Peking!"

"Why?" Fong asked, stunned.

"What if the Boxers, encouraged by Tsu Hsi, kill a foreign diplomat? They have already killed many missionaries and Christian converts in other provinces, you know. The killing of the missionaries may have been something the foreign powers manufactured as an excuse for invasion, but the killing of a foreign diplomat will be disastrous. It will be an open invitation for the worst invasion in Chinese history. Get your family out!"

"Where?"

"Get them out of the country. To America. To Europe. Anywhere but here."

"I don't know anyone in America or Europe."

"Paris or Boston. Take your choice. In both places I have nieces. I recommend the one in Paris. She is my favorite, married to a Parisian businessman. She will take good care of your family."

Fong stared at him, tongue-tied, his hands sweating. He had not realized the situation was so grave.

✻

Fong was at first hesitant to send his family overseas, but the next day he learned that the three ministers who had opposed the Boxers had been publicly executed. One of them was Li Shan, the Chairman of the Department of Revenue. If an official as high ranking as Li Shan could be decapitated like a common criminal for criticizing the Boxers in front of Tsu Hsi, Fong knew why Li Hung-chang wanted to get out of Peking. Fong decided to follow Father Barrington's advice. He must send his family away.

By 1900 Fong Yun had grown into a beautiful child. Her face, nose and eyes were almost replicas of her mother's. At seven, she was a stubborn and independent little girl who had definite likes and dislikes. Fong found it hard to influence her; nor could spanking change her habits or stubbornness.

To discourage her from sneaking into the street to play with the poor children, Fong started inviting some of the urchins into the house. Shao Mei had been horrified at first, but she had finally accepted some of the dirty boys and girls as Fong Yun's playmates. Agonizing over the situation, Shao Mei had tried to invite some rich boys to take the place of the ragamuffins, but Fong Yun always snubbed them. Fong found it amusing that his daughter treated the rich boys with such studied haughtiness and talked to them in stilted language, like a mistress addressing her servants. Without coaching, she could act like a terrible snob, tossing her head with a haughty air, grunting and snorting with disdain. She was quite an actress.

When Fong went to talk to Shao Mei about the trip abroad, he found her serving Fong Yun and one of her grimy friends an elaborate snack in the dining room.

The boy, about seven, had become Fong Yun's favorite playmate. He was dirty and dressed in rags, but was the best-looking boy of all the urchins. Fortunately he was healthy, with no sores on his skin or scalp. His thick black hair was neatly braided into a queue.

Fong smelled some of the tidbits Shao Mei was serving them. "Ah, hot buns and sesame dumplings!"

"Yun Yun," Shao Mei said gently, "don't you think you should take smaller bites?"

"Your mother is right," Fong said, sitting at the table beside her. "You don't want to choke on this delicious food, do you? Please eat like your friend."

"I am eating like him," Fong Yun said. "He ate fast and is full."

Fong looked at the boy, who was staring at the food almost cross-eyed. Obviously he was stuffed.

"Ah, I am glad he likes our food," Fong said with a little chuckle. "What is your friend's name?"

"Sticks."

"What?"

"His name is Sticks."

"Oh, well, it is a good name. Don't you have a family name, Sticks?"

"Sticks Kong," the boy said.

"Sticks Kong is a good name. From now on we shall call you Kong."

"No, I like Sticks better," Fong Yun said, stuffing another dumpling into her mouth and swallowing it without much chewing.

"Yun Yun," Fong said, "if you eat like a lady, we will call your friend Sticks. Agreed?"

"Agreed," Fong Yun said, her mouth still full of food.

"All right, enough eating. You two can go out and play in the courtyard. I want to talk to your mommie about something very important."

Fong Yun grabbed a few buns from a plate and crammed them into Sticks's pocket. After they had left, Shao Mei sat down and poured a cup of tea for Fong. "Tai," she said, "I am worried."

"About what?"

"About Yun Yun. She is learning everything from beggar boys."

"She will grow out of it," Fong said. "I have something important to discuss with you, Shao Mei. Peking is not safe. I want you and Yun Yun to take a trip to Paris. I want you to stay in Paris until the Boxer Rebellion is over."

"Paris? Where is that?"

"It is in Europe."

"A foreign country? I don't want to go to a foreign country."

"You will stay with Father Barrington's niece."

"I don't want to live with foreigners."

"They will be your friends, Shao Mei. Besides . . ."

They heard Fong Yun's laughter in the courtyard. Fong looked out the window. Fong Yun was kicking a Chinese shuttlecock. She kicked it up and down, using both her feet. Turning, spinning and doing acrobatics, she kept the shuttlecock flying in a variety of dazzling moves.

Fong watched her with a smile, his heart full of pride and love. Every move Fong Yun made reminded him of Rose.

As he watched, Fong Yun suddenly stopped kicking, took Sticks's hand and guided him to the side of the courtyard. She made him sit down on the curb under the eaves and sat beside him with a sigh.

"Do you like me?" she asked.

"Y–yes," Sticks said, blushing.

"Do you really like me?"

Sticks nodded, staring at his feet.

"I like you, too," Fong Yun said. "If you really like me, how much?"

"Very much," Sticks replied in a low voice that was almost inaudible.

Fong Yun bared one of her arms and said, "Give me a bite."

Sticks looked puzzled. "Come on," Fong Yun urged. "Give my arm a bite!"

"I don't want to bite your arm," Sticks said, staring at her round, white little arm, swallowing. "Why?"

"I want to find out how much you like me. Please bite!"

Sticks glanced at her, then at her arm. He took the soft little arm and gave it a gentle bite.

"Is that all?" she asked, disappointed. "You don't like me very much."

"I–I like you very, very much!" Sticks stammered. "But I don't want to hurt you."

"I am not afraid of pain. Try again. Bite!"

Sticks gave her arm another bite, a little harder this time. He looked at the toothmarks on her arm and winced.

"Is this how hard you can bite?" Fong Yun asked, still disappointed.

"I don't want to bite you anymore."

"You don't like me half as much as I like you," Fong Yun said. "Give me your arm."

Sticks looked at her, then at his own arm. Reluctantly, he rolled up his sleeve and revealed a dirty arm.

"Are you afraid of pain?" she asked.

"No."

Fong Yun held his arm and bit it hard. "Painful?"

"No."

Holding Sticks's arm with both her hands, she kept biting it, glancing at him between bites. "Still not painful?" Sticks shook his head, bearing the pain as best he could.

"Still not painful?"

"Ouch!" Sticks cried, withdrawing his arm suddenly. There was blood in the deep toothmarks. She had broken the skin.

"Sorry I bit you too hard," she said, hugging his arm and touching the bloody toothmarks with her cheek affectionately. "This is how much I like you."

"You've got blood on your face," Sticks said.

"Wipe it off for me."

Obediently Sticks wiped her face with a dirty hand. Watching them, Shao Mei was horrified, twisting a handkerchief nervously in her trembling hands.

"As I was saying," Fong said, "Father Barrington's niece and her family will be your friends. Besides, if you don't want Yun Yun to bite dirty little arms, you had better take her to Paris."

Shao Mei turned to him quickly. "When will we be able to leave?"

23

Fong Tai escorted his wife and daughter to Tientsin, where they took a French steamer to Shanghai and Paris. It was one of the last ships to leave China. He felt lucky, for his right eyelid had started jumping again. Right for luck and left for disaster, he decided. He laughed at himself for being superstitious, but still he was worried, dreading the day when the other eyelid might jump also.

Peking was in turmoil; nobody was sure of the Old Buddha's policy. Not too long ago she had sent General Yuan Shih-kai to control the Boxers in Shantung Province, and Yuan had killed many of them. Now she allowed the Boxers to attack the Foreign Legation in Peking, laying siege to it and endangering the lives of hundreds of foreign diplomats and their families. Tsu Hsi's paranoid mind seemed more ominous to Fong than the jumping of his eyelids.

He began to make entries in his logbook again with the information he gathered from Yao and the English-language publications in Father Barrington's house:

> June 2, Boxers destroy railway bridges near Liaoyang.
> June 3, Boxers burn down the British churches at southeast gate.
> June 5, All foreign churches in Fengtien are burned down by them; a French bishop is killed.
> June 6, Most of the foreign churches, bridges, stations, office buildings and mines in the northeast are destroyed.
> June 9, Governor Yu of Shantung, who was recently replaced by Yuan Shih-kai, is so awed by the powers of the Boxers that he entertains some Boxer leaders.
> June 10, Shrines have sprung up in every street and alley in Peking, and young female Boxers, the Red Lanterns, are active, dancing and chanting gibberish. A strange sight.
> With a heavy heart, I made the above entries, thinking of Fong Yun and Shao Mei. Have they arrived safely in Paris? Are they being cared for? Are they happy?

✳

One evening General Jung Lu sent for Fong. Dreading the meeting, Fong dressed quickly and entered the official sedan chair provided by the Governor. Four chair-bearers lifted him up and trotted away, swaying their arms and grunting in unison. The Governor's messenger, dressed in a blue uniform with a silk sash tied around his waist, walked ahead of the sedan chair, carrying a lantern with the Governor's name printed on it. Fong Tai expected the lantern to prevent the Boxers from searching him. Hoping for the best and trying to relax, he watched the streets through one of the small windows in the sedan chair.

But he was soon stopped by a mob of Boxers. Ignoring the Governor's lanterns, the leader ordered Fong to step out. Without arguing, Fong climbed out and confronted some two dozen of the rebels. Holding broadswords and long spears with tassels flying from them, they scowled at him disdainfully. Fong wondered if they also resented government officials.

The leader was a muscular man with a large oily mouth—as though he had just finished a greasy meal. Eyeing Fong up and down, he demanded, "Do you have anything foreign?"

"Nothing foreign," Fong said, knowing that every day there were bonfires built by Boxers to burn anything of foreign origin.

"Search," the leader ordered.

Two Boxers went through the sedan chair while another searched Fong. At first he tried to resist, but when he saw the messenger kowtowing to the Boxer leader, he was amused. If the new Governor's name on the lantern meant nothing to these fanatics, there was no reason why he should feel offended by this effrontery. Cooling his temper, he said to the leader, somewhat facetiously, "Eh, Older Brother, we are pleased that you can fight the foreign devils with magic power. What kind of magic power do you possess?"

"Come with me," the leader told him.

Fong followed him to an altar a short distance away. On it were tablets bearing the names of historical heroes whose magic powers and strength were legendary: the Pig Disciple of Monk Tang, the Monkey King who could travel eighteen thousand lis with one somersault, the Willow Spirit who could kill with an easy wave of its thousands of weeping leaves. Flanked by other minor heroes was the largest tablet of all, bearing the title in gilded characters: THE JADE EMPEROR IN HEAVEN.

There were offerings of incense, food and candles on the altar. Hundreds of buzzing flies were crawling over the spoiled fish and chicken. The leader picked up a few sticks of incense, lit them over a candle and ordered the Boxers to demonstrate their magic power.

They all knelt in front of the altar. After a few kowtows, they started murmuring prayers. The leader brought out from his pocket several pictures of demons painted on pieces of yellow paper. Murmuring prayers, he burned the pictures over a candle. As the ashes fell, he ordered the Boxers to fight.

Their mouths foaming, the Boxers jumped up and danced in a frenzy. Then they picked up their weapons and engaged in a furious combat, leaping and crying, "Sha, sha, sha!"

Soon the battle was over, with half of the Boxers hacked down by swords and spears. But there were no wounds, no blood. Lying on the ground, the wounded started to tremble and wriggle as if magic power were entering their bodies. Suddenly they leaped to their feet and were ready to fight again. "You see?" the leader said. "No one is hurt."

Fong was secretly amused by the bad acting, but he kept quiet. The leader wanted to recruit Fong, but Fong declined, saying that his mother had recently passed away and he was still in mourning. It was not until the leader had recruited the messenger and the four chair-bearers that they were allowed to leave.

Back in the sedan chair, Fong discovered that his pocket watch was missing. It was his antique Swiss watch, a gift from Third Uncle. He was grateful that the Boxer who searched him had stolen it. If the turtle's egg had handed it to the leader, Fong, as the owner of a foreign article, would have been branded a secondary devil and perhaps dragged away to God-knows-what punishment.

Fong arrived at the Governor's yamen on foot, an hour late. To his astonishment, the place was crowded with guards and chair-bearers. Soon he learned that Jung Lu's inauguration banquet was in progress and many of his colleagues had been invited to partake of the Governor's favorite seafood.

Luckily, being late to a banquet was traditional, a desired act of deco-rum. When Fong was ushered in to the middle hall, the banquet had just started. Uniformed servants carried food and drinks to a hundred or so guests seated at twelve round tables.

Jung Lu, a tall, rugged-looking man in a glittering Mandarin gown, was sitting at the head table, facing the entrance. He was about fifty and wore the dish-shaped Manchu cap with a large coral-colored button on the top. His whiskers were prematurely gray, but his eyes were bright and his voice deep and forceful. It was rumored that he was one of Tsu Hsi's lovers. Taking a close look at the man, Fong believed it. Such a virile man undoubtedly belonged to a special *pillow-talk* class that could communi-cate with the Old Buddha. He was definitely a power, and Fong hoped that what Li Hung-chang had said about him was true: ignorant but not stupid.

When he sat down at his reserved seat, far away from the head table, he was glad Jung Lu was busily engaged in conversation with someone else. He did not want to appear tardy, being the last guest to arrive.

The twelve-course banquet was superb. The courses were mostly sea-food—lobster, sea turtle, shrimp, seaweed, sea slugs, crabs, eels and fish, cooked in various ways. The last course was Jung Lu's favorite—sweet and sour crisp fish. When it was served, Jung Lu stopped his conversation and urged everyone to eat.

The guests fell silent and concentrated on eating, chopsticks clicking, lips smacking and crisp fish cracking between their teeth. The feast was occasionally interrupted by toasting and laughter.

Conversation, when resumed, was mostly about foreigners. Whenever Jung Lu spoke, the guests listened intently. "I ask you," he said, "do the foreigners know how to cook fish like this? You all know they only know how to cook fish three ways: boil, boil and boil!"

There was a ripple of laughter. He went on. "China has more than five thousand years of glorious history. It is unfortunate that we must deal with a bunch of foreigners who don't even know how to eat fish. I was once invited to one of their banquets. It was embarrassing to eat a meal with knives and prongs like primitive barbarians. And before they eat, they fill you with a thick soup that is only fit to feed hogs."

The listeners all grunted in agreement, nodding their heads significantly. One of the guests said loudly, "Your Excellency is absolutely correct. The uncivilized foreigners are not only ignorant about eating, their clothing is even more abominable. Look at their women. Two mountainous bulges, one in front and one behind, are considered fashionable. Can these indecent bulges compare with our women's tiny bound feet?"

An immediate cry of "No!" rose from the guests.

"And I heard," another man piped up, "when foreign men meet their women, they do the most horrible thing imaginable—they throw their arms around each other and rub noses and lips together!"

"How horrible! How horrible!" another official agreed. "And yet, only recently, those traitors who call themselves reformers even tried to imitate the foreigners. Just imagine what would have happened if they had been successful! Let us drink a toast to His Excellency Jung Lu, the new Governor, who single-handedly wiped out the turncoats!"

An echo of "Yes, yes, yes!" rose from the guests.

The food and wine made Fong Tai dizzy and courageous. He had to add something. Half in jest he asked, "What would have happened if the reformists had been successful, Your Excellency? Does anyone know?"

Heads turned to look at him; a few recognized this brash, arrogant man. One of the guests answered his question readily. "What would have happened? We would all imitate the foreigners by locking ourselves in each other's arms, walking back and forth like dogs in heat. Ignorant musicians would play revolting barbarian music—*eeyoo eeyoo yee.*" He imitated Western music, distorting his face comically, provoking an explosion of laughter.

A number of aged Mandarins shook their heads and sighed heavily. A few quoted Confucius and other sages to glorify Chinese virtues and belittle the barbarians' behavior. The consensus was that it was lucky the reformists had been routed in time.

Laughing happily, Jung Lu urged everybody to eat his favorite dish again. "Eat, eat!"

One guest, a man with a long beard, rose to his feet and proposed another toast: "Let us wish our new Governor ten thousand blessings!"

Everybody stood up and drank to Jung Lu. A bit tipsy now, Fong bowed to Jung Lu and said, "Your Excellency, everybody has heard that when Your Excellency eats your favorite fish, you eat everything—meat, fins, bones and all. Is that true?"

Jung Lu laughed. He seemed delighted by the question and eager to demonstrate how he enjoyed the dish. "I am glad you asked. Let me show you." He picked up a large fishhead and started to eat it, bones and all, crunching, crunching, crunching. In a few moments the entire head was devoured. Jung Lu smacked his lips with a broad smile, glancing right and left as if to invite applause.

The guests all applauded, grunted and sighed with admiration.

"Eat, eat, eat!" Jung Lu commanded with a sweeping hand. The guests obeyed happily. Once again hundreds of chopsticks clicked and flew. . . . Fong wondered if Jung Lu wanted to see him after the banquet, but after several courses he was too drunk to care.

✳

Fong Tai had heard so much about the Boxers' magic that he asked Old Liu if he had seen any real magic performed in the street.

"Yes, Master Fong! I saw one Boxer kill another with a foreign gun. The killed one leaped up and showed everybody the bullet wound; it was a little white dot on the skin. That's all! He was possessed by magic power, no doubt about it!"

Fong also learned from Old Liu that the Boxers were searching for secondary devils everywhere. If a suspect did not have foreign things on him, the Boxers still had a way to find out if he was guilty. They burned a piece of yellow paper with an incantation written on it. If the ashes flew up, the suspect was innocent; if the ashes went down, he was a secondary devil.

"They are testing people on Chien Men Street," Old Liu said. "Make sure you don't go there, Master Fong."

"What else have you seen lately?"

"An old woman called Heavenly Lady Wong," Old Liu said. "She is the leader of the Red Lanterns, the female branch. She is carried around in a yellow sedan chair by eight bearers. She is dressed in a yellow robe and carries a big yellow fan which has great magic power. If she fans at something, it will burn. She has burned many churches already. Many royal princesses have invited her to their palaces for magic demonstrations. It is said that if she blesses the house, the house will be protected by Heavenly Soldiers. No foreign devils can break in."

"Do you believe that?"

"Yes, sir."

"Why?"

"I have enlisted as a Boxer, sir. . . . Don't worry, Master Fong. If the foreign devils come, I can protect you and your house."

"It is very thoughtful of you, Old Liu. So you have learned some magic, too?"

"Yes, sir! Everybody trains and drills these days."

"Show me."

Old Liu turned to the south and paid obeisance with nine kowtows to the Jade Emperor in Heaven. Then he started to murmur with his eyes closed. Gradually he began to tremble and his face became distorted. After a little while, he leaped up and started to shadow-box. Suddenly his eyes turned upward, his mouth foaming. He said, "I am possessed by the Monkey King, the Pig Disciple of Monk Tang. I am invulnerable to firearms. I will not feel pain; I will not bleed; I am fearless! Sha, sha, sha . . ."

Before he finished, Fong delivered a vigorous kick to the old man's behind and Liu tumbled forward and fell on his face. Lying on the ground, he looked shocked and bewildered.

"Get up!"

Old Liu climbed to his feet, grimacing and wiping his bloody nose. Fong tried not to laugh. "Where is your magic, Old Liu?"

"Oh—I guess I have not trained enough," Old Liu stammered.

"Don't tempt me to shoot you with a gun. So stop training. By the way, how much did you pay to enlist?"

"No enlistment fee, sir, except I paid ten taels of silver for a uniform. It will be ready in a few days."

"Ten taels of silver for a uniform? It is worth no more than half a tael. What happened to your stingy nature?"

"I will not lose money, sir," Old Liu replied. "The Boxer leader told me that when I finish training, he will give me two hundred coins, and I will never finish spending these magic coins. They will also give me a rice cooker; when I cook rice in it, I will never finish eating it."

Now Fong had serious difficulty controlling his laughter. "I'll tell you what to do, Old Liu. Why have a rice cooker? Rice is cheap. Ask him to give you a magic pot to cook ham hocks in, so we can have a pot of ham hocks and never finish eating them. Both of us like ham hocks, don't we?"

*

Two days later, Fong found some magic that was in fact helpful. It was Old Liu's cheap Boxer uniform. Whenever he went out, he took Old Liu with him and the Boxers let them pass without harassment. Since Old Liu had never received his magic coins or rice cooker, Fong gladly paid for his uniform, which he thought was well worth the ten taels of silver.

With the servant accompanying him, he started visiting Yao and Father Barrington again. There was not much for anyone to do but wait for bad news. Able to come and go freely, Fong also began to make entries in his logbook again.

June 16. Tsu Hsi is heard murmuring something new every day. It is believed that she is reciting Boxer incantations that can drive away foreign devils.

June 17. A large fire, set by the Boxers, has burned the foreign racetrack. In that fire, many homes of Christian converts and secondary devils burned. Hundreds have flocked to the Foreign Legation seeking shelter and protection.

June 18. The Boxers attack the Foreign Legation. Foreign guards kill many Boxers.

June 19. In revenge, the Boxers burn more churches. Three hundred Christian converts are killed. Southeast wind helps the fire, which sweeps through the southern part of the city, burning four thousand homes.

June 20. The German minister, Klemens von Ketteler, is killed after he has kicked and caned a Boxer on the street.

June 22. Foreign diplomats demand that Tsu Hsi return power to the young Emperor, who is still under house arrest.

June 25. The angered Tsu Hsi declares war on *Faraway People,* which are the foreign powers.

June 26. Russia, France, Austria, Japan, Hungary and Italy attack Chinese seaports. Admiral Lo loses a fortress and commits suicide.

July 5. Foreign powers are planning a major invasion of China, with allied troops to be commanded by the German Field Marshal Alfred von Waldersee. Kaiser Wilhelm II has vowed vengeance. His order is to "Shoot the Chinese heathens on sight." May my right eyelid jump for China, jump for Fong Yun and Shao Mei; may it jump for their health and happiness.

Fong closed the logbook with a heavy heart. Again he was unable to fall sleep before dawn.

*

On July 28, Jung Lu summoned Fong to his office. Jung Lu was pacing the floor as Fong entered. The office was decorated with traditional weapons and Bannermen pennants. It was so different from Li Hung-chang's office that Fong found the change depressing and frightening.

Jung Lu came right to the point. "General Tung wants to shell the Foreign Legation. He wants to borrow my cannons. What do you think?"

Suspecting that Jung Lu was trying to find out where he stood, Fong decided to test the wind. Li Hung-chang wanted him to influence the man. Influence him he must—but he must also wait for the right moment. "Well, Your Excellency," he said, "the foreign missionaries have converted many evil landlords who use the foreigners as protection and to squeeze the poor. However . . ."

"Don't beat about the bush! Tell me what you think of the present situation."

Fong thought about Jung's dilemma. If the bandit general got the cannons, it would be the end of the Foreign Legation. "Well, Your Excellency," he said, his voice grave, "according to international law, a country cannot kill the diplomats of an enemy country . . ."

"Don't I know that?" Jung Lu complained irritably. "But that barbarian general and those pigheaded royal pumpkins supporting him don't believe it. Some of them don't even believe there is a country called America. What suggestions do you have? Li Hung-chang says you are clever."

"Thank you, Your Excellency. It is very nice of . . ."

"Speak up, speak up!" Jung Lu interrupted him impatiently.

Fong thought for a moment, taking his time, knowing that a quick answer lowered its value. He wanted to increase the suspense and add weight to his response. "Well, Your Excellency," he said, "I think the situation is rather . . . serious. Suppose you refuse . . ."

"I cannot refuse! The Old Buddha has already issued a decree ordering me to let that mutton-eating brute use my cannons."

"That will kill a lot of foreign diplomats . . ."

"Don't tell me what I already know. What is your suggestion? Speak up!"

But Fong again took his time. "Well, Your Excellency, you can say to General Tung that he can use your cannons . . . but on one condition."

"What condition? Speak up!" Jung Lu was now pacing the floor restlessly, his boots squeaking loudly.

"On condition that he let your own men, the Imperial Bannermen, fire them."

"What difference does it make? Cannons don't have eyes."

"Well, Your Excellency . . . you could secretly instruct your men to fire the cannons *over* the Foreign Legation, so that no cannonballs fall into the compound."

"Meeting adjourned. "You may go."

Fong was stunned by the abrupt dismissal. Feeling a chill run down his spine, he bowed and started for the door, wondering what he had done wrong. Suddenly Jung Lu called him. He froze for a moment, waiting for the worst. "Yes, Your Excellency?"

"You are a clever man, Fong Tai," Jung Lu said with a smile. "You may have saved your country—do you know that?"

✳

That afternoon the cannons roared in Peking, shaking the roofs. The excited Boxers were adding to the noise by marching and shouting even more energetically, "Uphold the Great Ching Dynasty! Extinguish the foreign devils! Burn, burn, burn! Sha, sha, sha!" Terror drove more citizens into hiding as they hid or buried their foreign possessions.

The next day a swarm of Boxers pounded on the front door of Fong's house. Old Liu, wearing his uniform, quickly admitted the Older Brothers and greeted them with low bows. Knowing that they were always hungry, he invited them to the kitchen for a bowl of noodles, but the Boxers did not have time to eat. They had an urgent mission—collecting animal dung, garbage, foot-binding cloths and other dirty objects to counteract the foreigners' magic. The Foreign Legation had been shelled for a whole day and a whole night, but nobody had been hurt! The Oldest Brother believed that the foreign devils were using their own brand of magic, and that the only way to break the evil spell was to throw dirty objects at them.

Since the maids at Fong Tai's house all had big feet, there was no foot-binding cloth to contribute, so Old Liu suggested that he dig up rags and old clothes, which the Older Brothers could soak in dirty water or urine and hurl over the legation walls. He was sure that these filthy clothes and rags would be just as effective as used foot-binding cloth.

The Boxer leader agreed. Besides food and money, they carried off almost all the discarded clothing in the Fong house.

The third day, the Foreign Legation still showed no sign of falling. The cannonballs were still flying over it, killing instead quite a few Boxers. In spite of the deluge of garbage and foul objects, the legation guards, with handkerchieves tied over their noses, had increased their firepower. Overwhelmed by the stench of the garbage, the Boxers had retreated momentarily to avoid more casualties.

*

Fong Tai had been keeping in close contact with Yao. From Yao he learned that Jung Lu had been protecting the foreign legations, only allowing the Boxers to make a lot of noise to impress the Empress Dowager. But Tsu Hsi, although appallingly ignorant, was not stupid. Someone had enlightened her as to the fact that international law did not allow any host country to kill foreign diplomats. So Her Majesty was getting worried. Some days she was even frightened.

Meanwhile, there was news that thousands of foreign troops had landed and were marching toward Peking. The Imperial family was ready to escape to Sian in the west. Government troops, such as the Moslem divisions, had been badly beaten and were turning into bandits, looting as they fled the city.

The day before the foreign troops started scaling the city walls, most of the Boxers escaped. Fong remained, his thoughts with his family. He wrote in his logbook:

> How are Fong Yun and Shao Mei? Do they like Paris? It is impossible to sleep while thinking of them. The only comfort is Father Barrington's assurance that they will be well cared for by his niece. But without hearing from them, how can I be sure? The doubt, the worry, the anxiety are killing me. When shall I see them again? Shall I ever see them again?

Early the next morning, Fong was awakened by urgent and angry pounding on the front door. He heard Old Liu calling in a pleasant voice, "Coming, coming, Older Brothers."

Fong turned in his bed, trying to go back to sleep, knowing that Old Liu's uniform would take care of everything. Ten taels of silver had been the best investment he had ever made. With it he had bought insurance and peace of mind.

But the angry voices outside made him sit up. They sounded like bandits demanding food and money. He got up quickly and threw some clothes on. Just as he was about to step out, half a dozen Boxers rushed in. One of them grabbed him and dragged him out unceremoniously while the others started searching his room.

Outside, in the courtyard, more Boxers were tossing things around. Through the open windows, Fong saw their heads bobbing in every room.

Some were hacking open locked cabinets and drawers with their swords.

Fong was dragged to the middle of the courtyard and ordered to kneel. He resisted at first but decided to obey, remembering the old saying *A genuine hero does not mind taking small insults.* It was also Li Hung-chang's philosophy, *Keep the hills green and one never worries about future firewood.* "Keep the hills green," he murmured to himself as he knelt.

The Boxer who had dragged him out was obviously the leader. There were several big bulges under his dirty but still gaudy uniform. Besides carrying a broadsword, he had two daggers tucked into his red sash and one in his red leggings. He was a stout man with several scars on his muscular, weather-beaten face. He stank of garlic and sweat.

"Do you own this house?" the man demanded.

"Yes," Fong said, glancing around to see where Old Liu was. Suddenly he felt a sharp blow on his cheek. The Boxer leader had struck him.

"Damn your mother!" the leader cursed. "Pay attention to me, you turtle's egg!"

Fong glared at him, controlling his anger. "I said, yes, I am the owner of this house."

"Where do you hide your jewelry and silver?"

"I have no jewelry. The silver is in a drawer in my bedroom. I am sure your men have found it already."

"I mean your hidden treasure and money."

"I have no hidden treasure or money."

The leader hit him again, this time harder. Fong felt a sharp pain and a burning sensation on his face, and he tasted blood in his mouth. The temptation to try to grab the man's sword was strong, but he still managed to control his temper. "Keep the hills green," he murmured.

"What are you mumbling about?" The Boxer chief raised his sword threateningly, looking worried. Obviously he was afraid of anyone who mumbled; it could be some kind of curse or incantation.

Fong smiled, trying to look confident and mysterious. He could try to fool this bandit by pretending that he too possessed magic powers. But on second thought, he quickly abandoned the idea. What if the Boxers tried to counteract his magic by urinating on him? The foreigners in the legation had already experienced such counteractions: showers of garbage and urine-soaked rags.

Fong decided to say something to divert the man's attention. The sword was not nearly as threatening as the garlic smell. He had to get away from him. His mind racing, Fong said with a smile, "Older Brother, I am a Jade Emperor–fearing man. I shall not lie to you. Everything I own is in this house; nothing is hidden. If you still waste time on me, I am afraid whatever I have will soon become hidden treasures under your men's uniforms . . ."

Before he could finish, he heard a woman's scream. It sounded like one of the maids. As the scream grew louder and more hysterical, his blood boiled. In his mind's eye, he saw the maid being raped and tortured. It could have been Fong Yun or Shao Mei. Unable to control himself any longer, he leaped up, grabbed the leader's sword, and cut him down with one mighty blow. Eyes bulging, the bandit chief sank to the ground, blood oozing from his neck.

The other Boxers who saw the killing were stunned. When they regained their senses, they rushed into the courtyard with drawn swords, crying, "Sha, sha, sha!"

Fong was surprised by his own strength and speed. His body fueled with unexpected adrenaline, he had become a fighting machine, his sword the blade of a windmill. He could hear the wind as the blade slashed the air and went through human flesh as easily as cutting beancakes. He could see blood spouting like fountains, swords falling with loud clangs and bodies toppling to right and left. Some of the wounded scrambled to their feet and fled; others crawled away on all fours. Were these Boxers? He wanted to laugh. What had happened to their martial arts? What had become of their magic power? If Rose were alive, she could have wiped them out with one hand.

Just as his sword was about to slice into a cowering Boxer, Fong saw a familiar face staring at him in horror. He stopped his weapon in midair. It was the face of Rose's brother Chin. He was the one who had spat on him when he was leaving Rose's house many years ago—the man who had wanted to kill him. Why did he hesitate now?

Fong couldn't bring himself to kill him. As they stared at each other, the courtyard fell silent except for an occasional low groan.

"Sha!" a voice cried behind him. Fong felt the heavy blow of a sword cutting into his neck. The last words he heard were, "Sha, sha, sha!"

24

On August 24, 1901, the Empress Dowager started her return trip to Peking. She had stayed in Sian as a refugee for almost a year, waiting for the foreign troops to withdraw.

Now she was anxious to see what the foreign devils had done to her Forbidden City. Judging from what Jung Lu had reported to her throughout the year, she could only dread walking into the Winter Palace, her favorite residence. The weekly message with its details about looting, killing and raping had deeply troubled her, but nothing was more upsetting than the thought of their dirty fingers touching her furnishings and pocketing her ornaments. She had no idea if they had unearthed her hidden treasure of diamonds and pearls—three trunkfuls hastily buried under a peach tree before she had fled.

Her entourage was almost a mile long, trailing thousands of pieces of luggage that she had accumulated during her one year's sojourn in Sian. First in the procession were Jung Lu's Bannermen, her personal Imperial guards dressed in bright uniforms, holding spears and swords with tassels; strapped to their backs were modern Japanese weapons. The officers rode on spirited horses, banners flying and four thousand hoofbeats clattering on the dusty road like muffled firecrackers.

Following the guards were the yellow Imperial sedan chairs of Tsu Hsi, the Emperor and Empress, each carried by two dozen uniformed bearers. Her Majesty wore her best satin gown, embroidered with a dragon and phoenix and bordered with peonies; she glittered with jewels.

The Imperial family was followed by ministers, the eunuchs and the ladies-in-waiting, many of whom had gone to Sian to escort the royal entourage home, riding in small sedan chairs. Bringing up the rear were the luggage carts, pulled by Shantung mules. Hundreds of coolies hired for the occasion carried red-lacquered trunks and baskets tied to long bamboo poles, which they balanced on their shoulders, swinging them rhythmically as they trudged laboriously on the uneven road.

Tsu Hsi was in an unusually good mood. In her spacious sedan chair she smoked her water pipe and talked easily with Chief Eunuch Li Lien-ying, who rode beside her, his magnificent stallion nodding and snorting.

When the caravan passed through a small town, it was prearranged that the mayor and chief magistrate were waiting on their knees at the roadside with gifts, welcome signs and good-luck sayings written on lanterns and banners. Also kneeling beside the road were townspeople—those who still could smile after the national disaster of the worst foreign invasion in Chinese history.

Nothing had marred the glorious return trip except the evidence of devastation during the last leg of the journey. Leafless trees and the remains of burnt-out buildings were still visible. Sometimes the stench from unknown sources was overpowering. Her Majesty would then cover her nose with her perfumed silk handkerchief and close her eyes.

It was during those moments that her mood changed and her hatred of foreigners returned. She had heard that Goldenflower, a famous prostitute, had even entertained the German Commander-in-Chief in the Imperial bed. The thought of it revolted her; she made a mental note to have her bed fumigated and evil spirits driven out with firecrackers. It angered her even more to hear that it was Goldenflower who had persuaded the German Field Marshal to end the foreign troops' atrocities. The fact that a prostitute had saved the city of Peking from complete ruin would haunt her forever.

According to Li Hung-chang's report, Mrs. Ketteler, the widow of the German minister who was murdered by the Boxers, had even demanded to slap Her Majesty's face personally as one of the peace terms. It was rumored that Goldenflower had also talked the widow into withdrawing the demand. Instead, a memorial gate would be built in Peking, lauding the German barbarian's heroism in China. Tsu Hsi wondered if an extra seaport leased to the Germans would have achieved the same result. Such news galled Her Majesty terribly, making her lose great face, especially when she was mentioned in the same breath with Goldenflower, a harlot. She wished Li Hung-chang had negotiated a better peace settlement. China was to pay almost a billion taels of silver in war indemnities to the foreign powers. An extra million, even an additional seaport or two, would have been nothing if they had saved her from all these personal insults.

Arriving in Peking in November, she was delighted that the day was sunny and breezeless. Yuan Shih-kai, the commander of China's modern army, was on hand to welcome her, along with the surviving ministers and princes. Lining the road to the Forbidden City were thousands of government officials and troops, paying Her Majesty the obeisance of nine kowtows.

Back in her Palace of Longevity, Tsu Hsi ordered Chief Li to reward all the eunuchs, ladies-in-waiting and serving maids who had not accompanied her to Sian. The palace was aglow with welcome lanterns that night; and the main opera stage was to be prepared for a five-hour program in celebration the next day. All the ministers and princes had been invited to attend Her Majesty's favorite operas.

The next morning, reviewing the list of high government officials seeking an audience, Tsu Hsi deleted some names. One name on the list, Tang San, was unfamiliar to her. She asked Chief Li who he was. The Chief Eunuch, who had been bribed by Tang San, gave her a glowing report. "He was the only son of Fong Tai, Venerable," he said. "He is a handsome young man fluent with the foreign talk. A charming man, knowing a good many influential foreigners. And his father was the one who invented the phrase that saved China: 'Use one foreign devil to repel another.' "

"Oh, I remember him," Tsu Hsi said. "He was murdered by the Boxers. I shall see his son tonight. Invite him to watch the opera with me."

"Yes, Venerable."

✳

In the afternoon, Tsu Hsi took a short nap on the kang, her favorite daybed, on which she used to smoke a pipe of opium every midafternoon. The nap refreshed her. Then she ordered her bath. Four serving maids helped her to the bathroom, where she soaked in the large, red-lacquered bathtub and allowed two ladies-in-waiting to wash her with perfumed soap. According to palace rules, no serving maid was allowed to touch the Empress's body.

Helped back to her kang after the bath, she enjoyed a bowl of a special tree-fungus soup, her favorite rejuvenating tonic. Then Chief Li, sitting on a little stool, massaged her feet with a secret skill that no other eunuch could match.

After the foot massage, another eunuch tapped her shoulders with the palms of his hands in the flowery rhythm to relax her. Sighing and groaning, she closed her eyes and allowed a lady-in-waiting to put on her three-inch-long fingernails, which were polished every day with a special herb ointment by a eunuch who specialized in such chores.

In the late afternoon, when it was time for her to get dressed, four serving maids displayed several dresses in front of Her Majesty. She selected a brilliant red and gold gown suitable for the occasion. Today was her theater day and she wanted to wear something showy enough to match the theatrical costumes.

After the two ladies-in-waiting had helped put her clothes on and dressed her hair with appropriate decorations—silk flowers, jewel-inlaid combs and a headband—she was ready to hold audiences.

Tang San was the last to appear. He had been waiting in the anteroom outside the reception hall for almost an hour. For the audience with Tsu Hsi, he had ordered special clothes from America. He was magnificently dressed in a long-tailed blue coat with gilt buttons, embroidered white waistcoat, dapper buff trousers and varnished boots. He carried a polished cane and wore a gold fob and diamond scarf pin. The foreign clothes had cost him almost fifty taels of silver. Luckily he had been fairly successful in the protection business since the invasion, selling his foreign connection to ignorant Manchus who were afraid of foreigners.

When he was shown into the reception hall, he straightened his coat, shot his cuffs and strode into the hall like a proud Westerner, head high and boots squeaking. Instead of throwing himself on the ground and giving Her Majesty the usual nine-kowtow greeting, he bowed deeply and said in his sonorous voice, "Ten thousand years, Your Majesty."

Tsu Hsi was enchanted by the young man's good looks and his strange, magnificent clothes. With a smile, she pointed at one of the chairs below the dais and bade him sit down. Tang San obeyed after another deep bow. Holding his bowler on his knees, he sat in the hard rosewood chair and looked straight into Tsu Hsi's eyes, a pleasing smile on his tanned face. Traditionally, nobody dared look into Her Majesty's eyes during an audience. But, again, Her Majesty accepted the affront, realizing that the world was changing. The West had won all the wars against China, and she must make adjustments to suit this Western trend.

"So you are the son of Fong Tai," she said amiably, gesturing for a eunuch to light her water pipe.

"Yes, Your Majesty," Tang San replied, feeling flattered that he had been asked to sit down. Nobody had ever been allowed to sit in the presence of Tsu Hsi before, not even Yuan Shih-kai. How he wished someone were there to take a picture of him.

"He was a good man," Tsu Hsi said between puffs on her golden water pipe. "I have ordered a belated funeral for him. He did a great service for our country."

"Yes, Your Majesty. He was the one who invented the foreign policy 'Use one foreign power to repel another.'"

Tsu Hsi did not want to hear what she had already been told many times. Showing a bit of displeasure by smiling, she asked, "I understand you speak some foreign language or other."

"Yes, Your Majesty. I learned English from my father, who was educated in America. I also went to the missionary school in Peking. At home, my father and I spoke nothing but English; we even ate with knives and forks."

"So you are familiar with all the Western customs and etiquette?"

"Yes, Your Majesty."

"Good. I would like to use you as my personal interpreter when I invite some foreigners here for tea next week. Are you available?"

"Yes, indeed. For such an honor, I would make myself available even if I were not."

"Good. Li Lien-ying will inform you of the time and the date. Do you have sisters and brothers?"

Tang San did some quick thinking. He decided to forget about his own low-class family and talk about Fong Tai's. "Yes, Your Majesty," he said, remembering Fong Tai's daughter. "I have a sister who has gone to Paris to study."

"Paris? Where is that?"

"It is in France, Your Majesty. One of the most advanced and civilized countries in the West."

"I understand that in diplomatic circles people use French; in social gatherings they often speak English. Is that true?"

"Yes, Venerable. That is why my sister is studying French."

"Good. Perhaps she will be useful when she returns."

"She certainly will be, Your Majesty. I shall tell her to study harder and pay more attention to diplomatic matters."

"What is your religion?"

Once again, Tang San did a bit of quick thinking. As a boy he had believed in ghosts and spirits and always rubbed the tummy of the Happy Buddha for good luck; but he had never offered a stick of incense to any god or prayed to any of them. Now it was time to be a bit religious. He said, "I am a Christian, Your Majesty."

"Oh? So you believe in that foreign god who died on a cross."

"Yes, Your Majesty." He held his breath, hoping that Tsu Hsi would change the subject. He did not know anything about the Christian god.

Tsu Hsi was pensive. She was not at all convinced that a half-naked skinny bearded man could be a god. Besides, how could a god die? And yet, all the foreigners seemed to have a lot of good luck; they were rich and won all the wars. Their god must have something to do with that. She had worshiped the Buddha all her life, but her life had been full of troubles. Was it possible that the foreign god was more powerful than the Buddha?

Perhaps she should order a statue of that skinny god and have it set up on a small altar beside her bed. She would offer him a few sticks of incense every morning—just in case. But she was not going to tell anyone about it. "Do you like the Chinese opera?" she asked, changing the subject.

Tang San hated Chinese opera, especially the screechy singing of the female impersonators and the thunderous roars of the villains. But he was not going to tell the truth in front of such a devoted opera lover as Tsu Hsi. "I love it, Your Majesty. It is my favorite pastime."

Tsu Hsi smiled. She had instructed Chief Li to prepare a dinner for those who would arrive early for the opera. "You may have dinner with the other invited guests here before the opera's opening gong," she informed Tang San. For this added honor, Tang San bowed. Tsu Hsi then waved him off with a bejeweled hand and withdrew to her living quarters with the help of two ladies-in-waiting.

Tang San stood watching them go, his eyes on one of the ladies-in-waiting, and wondered how many such beauties were being wasted in the Forbidden City. They were the best scenery in the palace.

*

While Tang San was waiting in the reception hall, savoring his promising future, other guests began to arrive. Most of them were richly robed ministers and Manchu princes. A few stared at him, but many smiled and tried to strike up a conversation. He was sure that the friendly ones had heard about him and his good relations with the foreigners, and that many government officials and royal family members had paid him for protection.

Maintaining his dignity, he kept himself a bit aloof, returning their greetings with a minimum of smiling and words. Familiarity never helped his protection business, he had learned; people always took advantage of each other when they became too familiar. He knew that many high government officials, mostly foreigner-haters, were now frightened. He remembered the old saying, "When they hear people talk about the tiger, the color of their faces changes." Even though a few of them had snubbed him, he was confident that in time they would come to him for protection. He would keep talking about the tiger and give them a good scare.

When he thought of his "foreign connections," he could not help smiling a little. His only connection was a British soldier from the British Legation who had been looking for prostitutes. They had become friends. The Britisher had sold him a gold watch, which further advanced his career as a self-employed security agent. The watch was now his badge, which he hung across his waistcoat on a gold chain. It ticked loudly and played music when it was opened. There was a secret compartment in the back that contained a photo of Queen Victoria. He often opened it to polish the photo and blow some imaginary specks of dust off. Who could own such a watch but someone who was well connected? That was the impression he wanted to give to those frightened chickens—and he had been successful.

Glancing around the hall, he made some mental notes about who would be good potential customers. He considered the fat, the nervous and the most gaudily dressed to be his first choices. He put his hand into a breast pocket and counted his calling cards. Yes, there were enough to go around.

When dinner was announced, he and some sixty-odd ministers and Mandarins were ushered into the dining hall and seated at six round tables. A horde of eunuchs rushed in and out serving food and wine. It was a delicious banquet of eighteen courses and two soups, including the most expensive delicacies such as bears' palms and monkeys' brains. The Mandarins, after a few jars of shao hsing and mao tai, became relaxed and unceremonious, making the necessary appetizing noises, laughing and chatting with each other loudly. They were grateful that the Empress Dowager was not dining with them. Obviously, Her Majesty wanted to give them the freedom of being themselves; otherwise they would have had to eat standing up and nobody would have been able to speak or laugh or make toasts in the presence of the Imperial family. Tang San passed out several of his business cards.

After dinner the guests were ushered to the open-air theater that was built in the enormous courtyard of the Palace of Longevity. The courtyard was brightly lit with thousands of lanterns; the stage was aglitter with colorful banners and silk draperies, some of them embroidered with dragons and phoenixes and bordered with peonies and chrysanthemums.

All the arrangements had been planned and executed by Chief Eunuch Li Lien-ying, for the party was considered private, given by Tsu Hsi in celebration of her return to Peking. Chief Li was a good manager, and Tang San could not help but admire the man. Knowing the Chief Eunuch's importance, he had gone out of his way to befriend him—which was simple, merely entailing expensive gifts and cash bribes. It was a known fact that this was one of the wealthiest men in Peking. Inside the Forbidden City, he was a servant, but outside he was a lord, owning several mansions staffed with servants. It was even rumored that he had several concubines. Being a eunuch, he was not supposed to marry or take concubines. The rumor, therefore, had set tongues wagging; people speculated that Chief Li was no more a eunuch than a duck was a goose.

Tang San had learned many stories about Tsu Hsi, too. Her Majesty had many idiosyncrasies. One was her annual act of mercy, personally releasing thousands of caged birds on a lucky day chosen by her favorite soothsayer. Another was her addiction to Peking Opera and handsome actors, and her daily foot massage by Chief Li.

He also knew that Tsu Hsi had started as a concubine of the late Emperor and clawed her way to the top by means of intrigue and murder. It was rumored that she had killed the late Empress with poisoned rice cakes.

Then, after she had become the Empress herself, she had started a relentless battle against the onslaught of age. Nobody in her presence dared even to hint that she had changed. A lady-in-waiting was assigned the exclusive job of plucking gray hairs from her head every morning; another was in charge of tightening her skin with herbs and tapes; a third was ordered to apply the right makeup. As a result, although in her sixties, she looked forty.

Tang San had also learned that Her Majesty was superstitious and suspicious. Once she had caught a nameless disease that no Imperial physician could diagnose; no medicine could stop her abdominal pain and hiccups. A soothsayer had found a cure through divination in a turtle's shell. He had told Her Majesty that the only cure was a piece of flesh cut from the inside part of a man's thigh. Cooked with certain herbs and eaten on an empty stomach, it would stop the pain and hiccups.

Tsu Hsi wanted to test the loyalty of her nephew, the young Emperor. She asked if His Majesty would donate such a piece of flesh, but the young Emperor flatly refused. There was no volunteer except Chief Li, who immediately cut a large enough piece of flesh from his thigh to make a good mouthful.

This story had been whispered among the people in Peking for years, but nobody had ever learned the result. However, since Her Majesty had long since stopped hiccupping, everybody speculated that Chief Li's flesh had probably cured her ailment. That was why the Chief Eunuch had become one of the most powerful men in the Forbidden City.

*

The stage curtain parted and the opening gong was struck. Chief Li, a spry man in his forties, announced the arrival of Her Majesty, the Old Buddha, and everyone sank to his knees and started kowtowing as Tsu Hsi entered the courtyard, helped by two ladies-in-waiting and followed by the young

Emperor, the Empress and two Imperial concubines. As Her Majesty approached the dais, the guests all started chanting, "Wan swei, wan swei, wan wan swei."

Smiling faintly, Tsu Hsi stepped onto the dais, settled down in her chair and gestured for everybody else to sit down. The guests climbed to their feet, bones cracking amid grunts of exertion. Tang San sat down with a secret sigh, shaking his head, lamenting the fact that China was being managed by so many rickety old men, each with one foot already in the grave.

After everyone was seated, the theater manager approached Her Majesty with a large gilded folder which contained the night's program. He knelt while Tsu Hsi glanced at the selections, then nodded her approval. A few minutes later, the cast appeared on the stage and paid the Imperial family the usual obeisance of nine kowtows. Then the opening gong sounded again and the program started.

Tang San could only vaguely grasp the characters in the traditional operas. A man with a black face was an honest magistrate who tried to solve a murder mystery; a man with a white face was a crook; a man whose face was painted in several colors was either a prime minister or a duke. Almost all the roles required ugly makeup except those of the heroes and heroines. Those were usually played by the stars and had the best-looking actor playing the woman's role.

As the program dragged on, Tang San began to feel drowsy. The only thing that kept him awake was the glittering costumes and the female impersonators. They were indeed good-looking and he fantasized about sleeping with them.

When finally the program was over, the actors once more trooped onto the stage to pay obeisance to the Imperial family. Tsu Hsi was pleased; she ordered Chief Li to invite them to the reception hall for some tidbits.

Tang San was one of the few in the audience invited for the midnight snack. Flattered beyond words, he followed a eunuch to the reception hall where Her Majesty was sitting on a dais with her family.

On both sides of the spacious hall, tables were loaded with food. A swarm of eunuchs were busy pouring tea into tiny cups. The actors were escorted in. They all knelt in front of Tsu Hsi, their heads bowed.

Tang San was escorted to the dais. Her Majesty gestured toward an empty chair next to hers. "You may sit beside me," she said pleasantly. He obeyed after a low bow.

"Did you understand all the stories in the operas?" Tsu Hsi asked.

"Y–yes, Your Majesty," he answered hesitantly, a bit worried. "But, having indulged in Western culture for so many years, I have not seen many Chinese operas. After tonight, I know how superior they are!"

Tsu Hsi looked pleased. "I am glad to hear that. I want you to meet my favorite actor. You two men may have a great deal to talk about. Lately, he has shown an interest in Western culture."

She pointed to a kneeling figure among the actors. "Bo Ho, you may come here and sit beside me."

Bo Ho, a handsome actor in his early twenties, rose quickly. When he reached the dais, he kowtowed once more and took the empty chair on the other side of Tsu Hsi. She introduced them and they greeted each other with a bow and a handshake.

"Li Lien-ying," Tsu Hsi said to the Chief Eunuch, "bestow upon all the actors three filled buns and a cup of tea."

"Yes, Venerable," Chief Li said. He promptly went to carry out the order. All the eunuchs were plunged into action, carrying food and tea to the actors. Each actor took three buns and a cup of tea from the trays. Chief Li came with a tray and served the Imperial family. Tsu Hsi took a bun and gestured for Tang San and Bo Ho to follow suit. After everybody was served, the room became quiet except for the noises of chewing and tea sipping.

When everyone had finished eating, Tsu Hsi dismissed the actors and bestowed on each three extra buns. They accepted the gifts and left the hall after more kowtows.

Turning to Bo Ho, Tsu Hsi said, "The program tonight was satisfactory. But that actor who played the pig did not squeal like a pig; instead, he bleated like a goat. Tang San," she said, turning in his direction. "Bo Ho is the best actor in Peking. He plays his roles with genuine emotion, and his singing has great quality, with clear and studied diction. It enters your ears and stays in your heart; it soothes your soul. A great artist, is he not?"

"No doubt about it, Your Majesty," Tang San agreed enthusiastically. "His art is monumental. I am deeply impressed, and I am grateful to Your Majesty for bestowing on me the opportunity to appreciate such a great artist."

"Good. I am glad that you are an art connoisseur. Do you think the foreigners will appreciate him?"

"No doubt about it, Your Majesty."

He glanced at Bo Ho, who was smiling with pride and gratitude.

"Good," Tsu Hsi said. "When I entertain the foreign diplomats' wives next week, I want Bo Ho to provide the entertainment. And I want you to interpret the program. I don't want the foreigners to miss the intricate stories. You two should get together and make some preparations."

"Yes, Your Majesty," Tang San said. "Please leave everything to us."

*

That night, Tang San was busy making plans. On the not too distant horizon he could see one of the most influential men looming up—Tang San, the Imperial Interpreter, businessman, friend of the rich and powerful. He wanted to become successful fast, and he knew that the only secret was money and connections. Having entered Tsu Hsi's inner circle, he was confident that he would now have both.

25

In fewer than six years, most of Tang San's dreams came true.
Fortune smiled at him like a courtesan. He acquired money and prestige and a large mansion in the Eastern City near the foreign legations. He hired uniformed servants who spoke rudimentary English with a British accent and addressed every male foreigner as "Sir" and every Western female as "Madame," regardless of age. He was the toast of Peking.

But he felt sorry for the Great Ching Dynasty, which was not so lucky. Cowering under the foreign guns, the country had become a sick dragon, timid and nervous, its body covered with wounds.

Tsu Hsi had become pathetic during her last two years. She had forced herself to give constant tea parties and sometimes elaborate banquets to please the ladies from the foreign legations. As long as she lived, Tang San was free to come and go in her palace without an appointment. Li Lien-ying liked him and told him that he was the number-one tipper. His generous gifts to Chief Li included Swiss clocks and government food notes in large denominations. Chief Li always shared them with his inferiors—lesser eunuchs, serving maids and even a few ladies-in-waiting.

Tsu Hsi had started smoking a few pipes of opium every day to relax her and to ease her back pain and headaches. To her, Tang San's visits had almost the same soothing effect as a drug. To him, she could pour out all her complaints and grievances without reservation. He was a good listener and agreed with her easily, adding comments instead of merely answering with a string of empty yeses.

The peace terms negotiated with the foreign powers after the Boxer Rebellion had hurt her deeply. The horrendous war indemnity was enough to wreck China's economy forever. In addition, there were other conditions which reduced China to a colony. She had shed tears when she mentioned Li Hung-chang; he had bargained with the oppressors for months, then died of exhaustion. She had worried about her own failing health and dreaded the possibility that she might die before the young Emperor, whose ailments had kept him confined in the palace as though he were still under house arrest.

She had been frightened by the foreign ships which sailed in and out of China's treaty ports like goldfish in her pond, leisurely and freely, protected by battleships and gunboats. Those merchant vessels brought hordes of foreign missionaries and traders and mountains of goods, all posing potential threats to her security.

Because of her fear of the foreigners, she went out of her way to please their diplomats, especially their wives, believing that women always controlled men, as she herself had done. For by manipulating men, she had become one of the most powerful women in Chinese history.

During her last year, only Tang San and Yuan Shih-kai were welcome visitors. Seeing Her Majesty almost every week, Tang San developed a fondness for the unusual and complex woman. She had always been the victim of her own unpredictable temper and moods, racked by fear and suspicion, obliged to entertain hated enemies, forcing herself to smile and buy favors with expensive gifts while her heart ached.

She had done everything possible to prolong her life. She had prayed to both Buddha and Jesus Christ, taken Chinese elixirs and foreign tonics, attempted to redeem her sins with acts of mercy and fasts, and eased her conscience by belatedly promoting dead ministers, many of whom she had wrongfully executed.

Tang San, who had never shed a tear for anyone in his life, had found himself sobbing at the news of Her Majesty's death just one day after the young Emperor died of consumption. She had died of stomach bleeding and lingering dysentery—a painful death—but she had smiled on her deathbed and said that she was relieved to finally pay her penalty.

On that fateful windy day, Tang San had rushed to the Forbidden City and found the Palace of Longevity full of mourners, all grieving with abandon over Her Majesty's death. The weeping shook the roofs; it was almost as deafening as the foreign guns that had shelled the city.

For a day the Forbidden City shook with people's grief. Goldfish dashed around frantically in ponds; birds took off in fright. Little Pekingese dogs hid under beds, whining pathetically, not knowing what was going on.

The next day, orders were sent out that all government officials must remove the red buttons on their caps to observe the official mourning period. Half a dozen High Ministers of the Funeral were elected. An elaborate Imperial ceremony was planned and the entire nation was informed of the lucky date chosen on the lunar calendar. It was also decided how many coffin bearers were necessary, what treasures would be buried along with the body and how much white cloth was needed for three thousand funeral gowns to be worn by the Imperial staff in the Forbidden City.

But the funeral was like a theatrical production that flopped. Nobody outside the Forbidden City really cared. Some even secretly celebrated. The foreign diplomats all sighed, "Good riddance!"

Soon after both the Emperor and Tsu Hsi were buried, the heir apparent, Pu Yi, was crowned. Again the nation regarded the ceremony as a joke. It saddened Tang San to watch it. The three-year-old Pu Yi did not care about the throne. He cried and kicked and made such a fuss that his father, Prince Chung, the regent, kept saying, "Behave, behave. It will be over soon."

This was considered a terrible omen and nobody expected the new dynasty to last.

Having witnessed the changes, Tang San made several predictions. One of them was that Yuan Shih-kai, the late Empress Dowager's trusted military commander, would be the most powerful man in Peking. His troops were equipped with the most up-to-date Western weapons; his uniform was a copy of the Japanese Emperor's. Physically, he was short and stout, like the Japanese Commander-in-Chief who had been terrorizing Manchuria. Tang San lost no time in worming his way into the inner circle of General Yuan.

Meanwhile, he also capitalized on his other activities, so that by 1909 he was a man of conspicuous wealth.

*

One morning that year Tang San had a grueling meeting with Kitchen God Tao, his new business partner. The spring air was still chilly, but the morning sun seemed to brighten the city, despite the influx of refugees from the southern provinces, where much of the farmland had been devastated by two years of famine.

The city of Peking was still in ruins almost nine years after the Boxer Rebellion. But time marched on. The car Tang San was riding in was an American import, a box on wheels, powered by Western magic that had been invented by modern science.

He tried to relax as he was driven along Chang An Boulevard, one of the main thoroughfares. The street was still scarred by the destruction wrought by the fighting. The country had been suffering constant flood and drought. Inflation was rampant; silver and gold had disappeared; the government frantically issued printed money called food notes.

The street was crowded. Peasants and coolies in rags bumped into each other, grimacing but apologizing with bows. Peddlers carrying their wares on bamboo poles balanced on their shoulders shouted and tinkled their bells or clacked wooden clappers. On the sidewalks small tradesmen conducted business under umbrellas or temporary shades made of patched burlap, weighing vegetables and bony chickens on hand scales. Buyers bargained and paid grudgingly with coppers or the new almost-valueless "food notes." Tattered beggars were everywhere, stretching out their dirty deformed hands to beg for scraps or leftovers or a copper or two.

Tang San congratulated himself that during the past nine years he had been one of the few who had prospered. He had made a fortune importing American firearms for warlords, smuggling the government-controlled salt and selling it without tax and lending money at high interest. The city was like an old man who was getting shabbier, his health deteriorating steadily. In the past year, only two things had seemed to increase in number— beggars and automobiles. He was one of the few people who owned a magical *fire horse*.

Tang San thought of Kitchen God Tao and felt a chill. The nickname seemed to fit the man quite well. Tao functioned like a real kitchen god, worshiped by all kinds of fortune seekers who wanted a bridge to great wealth; and Kitchen God Tao could provide that bridge.

Tang San remembered his mother and how she had smeared honey on the picture of her kitchen god before she burned it and sent it to Heaven. The honey sweetened the god's report on the family's behavior so that the Jade Emperor in Heaven would bestow more good luck on them in the new year. Like many others, Tang San had sweetened Kitchen God Tao with gifts and money in order to make more money. If anything went wrong, Tao always talked about *ching hung*—the use of violence. He supported a gang of hatchetmen that was headed by a brute who called himself One Stroke Cha.

Since the Boxer Rebellion the country had lost its grip on law and order.

The warlords who controlled the provinces wrote their own laws, as did business lords like Kitchen God Tao. Any wrong that was committed against him was punished by the loss of a limb or an eye. Tang San would ordinarily have avoided such characters, but in business everybody needed Tao's help and cooperation.

As soon as Tang San returned home, he ordered a bath. He knew that a long soaking in his American-made bathtub would soothe his nerves, which was especially necessary after his meeting with Tao.

His personal maid, nicknamed Double Pleasure, who sometimes did extra service as a mistress, informed him that he had a foreign visitor. The man had been waiting in the living room for almost an hour. Tang San looked at the calling card and realized that he had completely forgotten the appointment Father Andrew Barrington had arranged with him the week before.

"Go tell the foreigner I'll see him in ten minutes," he said to Double Pleasure. While he was washing, he wondered what Barrington wanted. He had met the foreigner only once in Fong Tai's house many years ago, but he had never forgotten him, a red-faced man with a big red beard who talked loudly in a deep, commanding voice.

When he went to the living room, Barrington was dozing on a sofa, his cane leaning between his legs and his clasped hands resting on his large stomach. Tang San coughed. Barrington's troubled snoring stopped. He opened his cloudy eyes and looked at Tang San like a bewildered, big-bellied Buddha, not sure where he was.

"Father Barrington," Tang San said, putting out a hand. "How do you do?"

Barrington tried to get up, but even after several attempts, he was unable to struggle out of the deep chair. "Don't get up, please," Tang San said. He sat down on the other sofa, surprised at how much the man had aged. "He must be near ninety now," he thought.

A servant poured tea. Tang San offered Barrington a Havana cigar, but he declined. "I'll tell you what I have come for, Mr. Tang," he said. "Do you remember Fong Yun?"

"Fong Yun . . . Fong Yun," Tang repeated, trying to place the name.

"She is called Brigid now," Barrington said. "Her name was Brigitte, but her mother always misspelled it, so Brigid became her name. She was Fong Tai's daughter who went to Paris with her mother during the Boxer Rebellion. Remember?"

"Of course, of course!" Tang San said with a laugh, remembering that he had mentioned her to Tsu Hsi eight years ago. He had long since put

her out of his mind. "She was that Sword Courtesan's daughter—born out
of wedlock."

"Well, she was adopted by Shao Mei, and she believes that Shao Mei
was her mother. Shao Mei died in Paris of a stroke. My niece likes Brigid
and wants her to stay, but I think she should come home so she will not
become a hundred-percent foreign devil." After a short laugh he added,
"Seriously, it would be a shame to cut her off from her roots and culture
altogether. What do you think?"

Tang San remembered the naughty little girl who had been spoiled
rotten by Shao Mei. He did not want the burden; besides, he had no use
for that relationship anymore.

"Yes, I remember her well," he said. "If Fong Tai were alive, I am sure
he would like her to stay in Paris. She likes Paris, does she not?"

Barrington fished a snapshot out of his breast pocket and handed it to
Tang San. "This is Brigid's last photo, taken on her seventeenth birthday.
She would be an asset anywhere; it would be a shame to lose her to
France."

Tang San stared at the beautiful young woman in the photo and became
speechless. It was a total surprise, an image exactly opposite to what he
had visualized. The stylish hairdo, the slightly coquettish smile and the
fashionable French dress tightly laced to accentuate her slim waist presented such an alluring picture that he could not take his eyes off her. He
swallowed twice and said, "Y–yes, you are absolutely right, Father. She is
Chinese and should not be cut off from her Chinese culture. If indeed she
returns, I shall be happy to be her guardian. After all, her father was my
father, too."

"That settles it," Barrington said. "I shall write to her and tell her what
you just said. I think she will be delighted to see you again. It will be a
load off my mind to know that she has a home to come back to."

"My home is her home; please tell her that. And I am most grateful
for your concern and for bringing her welfare to my attention. Of course
I shall bear all the expense."

"That is not necessary. I think her mother left her plenty of money.
According to my niece, the poor woman was gnawed away by unrequited
love. She wasted away before she died."

Barrington stopped. He wiped the corner of one eye and blew his nose.
"Well, time to go." With the help of his cane, he again tried to rise. Tang
San quickly took hold of his arm and lifted him up.

"You have no plans to visit your niece, do you, Father?"

Walking toward the door, Barrington said with a sigh, "At my age I can't even get out of a chair without help. I think I'll stop crossing oceans. If this is the last time I see you, I bid you farewell. God bless you."

*

That afternoon, when Tang San had barely finished a plate of noodles in his private chambers, a servant knocked. "General Yuan Shih-kai is here to see you, sir," the servant said through the door.

Normally he would have turned a visitor away with some excuse during such hours; but nobody refused to see Yuan Shih-kai, and it was a great honor that the General had come to see him instead of summoning him. He quickly got dressed and went to the living room, where Yuan was pacing the floor restlessly, his boots squeaking and his sheathed saber dragging on the floor. He looked nervous and agitated.

He stopped pacing the moment he saw Tang San. Without greeting him, he grabbed Tang's hand. "I need several automobiles. How many can you sell me?"

Tang was surprised by this abrupt request. "I can supply as many as you want, General. Please sit down and have an afternoon snack." He wanted to find out how urgent the need was before he decided on a price.

"No, no," Yuan protested. "I don't have time. I need the cars now— immediately."

"Immediately?" Tang said, feigning surprise. "In that case I have only three . . ."

"Three, then. Have them driven to my house and I'll pay you at my office."

"Why is it so urgent, General?"

"That turtle's egg Prince Chung has fired me! He said that I should go back to my home province to nurse my bad foot. Once, to avoid an assignment, I mentioned that I had a bad foot; now he is using it as an excuse to get rid of me. At this time, I don't have the support for a mutiny, but I'll repay him, you'll see!"

The news shocked Tang San. He knew that Yuan was taking the firing very hard. He thought Yuan probably wanted to buy a few cars while he was still able to pay for them with military funds. To soothe him he said, "I know you never cared for the job anyway, General. You always had your eye on the throne."

Yuan hushed him immediately and changed the subject. "About the cars . . . load them with spare parts. I'll see you at my headquarters."

Yuan marched out without saying goodbye. Tang watched him go, shaking his head, sorry that he had wasted so much time and energy cultivating this man's friendship. Power was fleeting, but nothing was a total loss. He was going to make quite a bit of money out of Yuan's misfortune. Sinking onto a sofa with a smile, he started calculating the handsome profit he was going to make from the three cars.

26

E very evening before sunset for the past week, a beautiful young woman sat on the stump of a date tree and stared blankly into space, her face sad, sometimes a tear creeping down her cheek. She was in mourning, dressed in a black Western suit and high-heeled shoes, her long black hair falling down her back almost to her waist.

Nobody knew who she was. Many passersby avoided the area, suspecting that the young woman was a phantom or a wronged ghost who had returned seeking revenge.

Word spread that Smoke Pipe Lane was haunted by all kinds of wronged ghosts and demons and spirits. People believed it, for during the Boxer Rebellion some ten years before, the entire lane had burned down and hundreds of people had died in the flames. This particular plot had belonged to Fong Tai, a man who had butchered eighteen Boxers single-handedly and then had had his head chopped off by a Boxer's broadsword.

It was almost winter. The wind from the Gobi Desert had begun to howl, churning up dust and debris on the desolate plot. By 6:00 P.M. the sun had sunk behind the distant glazed roofs of the Imperial City. Brigid Fong Yun, almost eighteen in 1910, was still sitting on the tree stump, undisturbed by the dust that was blown against her. She closed her eyes once in a while to keep out bits of debris, her face expressionless, her long hair tossing in the wind.

An old man approached her from the back, carrying a cane and a basket of groceries. He limped a little, shivering in the wind; his purple padded long-gown flapped below his knees. He stopped momentarily, took off his iron-rimmed glasses, blew on them and cleaned them with the large sleeve of his gown. After he had replaced them, he walked close to her, clapped a hand on her shoulder and coughed. "Fong Yun," he said as loudly as his cracked voice would allow. "It is time to go home."

Brigid Fong Yun rose slowly. She managed a smile and followed the old man to a carriage. After both of them had climbed into the vehicle, the old man poked the roof with his cane and the driver hit the bony old horse. The carriage began to move, increasing speed gradually, clip-clopping on the cobblestoned street toward the Eastern City. Outside, the wind howled, shaking the carriage.

"Listen, Fong Yun," the old man said. "This is absolutely the last time you will sit there like a fool."

"All right, Third Uncle," Brigid said. She was tired of Third Uncle's urging. If she wanted to visit the plot again, she would simply hire a carriage and come by herself without letting anybody know. But she did not think she would come here anymore. She had spent enough time, more than a week, recollecting her youth and all the fond memories she had of that house—the love and warmth of her family, her mother's indulgence, her playtimes with the street urchin Sticks, Old Liu, the giggling maids and, above all, her handsome father. When she thought of her father, tears burst out of her eyes again.

Third Uncle brought out a silk handkerchief and handed it to her. "Wipe your tears. Your face is as dirty as a street urchin's. Now, pull yourself together. When you were little I remember you were as strong-willed as a stubborn mule and naughty as a little brat, always saying no to everything. Now, ten years of foreign bread and butter have turned you into jelly and a water fountain."

Brigid dried her eyes. "Third Uncle, I promise you that I'll never shed another tear. From now on I will only hate!"

Her voice was so sharp and determined that it jolted Third Uncle. "What?"

"Hate, hate, hate!" she said between her teeth, her eyes glaring.

"Hate who?"

"Those who killed my father and burned our home."

"Now, now, now, Fong Yun," Third Uncle said soothingly. "What is the use of hating? The Boxers have gone long ago. It is like hating somebody who is long dead. Look forward, think of your future."

Brigid kept quiet. She knew whom she was hating—the Empress Dowager who had caused all the tragedies in China. Even though Tsu Hsi had been dead for more than two years, she still hated her and would never stop hating her. In France, she had read all about Tsu Hsi and what had gone wrong in China. Her father's death had demoralized both her and her mother so much that they had remained lifeless for months. Both had decided not to return to China; they could not bear to see the ruins of a house in which her father had been decapitated.

In the French daily papers she had read about the atrocities committed by the European troops during the occupation, their looting, killing and raping, the punitive expeditions that had wiped out entire towns. When she read those reports, she could smell the stench of rotting corpses and the cinders of burnt houses. When the French press condemned their own troops' brutality and their slaughter of innocent people in China, she had been moved to tears. From that day on she had switched all her hatred of the Boxers and the brutal foreign powers to one person—Tsu Hsi, the Empress Dowager.

Later, when she read Father Barrington's letter urging her to return home, she had not been able to make up her mind for a long time. She was still nursing her hatred. The tragedy had simply overwhelmed her, causing her to sit morosely and let the tears pour down her cheeks. By the time her mother died, she had no more tears to shed. She knew it was time to return. And now that she was back, she could not stop thinking about her youth in that house on Smoke Pipe Lane.

The carriage arrived at the palatial mansion with glazed green tiles, massive red walls and lion-dogs guarding the vermilion gate. Third Uncle stepped down and offered to help her out. He was still spry and energetic, but had lost the gleam in his eye and his hearty laugh. He no longer winked or shrugged philosophically. He treated Brigid as though she were a sick girl. She resented it, but she hated unnecessary argument. She let him hold her elbow as she stepped down from the carriage. Still holding her elbow, he guided her to the door and knocked three times with his cane. Almost immediately, a servant in a blue cotton long-gown opened the squeaking door and bowed.

Brigid stepped over the high doorstep into the spacious courtyard. Third Uncle handed her the basket of groceries. "Here are some Western groceries I bought for you—bread and butter, and some French pastries. I thought you were probably missing these things."

"Thank you, Third Uncle. Aren't you coming in?"

"No," Third Uncle said. "Another time."

This was Third Uncle's standard answer: "Another time." He had said it on numerous occasions, but he had never stepped over the threshold. Brigid knew that he would never come in. She suspected that he either held a grudge against Tang San or despised the man. Third Uncle would not tell the reason for refusing to enter that gate, and she would not ask.

"Goodbye, Third Uncle," she called after him. "Thank you again!"

"Take good care of yourself," Third Uncle said, lifting his cane in a salute and disappearing into the carriage.

The servant closed the gate and hurried to open the door in the east wing, where Brigid had lived since her return from Europe. Tang San had also had the entire east wing remodeled and furnished with Western sofas and chairs. Her bedroom was decorated with white velvet drapes, a white satin bedspread and a thick white carpet. The furniture was Louis XIV, and there were fresh flowers everywhere—in Ming vases and in cloisonné pots. He wanted to cheer her up, and she was grateful. He had even found Old Liu, the old family servant, in the slums and had rehired him as her personal servant.

After a bath, she put on a silk robe and sank into a deep sofa, trying to make some plans for her life. No more visits to that ruin, she told herself; that was final. She would spend more time practicing ballet again and making new friends.

There was a knock on the door. She knew it was Tang San, who always knocked with a flowery rhythm, like a drummer who sounded gentle, apologetic and a bit flirtatious. She was really in no mood to see him, but since she had decided to be more cheerful, she quickly tied her robe and said, "Entrez, s'il vous plaît."

Wearing an ingratiating smile, Tang San entered the room. He carried boxes wrapped with shiny white paper and decorated with red silk flowers. "How are you today, Brigid?" he asked cheerfully, laying the boxes on the dresser.

"Very well, thank you," she said a bit stiffly. She did not know why, but she always felt a little uncomfortable in his presence. And the stream of gifts made her even more ill at ease.

"Here are a few things that you might find useful," he said, indicating the packages on the dresser. He looked at her expectantly, waiting for her to open them and utter little cries of delight. But she only nodded appreciatively and awarded him a polite, "Merci beaucoup."

Trying not to show his disappointment, he sat down on a sofa and crossed his legs comfortably. Brigid considered this ill-mannered; but he was in his own house. She took a seat across the coffee table from him, feeling the tension building in her, dreading his next move. She tried not to look at him, and yet she did not want to appear rude.

He was looking at her intently. Fidgeting a little, she smiled. She was never shy, and hated to appear shy. She crossed her legs and folded her arms with a heavy sigh. "Well . . ." she said, breaking the uncomfortable silence. She was somewhat amused by her own ham acting.

"Brigid," Tang San said, his voice gentle and serious, "if you wish to rebury your mother in Peking, I can easily have her body shipped back from Paris. Being Chinese, she might prefer a Chinese burial."

Brigid was surprised that Tang San should mention her mother. She had been dead two years and had been buried in a lovely cemetery outside Paris, in gardenlike surroundings, lush and well cultivated with trees, bushes and lawns. There were flowers that bloomed at all seasons. Why would anyone wish to be dug up and returned to some strange place that was choked with incense smoke and weeping relatives who never got tired of kowtowing to the dead?

"It is not necessary," she said. "Besides, it is too expensive."

"Money is no consideration, Brigid," he said expansively. "For your mother I don't care how much I spend. She was very nice to me, you know."

"She liked Paris. If she were alive, she would definitely want to be buried there. Thank you, Tang San."

"All right." There was another brief moment of silence. Then he changed the subject. "Brigid, we have modern schools now. We even have a Western-style university. If you wish to enroll, I can discuss it with the president. And about your ballet and music lessons, I know just the right instructor. . . ." He rambled on. Did she know that he had been the Empress Dowager's personal interpreter? When she was alive, he had attended all her tea parties and banquets at which she had entertained the wives of foreign diplomats. He had become friendly with many of them; they in turn had introduced him to important foreigners—merchants, missionaries, artists and members of the nobility.

He had also ordered a grand piano from Shanghai. The middle hall in the east wing would make a perfect ballroom where she could practice ballet and the piano. If she wished to give a European-style ball, the remodeled hall would be ideal for such an occasion. "By the way," he said, his enthusiasm mounting, "why don't you decorate the middle hall? I am sure with your talent and feminine touch the place will be turned into a showcase. The talk of Peking. The foreign diplomats will rave about it."

Brigid felt increasingly uncomfortable as Tang San rambled on. But she did not try to stop him, lest she appear rude. She listened but remained noncommittal and unresponsive. She wished he would tire and go away.

Finally he closed his long monologue with an optimistic remark. "I am sure you will be happy here, Brigid. I promise!" He took a look at his gold watch and rose. She quickly rose with him. "Sorry, I must go," he said. "I'll see you tomorrow at breakfast." He started to kiss her hand but changed his mind. She was relieved and walked him halfway to the door.

As soon as Tang San was gone, Brigid called Old Liu. The servant limped to her room, but at the door he stopped, one of his feet hanging in midair over the threshold.

Knowing that he was afraid of the white color of her room, she took off the cross from her neck and gave it to him. "Old Liu, this is a cross, a symbol of the foreigners' god. He will protect you from evil spirits, foreign or Chinese. Wear it and come in!"

Old Liu looked at her, his mouth gaping, then at the cross. "Old Liu," she went on, her voice firm and irritable, "everybody is afraid of the foreigners in Peking. Don't you think that evil spirits are also afraid of the foreigners' god? So! Wear the damned thing and come in!"

Old Liu put the cross around his neck and stepped in reluctantly.

"Sit down. I have a lot of questions to ask you."

He sat gingerly on the edge of a sofa, grinning sheepishly and hoping that the foreigners' god could really protect him from those unlucky white objects and their evil influence. Besides, no master or mistress had ever asked him to sit down before, and he felt uncomfortable. "What would you like to know, Young Mistress?"

"Tell me what happened."

"What happened? Sure! I witnessed everything. I personally saw how Master Fong was hacked down by . . ."

"I don't want to hear that!" she interrupted. "Tell me what my father did when he was alive, what happened after he sent us away. Did he go to work for Jung Lu? Was it true that he saved the Foreign Legation from being shelled by Jung Lu's cannons?"

"That I don't know, Young Mistress. Nobody told me about these things."

"That is what I thought. Such important things as saving hundreds of foreigners' lives were totally ignored. Have you ever heard of a lady called Goldenflower?"

Old Liu rolled his eyes comically. "Ah, who has not heard about her? She is a fox spirit turned into a singsong woman. She slept with the foreign Commander-in-Chief in the Empress Dowager's Imperial bed. If I see her I will spit on her . . ."

"All right," Brigid stopped him sharply. "That's enough." Knowing that the ignorant and the common people were grossly uninformed, she realized that she would never get any accurate information from any of them. Third Uncle had told her quite a bit about Goldenflower, who had saved Peking from ruin by sleeping with Waldersee, the Commander-in-Chief of the Allied forces invading China. From Old Liu's reaction, she knew that nobody had told him of Goldenflower's accomplishment; all that interested him was that she was a traitor who had slept with a foreigner in Tsu Hsi's Imperial bed. If it had not been for her father, China would have been partitioned by the foreign powers; if it had not been for Goldenflower, their troops would still be in China.

"Tell me," she said to Old Liu, "what my father did when he was alive. What were his likes and dislikes? Where did he spend his leisure time?"

"Ah, it is a long story." Old Liu was a talkative fellow; now he warmed up to the kind of topic he enjoyed chatting about. He cleared his throat as an introduction to a long story. He told with relish all Master Fong Tai's habits, idiosyncrasies, likes and dislikes. Master Fong liked to eat barbarians' food with knives and prongs; he practiced martial arts in the courtyard every morning, waking everyone with his battle cries; he hated mahjong and kowtowing, which he did all wrong, kneeling on his right leg first instead of his left; he loved Eight Great Lanes . . . Old Liu stopped, realizing that he was touching on a forbidden subject. Stammering again, he went on. "He—he loved to go to Heavenly Bridge, Young Mistress. He used to go there every Sunday afternoon."

"Where is it?" Brigid asked.

"Outside the Chien Men Gate."

"Take me there."

Old Liu's mouth popped open. He stared at her as if in shock. "Go to Heavenly Bridge, Young Mistress?"

"Yes, I have heard about the place. I want you to take me there for a visit."

"Oh, no! Young Mistress! It is not the right place for a young lady to go."

"Will you take me? If not, I will go myself."

"Oh, no, no! All right, I will take you. When?"

"Right now. But don't tell anybody. Wait here."

She went to her bedroom and changed into a casual blouse and skirt, tied her hair into a pigtail and wound it around her head, then pinned it down tight. She still looked attractive, though a bit odd in the eyes of a Chinese. She liked to turn people's heads on the street, but today her only interest was to see Heavenly Bridge. She had no Chinese clothes; she hoped that the French casual wear would not attract too much attention.

But on their way to find a carriage, she did just that. Old Liu followed a few steps behind her, glaring at the gawkers. When they saw a carriage, she climbed in without bargaining about the fee. Old Liu climbed up beside the driver and told him an elaborate story to save face. He said that his Young Mistress wanted to go to Heavenly Bridge only to hire some coolies for some heavy construction work at home. Brigid heard the ridiculous and unnecessary excuse and shook her head. But she tolerated it. Old Liu, after all, was a product of the worst of feudal times.

Through the small window, Brigid watched the streets, thinking of her father. She understood why he had been attracted to a place like Heavenly Bridge. Regardless of what people said about the place, she felt a closeness to it; a sort of mysterious force that was tugging at her, urging her to do whatever her father had done when he was young and adventurous.

Heavenly Bridge was as lively as ever when they reached it and got out —crowded with humans, mules, donkeys, dogs and camels, all dusty and shabby. Old Liu was so embarrassed that he kept making loud excuses right and left. "We are here to hire coolies for construction work, hee hee hee. . . ."

"Stop that!" Brigid told Old Liu. "Toss a handful of brass coins to the people." Old Liu obeyed. As soon as the coppers fell, the beggars scrambled to pick them up and Brigid slipped away, disappearing into the crowd. Old Liu almost lost her.

The pungent smell of food sold in the stalls filled the air. The noise of peddlers hawking, babies crying, mothers scolding, street singers screeching, mixed with the music of drums and gongs, was deafening. Brigid was searching for Mongolian wrestlers. Third Uncle had told her that three Mongolians had saved her father's life.

"They stink, Young Mistress," Old Liu kept saying. "If you want to see a good show, I'll take you to a nice theater."

Brigid ignored him. She wanted to taste a bowl of coolie food, but changed her mind lest Old Liu faint from embarrassment.

Soon she heard a battle cry and a lot of grunting. She squeezed into the crowd, thinking it might be a Mongolian wrestling match. Inside the human ring she saw a man demonstrating martial arts. He was middle-aged, bare chested, wearing a pair of loose trousers and white leggings. His waist was tied with a black sash. With a cry, he hit a thick wooden board with the edge of his right hand but failed to break it. Standing beside him was a young man of about nineteen, also bare chested, with bulging muscles. He watched his master intently, his arms akimbo, a proud smile on his tanned young face. On the ground were several traditional Chinese weapons—broadswords, long spears, long-handled swords, and prongs.

After several tries, the man finally split the board with a tremendous blow. He bowed to the applauding audience, while the young man picked up the pieces and put them away. A few coins were tossed into the empty bamboo collection plate in the middle of the ring. The man bowed in all directions to thank the audience for its generosity.

"My name is Hu," he said. Pointing to the young man, he added, "He is Hu Yin, my student. Hu Yin, bow to the kind ladies and generous gentlemen." Hu Yin obeyed, bowing as his master had done.

"Now, Hu Yin and I are going to show you a weapons combat," Master Hu said. "If it pleases you, give us applause; if one of us is wounded or killed, give us applause, too."

There was some mild applause and laughter. "Hu Yin," Master Hu said, "pick up your weapon and be on guard!"

Hu Yin picked up a spear and with a battle cry leaped to the center of the ring. Master Hu grabbed a broadsword and assumed a fighting stance. Both men circled, staring at each other, moving their weapons threateningly, ready to strike.

Suddenly Master Hu attacked. Hu Yin fought back with the long spear. Weapons clashed; it was a choreographed battle, increasing in speed, with the combatants leaping, crying, whirling and tumbling. For a while there was a blur of sword and spear, red tassels flying, weapons slashing. It was a dazzling show of martial arts, brutal and yet graceful. Brigid had never seen anything like it before. She watched, wide-eyed, fascinated.

When it was over, both laid down their weapons and bowed low to the audience. Again the applause was enthusiastic, but only a few coins flew into the collection plate.

Brigid watched the pair demonstrate more feats, including a knife-throwing act with Hu Yin tossing half a dozen daggers at his master, each landing on a large wooden board, barely missing Master Hu. Brigid watched them tensely, her heart beating violently, her hands sweating. A large crowd had gathered. Their skills in weapon fighting, bare-handed combat, acrobatic feats and knife throwing earned a great deal of applause, but the collection plate remained almost empty.

"Old Liu," Brigid said, "toss all your coins into that plate."

"All the coins?" Old Liu looked puzzled. To him, one coin was enough to show generosity.

"Yes," Brigid whispered. "Empty your pockets!"

Knowing that it was not his own money, Old Liu broke into a broad smile and coughed loudly to attract attention. He fished out all the coins from his pockets, a large handful. Rattling them in his hands briefly to attract more attention, he tossed them into the plate with a flourish and a loud grunt. His aim was not good. The coins scattered wide and far around the plate. The audience was amazed. Many turned to look at the generous giver. Old Liu nodded casually and dusted his hands, pretending it was nothing.

Master Hu broke into a happy smile and bowed deeply, his tanned and leathery face shining with gratitude. "Hu Yin," he cried, "look at that! A lucky day! Thank this kind gentleman for his generosity! Heavens! We have not seen so much money in a whole year."

Both turned to Old Liu and bowed deeply. Old Liu accepted the bows, beaming, looking to his right and left to acknowledge the enthusiastic applause of the crowd.

"Ask them if they want a little extra program," Brigid whispered to the servant. "I'll dance for them."

Old Liu's smile disappeared. He stared at his mistress, deeply shocked. "I said, ask Master Hu if he wants me to dance for his show!"

Old Liu merely gaped like a goldfish. With a sigh, Brigid stepped into the ring and bowed to Master Hu. "I can demonstrate some of the foreign devils' martial arts for you. Will you allow me?"

Master Hu's face lit up. "What lucky wind is blowing today? Hu Yin, did you hear that? This . . . uh, this young lady will perform for us. Ah, what a blessing!"

He picked up a small gong and struck it a few times. As more people began to gather around them, Brigid took off her fur-lined coat and her overskirt and pinned her hair more securely. In her silk trousers, she did three somersaults, a brief excerpt from *Swan Lake,* four leaps and a tumbling roll.

The audience watched the strange show in awe, some gaping, some silent, unable to figure out what it was. When she took a bow, they burst into wild applause and showered the collection plate with coins, peanuts, watermelon seeds and buns. Master Hu, smiling happily, joined in the applause. He picked up some coins from the collection plate and offered them to Brigid, who accepted them graciously.

After the audience had dispersed, Master Hu invited Brigid to have a bowl of hot noodles. Hu Yin packed the weapons and other tools of their trade and followed them to an open-air restaurant nearby. Taking a corner table, they sat down. Master Hu ordered black dragon tea and four bowls of heart and lung noodles.

Brigid introduced herself, then introduced Old Liu, who still had not quite recovered from his shock. During Brigid's performance, he had wished there were a hole in the ground where he could disappear. Never in his life had he felt so ashamed, especially when his young mistress had accepted coins from a low-class street swordsman.

The hot noodles came quickly. Eating like a peasant woman, Brigid asked Master Hu if Hu Yin was his son.

Master Hu laughed. "I don't have such luck. Hu Yin was dropped from Heaven. I am very happy that he is now my student. And a good one, too!"

"The Master is like my father," Hu Yin said with a smile. He was a quiet and polite young man, obviously devoted to his master.

"How did he drop from Heaven?" Brigid asked with a laugh.

Master Hu swallowed a large mouthful of tea and chuckled, casting a fond glance at Hu Yin. "One evening," he said, "when I was enjoying a bowl of noodles in this restaurant, a dirty hand reached out and grabbed my bowl. I looked up and stared into a bony face with large sad eyes. The boy was about fourteen, pale and skinny. He looked at me pleadingly. He could have grabbed the bowl and run, but he did not. I pushed the food toward him and made him sit down to eat it. He devoured the noodles. He would have eaten the bowl and the chopsticks, too, if I hadn't stopped him."

"I was very hungry," Hu Yin said with a shy smile.

"His family died in the famine in the south," Master Hu said. "He had eaten nothing for three days except some grass roots and insects. Look at him now, all fattened up and pretty good-looking." He laughed and patted Yin on the shoulder fondly. "I gave him a new name, Hu Yin, a blessing dropped from Heaven."

"It was my lucky day," Hu Yin said.

"I would like to learn some martial arts," Brigid said.

"The teacher is sitting right beside you," Master Hu replied with another laugh, pointing at Hu Yin. "He is good! If we had a real match, he could beat me in every category—wrestling, boxing or weapons combat. If he exhaled deeply, he could blow me over."

Hu Yin laughed with embarrassment. "You know my master is joking. He is the best joker at Heavenly Bridge."

"I'll learn from you both," Brigid said. "Besides martial arts, I'll learn from Master Hu how to joke; you, Hu Yin, can teach me how to exhale."

While they were all laughing, Old Liu fidgeted on his bench, his face distorting in agony.

27

When Brigid returned home, she was surprised to find cars and soldiers outside the gate. There were five automobiles, half a dozen fancy horse carriages and several sedan chairs. Dozens of armed soldiers were wearing new gray uniforms. Some even wore decorations, oversized gunbelts and red armbands with Chinese characters sewn on their sleeves.

For a moment Brigid stood a few yards away, wondering if she should go in. Was the house being invaded and Tang San arrested?

"Don't worry, Young Mistress," Old Liu said, smiling broadly. "Big generals' cars. It is a party. You will have a good time."

Brigid remembered that Tang San had mentioned a party a few days earlier. She followed Old Liu to the door, but one of the soldiers, apparently an officer, stopped them. A servant rushed out and told him who they were. The officer stepped back quickly, saluting.

Inside the courtyard, the lanterns were lit. Six tables were set up for a banquet and a group of uniformed servants was running around making preparations, carrying chairs and setting the tables with shining Western dinner plates and flatware. A six-man orchestra was playing a Viennese waltz on the terrace, where couples were dancing. The other guests, mostly foreigners, were milling around, smoking and drinking champagne. The pungent smell of Chinese food was already drifting to the courtyard from the kitchen.

As Brigid went across the yard to the east wing, Tang San rushed out of the reception hall. "Ah, Brigid," he called excitedly. "I have been looking for you. Some of my friends are anxious to meet you."

He was wearing a white suit. His shirt was a mass of fringe and his shining boots were silver-tipped and clamped with large, noisy spurs. His tall hat was sitting on his head at a jaunty angle. Tang San took her arm and guided her into the reception hall. About a dozen people were sitting there, talking and drinking champagne. Three of them were dressed in glittering military uniforms, two in silk Mandarin gowns and the rest in Western clothes. Tang San presented Brigid as his sister, repeating to every guest that she had just returned from Paris.

Brigid enjoyed the bows, the clicking of heels and the few hand kisses. She decided to play the charming hostess and exchanged pleasantries with each of them. They were people with impressive titles: General Tuan and General Feng, both division commanders of General Yuan Shih-kai's modern army; Colonel Yamamoto, of the famous Japanese Kwantung Army; a Mr. Johnson from the American Embassy; Colonel Hopkins, military attaché from the British Embassy; Prince Fu, the boy Emperor Pu Yi's cousin, and his sister Princess Lan; Sir James Somerville, a retired admiral of the British Navy; Lord Tao and a few other men of lesser importance. After the introductions, Tang San whispered, "Lord Tao is known as the Kitchen God. He can grant anybody any wish in Peking. I want you to know him better."

Brigid shrugged. "Why not?" She went over to the Kitchen God and sank down into the French couch beside the immense man. Lord Tao was wearing a purple Mandarin gown. His brooding dark face broke into a wide smile, pleased that she chose to sit beside him.

All the male guests were smoking cigars and drinking champagne except the Kitchen God, who was puffing on a long bamboo pipe and sipping tea noisily from a covered cup. Third Uncle had told Brigid that those who smoked long bamboo pipes were usually farmers and coolies; the upper-class Chinese always smoked water pipes. Suspecting that the Kitchen God was a self-made man of humble origins, she became more curious about him. She knew how to talk to unsophisticated types.

"Lord Tao," she said, "are you the richest man in Peking?"

The Kitchen God was taken aback by such a frank question, asked without any preliminary flattery. But this pretty young lady with rosy high cheeks and sparkling eyes intrigued him, even though her Western dress was an eyesore.

"The god of wealth liked the shape of my head," he said with a laugh. "It is square, is it not?" He moved his head right and left for her to inspect. The head was indeed large and square, set on a thick neck that seemed even larger. The man must have weighed more than three hundred pounds.

"Yes, Lord Tao," she said, laughing. "It is the most unusual head I have ever seen."

"When you look for a husband," Lord Tao said seriously, pointing a stubby finger at her as though he were a concerned uncle, "try to find one with a square head. Round things are slippery; only square things are solid. The god of wealth blesses only those who are solid. Remember that! So you are Tang San's sister."

"Y–yes," Brigid said hesitantly. She hated to explain their relationship.

"You don't look like him. Let me read your face." He put a finger under her chin and pushed it to the right and then to the left a few times, as if he were inspecting a Ming vase.

"According to your physiognomy, you have a long life ahead of you, blessed with many good fortunes. You will marry very well the first time, but your high cheekbones might cut your husband's life short. To remedy that, you should wear your hair differently. Let it fall on the sides and grow a bang here. Make a frame to contain the ill influence of your high cheekbones."

"You mean I am going to have more than two husbands?"

Lord Tao tipped her chin and studied her neck, then felt her skull with two fingers. "You will have three if you are not careful," he said gravely. "If you can contain the evil force of the high cheekbones, you will live with your first until you have four generations under one roof."

"Four generations under one roof! God!" she said, wincing. "You mean I'll have a lot of little feet running around under my skirt when I am old and tired?"

She noticed that Tang San, who was talking to General Feng nearby, was glancing at her and looking worried. Nobody talked to Lord Tao so casually and so flippantly. But she found Tao rather funny and easy to talk to.

"Old and tired?" Tao was saying, his small triangular eyes squeezed into two little slits in merriment. "You will survive everybody—even some of your own grandchildren." He tugged at one of her ears and added, "Look at those earlobes—as long as a goat's. They are the unmistakable sign of longevity. Not very sightly, though. But . . ."

"Lord Tao," she interrupted, "how rich will my future husbands be?"

The Kitchen God took a deep breath, took one of her hands and inspected it. "See this hump at the base of your thumb? Unusually high, is it not? It represents wealth. You will be very rich."

"I guess it is not as high as yours," Brigid said with a giggle.

Lord Tao opened one of his own pudgy hands and, sure enough, there were several high mounts on the palm. He chuckled. "All these signs are designed by Heaven, understand? Nobody can alter them."

"Good," she said, her voice almost a trill of joy, attracting the attention of a few guests sitting nearby. "You mean it is my destiny. I don't have to go out and chase the dollar. Simply marry a rich man and voilà! I am rich forever."

"That is right."

"Bien! If I become too tired of my husband, I don't even have to do anything to get rid of him. Just let my cheekbones do the dirty work."

"Brigid, darling," Tang San said, rushing over with a forced laugh. "You are joking, of course. Lord Tao, Brigid can't drink. Two sips of champagne and she is no longer herself."

"Champagne? Nobody even offered me any."

"I told the servants not to serve you, darling. You are still underage."

"In France I started drinking wine when I was nine."

"Did you?" Tang San looked surprised. "Of course you are joking, Brigid."

"I believe her," Lord Tao said. "Offer her a glass, Tang San. She is different. Much more lively than those shy and demure women her age. Maybe the French wine had something to do with it. Not a bad thing to import, eh, Tang San?" He chuckled.

Tang San relaxed. Laughing and agreeing with the Kitchen God, he hastened to pour a glass of champagne for Brigid.

Tang San was delighted that Brigid was getting along so well with Tao. The old lord had never before carried on a conversation with a woman; all his life he had treated them as toys and played with them according to his whims. If Brigid could make Lord Tao drink the foreign champagne, she could probably bend him at will in other areas. There were many areas where Tang San wanted the lord to cooperate. Brigid certainly would be an asset.

So as not to ignore other important guests, Tang San took Brigid's hand. "Come, Brigid—let me introduce you to some of my other friends on the terrace. You can come back and chat with Lord Tao after you have greeted everybody."

He clicked his heels at the Kitchen God. Tang San had adopted the salute from the Germans, and he used it regardless of the occasion or what he was wearing. Sometimes, when he was in pajamas and slippers, he clicked his heels as he and Brigid met for breakfast. Now he guided her to the terrace. She resisted a strong desire to tell him how ridiculous he looked.

The orchestra was finishing another waltz when they reached the terrace. Several couples were returning to their seats. Tang San first introduced Brigid to a pretty young Chinese woman and her bearded foreign escort. The woman was wearing a modified Mandarin gown of green silk that flattered her excellent figure. Its high slits showed her slim, shapely legs.

"Brigid, I want you to meet Ding Fei, a famous reporter. This is her friend, Mr. Sam Cohen, a very successful American businessman. Both are my good friends."

"Correction," Ding Fei said with a short laugh. "I am not famous. I am only a dreamer dreaming of becoming a famous reporter. Pleased to meet you, Brigid. Your famous brother has talked about you so often, I feel that I've already known you for years."

"A pleasure to meet you, Miss Fong," Sam Cohen said, shaking her hand. He was a muscular man about thirty years old, rather good-looking despite his full black beard. Brigid almost winced when she felt the grip of his powerful hand.

Behind Ding Fei and Sam Cohen, she saw a handsome man sitting alone in a garden chair looking at her with a faint smile. Fascinated, she could not take her eyes off him.

"Oh, here you are, Bo Ho," Tang San said. "Meet my sister. Brigid, this is Bo Ho, the famous actor who plays the roles of both heroes and heroines with equal excellence. He was the late Empress Dowager's favorite and a very good friend of mine."

Bo Ho rose quickly and bowed. Brigid offered him her hand and he shook it. His grip touched off a thrill that shot through her body. She wished he would hold her hand longer, but the handshake was brief and polite.

While Tang San introduced her to a few others, she only heard the names but did not listen, forcing a smile and greeting them automatically. In her mind's eye she was seeing Bo Ho: his bright eyes, straight nose and sensuous mouth. She longed to talk to him and find out more about him.

He was wearing the male version of a modified Mandarin gown in blue silk, the new fashion that was gradually becoming popular among the well-to-do. It was slimmer than the old-style gown, with shorter sleeves and lower collar; the slits were higher and it was often worn without the short black jacket. Brigid could tell that he had a strong, athletic body with smooth muscles and skin. She imagined that their two bodies were touching, and a thrill ran through her. For the next few moments she did not hear a word that Tang San was saying.

"What's the matter?" he whispered. "Are you sick?"

"Oh, no," she said, a little embarrassed. "When is dinner?"

To her relief, Ding Fei came over and took her arm. "Come talk to us, Brigid," she said, guiding her over to a group of chairs where Sam Cohen was relaxing and puffing on a pipe. As he rose to greet her, she glanced at Bo Ho, who was now engaged in an animated conversation with Tang San and another man.

"Sam," Ding Fei said to her escort, "you said that a Chinese woman never looks good in Western dress. But you were wrong: look at Brigid."

Sam Cohen leaned back and appraised her, puffing on his pipe. "Miss Fong," he asked, "are you by any chance a ballet dancer?"

"What makes you think that?"

"The way you walk. Dancers have a certain way of walking that is different."

"I hope we don't swagger," she said absentmindedly.

Cohen laughed. "Something between swaggering and a Chinese lady's teetering on small bound feet."

"Sam," Ding Fei said, as though she were a mother reprimanding a child, "are you practicing your comedy act again?"

"Are you, Miss Fong?" Sam insisted.

"Am I what?" Brigid asked, stealing another glance at Bo Ho.

"Are you a dancer?"

"I studied ballet in Paris."

"I thought so," Sam said with a grin. "You must give us a performance on the terrace."

"Not until after dinner." She was busily planning a way to sit beside Bo Ho at the dinner table.

A uniformed waiter came with more champagne and both Western and Chinese hors d'oeuvres.

"How can anyone eat dinner after all these?" Ding Fei said, helping herself generously to the meat dumplings and buns. Brigid picked up a glass of champagne. She thought the Western hors d'oeuvres tasted a bit peculiar, but the Chinese guests probably did not know the difference. Many of them, in order to Westernize themselves, ate the black caviar valiantly, smirking and praising its taste.

"Brigid," Ding Fei said, putting her food on a tray and moving her chair closer to her, "I would like to discuss women's fashions with you, but time is crucial. Let's talk about something more important." She made a sweeping gesture with her hand. "There are sixty-odd people here tonight. Have you met everybody?"

"Only a few. They are all famous, I suppose."

Ding Fei laughed. "That's the way your brother introduces people—everybody is famous. At least, I'm not."

"Who are you, really?"

Ding Fei cast Sam a glance. He was puffing contentedly on his pipe in his chair, pretending he wasn't listening. "Sam and I have a business," she said. "We are also in politics. One supports the other. . . . Are you interested in politics?"

Right now Brigid's only interest was to talk to Bo Ho. She cast a quick glance in his direction and her heart sank. He was gone. She hoped that Tang San had taken him to the reception hall to show him off. Would he come back? She hoped he would reappear before dinner was served.

"What do you want to talk to me about?" she asked, still absentmindedly.

Ding Fei was watching her carefully. "Tell me—are you interested in politics?"

"Very much so," Brigid said, still wondering where Bo Ho had gone. "I want to see something happen in this country—like the French Revolution."

Ding Fei and Sam Cohen exchanged a quick glance. "Now," Ding Fei said, moving her chair a little closer, "I feel we are breathing through the same nostril, as the old saying goes. Do you know that everybody here has the same ambition?"

"What is that?"

"To overthrow the Ching Dynasty. Everybody here wants to replace the boy Emperor, Pu Yi, with his own man."

"That's interesting," Brigid said, trying to forget about Bo Ho, who had probably slipped through her fingers, at least for that evening. "What man? The same man? Or different ones?"

"Everybody has his own man," Ding Fei said.

Now Brigid was more attentive. Ding Fei sounded a bit mysterious. Brigid had never met anyone so eager to discuss politics with her. "What business are you in?" she asked.

"Gold and jewelry," Ding Fei said, casting another glance at Sam. "Sam is an expert; he is the business brain. I'm his errand girl."

"I'll leave you two ladies to your girltalk," Sam said, rising. "I'll find someone to waltz with."

Ignoring him, Ding Fei went on. "Sam is a member of the International Gold and Diamond Dealers' Club, with headquarters in New York and London."

"Really?" Brigid began to warm to the subject. "Where is your headquarters in China?"

"In China they meet in synagogues. They always retain a low profile, so the warlords and the Green and Red Gang chieftains won't rob them."

"What do you do?" Brigid asked, her curiosity increasing. "What kind of errands do you run?"

"I gather information. Find the sources of supply and demand. Who wants to buy and who wants to sell. With the present rate of inflation, everybody wants to buy or sell, out of necessity or greed. Business has been excellent."

"Why did Tang San call you a reporter?"

"I do write about gold and diamonds for newspapers and magazines, chat about prices and industry trends. Occasionally I throw in an article or two on politics, using a pseudonym. To tell you the truth, politics is my main interest. But I must work in the shadows of Sam and his Jewish friends. I mingle a lot with long beards, white shirts, black coats and hats."

"What do you mean?"

From Brigid's sparkling eyes and her eager voice, Ding Fei knew that she was warming to the subject. "Most of the gold and diamond dealers in China are Hasidic Jews," she said. "That's how they dress. Nobody suspects a Chinese revolutionary to mingle with such strange foreigners, eat their food, shake their hands and say, 'Mazel un brucha.' People just laugh at me thinking I'm crazy."

"Mazel . . . mazel un brucha? Is it a kind of revolutionary secret code?"

"No," Ding Fei said with a little laugh. "Simply a parting phrase, like 'Luck and blessing.'"

"Is Sam involved in the revolution, too?"

"Up to here," Ding Fei said, raising a hand to her chin.

"Why should he be involved? He is not Chinese."

"Sam is a world citizen. His feelings have no nationality. He never talks about it, but he's all action. That's one of the reasons I love him." Ding Fei jerked her head toward a few men standing in the courtyard, looking grim and aloof. "See those men? They are the Kitchen God's bodyguards. See that big fellow with the turban and a big bulge under his gown? That's Kitchen God's number-one hatchetman, One Stroke Cha. He chops people's heads off with one stroke and enjoys watching them roll like melons. Somebody said he drinks human blood while it is still warm. Sam says he is dying to castrate him with one shot."

She stopped, took a drink of champagne and went on. "Brigid, I'm not here to gossip about gangsters. I want you to know that some of the guests here tonight are not ordinary people. They are rich, powerful and violent —full of intrigue."

Brigid's eyes widened. "What intrigue?"

"Remember those two generals you met? They are General Yuan Shih-kai's right-hand men. They want to put Yuan on the throne. See that Japanese over there?" She jerked her head.

Brigid saw Colonel Yamamoto standing several yards beyond the terrace, rocking on his heels and slapping his boots with his riding crop. He was a short little man with thick horn-rimmed glasses.

"Those glasses are telescopic," Ding Fei whispered. "So don't stare at him."

"What about him?"

"He has somebody else in mind for the throne—Marshal Chang, a Manchurian warlord. He would be a good puppet for the Japanese."

"What does the Manchu Prince want?"

"To usurp his cousin's throne. What else?"

"How about the foreigners?"

"That American is a spy, trying to find out who is doing what. The British Military Attaché is also here to get information. They have nobody particular in mind, but they will back the right man on the throne so they can work out deals that will profit their own government. They know that most of the men here are courting the Kitchen God, the number-one arms smuggler, the source of violence. In better terms, the kingmaker."

"Who is your man?" Brigid asked.

"Have you heard of Dr. Sun Yat-sen?"

"No."

Ding Fei moved her chair even closer. After another quick glance around, she told Brigid about Sun Yat-sen, talking in a low, confidential voice. Sun was a medical doctor whom she had met a year earlier on a steamer going up the Pearl River to Canton. During the short trip from Hong Kong, the Chinese passengers were repeatedly searched by tax collectors, then by opium inspectors and finally by customs officers. Each time some of their possessions were confiscated. When the fourth group of soldiers came aboard, Dr. Sun refused to open his suitcase. He was thrown overboard by the soldiers. He could not swim. As he was struggling in the water, an American plunged in and rescued him. After they were pulled back onto the boat, this young doctor, shivering in his wet clothes, stood on a bench and gave an impassioned speech, accusing the government of oppression and corruption.

"Luckily the soldiers were gone," Ding Fei said. "Otherwise they would certainly have shot him on the spot. I admired his courage. So did the American. We became his friends."

"Who was the American?"

Ding Fei looked across the room. "Sam Cohen."

Cohen was now waltzing with Princess Lan, who was laughing and protesting as she followed him awkwardly.

"A week later Sam rescued him again," Ding Fei went on. "At a temple of many gods. Dr. Sun was denouncing superstition and dismantling an idol on the altar. Some locals grabbed him and beat him up. Sam happened to be there. If Sam hadn't drawn his gun, Dr. Sun would have been dismantled himself, by those roughnecks. Sun wanted to hire Cohen as his bodyguard. Because white men enjoy special privileges in China and are feared by the Manchus, they are the best protection. So Sam became Dr. Sun's bodyguard."

Brigid cast another glance at Sam Cohen. "Why is he not with Dr. Sun right now?"

"Dr. Sun is in America, raising money for the revolution. Sam and I have other errands."

"For the revolution?"

Ding Fei nodded. She whispered, "Sam has known your brother for a long time. They did some business together. This time we want your brother to do something for China. We want him and the Kitchen God to smuggle arms for the revolution. Your brother is hesitant. We need your help, Brigid. Your influence will probably sway him. We have to win him over. All the others here are trying to get his help—especially those two generals."

"Do you want Tang San to donate the arms?"

"No, no! We want him to sell them to us. We may not be as rich as the generals or the Manchu prince, but we can pay. China's fate depends on this, Brigid. The choices will be: a bandit warlord from Manchuria for the new Emperor—a Japanese puppet. Or Yuan Shih-kai, the man who staged a coup and put the Empress Dowager back in power—he is nothing but a traitor. Or Dr. Sun Yat-sen, a courageous patriot who wants to turn China into a democratic republic. From now on there will be uprisings everywhere. Thousands will die. But if Pu Yi is replaced by a bandit, or a traitor, or his treacherous cousin, all the blood will have been shed in vain. Will you help?"

Ding Fei looked so earnest, her voice sounded so sincere and urgent, that Brigid was moved.

"Sam and his Jewish friends have donated some money, too," Ding Fei went on. "They want a stable China; they want Dr. Sun to get rid of the feeble government, wipe out the warlords, the Green and Red gangsters, so that the Jews can keep doing business in China safely and peacefully. So you see, they are not working for the revolution for glory or out of charity. . . ."

Brigid did not know what to say. She felt a little ashamed of being a Chinese and yet indifferent to China's conditions. Even foreigners were involved. "I'll help, Ding Fei," she finally said, trying not to sound emotional. "I'll do everything I can. I'm glad you asked."

*

A gong sounded and dinner was announced. Tang San came out of the reception hall and personally guided the important guests to their honored seats, one at each table. All the honored seats faced the entrance, according to Chinese tradition.

To Brigid's surprise, Bo Ho appeared from nowhere and hurried over to take a seat beside her, while Ding Fei and Cohen sat at her other side. The guest of honor at their table was Sir James Somerville, whom Cohen knew fairly well. According to Ding Fei, Somerville had made millions in the opium trade after the Opium War. He had even taken a Chinese concubine in Canton and begotten two children, whom the Admiral had given the best education money could buy. He had set them up in business in Hong Kong on the condition that they take different names and never reveal their paternal identity.

The little orchestra was now playing dinner music. They played loudly enough so that Ding Fei felt safe to gossip, even though Sir James sat only four places away.

Brigid was fascinated by Ding Fei's stories about Yuan Shih-kai, the dismissed warlord—how he had betrayed Emperor Kwang Hsu and staged the coup, how he had invented a foot ailment to avoid duty, and how Prince Chung, the regent of Pu Yi, had used the imaginary bad foot to force him to retire. That bad foot, she predicted, would cause a lot of trouble for the boy Emperor, Pu Yi; for Yuan was a venegeful man, full of intrigue and ambition. Nobody among the Manchu nobles was his match. Although retired to Honan Province, he was still in command of the modern army. He had placed two of his trusted men, General Tuan and General Feng, in key positions. "You will see," she said, indicating the two generals, who were sitting at another table. "These two actors will play important roles in the forthcoming play, which I'll call 'The Juggling of the Boy Emperor.' "

Brigid smiled at Bo Ho from time to time, but waited for him to start the conversation. She suddenly felt awkward. Perhaps she was too excited and anxious. Her heart racing and her hands wet, she searched for something appropriate to say. She had always felt at home with people she liked, and conversation had always come easily; why did she feel different with this man?

"What shall I call you?" Bo Ho asked at length, "Brigid or Fong Yun?"

"It depends," she said, delighted. "I like my intimate friends to call me Brigid; formal friends and acquaintances call me Fong Yun."

"All right—I'll call you Brigid."

Brigid felt the same thrill again; she was flattered by the star's desire to be more intimate.

"What does Bo Ho mean?"

"Bo Ho is a herb—very soothing. It is the basic ingredient in a medicine called the Pill of a Thousand Cures. Do you have a headache or a belly-ache?"

"Not yet," Brigid said, laughing. "If I have, I'll ask for a Pill of a Thousand Cures."

"Here is my calling card," he said, placing a small red card beside her plate. It had Bo Ho's name and address printed on it in gold characters.

"That bearded foreigner wanted you to perform after dinner. Are you going to?"

Brigid looked at him, an amused smile on her closed lips.

"Why do you look at me like that?" he asked. "Is there a speck of food on my nose?"

"I wonder if you have *an ear of a thousand miles*. You have heard everything, have you not?"

"Only the interesting parts. I would like to see your performance."

"I will perform for you if you ask."

"I will, if that bearded American has not beaten me to it."

"Your request will be granted first. But not too soon after dinner. It usually takes two hours to digest a rich meal."

"How can I wait that long?"

Brigid expected to hear some flattery and flowery compliments, but he did not say anything more. He just looked at her. His eyes seemed to do all the talking. She wanted to put a finger on his lips and whisper, "Stop pouting. I will entertain you for two hours before showtime."

"Do you drink coffee?" she asked.

"I certainly do," Bo Ho said. "But where?"

"I have a coffeemaker in my quarters—and I make good coffee, French style."

Bo Ho was noncommittal. "Did you like France?"

"I loved it."

"The country or the people?"

"Both."

"The French troops were brutal," Bo Ho said. "During the last invasion they were ranked third in looting and raping, only after the Germans and the Italians."

"The French press rated them second," Brigid replied. "Only after the Russians. That's why I like the French. They don't hide anything. When something goes wrong, they come right out and point an accusing finger at themselves."

Bo Ho did not pursue the subject as the dinner had begun to arrive. The food was excellent, a Chinese banquet served and eaten Western style. A waiter came with a large plate of red-cooked sea slugs. Bo Ho helped himself to several spoonfuls. Brigid winced.

"Do you enjoy that?" she asked.

"My favorite," Bo Ho said. "Better than French snails. Try it."

Brigid swallowed hard. Since she had eaten French snails, there was no reason why she could not eat a few Chinese sea slugs. She took a generous helping of the black, slippery stuff and swallowed a few chunks without chewing, holding her breath. She had been told that any food from the sea was healthful, so she considered it a tonic and decided that she would not mind swallowing more if pressed.

"I was told that you were the Empress Dowager's favorite actor," she said, trying to suppress a twinge of nausea.

"Being her favorite actor was no different from being her favorite Pekingese. We got a few more meat buns forced on us during her receptions after the performances. That was all."

"I would like to attend one of your performances sometime."

"Be my guest anytime."

"Thank you. What was the Empress Dowager's favorite opera?"

"Anything in which I played the role of a woman. I played all the tiger ladies in Chinese history—beautiful women who manipulated men and reached the pinnacle of power."

"You must be very good."

"I hated it," Bo Ho said. "It made me feel like those half-man, half-woman eunuchs. After the Empress Dowager died, I never played a woman again. I'll never squeal or titter mincingly or wave a handkerchief coquettishly on the stage again."

"Too bad. What roles do you play now?"

"Anything with action. I happen to be a good acrobat. The older I get, the higher I leap."

"It must be the sea slugs," she said, laughing. "Where are you from?"

"I was born in Hunan, but raised in Peking."

"Hunan! That's where my mother came from! Have you been there?"

"A few times. The food is too hot."

"I was told that the province is famous for three things: hot peppers, ill-tempered soldiers and passionate women—all because of the hot peppers."

"No doubt about it," Bo Ho said, finishing his sea slugs. He raised his wineglass and proposed a toast. "To hot-tempered and passionate Hunan people. Without us there will be no revolution."

"Agreed," Ding Fei chimed in and took a drink from her glass. "Brigid, we are going back to Hunan in a few days. Here is our Hunan address. If you should happen to go there, please look us up."

She pushed a card toward her. There were two addresses on the card, one in Peking and one in Changsha, the capital of Hunan. Both were rice stores.

"Is your father a rice merchant?" Brigid asked.

"These are our stores," Ding Fei said. "Yours and mine." She lowered her voice and added, "They are a front for our political activities."

＊

After dinner, the dance music resumed. It was no longer waltzes. Brigid recognized some American numbers. The honored guests had returned to the reception hall. A few especially important ones, such as the generals, the Manchu prince and his sister, had left early, according to custom. They were expected to arrive late and leave early to show their busy schedules.

Brigid had lost Bo Ho again. She hoped that he had gone to the washroom and would eventually come to claim his French coffee.

Tang San approached and sank into a chair beside her on the terrace. "Brigid, I have been looking for you. Quite a few guests have requested that you dance a ballet for them. I think it is a good idea; I want to show you off tonight. Will you do it?"

Brigid shrugged. "I don't mind. When?"

"We have other entertainment—a fan dance, a ribbon dance and such. Bo Ho may do a monkey dance. You will be the star. Yours will be the curtain number. How is that?"

"Whatever you say, Tang San."

"It's settled, then," Tang San said excitedly. "The musicians will be happy to play anything you ask. They are the best, from the Shanghai Symphony Orchestra. Tell them what you want. Did you enjoy the dinner?"

"Yes, I did."

"Tonight I have coined a phrase: Eastern food eaten the Western way. The foreigners like it—the Jews and Russians especially. They love Chinese food but hate chopsticks. Besides being unsanitary, chopsticks are hard to handle. And we must do business with the Russians and the Jews."

"Why?" Brigid asked automatically; she was not really interested in business.

Tang San cast a discreet glance around and said, almost whispering, "The Russians will keep the wolves from China's door—which is Manchuria."

"Who are the wolves?"

Tang San put his mouth close to her ear. She could smell his heavy liquor breath but refrained from recoiling.

"The Japanese," he whispered.

"What about the Jews?"

"They are shrewd; they can get anything you want. I have ordered a diamond for you, Brigid. One of my Jewish friends has promised that it will be the largest I have ever seen."

As he talked, his mouth was getting closer, almost touching her ear. She pulled her head away. "Well, since I have to dance," she said, rising to her feet quickly, "I must talk to the musicians and change my clothes."

"Go change into your little skirt," Tang San said. "By the way, the Kitchen God is still here. I told him that you are going to perform. He even canceled an appointment so he could watch you. You can wrap him around your little finger." He pointed at her, then at himself, and added confidentially, "Brigid, you and I will make a great team. Together we can conquer the world!"

✳

The show started shortly thereafter. A young woman in a Chinese costume consisting of a red blouse and matching trousers and shoes pranced around, waving two folding fans, smiling and squeezing her eyes coquettishly. Accompanied by two musicians who played a flute and a fu chin—the two-stringed Chinese violin—she burst into song. She had a high-pitched, beautiful voice and delivered the song with a variety of expressions, the audience punctuating her performance with laughter and "Hao, hao!"— a loud Chinese *bravo* that drowned out the music.

Brigid anxiously waited for Bo Ho's appearance. After a short ribbon dance, a gong was struck and a fu chin started wailing. Suddenly Bo Ho, dressed in a glittering costume of red and gold that was pulled tight over his slim, beautiful body, leaped out. Wearing the mask of a monkey, he did a succession of dazzling somersaults. In a few minutes of brilliant performance, but without saying a word, he related the story of the monkey king who tumbled his way to Heaven to steal the heavenly peach, which could turn a man into an immortal. He fought several battles with imaginary enemies on the way. When he finally stole the peach, he started to take a bite. But he hesitated, torn between the desire to become an immortal and the wish to sell the peach for a profit.

Brigid was entranced. "He's a genius," she thought.

When her turn came, Tang San leaped onto the center of the terrace and quieted the audience, many of whom were still applauding Bo Ho's performance. He raised both his hands and gave a special introduction, his face flushed, his voice tense with emotion. His brief introduction described his sister as green and inexperienced—but his voice trembled with excitement. Without saying so, he was promising an outstanding performance.

Feeling a bit overwhelmed, Brigid took off her silk robe and leaped onto the terrace. She did excerpts from *Swan Lake* and *Sleeping Beauty*. The musicians accompanied her skillfully as she executed her leaps and turns. She knew that her *pas de chats, jetés* and *glissades* were not perfect, but she hoped she retained the natural grace that her French ballet teacher had often praised her for. Besides, she loved to dance and executed her turns with real feeling.

When she bowed at the conclusion of her performance, she felt she did not deserve such an enthusiastic response—the applause was even louder than that accorded Bo Ho.

Tang San rushed over and congratulated her. The Kitchen God, too, was delighted. Brigid always enjoyed praise. It gave her a sweet taste of triumph.

She hoped that the riotous bravos had not been planted by Tang San.

28

It was almost like spring—the air breezy but not cold. Looking through the large glass window, Brigid saw the clear sky dotted with kites of all shapes and designs—dragons, phoenixes, butterflies and even houses. The distant street noises floated to her pleasantly, bringing life from the city that had been saddened by war and brutality. She especially liked the camel bells, ringing rhythmically under the animals' long necks as they lumbered along carrying heavy loads of firewood and water.

She finished her coffee and got dressed. Bo Ho would arrive in about an hour to pick her up for dinner. That evening, she would go to the Kwang Ho Theater to see his opera, in which, she had heard, he played a warrior who killed a tiger with his bare hands. It was her favorite legendary story adapted from the novel *All Men Are Brothers.*

Whenever Bo Ho appeared on stage, the audience watched, entranced, as if they were hypnotized. At the correct moment they burst into spontaneous applause and cried, "Hao, hao, hao!" at the tops of their voices. During those moments Brigid felt surging excitement, as though the thunderous ovations were meant for both of them.

As she was thinking of Bo Ho, there was a gentle knock on the door. She knew it was Tang San, whose knocking was like his voice, overly friendly and a bit apologetic.

"Come in, please," she said after a pause, hoping he would not stay too long.

Tang San brought several packages wrapped in shiny white paper and decorated with red silk ribbons and bows. As usual, he laid them on her desk and came over to kiss her hand. This morning he neglected to click his heels: perhaps some foreigner had advised him not to do it every time he greeted a relative.

"How are you, Brigid?"

"Very well, thank you. You don't have to bring me gifts every time you come here, you know."

"What is money for?" Tang San said, spreading his hands expansively. "Money is to make people happy, is it not?" He was dressed formally, wearing a top hat. He flipped the tails of his coat and sat down on a sofa with a contented sigh. "I have brought you good news, Brigid."

"Again?"

"Yes. From now on we'll have nothing but good news. As I told you, I planted many seeds during that party I gave a few weeks ago. Now some of them have sprouted. Remember Ding Fei and Sam Cohen? I heard from them this morning. They have placed a big order for merchandise."

"You mean arms?"

"Yes. You talked me into doing business with them, remember? The deal means tens of thousands of dollars. At ten percent commission . . ."

"What is the other good news?" she interrupted.

"Colonel Yamamoto has also heard from his government. The Kwangtung Army will support General Yuan Shih-kai, and a loan of one million taels of silver is being considered. Again I am counting on a fat profit. Of course, the Kitchen God will have the lion's share. But that isn't all, Brigid. Remember Prince Fu? He has sold some real estate and raised two million taels. He is thinking of organizing a private army. He has asked me to contact a few northern warlords to see if any of them would be interested in training the troops."

"Private army? What for? Fighting a civil war?"

"Usurping the crown," Tang San whispered. "Get rid of that boy, Pu Yi. I believe that his cousin, Prince Fu, will make a better Emperor. He is thirty-three years old, he is Westernized and he no longer wets his pants." He laughed. Seeing that Brigid remained grave, he stopped. "Brigid, do you know what all this good news means? It means diamonds on your fingers and furs on your back."

"Furs on my back? Am I going to become an ape? It sounds horrible!"

Tang San laughed. "You have a tremendous sense of humor, Brigid. But this is not a joke. This has to do with the future of China. We are helping China choose the right leader."

"Which side are you on, Tang San? Who is your choice?"

"That's funny," Tang San said brightly. "This is exactly the same question I asked Sir James Somerville, my British consultant, who knows quite a few arms dealers. He said a famous European named Darwin has discovered a theory. It is called the Survival of the Fittest. He said the world will one day belong to the fittest through the fighting process: the weak and incompetent will be eliminated. Let the best win, Brigid. And we will support the winner. In the meantime, we will pocket a big chunk of profit. We help China select the best ruler and at the same time line our pockets."

Brigid merely looked away. "I must finish dressing, Tang San."

"Going out?"

"Yes."

"By the way, I have two cars and two drivers. I can't use both of them at once, can I?"

"No."

"So! You are welcome to use one of them. Just tell the driver where you want to go."

"Thanks. When I want a car I'll let you know. I must get ready now. Will you excuse me?"

She went to the door and opened it. Tang San looked displeased. He departed with a frozen smile on his face.

✳

After consuming several more cups of coffee, Brigid became restless waiting for Bo Ho. As she was picking up her coat to go outside, she heard the front doorbell ring. Knowing it must be Bo Ho, she sat down again. If Bo Ho was accustomed to being late, she was not going to look too anxious, either.

Her heart pounding, she waited for Bo Ho to knock. She kept glancing at her watch. Her heart finally sank. It would not take a turtle ten minutes to crawl across the courtyard to the east wing. Would Bo Ho never show up? After twenty minutes, she anxiously called Old Liu.

Old Liu shuffled into her room, looking gloomy. "I heard the front doorbell," she said. "Who was it?"

"It was Master Bo Ho, Young Mistress," Old Liu said unhappily.

"Why didn't you tell me?" Brigid asked sharply. "Where is he?"

"He is gone."

"Why?"

"Master Tang San has instructed all the servants that if Master Bo Ho calls, we are to tell him that you are not in."

"Go get me a carriage," she said, feeling her anger rising.

"Carriage? Where are you going?"

"Just do as I tell you!" she snapped.

Vaguely understanding what was going on, Old Liu quickly withdrew. He wondered if he should defy Master Tang San's orders and hire a carriage. He did not stop at the front gate. After all, an old servant was supposed to be loyal to only one master, for better or for worse.

When Brigid arrived at Bo Ho's apartment, he was lying on a couch in the living room. The upstairs three-room flat, the best in the theatrical troupe's dormitory, was tidy, decorated with couplet scrolls of watercolor and calligraphy. Bo Ho's awards and trophies were displayed neatly on his desk and shelves; a teakettle was humming on the potbellied stove.

"Bo Ho," she called softly.

He did not stir. Alarmed, she sat on the edge of the couch and felt his pulse. With a sigh, Bo Ho turned to face her. "Did you think I was dead?"

"Yes, I did," she said with a laugh. "Killed yourself for unrequited love."

"I shall never visit you again, Brigid," he said with a sigh. "People used to roll out the red carpet and set off firecrackers to welcome me. Being told off at your brother's gate like a beggar was too much for me. That's why I am here licking my wounds."

"You don't sound very sad."

"It taught me a lesson; it gave me a chance to feel rejection for the first time. No wonder lovers swallow gold or opium to end it all."

Brigid put a finger on his lips. "Don't say that. It will never happen to you. From now on I'll come to you. I might even bring my coffeepot." She kissed him gently on the cheek. He returned the kiss on her mouth, lingeringly. Taking a breath, she said, "I thought you would never stop treating me like a sister."

"It was hard, believe me. I'm so much older than you."

"I don't mind."

"I'm glad." He held her at arm's length and stared at her for a moment. "Anyway, you don't look seventeen."

"I'll be eighteen next week."

Bo Ho didn't believe her, but he didn't argue. "What do you want to do?"

"Whatever you choose."

"Whatever we do, let's do it comfortably. Here are the choices: first, dinner at the Peking Pavilion, then the theater; second, dinner at the East Wind Restaurant, then come back here and continue what we are doing. Take your choice."

"What about your performance tonight?"

"My favorite disciple can take my place. He will be grateful."

Brigid thought for a moment. "If we take the second choice, why the East Wind? Why not the Peking Pavilion?"

"The East Wind is a Moslem restaurant. You know those mutton dishes. They do wonders in . . ."

She stopped him. "I don't need those mutton dishes. May I suggest a third choice?"

"This is your night. Suggest anything you want."

"Let's continue what we are doing, then have dinner at the Peking Pavilion. I have heard endlessly about the place, but nobody has ever taken me there. Maybe you can afford it."

With a smile Bo Ho picked her up, and, carrying her to the bedroom, placed her on the double bed. The spacious room was simply decorated, full of house plants and ancient pine bonsai. There was a faint fragrance of tuberose in the air. Brigid had imagined such moments many times—being swept off her feet by someone handsome and famous.

Bo Ho was the kind of man who did everything very well. His gentle touches and kisses made her feel like a precious, delicate vase being savored by a connoisseur. He dispelled her fear and tension with soothing words.

His confession of love, which first relaxed her and then excited her, aroused in her a mounting passion.

When it was over, she lay in his arms, exhausted. Though she had fantasized about such moments, the reality far surpassed her dreams. Her body continued to tingle with the pleasure of the experience. This was happiness! She knew she would never ask for anything else for the rest of her life.

"Hungry?" Bo Ho asked.

"Yes!" She planted a kiss on his lips and climbed out of bed. "Please show me Peking, Bo Ho. I want to see things and taste foods I have never seen or tasted before."

✳

The Peking Pavilion was one of the oldest and largest restaurants in the Imperial City. When they arrived in Bo Ho's private carriage, the gaudy palatial building with its large gilded signboard, massive vermilion doors and gleaming glazed tile roof was already surrounded by automobiles, carriages and sedan chairs. Several armed soldiers were keeping beggars and gawking peasants from approaching the gate. The pungent smell of food had attracted several homeless dogs to the vicinity.

"Inside this restaurant you will see things that many Westerners have never seen," Bo Ho said, helping her out of the carriage. "It might be your first experience, too."

Squeezing his hand, she held his arm and mounted the marble steps to the door, which was guarded by two ferocious marble lion-dogs. A tall doorman dressed in blue silk gown and satin cap recognized Bo Ho. He greeted him with a low bow and called out, "Welcome, Master Bo Ho."

"You must be a regular customer," Brigid said.

"More like a regular guest," Bo Ho said. Lowering his voice, he added, "We actors are like prostitutes and police officers, we seldom pay our bills. Sometimes two or three parties will fight to pay for our dinners. You will see."

"Who are those soldiers outside?"

"They are the bodyguards for some important people. Looks like someone is giving a big banquet here tonight."

The restaurant was brightly decorated with red and blue lanterns, carved beams and silk embroidered landscapes in gilded frames. It was crowded, noisy and warm, with waiters darting about carrying food, drinks and hot towels, their pigtails neatly oiled and braided and swaying against their blue cotton uniforms with red borders.

The manager, a fat man wearing a dark silk gown, greated Bo Ho warmly and escorted them to one of the private dining rooms that lined both sides of the enormous building. Each room had a poetic name written on a gilded signboard hanging over the curtained door. In the front part was the general dining area; in the back were the banquet halls, glittering with more lanterns, all filled with people dining, chatting, laughing and playing the finger-guessing game. The noise was deafening.

Brigid liked the name of their private room: Sunrise on Lotus Pond. Inside was a small, marble-topped, carved round table surrounded by four straight-backed chairs with thick satin cushions. The manager exchanged a few customary pleasantries with Bo Ho and withdrew. Almost immediately, a waiter entered with a tray of tea, watermelon seeds and hot towels. Smiling pleasantly, he asked which drink Master Bo Ho preferred.

"I am going to select the menu," he said to Brigid. "Do you mind?"

"Surprise me," she said with a smile.

She watched Bo Ho read the enormous menu as though he were perusing a book of poetry, shaking his head rhythmically like a scholar reading the classics. When he had finished, he cleared his throat and ordered, mentioning the names of several dishes that sounded like classical poems.

"Are we dining or attending a poetry class?" Brigid asked with a laugh.

"The lunar New Year is coming. All the restaurants have changed the names of their dishes for good luck. Now all the items have poetic names. Chickens are no longer chickens but phoenixes, and so on."

"I heard you mention phoenix in one of the orders. At least I know we are going to have a chicken dish. What else did you order?"

"You want surprises, so you will have surprises. Let's drink a toast."

It was the first time Brigid had drunk mao tai, and the fiery liquor burned her throat. Trying not to grimace, she valiantly downed her cupful. This was a special occasion and she felt like a bride. She would not spoil it by refusing anything.

The party in the next room was growing boisterous; two people were shouting at each other, but bursts of laughter indicated that it was not a fight. As she listened, she discovered that they were shouting poems at each other. She laughed. "Is that a poem-shouting contest?"

"That's a finger-guessing game," Bo Ho explained. "You certainly have become a foreign devil, Brigid. Don't you know the finger-guessing game?" He flung two fingers at her and shouted, "Five sons all pass the Imperial examination!"

"What do I do?" Brigid asked.

"You do the same, putting out any number of fingers on one hand, and at the same time shout a phrase with a number in it. Not just any phrase, but a poetic phrase taken out of poetry or old sayings, such as Prosperity in Four Seasons. If the combined number of fingers coincides with the number you have shouted, you win. Shall we try?"

Brigid made sure she understood. Then Bo Ho put out four fingers and shouted, "Five generations under one roof!"

Brigid threw out one finger and shouted, "My two aching feet."

"You lost," Bo Ho said, laughing. "My four fingers plus your one finger are five. I said, 'Five generations under one roof.' If you had shouted, 'Five aching feet,' we would have had a draw. Drink up. The one who loses always drinks. That's the rule of the game."

Brigid gulped down her cup of mao tai.

Before dinner was served, she felt the effect of the drink. She was flying and her head spinning. She heard a disturbance in another room. "A fire, Bo Ho!"

Bo Ho laughed. "Listen again, Brigid."

She listened. It sounded like a loud argument. There were rapid-fire voices from several people, mingled with noises of jostling, pushing and yelling. "My God, a fight! Bo Ho, I thought you had brought me to a high-class restaurant!"

Bo Ho leaned back in his chair, lit a cigarette and stared at her, looking amused. "Brigid, those noises are a show of Chinese politeness."

"Do you think I am drunk?" She blew the front part of her hair and laughed.

"This is the way a dinner ends," he said seriously. "Everybody is fighting to pay the bill. The waiter is going to decide whose money to take. The one who pays will gain big face. Of course, a few might just make a gesture of paying, holding out their money tightly, hoping that the waiter will look elsewhere. But the fight is a show of hospitality just the same, can't you see? A lot more civilized than when we actors and prostitutes simply wipe our mouths after dinner and say, 'Thank you.' Listen, you are going to hear something else that will introduce you to more Chinese culture."

While they were drinking and chatting, they heard more quarrels in other rooms. "The people in the next room are leaving," Bo Ho said. "Listen to this."

Brigid listened. She heard people talking and laughing. Presently someone was shouting at the top of his voice, "See the guests off! Master Wong has tipped twenty dollars! Thank you, Master Wong!" Then there was a chain reaction of shouting, "Thank Master Wong!"

"That is a waiter's voice," Bo Ho said. "Now all the other waiters are bowing as Master Wong waddles out in style, followed by his proud companions. If you want to have your name announced, just tip heavily. Don't shudder, Brigid; that's the tradition in Peking."

The waiter was now bringing in the dishes. With a smile, he laid several steaming bowls of food on the table and began to serve Brigid. But Bo Ho waved him off. "I am not going to give him the pleasure of serving you, Brigid," he said, helping her to the food.

"Tell me what they are. They look peculiar but smell good."

Bo Ho filled her bowl with a thick soup. "This is the restaurant's famous delicacy. Its main ingredients are turtle meat and chicken feet." He opened the cover of a large plate. Resting in the middle were two tiny roasted birds and two small eggs the size of thumb joints. "These are a pair of golden birds and their two eggs. The whole family."

A waiter came in with a bottle of champagne. "Master Tang San's compliments, sir," he announced, beaming.

Another waiter lifted the door curtain and Tang San entered, smiling broadly.

Brigid's heart sank. She greeted him coldly. "How did you know I was here?"

"Bo Ho is the most famous man in Peking. Even beggars recognize him. How can you avoid me?" He laughed. "By the way, General Feng and General Tuan are hosting a party in the banquet room. Remember them?"

"How can anyone forget them? Their chests are decorated like the walls of a picture gallery."

Tang San laughed again. "Anyway, I want you to meet some of their guests."

"Sorry, Tang San," Brigid said, her voice firm. "Not tonight."

Tang San kept smiling, but his eyes turned icy. After a quick glance at Bo Ho, he clicked his heels. "I understand. Have a good time." Raising his cane in a salute, he flung the curtain aside and marched away.

"He sounds like a very jealous brother," Bo Ho said.

"He is not my brother. Just someone my father befriended."

"Oh?" Bo Ho raised an eyebrow. "He certainly fooled the Empress Dowager. Tell me about it."

"No. I don't want to talk about the past."

"All right," Bo Ho said, helping her to more food.

Brigid ate without tasting anything. She was worried now. Tang San's bitterness was audible in his voice, in spite of his smile. She felt he was spinning a web around her. A trap was getting ready to be sprung and she must do something about it.

"Bo Ho," she said after taking a large mouthful of mao tai, "why are you not married?"

Bo Ho looked surprised. "Why are *you* not married, Brigid?"

"I haven't found the right man, I suppose. But by Western standards, I am still young."

"By Chinese standards I am already too old," Bo Ho said with a chuckle. "Who would marry an old man almost thirty-five?"

"I would," Brigid said quickly. "My Third Uncle said that age differences do not matter if the couple is married on the right date selected from the lunar calendar. There are certain lucky dates that are suitable for such matches, you know." She also laughed, but it was halting, almost timid. "I am getting superstitious, am I not?"

Bo Ho didn't respond. He filled her cup with mao tai. "Your capacity for this fire liquor is improving, Brigid. I have seen women pass out after two tiny cups."

They ate quietly until Bo Ho poured some tea and asked for the bill. The waiter smilingly fished out several pieces of paper from his pocket. "Master Tang San has already paid your bill, sir. And here are messages from other guests."

Bo Ho read them and smiled. "Brigid, tonight we can eat five dinners. Five people have offered to pay for our meals."

Before he finished, another waiter came in with a tray containing four bottles of mao tai. They were from other guests, each accompanied by an impressive calling card. Without reading them, Bo Ho waved the gifts away and told the waiter to return all of them with his thanks. Then he turned to the first waiter and added, "Please tell Master Tang San and the others that today I must pay for the dinner myself."

He brought out a handful of silver dollars and handed them to the waiter. "This ought to cover everything, including the tip."

The waiter broke into a happy smile. "Master Bo Ho, this is too much!" He started to shout, "See the guests off . . ." but Bo Ho stopped him quickly. He tossed another dollar on the table.

"The extra dollar is for you not to shout my name when I go out, understand?"

The waiter bowed and nodded.

On their way out, Brigid walked beside Bo Ho without holding his arm. She was quiet, her heart heavy with frustration and shame. She had completed the ruin of the evening by shouting out her thoughts about marriage, and to make things worse Bo Ho hadn't even responded. She had spoken in desperation, but his rejection was too much. It made her feel cheap.

Bo Ho took her arm and walked with her to the waiting carriage. The moment they settled down inside, Bo Ho sighed. "Sometimes I wish I had a different face. No matter where I go, I feel like an expensive harlot parading on the street."

Brigid was quiet. He reached for her hand. "Would you like to go back to my apartment?" he asked after a pause. "I have the best mao tai if you feel like having another cup."

She was tempted to withdraw her hand but did not. The shame and frustration felt like a rock weighing heavily on her heart. "No, thank you, Bo Ho," she said, trying not to sound too unhappy. "You had better take me home."

"All right," he said, sounding rather relieved. He knocked on the roof of the carriage and told the driver the address.

During the short ride to Tang San's house, Bo Ho tried to be cheerful, but the effort showed through his forced laughter. When the carriage stopped and he helped her out, she was almost in tears. Saying a hasty, "Good night," she ran to the gate. Before the doorman responded to her knock, she heard Bo Ho's carriage leave.

Back in her living room, she threw herself on a sofa, buried her face in a cushion and cried. Who would have guessed that a happy evening would end like this? Her first serious romance had been like tiger head and snake tail, a Chinese expression she had often heard people use to describe anything short-lived. After she had cried, she felt drained physically and emotionally. Blessedly, she fell asleep.

29

I n the morning Brigid woke up on her living room sofa with a headache. The first thing that caught her eye was a bouquet of roses in a cloisonné vase on the coffee table. She grimaced. "Oh, not again!" Tang San had been showering her with gifts of clothing and art objects, which she had often wished were diamonds or flowers. This morning even roses did not excite her.

She had not recovered from last night's disaster; she felt acute pain, accompanied by utter loneliness. On top of that, she had a splitting headache.

She resolved to forget about Bo Ho. From now on she would go to Heavenly Bridge more often, increasing her regular martial arts lessons with Hu Yin and Old Master Hu.

As she stretched, ready to take a shower, she heard the familiar knock. Without waiting for her to respond, Tang San opened the door and came in. He was dressed in one of his Western suits, a bowler sitting on his slick, oily hair at the usual studied angle. For the first time, he was unsmiling and businesslike. "May I sit down?"

"Please," she said, smoothing her clothes.

"I see you are dressed up. Ready to go somewhere?"

Brigid didn't want to tell him that she had slept on the sofa. "What do you want, Tang San?"

"You have been going out so often," he said, his voice carefully controlled. "I am worried. You are still my responsibility, you know."

She took a deep breath. "Tang San, I am almost eighteen. I am no longer a child."

"But this is China. You are my charge until you no longer live in this house. I am entitled to know what you have been doing and what people you are seeing. Is Bo Ho the only one?"

"What do you mean, *only one?*"

"I mean is he the only lover?"

"I don't have to answer that!"

"Do you see others?" he asked sharply. "Answer yes or no."

"I see a lot of other people—Third Uncle, Hu Yin, Master Hu . . ."

"Who are Hu Yin and Master Hu?"

"They are performers at Heavenly Bridge."

Tang San looked stunned. "You mean beggars?"

"They are experts in the martial arts. They entertain people. They don't beg!"

"Why do you see them? How did you become their friend?"

"I learn martial arts from them." She took another deep breath, a sign of impatience. "Tang San, I am not going to answer any more questions. If you don't like what I am doing, just tell me and I will move out of your house."

Tang San smiled. He leaned back on the sofa and crossed his legs. "Listen —you don't have to take such drastic action. I am only concerned, that's all. I have your welfare at heart. I just wish you would stay home more often.

There are many worthy things you could do. Why waste your time meeting swindlers and medicine peddlers at Heavenly Bridge? Are you seriously interested in martial arts? I can introduce you to a real master . . ."

"Tang San, I have already engaged a teacher. I have a headache, please."

"How often do you see Bo Ho?" he interrupted.

Brigid rose to her feet, her face flushed. "Tang San, I said I am not going to answer any more questions. Will you please excuse me?"

Tang San stared at her for a moment, trying to make up his mind about what to do with her. Finally he smiled again. "All right, I won't ask any more questions. I mean well, Brigid. Please don't misunderstand me. Just think about what I've told you."

As he left, he did not click his heels. At the door he turned and in a cold, ominous voice he added, "I can see that you have accepted some roses from someone this morning. Or did you bring them back last night?"

After he was gone, she quickly picked up the cloisonné vase of roses. Attached to it was a small card that she had neglected to read. The message on the card was written with a brush in fine, masculine strokes: *Thank you for a wonderful day. Please ask your Third Uncle to select that lucky date from his almanac. Out of town today. See you tomorrow. Bo Ho.*

She held the roses close to her bosom and read the message several times. The roses had suddenly and miraculously cured her headache. She kissed them as she waltzed into her bedroom.

*

After breakfast Brigid called Old Liu, who shuffled into the living room, smoking a bamboo pipe. He still wore the cross she had given him; it dangled against his blue cotton coolie blouse. He had by now become accustomed to Brigid's peculiar Western habits and superstitions, and was no longer afraid of the funereal white of her apartment. Since no ill effects had befallen her, he concluded that her foreign ways might not be all that bad.

"Old Liu, go hire a carriage," she ordered, tucking her hair into a knot. "We are going to Heavenly Bridge."

"Again?"

"Yes. Master Hu is teaching me double swords and monkey fist three times a week, remember?"

Old Liu had a good memory, but he always managed to forget things that he did not like or approve of; going to Heavenly Bridge was one of them. But, since he could not possibly talk the Young Mistress out of doing anything, he had long since stopped protesting.

Heavenly Bridge was unusually busy that morning, for General Tuan and General Feng were recruiting soldiers. Hundreds of people, even elderly men, children and beggars, were trying to sign up at several long tables manned by officers wearing red armbands. Banners were flying on long bamboo poles nearby, advertising enlistment.

Closely followed by Old Liu, Brigid shouldered her way into the crowd and finally reached the spot where Master Hu and Hu Yin were unpacking the tools of their trade. Hu Yin had just spread a worn blanket on the ground; Master Hu was taking their various weapons out of a bundle. When he saw Brigid, he straightened up with a smile and waved. Hu Yin's face brightened. He bowed and returned to his chores, a shy smile on his square muscular face.

"Have you eaten, Fong Yun?" Master Hu asked.

"Yes, I have," Brigid answered. "Have you?"

"Yes," Master Hu replied politely.

The exchange was the common greeting at Heavenly Bridge, and Brigid had a hard time getting used to it. She still thought it was silly, as though eating were the only thing on people's minds. "I have come for my new lessons, Master Hu," she said.

"Good," Master Hu said. "Today Hu Yin will teach you eighteen ways of kicking, another fighting skill that is popular in both the south and the north."

For the next ten minutes, Hu Yin demonstrated shadow-boxing, blocking and attacking. The moves were fast and strong, creating a wind as his fists and feet flew.

When he started teaching Brigid, she was ready and eager. With her ballet and gymnastic training, she learned fast, memorizing the moves and copying the style. It was almost like an energetic dance, executed with power and grace. By the time she finished the first lesson, a large crowd had gathered to watch them.

Master Hu struck the opening gong and made the show's customary introduction, including some humble remarks about Hu Yin and himself. "Hu Yin," he shouted, "prepare yourself for attack!"

With a battle cry, Hu Yin, stripped to the waist, leaped into the middle of the ring, his eyes bright and sharp, his lean muscles rippling, his mouth tightly closed, his hands extended and legs apart in a fighting stance.

Master Hu, wearing a kung fu blouse with eighteen cloth buttons and a wide red sash tied around his waist, started prancing around, shadow-boxing. Suddenly, with a cry, he attacked. In a flurry of blows and kicks the two engaged in a beautifully choreographed barehanded battle, dodging, feinting, blocking, kicking and leaping, punctuated by ear-rending shouts. The audience watched them tensely, their eyes following the fast action.

When it was over, both took a deep bow. Hu Yin picked up their bamboo plate and placed it in the middle of the ring. Brigid nudged Old Liu, who brought out a handful of brass coins and tossed them onto the plate. A few others in the audience followed suit. Master Hu bowed and thanked the kind ladies and generous gentlemen, then introduced their next program—Hu Yin's knife-throwing act.

Brigid had watched the act a few times before. She hated it. Every time the knife flew out of Hu Yin's hand, her heart leaped. She knew that the knives would land on the wooden board, barely missing Master Hu's body, but each time it happened, she jumped. Often she had to close her eyes and look away until the audience started to applaud.

When she had braced herself for the act, she heard a disturbance behind the crowd. Four men pushed themselves into the ring, cursing the audience for not making way fast enough. "There she is, there she is!" one of them shouted, pointing at Brigid.

He looked familiar, a large man wearing a turban, his face the color of liver, a scar running through one of his thick eyebrows. Suddenly she remembered. He was Kitchen God Tao's hatchetman, One Stroke Cha. He stood almost a head taller than the others. He wore a blue cotton gown with a fur collar, and there was a bulge under the gown on his right-hand side. The other three men, dressed in blue cotton blouses and trousers, had short weapons tucked in their waistbands. One of them had a hatchet handle showing, the other two, purposely or otherwise, exposed the sharp points of the daggers half concealed under their blouses.

Master Hu bowed politely to One Stroke Cha. "She is our guest. Do you wish to speak to her?"

"We want to take her away," One Stroke said gruffly. He turned to Brigid and bowed. "Young Mistress, Lord Tao has invited you. He wants you to provide some foreign devils' entertainment at his luncheon party."

Brigid stared at him, trying to suppress her rising anger. She had never heard of such a rude invitation before. But then she realized that it was a gangster's way of doing things. She was sure Tang San was behind it; otherwise how would Lord Tao know she was at Heavenly Bridge? She might as well play the gangster's game, she thought. Stepping forward, she bowed and told Cha to tell Lord Tao that she could not attend his luncheon party because of a previous engagement.

One Stroke Cha looked surprised. Nobody had ever turned down Lord Tao's invitation before. For Lord Tao, a corpse would rise from the grave if it were invited. "You refuse to go to Lord Tao's party?" he said incredulously.

"Yes, I refuse to go," Brigid told him with an icy smile. "Please thank him for inviting me."

The hatchetman took a long breath. For a moment he did not know what to do with this beautiful, defiant woman. She was no ordinary peasant or coolie girl, but Tang San's sister, so rough handling was out of the question. He took a step forward and bowed again.

"Young Mistress, please have mercy on me. If I don't bring you to Lord Tao's house, I will lose face, I will lose pay, I might even be out of a job." He jerked his head. The other three men came closer, ready to follow orders. They stood with their arms akimbo and legs apart, looking ominous.

"Take her!" One Stroke Cha ordered.

As the men were closing in on Brigid, Hu Yin, screaming a battle cry, delivered a vicious kick at the nearest one, sending him tumbling backward. The other two gangsters immediately turned their weapons on him. Wielding a four-section flying stick, Hu Yin became a fighting machine, wild and yet methodical, blocking and hitting. The four short sections of hardwood became a blur, flying and hissing in the air, then landing with bone-crushing force. In a few seconds the three men were bloodied and were making a last-ditch fight.

One Stroke Cha abandoned protocol. He grabbed Brigid by the arm and tried to force her to go with him. While she struggled, Old Liu started beating him over the head with his oilpaper umbrella. Master Hu also joined the fray, grabbing One Stroke and choking him. One Stroke turned purple, blood vessels standing out on his face and neck like mountain ridges. He cursed while Brigid kicked him and Old Liu whacked his bald head ineffectually with his old umbrella. But One Stroke Cha was so strong that he finally broke free and turned all his fury on Master Hu. The two battled each other with their bare hands until Hu Yin came to Master Hu's aid, sending out the end section of his weapon like a missile. It struck One Stroke's head with a sickening thud. One Stroke staggered backward; his eyes turned white and his face distorted in shock. As he fell, Master Hu leaped forward and followed that fall with his sword, pointing it at his throat. Lying on his back, One Stroke stared at the sword, blinking in pain, a trickle of blood creeping down his cheek.

"If you come to bother this young lady again," Master Hu said, "I will chop your head off." He delivered the line dramatically, like an actor in an opera, and the audience loved it. To the sound of cheers and applause,

One Stroke Cha climbed to his feet and fled, hastily followed by his fellow thugs.

Master Hu announced that there would be no more shows that day, but the audience had enjoyed a real tussle and seemed to be satisfied. Some people even tossed brass coins, paper money, fruit and nuts into the ring. One man laid half a dozen eggs at Brigid's feet in appreciation: after all, she was the cause of the entertaining battle.

After packing their gear, Master Hu said to Brigid, "Tonight, I'm going to cook a Shantung dinner. My humble home is shabby and dirty, but it will be better than inviting you to an open-air restaurant and eating the same old heart-and-lung noodles. Besides, Hu Yin may want to show off his arts and crafts. Hu Yin, do you agree or not?"

Hu Yin nodded eagerly. He turned to look at Brigid as if to see how she would react. He kept looking, his eyes almost pleading. When she smiled her acceptance, he broke into a happy smile and hurried to pick up his gear.

*

Master Hu lived in a little nameless alley off Chien Men Street, not too far from Heavenly Bridge. Through years of hard luck and economic depression, the area had been reduced to a slum. Brigid had never seen or imagined a place so poor and depressing. The road was full of mudholes and strewn with filth. "Shade your eyes and close your mouth when the wind blows," Master Hu said apologetically. "Sometimes it churns up dirt. I have heard stories about dead centipedes and crickets blowing into people's mouths. I like crickets roasted, but not raw." He laughed.

Toward the end of the lane Hu Yin hastened his steps and, stopping at a small dilapidated gate, pushed at the double doors, which opened with a loud squeal. It was a small building with a broken tile roof. The white paint on the walls was peeling and the red paper lucky sayings of BLESSINGS and LONGEVITY posted on doors were torn and faded with age.

But inside the gate the narrow courtyard was neat and clean, with pots of chrysanthemums and azaleas artistically arranged in clusters. In the middle was an old date tree covered with lush leaves. Three clotheslines were tied to it from the three houses in the yard.

Hu Yin opened the door of the smallest house in the yard and bowed. Old Master Hu stood aside and gestured for his guests to go in. "A dirty place," he said, smiling, "but it is home."

The small front room was cluttered but very clean. In the center was an unpainted table surrounded by four benches. Along the walls piles of firewood were stacked knee high. A picture of the famous warrior Kwang Kung was scowling at the world. The rest of the walls were covered with modern calendars of legendary beauties and lucky sayings written on strips of red paper. In the back was an altar with an incense bowl and two candleholders. Behind them was a wooden tablet bearing the words SEAT OF HEAVEN, EARTH, COUNTRY, ANCESTORS AND TEACHERS. Beside the altar was an unpainted shelf on which wood and soapstone carvings of animals were neatly displayed—cats, dogs, water buffalos, goats, eagles and tigers —all lifelike and carved in great detail.

"All are Hu Yin's creations," Master Hu said, indicating the shelf. "The boy is rough with a weapon; who would guess that he also has such fine hands?"

Looking a little embarrassed, Hu Yin pulled the benches out and asked everybody to sit down. Master Hu lit a few sticks of incense at the altar while Hu Yin brought out plates of watermelon seeds and dried dates and laid them on the table. Brigid inspected the carvings. She especially admired a little dog. When she handled it fondly, Hu Yin looked delighted, casting secret glances at her.

Master Hu made some Shantung chiao tsu, a kind of northern Chinese ravioli Brigid always enjoyed. He also stir-fried some minced ham with cabbage, steamed some eggs and sprinkled them with sesame oil and green onions. He and Hu Yin had grown the vegetables in a plot in a corner of the yard.

Brigid had never observed the lives of the poor, and their simple lifestyle intrigued her. "You have not told us much about yourself, Master Hu," she said. "Where are you from? What did you do before?"

"It is a long story," he said with a sigh. "A famine in Shantung killed my family. I was drafted by a warlord, but I don't like civil wars, so I escaped. You might say I was a refugee from famine and war. I told myself, 'Don't worry; with a carrying pole I can manage. People can hire me to carry things or I can defend myself against dogs when I beg.' But Heaven has eyes; it sent me this young fellow. He is not only a good student, but does all the chores—cleaning, washing and taking care of me. And carving all these beautiful things! It is a blessing!"

Hu Yin smiled. "I am the one who is blessed, Master."

"All right, we are both blessed. First I thought of opening a kung fu studio, but who had money to study kung fu? So I started the little show at Heavenly Bridge to collect a few coins."

When they finished dinner, Hu Yin served tea, a smoke-flavored black tea which he poured into tiny cups, scalding hot. For a while there was no other noise but tea-sipping. Then Hu Yin got up. In a few minutes he came back with a basket and a handful of coins. He laid them on the table. "We have collected a hundred and twenty brass coins. Here is your share of sixty. In the basket are fruit and nuts, and six eggs . . ."

"No, no!" Brigid said hastily. "We can't accept all these. No!" Her voice was so firm that Master Hu did not insist.

Hu Yin hurried to the shelf and brought back the carved dog that Brigid had admired. "For you," he said.

"Let me buy it," Brigid said.

"Young lady, if you don't accept his gift," Master Hu protested, "you will break his heart."

She turned to Hu Yin, who was looking at her with pleading eyes. "All right," she said. "I shall always treasure it, Hu Yin."

He broke into a smile. Master Hu looked between them and nodded with a chuckle. "We have good luck with the show. Why don't you join us on a permanent basis? You and Hu Yin will make a fine team, a combination of muscle and beauty."

Brigid was touched. She did not know how to decline, but perhaps honesty was the best policy. She said, "Thank you for your invitation, Master Hu. But there is a man who . . ." She stopped, regretting that she may have spoken too soon.

"Ah, I understand," Master Hu said, casting a quick glance at Hu Yin. "When is the lucky date?"

"We have not selected a date yet."

"Don't forget to invite us to the ceremony," he urged, trying to sound cheerful; but she could detect the sadness in his voice.

She glanced at Hu Yin, who looked away. His face was expressionless, but she could sense his disappointment. She rose quickly. "Well, it is time for us to go. Thank you so much for the dinner."

Master Hu rose with a sigh. "I always believe in fate. I hope we shall meet again."

"What do you mean? Am I dismissed as your student?"

Master Hu laughed. "We will see you the day after tomorrow." He walked his guests to the front gate.

Hu Yin rushed out with a lighted lantern. "It is dark; you need this." He pressed the lantern into Old Liu's hand and they waved goodbye.

As Brigid returned their wave, she held the carved dog close to her breast. Her goodbye did not sound as cheerful as it should have; she had never felt so much warmth as in that little house.

*

Walking across the courtyard to Tang San's, she heard him greet her. His footsteps were heavy; he had by now even adopted a foreigner's gait, his boots striking the ground heavily as if on military drill. Without turning, she stopped and waited.

"You missed dinner," he said behind her.

"I have had some chiao tsu," she said stiffly, wondering if he knew that his gangster friends had been soundly beaten at Heavenly Bridge. She hoped it would be a lesson for the Kitchen God not to push people around again.

Tang San put his hands on her shoulders, standing so close to her that she could smell his tobacco breath. "Come, Brigid," he said sweetly. "Let's talk in my living room."

"What about?"

"Your future, the plans I've made for you, and the things I . . ."

"Tang San," she interrupted, "I am tired tonight. Can we talk tomorrow?"

"Tired? Why are you so tired?"

"I've had an exhausting day."

"An exhausting day? What exactly did you do that exhausted you?"

Brigid decided to confront him with the Heavenly Bridge incident. "You ought to know, Tang San. You would have had me kidnapped if my friends hadn't protected me."

There was a moment of silence. Suddenly Tang San laughed uproariously. "What are you talking about? Did you say you were almost kidnapped? How absurd. Where?"

She turned to face him, her voice low and angry. "Please tell me why you did it. You could have killed or maimed people, using those brutes to do your errands. From now on, if you have something on your mind, just say it instead of using gangsters to enforce your will."

Tang San threw his head back and laughed again. Brigid had no idea if he was amused or angry and decided that the forced hilarity was only an expression of contempt. Without another word, she ran to her quarters, went to her bedroom and threw herself onto the bed. She expected Tang San to rap on her door and demand to come in, but there was no sound except the singing of crickets outside her window. Tang San did not knock that night.

30

T hird Uncle made a pot of aster tea and served it in large bowls instead of the customary tiny cups. He believed that aster tea was good for the eyes, and said that even at his age he never needed eyeglasses, which he used only as decoration on important occasions.

"I don't know about coffee," he said to Brigid. "If you switch to aster tea, in two years you will be able to count ants' legs ten feet away."

"I want a tea that will help me tell my fortune ten years from now," Brigid said, sipping the bittersweet brew and wincing at its taste.

She was visiting Third Uncle that morning in his modest apartment in the Western City of Peking. He had come down in the world with the slow decline in family fortune, but he was still as undisturbed as ever. Brigid shifted in the hardwood straight-backed chair, remembering what Third Uncle had said about Western sofas: "Like sitting in a fat woman's lap." Third Uncle was modern in many ways, but not in his taste in furniture. Nevertheless she enjoyed visiting him, and valued his opinions and wisdom. She thought it was unfair that a man like Tang San was so prosperous and a man like Third Uncle was so poor, barely making a living by carving people's names on their seals and by writing lucky sayings on strips of red paper.

"Do you have something on your mind this morning?" Third Uncle asked, refilling her bowl with tea.

"I have a confession to make. I borrowed your name and told a lie. But it brought me good results."

"If my name is that useful, borrow it anytime. Tell me about it."

"I told a man that you could find a lucky date for people to get married, regardless of their difference in age. Now he wants you to find the lucky date for him. Do you have an almanac?"

"I do!" Third Uncle said. He rose from the table and went to his bookshelves to search for it. The small room was full of bookshelves. He fished out a dog-eared book with a faded red cover and brought it to the table. He opened the book at random. "Here, the twenty-fifth day of the second moon is lucky for taking a bath. The third day of the third moon is suitable for a haircut. Let me find a lucky day for a wedding."

Suddenly he shut the book, laid it on the table and stared at Brigid. "You haven't told me who he is. The date is not important. The man is."

"Bo Ho, the actor. Do you approve of him?"

Third Uncle took a deep breath and folded his arms. Brigid looked at him, wondering what kind of reaction this was. He had been enthused about it; why had he become so withdrawn all of a sudden?

"What is it, Third Uncle?" she asked, a bit fearfully.

"If your ancestors were alive, they would jump into the Yellow River if you told them you were marrying an actor. However, never mind about the dead ancestors—let them turn in their graves. But I approve of it. What date do you want me to give you?"

Brigid heaved a sigh of relief. "It is your job, Third Uncle. Find a lucky date in the almanac."

"There is no such thing as a lucky day for this or that. Five years ago I did everything on lucky days; look at me now." He glanced around and laughed. "Do you still believe in lucky days? Find a day that is comfortable and convenient. I'll sign my name to it."

"I want to get away from Tang San, so the earlier the better."

"You mustn't look too anxious. How about two weeks after the fifteenth of the third moon, in the Year of the Dragon—a good year, so nobody will criticize me for selecting it. It's soon enough so he has no time to change his mind, yet it's far enough away to make him anxious." He stopped with a frown.

"What is it, Uncle?" Brigid inquired, staring up at him, afraid that something was wrong.

"You have no dowry," he said, his voice grave and sad.

"Is that important?"

"It depends on how old-fashioned Bo Ho's family is. Too bad your father's properties have all been confiscated for nonpayment of taxes. Will Tang San . . ." He shook his head. "No, no, it would be like asking a wolf to give away not only his chicken but a supply of chickenfeed as well. I know how he feels about you."

"I don't think Bo Ho really cares. If he thinks a dowry is more important than me, I would rather jump into the Yellow River." She laughed. "Will you give me away, Third Uncle?"

"Certainly. I may have to do that over Tang San's dead body, but I will." He refilled her bowl.

"I have another request. If you have a bottle somewhere, I want you to say, 'This calls for a drink!' "

Third Uncle was taken aback. Modern women were so forward, it was shocking. But times had changed. Bursting into laughter, he said, "I happen to have a bottle of mao tai under the bed."

*

Brigid woke up in Bo Ho's bed without knowing what time it was. Bo Ho had stepped out of the room. She turned and moved closer toward his side. She could smell the scent of his body on the sheet and a faint jasmine perfume on his pillow. She thought about her approaching married life. How peaceful it would be—peaceful because marred by no jealousy or suspicion, yet often exciting because there would always be something interesting to do together.

Bo Ho returned to the room. He was dressed and had ordered lunch from nearby. "Let's eat in bed," he said, placing a low table in front of her, "just as the foreigners do on their honeymoons."

"How do you know so much about foreigners?" Brigid asked.

"I entertained a lot of foreign ladies when the Empress Dowager was alive. I learned all about their habits and customs. Some of them even told me about their secret lives."

"Bo Ho," Brigid said, "you don't mind people finding out that we sleep together, even in the morning, do you?"

"What do I care? I am an actor. An actor's reputation is ruined before he is born. You are the one who should worry."

"I am an orphan. Let my dead ancestors turn in their graves."

Both laughed. There was a knock on the front door. "It's the servant with our lunch," he said, hurrying out of the bedroom. A few moments later he returned with a tray laden with steaming rice and four dishes, two meat and two vegetables. He served them on the low table and climbed back into the enormous bed to share the food.

Brigid found herself ravenous, and the red-cooked pork and stir-fried oyster beef tasted better than any restaurant food.

"You know," she said, "a moment ago I imagined we were terribly poor, sharing a bowl of soup with nothing in it except some old cabbage and a few chunks of pork skin floating on top. You know what? I was happy. Would you be?"

"Heavens, no!"

"What?" Brigid said, disappointed.

"If I could only afford pork-skin soup, would I be happy? I would sell myself to buy you a better meal."

She pinched him fondly with a chuckle. "You always have the right answer, don't you? By the way, you made a request a week ago. It is granted."

Bo Ho raised an eyebrow, looking puzzled. "Request?"

"Yes, you wanted my Third Uncle to find a lucky date. He did. The fifteenth day of the third moon in the Year of the Dragon. And I won't let you wriggle through my fingers. So don't plan to escape."

Bo Ho planted a kiss on her lips and pulled out a jade fish on a gold chain. He put the chain around her neck. "I hope this will tie a hundred knots. Fish is a symbol of prosperity, so you will never eat pork-skin soup. I promise!"

Brigid pressed the fish close to her heart. "How about your family, Bo Ho? Will they approve of me?"

"I am an orphan like you. My distant uncles and cousins never mention our relationship to anybody."

"Why?"

"Because I am an actor."

"Even if you are famous?"

"Worse! The more famous I become, the more vigorously they deny their relationship to me. Especially in Hunan. I admire your courage, Brigid; for that I am grateful!"

Brigid looked at him tenderly. "Is that why you are not married?"

Bo Ho nodded. "Yes. I don't want to marry just anybody. She must be *somebody.* But *somebody* will never dream of marrying an actor. So there you are. A middle-aged bachelor."

Squeezing his hand affectionately, she whispered, "I love you, Bo Ho. I'll always love you, regardless of what I am or how old you are."

After they finished their lunch, Brigid suddenly remembered her kung fu lesson. "What time is it?" she asked.

Bo Ho glanced at his watch. "Two-thirty," he said. "We can spend the whole afternoon making love."

"Oh no!" she said, jumping out of the bed and throwing her clothes on. "I am late for an appointment. I have a date with Master Hu at Heavenly Bridge."

"Master Hu? Heavenly Bridge?" Bo Ho raised an eyebrow. He was puzzled but not surprised.

"I want to be an actress. I have a lot of secrets, don't I? Well, I'll tell you all about it later." And like a whirlwind, she was gone.

✳

On her way to Heavenly Bridge in a hired carriage, Brigid decided that this was the best day of her life. She hummed and whistled, something she had not done since her high school days in Paris. She was lost in a cloud of happiness.

The carriage stopped. The noise and smell of Heavenly Bridge gave her a jolt. Coming out of her trance, she quickly stepped out of the shabby carriage, paid the driver and plunged into the crowd.

As Brigid walked past several familiar sights, she tried to remember where Master Hu and Hu Yin gave their daily performance. She had always followed Old Liu and had never paid any attention to where they were going. She moved along with the crowd until some people started rushing in a different direction from hers, chattering and gesturing. Others turned to follow them. She allowed them to carry her along, enjoying the sensation, as if she were riding in a human sea. Then she realized that she was being carried in the right direction—they were going toward the spot where Master Hu performed. A crowd had gathered, all talking excitedly, craning their necks to get a better view of what was happening.

She pushed harder, her heart pounding. As she neared the center of the crowd, she had a glimpse of Hu Yin. He was bending over Master Hu, calling, "Master! Master!" in an anguished voice.

A man shouted, "Call a doctor! Hurry, Hurry!"

A few other men were trying to make Master Hu comfortable. One was covering him with a blanket and another was cushioning his head with a roll of clothing.

Brigid pushed and yelled, "Let me in! Let me in!" With a desperate shove, she broke through the crowd. Master Hu was lying in a pool of blood, his face ghastly pale, his eyes almost dead. He was groaning, "Don't worry, I'll be all right. Hu Yin, it is not your fault . . ."

Suddenly Brigid saw the knife. It was embedded in Master Hu's chest almost to the hilt.

Brigid knew what had happened. She had hated that knife-throwing act and had always dreaded it. Now it had happened. She threw herself beside Master Hu and called to him. He did not respond. She choked, buried her face in his shoulder and sobbed.

"It is not Hu Yin's fault!" a man shouted. "Somebody else did it."

She looked up. There were many sympathetic and sad faces around her. She did not know who had spoken. She turned to Hu Yin. "What happened? Tell me what happened."

Hu Yin looked like a man who had lost his mind, his chest heaving, his eyes unblinking, a distraught look on his rigid face.

"Will anybody tell me what happened?" Brigid pleaded.

"It was One Stroke Cha," an angry old man said in a cracked voice. "Everybody saw it. He hit Hu Yin's hand with a stone from a slingshot, and Hu Yin's knife went wild. Ask anybody!" He turned to another man. "Did you not see it?"

The man, looking frightened, turned and disappeared. The old man pointed at some others.

"You saw it, did you not? You! You saw it! And you! And you!"

No one wanted to admit anything. One by one they sneaked away to avoid being questioned. The old man shouted after them, "Cowards! Frightened turtles' eggs!"

A doctor arrived—a middle-aged man wearing a blue silk gown and carrying a little cloth bundle under his arm. He laid it down, squatted beside Master Hu and felt his pulse. Shaking his head, he closed Master Hu's eyes and rose to his feet.

"He has entered the other world. Take him home now. Let a Taoist priest console his spirit with some incense sticks and a few prayers."

31

B rigid was awakened by a pounding on the door. She looked at her bedside clock. It was almost 11:00 A.M. She had slept soundly. It was unusual, for most nights lately her sleep had been restless with disturbing dreams. Sometimes she had even been jolted awake by nightmares.

"Who is it?" she called.

"Brigid, I have something to tell you." It was Tang San's voice. He had already come into her living room. Afraid that he might burst into her bedroom, she quickly threw on her clothes.

"I'll be right out," she called through the door.

When she came out, she found Tang San sitting on a sofa, his legs crossed, one of them shaking nervously. He picked up a piece of paper from the coffee table and shook it at her. "Lord Tao just sent this. Read it!"

Brigid took a look at the message in Chinese characters and returned it to him. "You know I don't read free-style Chinese."

"Lord Tao's message says there was a massacre last night. Lord Tao's lieutenant, One Stroke Cha, was murdered along with two of his followers. There was one survivor. He identified the killer. It was your beggar friend,

Hu Yin. One Stroke Cha was decapitated." He glared at her, waiting for her to respond.

She was stunned; her heart started pounding. She had had a premonition that Hu Yin would do something drastic—the glare, the flaring nostrils, the constant working of his jaws. "What does Lord Tao want?" she asked fearfully.

"He wants to capture the murderer, naturally. And since the crime was committed by your friend, you may know where he is."

"Tang San, he did not tell me what he would do or where he would go. How would I know?"

"You went to his father's funeral last week, did you not?"

"Yes, I did."

Tang San took a deep breath. "Listen," he said despairingly, "you had better help. The Kitchen God is angry."

"How can I help? What can I do?"

Tang San tapped the palm of his hand with the piece of paper. "This is the Kitchen God's request. He wants me to question you and find out all you know about that murderer. That's what you can do—tell me the truth."

"Tang San, I'm just as anxious as you are to find out what happened."

"Just tell me what you know," he said irritably.

"All I know about him is that he loved his master. He is a good artist who carves animals out of wood and soapstone. He is kind and shy; he is nonviolent. He would never hurt anybody. That's all I know."

Tang San rose to his feet and pocketed the piece of paper. "Brigid," he said, his voice softening, "I hope you are telling the truth. This is what I'm going to tell the Kitchen God. As long as you wash your hands of Heavenly Bridge beggars and medicine peddlers, you will be all right; otherwise you will not only bring trouble to me, you are also going to endanger your own life. Why be foolish? Why lower yourself by mingling with these people? Sometimes I just don't understand you, Brigid."

He looked sad and concerned, his voice earnest. Brigid wondered if he was genuinely worried or simply pretending. "All right, Tang San," she said with a smile. "I'll be careful—don't worry."

Tang San tried to kiss her, but she flinched. "Thank you, Brigid," he said, swallowing. He looked at her longingly for a moment, then turned abruptly and walked out.

Brigid was worried about Hu Yin. She wanted to find out exactly what had happened and if he had safely escaped. Without telling Old Liu, she hurried out and hired the first carriage she saw on Chang An Boulevard.

The thought of the massacre began to disturb her. Violence appalled her, and Hu Yin's brutal revenge disappointed her. It was an act of a madman. She couldn't believe that Hu Yin, quiet and gentle—even timid —could be so violent. Had he gone insane? It could also be a false accusation. The survivor could have been wrong. A man like One Stroke Cha must have had many enemies. He could have been murdered by anyone who had hated him enough to decapitate him.

Arriving at Hu Yin's house, she was not surprised to see soldiers guarding the front door. They were braves from the city's security bureau. They wore gray uniforms with the character *brave* sewn on the chest and back and carried swords and pistols. A few had rifles strapped on their shoulders. One of them, apparently an officer, stopped her and demanded to know what she was doing there.

"I have come to visit a friend," she said haltingly. A group of braves was inside the gate. They were talking loudly, and the landlady, Mrs. Shun, was pleading. Brigid tried to go in, but the officer grabbed her roughly. "Don't move!"

Presently, Mrs. Shun, her hands tied behind her back, was pushed out of the gate, followed by three other neighbors—a middle-aged couple and their fifteen-year-old daughter, who was sobbing. The braves pointed their bayonets at them and ordered them to hurry.

"You, too," the officer said to Brigid. "Follow them!"

"Why me?"

"Just follow!" he said, shoving her toward the others.

"Where are you taking us?"

"The magistrate's yamen."

"What have we done?"

"The magistrate will find out. Hurry up!"

Brigid protested. One of the braves threatened her with his bayonet. Suppressing her anger, she followed them. "What luck," she thought with a sardonic smile. She should have taken a bath this morning and played a hand of solitaire at home instead of walking into this trap.

Mrs. Shun started to cry, swearing that she had done nothing wrong and calling for Heaven's help. The security braves ignored her, and escorted the prisoners as though they were marching them to the execution grounds. Brigid shuddered. It was entirely possible that they would be executed after a trial at the magistrate's yamen.

The magistrate's yamen was in the Imperial City, not too far from the

Forbidden City. It was an immense palace built by one of the royal families and sold to the government. The building, complete with the usual vermilion gate guarded by two lion-dogs, red-laquered pillars, carved eaves, green tiles and red-painted walls, was aged and in bad repair.

The braves brought them into the main building in the courtyard and made them wait in the chilly hall. Brigid vaguely remembered similar buildings she had seen in storybooks, where a just, scowling judge tried incorrigible criminals. His Honor would sit behind a large table, a straw cushion placed below it and a court guard standing at attention, holding a bamboo stick. He was the bottom-beater. The prisoner would kowtow to the judge and answer questions while His Honor blew his whiskers and angrily accused the prisoner of lying. As Brigid looked at the ominous table, she had a terrible sinking feeling.

Presently, a court clerk, a middle-aged man wearing a loose silk gown, entered from a side door and glanced at the prisoners. The landlady sank to her knees and kowtowed to him, pleading her innocence. The clerk told the officer, "Keep her here. Take the others to the waiting room."

The waiting room contained a black-laquered table with a few chairs beside it. It was just as gloomy, with a high window and another door in the back. There were cobwebs hanging from the four corners. The walls were blackened with age. Brigid and the other prisoners were ordered to stand in the back. Were they witnesses? Brigid wondered.

"What are you going to do to us, officer?" she asked, trying not to show her fear.

"Quiet!" he ordered, dusting off one of the chairs. The clerk wandered in. The officer pulled out the chair for him and the clerk sat down, eyeing the prisoners one by one. A brave came in with a cup of tea and served the clerk with a bow. The clerk kept looking at the prisoners, sipping tea noisily through the covered cup.

The young girl was still sobbing. Her mother tried to comfort her by putting her arms around her. The father kept shaking his head, quietly lamenting his bad luck.

The clerk put the teacup on the table and cleared his throat. "You," he said, pointing at the father. "Tell me your name!"

"My name is . . ."

"Kneel!" the officer shouted.

The man, still shaking his head, knelt down with a sigh. "My name is Tung Wei, nickname Water Bucket."

"Do you live in the same building as the accused?"

"Yes, Your Excellency. We are neighbors."

"What do you do for a living?"

"I am a carpenter, Your Excellency. My specialty is making water buckets."

"Do you know the accused?"

"Not very well, Your Excellency. We hardly spoke to each other."

"Did you help him in any way when he committed the crime?"

"No, no, Your Excellency," the carpenter said, his voice rising. His face twisting in anguish, he started knocking his head on the ground, pleading his innocence and denying any connection with the accused.

The clerk questioned the others. He repeated the questions, and they all denied any knowledge of the crime.

Brigid answered the questions without kneeling. To her surprise the officer did not force her to kowtow. She wondered why the landlady had been tied like a criminal while she and the others were not. Where was the woman? Why were they separated from her? Was Mrs. Shun involved in the massacre?

Another clerk came in. He was older and wore a faded silk gown with longer sleeves. He was clicking two walnuts in his left hand. Brigid wondered if he was a grade higher in rank than the first, since his sleeves were longer and the red button on top of his cap was bigger. Peering over his steel-rimmed glasses, he asked the first clerk if he had extracted any confessions from the prisoners.

"Not yet," the first clerk said.

Without a word, the second one took a seat and a brave came in with a cup of tea and served him. Sipping tea and taking his time, the second clerk made himself comfortable in his chair and coughed a few times to show his authority. Brigid wanted to knock the tea out of his hand and shout at him to hurry up and get it over with, whatever they wanted to do with her.

Suddenly a woman's voice could be heard screaming in the main hall. Brigid knew it was Mrs. Shun. The young girl, terrified, caught her breath and started to whine. Her mother hugged her protectively, whispering soothing words into her ear.

The woman's screams subsided. The senior clerk spoke, his voice calm, almost kind. "His Honor the judge is trying the landlady. She is stubborn and refuses to tell the truth. You can spare yourself pain if you tell the truth now."

The carpenter knocked his head on the ground again and pleaded, "Your Excellency, my family and I have nothing to do with the crime. Let Heaven above be the witness! Lord Heaven has eyes. We are only neighbors. We pay our rent and taxes; we mind our own business."

The landlady started screaming again, this time louder. Then she stopped abruptly. Obviously she had fainted. The carpenter kept kowtowing and pleading, "Spare us, spare us, Your Excellency! We are innocent! We have nothing to confess."

"You will confess when needles are inserted under your fingernails," the senior clerk said quietly. "But if you confess now you will spare yourself the torture." His voice was still kind but firm, his face serene, even a bit fatherly.

Brigid cringed each time Mrs. Shun started screaming. Obviously, they revived her repeatedly and then tortured her until she fainted again. Brigid found her anger rising. It finally overpowered her fear. She felt a tingling sensation on her skin, as though she were suddenly possessed by the devil.

She shook a finger at the senior clerk and yelled, "You animals! You barbarians! I hate you! Shoot me! Kill me!"

As Brigid leaped forward to scratch the man, the officer grabbed her by the hair. She shouted and struggled, her legs kicking and arms flailing. Two more braves rushed in and pinned her down. One of them hit her with the butt of his pistol and she blacked out.

When she woke up, she was lying on a bunk in a cell. Her face and clothes were wet. A brave dashed another bowl of water onto her face. She shook her head clear and vaguely realized what had happened. When she sat up, she found Tang San standing in front of her, scowling.

"Hello, Brigid," he said, his voice icy cold. "I have come to take you home."

Her head aching, Brigid struggled to her feet and followed him out of the dungeon, saying nothing. Tang San did not help her. He climbed into his automobile without waiting for her, abandoning his Western manners. Brigid got in and sat beside him, hugging herself for warmth. She was so depressed that she did not even bother to wipe her dripping face and hair.

They rode home through unfamiliar streets. Tang San was quiet until the car reached Chang An Boulevard, then he broke the silence. "I am disappointed with you, Brigid."

Brigid had nothing to say. The headache was worse. She closed her eyes, trying to remember what had happened. When the car stopped in front of their house, Old Liu hobbled over to help her out. Tang San went inside without another word.

Back in her apartment, she changed into dry clothes, sank onto the nearest sofa in the living room and ordered a bowl of hot ginger soup.

After the servant had gone, she sipped the soup slowly, trying to pull herself together and put her thoughts in order. The experience had devastated her, and she tried not to think about it.

When Tang San knocked, her distraught feeling returned almost immediately. She wished she had gone to Bo Ho's apartment.

Tang San came in, unsmiling. He closed the door and stood there staring at her, arms akimbo, looking like an angry schoolmaster glaring at a naughty student. Brigid decided to be friendly. "Please sit down, Tang San," she said.

"I am very disappointed with you, Brigid. You betrayed me."

"What do you mean I betrayed you? What did I do to betray you?"

"You promised me to wash your hands of those Heavenly Bridge characters. Why did you go to the slums to see him again? Did you worry about him?"

"I went there to find out what really happened. I don't believe Hu Yin did it."

"You don't?" Tang San shook his head incredulously. "There is an eyewitness who survived the massacre. There is his landlady, who confessed her involvement, and there are his neighbors who saw him . . ." He stopped, shook his head and sat down with a sigh.

"Saw him do what?"

"Saw him commit the murder. With all those witnesses, you still don't believe he is guilty?"

"Those people were tortured. Do you call them witnesses? Needles were driven under their fingernails to make them confess! Do you call that confession? I would have confessed, too. I would rather have a quick death than go through that barbaric torture."

"Brigid," he interrupted, "I don't know if you were involved or not, but I have rescued you. It wasn't easy. Without the Kitchen God's interference, you would have been tried like the rest. Anybody involved with the massacre will be beheaded, and his head will hang on Chien Men Gate for three days for everybody to see. You don't know how lucky you are!"

"Master Hu was murdered, too," she said, trying to suppress her anger. "Why didn't those security braves arrest anybody? Why was there no trial?"

"Master Hu was murdered by his own son, Hu Yin. Before they could find him, he committed another crime—a massacre. Now the security forces are looking for him everywhere, and they need our help to bring him to justice. The Kitchen God has posted a thousand taels of silver for his capture, dead or alive. I understand that your lover, Bo Ho, is also involved."

"Why do you say that?" she asked after a pause, feeling the blood draining from her face and hands, her knees weak and her head spinning.

"He financed that funeral, did he not? Who would spend money on a lavish funeral for a total stranger?"

"Bo Ho donated to the funeral because of me! Because I requested it!"

"Oh?" he said, raising an eyebrow. "Who is your lover, anyway? Bo Ho or the murderer? Or did they share you?"

Brigid slapped him so hard that her hand burned afterward. Tang San started to hit back but controlled himself. He felt his reddened cheek with a hand and smiled. "Don't worry, I will not strike you. Not only will I not strike you, I will also protect both you and your lover. But on one condition."

He fished out a piece of paper from his pocket and tossed it on the coffee table. "Copy this message and sign it. I'll have it delivered to your lover immediately."

She glanced between Tang San and the paper, then picked it up and read what was on it. The writing was Tang San's, crude but legible. It said:

> Bo Ho: I have decided that our relationship is a terrible mistake. Since I don't really love you, there is no point in continuing to see each other. From now on, please stop sending me flowers or writing to me. I will soon marry somebody else and it is better that we forget each other completely. Signed, Brigid Fong Yun.

When Brigid finished reading it, she crumpled the paper in both hands. "You bastard! You animal. . . ." Tears welling in her eyes, she looked for something to throw at him. Tang San watched her and kept smiling, enjoying her helpless fury.

"It is up to you, Brigid," he said calmly. "If you copy it, I'll see to it that he gets the message safely. If you refuse, I guarantee that he will be arrested, tried and convicted as a partner in the heinous crime committed against Lord Tao's employees. And in two days you will see Bo Ho's head dangling from Chien Men Gate. It will be displayed for three days as a warning against lawlessness and random killing of innocent citizens."

"Innocent citizens! You call One Strike Cha an innocent citizen?"

"No lectures, please," Tang San said, wagging a warning finger. "You must understand the power of the Kitchen God. If he wants people to die, they die. If he wants somebody to pay for his crime, he pays. There is nothing you or I can do. But I can always try. If I am lucky, I might be able to save Bo Ho's life. I hope it is not too late."

Without a word, Brigid brought out stationery from her desk drawer and copied the message from memory, then scribbled her name under it in bold, angry strokes.

"Take it," she said, tossing the message on the coffee table. She ran into her bedroom, slamming the door.

*

Next morning Brigid woke up from a night of troubled sleep. She made coffee and drank several cups, feeling increasingly depressed and nervous. Perhaps Third Uncle could give her some advice. She threw on some casual clothes and sneaked out.

Third Uncle was making noodles on his tiny stove when she arrived. He took a look at her and scowled. "Are you sick?"

"I didn't sleep well last night. I have some problems, Third Uncle."

"Sit down and have a bowl of hot noodles. But first a cup of aster tea."

He made her sit at the table on the only cushioned chair. Third Uncle joined her at the table. "The moment you came in I knew you had troubles," he said. "Now tell me the details. I may not offer solutions, but at least I can analyze them."

Brigid told him what had happened and how Tang San had forced her to write the note to Bo Ho. The note was the most painful part, torturing her like a knife in a wound. She finished her story in a choking voice, her eyes filled with tears.

Third Uncle listened intently. He asked no questions, nor did he make any comment. He got up and served her a bowl of noodles and urged her to eat. They ate quietly and she felt better after several more cups of tea and another bowl of spicy noodles, cooked with leftover vegetables and red-cooked pork.

When they had finished, Third Uncle said with a smile, "Nothing to worry about. I always say, 'If you keep the hills green, you never have to worry about firewood.' If you are healthy, the hills are green. If you can eat, you are healthy. Now, let's analyze your problems. First, forget about Hu Yin. Obviously the man can take care of himself. Forget about the landlady and the neighbors. You know the old saying, 'Heaven has eyes.' Everything will turn out correctly, because Heaven is not blind. Now, your unhappiness is caused by that note to Bo Ho. If Bo Ho is clever, he should know that you did not mean what you said in the note and that you had been forced to write it. If he is stupid, then leave the result to Heaven; he deserves that note. However, my philosophy is, do your best first, then leave the result to Heaven."

He stopped. Then, lowering his head and swallowing hard as though an unpleasant thought had suddenly struck him, he remembered Fong Tai, her father. It was the same advice he had given Tai years ago. He had no idea if Fong Tai had followed it. His tragic end seemed to refute this philosophy. Heaven did not have eyes in Fong Tai's case; the result devised by Heaven had been horribly wrong. He started to speak but couldn't find his voice. He picked up his bowl and finished the noodle soup.

"Well, Brigid," he went on after a long silence, trying to sound casual and cheerful, "I am sure Bo Ho still loves you, no matter what you wrote. But when the house has caught fire, you must do everything to save it. Go to him. Tell him what happened. You two don't have to stay in Peking. The city is ruled by that overlord Kitchen God Tao, but his power does not reach beyond Chi-li Province. Go to another province with Bo Ho. If necessary, go back to France. Take him with you. Go, Brigid, before it is too late!"

Almost before he had finished, Brigid had picked up her coat and was flying out of Third Uncle's apartment. She felt energy surging through her. Why hadn't she thought of that herself? China was so big; they could easily disappear like two fish in a vast ocean.

She paid the carriage driver a double fee. The carriage arrived at the theater in record time. She ran upstairs in the dormitory building and burst into Bo Ho's flat.

There was nothing left but empty boxes and wastepaper strewn on the floor. The books, the trophies and awards, were all gone. She staggered toward the bedroom. The bed had been slept in, but all Bo Ho's belongings had disappeared except for a pair of old slippers. She picked them up, stared at them, and felt tears creeping down her cheeks.

She hurried downstairs and went in to the theater. The manager was in his cubicle, holding a meeting with two other men. When they saw her they rose quickly, their faces brightening.

"We were trying to find you, miss," the manager said. "Where is Bo Ho?"

"I am here to ask you the same question. Where is he?"

"The servant found his flat empty this morning," the manager said, rubbing his hands nervously. "He must have moved out last night. We don't have the faintest idea where he has gone."

*

Brigid returned home in utter despair. The loss of Bo Ho was so over-whelming that her anguish seemed unbearable. Bo Ho's image kept flash-ing in her mind's eye. She found it hard to breathe and her heart felt tight, as though it were being weighted down by a rock.

Unable to bear it anymore, she went to the liquor cabinet and took out a bottle of mao tai that Bo Ho had given her. Sitting on a sofa, she began drinking it down from the bottle. She wanted the burning sensation to counteract her pain. The 120-proof liquor rushed to her brain, wiping out her loneliness and depression. Soon she began to feel a flowing sensation; the ceiling and the walls waved and spun.

Brigid stripped off her clothes, tossing them at the ceiling. "Hooray, hooray!" she shouted. Singing, she staggered, naked, to the courtyard. "Let's celebrate!" she called defiantly. "Life is a party! Hooray, hooray!" She started dancing drunkenly, kicking and turning haphazardly. Finally she tumbled and fell, and everything blacked out.

When she woke up, she found herself in her own bed. She blinked and tried to remember what had happened. When she finally saw a man sitting on her bed, she bolted up and started to scream. The man quickly put a hand over her mouth and said soothingly, "It's me, Tang San. You are all right; you are fine."

Tang San was stroking her arm affectionately, his face red, his eyes bloodshot and his breath smelling of whiskey. He was thoroughly drunk.

"You had a good sleep," he went on, his voice low and a little breathless. "I watched you for a long time, Brigid. You look beautiful in your sleep, like a painting. The servants were shocked. They wanted me to set off a string of firecrackers to drive away evil spirits. They believe it is bad luck to see a naked woman in bright daylight. I told them you are a Western woman. In Western countries nudity is beautiful. Artists paint it. What a beautiful body you have, Brigid, absolutely stunning. I wish I could paint it."

He started stroking her. She shook her head clear and remembered what she had done. "Please stop," she said, brushing his hand away. "Leave me alone!"

Tang San withdrew his hand. "I have waited a long time for you to wake up, Brigid. I have a few proposals to make. First, I want to make love to you tonight." He started to uncover her, but she grabbed the blanket and refused to let go of it.

"Tang San, leave me alone! I mean it!"

Again Tang San withdrew his hands, grinning. "I also want to marry you, Brigid," he droned on in the same monotonous voice. "We are two of a kind. We both are of low birth and both are lucky. We will make a good team."

"Tang San," she said, glaring at him, "I don't love you. Please don't ask!"

"Love will grow, Brigid. I promise I'll help it grow. I'll treat you like a queen."

"I don't want to be a queen! Let me go! Please leave me alone!"

"Now you are forcing me to do something that is not nice," he said, bringing out a pistol from his pocket and aiming it at her temple. "I want you now, Brigid. . . . If you refuse to cooperate, I will kill both of us. I can't live without you. If I go, I must take you with me!" Hand shaking, he held the gun and stared at her, his bloodshot eyes like those of a madman.

She shuddered. "Put the gun away," she said, cringing from the muzzle.

"Not until you say yes, Brigid."

"Yes, yes!" Brigid said quickly. "Just put the gun away!" She tore the blankets off and lay naked. "Go ahead! Hurry! Get it over with!"

Surprised, Tang San took off his clothes nervously. Grunting, he climbed on her and clumsily tried to make love. She lay passively, without a sound, staring at the ceiling and praying that it would be over soon. She wanted to shorten the ordeal as much as she could. When he was inside her, she started to move violently. A few seconds later, Tang San let out an agonized groan. Then he lay on top of her, limp and breathing hard.

She pushed him off, pulled the blanket back over her and turned toward the wall. She wanted to cry, but instead she bit her lip until she tasted blood.

"Thank you, Brigid," Tang San was saying. She heard him putting his clothes back on. "Now that I have something inside you, Brigid, I feel that you are mine and I am yours. I promised you a diamond, did I not? I have brought it. It is all yours."

She heard him unwrapping something. "Here it is, darling," he went on. "You will find it on your bedside table. Have a good sleep. Sweet dreams. But remember, we are engaged to be married."

She heard the door open and close. Just as she was about to get up, she heard the door open again and Tang San's voice said, "From now on you will only go out with me. Remember that!"

32

B rigid climbed the ladder and stepped nimbly over the eight-foot wall. Climbing down the other side, she found Old Liu and the other man standing below waiting to aid her. Without their help she leaped off the ladder and dashed to the waiting carriage.

Through the window, she saw the other man climb back into the yard. Old Liu lifted the outside ladder and helped him take it over the wall. It was fast work, and done with a minimum of noise. "God," Brigid thought, "we are as good as professional burglars!"

It was a dark night with a half-moon almost hidden in clusters of clouds. The street outside was quiet except for the singing of crickets. As soon as Old Liu climbed in, the carriage started to move. From the beat of the horse's hooves Brigid knew it was not an old, broken-down animal that was pulling the carriage. It bumped over the uneven road at high speed, shaking and rocking so violently that Brigid had to hold on to the window frame with both hands.

"How far is the railway station?" she asked.

"Not too far," Old Liu said. "We shall catch the five o'clock morning train to Tientsin."

Brigid looked at her watch. It was 3:30 A.M. "Who is the other man who helped us escape?"

"One of the servants. Don't worry, Young Mistress. He is my nephew."

"I hope you have paid him well."

"Blood is more dependable than silver dollars. He was helping me and he will never tell anybody. A good thing that you have big feet, Young Mistress. A woman with small bound feet could never climb over a wall as easily as you did."

"I am a dancer and gymnast," she said with a smile. "At your age you are as nimble as I am. How long does it take to reach Hunan Province?"

"It depends. If Heaven is looking after us, we can reach Changsha, the provincial capital, in three weeks."

"Old Liu," she said after a pause, "you still have time to change your mind. You don't have to give up a comfortable life to follow me. In Changsha I have my mother's relatives. I also know a woman who operates a rice store."

Old Liu looked at her as if he were offended. "Young Mistress, I am an old servant whose family has worked for your family for three generations. If I desert you now, how can I face my ancestors when I . . ." He stopped, trying to avoid any unlucky words early in the morning.

"Thank you, Old Liu. I would be disappointed if you deserted me now. I have never traveled in China. I would feel lost without you."

"I hope Master Tang San won't find you missing too soon this morning."

"Don't worry. Last night I told the maid not to disturb me until noon. I think we have enough time to get away."

"Too bad you have brought nothing with you, Young Mistress," he said, looking worried.

She laughed. "Don't think I am still a rich man's daughter, a helpless *thousand gold.* I can rough it if necessary. Besides, I have brought a bag with a change of clothes and a diamond. A big diamond is like a roof over your head and food in the stomach. My Third Uncle used to say, 'If you keep the hills green, you never have to worry about future firewood.' This diamond is our green hills."

The train station was busy and noisy when they arrived. In front of the ticket window people climbed on each other's backs to buy tickets. The noise was deafening—peddlers hawking their wares, babies crying, mothers calling for their lost children and fathers scolding. Peasants and petty merchants, carrying their meager belongings in bundles and baskets, had already gathered along the tracks, some sitting on their luggage, others standing close to the tracks, looking both ways, anxious for the train to arrive.

After a long struggle Old Liu finally purchased two third-class tickets. All the first- and second-class tickets had been sold "under the table," but Old Liu assured Brigid that traveling in third-class was much safer, for no security braves would bother to look for her among peasants and coolies. Furthermore, those who were going south were mostly southerners, not the garlic-eating northerners.

While waiting for the train, Old Liu kept chatting. Brigid saw a man sitting on his battered trunk, eating a persimmon. Close by was a beggar boy, watching him hungrily, an emaciated arm stretched toward him, his lips moving, begging for the skin.

It reminded her of the story Ding Fei had told her about a beggar boy begging for sweet potato skins from a coolie at a railway station. When the coolie finished eating the potato, he tossed the skin under the train. The beggar boy dashed after it and disappeared just as the train began to move. As the train gathered speed, there was a loud scream. Nobody was shocked. Just another beggar boy had died, like a sowbug crushed under somebody's foot.

Before the train stopped, bedlam broke out. People started climbing in the windows, pushing, dragging in bundles, bedding and clothing, baskets of cackling chickens and squawking ducks. Brigid climbed into the nearest window after Old Liu, who jerked her in like a piece of luggage. They grabbed a window seat, letting the others climb over them, stepping on their knees and holding their shoulders for support.

Brigid clutched her handbag, in which she carried some toilet articles and money. The diamond was safely sewn into her coat.

✳

Brigid and Old Liu arrived in Changsha, the capital of Hunan Province, after three weeks of torturous journey on land and water. On water they had traveled on filthy junks and tramp steamers. On land the refugees from famine had trudged for days, seeking food and hope. Brigid had seen old men drop and die, mothers bury their dead children at the roadside, some weeping and others dry-eyed. Once she had dashed to a baby that a woman had tearfully left under a tree. She had heard about girl babies being abandoned or even killed. But it was a boy, three or four months old, and the corpse had started to smell. Obviously the mother had kept it for days before she decided to abandon it. Brigid and Old Liu covered the remains with rocks so wild dogs would not devour it. By the time she reached Changsha, she was so tired and shaken that she had trouble keeping her food down.

Changsha was a busy city, buzzing with activity. Everywhere a sea of energetic humans hurried along with loads on their shoulders or under their arms and oil-paper umbrellas over their heads. The smell of spicy food and odors from the gutter drifted with the breeze, and the din of voices calling, quarreling and laughing never seemed to stop—like the incessant drizzle, which was so constant that the Hunan artists had forgotten how to paint the sun. "Awful," Brigid thought. She already missed sunny Peking.

She was anxious now to meet her mother's relatives. Shao Mei had told her that her family lived in several big houses hidden behind a tall red wall. Inside the wall there were three courtyards leading to an enormous garden with lotus ponds, teahouses, bamboo clusters, honeycombed rocks, and waterfalls. Potted orchids, chrysanthemums and peonies were artistically arranged beside each moon gate in the red wall. Each courtyard contained three palatial buildings occupied by different branches of the large family, which was ruled by Shao Mei's father, the patriarch. Each member had his or her private servant, a nursemaid or a slave girl.

Old Liu did not like the chilly wet weather; his shoes had already soaked through.

"Cheer up, Old Liu," Brigid said. "When we find my grandfather, you can soak your feet in a basin of hot water and fill yourself with red-cooked pork. Let's find a carriage."

They walked in circles for a while and finally saw two sedan chairs for hire. The bearers couldn't read the address, nor did they understand Mandarin. When a passerby read the address aloud for them, the bearers said it was five li outside the city gate.

After two hours of sloshing through the mud on a narrow trail that wound through paddy fields, they finally sighted an enormous building nestled in clusters of trees and bamboos. It was almost dark.

The sedan-chair bearers quickened their steps, splashing mud and chanting in unison. Brigid felt relieved. The unbearable torture had finally come to an end. She visualized herself diving into a hot tub and submerging herself until the smell of cow's dung was washed away. Her grandfather might even assign her a slave girl to bathe her and serve her a hot meal in bed. What a life she was going to have in Hunan, pampered by servants and relatives! She would read and write letters in bed, telling all her friends in Paris about Hunan hot pepper, temperamental soldiers and passionate women.

When they arrived at the palatial gate of her grandfather's house, they were greeted by the fierce barking of dogs behind the wall. Old Liu discharged the sedan-chair bearers and knocked on the vermilion double door. Then he picked up a stick that was lying by the roadside and asked Brigid to stand behind him.

"Country dogs," he said. "They prefer human legs to dog food. When they grab a leg they never let it go."

Presently, the gate opened a crack and an old man's beady eyes showed through. The long-winded Old Liu asked to see the master of the house, the father of Madame Shao Mei, who was the late wife of the late Master Fong Tai of Peking. "Tell the Old Master that his granddaughter has traveled three thousand miles from Peking to visit him."

Brigid tugged at Old Liu's sleeve to cut short his introduction, but the servant was determined to have his say, so he rattled on, describing the hardships of the long journey with considerable exaggeration, as though he had hoped that the Old Master would rush out with tears in his eyes when he learned how his loving granddaughter had suffered.

But before he could finish, the old man behind the door interrupted. "Sir," he said, "the Old Master died long ago, and the place was sold to General Ho."

"Who is General Ho?" Brigid asked, crushed.

Without answering the question, the old man shut the door and bolted it and the dogs raised another hullabaloo.

"Well," Brigid said with a shrug, "probably another warlord." The dogs kept barking and scratching at the gate. Brigid shuddered. "Those damn dogs! Maybe they have eaten too much hot pepper, too."

"What are we going to do?" Old Liu asked, looking lost.

"Let's go visit my friend's Forever Prosperous Rice Company," she said, glad that she still had Ding Fei's calling card.

"We have lost the sedan chairs," Old Liu said, straining his eyes to see how far the bearers had gone.

Brigid, recovered from her disappointment, stepped out. "If you are tired, Old Liu," she said cheerfully, "I'll carry you," whereupon she marched away from the gloomy mansion, splashing mud.

With a sigh, Old Liu followed her. "Just like her father!" he mumbled.

33

The Forever Prosperous Rice Company was located on the Great South Gate Street in Changsha. The storefront was small with a gaudy gilded signboard hanging horizontally over the door. The red strips of lucky sayings posted on the double door were new, but the walls were darkened with age and the furniture was old and worn. The store didn't seem very prosperous.

Behind the counter a bespectacled young man in a blue cotton gown was reading a Chinese-language paper when Brigid and Old Liu came in and inquired about Ding Fei. The young man glanced up from his paper indifferently and shook his head.

"No Ding Fei here," he said and returned to his paper.

"Do you know Sam Cohen?" Brigid asked. "He is an American."

"No."

"Mister," Brigid persisted, "Ding Fei owns this rice store. She is a pretty young woman—a reporter."

The last word gave the young man a jolt. He quickly put his paper away and rose to his feet. "Come with me," he said in a lowered voice. "Here she is called Oldest Sister. So you are her friend. . . ."

"Yes."

"Only her friends know what she is doing. So we are cautious. You understand."

The young man introduced himself as Second Younger Brother and took them to the back of the store. The drizzle had stopped, but the cloudy sky was dark and gloomy. In the large backyard, coolies were unloading burlap sacks from pack mules. A middle-aged woman was squatting in a corner scrubbing clothes in a wooden tub. Sleeping beside her was a bedraggled yellow dog that raised its head and growled at the strangers, but was pacified by the woman with a few words in the Hunan dialect.

Inside the dingy building several people in blue cotton blouses were sitting on benches at a long table, eating breakfast. Ding Fei, dressed as a peasant woman, recognized Brigid immediately. She threw down her chopsticks and rushed to meet her friend.

"Brigid! I dreamed about you last night. What a coincidence!"

"How are you, Ding . . . uh, Oldest Sister," Brigid said with a laugh. "It took us all day to find you."

"A little store with a big backyard. People don't even know we exist. Let me introduce you to my 'family.' " Turning to Old Liu, she asked, "Who is this gentleman?"

Brigid introduced her servant as an old family friend.

Ding Fei's *family* was large. She had five *brothers*, two *sisters*, three *sisters-in-law* and one *brother-in-law*. Everyone had a number. Eating breakfast in the middle room were her *Second Older Brother, Third Older Brother* and their wives. Outside, busy unloading rice, were the rest of the brothers. Her *mother* was the scrubwoman. Her *father* and the others were out.

One of the sisters-in-law brought extra chopsticks to the table; another came with fresh bowls of steaming rice. Brigid and Old Liu were seated in the honored seats facing the entrance. Ding Fei started heaping food in their rice bowls, complaining about the miserable Hunan weather and urging them to eat. Brigid was hungry. It was the first time she had used such extra-long chopsticks and such large bowls. The food was so hot that everybody kept sucking in air to cool their tongues.

"Where is Sam Cohen?" Brigid asked.

Ding Fei's smile vanished. She looked pained. But she recovered quickly and explained that she and Cohen had separated. He had been offered the presidency of a railroad company in Chungking.

"What do you expect?" she added bitterly with a shrug. "Money to some men is like honey to a bee. The railroad company offered him a lot of money."

"Even love wouldn't hold him?"

"Ha, love!" Ding Fei laughed. "I see that you are still a starry-eyed romantic."

Brigid was disappointed. She had gotten the idea that Sam Cohen was serious, loyal and romantic, a kind of mysterious swashbuckling musketeer, popping in and out to right the world's wrongs, indifferent to money or high position. He and Ding Fei had seemed to make a perfect team, capable of outsmarting the world.

"By the way," Ding Fei asked, "what happened to you and Bo Ho?"

Brigid felt a stab of pain whenever she was reminded of Bo Ho, but she managed to hide it. Bo Ho was different from Sam Cohen; she had driven him away.

"The flower closed and the bee went elsewhere," she said with a smile. "So I left. There isn't much to tell."

"It was good while it lasted, wasn't it?" Ding Fei said, her voice bitter. "Anyway, it's water under the bridge. We have greater things in life that need our attention. Is this a visit? Or have you come to join us?"

"Do you need extra hands?"

"In this business no hands are extra; every hand is needed and everybody belongs. Old Liu will be our *Oldest Uncle;* you will be my *Third Younger Sister,* new family members visiting from the north. We have a lot of bunks in these buildings. The rooms are not too warm, but the food is so hot that it drives the chill out of your body."

*

After breakfast Ding Fei showed Brigid and Old Liu their sleeping spaces. Brigid shared the room with Ding Fei in the main building, and Old Liu bunked with Second Older Brother in the side building. There were holes in the walls, hidden by couplet scrolls of calligraphy and watercolor paintings, and pistols and ammunition were stored in them. Everybody in the *family* had learned how to handle a weapon. Ding Fei promised to take Brigid and Old Liu for target practice in the countryside twice a week. Not everybody was a fighter in this organization, she said, but it wouldn't hurt to be able to use a gun in an emergency.

*

That night, about eight, all activities in the rice store stopped and the doors were bolted. More *relatives* arrived. They were admitted through a small back door into the main building. Everyone looked grim. They wore dark cotton padded clothes and hats with padded flaps turned down to cover their ears and the backs of their necks. Each had a cotton or woolen shawl wrapped around his or her face, hiding the face except for the eyes. Some were dressed like peasants, carrying a hoe or a basket. Quietly, they went to the meeting hall upstairs in the main building.

Under kerosene lamps that hung from the ceiling, a meeting was held promptly at nine o'clock. All the *family members*—more than thirty strong —were seated on rickety chairs around a long table, with the younger members on the floor against the walls. Sitting at the head of the table was a tall man wearing a peasant turban and a heavy padded cotton coat. He pulled his shawl down to reveal his mouth and chin. He was a darkish man with a muscular face, thick eyebrows and deep-set sharp eyes. Ding Fei had already introduced Brigid to him. He was Sun Woo, the regional leader, known as *Oldest Brother*. Glancing around several times as if to count heads, he took out a piece of paper and laid it on the table.

"Comrades," he said quietly, his voice clear and commanding, "the news from Wuhan is not good. Two weaknesses have been plaguing the comrades. One, the ammunition supply is not adequate. Two, the explosives are not as powerful as they should be. However, Dr. Sun Yat-sen has recruited more experts to correct these problems. In the past several months, throughout 1911, all our anti-Manchu uprisings have failed miserably. During the last major effort, in Canton, seventy-two of our comrades died. We in Hunan cannot afford this kind of failure, for the government troops here are strong and they are commanded by two brutal traitors: Shih Ling, the Governor, and Mao Wing, the garrison commander. Luckily we have infiltrated the New Army. In case of trouble, the ranks of the New Army will growl, but not bite, so we can concentrate on dealing with other Imperial troops.

"Dr. Sun's Wuhan headquarters has planned a national uprising in October. All of us in the provinces must respond. Live or die, we must bring the Ching Dynasty down this time. There are more than ten thousand Hunan soldiers in the New Army of Wuhan, and they are ready to revolt on that day. The secret societies in Kwantung, Hupei, Yunnan and Kiangsi provinces have sharpened their weapons for a fight. So have many of the New Army infiltrators who are scattered in these areas. When one explosion is heard, all the mountains will echo. This is our goal!

"Dr. Sun Yat-sen hopes that every major city will have a five-hundred-member suicide squad to seize the government buildings and capture the government heads. The rest of us will help our other fighters in resisting the Ching troops. I must inform you—in some provinces the mission of the suicide squads may be less dangerous, for most of the Ching governors and yamen heads are only scarecrows. A few are nothing but useless meatballs who will be frightened and run at the sound of gunfire.

"But the bad news in Hunan is that we have no meat dumplings here. However, the Imperial Garrison commander has a weakness that makes him vulnerable. He is a licentious womanizer, a self-styled conqueror in bed. No amount of action in that area can satisfy him. Besides having numerous concubines, he is constantly on the lookout for fresh, spicy dinners. To capture this man, we must set bait. His personal guards are all armed with the best Japanese rifles and pistols. If we can devise a plan to disarm these men at the right time, we will have achieved the goal of shooting two vultures with one shot.

"Comrade Liu Kwei has taken the task of organizing the suicide squad. I have volunteered to capture the womanizer. Remember, his weakness is our best ally. I have thought of a plan and I want a volunteer—a female comrade in this *family* who is not afraid of this type of service. Anyone?"

He looked at the women in the room, but there was no response. "Perhaps I should emphasize that the bait will not be swallowed by the vulture," he went on. "According to my plan, he will not have a chance to touch it. But I need a younger sister who is courageous and not afraid of exposing a bit of flesh."

"How much flesh?" one of the young women asked.

"He is a connoisseur of the old school. He likes a woman's small bound feet."

"Who has small bound feet?" another young woman asked sarcastically. "If we had those, we wouldn't be revolutionaries."

"Lure him with a woman's second best asset," a man piped up. "Breasts."

"Who wants to look at a woman's breasts?" Oldest Brother said. "Mothers are breast-feeding babies everywhere. Legs—show him your legs." When nobody responded, Brigid raised her hand.

"Ah, a volunteer!" Oldest Brother said, pointing at her proudly, as though he had found someone who deserved a medal. "I'll tell you my plans after the meeting, Younger Sister. But be assured this is a safe mission. Before he has a chance to touch you, he will be begging for mercy."

34

I t was a rare sunny morning. Inside the main building the *family* was partaking of a Hunan lunch of hog-blood soup, ham hocks and fried eels plus two vegetables spiced with the fiery-hot red pepper. The noises of eating were suddenly interrupted by a loud "Hello!" in English. Everybody looked up. A strange-looking man in patched coolie blouse and fisherman's broad-brimmed oil-paper rainhat had walked in. Ding Fei immediately recognized him.

"Sam!" she yelled, rushing to meet him. They embraced long and hard.

Brigid was happy for Ding Fei. But she was surprised to see how much Sam Cohen had changed. Without the beard, and with his face smeared with a bit of dirt, he looked like a coolie—except for his nose, which was perhaps twice the size of that of an average Chinese.

Though obviously still in love, Ding Fei could not forget her grudge. She pushed him from her and returned to her seat at the dinner table. "Sam," she said coldly, "why have you come back?"

Cohen followed her to the table, grabbed a chair and sat down beside her. Second Oldest Sister brought him a bowl of rice and a pair of chopsticks.

"Dr. Sun Yat-sen wants me," he announced. "I'm on my way to Wuhan."

"Oh?" Ding Fei said, arching an eyebrow. "Even a fortune couldn't hold you in Chungking?"

"Ding Fei," he said, looking a bit hurt, "I'm disappointed that you still don't know me. I'm an ill-tempered bastard. When I'm mad enough, I'll do anybody's dirty work. But, listen, no fortune is worth more to me than what you and Dr. Sun are doing."

Ding Fei's eyes softened. "What makes you so mad this time?"

"We've been betrayed. All the Americans in Chungking are up in arms."

After Sam had finished eating, he revealed what had gone wrong in Chungking. The American-China Development Company, of which he was the president, had bought China's railroad-building rights. Last week they suddenly found they had lost the rights, for the Ching government had sold them again, this time to France and Germany.

"We've petitioned President Taft," Sam said, fuming. "The President has promised to raise hell in Peking! Meanwhile, I'm going to do some dirty work in Wuhan for Dr. Sun."

"What does he mean by dirty work?" Brigid whispered.

"He means explosives," Ding Fei confided. "Sam's an expert."

Brigid guessed Sam's mission. Ding Fei had told her of the carefully planned uprising in Wuhan. Dr. Sun, on whose head the Ching government had put a price, had been directing the operations from Tokyo under assumed names. Sam's expertise in explosives was in great demand. Brigid's heart started thumping as she thought about it.

"God bless you, Sam," Ding Fei said. "I like an ill-tempered bastard who has principles." She planted a kiss on his mouth. The revolutionaries all applauded.

*

Besides antitaxes, anticorruption and rice riots, a railway-agitation demonstration had been added to the agenda organized by the revolutionaries in Changsha. Now, after six months of thorough preparation, the stage was set for the big event. Through Changsha's regional revolutionary group, secret societies, gentry-merchant groups, farmers' associations, labor unions, army infiltrators and student activists had coordinated their efforts to implement their programs.

The riots and demonstrations were calculated to stir up anti-Manchu feeling in preparation for the national uprising in Wuhan. On the day scheduled for the local demonstration, organizing groups started gathering along the Hsiang River. They paraded with banners and slogans, shouting, "Drive out the Manchus! Revive the Chinese nation! Establish the Republic! Down with the traitors!"

Thousands of people gathered, listening to speeches by revolutionary leaders. Sun Woo, Oldest Brother, climbed onto a table and declaimed against the Ching government, which, he said, plunged deeper into treason in external affairs and stepped up exploitation of the people within the country.

His speech was constantly interrupted by angry patriotic slogans: "Arise, arise! Down with the rotten Ching Dynasty! Long live the revolution! Arise, arise!"

A man jumped out of the crowd, shoved a stool in front of Sun Woo's table, produced a meat cleaver from under his blue cotton gown and chopped off one of his index fingers. While the blood was spurting out of his wound, he picked up the severed finger and shouted, "Your Honor, this is my show of determination! I am ready to sacrifice my head the same way for the revolution!"

The crowd roared its approval. Angry shouts echoed in all directions, attracting even more people to the riverbank.

Brigid watched the revolutionary fever grow and felt her own blood boil. She was glad she had volunteered. If she had had a gun, she would have immediately marched with the suicide squad—anywhere, without fear, and died gloriously.

"Down with the rotten Ching Dynasty!" she heard herself scream with the crowd. "Kill the traitors! Arise, arise!"

Suddenly an old woman appeared, bobbing toward Sun Woo's table on a cane. "Your Honor, Your Honor!" she shouted tearfully at Sun Woo. "Save my son's family! They are drowning themselves in the river. Heaven has eyes—they must not die! Save their lives, Your Honor! Hurry, hurry!"

Pushing and shoving, Brigid rushed with the crowd to see what was happening. Hundreds of people had already lined the bank to watch the mass suicide. On a junk anchored about a hundred yards offshore, an entire family—mother, two sons, a daughter-in-law and two children of about ten and eleven—were sitting on the deck in a circle. They had tied themselves together with heavy rope and fixed the rope to cement blocks. The father, a middle-aged man in tatters, was scuttling the junk by hacking holes in the bottom with a hatchet.

The old woman had now crawled back to the bank and was knocking her head on the ground in grief, alternately crying for mercy and shouting at her son to stop. Nobody paid any attention to her. They stared at the slowly sinking junk, dumbfounded. Some were in shock. When water had reached the father's ankles, he sat down, picked up the rope and tied himself to the nearest cement block.

The boat sank quickly when water flooded in, and the family calmly allowed itself to sink with it. Soon the entire boat disappeared, leaving nothing afloat but a few pieces of clothing, some wooden kitchen utensils, two buckets and a mound of bubbles.

The old woman had stopped crying and kowtowing. Whimpering and murmuring prayers, she produced a roll of paper and opened it. Obviously her son had requested her to show it to the public. On the paper he had written in bold and uneven strokes

> I am a water carrier. My family is facing starvation, like 100,000 others in this province. Rich men and officials are hoarding grain to push up the price. Life has become impossible for the poor. We take this action

to dramatize our plight. I pray that Heaven will have mercy and stop this curse on others. Tang Kang and his family of Changsha kowtow.

The old woman spread the paper on the ground. Kneeling beside it, she whimpered and prayed, her eyes tightly closed in anguish. "Heaven have mercy! Please forgive my son for his foolish action. Oh, merciful Buddha, forgive him, forgive him."

35

During the weeks following the riverside demonstration, Brigid witnessed many revolutionary actions. Rice riots occurred spontaneously after government warehouses were raided, and though people were killed, the message of revolution was spreading far and wide.

In the summer of 1911 thousands of boards, varnished with tung oil and wrapped in oil paper, were thrown into the river, to float downstream as "water telegrams." It was the plan that people would pick them up, read the messages and learn what had happened in Changsha; the recipients were urged to arm themselves and join the revolution.

It was hoped that the Changsha uprising would fan the revolutionary fever all over China. Everything was planned to provide favorable conditions for the impending Wuhan revolt.

Brigid followed her instructions carefully, and constantly reminded herself of what Sun Yat-sen had said: "This time we must not fail!"

Meanwhile the trap for the Changsha Garrison commander had been set. After several meetings with Ding Fei and Oldest Brother, Brigid had been introduced to a man called the Monkey Player and his two young assistants. They spent a week rehearsing in a pine woods close to the city.

She was becoming increasingly nervous as the date to capture the womanizer neared. She remembered the night she had volunteered to be the bait. She had awakened in the middle of that night in a cold sweat, stared at the ceiling and moaned, "Oh, my God! What have I done?"

The Monkey Show was scheduled for a Sunday morning. That day a team of four people, the Monkey Player, his two young assistants and Brigid, got up early and left the woods before dawn. The two assistants were in their twenties, muscular and quiet, and anonymous except for code names: Second Nephew and Third Nephew. One took care of two large Mongolian dogs and the other handled some props.

It was another rare sunny day. They arrived at the marketplace after a hearty breakfast at an open-air restaurant nearby. One of the assistants who handled the props spread an old blanket on the ground, took out a cracked gong from a basket and beat it several times to attract a crowd. As soon as Third Nephew started beating the gong, a monkey leaped out of a basket. It put a red cap on and saluted the crowd a few times, then it leaped onto a wooden trunk, looking around and scratching its belly. The Monkey Player tossed a few peanuts to the monkey, which picked them up and shelled them with its teeth, then ate them, saluting the audience once in a while by tipping its cap.

"Be polite, monkey, be polite," the Monkey Player said, like a father chiding a child. "Stand up and bow. And stop scratching your ugly stomach!"

But the monkey ignored him and kept scratching. The audience laughed.

"Spoiled brat!" the Monkey Player said, shrugging. "Incorrigible beast! Nobody likes him but fleas. Next time I'll get a snake. No hair, no fleas!"

The Monkey Player then performed a number of tricks using his various props, not only the scrawny monkey, but a snake and the two mangy sheep dogs—all to the great delight of the audience, which kept laughing and clapping for more. Brigid watched from the sidelines. At the conclusion of his act, the Monkey Player turned to the monkey, which was again enjoying its peanuts on the wooden trunk.

"You little ugly," he said, "how is the world treating you?"

The monkey showed its teeth. The Monkey Player winced. "I have known this monkey for seven years, and I still don't know if that's his smile or a snarl of disgust. Anyway, he is our banker, he collects all the appreciations at the end of the show and only wants peanuts for his pay. We really shouldn't complain. Now, kind ladies and generous gentlemen, I have a few miracle herbs that will cure headaches, common colds, open sores and upset stomachs. Does anybody have arthritis or a fractured bone?"

Before he finished, a dozen soldiers arrived with a flashily dressed officer. One of the soldiers, a sergeant, started pushing people aside.

"Make way for the commander!" he shouted. "Make way! Make way!"

The crowd opened up quickly. Brigid, standing behind some people, saw the stout officer and her heart thumped. She knew it was the Changsha Garrison commander, Mao Wing—the womanizer. He wore a spotless gray uniform with gold buttons and gold epaulettes, a shiny officer's belt and knee-length leather boots. Like many others, he liked to imitate Japanese Army officers. Flourishing a riding crop, he stepped forward and glanced around, his arms akimbo. The soldiers stood behind him, keeping the onlookers from crowding him. Mao Wing scowled as though he had seen something not to his liking. He glanced around again, beating his boots with his crop.

The Monkey Player finished his sales talk and told his assistants to show the items. Second Nephew and Third Nephew fished out some jars and little packages from one of the baskets and walked around, waving the items in the air.

"Cold medicine, ten coppers a jar," the Monkey Player called. "Stomach Soothing Pill, twenty coppers a jar. All guaranteed to provide a miracle cure in three days or your money back."

As he called out the names of various jars and packages and talked about their functions, money and merchandise began to change hands. The assistants collected the money and handed it to the monkey, who ran between the two men, busily stuffing it into an enormous pocket. Each time it put money into the pocket, it tipped its red cap.

The Monkey Player spotted Brigid and gave her a secret nod. She nodded back and started unbuttoning her loose cotton gown.

When the audience finished buying the miracle medicine, the Monkey Player picked up the gong, raised it over his head and beat it a few times. "Now, kind ladies and generous gentlemen, you are going to see our star performance. Our Younger Sister is going to open your eyes with something that you have never seen before. Younger Sister, are you ready?"

Brigid stepped out, took off her long gown and tossed it on the blanket, revealing a homemade red costume of tight blouse and short skirt, which showed quite a bit of her shapely legs. The audience reacted to this scanty dress with excited throaty noises and sighs. A few caught their breath as though they had seen the phantom of a heavenly maiden. After a graceful bow and smile, Brigid did somersaults, then performed ballet excerpts. The audience watched her with their mouths open, unable to comprehend just what they were watching. Just as the Monkey Player said, they had never seen anything like it before.

The garrison commander was intrigued. He watched her with narrowed eyes, a row of gold teeth gleaming through his smiling thin lips.

When she finished, she curtsied all around, dipping her knee gracefully like a ballerina accepting curtain calls. The audience applauded politely, a bit uncertain about how to respond to this strange show. But the commander liked it. He did not stop smiling until he remembered his duty. Then, beating his boot with his crop, he said to the Monkey Player, "You —come here!"

"Me, Your Excellency?" the Monkey Player said with a big smile, pointing at himself.

"Yes, you. What is your name?"

"Name? Everybody calls me the Monkey Player."

"Do you have a license for this show?"

"License, Your Excellency?"

"Yes, license! All peddlers and medicine salesmen must have a license. It is for the protection of the public."

"If Your Excellency will tell how to get it, I will . . ."

"How many people do you have?" the commander said, beating his boot, his face grim.

"Four, Your Excellency: myself, my younger sister and my two nephews."

"Where are you from?"

"From Hsiangtan County, Your Excellency."

"Some peasants have reported that their chickens have been stolen," the commander said. "We don't allow monkey players to perform here without a license."

"We never touch anybody's chickens, Your Excellency," the Monkey Player said earnestly. "We bring our own chickens and eat our own eggs. If anybody has lost his chickens, I can prove that our ugly chickens are not his . . ."

"You have violated the law by performing your monkey tricks without a license—do you understand?"

"Yes, yes, Your Excellency. How much does a license cost? I have the money right here."

"Where do you live?" the commander asked, casting a quick glance at Brigid.

"In the pine woods outside the south gate, Your Excellency," the Monkey Player said, digging out several strings of brass coins from his pocket. "We don't have money to stay at an inn, so we pitched a tent in the woods. Are two strings enough for a license, Your Excellency?"

"You are under arrest," the commander said, and turned to the sergeant. "Bring him to headquarters." Beating his boot, he strode toward his horse and rode away.

The sergeant pointed his rifle at the Monkey Player. "You! Come with me!"

*

It was a chilly night, with a few large dark clouds hanging in the sky. When they moved under the moon, hiding it, the woods became ominously dark. Frogs croaked mournfully nearby; in the distance, dogs barked.

Inside the tent, Brigid sat on the ground on a blanket and played with the monkey. She had learned a few tricks and was now making the monkey sit down, stand up and do somersaults, then snarl. She laughed and tossed peanuts at it each time it did a little trick correctly.

Outside, Third Nephew was cooking a late dinner. Second Nephew was in the back of the tent, feeding the dogs. Brigid could smell the pungent odor of salted fish drifting into the tent.

They had returned to the woods more than ten hours earlier. Brigid was beginning to worry about the Monkey Player. Had he been thrown into jail? Second Nephew and Third Nephew were not concerned. They had complete confidence in the Monkey Player, who, they said, could handle any situation and come out unscathed. Brigid would have liked to know more about the three men, but they steadfastly refused to say who they were and where they had come from.

It was not until she heard the beat of a horse's hooves that Brigid knew the Monkey Player was back. She quickly turned the kerosene lamp low. The tent was now almost dark. She had planted knives in certain strategic places, just in case. The scheme must be carried out successfully, she told herself, breathing deeply several times to calm her nerves.

The monkey jumped onto a chest and rocked it, screaming for more peanuts. Second Nephew came in, picked it up and rested it on his shoulder. "Back to the cage, monkey," he said gently.

"How many are coming?" Brigid asked.

"About a dozen."

The dogs were heard barking. "Where will you be?" she asked.

"Third Nephew and I will be in the back, taking care of the animals. The Monkey Player will take care of you, so there is nothing to worry about."

He left with the monkey through a hidden opening in the back of the tent. Voices were heard outside. Someone lifted the tent curtain and the Changsha commander entered, a crop under his arm and a big smile on his tanned face. The Monkey Player followed, carrying a large kerosene lamp.

"Everything is all right, Younger Sister," he said. "His Excellency has issued us a license. We can continue our show as long as we want to."

"Right, right," the commander said, beating his boot as usual.

"His Excellency wants to have a little conversation with you," the Monkey Player said. "Entertain His Excellency the best you can, Younger Sister." With a bow to the commander, he started to withdraw.

"Wait," the commander said. "Leave the lamp here."

"Yes, Your Excellency." The Monkey Player placed the lamp on the ground near the entrance and left quickly.

The commander took the lamp and shone it on Brigid's face. Grunting with satisfaction, he put it down and turned the other lamp up. "I like a lot of light when there is something pretty to look at." Chuckling, he pulled Brigid to her feet and made her stand between the two lamps. He walked around her a few times and looked her over from head to toe. "Nice, nice," he chuckled. "Very nice. Built to perfection. A gem. A lotus flower fresh out of water. How old are you?"

"Eighteen, Your Excellency," she said, her heart thumping violently in anticipation of violence.

"A few years too old, but still young enough to be interesting. Sit down."

Brigid obeyed, pretending to look a bit frightened. She was wearing her tight dancing costume. She hugged her knees to hide her bare thighs. The commander tossed his crop away and squatted down to touch her. She could smell his strong garlic and liquor breath and decided to get the job done as quickly as she could.

"Your Excellency," she said timidly, knowing from instinct that this type of man liked shy girls. "Will you be gentle with me?"

"Gentle?" He laughed. He grabbed her bare arm and started kissing and biting it. "Of course I'll be gentle. When a man eats soft beancake, he is always gentle. . . ."

She felt a surge of revulsion and wondered if she should grab his pistol and get it over with the easy way. But she had never killed anyone and wasn't sure she could do it. She decided to proceed as planned and let the Monkey Player finish the job.

"Now, my little heart and liver," the commander said, "give me a little kiss." As he attempted to kiss her, she turned her head away and giggled. "Too much light, Your Excellency."

"I know, I know; but that's what I want! Can't enjoy a flower if I don't see it, can I? Let me undress you . . ."

"No—I don't want to be undressed unless you are undressed first!"

"A little shy, eh? All right, I don't mind." Chuckling, he took off his gunbelt, then his officer's belt. As soon as he had removed his coat, the Monkey Player entered through the opening in the back as quietly as a panther. Moving up behind the commander, he clamped an arm around his neck and pressed a knife at his throat.

"Sorry, Commander," he whispered. "I want you to do us a favor. Go out with me and tell your guards to lay down their arms."

Mao Wing, his eyes bulging from shock and the arm's pressure, tried to say something, but the armlock was so strong that he choked instead. "Just do as I say, Commander," the Monkey Player said, dragging him toward the tent door. "If not, there will be a hole in your windpipe and you will never chuckle again."

He jabbed the knife at Mao Wing's throat and forced him through the door. As they stood outside the tent entrance, the Monkey Player shouted at the stunned guards, "You have a choice. Either shoot both of us or follow his orders!"

"Lay down your arms!" the commander shouted. His men hesitated and he shouted again, his voice almost hysterical, "Lay down your arms, you idiots! All of you!"

The thirteen soldiers, including the sergeant, put down their rifles and small arms. Second Nephew and Third Nephew jumped out from behind the tent with the dogs, which started barking fiercely, straining at their leashes. Third Nephew collected the arms and put them in a pile beside the tent, while Second Nephew tossed a bundle of ropes at the feet of the soldiers.

"Now, tie each other up!" the Monkey Player said to the soldiers, jabbing his knife, which broke a bit of skin under the commander's chin and drew blood.

"Tie yourselves up, tie yourselves up!" Mao Wing shouted frantically. "Sergeant, you know what to do! Hurry! Hurry!"

Under the direction of the sergeant, six men tied up the other six, first their hands, then their feet; then three men proceeded to tie up the other three in the same manner. Finally everyone was tied except the sergeant. Second Nephew picked up the last piece of rope and completed the job. He and Third Nephew examined the knots. Satisfied, they pushed the soldiers to the ground. They lay on their backs and stared at the darkened sky, awaiting their fate.

Brigid had come out of the tent with the commander's pistol. She aimed it at his mouth and cocked it. The commander stared at the pistol, his eyes wide, face ashen. Suddenly he sank to his knees and begged, "No, no! Please don't shoot! Please! I'll give you anything, anything!"

He tried to grab her feet but she backed away quickly. As Brigid watched the wretched man knocking his head on the soggy ground, begging for mercy, she felt a peculiar sadistic satisfaction and an itch to correct old wrongs. She wanted to avenge every suffering, personal and collective, upon this disgusting wretch.

"Wait, Younger Sister," the Monkey Player said, gently removing the pistol from her hand. "Our orders are to capture this man alive. He might supply some useful information."

"Anything you want—anything, anything!" Mao Wing stammered, wiping his sweaty face with a trembling hand.

Brigid restrained an urge to spit on him. But, having given the man such a fright, she felt better. The job had been done, and her contribution, no matter how insignificant, had helped.

Suddenly there were gunshots nearby.

"You had better let us go," the commander said. "You know you can't get away. You are surrounded. I am the only man who can save your lives."

More shots pierced the still, cool air. They sounded closer, echoing in the valley beyond the forest. A group of people came into the woods, running and occasionally firing their weapons over their shoulders as though they were being pursued.

The bright half-moon emerged from a dark cloud and Brigid immediately recognized Ding Fei, Oldest Brother and other members of the *family.*

"Run, run!" Oldest Brother ordered Brigid, gesturing at her wildly. His left hand was bleeding from a bullet wound.

"Follow me," Ding Fei said, rushing past Brigid. "Something has gone wrong. The Ching troops have been tipped off. Follow me. Hurry!"

As Brigid followed Ding Fei, the Monkey Player picked up two rifles from the pile and tossed them at Second Nephew and Third Nephew, who caught them and took positions behind the trees. The Monkey Player strapped a rifle on his shoulder, picked up another and dashed behind a rock. Almost immediately, shots were exchanged. Dark shadows appeared, guns blazing. Oldest Brother stood up, raised his hand and yelled, "Stop shooting, stop shooting!" His hands raised high, he walked toward the approaching troops. "Brothers, we are all Hans. Please join the revolution and revive the Chinese nation . . ."

Before he finished, a volley of gunfire exploded. The force of the bullets threw Oldest Brother backward several feet. As blood spurted from his wounds, Brigid stood petrified, feeling nauseated and faint. "Another failure," she moaned.

"Hurry!" Ding Fei called after her.

Without looking back, she fled after Ding Fei.

36

The unscheduled tramp steamer sailing from Changsha to Hankow reminded Brigid of a wet dog, hungry and sad. But she and Ding Fei considered themselves lucky to have gotten aboard. They had eluded the Ching troops and hidden in a clothing store for two days until the owner had smuggled them to the steamer in a sampan. The owner was a generous sympathizer. He had stuffed some cash and several changes of clothing in two bags, which they carried strapped to their shoulders. Mingling with the third-class passengers like peasant women, they felt safe.

Nobody was sure what the dilapidated five-thousand-ton ship carried, except the fifty-odd third-class passengers and some first-class travelers on the top deck. It chugged along the Hsiang River toward the Yangtze at a snail's pace. The berths were infested with bedbugs, but the food was abundant and delicious. The passengers were relaxed, eating and sleeping most of the time, snoring loudly.

During the voyage, both Brigid and Ding Fei shed their educated manners and refined language. Brigid was secretly amused by their acting. Ding Fei even tried to talk out of the corner of her mouth and made unnecessary noises at the dinner table, sucking in air and blowing her food at the wrong times. It occurred to Brigid that an honest woman made the worst actor. Having associated with Ding Fei for several months now, she believed she had never known a more upright person. If more treacherous people had been involved in the revolution, perhaps the uprisings would have been successful. The failures had made Brigid cynical, but she was amused.

"What are you chuckling about?" Ding Fei whispered.

"I am wondering if our *family members* are too nice. Maybe we need some gangsters and crooks in our organization. You know the old saying, 'The best thing to counteract poison is poison.' "

Ding Fei hushed her quickly and Brigid stopped with an apologetic smile. They were listening to a blind storyteller who entertained the third-class passengers. Brigid could hardly follow the lyrics, but she enjoyed the man's high-pitched thin voice, his gentle style and the rhythmic clicking of his wooden clappers.

"Did you just notice something?" Ding Fei asked.

"No. What did you see?"

"The last time he picked up his teacup, he knew exactly where it was. This time he groped for it. The last time he forgot he was blind, this time he remembered."

"Then he's not blind. So what?"

"It worries me. We had better get out of here." Muffling a yawn, Ding Fei got up and left the room. Brigid thought the yawn was unnecessary. Besides, it was so overacted that it looked as though she were burlesquing it. She dropped a few coins into the storyteller's cup and followed Ding Fei out of the dining room.

"Did he smile at you?" Ding Fei asked.

"I didn't look."

"I heard you drop a lot of coins into his cup. Why so generous?"

"If he can see, his feelings might have been hurt by your big yawn. A few coins may soothe his injured ego."

Ding Fei merely smiled.

                    *

As they approached the Yangtze, the river grew wider and muddier. There had been a flood in several nearby counties. When Brigid saw the first corpse float by, she lost her appetite for breakfast. By lunchtime, she had seen not only the bodies of humans, but bloated dogs and horses riding on the undulating yellow water, some of them bumping against the side of the slow-moving ship. Ding Fei said that seeing corpses every day would develop Brigid's immunity to the sight of death, and she was right. Brigid found herself enjoying an enormous lunch of hot dishes while bodies floated by.

The sky was as murky as the river water, but there was no sign of rain. The banks were barren; the few trees had died either through drought or war. The low hills had become desolate mounds of brown earth. Ding Fei said that this part of the country was supposed to be the rice bowl of Central China, the pride of Hunan, Hupei and Kiangsi provinces, irrigated by the mighty Yangtze and the beautiful Tung Ting Lake. Ancient poets had praised the scenic beauty and wealth of the region in songs and poems; they had boated and fished on the lake's clear blue water, dined and wined on flower boats with friends, been entertained by singsong girls. In boats or in pavilions, the retired scholar-officials had played musical instruments, practiced calligraphy, composed eight-legged essays and enjoyed games of chess. Those idyllic days had been recorded in Tang poems and Sung paintings. But where were those marvelous sights and sounds now?

Ding Fei talked with tears in her eyes. Brigid enjoyed her friend's descriptions, thinking that Ding Fei would make an excellent professional storyteller.

As soon as they finished their lunch, Ding Fei nudged Brigid in the ribs. The storyteller had started to sing again. His song was one of those describing the good old days, echoing Ding Fei's sentiments. His voice was forlorn and sad. For the first time the audience listened quietly. When he finished, a few elderly people wiped tears from their wrinkled faces.

"My God, he's one of us," Ding Fei whispered. "He heard everything we talked about." She got up, went over to him and dropped a handful of coins into his cup. The storyteller nodded with the same flicker of a smile, which, however did not interrupt his singing. But to Brigid and Ding Fei it seemed as if he were saying, "The revolution must not fail!"

✳

In the evening the boat reached a small town in Hupei Province. As soon as it docked, a band of soldiers rushed on board shouting, "Off, off! All of you, off!" Then they started pushing and dragging people toward the gangplank, threatening them with bayonets. Some passengers were forced ashore without their luggage; a few protested and were promptly thrown overboard. On the dock, hundred of soldiers were waiting to come aboard. They were a filthy band of skeletons, dressed practically in rags. They wore red armbands and carried all kinds of weapons—rifles of different makes, assorted pistols, broadswords and spears with red tassels. Some of them sat on small unpainted coffins, eyes sunken and sallow skins covered with sores.

"A warlord is seizing the ship," Ding Fei said. "Let's get out of here!"

Brigid followed her to their cabin, grabbed their clothing bags and rushed ashore just as a second mob of soldiers started coming aboard, carrying supplies and crude pine boxes.

Everybody was shouting, trying to salvage what they could reach. When the passengers had cleared out, more soldiers arrived. Judging from their smell, sunken cheeks and bloodshot eyes, Brigid decided they were all diseased and starved.

Ding Fei and Brigid hurried away from the steamer. Ding Fei said she could almost tell from the looks of the soldiers that this warlord was one of the bandit-generals of Central China. Raping, looting and kidnapping slave laborers was their usual practice.

"Where are we going?" Brigid asked.

"We'll catch a junk to Hankow," Ding Fei said. "Brace yourself for worse troubles."

"Why do you say that?" Brigid asked, following her closely, more worried now.

"Warlords seize trains and steamships, but pirates like junks and fishing boats. Compared to pirates, warlords are gentlemen."

Brigid cringed at the thought. Refusing to think about the pirates, she touched the diamond sewn inside her cotton padded gown. As long as she still had it, she felt secure. She had been told that Hankow, the capital of Hupei Province, was a modern industrial city, and all the foreign powers had concessions and consulates there. "How far is it to Hankow from here?" she asked.

"Three or four more days by junk. We could have reached it by tomorrow if the steamer hadn't been captured by that damned warlord."

"Who is this warlord?" Brigid asked. She had almost become allergic to the word warlord. Every time she mentioned it she felt a headache coming on.

"One of the southern bandit-warlords called Hunan Wild Dog," Ding Fei explained. "They are all the same. They seize cities like they seize ships. They rob and levy their own taxes."

"Which side are they with?"

"They are like dogtail weeds on a muddy wall, bending with the wind. If revolutionaries are winning, they will join us; if the government troops are ahead, they will do errands for the government for a fee, including fighting, like mercenaries."

Suddenly they noticed people rushing toward a junk about two hundred yards away. A weather-beaten middle-aged man was gesturing at them wildly.

"We are in luck," Ding Fei said. "A fisherman is picking up yellow fish."

"Yellow fish?" Brigid asked as they followed the crowd.

"Yes," Ding Fei panted. "That means us. Slang on the docks. Hurry! It will be filled in a few minutes."

The fisherman was not greedy. As soon as Ding Fei and Brigid climbed aboard, he leaped on the deck and pushed the boat away from the bank with an oar, leaving a group stranded on the bank, clamoring to be taken away. Some sank to their knees, begging.

It started to drizzle again. The fisherman had taken twenty-odd passengers. He put the six women and five children in the cabin, which had a bamboo matted cover. The men were told to sit on the front and back decks. He collected a passage fee of one dollar a head. Children free. He and his sturdy young son, a lad of about twenty, sculled the boat with strong rhythmic strokes, while his wife, at the stern, cooked a rice gruel on an earthen stove.

When it was ready, the fisherwoman dished the soup out into wooden bowls and fed everyone. Then she made a large pot of tea. For a while nobody talked; the boat was full of sucking noises, made amid sighs of satisfaction and gratitude. When the bowls were empty, the fisherwoman poured a thick black tea into them.

They were all grateful for the meal and praised the fisherman and his wife profusely, wishing them prosperity in both this life and the next.

"Everybody has hard times," the fisherman said after acknowledging the praise. "You may do me a good turn one of these days."

"Not likely in this life," an old man said. "But after I die, my spirit will never forget your kindness."

"O mi tu fu," the fisherman's wife said quickly, putting her palms together and saying a prayer. "Please don't speak of death, sir. You will live a long time. Your long earlobes indicate that."

"Longevity is not my wish in this life," the old man said with a sigh.

A few other men nodded in agreement. Brigid watched them and wondered how they had survived the never-ending war and starvation. Suddenly she felt terribly depressed. When a group of men who had been toughened by such misery all their lives no longer wished for longevity, the greatest blessing in Chinese life, she knew it was the end of her hope. She would never be able to make the adjustment. Perhaps she should get out of China; the country had become too alien to her.

"Ding Fei," she said, her voice trembling with emotion, "you are still young. You can seek a better life elsewhere. Why don't you go to France with me?"

Ding Fei looked surprised. "No," she said. "I am devoted to what I am doing. Haven't you found that out?"

"What if it fails?" Brigid asked, avoiding the word revolution.

"We will try again, of course. We always hope to win. If not, each of us carries a red pill in our pocket."

"Suicide?" Brigid asked, shocked.

Ding Fei nodded.

Brigid was silent for a moment. She did not know what to say. It sounded almost like a melodrama, one of the stories she had read in school about unselfish heroes and heroines who died bravely for a cause. She had always thought them a bit silly, like those high-sounding patriotic slogans on wall posters: GIVE ME FREEDOM OR DEATH!

"What a pity," she thought. "Ding Fei is too young and too pretty to give up her life like that." She remembered her at Tang San's party—so lively and so full of vigor and optimism. Now she was haggard and thin, and was carrying a suicide pill. . . . What a waste if she took it! In France they could have been happy together. Brigid watched her friend and swallowed a large lump in her throat.

37

The junk arrived in Hankow on a foggy morning. In the distance, the skyline of the tri-cities of Hankow, Wuchang and Hanyang on the Yangtze resembled a sprawling Western city, but as the boat came closer, Brigid could see sampans, junks, barges and small steamers plowing through the yellow water, fishing or carrying cargo and passengers.

The fisherman docked his junk away from the main harbor. He, his wife and his son helped the passengers step off the boat and onto a beach. The fishing dock was shabby, crowded and chaotic. The charm of Chinese life had fascinated Brigid in Peking when she first returned to China, but not anymore. Now she found it irritating. And when she saw greasy stews in huge caldrons at the coolie market on the dock, she found nothing especially appealing or exotic about them.

After stepping off the dirty, smelly fishing dock, they wandered through a maze of cobblestoned streets in which crowds hurried along, bumping each other, talking, calling and coughing. Coolies carried muddy water from the river in buckets, which they balanced on their shoulders on bamboo poles, synchronizing their steps with heavy grunts. Peddlers carried their wares in baskets, ringing bells or beating sticks of wood while they chanted their wares.

The narrow streets were lined with stalls; fruit, eggs and trinkets were spread on blankets in every available space, and all sorts of unappetizing tidbits were displayed in trays and baskets, with flies hovering over them.

In the better sections of the city, the buildings were a little less shabby. Some had Western façades and glass windows. Buyers and sellers conducted business inside tiny shops, bargaining, weighing, sipping tea and chatting. Tailors wearing dark eyeshades sewed; sick old men dozed in bamboo chairs, all in plain sight of the street. There were dogs roaming about and children playing underfoot. Only a year ago, Brigid would have regarded such typical Chinese scenes as picturesque, but now they were nothing but an indication of hopelessness—lives that would never rise above chronic misery.

Ding Fei had become alive again since their arrival in Hankow. She talked animatedly, her face flushed with color, her voice strong and excited —as though anticipation of the Wuhan uprising had revived and energized her.

Ding Fei now revealed the plans of the Wuhan uprising to Brigid. The New Army infiltrators would play the most important part because they had modern weapons. They would engage other Ching troops and let the revolutionary fighters, disguised as peasants, attack the government buildings. Meanwhile women volunteers, secret societies and propaganda specialists would step up the effort to reduce Ching power by spreading infiltration rumors in the hope that the government would disband infected contingents.

Brigid soon felt her own blood begin to stir. The patriotic slogans didn't seem ridiculous anymore. If she had been asked to shout "Give me freedom or death!" she wouldn't feel uncomfortable.

"Where are we going?" she asked.

"To our Wuchang headquarters," Ding Fei said. "Sam Cohen is there."

The Wuchang revolutionary headquarters was also a rice store, no larger than the one in Changsha. It also had a flashy name on a gaudy signboard: A THOUSAND PROFIT RICE COMPANY.

The man behind the counter, another young man in a threadbare long gown, immediately recognized Ding Fei as she and Brigid walked in. After the usual greetings, he took them to the back of the store. To Brigid's surprise, the courtyard and the buildings in the back were almost identical to those in Changsha. They went into the main building and climbed rickety stairs to a large room where a meeting was in progress. There were about thirty people in the room, sitting on benches and assorted chairs, with some squatting along the walls. A moon-faced stout man in his early thirties, wearing a wrinkled Western suit, was talking behind a schoolroom desk, a piece of chalk in one hand. He had just finished writing something on the blackboard.

Ding Fei nudged Brigid. "That is Hwang Sin," she whispered, "our national leader and Dr. Sun Yat-sen's right-hand man. He is missing three fingers because of a recent encounter."

Hwang Sin caught sight of Ding Fei and his face brightened. He tossed the chalk into the blackboard trough and dusted his hands without interrupting his talk. "The suicide squads will attack the government yamen in Wuchang and get rid of the top officials. 'When the dragons are deprived of their leader,' as the old saying goes, 'they are no longer dragons but little eels.' The Wuhan arsenal has been infiltrated, so we will have access to most of their small arms. What we need desperately is explosives, but we have an American friend who knows how to manufacture bombs and hand grenades from available materials."

"He means Sam Cohen," Ding Fei whispered, giving Brigid another nudge.

Hwang Sin paused for emphasis, then continued in a more dramatic voice. "The Wuhan uprising is most crucial! It must succeed! Only then will all the provinces respond by declaring independence. Only then can we toss the Manchus out of the Forbidden City. Let me repeat: *the Wuhan uprising must succeed!*"

He spoke with such conviction and determination that many of the revolutionaries responded by shouting and waving their fists. "It must succeed! It will succeed!"

When the meeting was over, quite a few people, including Hwang Sin, hurried to greet Ding Fei. Ding Fei introduced Brigid. Many others came over to shake Brigid's hand. Hwang Sin said that everybody already had his or her assignment for the Wuhan uprising, but he would like Ding Fei and her friend to supervise and coordinate the propaganda work before the scheduled national revolt. Then Hwang Sin hurried out of the room.

Brigid and a woman named Shun were assigned the job of painting signs and writing slogans on posters in Chinese, French and English. Shun was a thin schoolteacher and writer who dressed as a peasant. The tri-city of Wuhan, astride the Yangtze, had thousands of foreign residents—missionaries, traders, government officials, military personnel—and Hwang Sin wanted all of them to know that the revolution was the only salvation for China.

Suddenly while they were talking there was a roof-shaking explosion. The impact sent Shun to the floor. Ding Fei ducked under a desk.

"Stay down, stay down!" Ding Fei yelled. Brigid threw herself to the floor and crawled under her desk. There was another blast. She felt the ground tremble and heard plaster fall onto her desk. She wrapped her arms around her head and put her head down.

Outside, bedlam had broken out. Brigid could hear running feet and shouting. A messenger burst in and asked everybody to go to the assembly hall immediately.

When Brigid, Ding Fei and Shun arrived in the large hall downstairs, it was almost full. Everybody was talking at once, speculating as to what had happened. The scheduled uprising was still two days away. Had there been another blunder? Had something happened to upset everything again? A distraught man next to Brigid was almost in tears. Was the revolution destined to fail, he lamented? Another man rushed in and quieted everybody. He was Kan Ming, Hwang Sin's deputy.

"There has been an accidental explosion," he said, his voice charged with emotion. "It has prematurely disclosed our preparations. There is no choice but to act now."

There was a tense silence, then the room filled with heated argument. Kan Ming raised his hands, demanding discipline and order at this critical moment.

"There is a rumor," he said, "that a list of infiltrators in the Wuhan New Army has been captured by the police. Our members have decided to revolt now."

Hwang Sin, he said, had issued an order for an all-out attack. The suicide squads had been dispatched to seize the Viceroy's headquarters. Hwang Sin himself had gone with them to direct the operation. The revolutionaries who had infiltrated the Imperial regiment in Wuchang were ready to attack the Hanyang arsenal.

"What are we going to do here?" someone shouted.

"The triple city of Wuhan is in total chaos," Kan Ming said. "There is nothing we in this building can do but wait for news."

"We cannot sit here waiting to be slaughtered," another man shouted. "If we die, we might as well die fighting!"

Many of the revolutionaries agreed with him, and they started shouting angrily. Kan Ming waved his hands, trying to quiet them, but the majority clamored for action.

"We don't have enough arms," Kan Ming protested. "Leave the fighting to the fighters. Besides, you are some of the best brains. I don't want you to become cannon fodder."

"We don't want to be sitting ducks, either," a third man shouted. "Let us go, Kan Ming!"

Now there was total disorder. A handful of men rushed to the door, waving their arms wildly, imploring others to follow them.

"All right—go. Go!" Kan Ming ordered. "Take whatever weapons you can find."

"Should we go?" Shun asked Ding Fei, her lips dry and her face ashen.

"Where are the weapons?" Brigid asked.

"Forget the weapons," Ding Fei said. "Follow me!"

Gunfire and explosions could be heard in the distance—obviously heavy fighting had broken out. They rushed to the street. People were running in all directions; shopowners were closing their doors frantically; women, shielding their babies in their arms, were begging for shelter. Peddlers were abandoning their pushcarts. The gunfire was getting closer. There were several loud explosions that drowned out all the other noises, followed by women's screams, babies' crying and dogs' barking.

Brigid followed Ding Fei closely, running against the crowd, with Shun tagging behind, panting and coughing. "Where are we going?" Brigid asked breathlessly.

"Don't ask," Ding Fei said. "Just follow me." She stopped momentarily to wait for Shun. When Shun finally caught up with them, she looked ghastly pale. She was coughing and gasping for air. Ding Fei helped her to the side of the street and made her sit on the doorstep of a closed store.

Shun kept coughing. Ding Fei patted her on the back to ease her distress. Suddenly Shun bent down, put her head between her knees, and a mouthful of blood gushed out.

"My God!" Ding Fei said. "I didn't know she had tuberculosis. She shouldn't have run like that."

Brigid started pounding on the closed door. There was no response. She went to the next door and pounded on it with both fists. "Open up! Please open up! We have a sick woman!"

She knocked on several other doors but nobody responded. By now Shun had vomited a great deal of blood. Her coughing finally stopped. Ding Fei wiped Shun's mouth with a handkerchief, then dried her perspiration.

"Go on, go on," Shun said, still gasping for breath. "I'm all right. Leave me alone."

"Don't talk; just keep quiet," Ding Fei said firmly.

"I don't want to be a burden," Shun said. "Go on, please!"

"Burden or no burden, you are stuck with us," Ding Fei said. "Please shut up!"

Shun looked relieved. She put her head against Ding Fei's shoulder and closed her eyes. Brigid banged on a few more doors. When she saw blood on her knuckles, she started kicking at the doors.

"Brigid," Ding Fei called. "Nobody will open his door now, you know that! Come over and help Shun; we'll continue."

Both of them helped Shun to her feet. They practically carried her as they turned into an alley. By now the streets were almost deserted, but the gunfire continued. It could be heard in all directions, increasing in density. There were also thunderous explosions, and trails of smoke rose in the distance. Some of the fires were so close that flames could be seen licking the sky.

With Shun dragging her feet between them, they plodded on without speaking. Brigid wished she knew where they were going, but she refrained from asking. She knew Ding Fei was methodical. Everything had been planned.

But they did not go far. The gunfire was getting closer every minute. Presently they heard running footsteps behind them. "Halt! Halt!" someone was shouting, and almost immediately bullets smashed into the ground near their feet.

They stopped. Brigid did not even look, knowing it was the Ching troops. She did not panic, nor did she despair. She remembered Third Uncle's favorite saying, "Leave everything to Heaven."

Soon they were surrounded by a dozen soldiers, their bayonets pointing at their throats. "Why are you running away?" demanded the officer, a small man wearing an armband with the character *Great Ching* written on it.

"Isn't everybody?" Ding Fei said, her voice defiant.

"Where are you from?"

"Right here. We are natives. Can't you tell from my accent?"

"That is Shun Mei, a writer," a soldier said, pointing at Shun. "She's a revolutionist!"

"Ah, so you are from that Thousand Profit Rice Company," the officer said with scornful glee. "A business that hangs out a goat head but sells dog meat. You are under arrest!"

*

The jail was behind the Viceroy's yamen, a stone structure in which criminals and political prisoners were confined in large cells. Brigid, Ding Fei and Shun were thrown into the biggest one, already crowded with fifty-odd revolutionaries and a dozen or so thieves waiting to be executed. The thieves were excited about the newcomers, feeling honored to have such prestigious fellow prisoners to share their fate. A one-eyed man with a shaved head expressed his pleasure as soon as the guards had slammed the iron door shut. Using the most learned language he could manage, he said happily, "Honorable sirs and madames, welcome! We are only petty thieves, humble at birth and humble at the end. But you are the noble sort. Instead of stealing somebody's chickens, you tried to rob the Emperor's big dragon throne. Your honorable presence has made this place high class. It will be a great honor to die in such august company. Welcome, welcome! We are delighted to share your fate."

When he finished, the thieves all applauded. The revolutionaries did not know how to respond. A few grinned. Most turned away unhappily, unwilling to have anything to do with common criminals. One of them shook all the thieves' hands and started preaching the revolution.

Shun tried not to cough. She covered her mouth with a soiled handkerchief and convulsed. Ding Fei begged everybody to make a little room for Shun to lie down. A few of them got up and yielded their squatting space. They helped Shun down and covered her with cotton padded coats donated by two of the revolutionaries. Shun thanked them with a thin smile. Ding Fei sat beside her and tried to encourage the sick woman whenever she opened her eyes. Nobody had much to say. Their fate was uncertain. A few believed they would be shot with the common criminals in the morning, and accepted this philosophically.

"Everybody goes sooner or later," one said, "like taking a ship to another world. I'll be glad to catch an early one."

After a long rest, Shun opened her eyes. Both Ding Fei and Brigid smiled at her. "How do you feel?" Ding Fei asked.

"Better." Shun managed a smile, trying not to cough.

"Wei, brother," one of the revolutionaries asked the one-eyed thief, "how is the food in this hotel?"

"A three-course dinner every evening—pork-skin soup, a rice ball and a cup of tea."

"No meat?"

"If you look carefully in the rice ball, you may find a crushed cockroach or two. That's meat."

Brigid felt a sudden attack of nausea after that comment. She quickly turned her thoughts to Bo Ho and it subsided. It worked like a miracle. If she were to be shot in the morning, she thought, she would do the same. Who could tell, maybe death wouldn't be such an unpleasant experience.

The gunfire in the distance continued. The big guns reminded her of heavy fireworks. Brigid closed her eyes and visualized the brilliant display of pyrotechnics during the Chinese New Year. She remembered her father, her mother, Third Uncle, Old Liu. . . . Whatever had happened to him?

She could smell the New Year's dinner prepared by the fat chef who was chronically grouchy except during the New Year. She loved the feast, usually a twelve-course banquet shared by relatives she had hardly seen. She had kowtowed to all the elders, always in anticipation of a big red packet, which the elders passed out to children after accepting a kowtow. Once in a while she would run to her room with all the red packages, open them anxiously to find out how much money was in each, trying to remember who was generous and who was stingy. Her mother was always the most generous. In her red packet there had always been several silver dollars instead of a string of brass coins.

The explosions sounded louder and closer. "That's the government troops," one revolutionary said. "We don't have that kind of nice big modern guns."

"Well, we go sooner or later," the philosophical one insisted. "It is only a trip. Who cares if you are done in by a nice big gun or not."

"Come on, come on, all you turtles' eggs!" the one-eyed thief shouted at the door. "Hit us with a big one! That will save you some bullets in the morning."

"Bullets? No such luck," another condemned criminal said with a snort. "Since when do they execute the condemned with bullets? They chop our heads off. Just pray for a good executioner, brother—one with good aim who can finish the job with one quick clean stroke!"

Again Brigid turned her thoughts to Bo Ho. He appeared in her mind's eyes, miraculously, shielding her from a gruesome decapitation. "Oh, God," she thought, "how long is this ordeal going to last?"

Shun started fumbling in her pocket. She brought out a little box with a trembling hand, opened it and took out a red pill. Just as she was about to put it into her mouth, Ding Fei grabbed her fragile wrist.

"No, no! It's too early to end it all, Shun. I'll tell you when. I have one too. . . ."

Brigid knew what they were talking about—the suicide pill. She felt a sudden anguish; even the thought of Bo Ho couldn't drive it away. Ding Fei gently removed the box from Shun's shaking hands, slipped it into her own pocket and gave Shun another encouraging smile. Shun closed her eyes tightly, trying to control her sobs.

An explosion shook the roof, followed by several fusillades which sounded so close that the prisoners paled. Everybody sat up and waited, expecting the worst. A few Christian converts made the sign of the cross; the Buddhists started praying, mumbling, "O mi tu fo," with their palms together.

Suddenly the shooting stopped and shouts were heard. "Down with the Ching Dynasty! Revive the Chinese nation! Long live the revolution!"

Ding Fei leaped up. "The revolutionary brothers are coming! We have won!"

Bedlam broke out in the dungeon. Everybody was on his or her feet, shouting, laughing and embracing one another. Heavy footsteps sounded and a group of revolutionary fighters rushed into the building. They knocked the lock off the cell door with their rifle butts and threw it open.

"Brothers, we have made it!" one of them shouted. "Long live the revolution!" After another round of slogan-shouting, some wept, others danced. One soldier sang an aria from a Chinese opera depicting the mood of a triumphant warrior.

"Don't go yet, don't go!" a revolutionary yelled, trying to stop the prisoners from leaving. "The Ching troops are still firing back. Don't go out and get killed. We want you to help build the Republic. . . ."

Before he finished, a man who appeared to be European pushed his way into the cell, his face dirty, his clothes torn and covered with powder burns. He was in tatters, but Ding Fei recognized him immediately.

"Sam!" she called, rushing toward him, arms outstretched.

A few people quickly stepped aside to avoid being knocked down. Now all the attention was on Ding Fei and the foreigner. In stunned silence, they watched the couple fling their arms around each other and kiss. Some had never seen anything like that before—rubbing noses in the daytime in plain sight of everybody.

"Sam," Ding Fei said, taking a breath. "I thought I would never see you again! You look like a ghost. What did you do?"

"Taught some dumbbells how to use explosives. One fellow blundered, two explosives went off prematurely. Thank God it's over! The success is a miracle! Nobody expected it . . ."

"It was no miracle, sir," the revolutionary chimed in. "We infiltrated the Ching troops. A regiment mutinied, the Viceroy and the garrison commander fled in panic. Everything was well planned in advance. No revolution can succeed without sweat and blood and well-thought-out plans." He stopped to listen. Outside, drums and gongs could be heard. People were cheering.

"All right, brothers," he said. "You all can go now."

Raising his rifle over his head, he led the other fighters out, cheering and shouting slogans. The prisoners rushed out to join the celebration. Ding Fei ordered two men to carry Shun to the hospital.

The street was jammed with revolutionaries and celebrants. Firecrackers exploded and lion dancers pranced around.

Ding Fei and Sam Cohen joined a passing parade, singing revolutionary songs. Brigid also fell in, marching with the others, singing and cheering. She had never experienced such excitement and exhilaration before; she felt as though she were walking on air, her spirit soaring, oblivious to worry and pain. Before her she saw Sam Cohen, a head taller than the others, shouting at the top of his lungs, "Down with the Ching Dynasty! Long live the revolution!"

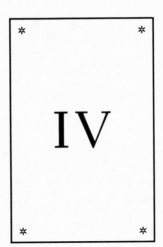

38

When Brigid returned to her modest apartment on Tung Hu Road one warm evening, she saw a note on her door. It said,

To celebrate the signing of the Treaty of Versailles and the triumphant conclusion of the brutal world war, would the charming lady honor me with her delightful company for dinner at Peter's, the horrible but the one and only American eatery in Wuhan? We might also indulge in a discussion of the follies of the earthly creatures called humans, that odd species of animal with an innate tendency toward sadism and masochism. If the above balderdash is acceptable, your humble servant will be most happy to collect his guest at 6:00 P.M. sharp on the nineteenth day of May, 1919, and let our friendship flourish through the evening and beyond. Signed, Michael D. Steward.

Brigid took down the note and smiled. She liked Steward very much and always enjoyed the "mad" journalist's company. He had been fighting stuffed shirts and stilted language all his life, and he often ridiculed them by using exaggerated language in his casual notes. He said it was the Western eight-legged essay.

Though Steward was scholarly and well read, Brigid liked him only as a friend. She sometimes felt reluctant to see him. Steward, thirty-nine, Hearst's foreign correspondent in Central China, married, with three children, had been chasing her earnestly since their meeting at the Foreign Press Club in Wuhan the year before.

Although Brigid did not find him attractive, she did find him amusing. He was a sort of intellectual clown with serious pretensions, a devoted lover of Chinese culture and Chinese women. Somewhat alcoholic, he harbored a great resentment against the wrongs done to China by the foreign powers and lately the wrongs done by the foreign powers to themselves. His articles and news reporting were often tinged with pro-China sentiments. To her, he was a true champion of the Chinese revolutionary cause, deploring the Imperial pretensions of President Yuan Shih-kai and supporting the republican aims of the provincial governments loyal to Sun Yat-sen. For that reason, she had seldom declined his invitations and tolerated the overdone and heavily spiced New York steaks at Peter's.

Many times she suspected afterward that they had dined on well-disguised water buffalo or donkey meat.

Brigid lived in a small three-room place in a two-story Western-style building in the "arty" section of Hankow, not far from the foreign concession. Steward arrived at six o'clock sharp. He had a pleasing smile, but his preoccupations often brought a frown to trouble his otherwise friendly, bearded face. Brigid had never seen him relaxed. His sarcasm was biting, and occasionally he did outlandish things to show his rebelliousness. After greeting her, he complained, "Brigid, why do you do this to me?"

"What do I do to you?" she asked, surprised.

"You always make yourself so attractive. It's cruel, you know."

Brigid laughed. She was wearing a tight new Chinese gown, a modified Manchu robe known as a cheongsam, with high slits—a new fashion that the Wuhan ladies had not yet adopted. They thought it was too revealing. "Just keep your eyes at eye-level," she said. "You'll be all right."

He planted a kiss on her cheek. "When will you let me greet you properly, Brigid?" he asked.

Without answering his question, she picked up her purse and started for the door. "Let's go."

She felt guilty for being unable to let him greet her "properly," which meant a kiss on the mouth. Steward had often looked at her like a hungry street urchin staring at food in a store window.

Riding in a hired carriage to Peter's, Steward kept glancing at her legs and swallowing. The sexual tension made him quiet and nervous. In turn it made Brigid uncomfortable.

"Speaking of balderdash," she said with a smile, trying to divert his attention from her legs, "why do you call humans the odd specimen of animals with a born tendency toward sadism and masochism?"

"We love to kill each other. If we loved each other instead, there wouldn't be constant war."

Brigid didn't want to get into a discussion about that. "By the way," she said, "I have a performance tonight. The curtain is eight-thirty. If you don't mind seeing Ibsen's *A Doll's House* in Chinese, you're invited."

"Five horses couldn't keep me from going," he said, squeezing her hand. "Chinese saying. What part do you play—Mrs. Warren?"

"What Mrs. Warren?"

He snapped his fingers. "Sorry. I got it mixed up with *Mrs. Warren's Profession*. Aren't you a bit too young for Nora?"

"Thanks, but the audience doesn't seem to think so. Anyway, being a ham, I'm grateful for the chance."

"Haven't you thought of doing a play in English? *Mrs. Warren's Profession* would pack the house."

"What house? Where?"

"The Foreign Legation, of course. Most of the foreign devils don't understand Chinese. It would be marvelous to provide them with some cultural entertainment. So far their pastimes have been limited to cricket, horse racing and sport in bed."

"Who is going to produce it?" Brigid said. "It takes a lot of money to mount a play, you know."

"I know how to get it mounted. All I have to do is corner one of those profiteering Imperialists in the foreign concession. And voilà, there will be a play."

"I'll think about it." She looked away, a bit amused by Steward's constant swallowing.

Peter's was crowded with Americans and Europeans. It was smoky, the air heavy with cigar smell and men's cologne. Because of the shortage of water in Wuhan, men had reduced their baths to two a week and perfume was used instead.

Steward took her to a corner table, greeting acquaintances as they wove between small tables covered with spotless white linen tablecloths. Everybody seemed to be talking about the Treaty of Versailles.

Steward ordered a bottle of red Bordeaux with their food and proposed a toast. "Let's make this a double celebration," he said, raising his glass. "Kan pei—bottoms up!"

"Why a double celebration?"

"In China, you have red happiness and black happiness. One is a wedding, the other is death. You celebrate both. . . ."

"Who is getting married?"

Before he answered, a fat American with bushy hair and a wrinkled tweed suit came over, grabbed a chair and sat down beside Brigid. "Michael, you lucky dog," he said, switching his bulging eyes between them. "Where did you meet such a delicate Ming vase? How about an introduction?"

Steward grudgingly introduced them. George Gordon was a reporter from a Philadelphia paper. He had just finished his dinner and his mouth was still greasy from Peter's famous steak. Brigid refused to let him kiss her hand but accepted his limp handshake. Gordon was loud and laughed constantly. "What do you think of the Versailles Treaty, Michael?"

"It stinks. The death knell for humanity."

"I knew you would say that," Gordon said with a laugh. "That's your standard remark. But I agree with you this time. It gives practically everything the Germans owned in Shantung to the Japanese. China got rid of a fox and got a wolf instead."

Steward wasn't keen about discussing China's problems with Gordon and responded with only a few indifferent grunts. But Brigid was interested and asked why the peace settlement with the defeated Germans had so much to do with China.

Gordon talked like a schoolteacher lecturing a pretty but not-too-bright pupil. He said that Shantung had been a German concession. Now that Germany had lost the war, China was entitled to regain the territory. But at the peace conference, the Japanese, free at last of the Czarist incubus, had manipulated the Allies and made them hand Shantung over to Japan. Woodrow Wilson had objected but had finally caved in under pressure.

By the time Gordon had finished his lecture, Steward had consumed several glasses of wine. Somewhat tipsy, he refilled his glass, rose to his feet and shouted, "Ladies and gentlemen, may I propose a toast to celebrate a double occasion: the signing of the Versailles Treaty and the rape of Shantung! America, by conspiring with the other Western powers, has betrayed China and sold the country down the river! Let's celebrate the Allied victory in Europe and the death of integrity at the conference table. Bottoms up!" With the wine dripping down his chin, he finished his drink in one big gulp, then smashed his glass on the floor. "Ladies and gentlemen, I hereby disavow my loyalty to Mr. Wilson, one of the butchers of China!"

The other diners all turned their heads away, looking embarrassed. George Gordon sneaked away quietly.

Brigid got up quickly and picked up her purse. "I have to rush, Michael. I have a performance, remember?"

"I'm sorry, Brigid," Michael said, throwing some bills on the table. "I meant to tell you everything after dinner, but that big mouth spilled it too soon. I hope it didn't spoil your dinner."

Brigid pushed her empty plate toward him. "Not at all. I enjoyed every bite of your American coolie food!"

*

They arrived at the Kunming Theater an hour before curtain time. Brigid rushed to her tiny dressing room while Steward went to do some errands, promising to return shortly before the play began.

Mrs. Wang, Brigid's assistant, helped her with her makeup and change of clothing. They had studied theater together at the Drama Department of Wuhan University. Eight years after the Wuhan uprising, Brigid had realized her ambition of becoming a stage actress. But the less ambitious Mrs. Wang wound up in somebody else's dressing room.

They enjoyed the usual chitchat, with the plump and amiable Mrs. Wang doing most of the talking. In the distance, they could hear what sounded like someone shouting slogans.

"What can that be?" Mrs. Wang asked, helping Brigid into her costume. "Sounds like student rioting again, doesn't it?"

"I haven't heard students riot for quite a while," Brigid said. "I almost forgot what it sounds like."

"I'll never forget," Mrs. Wang said. "My son participated in every riot during the past five years. Thank God the revolution is over! The only memento of his riot days is his cracked voice."

Brigid listened to her quietly, wishing Mrs. Wang were a little less talkative and a lot less repetitious.

The play had proved a success. Because she had been acting in it for almost three months now, she could do the performance automatically. Sometimes she searched the audience for familiar faces. She secretly prayed that one day she would spot the right face, one she had been longing to see all these years. In her daydreams she saw his handsome visage beaming at her from the front row, his clear, deep-set eyes fixed on hers, radiating love and tenderness. In her imagining she could hardly control her desire to leap off the stage, fall into his arms and smother him with kisses.

While Brigid took a bow during the curtain call that night, her mind still kept wandering. She imagined she was having dinner with Bo Ho in her favorite restaurant, where she showed him off to her friends. During the second curtain call, she desperately searched the audience, but when she saw Steward in the third row, giving her a standing ovation, applauding wildly and yelling "Bravo!" her heart sank.

After the final bow she withdrew to her dressing room quickly, feeling a terrible letdown. The props, the grubby backstage and the tiny cluttered dressing room—all reminded her of the daily grind. She quickly changed into her street clothes, dreading what lay ahead. In a little while she would face a cold night and an empty apartment. The only prospect was Michael Steward, who might drop in and offer to take her for a midnight snack at the Cricket Club, where at least they served good coffee.

Trying to stop Mrs. Wang's ceaseless talk about her son, Brigid asked, "Why did the students make such a racket tonight?"

"Who knows?" Mrs. Wang said, shaking her head. "Maybe they have itchy throats—just like my son a few years ago. Thank Heaven he finally married a good woman who does not believe in all that foolishness. She pinned him down and demanded that he raise a family instead. She is expecting her third child now, bless her."

While Mrs. Wang was chuckling, Michael Steward knocked on the dressing room door and walked in with a bouquet of roses.

"I love roses!" Brigid exclaimed, planting a quick kiss on Steward's lips. He looked surprised. He wanted to return the kiss but was stopped by Mrs. Wang.

When they left the theater it was still early. Outside, the air was cool and the half-moon bright above the Wuhan rooftops. The street was still crowded with pedestrians, strolling, shopping and hunting for pleasure. Wuhan, the second-largest city after Shanghai, the Chicago of China, was growing prosperous. Refugees, profiteers, foreigners, prostitutes and thieves all flooded to the big tri-city to find misery or fortune.

Brigid walked leisurely among the crowds, her right arm resting loosely on Steward's.

"What amuses you?" Brigid asked when Steward chuckled.

"The Chinese saying about a guy who hasn't tasted goat meat but already smells like a goat."

"You one-track-minded devil," Brigid said, pulling her arm away.

As they turned into Hankow Road, the main thoroughfare, they saw people running. Many of the stores had been closed, and the owners of others were frantically taking down their signs and boarding their doors. They could again hear shouting. Presently groups of students holding anti-Japanese placards marched by.

"Down with the Japanese bandits! Down with the American Imperialists! Boycott those who sell their goods! Burn their merchandise!"

Brigid and Steward quickly backed into a doorway. After the noisy groups were gone, they walked quietly to Brigid's apartment. They did not speak until after Brigid had unlocked her door.

"Good night, Michael," she said. "And thanks for the roses."

"It's a shame!" Steward said, his voice low but tinged with anger. "Since the Boxer Rebellion, America has been sympathetic with China, championing China's right and independence. Now a stroke of Mr. Wilson's pen wipes out everything. I hope it doesn't affect our friendship."

"Why should our friendship be tied to the Versailles Treaty?"

"I hope you really feel that way, Brigid," he said. Looking depressed, he turned and walked away without saying goodnight.

39

The sun had set behind the forlorn cluster of low houses. Stopping at a crossroad, Hu Yin contemplated the distant scenery, wondering what this desolate little village had to offer that evening. He could almost smell the cooking. A hot dinner at a small inn would be good, perhaps with a jar of warm wine to go with it. But the lone leafless tree outside the village, silhouetted against the flaming sky, made him hesitate. The tree was dead, another sign of the famine that had devastated the northern plains for decades.

He remembered what Master Hu had told him years ago: "Never enter a village that has dead trees." Master Hu should know. He had grown up in famine areas in the north.

"A hot chicken dinner?" Master Hu had once said outside a village with dead trees during their traveling days. "Yes, the innkeeper might serve you a chicken dinner. More likely he will call it a rabbit dinner, for in the famine country nobody has seen a chicken in years. When you are wondering why the meat tastes so funny, you might also find a few human fingernails in it. Have you ever seen a rabbit with human fingernails?"

Hu Yin shuddered. Master Hu's voice still rang in his ears. He quickly turned into the small dirt road that led to the barley fields. Some shoots were growing, indicating that the famine was not so bad this year. Even so, he was not about to go to the village looking for a chicken dinner.

In the past he and Master Hu had often stayed in temples. In the countryside there were all kinds of temples—temples for Kwanyin, for the god of wealth, for Confucius, for regional gods. Every village had a regional god, like a district magistrate who oversees people's welfare. Master Hu had always preferred the temples of such gods, where there were no keepers, no priests or monks to demand rent in the name of incense money. Besides, there were always food offerings on the altar that one could eat without wondering what it was.

"Free food and free rent," Master Hu had said. "No lice, no bedbugs or mosquitoes. What more can you ask?"

*

The ancient, dilapidated temple was large; in fact too large for a regional god. The characters over the entrance had faded away. Perhaps it was a Confucian temple. Despite their bare limbs, a few old pine trees in front of the temple were still alive. A flock of crows took off noisily from the trees as Hu Yin approached the building.

He mounted the cracked stone steps and knocked on the peeling door of the temple. He hoped there was no keeper. Famished, he also hoped there were food offerings on the altar. Hu Yin studied the façade of the temple. He liked the elaborate carvings—a wooden crane with a long beak perched below the eaves, symbolizing longevity. On each corner of the roof, a fierce stone lion guarded the building. There were hideous figures on the walls, faded and worn by time. There were mythical creatures, half man–half animal, painted on the walls to frighten evil spirits. A pretty safe place to spend the night, he decided.

He knocked on the gate once more. No response. "Good," he said, and pushed at the double doors, which opened slowly with a loud squeal. Several dark objects darted at him like little cannonballs. He ducked quickly and they shot out the door, flapping their wings, narrowly missing his head. Bloodsucking bats.

There were several idols on the altar—it was one of the rare temples that had a collection of gods. He struck a match and lit a half-burned red candle. A few sticks of incense were still burning in the incense urn in the middle of the long offering table. He looked for food offerings but there were none.

"No disaster," he said philosophically with a shrug. He slipped the bundle off his shoulders and dropped it on the ground. He could identify the goddess of mercy in the middle, flanked by the two gods of wealth, one good looking and the other ugly. The other ugly god was probably Chungkwei, the ghost chaser. He had a dark face with bulging eyes and a full beard. Sitting beside him was a goddess with almond eyes. She might be the baby goddess or the lotus goddess; both had the power to send babies to earth.

Hu Yin studied the row of figures and gave them a collective bow in lieu of rent. He had decided to spend the night directly below the altar. Leaving ten coppers of incense money under the urn, he lighted a few more sticks of incense to ward off mosquitoes.

He made a bed, using his well-folded army uniform as a pillow. He kept the uniform neat with the right creases. It was his passport and meal ticket. Wearing it, he could get almost anything free, for the civilians were always afraid of soldiers, especially officers. At twenty-nine, he was a captain, a pretty awesome rank.

During the past ten years, Hu Yin had had many ups and downs; but on the whole he had done well despite the disappointments. He had joined a secret society and had participated in the revolutionary uprising in Shantung Province. He had risen to the rank of captain in Warlord Chang Tso-ling's army in Manchuria. He had marched to Peking with the warlord, who had a secret ambition to become the President of the Republic. Because of his height and good physique, Hu Yin had become a member of Warlord Chang's ceremonial guards.

All China's warlords wanted to be President of the Republic—the bandit warlords from Manchuria, the gentleman warlords from the central plains, the Christian warlords from the north, the fabric-salesman warlord Tsao Kwen, and many other lesser men, including President Yuan's own generals. But Hu Yin only laughed at them. He thought that only one man —Dr. Sun Yat-sen—should be President of China.

He was bitterly disappointed with the revolution. Ten years after the founding of the Republic, the Manchu Imperial family was still living in the Forbidden City: the boy Emperor, Pu Yi, now a teenager, was still treated like an emperor, riding his fancy bicycle and kicking rubber balls next door to the President's office, as though the country were ruled by two governments. Meanwhile, hordes of warlords were waiting in the wings like hungry wolves, ready to pounce.

Chang had recently sent Hu Yin to his son, Marshal Chang Hsueh-liang. Hu Yin liked the good-looking Young Marshal, a man of action who played golf instead of mahjong and who danced the foxtrot instead of smoking opium. But when Hu Yin discovered that the Young Marshal was in fact an opium addict, he became disillusioned.

If he could work for Sun, Hu Yin would certainly resign from the Young Marshal's army. He disliked the freezing weather of the northeast; he hated the Japanese, who were everywhere in Manchuria, walking with a swagger and kicking Chinese on the street. Everybody in Manchuria called the Japanese bandit dwarfs behind their backs. He hoped that someday someone would kick them out, chop the heads off the warlords and put the country back in order. Perhaps Sun Yat-sen was the man. Heaven knew that none of the warlords then effectively running China was.

The more Hu Yin reflected about the comical President and the warlords, the more he felt compelled to go south to Canton to serve Sun Yat-sen.

✳

Hu Yin was awakened that night by a strange noise. He sat bolt upright.

"Heh, heh, heh . . ." Someone was chuckling nearby.

Hu Yin grabbed his revolver from under his shirt, his eyes searching the darkness. "Who's there?"

"Me, Elder Brother," a low, cracked voice said. "Ease your mind. I am no ghost, just another traveler. . . ."

Hu Yin squinted. A few feet away, sitting on the ground in the semidarkness, was a large man, his legs tucked under him, his back resting against the wall. He was almost in rags, chuckling and taking swigs from a wine bottle. "A drunk," Hu Yin thought, putting his gun away. He lay down again, turned toward the altar and tried to go back to sleep.

"Well, Elder Brother," the man said again, "any food to spare?"

"No," Hu Yin said irritably. But he remembered that he still had a bun left. He fished it out of his bag and tossed it to the man, thinking that if he did not give it to him, the drunk would probably steal it anyway. Besides, when traveling it was always a good idea to make friends. It had been Master Hu's motto.

"Thank you, Elder Brother," the man said cheerfully, eating the bun noisily. "Good food. I haven't eaten anything made of white flour in years. Quite a treat. Much obliged!"

Hu Yin was quiet. He wanted to tell him to shut up and go to sleep, but on second thought he changed his mind. No use offending the man after he had just bought his goodwill with a bun. He turned and tossed, trying to sleep, but soon he heard the man chuckling again.

"What are you laughing about?" Hu Yin asked, trying to sound as polite as possible.

"You would laugh, too, if I told you, Elder Brother. Call me Ah Hung, milk name Iron Rooster. What's yours?"

"Ah Hu," Hu Yin said.

"Now, Ah Hu," Iron Rooster said, "we are brothers, both down on our luck. Correct? But I am not a beggar. I have done a lot of things in my life, but never robbed a blind man or a cripple, just a few rich rotten officials. Killed a few, too. Do you want to hear my funny story?"

"No, I don't!" Hu Yin said. "Another time."

"Sure, another time then."

There was a moment of silence. Suddenly the man chuckled again. "Wei, Elder Brother, do you want to make some money?"

"No, thank you," Hu Yin said. Then he turned and added, "How?"

"Rob a grave," Iron Rooster said.

"No, thank you," Hu Yin said, pulling the cover over his head.

"It's the grave of Tsu Hsi, the Empress Dowager, Elder Brother. You can throw away the gold and silver bars and keep the pearls and diamonds. You can become a very rich man."

Hu Yin ignored the man. He knew that Imperial tombs were built like fortresses. It would take army engineers to open them.

"Have you heard of General Sun Tien-ying?" Iron Rooster asked. "He wants to rob the Empress Dowager's grave. He is recruiting soldiers to do the job."

Hu Yin knew that Sun Tien-ying was a warlord who was famous for looting the rich. Since there were not many living rich to bother with, he could have decided to rob the dead.

"Robbing the dead is supposed to be kept a secret, mind you," Iron Rooster went on. "We are supposed to join the warlord's army only for good pay and smart new uniforms."

"How do you know all that?" Hu Yin asked.

"I am one of those who have long ears," Iron Rooster said. "No more questions. Just get up early tomorrow and follow me. I am telling you all this because you are a friendly fellow. One day you might do me a good turn."

✳

Next morning Hu Yin was awakened by Iron Rooster's loud snore. He glanced at his watch. Ten o'clock. People might arrive at any moment to pray for sick relatives or to shake the fortune holder to see which fortune sticks would fall out. He leaped up and gave Iron Rooster a kick in the behind.

Iron Rooster stretched, yawned, coughed and asked what time it was. Hu Yin told him.

"Terrible, terrible! We should have been there before dawn!"

"Then hurry up!" Hu Yin ordered, hiding his bedding and clothes behind the altar. Judging from the thick cobwebs, he knew that nobody had ever used the little space. Perhaps nobody had even looked behind there. Iron Rooster had nothing except the clothes on his back. He took off his padded coat and shook it vigorously a few times. It occurred to Hu Yin that the fleas shaken out of his coat were probably all this man was going to leave behind.

He followed Iron Rooster to a little valley in the hills about two miles away. The place was surrounded by brush and half-dead trees. Soldiers could be heard drilling in the distance, shouting, "One, two, three, one, two, three . . . kill, kill, kill!" In the desolate little valley some coolies had gathered. They were standing in a circle, listening to a tall, thick-necked officer's instructions. Judging from his collar insignia, the man was probably a captain in the warlord's engineering battalion. A dozen soldiers holding bayoneted rifles were patrolling the hills. When one of them saw two men approaching, he shouted, "Halt!"

"We have come to join the new army, Your Excellency," Iron Rooster said with a broad smile and a low bow.

"You are late!"

"Sorry, Your Excellency. My brother here and I have a sick mother . . ."

"Hurry up, you turtles' eggs!" the soldier shouted, gesturing for them to pass.

Saluting the soldier, Iron Rooster scrambled down the hill and joined the fifty-odd coolies in the valley. Hu Yin followed. The officer in the center of the circle ignored them and kept talking.

"When you have finished the job, I want all of you to come back here to collect your pay, understand?"

The coolies nodded and grunted in response. One of them asked, "No uniforms? No guns?"

"You are going to dig a grave this morning," the officer said. "Military drill starts tomorrow."

"Digging all day?" another coolie asked.

"Yes," the officer said, glaring at him. "For thirty yuan a month, what else do you expect? Sitting under a tree picking your teeth? Now, get your canvas bag, the tools, and go to work!"

There were piles of picks, shovels, Chinese hoes and canvas bags. The coolies picked them up and followed the officer to a large tomb a short distance away behind a hill. The area was surrounded by ancient pines and a stone wall. The impressive entrance was decorated with a yellow pagoda roof, complete with lucky sayings engraved over the door and on the sides. Two mythical lions sitting on pedestals guarded it.

The officer ordered two of the coolies to break down the red-lacquered front door. They swung their picks and the brittle door crumbled easily. But inside there was another, made of rock. It was so thick that several coolies failed to make even a dent in it, let alone break it.

The officer decided to dynamite it. He ordered the coolies to dig two holes near the door. Two soldiers buried a stick of dynamite in each hole and another one sent up a flare into the sky. Presently, guns were heard in the distance: the warlord's artillery battalion had started practicing, to drown out the noise from dynamite explosions.

As the big guns boomed, the dynamite was ignited and two blasts rocked the area, sending rocks and dirt sky-high. After the debris had settled and the coolies and soldiers had emerged from cover, they found the stone door demolished. But inside there was another. The engineers repeated the process until three more stone doors had been breached. It was a well-planned operation.

When the coolies had removed the debris, they found the tunnel. It was dark and long, with stone steps going down to an underground chamber. The officer went in with half a dozen soldiers holding torches. The coolies followed.

Hu Yin and Iron Rooster, each carrying a pick, were among the first to enter the tomb. Some of the coolies prayed and asked Heaven's forgiveness for having entered this sacred place.

Inside the chamber, the first thing they saw was an enormous redlacquered coffin placed on a stone dais, surrounded by solid stone walls on which lucky sayings were engraved and painted red.

Below the lucky sayings were stacks of treasure boxes of various sizes, some containing satin and silk robes, others gold and silver bars. After the treasure boxes were removed, the officer ordered the coolies to smash the lid of the coffin, but none was willing to do so. Some even knocked their heads on the ground, begging to be excused. They had come to join the army, not to rob the dead.

Disgusted, the officer asked for volunteers. Hu Yin and Iron Rooster raised their hands. "Good!" the officer shouted. "Do it! We have wasted enough time!"

After spitting on their hands, Hu Yin and Iron Rooster hacked at the coffin with their picks. The lid broke easily. To everyone's surprise, the body inside was well preserved. Tsu Hsi appeared almost alive, her skin tight and her flesh supple. Although pale, she looked peaceful. Her eyes were closed and her hands were folded on her stomach. The body smelled of lime and camphor. It was gaudily dressed in an elaborately embroidered gold dragon robe and was practically buried in glittering treasure—diamonds, pearls, jade and other precious stones, many of them exquisitely carved.

The fifty-odd coolies, each with a canvas bag tied to his waist, started filling the bags, making nasal noises of surprise and awe. A few refused to look at the corpse, believing it would bring bad luck. Hu Yin and Iron

Rooster worked fast, scooping up shiny jewels with their quick hands.

"Hurry, hurry!" the officer kept shouting. He and the soldiers also refused to look at Tsu Hsi's body, thus allowing the coolies to slip a few things into their pockets.

Knowing that more precious stones had been stuffed inside Tsu Hsi's body, the officer ordered the coolies to dig into Tsu Hsi's mouth, nostrils and ears for them. Again nobody was willing and again Hu Yin and Iron Rooster volunteered.

As they tried to pry the Empress Dowager's mouth open, her skin tore easily and her flesh crumbled in their hands like soft dough. By the time several large red pearls were removed from her mouth, part of her face was destroyed. The peaceful Tsu Hsi began to look gruesome.

It took almost an hour to remove all the treasure from the coffin. Most of the coolies' canvas bags were full. They filed out of the tomb, some looking sick and pale, a few murmuring prayers. The officer and the soldiers, still avoiding looking at Tsu Hsi, hastily withdrew from the chamber. While leaving, one of the soldiers reminded the coolies to regroup in the valley to receive their pay.

Outside the tomb, the coolies talked excitedly, some laughing and some still praying. They rushed toward the valley. Hu Yin and Iron Rooster were the last to come out of the tomb. But instead of following the others, Hu Yin tugged at Iron Rooster's sleeve and jerked his head, indicating that they should take another path. Iron Rooster, looking bewildered, started to speak, but Hu Yin hushed him.

"Just follow me," he whispered.

He quickly ducked behind some bushes and disappeared. Iron Rooster followed him reluctantly, shaking his head. Inside the brush, Hu Yin threw himself down.

"Stay low!" he said. Iron Rooster obeyed, lying down beside him. When he attempted to speak, Hu Yin again hushed him. They stayed quietly in the bushes until all the coolies had left the area.

"All right, we can come out now," Hu Yin said, climbing to his feet.

Iron Rooster got up with a sigh. "Ah! Let's get going, Elder Brother."

Hu Yin grabbed him. "What are you doing? This area is surrounded by Sun Tien-ying's soldiers. Come here and watch." He cautiously climbed to the top of a hill and hid himself behind a large bush. "Look down there," he said.

Iron Rooster crouched beside him and peeked through the leaves. In the valley, the coolies were returning the tools to one group of soldiers and handing their canvas bags to another. After the soldiers had collected the tools and the treasure bags, they started searching the coolies. Some protested, but the soldiers smashed at them with the butts of their rifles. They took all the stolen treasures out of the coolies' pockets and tossed them into a large bamboo basket held by a grinning officer.

In the distance beyond the hills, other soldiers were still drilling, making a lot of noise. Besides rifle shots, machine guns also rattled. Soon the coolies were herded into a tight group. Hu Yin saw the officer talk to them briefly. Then he ran up a hill, gesturing wildly. The soldiers followed him. Suddenly machine-gun fire flashed from a hilltop, followed by a loud rattle that sounded like firecrackers at a New Year's celebration. The coolies scattered frantically, screaming, trying to escape. There were more flashes of machine-gun fire from another hill. More coolies fell. *Tet tet tet . . . tet tet tet,* several more machine guns rattled from nearby hills. The massacre lasted only a few minutes. To make sure that all the coolies were dead, one of the machine gunners sprayed more bullets into the scattered bodies.

Hu Yin and Iron Rooster hid in the brush until the soldiers had left the valley, carrying the tools and the loot but leaving the dead behind. In the distance the drilling and marching went on, but the gunfire had stopped.

"We can't go yet," Hu Yin said.

Iron Rooster looked pale and sick. It took him a while to find his voice. "Elder Brother," he said chokingly, "you saved my life. How did you know those turtles' eggs would shoot us?"

"For one thing," Hu Yin said, wiping the sweat off his face, "no warlord would pay new recruits thirty yuan a month. Three yuan is the going rate. Number two, they know we are all thieves. Three—dead men don't talk."

"Curse their mothers!" Iron Rooster spat. "I never thought of that. Did you steal some?"

Hu Yin patted the bag tied around his waist. "This is what I stole."

"Didn't you put some in your pockets?"

"Why would I do a stupid thing like that?"

"You're right," Iron Rooster said, shaking his head sadly. "None of the poor devils got away with anything. I thought I was clever. I thought nobody would know where I hid mine."

"Where did you hide yours?"

Iron Rooster patted his belly. "Here. I swallowed them. Now I'm going to have a bellyache for a week."

"Look at it this way, Iron Rooster," Hu Yin said sympathetically. "You're still alive."

"Yes, yes," Iron Rooster said with a bitter grin. "Elder Brother, you are smart. I owe you my life."

"Help me collect some rocks," Hu Yin said, picking up rocks the size of goose eggs.

"What for, Elder Brother?"

"To kill some rabbits for food. We have to stay here for a few days until it's safe to leave."

"You're right, Elder Brother," Iron Rooster said with a groan. "Oh, my bellyache! It's coming." Grimacing, he stooped to pick up the rocks.

✻

They roasted a rabbit in a little clearing in the hills. Hu Yin had killed a dozen rabbits and some lizards with rocks. His aim was so deadly that he might have exterminated the entire rabbit and lizard population in the area.

"Curse their grandmothers!" Iron Rooster said, tearing meat off a rabbit leg like a savage. "One of these days I'm going to kill that bandit Sun Tien-ying. Wei, Elder Brother, did you ever kill a man?"

Hu Yin decided to tell him the truth. That would earn more respect from somebody like Iron Rooster. "Yes, I did," he said, swallowing a mouthful of rabbit meat and wishing he had some salt.

"Who did you kill?"

"One Stroke Cha. I also sent a few of his followers to the ghost world along with him so he wouldn't feel lonely."

"One Stroke Cha?" Iron Rooster exclaimed, his eyes bulging with surprise and admiration. "Did you really kill One Stroke Cha?"

"Like this," Hu Yin said, making a sweeping gesture with a hand. "His head rolled like a melon."

Without another word, Iron Rooster threw himself on the ground and gave Hu Yin three kowtows.

"What's that for?"

"Anybody who chopped the head off One Stroke Cha deserves my kowtows. You are Number One, Elder Brother. You are the greatest!" He was about to kowtow some more, but Hu Yin stopped him.

After that, Iron Rooster treated Hu Yin as his master, bowing and serving him berries and frogs' legs. He even offered to wash Hu Yin's clothes in a nearby creek, but Hu Yin declined.

They spent several more days in the wilderness until they had eaten all the animals and were beginning to starve. For two more days they ate insects, grass roots and tree bark. Meanwhile, Sun Tien-ying's troops continued drilling and marching. Hu Yin and Iron Rooster could hear their battle cry: "Kill, kill, kill!"

On the sixth day Iron Rooster disappeared. When Hu Yin found him gone, he quickly examined the contents of his treasure bag. Nothing was missing. "Not a bad turtle's egg," he said with a smile.

On the eighth day the drilling stopped. About noon a single shot rang out. It echoed in the valley. Hu Yin tensed, knowing that Iron Rooster had joined the coolies in the other world. Somehow he missed the man. "Some people are just not destined to be rich," he thought, shaking his head sadly.

*

That night he decided to visit the tomb again. He had been told that in Imperial tombs the dead Manchu's platform shoes were ordinarily stuffed with rare pearls. He remembered that Tsu Hsi had worn such shoes and the warlord's soldiers had ignored them.

It was a chilly night. The bright full moon was shining on the pine hills, but on the horizon an ominous dark cloud was looming, with an occasional lightning flash across the sky. Insects were singing loudly, drowning out the crunching noise his shoes made as he waded through the dead grass and dried brush. Outside Tsu Hsi's tomb, the debris was still scattered around, giving the area a haunted look.

He entered the tunnel cautiously, holding a torch that he had made from tree branches and twigs—which attracted a lot of flying insects.

Inside the chamber a putrid smell suddenly choked him, and several huge rats scattered away from his feet as he approached the red-lacquered coffin. Nothing had changed except for the smell and the rats. The ground was still littered with broken boxes and torn fabric: the coolies had done a thorough job looting the place. He surveyed the damage and shook his head sadly. If Tsu Hsi's spirit knew what had happened, he thought, she certainly would have turned in her coffin.

When he raised the torch and looked into the coffin, he shuddered. Tsu Hsi had not turned, but she had become horribly different. Her broken face had grown fuzzy white hair almost half an inch long. There were large gaping holes in her cheeks and neck, probably gnawed by the rats. The stench was overpowering.

Hu Yin was so shocked that he froze for a moment. Then, regaining his senses, he began to back away. Tsu Hsi's grotesque skull with the rotting flesh and white hair seemed to stare at him. Shuddering, he tossed the torch into the coffin and ran. Climbing out of the tomb three steps at a time, he felt a chill running down his spine and goose pimples crawling over his body. Spitting repeatedly, he ran all the way back to the hills.

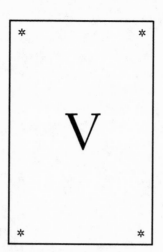

V

40

Wuhan was an ugly triple-city in 1925. To Brigid, Hankow was like a playboy—gay, fun-loving and hungry for money; Wuchang was a politician, poor, tricky and unclean, infested with lice and other vermin; Hanyang was a workaholic, industrious but sloppy, terribly dreary and humorless. But Brigid found herself growing used to Wuhan. Like a mother who had adopted an ugly child, she couldn't help loving him a little after so many years.

She considered herself lucky, living fairly comfortably in a nice district in Hankow, having many friends and enjoying what she was doing professionally—acting. The troupe was doing well. In spite of misery, disease and poverty, the cultural life of the city was still in existence, nourished by the Wuhan intellectuals, who wore threadbare clothes and skipped meals to save money for a theater ticket or a book.

Brigid had met many of them. They congregated in teahouses and reading rooms in the YMCA and YWCA. Money was always tight, but the theater owner, Mr. Lung, was a good patron of the arts. The troupe couldn't have survived without the five-hundred-seat theater, which Mr. Lung rented to them for a dollar a month on one condition: Lily Han, Mr. Lung's adopted daughter (or mistress), must appear in a play at least twice a year. Miss Han was no actress; in fact, her overacting was so horrible as to be ludicrous.

Still, the members of the troupe pampered her, not only because she was the *rice in the pot* but because she was also fun to be around, with her practical jokes. Moreover, by playing a poor hand of mahjong, she gave everybody a chance to win some pocket money.

Brigid was the only one who refused to play mahjong. She would rather spend the time practicing the piano or ballet at the YWCA or sitting on the roof terrace of her apartment building, sunbathing and daydreaming. She had many suitors—military men, politicians, merchants, soldiers of fortune, smugglers, cutthroats from secret societies, entrepreneurs and pseudointellectuals—including Mr. Lung, the theater owner. The rich ones were fat and the poor ones thin, and most of them were married.

Among her other suitors were many foreigners. Some of them were serious. Michael Steward had disappeared for a while. When he returned to Wuhan, he claimed that he had finally obtained a divorce from his pleasant but unfortunately frigid wife. But the divorce had not changed anything. Brigid still refused to be "greeted properly." But Steward's patience was as long-lasting as his infatuation.

Brigid still found him amusing, especially when he misquoted mildewed Chinese wisdom. Of all her suitors, he was one of the few she could tolerate. Most of the time she found her women friends less taxing, and there was no ulterior motive in their friendship. Over thirty, she was still a prude, refusing to have casual sex with anyone.

For years she and Ding Fei had met for lunch and gone to parties together. But since the death of Dr. Sun Yat-sen in Peking that year they had seldom seen each other. Ding Fei had accompanied Madame Sun, the former Miss Sung Chin-ling, to the funeral. Dr. Sun's death had hit both of them hard. After the funeral, they had mourned their loss and nursed their anguish together. Ding Fei had said that in all her life she had admired only two people—Dr. Sun Yat-sen and Madame Sun.

Brigid missed Ding Fei's companionship and the stormy days during the revolution. Even misery, as she recalled now, had sometimes been enjoyable. She often wondered what had happened to Sam Cohen. She had once asked Ding Fei when the wedding bells would toll. Ding Fei only shrugged.

Brigid had been fascinated by the mysterious soldier of fortune, who had come and gone in China like a phantom. Sam had risked his life, not necessarily for money, and had tried a lot of things on a dare. Ding Fei had once told her that perhaps Cohen's daring had turned her off and killed her desire for a permanent commitment. The last caper was probably the straw that broke the camel's back, she said. It had happened a year earlier. A Hunan snake peddler had dared Cohen to suck fresh blood from a mutilated rattlesnake . . .

Brigid had stopped her. She didn't want to hear about it. She had once thought Cohen a serious man. The snake story made him seem childish. She didn't want to hear.

Brigid mused about these events on the roof terrace of her apartment house one hot summer day. The sun was burning her slick, oiled body. Finally she wrapped herself in her bath towel and climbed down from the roof on an almost perpendicular ladder through a square hole.

As she approached her apartment door, she saw a note, written in a bold, slapdash hand. She immediately recognized it as Michael Steward's. It was another invitation to celebrate something—he did not say what. He would come to collect her at 6:00 P.M.

Ever since Sun Yat-sen had died of cancer, the warlords had been clamoring and fighting, trying to seize power and territories, trying to wreck his republican organization, the Kuomintang. She liked to hear Michael's analysis of the chaotic situation. So she was ready on time.

For the first time, however, Steward was late. He arrived looking exhausted, his hair windblown and his tie awry. That, too, was unusual, for he always groomed himself whenever he took her out.

"What's the matter, Michael?" Brigid asked, surprised. "You look as if you have just escaped from kidnappers."

"It's not safe to go out tonight. If you don't mind, let's send for some food and eat here."

"Come on," she said with a laugh. "Tell me what kind of disaster you're predicting."

With a sigh, Steward sat down heavily on a sofa. He brushed some blond hair out of his eyes and straightened his tie. "The Russians are coming, Brigid."

"Is that a disaster?"

"Mikhail Borodin and company. All of them are Stalin's secret agents. They are here to undermine the Kuomintang government."

Brigid was not in the mood to discuss the Russians.

"Michael, I'll fix something for us to eat. But remember, I have a performance tonight. *Romeo and Juliet,* curtain eight-thirty."

In the kitchen that adjoined the small living room, she started making some sandwiches. "By the way, what kind of trouble are the Russians trying to stir up? They can't possibly start a world revolution in Wuhan."

"You just wait and see."

After the sandwiches and a quick cup of coffee, Michael accompanied Brigid to the Kwangming Theater. Somehow Brigid had made him forget the Russians and cheered him up a bit, describing the production of the play, which Professor Liang Shih-chu at Peking University had translated into Chinese. Many troupes in China's big cities had been presenting it in churches, school auditoriums and rented warehouses, for Shakespeare had almost taken the place of Confucius in modern China. Nobody really understood the Chinese blank verse, but it was fashionable to attend.

At the final curtain, as usual, Michael Steward gave Brigid a standing ovation, applauding wildly, ignoring the stares and frowns of the Chinese audience sitting near him. A few ladies giggled and some disgruntled men mumbled racial slurs. Anti-West feeling was strong after the Versailles Treaty, and even Russians had been harassed.

In these days of turmoil, everybody wanted to believe in something, like survivors in a stormy sea reaching for something to hang on to. Lenin and Marx were popular among some of the intellectuals, but the Chinese translation of Communism—*sharing property*—was scary. The average poor, who owned some livestock, were afraid that Communists might drop in, make themselves at home and say, "Wei, neighbor, let's share your hogs and chickens!" There was also a rumor: some Communists even believed in sharing people's wives. Shakespeare was much safer than Karl Marx, although he was just as hard to understand.

Mrs. Wang, Brigid's dressing room assistant, was getting more aches and pains. But she had not become less talkative. As Mrs. Wang's voice droned on meaninglessly in Brigid's ears, a welcome noise interrupted: Michael knocked briskly a few times on the open dressing room door. Entering with a large box of chocolates, he aimed his kiss at Brigid's mouth but landed on her cheek.

"Michael," she said, "why must you spend your hard-earned money? You don't have to bring me things every time, you know."

"Why shouldn't I?" he protested. "I have no family to support now."

Brigid dropped the subject quickly. Whenever Steward had a chance, he never failed to remind her that he was divorced and fancy free.

"Sit down," she said. "I won't be long. By the way, are you still learning to write Chinese?"

"Not anymore," he said with a sigh. "The teacher used the Chinese translation of Marx and Lenin as my textbook. I booted him out."

There was another knock on the door. Framed in the doorway stood a tall, muscular army officer holding his cap in one hand and with a smile on his deeply tanned broad face. He stood looking at Brigid admiringly, waiting for her to say the first word.

Brigid stared at him in stunned disbelief. After so many years the stranger had not changed much, except for his clothes. She would have recognized him anywhere in spite of his deep tan and higher brow. Quiet but no longer shy, he still had his air of honesty and devotion, although the old boyishness, mainly in his looks, had gone. Suddenly she felt like a doting sister who had found her long-lost brother.

"Hu Yin!" she cried, flying to him with open arms. She held him tightly, choking back tears.

Mrs. Wang stared at them, making gargling sounds, as though she were witnessing a miracle. After a brief introduction, Michael Steward made a polite departure. He sensed he was no match for a man whom Brigid greeted so warmly.

Brigid guided Hu Yin to the empty chair and made him sit down. When she found her voice, questions poured out.

"May God forgive you, Hu Yin, what did you do? Why did you disappear like that? Where have you been?"

Hu Yin smiled, not knowing where to begin.

"Never mind," Brigid sighed. "Just tell me where you have been. Wait, let me guess. From this tiger skin and fancy insignia, you've joined the army. A colonel, right? Which horrible warlord are you serving?"

"Marshal Chang Hsueh-liang of Manchuria. Have you heard of him?"

"Have I heard of him! He's the famous playboy son of Marshal Chang Tso-ling, who wants to be the next Emperor of China. I'm glad you're serving his son, not some bandit or dog meat warlord. How did you know I was here?"

"I saw your photo outside the theater. And I saw the play, too." He smiled.

Brigid was disappointed that Hu Yin was so relaxed and casual; he could have shown some excitement about having found her in Hankow. But then she knew that Hu Yin had always been calm, never too expressive.

"Close your eyes," she said. "Wait while I change. Then we'll discuss what we do next."

A few minutes later Brigid took Hu Yin to her apartment and plied him with tea and her favorite French pastry. She wanted to pump all the information out of him about those missing years. Hu Yin was more talkative now. His voice was deep and confident; he used refined language, sometimes he was even eloquent. Brigid was surprised at how much he had changed intellectually. He gave her a brief account of his past fifteen years. He had been a vagabond and a member of secret societies. After that he had joined the army, rising from private to major, and had recently been promoted to lieutenant colonel. He had fought in many wars, served as personal bodyguard to warlord Chang Tso-ling and President Yuan Shih-kai. Now he had orders to keep an eye on Marshal Wu Pei-fu.

"The Gentleman Warlord," Brigid said. "Why watch him?"

"We think he has great ambitions."

"Does Marshal Wu want to become Emperor?"

"Name a warlord who doesn't."

Hu Yin was not inquisitive. Brigid was again disappointed that he was not curious about her life. But, in a way, she was glad. She had done a lot of things she would rather lock up in her heart permanently.

Suddenly Hu Yin fished out a handful of jewels and offered them to her. He also said that he had just bought a house in Hankow, a vacation home of a Hupei bigwig who had been assassinated. The house was supposed to be haunted, but it was cheap.

Brigid stared at him, then glanced between his face and the glittering jewels in the palm of his hand. She was flabbergasted for a few seconds.

"What did you do? Rob a bank?"

"I robbed a grave," Hu Yin said offhandedly. "I want you to have these jewels. And you are welcome to move into my house."

"Hu Yin!" she said, shocked. "Have you become a professional grave robber? How many graves have you robbed?"

"Just one. And I won't do it again. Will you move in?"

"Thank you, but I can't. I'm happy in my little nest." She tried to change the subject. "Robbed only one grave? How can you become so rich by just robbing one grave?"

Hu Yin picked up his cap and rose. "My house is always yours," he said, his voice calm, but she could detect the touch of sadness in it. "You know how I've always felt about you, Fong Yun."

When he reached the door, she called, "Hu Yin, will we see each other again?"

Hu Yin stopped. "Of course," he said without turning his head. After he had opened the door, he turned. "Fong Yun," he said quietly, "I robbed the Empress Dowager's tomb. Everything I got from her represents people's sweat and blood."

She stared at him incredulously. Then suddenly she burst out laughing. She laughed so hard that Hu Yin began to look alarmed.

"Hu Yin, what made you do a crazy thing like that?"

Hu Yin shrugged.

Brigid suddenly felt vindicated, but she controlled a desire to fling her arms around him and kiss him for his crazy deed. Whenever she thought of Tsu Hsi, she wanted to boil her alive. She had always believed that the horrible Manchu woman had murdered her father. "I'm glad you robbed her," she said. "I'd have done it myself! Give me the jewels. I want them!"

Still laughing, Brigid cupped her hands and Hu Yin dropped them into her waiting palms.

41

B rigid still had Tang San's diamond, which had been lying in an old tea can on the top shelf in the kitchen along with Hu Yin's jewels. But what if they were stolen?

Suddenly she became concerned. If they were, she would hate herself for not having taken better care of them.

She brought the container down from the shelf, poured the contents onto the kitchen table and examined them. For the first time she discovered how beautiful Tang San's diamond was—two carats at least, perfectly cut. The jewels that Hu Yin had brought her were also lovely—large ruby and jade rings, earrings, black jade bracelets, necklaces of pink pearls and pendants of other precious stones which she could not identify. She shined each piece carefully and packed it in a brocade jewel box that one of her suitors had given her the previous Christmas.

She had no idea how much the lot was worth. She could probably retire if she sold them.

She tried several hiding places—under the bed, behind her books, in the closet, in the rice tub, in the bottom of her trunk, in the hamper under her dirty clothes. Finally, she laughed. The safest place was still in the old tea can on the kitchen shelf. Some time ago, a banker friend had said that the safest way to transport money in Wuhan was to carry it in an old paper bag.

Brigid tidied her apartment and tossed some old correspondence into the wastebasket. She still had some neglected mail, one piece of which she had not even opened. It was an invitation to a party at the Foreign Press Club, and it was for tonight. She had no idea who had sent it.

She wondered if she should go with an escort. There were so many unattached men in Wuhan that a wink from an attractive woman was enough to collect an army. But not many of the men were honorable. She decided to go alone and enjoy an evening without jealous males fighting for attention or hovering over her like bodyguards.

She thought of Hu Yin, but she doubted that he would enjoy an evening at a Press Club party. These affairs were usually attended by foreigners and sophisticated Chinese who liked to discuss politics, philosophy and European literature. Hu Yin would probably feel uncomfortable mingling with them.

*

She arrived at the party in one of her bright-colored silk cheongsams, the tight gown that was gradually becoming fashionable in Wuhan. It revealed a woman's contours very nicely, showing her best assets.

The party was in full swing when Brigid arrived. She was greeted by three smiling ladies sitting at a long table just inside the door. One of them collected her invitation, another requested her signature. When the third lady saw Brigid's name, she let out a little shriek of excitement.

"Brigid Fong Yun! The star at Kwangming Theater!"

The other two ladies responded with warm greetings and a flurry of ohs and ahs. Brigid liked the appreciation, and wrote her name again with a flourish on her little name plate.

The club was noisy and crowded. On one side of the spacious hall were several long tables loaded with food and drinks, which a horde of waiters in red uniforms were serving. On the other side was a five-man band playing dance music—five White Russian exiles in ill-fitting dark suits. Brigid had no idea how many people were attending the party, but the hall was full, some standing around, chatting and drinking, others dancing or eating little sandwiches and chunks of cheese.

"Look who's here!" someone said. Before Brigid could turn, Ding Fei hugged her. Standing beside her, puffing on a big cigar, was Sam Cohen. "How are you?" Ding Fei exclaimed. "Sorry I've been out of touch so long."

"I've been hurt," Brigid said, feigning anger.

Sam looked her up and down, appreciating her cheongsam and her pretty figure. He was well groomed and wore a tuxedo. An agreeable whiff of men's cologne greeted her as he kissed her hand.

"Come join us," Ding Fei said, dragging her to their table nearby. "Now tell me everything."

"I have too much to tell—I don't know where to begin."

"First let me apologize for the long silence," Ding Fei said.

"And for the broken promises," Brigid said reproachfully.

"Oh, yes—promises, promises. What did I promise you?"

"First you promised to introduce me to Madame Sun Yat-sen."

"Too bad. She has gone to Shanghai. She will be back. Shanghai is a horrible place, a mad world; she'll hate it. She'll sell her house and rush back to good old Wuhan before the year is out. You don't have to tell me what you have been doing, Brigid. As the old saying goes, 'Your name is like thunder, rumbling in everybody's ears.' Listen, I've got a lot of friends who are dying to meet you. Sam said if we set an introduction fee, we'll be wealthy."

"Sam," Brigid asked jokingly, "what mad deeds have you perpetrated lately?"

"I've retired from anything daring. Actually, I'm never foolhardy, only romantic."

"Do you call drinking fresh blood from a cut-up snake romantic?" Brigid asked with a wince.

"I don't know what you two have been saying about me," Sam said. "A Hunan snake peddler said that fresh snake blood is the best aphrodisiac in the world and dared me to try it. Before he cut the snake in two, I dared him to swallow it whole. By golly, he did! Five minutes later he pulled it out of his mouth and the snake was still alive. I lost a five-dollar bet, that's all. I never got to drink its blood."

Brigid leaned forward and gave him a peck on the cheek. "Sam, I've wronged you. The moment I heard about the snake story I thought you were so childish that I stopped my hero-worship. From now on I'll not jump to conclusions. By the way, who is giving this party?"

"Why should you care?" Ding Fei said. "You'll be invited everywhere. Just go and enjoy yourself." She rose and took Brigid's hand. "Come—let us introduce you to some people."

"Uh uh," Sam said quickly, wagging a finger at Ding Fei. "Not before I've had my dance with her first. After the introductions, she'll be mobbed and we probably won't see her again for the rest of the evening."

Sam and Brigid danced a foxtrot to the lively music of the five White Russian musicians. Sam was not a very good dancer—a bit too forceful in his leading and too tight in his clutch—and he always danced cheek to cheek. Brigid did not object, except that his beard scratched.

Just as they were about to begin a waltz, somebody cut in. "Michael!" Brigid exclaimed.

"You lucky dog," Sam said, giving up his partner reluctantly. Steward thanked him.

Brigid and Steward greeted each other as they waltzed away. "Do you know Sam Cohen?" Brigid asked.

"It's my business to know everybody who comes to the Press Club. But Sam Cohen is a tight-lipped turtle's egg. I don't really know him very well. Is your friend one of his mistresses?"

"Don't pump me, Michael. Tell me—were you mad at me?"

"I'm not mad. Just jealous. I've had a lot of sleepless nights. By the way, who is that lucky fellow?"

"Hu Yin? Just a long-lost friend. We're like sister and brother. Tonight I've learned not to jump to conclusions. So should you, Michael."

"I did."

They danced quietly for a while. Then Brigid asked, "Michael, who got me the invitation to this party? Did you?"

"I thought of asking you out many times, but I was afraid of your long-lost friend . . ." He stopped.

"You men are all the same, aren't you?" Brigid said with a little chuckle.

"Well, I'm glad it was a false alarm. If you don't mind, I'll continue to leave notes on your door."

"I don't mind as long as you understand it's Platonic."

Again Steward became quiet. Brigid changed the subject. "Who gave this party, Michael?"

"The Russians, who else? But they have a front, of course. The official host is supposed to be . . . listen to this: the Coordinating Committee for International Friendship and Goodwill in Central China. Quite a mouthful. Nobody had ever heard of it until the Russians borrowed it."

"Did you get me the invitation?"

"It was easy. I gave your name to the club secretary and here you are."

"I almost threw it away without opening it."

"I didn't expect you to come. I was about to leave when suddenly I saw you. Who did you come with?"

"I came by myself."

"In that case I'll change my plans. I'll stay. Shall I?"

They waltzed once more and returned to Ding Fei's table. Ding greeted Steward warmly.

"I thought you would never bring her back, Mr. Steward," she said. "May I borrow her for a few moments?"

"She's all yours," Steward said, smiling. He sat down in a chair. Sam cringed comically, as though he had been attacked by a monster. Brigid smiled. Obviously they were acquaintances, but did not care too much for each other's company.

Ding Fei took her over to a group of people who were listening with rapt attention to somebody's discourse. In the middle of a small, tight ring was a handsome man with thick eyebrows, deep-set bright eyes and a full, delicately shaped mouth. He had a warm smile; his voice was soft but firm; his words precise. When he saw Ding Fei, he interrupted himself to greet her.

"Brigid," Ding Fei said, "I want you to meet Mr. Chou En-lai."

As Chou and Brigid greeted each other, their eyes met and lingered. Brigid felt a thrill running through her; she had never met anyone who had affected her like that except Bo Ho. She wanted to listen to Chou's talk, but Ding Fei pulled her out of the ring and dragged her to another group of people who were engaged in lively conversation in Russian. Ding Fei propelled Brigid into the group and introduced her, in English, to a bear of a man.

"Brigid, I want you to meet Mr. Mikhail Borodin, alias Mikhail Mikovich Grusenberger . . ."

"No, no, no!" Borodin interrupted her quickly. "Just Mikhail Borodin. You study too much, Miss Ding." He laughed.

Borodin had a round beefy face with bushy dark hair and wore a Stalin mustache. He was dressed in a dark, rumpled suit. He always spoke in a booming voice and had a hearty laugh. He greeted Brigid with a strong handshake.

"Mr. Borodin is a political adviser from the Comintern," Ding Fei said. Then she turned to a tall lady who was standing beside him and introduced Brigid. "This is Mrs. Borodin . . ."

"No, no, no!" Borodin interrupted again. "This lady is an American reporter, Miss Anna Louise Armstrong. Just a good friend, that's all. Aha! Miss Ding, you did not study too much this time."

They all laughed. Then Borodin introduced Brigid to the rest of the crowd, two Russian correspondents, a Chinese interpreter and three more Russian advisers, one of them a large man in military uniform with two enormous red epaulets, named General Galen.

Brigid was a big attraction. The men immediately abandoned their discussion and turned all their attention to her, chatting and asking silly questions in English, which Brigid could understand only vaguely because of their thick accents. Ding Fei quickly steered her out of the circle.

"Why are we in such a rush?" Brigid asked.

"What if they start asking you to dance? Those big Russians have breaths that smell like cheap vodka and yesterday's fish dinner."

"Thanks. My first Russian encounter. I'm glad they all have short names."

"They all use aliases in China so their real names won't break our jaws. Galen's real name is . . . ready? Vasily Konstantinovich Blücher."

"Amazing that you remember it!"

"I happen to have a good memory for names. Most of the Bolsheviks were peasants, and they're terrible dancers. Besides bad breath, they stomp on your feet. They could break your toes."

Back at their table, Sam Cohen was alone, smoking and drinking beer. "Where's Michael Steward?" Ding Fei asked.

"Don't worry, he'll be back," Sam said. He pulled out chairs for both of them.

"Brigid," Ding Fei said, "everybody knows that Michael Steward has fallen under your *pomegranate skirt.*"

"What does that mean?" Brigid demanded.

"It's Steward's famous quote of an old Chinese saying, meaning that he worships you. I'm afraid he's hopelessly in love with you."

Brigid changed the subject abruptly. "Sam, where have you been? I haven't seen you for months."

"You'll never find out anything from him," Ding Fei said. "I'll tell you. Sam, may I?"

"How can I stop you, darling?" Sam said with a grin. "Guess I'll go wash my hands." He rose, lit a new cigar and left.

"You still haven't told me where you've been," Brigid said.

"A warlord invited Sam to visit him. I went along. He is in the diamond business. Sam sold him a few things and I talked him into joining the Kuomintang. We made him useful. An arrow for two vultures, so to speak. Besides, we had a good time. . . ."

Puffing on his cigar, Sam returned with a young man in a well-cut dark brown suit. "Ladies," Sam said, "may I have the pleasure of introducing my good friend Charles Hong?"

He described Hong as a businessman from Honolulu who worked for an American company that sold scrap iron to China. Hong looked more like a well-groomed college student than a businessman.

"Charlie's father donated a lot of money to Dr. Sun's revolution," Sam said. "A good friend of the Suns'."

"Scrap iron?" Brigid said. "What kind of business is that?"

"We collect junk cars and mothballed ships," Charles said. "China buys them to make weapons. Very good business."

"Family business?"

"God forbid!" Charles said. "My father is in the grocery and haberdashery business. Small potatoes compared to scrap iron. But he's old-fashioned, not very happy about my working in junk. He says he loses plenty of face. No nice Chinese girl will ever marry me."

"We'll take care of that, Charlie," Ding Fei said with a laugh. "How old are you?"

"Twenty-one."

"A young pup. Don't you worry, Charlie. Tell your father I'll see to it that in two years he'll bounce a fat little grandson on his knees."

Charles looked embarrassed; he didn't know what to say. Sam gave him an affectionate pat on the shoulder. "Well, Charlie, stick around. We'll toughen you up a bit. The first thing is to get you deflowered."

Ding Fei delivered a kick under the table and Sam stopped. "Sorry, censored!"

Brigid laughed. She always liked polite young men, a bit shy, somewhat like Hu Yin in his younger days. Just as she was about to find out more about Charles, Michael sauntered over and requested another dance.

After the waltz, Steward suggested that they go somewhere else. He said the Russians were like nails in his eyes, quoting another Chinese saying. "Besides," he added, "tomorrow is Valentine's Day. I'd like to take you somewhere for a drink."

Brigid declined the drink, so Steward suggested a cup of coffee at the Cricket Club.

"My coffee is better than the Cricket Club's," she said, and offered to make a pot.

Back at Brigid's apartment, she served coffee and French pastry. Steward fished out a little package from his coat pocket.

"For you. Happy Valentine's Day."

Brigid was surprised. He must have planned everything ahead.

"I got it a week ago, but I didn't have the nerve to give it to you."

Brigid opened the package. It was a bottle of her favorite French perfume, Chanté. She leaned across the coffee table and gave him a kiss on the forehead. "Thank you, Michael. You are always so sweet and considerate. Calculating, too, I must say." She poured a cup of coffee for him. "Tell me, what have you been doing during your absence?"

"Red-hunting."

"What?"

"There's something brewing in Wuhan. One of these days there is going to be a massacre."

Brigid laughed, knowing that Steward was getting even more paranoid. "No wonder you look so worried. What kind of massacre? This city is infested with rats and cockroaches, you know. I'm in favor of a massacre."

But Steward was dead serious. He said that the Kuomintang government was badly split. The right and left wings had been fighting. Soon a civil war would explode, and there would be bloodshed all over China. "A time bomb is ticking away, Brigid!"

"How do you know that?"

Steward said that he had gone Red-hunting with the Wuhan police the previous week. The secret police had carried out the job like a treasure hunt. They took a tortured and confessed Communist to Long Street in Wuchang, where most of the Communist underground organizations were located. Hiding in a car, the police ordered the Communist prisoner to point out and identify other Party members on the street, then the plainclothesmen jumped out, seized them and carted them away in unmarked cars.

"Have you changed sides?" Brigid asked. "You used to oppose Communism."

"I still oppose Communism, but they deserve a fair shake. Even criminals are protected by criminal laws." After a pause he added, "I'm disillusioned, that's all."

"Michael, this is not your country. Why are you so concerned?"

"China is my country! My parents were missionaries here. I was born in Shanghai. I love . . ." He stopped, his eyes becoming moist and red.

Michael's deep feeling for China touched her; he somehow reminded her of her mother—someone with a strong sense of fairness. "Michael," she said, "would you care for a drink?"

"No, thanks." He closed his eyes, trying to pull himself together.

"I still remember a short speech you made at Peter's a few years ago," Brigid said. "I thought you were a bit phony at the time. Now I know better."

He opened his eyes and stared at her, looking hurt. "In 1919," he said, "I was terribly impressed by Woodrow Wilson's Fourteen Points on the rights of self-determination for small and weak nations. I was convinced that the United States would insist that other Allied powers respect Chinese sovereignty. But when he signed the Treaty of Versailles and sold China to Japan, his hypocrisy upset me. I am sorry that you thought I was a phony."

"I've changed my mind," Brigid said. "I apologize."

Steward shook his head, pinched the bridge of his nose and sighed. "I was sympathetic with Stalin and the Bolsheviks, too—until I read about the Cheka terror. Cheka agents bayoneted, shot and beat to death half a million people and proudly announced that terror was the only cure for a country's illness. Even Lenin once said, 'Merciless mass terror must be encouraged.' That was the beginning of my revulsion to Communism." He looked up at Brigid and warned, "The same thing is going to happen to China. The Nationalists and Communists in this country are ready for a bloodbath. Millions of innocent people will die. Let me have that drink, please."

Brigid poured him a stiff drink. She looked at him sympathetically, wondering what kind of Valentine gift to give him. He was such a decent man, so adoring and yet so well behaved. How sad, she thought, that she didn't love him.

42

By early 1927, China had become even more split; the infighting between the Kuomintang's right and left—the Nationalists and the Communists—had come out into the open. Brigid wasn't alarmed until her maid, Liu Mah, asked for a long sick leave. Then she recalled having been told that if rosy-cheeked maids with robust health were suddenly sick and wanted to go home, something dangerous must be brewing.

After the Press Club party, Brigid had met Ding Fei a few more times. Ding Fei had confirmed Michael's suspicions. Two leaders were emerging in China, Chiang Kai-shek and Mao Tse-tung, the former representing the right and the latter the left. While Chiang's secret agents had been carrying out Red-hunting campaigns, the Communists had been stirring up trouble in the countryside and in the big cities, organizing strikes and demonstrations against capitalists and landlords.

Ding Fei said that the May 4 massacre of five hundred Communists in Shanghai was the beginning of an open war.

Generalissimo Chiang had organized the Nationalist government in Nanking to exclude the Communists. The political turmoil worried everyone in Wuhan. Brigid's troupe had been disbanded. She faced a bleak future. She had no job, no maid, and her savings were running low.

Presently she wrote Hu Yin a note. She said she would like to accept his offer to move in with him. She drafted the note several times, changing the wording from "move in with you," to "rent a room from you," then to "borrow a room from you," and finally settling with, "May I move into your house?," which seemed less cold and yet not intimate enough to be misleading.

For two weeks she did not hear from him. Then, while she was wondering if she should pay him a visit, a messenger arrived with his letter, apologizing for not having replied to her request sooner. He had been in and out of Wuhan and had just returned from Canton, where he had received six months of officers' training at the Whampoo Military Academy. Unfortunately, he was ready to leave Wuhan again. Accordingly he asked her to have everything packed by morning. A coolie and sedan chair would be sent to her early the next day to help her move. He might not be at home to welcome her, but a maid and a servant would be there to take care of all her needs.

Brigid marveled at Hu Yin's elegant handwriting and fluent language. Was he the same Hu Yin? It seemed only yesterday that he had tried to sell himself like a beggar on that dirty street in Peking. Today he was the owner of a house that was staffed with two servants, and he could write like a college professor.

Hu Yin's house was not big, but it stood on a nice clean street and was well constructed, with brick walls and tile roofs and a vermilion double door that was guarded by two mythical stone lions. Inside the gate was a small courtyard. The main building, which faced the courtyard gate, had two wings. Old Woo, the male servant, and his wife, Woo Mah, greeted her with low bows and escorted her to the main building.

The main hall, which doubled as the ancestral hall, living room and dining room, was furnished with unmatched, assorted furniture, some modern and some old. There was a traditional ancestral altar but no ancestral tablets, incense bowls or food offerings. Hu Yin had said that the house was haunted. Jokingly, Brigid dared the ghost to visit her at night. It would be something interesting to report to Ding Fei and Sam.

Her bedroom was behind the main hall. The best piece of furniture was the antique double bed, whose wood frame was intricately carved with birds and flowers. The bedding—quilted mattress and comforters with attached sheets—smelled of mothballs. To air the stuffy room, she threw the latticed windows open and ordered the sheets washed to get rid of the mothball smell. Woo Mah was surprised. To her, mothballs were a status symbol. All the affluent modern people used them. It meant cleanliness and hygiene, a bed without bedbugs.

Brigid learned from Woo Mah that Hu Yin slept in the east wing. It was half the size of the main building and unfurnished. Hu Yin's room, behind the middle hall, had only a mattress on the floor and an old rattan chair beside it. The room made Brigid uneasy—but Hu Yin was accustomed to a spartan life-style.

She toured the house. Most of the rooms were empty, dark, smelly and damp—almost ghostly. The servants occupied the west wing, also sleeping on the floor. Back in her own room, she unpacked and decided to make the best of it. She made a few changes, removing some of the vulgar calendar pictures from the walls. She also had some of the old furniture thrown out.

She had no idea if Hu Yin had left household money with the servants, but she decided to pay her own way. She went to a pawnshop that afternoon and tried to pawn her diamond ring. The pawnbroker, sitting high behind the six-foot-tall counter, was out of sight so the customers would not have to see him and lose face.

On tiptoe, she put the diamond ring on the counter. A moment later, a high-pitched voice offered her $500. The interest was five percent per month. She was disappointed, but accepted it. After all, she was not selling the ring.

Then she visited Ding Fei in her cozy little apartment in a pleasant Chinese section near the foreign concession. Ding Fei was always happy to see her. She served her a glass of Shanghai beer, Sam Cohen's favorite. Brigid had no idea if Cohen was living with her, but she saw a necktie lying on the back of a sofa. That put her at ease. She told Ding Fei that she had also moved in with a man, but they were like sister and brother.

"Forget that," Ding Fei said. "In Wuhan, people are obsessed by two things—politics and sex. Whenever they see an attractive woman, they invariably ask themselves two questions: Is she right or left? And whom did she sleep with last night?"

Brigid laughed. "I should put a sign on my back saying, 'I'm in the middle and I sleep with my fantasy.'"

"Why don't you say you're living with a warlord? Wuhan is not the same anymore. Today you don't worry about your morals, just your safety. See that necktie on the sofa? That's my protection. Sometimes I drape a man's shirt over a chair. That's even better."

"Does Sam live with you?"

"Heavens, no! What if someone took a shot at him some night?" Ding Fei laughed. "No, he sleeps in a hotel room. Hotels are his home. He feels lost when he's not tossing and turning in a squeaky hotel bed. But that doesn't mean we don't sleep together."

"Can you help me find a job?" Brigid asked. "The theater's been closed down."

"Join Madame Sun Yat-sen's China League for Civil Rights. The organization is poor, but we hope to get support."

"I would work for Madame Sun for nothing. Do you know anyone who wants to buy a diamond ring?"

"That's Sam's territory. He knows all the jewelers in China. Have you brought it with you?"

"I just pawned it."

"Brigid, are you broke?"

"No—I just want to have some emergency funds on hand. Everybody is talking about Wuhan being unsafe. People say we're sitting on the edge of a volcano."

"Where else is safer? Bandits, warlords and famine are everywhere. No matter where you go, you carry your life in your hands. Are you sure you're not short of money?"

"To tell you the truth, I have a lot of jewelry. When it's turned into cash, I'll be quite wealthy."

Ding Fei stared at her in surprise.

Brigid laughed. "I know you want to ask me where I got it. Well, from men, of course!"

"I knew you were popular, but I didn't know you were *that* popular," Ding Fei murmured, looking at her askance.

"Just lucky, I guess," Brigid said, laughing.

*

Back in her new home, Brigid ordered a bath. The bathroom was small but had an enormous Victorian bathtub with cold running water. Woo Mah filled it with hot water. Brigid soaked in it luxuriously, kicking slightly to make the water caress her body.

She thought about her job possibility. Ding Fei had told her that the China League for Civil Rights was so poor that Madame Sun had been supporting it by selling her meager assets. It seemed that Dr. Sun had left her almost nothing but stacks of books and a modest house in Shanghai's French Settlement.

According to Ding Fei, Madame Sun could have joined her rich sisters in Nanking. One had married Dr. Kung, a multimillionaire; the other was married to Generalissimo Chiang Kai-shek, the head of the Nationalist government. And her brother, Dr. Soong, was the Premier and Minister of Finance. But Madame Sun refused to have anything to do with her rich relatives. Her opposing political philosophy had strained family relations, and some family members had even accused her of being a Communist.

It was dark outside by the time Brigid was done with her bath. Woo Mah came in to announce dinner. Brigid put on a brocaded robe over her silk nightgown and went to the main hall.

Entering the room, she found Hu Yin at the table, waiting. He rose quickly. He was wearing a green army uniform, complete with an officer's belt, holster and gold collar-insignia.

"Hu Yin!" she cried excitedly. "If you keep surprising me, I'm going to have a heart attack! When did you come back?"

"A little while ago. I didn't want to disturb you. I'm sorry the house is not very comfortable."

"Comfortable enough. And I'm anticipating my meeting with your ghost."

Hu Yin laughed. "It's rats. But don't worry; I'm going to get rid of them."

He was such a serious person that Brigid was surprised by his hearty laughter. "I have brought you a few things from Manchuria," he went on, pointing at a pile of packages on a tea stand.

She opened them immediately—a short white fox coat, a pair of high-heeled shoes, a leather purse and some cosmetics.

"Women's best friends!" she said happily and gave him a resounding kiss on the cheek.

The dinner was hot and spicy. Hu Yin was a lot more talkative than before. Brigid was surprised that he still treated her like a princess and put her on a pedestal. He worshiped her, as always, and she loved it.

"Tell me where you disappeared to," she said.

"After I completed my training at the Whampoo Military Academy, I went back to Manchuria."

"So you still work for Warlord Chang's son, the Young Marshal?"

"Yes."

"Everybody is talking about right and left," she said. "Is there any threat of civil war?"

"The only threat is Japan," Hu Yin told her. "In Manchuria I saw every danger sign. Japan's Kwantung Army has been ready to strike for years. Have you ever heard of a snake that swallowed a whole cow? Japan is like a snake; China is a big sick cow. The Young Marshal never stops talking about it."

"A lot of people say the Young Marshal is a decadent playboy. Is that true?"

Hu Yin swallowed a mouthful of food and sighed. "He dances and plays golf; he womanizes and smokes opium. Whether he enjoys all that or not I don't know. But one day I saw him sitting under a tree in his garden, sobbing. I was shocked. I had never seen a grown man cry, let alone a field marshal who commands a quarter of a million well-equipped troops. It tore my heart apart."

"Why did he cry?"

Hu Yin did not answer immediately. He chewed his food. Then suddenly he broke the silence. "Next day, the Young Marshal disappeared. I was alarmed, but his wife was not. Two months later he returned home a different man, spirited and healthy. He had gone to Paris and had his opium addiction cured. Nobody has ever accomplished that before in only two months, but he did." Hu Yin sounded very proud of the Young Marshal, and Brigid even detected a bit of reverence in his voice.

When tea was served, Hu Yin changed the subject. He chatted about nonpolitical matters, about the house and the servants. They reminisced, wondering what had happened to their old acquaintances in Peking. Brigid had always wanted to ask him one question but never had. Now she did. "Hu Yin, did you kill One Stroke Cha and his henchmen?"

Hu Yin took a sip of tea and swallowed it noisily. "If I say yes, you will think I'm a killer; if I say no, you'll think I'm a liar. Either way, I'm no good. I'm a better man without the answer."

"All right," Brigid said with a smile. "Let's leave it at that."

Hu Yin looked at her longingly. Brigid had never seen his deep-set eyes so tender. Feeling a bit uncomfortable, she lowered her eyes. There was an awkward pause.

Slowly, he rose from the table. "Good night, Fong Yun," he said. He bowed slightly and was gone.

Back in her own room, she changed into her silk pajamas and went to bed. Hu Yin's hungry eyes bothered her. She got up and bolted the door. She tossed in her bed, trying to sleep, but could not. She thought of Hu Yin again and felt guilty for having bolted her door.

She got up and unbolted it. After she returned to bed, she wondered if Hu Yin would come and knock. He never did.

43

It was a rare beautiful morning in 1927. The bright sun had driven the winter chill away. Brigid felt restless. She decided to visit Wuchang again. The city across the river was noted for being the birthplace of the Republic. It had been dirty and poor, as she remembered it; later it had become the Red-hunting grounds for Kuomintang secret agents. It was a depressing city and yet exotic. But she had some fond memories of the place after the Wuhan uprising in 1911. She and Ding Fei had wandered in the native marketplace, enjoying jasmine tea at Cantonese teahouses, and had had long political discussions with other young revolutionaries.

That was almost sixteen years ago. She wondered if the revolution had changed it much. She was curious.

Just as she was about to leave the house, Woo Mah brought her a letter from Hu Yin. It was the third time she had heard from him since he'd left suddenly one morning four months before. Each time he wrote, he'd enclosed a money order for $600. This time it was $1000. He said that he had planned to return home for the Chinese Lunar New Year, but an unfortunate event had compelled him to change his plans. Marshal Chang Tso-ling, the old Tiger of Manchuria, had just been murdered. The Japanese Kwantung Army's secret agents had blown him up in a railway station along with his one hundred bodyguards and several of his concubines. His son, the Young Marshal, was beside himself with grief. Hu Yin said that, being one of the Young Marshal's close aides, he must remain in Manchuria for a while and help the Young Marshal make the greatest decision of his life—whether to fight or withdraw.

Brigid was disappointed. She had hoped to spend the Lunar New Year with Hu Yin. But she was glad that money had not changed him. He was still hardworking, loyal, serious about his job and concerned about others' welfare. And he seemed always politically involved.

She tossed the $1000 money order into the tea can. She had put all of Hu Yin's remittances in it, untouched. She did not need it. Sam Cohen had sold her diamond ring for $5000.

Wuchang was still the same, dirty and poor, but more crowded. The Long Street was forever wet and muddy, as thousands of people carrying water from the river constantly spilled from their swinging buckets.

Brigid crossed the Long Street to the busy marketplace, which she had visited a few times immediately after the revolution. The stalls, the open-air restaurants, the traveling barbers, the peddlers hawking their wares and ringing their bells were still there. Farther down the street, away from the river, the better shops had already started their New Year's preparations. Owners were busy washing their storefronts and posting New Year's lucky sayings on their doors. A few even displayed their New Year's goods—pictures of door gods, money gods and kitchen gods, New Year's cakes and firecrackers.

The marketplace reminded her of Peking's Heavenly Bridge, making her nostalgic. She went into a Cantonese teahouse, ordered a pot of chrysanthemum tea and watched the rosy-cheeked teenage girls thread their way between crowded tables with trays of dim sum. She picked a few of her favorite dishes—braised ducks' feet, black bean spareribs and barbecued pork-filled buns, all steaming hot. The waitresses were always smiling, their eyes roving and glancing around. A wriggle of a customer's finger would bring one of them to his table in a hurry. Flirting was a game. Brigid sipped her tea, ate the tidbits and watched the game with an amused look. It was a different world; it made her forget about bandits, warlords, famine and all the other miseries China was suffering.

After finishing the pot of tea, Brigid toured the open-air restaurant row, where herb stews were simmering in large caldrons—stews made of pork gristle, armadillo and wildcat meat. She had been told that those concoctions were extremely healthful. Eating them regularly, one would not even catch cold for the rest of his life.

She decided that she wouldn't have minded trying a bowlful—if she could be assured there was no dog meat in it!

Brigid passed a wineshop that featured a snake drink which was supposed to be good for the eyesight. She stopped to watch a richly dressed lady being served. The lady had bloodshot eyes from all-night mahjong games, and the waiter knew exactly how much to serve her. He fished a five-foot-long king snake from a burlap sack, cut open its belly and squeezed out the gallbladders. Then he pricked the two little pouches and let the black juices dribble into a small wine goblet. He mixed the juice with some hot rice wine and stirred. The lady drank the mixture in one big gulp, paid quickly and disappeared into her waiting ricksha, hiding her eyes with a tiny folding fan.

Next door was a barbershop for men. Several customers were sitting on benches, submitting to a lengthy treatment that included haircut, shampoo, scalp massage, shave, trimming of eyebrows and nostril hair, a thorough cleaning of the ears with a silver ear-digger, and a beating of the shoulders in a flowery rhythm as the finale—all for fifty cents.

While touring the clothes mart, she wanted to purchase some clothes for Old Woo and Woo Mah. Since everybody was bargaining, she couldn't resist trying it herself. Having watched how it was done, she opened the game by cutting the merchant's asking price by half. After almost half an hour of haggling, walking away and turning back, she hit the bottom and a deal was made. It was almost like a street quarrel without coming to blows; but invariably money and goods changed hands with no hard feelings, sometimes even with a smile.

Brigid thoroughly enjoyed herself. Once again she felt close to the people.

＊

In the afternoon, Ding Fei came to visit in a new ricksha. She said it was a gift from Sam. She took Brigid for a ride around the corner, attracting stares and turning heads as the young puller trotted proudly in the middle of the street, honking the loud horn repeatedly.

Brigid told Ding Fei about Hu Yin's letter.

"Good," Ding Fei said. "After the New Year's dinner at my Aunt Liang's, I have a surprise for you."

She said the China League for Civil Rights was sponsoring a variety show to entertain the North Expedition Army, which had routed some of the warlords in the Yangtze Valley. "By the way, if the show is successful, we might organize a touring company. We want you to join us."

"I'd give my right arm for a chance to go back to the theater," Brigid said excitedly. "I'd even donate my five thousand dollars."

She told Ding Fei about her visit to Wuchang. Ding Fei looked horrified. "Never go there again," she warned. "Wuchang is full of spies, gangsters and kidnappers. A good-looking woman like you could be kidnapped and sold into prostitution."

"I'll never see thirty again. Who'd want me?"

Ding Fei stared at her, shaking her head. "Brigid, you sound as if you were disappointed that you're too old to be kidnapped and sold. Listen, you'd be worth a lot more than some teenager. Today, the pleasure seekers demand that a woman not only know how to make love but also speak several dialects. As for age, the old saying is back in vogue: Women are like sugarcane—the older the sweeter. You're valuable merchandise."

*

The Year of the Dragon ended on a chilly day in February 1928. Early in the morning, Brigid, Ding Fei and Sam Cohen took a horse carriage to Madame Liang's home in a high-class Chinese section of Hankow. The house was almost like Hu Yin's, except larger. Madame Liang, Ding Fei's aunt on her mother's side, was a plump lady in her fifties, widowed, with only one son, who had been killed during the May 4 demonstrations. She had not believed in political activities, but since the death of her son she had begun to take sides. She was not sure what was going on, but it was easy for her to tell who her enemy was—those who shot students.

Her closest relative was Ding Fei, whom she now treated like her own daughter. She worried about Ding Fei's health, her income and her love life. She was as old-fashioned as a pigtail, and it took her a long time to accept Sam Cohen as Ding Fei's boyfriend. But Cohen had finally won her over by his attentiveness and his big show of Chinese knowledge.

When they arrived, Aunt Liang was standing at the front gate, waiting. Ding Fei avoided kissing and hugging in front of her aunt, greeting the elders with a bow.

The elders were Aunt Liang's distant aunts and uncles. They had come for the New Year's family reunion dinner. When being introduced, they all stuffed little red packages of lucky money into the hands of the younger generation.

Sam Cohen was treated like an American son. He knew all the New Year's traditions and ceremonies. Before dinner he voluntarily swept the middle hall for a few minutes as a symbolic gesture, for every New Year was a fresh start; one must pay all his debts, clean his house and give the kitchen god a seven-day leave. While sweeping, Cohen took care that he swept only inwardly, so that he would not sweep out any good luck. That pleased Aunt Liang enormously, and she kept commenting to Ding Fei, "This foreign devil son is better than a lot of Chinese sons."

During the New Year, the kitchen god, a ferocious-looking picture pasted above a little shrine in the kitchen, was supposed to go back to the Jade Emperor in Heaven to report on the family's behavior and morals. Each year the family gave the kitchen god a royal send-off, with offerings of food and incense and a rich dessert as bribes. The dessert was made of sticky rice, which served to glue the god's mouth so he would not talk too much. Some cautious housewives even smeared honey on the god's mouth.

Before the New Year's dinner, the middle hall was cleared of furniture and a fourteen-course banquet was served on three large round tables, with the young people all sitting at one.

Nobody in the family was forgotten. At Ding Fei's table, several pairs of chopsticks were placed at vacant seats. They were for Aunt Liang's younger brother and his family, who had moved to Manila.

The food was sumptuously prepared. Everything was finely sliced. Some dishes, such as pork kidneys and bamboo shoots, were cut in flower patterns. All the dishes were elaborately designed, with emphasis on shape and color. To Brigid, the most colorful of all was the famous Eight Treasure Rice, decorated like a jeweled mountain, inlaid with red dates, lotus seeds, melon seeds and litchi nuts. The main course was an enormous fish; but Aunt Liang confessed sadly that this year's fish was made of wood, because all fishing boats had been requisitioned by the government to transport ammunition. But a fish was a must at a New Year's banquet; it signified abundance, as *fish* and *abundance* sounded alike.

At dawn, a long string of firecrackers heralded the beginning of the Year of the Snake. Everybody helped Aunt Liang put up more lucky sayings written on strips of lucky red paper. Brigid pasted on the family rice barrel the words ALWAYS FULL, then stuck a poster beside the stairway that said, UP AND DOWN WITH SAFETY. Ding Fei posted in the middle hall a large sign saying GOLD AND JADE FILL THE HALL and another one saying HARMONY BRINGS WEALTH. Sam Cohen pasted the lucky word BLESSING upside down over a door. Everybody laughed until Aunt Liang informed them that the word blessing was supposed to be hung upside down, because upside-down *blessing* and *arrival of blessing* sounded alike. Cohen, leaning against the door with a hand on his hip and one leg crossed over the other, winked with a cocky smile.

After lunch the next day, Aunt Liang said there would be a little extra ceremony. It was called the Great Fortune Day Walk, which could be accomplished by walking in circles a few times. The walk would bring good luck because circles symbolized money. They all performed the ceremony in the courtyard.

Laughing, Ding Fei said to Sam, "I wonder which race is more money-crazy, the Jews or the Chinese."

"The Chinese, of course. Even your New Year's greeting, 'Kung hee fat choy,' means 'Hope you make a lot of money.' "

Shouting "Kung hee fat choy!," Ding Fei and her friends said goodbye to Aunt Liang.

     *

The tent theater was in an army camp in the suburb of Hanyang, not too far from the arsenal. When they walked into the theater that night, it was packed. There were at least two thousand troops sitting on the ground, waiting quietly for the curtain to go up. They were weather-beaten men in dark-green uniforms, well nourished and disciplined, their duck-tongue caps shading their eyes. They were part of the Nationalist troops engaged in Generalissimo Chiang's Northern Expedition to wipe out the warlords.

Brigid followed Ding Fei and Cohen to the two rows of folding chairs in front of the stage. They took the three reserved seats in the middle of the second row. They were the only civilians. The higher-ranking officers, occupying most of the other folding chairs, watched the two women and the foreigner without moving their heads, pretending that they were not curious. The stage was constructed of roughly cut lumber; the curtain, made of bedsheets, hung loosely on an electric wire across the thrust stage.

Ding Fei, sitting between Cohen and Brigid, whispered, "Don't expect too much from the show. All soldiers care about is pretty girls and the star."

The music started and the curtain opened. Hanging across the stage was a long banner saying THE VARIETY ARTISTS' ENSEMBLE FOR COMFORTING PATRIOTIC SOLDIERS. Sitting in a little cluster at the back of the stage were five musicians, playing flute, two-string violin, Chinese trumpet, drum and gong.

The first number was acrobatics. Both men and women, wearing glittering red and blue tight costumes, gave a dazzling exhibition of somersaults, tumbling and high leaps. A ribbon dance followed. After that, a magician swallowed fire and a sword. Then there was an animal show featuring a talking bear riding a bicycle with a dog.

The second half of the show was mostly music and dance. In the lantern dance, six girls in colorful Ming Dynasty flowing silk gowns gestured coquettishly in slow motion. The number performed by members of a minority race had a man and woman stomping, clapping, wriggling and flirting with each other. There was a Western number with eight girls wearing bathing suits doing the cancan. It was the most popular. The soldiers went wild, applauding and yelling, "Hao hao hao!"

Suddenly the bright bare lights on the stage went out and the musicians started playing more vigorously. "The star is coming out now," Brigid whispered.

The audience became quiet, waiting tensely. When the drumbeat reached a crescendo, the lights were turned on and the star leaped out from the wings. He was wearing a tight shiny costume and a monkey mask.

"This is the surprise," Ding Fei whispered, nudging Brigid.

Brigid's heart leaped. She almost cried out, "Bo Ho!" Her face flushing and tears filling her eyes, she watched Bo Ho's monkey dance in rapturous silence. He played the monkey king as he always had, acrobatically, vigorously, gracefully. His every gesture, every turn of head and every leap brought thunderous applause.

When the number was over, Brigid was the only one not applauding. She was overwhelmed by the surprise, choking and wiping away her tears. She controlled an unbearable desire to leap onto the stage. But she was stopped by a sudden fear; what if he had lost interest in her? What if he had already married?

"Let's go meet him," Ding Fei said after the repeated curtain calls.

"No, no, I can't," Brigid protested.

Ding Fei was perplexed. "Why not? Don't tell me I've wasted all that time and energy finding him! Come on, Brigid. He's anxious to see you again."

"Is he? Is he really?"

"Of course!" Ding Fei said peevishly. "Otherwise I wouldn't have gone to all this trouble to surprise you."

Brigid forgot she was Chinese, forgot she was over thirty. She became French again, flying to the stage like a teenager who had been invited to meet her idol.

*

Sound asleep, Bo Ho looked lean and pale, but his strong handsome features were the same, framed in the soft, cream-colored pillow like a sculpture. Brigid, lying beside him under the matching down comforter, felt his warmth. The mixture of a faint gardenia scent and the odor of his body excited her, making her desire him again. But she refrained from waking him, even though it was late. She could almost tell the time from the full moon, which shone brightly through the open window.

She felt a little uneasy about the wide-open window that opened to the back garden. In their haste to undress two hours earlier they had been oblivious of everything but the bed and each other. It was not until it was over, with her lying on top of him, totally exhausted, that she had remembered Ding Fei and she had mumbled gratefully, "Thank you, Ding Fei, thank you!"

Now, as she lay beside Bo Ho and watched his handsome profile, she felt even more thankful. Ding Fei had gone through a great deal of trouble to track him down. Without her wide connections, who would have known that he had joined a small traveling troupe wandering in a vast, chaotic country under assumed names? He had always been a big attraction no matter where he was, on stage or off, but for many years he had been a nobody. "Brigid," he had said after the lovemaking, "I was so heartbroken after I read your note that I had given up fame and fortune altogether. . . ." Those words had touched her so deeply that she had wept.

This unexpected reunion had pumped new energy and happiness into her drab life in Wuhan. How they had hungered for each other! She couldn't help feeling amused by the saying that thirty is like wolf and forty is like tiger. Still in her thirties, she had already felt like a tiger, greedy and ferocious. She and Bo Ho had almost devoured each other. Years of longing and uncertainty had made her all the more hungry and insatiable. She rested her head on his bare chest and could hear his strong heartbeat.

Bo Ho turned. She did not want him to go back to sleep again. She whispered, "Good morning."

Bo Ho took a deep breath and stretched. "Good morning? What time is it?"

"It must be two or three in the morning. You slept two hours. I watched you all the time. You might as well stay."

"What will your friends think of you?"

"Let them think whatever they want to think. I don't care." She planted a kiss on his lips and went on, "Bo Ho, what if I'm pregnant?"

Bo Ho was wide awake now. He kept quiet for a moment, then turned and kissed her back. "If you're not pregnant," he whispered, "we'll do it again and again until you are!"

His remark gave her another thrill. She nestled closer to him, tightly clutching his muscular body between her thighs. Yes, she could do it again and again.

A knock on the door startled both of them. "Woo Mah," she called, "I don't want to be disturbed!"

"It's me!" a male voice said. It was Hu Yin.

Brigid's heart almost stopped. "Oh, my God!" she cried, leaping out of bed.

The door was bolted but it was soon kicked open. Framed in the doorway, Hu Yin glared at her. He was breathing heavily.

Bo Ho was now out of bed, throwing on his clothes frantically.

Paralyzed by fear and shame, Brigid couldn't speak. With a moan of agony, Hu Yin picked up a chair and threw it at her. It knocked her down. Enduring the pain, she picked herself up from the floor and tried to say something, but Hu Yin was gone.

44

Ding Fei came to the coffee table with a jar and two wineglasses. "This is genuine mao tai, brewed in Kweichow Province from a secret recipe, guaranteed twelve proof," she said to Brigid as she filled the glasses. "It will give you an immediate high, like a pipe of opium—and then a nightmare."

She attempted to cheer her guest, but Brigid was deeply depressed. Nothing could raise her spirits this morning, certainly not mao tai, which could only make her drunk.

"Well, it's better than feeling sorry for yourself," she thought and downed her glass.

Ding Fei looked sympathetically at her tired and haggard friend. "Tell me what Bo Ho said when he was leaving you. We'll analyze it. As the old saying goes, 'Two stinking shoe repairmen are better than one wise man.'"

"He said one word, 'Goodbye!'" Brigid said, blowing her hair, out of habit. "With a word of encouragement, I would have gone with him . . . or a little gesture—a kiss, a hug. . . . I was dying to hear him say, 'Come with me, Brigid.' But he said nothing. Just a hasty 'Goodbye.' May I have another?"

Ding Fei refilled Brigid's glass. "Well," she said, "maybe you should have asked him. Men have such false pride, you know."

"I would never go with a reluctant man. It would never work!" She picked up her wineglass and drank again. "Don't worry about me. I'll be all right."

Ding Fei stared at her friend, worried. She had never known her to drink so much. It reminded her of a woman frantically trying to quench a fire with small cups of water.

"Listen," she said. "There are two kinds of men a woman must not get serious about. One, the suspicious rich man who is afraid of losing his money; two, the spoiled Casanova who is afraid of losing his freedom. With those stinkers you can't get anywhere beyond the bedroom. I think Bo Ho's flight is a blessing in disguise. He is not worth your heartache, Brigid."

"Bo Ho?" Brigid blew her hair with a snort. "He has said goodbye for the last time. Ding Fei, as the old saying goes, 'Thirty is like wolf and forty is like tiger.' I still have a few years to go; I still have a future." After a pause, she asked doubtfully, "Haven't I?"

"Of course you have!" It pained Ding Fei to see Brigid so anxious. "Brigid, go to Shanghai with us. We can leave tomorrow if you are ready."

"Ready? I can go right now! I'm rich! Shanghai, Shanghai, here I come!" She started dancing around the room, waving her wineglass with one hand and flipping her hair with the other. When she stumbled, Ding Fei helped her sit down and put the bottle of mao tai out of sight.

Brigid again waved her glass and started to sing, then she laughed ruefully. "Ding Fei, I'm proud of my record. Could any battered woman do better? One man raped me, another hit me with a chair, a third has deserted me. I'll give any woman five thousand dollars if she can better that record!"

Ding Fei had not realized the liquor worked so fast. Her heart aching, she went to the kitchen to make some strong coffee.

✳

A week later Brigid arrived in Shanghai with Ding Fei and Sam Cohen by one of the few small steamers that plied the Yangtze.

Shanghai was like Hankow, except that it was bigger and busier. The buildings were taller; the poor poorer and the rich richer. Automobiles and rickshas poured in and out of the foreign concessions; pushcarts, peddlers and beggars milled in the Chinese section, pushing, quarreling and pan-handling; the dead and the dying lay in the streets, waiting to be collected and buried in a mass grave. The stench was appalling. Brigid, riding in a hired carriage with Ding Fei and Sam Cohen, stared out the window and wondered why life was still so miserable eighteen years after the revolution.

China had been horribly abused and mistreated. If she regarded China as a battered woman, then her own fate was not nearly so bad. While the carriage was passing the British Concession, she saw a sign at the gate of a park that said CHINESE AND DOGS ARE NOT ALLOWED. It hit her like a blow. Immediately, her own problems and unhappiness did not seem important. In the past, when she had thought about those who had sacrificed them-selves for the revolution, she had often wondered if some of them had died for other, ulterior motives. Now she believed that signs like this one must have stirred up a lot of skeptics and turned them into patriots and martyrs.

Nobody spoke as the carriage went through the crowded streets at an uneven pace. The horse's hooves hit the dirt road, the muddy street and the asphalt like a drummer beating different drums. When Brigid closed her eyes, she could almost tell where they were—the slums, the busy native streets or the tree-lined avenues of the foreign concessions.

The French Concession looked like a different world. A miniature Paris, it boasted pleasant homes in the residential area and magnificent buildings in the business section. The streets were crowded with foreigners and well-dressed Chinese, many wearing silk and satin gowns and jackets, a few in fashionable Western suits, swinging canes and sporting rosebuds in their lapels. Ding Fei said that those were the tai pans—the money- and busi-ness-brokers of Shanghai.

Madame Sun lived in a modest house on Rue Molière. She had ex-tended a standing invitation to Ding Fei and her friends to stay with her. Ding Fei had wired Madame Sun three days prior to their departure from Wuhan, but there was no definite date of arrival, for nobody was sure of the ship's schedule. As expected, when they arrived, Madame Sun was not at home. The maid received them and showed them their rooms.

Brigid shared the upstairs guest room with Ding Fei. A male servant brought up their luggage, which was mostly Brigid's. It was the first time Brigid had traveled with so many bags and suitcases, and so comfortably. A week in the first-class section of the steamer had been a real vacation. The shipboard activities and the congenial companionship of Ding Fei and Sam Cohen had kept her problems out of her mind. She had told Ding Fei that if she liked Shanghai, she would stay and find a job. She was sorry that Ding Fei's plan for a theatrical touring company had not materialized —through lack of government support.

Madame Sun returned before dusk. She had brought home two dinner guests, Mr. Teng and Miss Hwang. Mr. Teng, a handsome man in his thirties, was a strong supporter of the China League for Civil Rights. Miss Hwang was Madame Sun's part-time secretary. Madame Sun had had a busy day, attending meetings and fund-raising events.

"I've declined all activities for tomorrow," she said after greeting her guests. "I've told everybody that I have friends visiting me. People all know the old saying, 'How delightful it is to have friends coming from afar.'"

Brigid found Madame Sun close to the image she had admired: warm, delightful, earthy and yet serious on serious subjects. Ding Fei had said that Madame Sun had a crisp laugh that sounded like a bell, dispelling dead air and bringing cheer to gloomy people. There was only one surprise: Brigid had not realized that the woman was so young.

Madame Sun felt like cooking that evening. She invited everybody to the kitchen to have a cup of woolung tea while she chopped and sliced. The maid was happily demoted to fry cook, making rice and vegetables.

Miss Hwang was a young lady who reminded Brigid of Miss Shun, the free-lance writer who had written revolutionary propaganda during the Wuhan uprising. Miss Hwang was not consumptive, but her thick glasses, her short hair, her deliberate mannerisms and even her weak voice were like Shun's. But Miss Hwang said she did not know any Miss Shun.

Brigid chuckled to herself. In these tumultuous days it was entirely possible that sisters and brothers were born in different cities and to different mothers, while the fathers were busily sowing wild oats everywhere.

Mr. Teng was a serious young man who seemed to have one thing in mind—politics. He and Madame Sun agreed totally about the problems of China—the left was too left and the right too right. That was why the moderates had created a third faction championing the middle way.

"Every day I go out to promote the middle way," Madame Sun said with a laugh. "Mr. Teng does the dirty work; he goes out to attack the extremists. But Mr. Teng is luckier than I am. He loves to give speeches, while I freeze and tremble on a stage. I have no idea what good I have done, but I've decided to start a magazine which will do all the talking for me."

"I never saw you freeze and tremble," Mr. Teng said. "You are an excellent speaker."

"Maybe so, but the anxiety tears my insides to pieces when I'm speaking. From now on I'll beg off all invitations to give speeches."

Madame Sun talked as she cooked. The dishes she made were delicate and tasty, mildly spicy, true to her middle-way philosophy. She said that if she were forced to choose sides, she would lean toward the left, because the left was for the poor, and ninety-nine percent of the Chinese people were poor. But she did not trust the Russians.

"What is your middle way?" Brigid asked.

"We work for everybody. That means we want China to be strong. In a strong country, everybody benefits. But you cannot build a strong body until you've got rid of your horrible diseases. And China has too many such diseases."

Brigid wished Madame Sun would be a little more specific, but she was not going to pressure her for details at their first meeting.

"Do you dance?" Madame Sun asked after dinner. Everybody nodded. "Good. It's the best exercise there is. And enjoyable."

Some pieces of furniture were removed from the living room and everyone danced to music from a little Victrola. For the rest of the evening, politics was forgotten.

*

During the next two weeks, Madame Sun was seldom home; she was still giving speeches. Brigid attended some of them and was convinced that Madame Sun would turn her middle way into a strong political force independent of the Nationalists and the Communists, a third force that many people like her would like to embrace.

Meanwhile she went out often with Ding Fei. Cohen, however, did not always join them. Sometimes, he would go out alone and return very late. Ding Fei never questioned him. "He's a businessman," she said. "Unless he's wheeling and dealing, he's a fish out of water."

To soothe Brigid's lingering pain of a broken romance, Ding Fei often took her to movies, theaters, beauty salons and coffeehouses. "Shanghai is a great playground," Ding Fei said during lunch one day. "If you can block out all the poverty, misery and danger, that is."

"What danger?"

"Danger always lurks somewhere in the darkness here. It sometimes leaps out unexpectedly and seizes you by the throat, like a mugger."

Brigid didn't think about it much. But on the third Saturday afternoon after their arrival, terror struck. Everyone was home except Sam Cohen, who had gone to a synagogue for his Saturday services. He returned suddenly, his face grim and perspiring.

"Pack your things," he ordered. "We've got to leave Shanghai immediately!"

"Why?" Brigid asked, horrified.

"Don't ask why. Just do it!" Madame Sun added, hurrying into her bedroom to pack.

In ten minutes everybody met in the living room. Without a word, Sam took a quick peek out the window and gestured for the three women to follow him. Outside, a Ford was waiting, its motor running. The driver, a cap pulled down over his eyes, did not look at them or speak. Sam opened the back door and helped the women in. The moment he jumped into the front seat beside the driver, the car took off.

Half a block away, a small group of suspicious-looking men appeared. They were dressed in dark long gowns, their felt hats pulled over their eyes. They approached the car from both sides of the street.

"Slow down," Sam whispered to the driver. The driver obeyed.

Sam rolled the window down and called out, "All right, brothers, we surrender. Here is my gun!" He opened the car door and extended the handle of his automatic toward the man who was sauntering slowly toward them, one of his hands in his pocket. When he was close enough to reach for Sam's gun, Sam grabbed him and hauled him into the car, stuck a second gun to his throat and pulled the car door shut.

"Tell them not to shoot," he said fiercely, "or you die first."

"Don't shoot, don't shoot!" the captured man shouted. His frantic voice immediately stopped the others. They stood and stared helplessly at their leader.

"Go!" Sam said to the driver. The Ford roared out of the street at top speed.

They rode quietly. Some distance from the wharf, Sam suddenly struck the gangster on the head with his gun butt. It made a sickening thud. The captive's eyes turned white and his head dropped. He did not even have time to groan.

Sam opened the door and pushed the man out, like a sack of potatoes. The car sped on. A few minutes later it stopped at the wharf, where a large ship flying an American flag was docked. Sam leaped out, opened the car door for the women and said, "Go aboard. Don't look back! Hurry!"

The women, each carrying a bag, obeyed, running up the gangplank as fast as they could. Sam stuffed a handful of money into the driver's hand and bolted up the gangplank himself.

In the nearly empty first-class saloon of the liner, they settled at a round table, breathless from fear and exertion.

"Where are we going?" Brigid asked.

"Back to Hankow," Sam said.

"But this is an oceangoing ship!"

"It sails for Seattle in three days. But we'll hide here for a night and catch the next ship to Hankow in the morning. A drink?"

The women nodded. Sam went to the bar to order drinks.

"Brigid," Madame Sun said, "I don't know if Ding Fei has told you, but Sam Cohen was my late husband's bodyguard. He always knows what is going on and what to do. We used to call him Two Gun Cohen."

"Thank God he had two of them! Who were those gangsters?"

"The Red and Blue Gang," Madame Sun explained.

"What did they want?"

Madame Sun sighed. "You know that the right wing hates me. I am giving them much discomfort. They probably hired the gang to kidnap me and get rid of me."

"And yet you are so calm, Madame Sun," Brigid said admiringly.

Madame Sun merely shrugged.

Sam came with the drinks. "Double scotch for everybody," he announced. "We all need it."

"Sam," Ding Fei said, "will they let us hide here for the night?"

"The captain is my poker partner. Besides, money can make a ghost turn windmills. Old Chinese saying."

The women laughed delightedly.

"Am I quoting it correctly?"

"Not quite," Ding Fei said, "but it'll do."

✳

Back in Hankow, Brigid found the atmosphere in Hu Yin's house unchanged. She had expected the servants to be quiet and unsmiling, doing their chores without much enthusiasm. But Woo Mah acted as though nothing had happened. She performed her duties as before, fetching water and cooking the meals cheerfully. Brigid suspected that the maid was secretly enjoying what had happened in the House of Hu, like a reader enjoying a novel of sex and intrigue.

Hu Yin had not returned since he'd left the house that fateful night three months earlier. The servants did not know where he had gone, nor had he written to anyone. Brigid had sent a brief note to Manchuria before her Shanghai trip, asking him if he wanted her to move out, but Hu Yin had not replied.

Brigid had not been feeling well. On the third day after her return, she asked Woo Mah to find a doctor. Woo Mah personally escorted her to Dr. Tang, a herb doctor two blocks away. Brigid did not object to herb doctors; in fact her mother had always trusted them and had often told her of miracle cures she had experienced during her childhood in Hunan.

Dr. Tang also owned the herb store in which he practiced. On the door was a black-lacquered signboard that said in golden characters, SAVING THE WORLD BY HANGING OUT MY KETTLE. It was the standard advertisement of herb doctors in China.

The store was ancient and cluttered with shelves and jars and little drawers. Dr. Tang's desk was in the back. His wife managed the store in the front, filling her husband's prescriptions and weighing herbs with a little hand scale.

They welcomed Brigid with smiles. A teenage son served her a cup of tea. Sitting on a thickly cushioned chair across from Dr. Tang's desk, she listed her symptoms. The doctor listened carefully, then asked her to rest her hand on a little cushion on the desk. Closing his eyes in intense concentration, he felt her pulse, tightening and loosening the pressure of his fingers alternately, his face expressionless. After a few minutes he felt the other wrist, still saying nothing.

When this was done, he took out a piece of thin rice paper, wet his writing brush in an ink stand and started writing, humming and shaking his head slightly, as though he were composing an eight-legged essay during the Imperial examination. Brigid had read about such examinations and wondered if Dr. Tang was a bit out of date.

It was a lengthy prescription, with the symptoms carefully described in poetic language. The names of the herbs followed, written in grass style, almost unreadable to laymen's eyes.

Dr. Tang finished the prescription with a flourish, put his writing brush carefully on a brass rack and took a deep breath. Then he looked up, his face breaking into a broad smile.

"Congratulations, Mrs. Fong," he said. "In six months your house will be blessed with a precious addition. All signs indicate that a healthy boy will glorify the Fong surname and bring great . . ."

"How much do I owe you?" Brigid interrupted politely but firmly. Her pregnancy was a foregone conclusion, and she was in no mood to hear a poetic-sounding report. If allowed to go on, Dr. Tang might even tell the unborn baby's future, with lengthy details: he looked like the kind of herb doctor who also doubled as a fortune teller.

"No charge, please," Dr. Tang said. "We never charge anyone who is blessed with such good tidings. The prescription will be carefully filled out by my humble, worthless wife, and instructions for how to brew the medicine will be explained . . ."

"I'm pregnant," Brigid said flatly. "What is the prescription for?"

"For the lucky woman who is bestowed by Heaven with such happiness. Everything in the prescription is designed to balance the ying and yang, Mrs. Fong, so the precious little treasure in your belly will . . ."

"Thank you," Brigid said quickly, rising from her chair.

As Brigid walked home, her mind was at first almost empty of emotion. Abortion occurred to her, but she soon ruled it out, thinking that this was probably her last chance to become a mother. But the moment she decided to have the child, she suddenly found herself bursting with happiness. She felt like going back to the herb store to thank Dr. Tang for his free diagnosis.

Turning around, she hailed a ricksha and told him to take her to Ding Fei's address. She wanted Ding Fei to be the first friend to hear the tidings.

45

H u Yin did not like Nanking very much. The streets were narrow and old and the weather unpleasant, with unpredictable rain that dampened a man's spirits. He had been staying at the Nine Peaks Inn, a native hotel in a convenient location where all the government bureaus were within easy reach. Busy with assignments, he made daily reports to Young Marshal Chang, who had finally decided to join Generalissimo Chiang's Nationalist Army. The Young Marshal had told Hu Yin that the Nationalist government in Nanking was China's only hope; it was recognized by foreign powers and most of the major warlords whom the Northern Expedition had failed to tame. The expedition had been launched by Chiang Kai-shek to wipe out the rebellious warlords.

Tired from meetings and briefings with the Nationalist Army officers and from hunting an official residence for the Young Marshal, Hu Yin returned to Nine Peaks Inn late one evening. Several letters were awaiting his attention on his desk. The airy room had been tidied by the hotel attendant, the teapot in the tea warmer refilled with fresh hot water and the cuspidor cleaned. A basin of water was sitting on the washstand, still warm. The attendant brought in hot water regularly several times a day, regardless of whether he was in or not.

He poured himself a cup of tea and glanced at the mail. It was mostly official correspondence from the Young Marshal in Manchuria, but at the bottom of the pile he found a small, Western-looking envelope. He recognized Brigid's delicate slanting handwriting. He was tempted to tear it open, but changed his mind. Her letters always troubled him, reminding him of the pain and jealousy he had suffered. And yet the sight of her handwriting always excited him, making him anxious to read the letter to learn how she was and what she had been doing.

He had received several letters from her, the last two of which he had tossed into the wastebasket without opening. This one was dog-eared from having been forwarded from Manchuria. The postmark was more than a month old. He felt all the pain and anger rising again as he held the letter, wondering if he should read it. Deciding again not to, he tossed it into the wastebasket beside his desk.

Forcing himself to forget, Hu Yin went to the washbasin and scrubbed his face vigorously. Hard scrubbing of his face and neck usually refreshed and relaxed him. When he had finished, he lay on the double bed. Tense and perturbed, he kept glancing over at the wastebasket. It had been a long time since he had thrown her previous two letters away. Although he seldom heard from her, he wished she would not write at all.

"Oh, damnation!" He tossed on the bed, fighting the unbearable desire to know how she was.

Finally, he got up and fished the letter out of the wastebasket. His heart pounding and with trembling hands, he tore it open. It was brief and straightforward, written with restraint:

> Dear Hu Yin,
> I just had a baby girl. It is Bo Ho's child. I wish I could wipe out the painful past with a magic stroke; but since it is impossible, I must carry on and love this baby, for it is not her fault that she has arrived. I have always been grateful to you for your help and concern. Please tell me if you want me to move out of your house. This house is a great convenience to me, especially now; but I will feel miserable if my presence has stopped you from returning to your own home. Please write.
>
> > Sincerely,
> > Brigid Fong Yun

With mixed feelings, Hu Yin read the letter twice. The name Bo Ho angered him, but he could not hate the baby. Should he tell her to move out? Or should he ignore the letter? He decided to ignore it, but he did not toss it back into the wastebasket.

*

During the next few weeks, Hu Yin kept his mind totally occupied so that there would be no room for any old memories to seep in. A lot had been accomplished. Through Hu Yin's initial negotiations, the Young Marshal would have a high position in the Nationalist Army and his troops would remain in Manchuria under the Nationalist banner and enjoy their own taxation. In case of war, extra aid would be allotted by the Nationalist government. The Old Marshal, murdered by the Japanese, would be honored with an elaborate funeral, and a stone arch built to immortalize his deeds.

Hu Yin had wangled the last promise from the Nationalist Defense Department to boost the Young Marshal's spirits. Despite all his worldly faults, the Young Marshal was extremely filial, a devoted son who had worshiped his father.

*

The Young Marshal did not move to his new mansion in Nanking until the early autumn of 1931, when the Japanese started a new war in Manchuria. Immediately, he and Hu Yin rushed back to the headquarters of the Young Marshal's Northeastern Army in southern Manchuria. The Young Marshal was ready to fight, but Nanking restrained him, ordering him to retreat as soon as possible.

He obeyed reluctantly. In rapid succession, the Japanese Kwantung Army marched southward and seized the Autung arsenal and the key cities of Mukden, Changchun and Kirin. A few weeks later the entire northeastern three provinces were on the verge of being overrun. Refugees poured into the provinces inside the Great Wall. The nation was torn by riots and demonstrations protesting the Japanese invasion. Mao Tse-tung's Communists were rising up, clamoring to fight the invaders on a united front and gaining public support. But Generalissimo Chiang restrained his own armies, like a man holding back the leashes of his fighting dogs.

It broke Hu Yin's heart to see the Young Marshal going through the pain of withdrawal from his beloved homeland without a fight. His face white, he had refused to eat for two days. Hu Yin watched him helplessly as their train sped southward, over the same tracks where his father, the Old Marshal, had been blown up by the Japanese only two years before.

"Why, why, why?" the Young Marshal moaned in his private dining car, his breakfast untouched. Hu Yin and several other aides sat close by, agonizing with him.

The train sped through the green farmland of the northeast, the lush forests, the beautiful blue rivers and the neat villages that nestled among the tall pines. Manchuria was a rich land with tremendous underground coal and oil reserves. All this wealth would soon be lost to an enemy which would one day use its resources to destroy China.

Hu Yin sat near a window and watched the landscape roll by. "Why, why, why?" he heard the Young Marshal's choking voice behind him. He could not bear to look at him, nor could he find anything appropriate to say. He wished he had a magic pill that would relieve the man's misery.

✻

Thereafter the Young Marshal settled into his new mansion in Nanking with his beautiful modern wife, Yu Feng-chi. His close aides, including Hu Yin, occupied the fifty spare rooms in the building, which had been built like a museum, with large pillars and high ceilings. It was cold and gloomy; no amount of decoration could change its depressing atmosphere.

The Young Marshal's wife, who preferred to be called Miss Yu, had her own living quarters filled with pots of houseplants and bonsai. She and the Young Marshal had lost all their antiques and European works of art. With no decorations other than plants, the mansion looked like a nursery about to go out of business.

The Young Marshal liked to spend time with Hu Yin in his room, chatting and sipping tea. He claimed that his wife's flowers made him sneeze. Hu Yin suspected that the Young Marshal and Miss Yu had domestic problems. The Young Marshal was trying to get away, and Miss Yu's lush plants got the blame.

Sipping tea and chain-smoking one day, the Young Marshal, thin, tall and handsome with a small mustache, sat at Hu Yin's table and poured out his laments to Hu Yin's sympathetic ears. He could not stand the inactivity, he said; his troops were hundreds of miles away in the northwest, waiting for action.

"I'm like a leashed wild dog," he complained. "I can only snarl and bark, but I can't grab my enemy and tear him apart."

Hu Yin served him another cup of tea. "You had a long meeting with the Generalissimo this morning," he said. "What did he say?"

"He wants me to fight the Communists," the Young Marshal said. He sighed. "But I told him I want to fight only the Japanese. It has been a never-ending argument. When each meeting is over, he pats me on the shoulder and says, 'Han Ching, your father died not too long ago. You are still young. Let me treat you like my own son and tell you what is good for you.'" The Young Marshal shook his head. "I don't want another father! I don't want to know what's good for me. All I want to do is fight the dwarfs from the East Sea!"

The next day the Young Marshal looked a little better and happier. He said he had requested a communiqué service from the Defense Ministry.

He had just heard from the Defense Minister, General Ho Yin-ching, that his request had been granted. The communiqué service would supply all the pertinent information to him without censorship.

"Hu Yin," he said after several gulps of tea, "this granting of a communiqué service is a small favor. To tell you the truth, I couldn't care less, but it means that they are beginning to trust me. I want you to read every communiqué they send me. I want you to brief me on the important items. Most important of all, find out if some of the news has been censored."

"Leave everything to me, Young Marshal," Hu Yin said. It was good to see his superior gradually shaking off his depression. Hu Yin suspected that he had a secret plan of his own.

After several weeks in Nanking, Hu Yin felt that he knew the city well. He knew that it was full of Westernized people, especially at the universities. Most of the students at Ching Ling University wore European clothes. It was said that they even kissed in public, like the actors and actresses in American movies. Undoubtedly, they all knew how to dance. "If you wish, Young Marshal," he said one day, "I can invite some university students here and give a tea dance. I don't know how to dance, but I can always pour tea and operate the phonograph."

"No, no," the Young Marshal protested, shaking his head as if he had just awakened from a dream. "I have sworn that I'll never dance again until the Japanese are driven out of the country."

Hu Yin was a little tired of his commander's constant preoccupation with the Japanese. It was almost as though he were putting a daily curse on his enemy.

"Let me tell you what the Generalissimo told me this morning," the Young Marshal said in a lowered voice. "He said he was thinking of appointing me his Deputy Commander-in-Chief, to be stationed in Wuhan. He even has found a house for me in Wuchang. What he did not say was, 'Han Ching, I want you to be the Deputy Commander-in-Chief of the Bandit-Suppression Army. As for the house, it has a swimming pool, ballroom, massage room and all the facilities for good living.'"

Hu Yin congratulated him, but the Young Marshal only grimaced.

＊

Young Marshal Chang Hsueh-liang stayed in Nanking for three years. In the interim the government conducted four more campaigns to exterminate the Communists without involving him. No longer complaining about the inactivity, he gave everyone the impression that he was ready to go back to his old habits—gambling, dancing, even smoking opium.

Only Hu Yin knew better. The Young Marshal took frequent trips out of town—supposedly pleasure jaunts.

Early one afternoon he walked into Hu Yin's room and announced that he had received a new title and a new assignment. "Very flattering to a playboy," he said with a laugh.

The title was Commander-in-Chief of the Northwest Bandit-Suppression Army. His assignment was to have a face-to-face talk with General Yang Fu-cheng in Shensi Province. "Do you know General Yang?" he asked.

Hu Yin had followed Yang's career for a long time. The General had started as an orphan and a beggar, almost like himself. "He is known as Tiger Yang," he said. "He has been a thorn in the Generalissimo's side for quite a while."

"The Generalissimo has given him a big title, too—Commander-in-Chief of the Shensi Bandit-Suppression Army. But he is unreliable."

"That's understandable," Hu Yin said. "Are you going?"

"Of course!" the Young Marshal said. "But before I leave, I want you to find out everything you can about the Red Army—their positions, their strength, their best units and, above all, their intentions."

It was the winter of 1935. Hu Yin had already learned a great deal about the Communists. They had survived all the government's bandit-suppression campaigns. After their one-year Long March to Shensi Province to avoid encirclement by the government troops, they had settled in Pao-an, a desolate little town in Shensi where they lived in tents and caves. They had organized the poor peasants and were winning public support through their eagerness to fight the Japanese. Their battle cry was "Stop the civil war! Organize a united front to resist the Japanese invasion!"

When Hu Yin finished his report, the Young Marshal praised his good work. "Now, what I am going to tell you is strictly confidential. I was told that General Tiger Yang might have cooperated with the Communists. My job is to order my commanders in Shensi Province to keep an eye on him. Here is my plan. If I find that this Tiger Yang is interested in fighting the Japanese, I'll shake his hand and tell him that he has nothing to worry about from me." The Young Marshal stopped and grinned mischievously. "I'll even go a step further. I'll even tell my commanders to accept him, and talk him into cooperating with me and . . ." He stopped again, chuckling.

For a moment Hu Yin was horrified. Was the Young Marshal thinking of mutiny? "And what, Young Marshal?" he asked gingerly.

The Young Marshal took a sip of tea and a bite of a Western cookie. "We will organize a united front ourselves—the Red Army, the Tiger's

Northwest Army and my Northeast Army. It will be a formidable force. We can kick the Japanese out of the country without the government's help."

The next day the Young Marshal disappeared. Hu Yin's first thought was that he had been kidnapped by government secret agents. But then he relaxed. He knew that he must not underestimate the "playboy." He had doubtless gone to the Northwest Territory to carry out his secret mission.

46

Hu Yin had bought a stack of war books. One about the 1932 Battle of Shanghai was the most popular. It described in great detail the Chinese defenders' heroism and the Japanese invaders' brutality. The entire Chapei section of Shanghai had been destroyed. Rich people had poured into the International Settlement for protection. When the Japanese artillery bombarded the Chinese positions, they sometimes missed the targets by miles, killing thousands of civilians.

But the Chinese defenders refused to abandon their positions. The Japanese sent tanks to block all the streets, then set fire to the area. It burned for days. Everything was destroyed—houses, soldiers, civilians and animals. Nothing escaped. The stench permeated the entire city.

Another popular book was about Henry Pu Yi, the former boy Emperor of China who had become the Emperor of Manchukuo, the Japanese puppet state in Manchuria. Hu Yin remembered how the news had affected the Young Marshal. The commander had gone into a deep depression. For days he had not come out of his quarters. And when he finally emerged, he was drunk.

"Pu Yi?" he had sneered hoarsely, staggering around Hu Yin's room, hitting his palm with his fist. "The last time Henry Pu Yi made news was when he wet his pants on the dragon throne in the Forbidden City. Now he's back. Emperor of Manchukuo! I suppose I must give him nine kowtows when I return home to sweep my ancestors' graves."

The summer in Nanking was hot and humid. But there were many beautiful spots in the city. Gradually Hu Yin grew fond of both its beauty and ugliness. Six times Nanking had been the nation's capital. It had mountains and lakes. The city itself had eighteen gates without a city wall.

It wouldn't be too difficult to escape Nanking if the city were attacked. One of the warring emperors over a thousand years ago had easily escaped his enemies by disguising himself as a Buddhist nun.

The only place in Nanking Hu Yin avoided was Tung Chi Gate, where professional beggars were always present. If refused money, they cut their heads and bodies with broken glass, then reappeared with blood dripping down their faces and bodies.

Hu Yin liked to visit the Chung Yang Gate—formerly the famous Ghost Gate. He would sit in a teahouse and listen to tea sippers telling each other ghost stories. The Lake of No Sorrow was another scenic spot he loved to visit. He enjoyed boating on the lake and letting the carp nibble his fingers. When he dropped his hand into the clear blue water, he always felt that the fish were nibbling his sorrows away.

Then he would climb a rock named Thousand Bows. Standing on the rock, he could see fishermen in the distance, sculling their boats toward the city on the Yangtze. It looked as though they were bowing. An honest Ming Dynasty official had been buried behind this rock by the Emperor, so that the official would receive a thousand bows every day.

*

Hu Yin had not seen the Young Marshal for quite a while when one day the commander walked into Hu Yin's room and announced that he was moving to Wuhan. He had accepted a new assignment, he said, Deputy Commander-in-Chief of the Bandit-Suppression Army of Hupei Province.

Hu Yin told the Young Marshal that if possible he would prefer to stay in Nanking. When the Young Marshal learned the reason for his reluctance to go to Wuhan, he laughed.

"Who does not have woman trouble? Not too long ago I met a charming woman, Miss Fourth Chow, and I've been having trouble with Miss Yu ever since."

The next day the Young Marshal left for Wuhan to look over his new headquarters. He had been restless, but had recently shed his gloom. Now he chatted and laughed, and humor returned to his conversation. He had also stopped reminding people how much he hated the Japanese. Hu Yin wondered if he had started a new romance with Miss Fourth Chow.

One day Hu Yin received another letter from Brigid. It had been five years since he had last heard from her. He still had the letter reporting the birth of her child. He had almost forgotten Brigid, except when he occasionally heard Wuhan mentioned in conversation or in news reports. At first any of the names of the triple city—Hankow, Wuchang and Hanyang

—had caused him pain, but as the years went by, the pain disappeared. Now, whenever he was reminded of Brigid Fong Yun, he felt only a small pang.

When he opened the letter, a whiff of perfume greeted him. It was a long letter, written carefully in her slanting hand. He took it to a chair, sat down and read it. The old anxiety was gone; what was left was curiosity.

Dear Hu Yin,

I suppose you have been wondering what has happened to me. A few letters I addressed to you at your old address in Manchuria have been returned. When I read about the Young Marshal in the newspapers, I knew that you had moved to Nanking. I was disappointed that you failed to inform me of your move, but I understand.

The reason I must write to you is manifold. First of all, since you have not kicked me out of your house, I suppose I am still your tenant, even though I have not paid any rent. I still hope that you will tell me if you want me to live in your house, of which I have grown very fond. But I will move out if you say so, and all the past rent will be paid if you simply mention the amount.

Secondly, my daughter, May Po, is growing up fast. Her English name is Mabel, close to May Po. To our foreign friends, May Po means Beautiful Wave, a name she loves. But she does not have a last name, so when a last name is required, we simply borrow yours. In school she is Hu May Po, or Mabel Hu.

She knows about you, of course, and thinks that you are her real father. But if you do not object, it would thrill her if you would be so kind as to drop her an occasional note, addressing her as "daughter." I shall be most grateful, for I hate to tell her the truth about us. She is sweet, warm and full of life. Breaking her heart would also kill me.

However, if you decide to ignore this request, I shall also understand. Since Hu is a common name, we shall keep it, and I assure you that we shall never bother you or claim any relationship with you if that is your wish. But since you have always been kind and a gentleman, I have no doubt that you will let us use the name.

This is a lengthy letter and I hope it does not bore you. Thank you and God bless you.

Sincerely,
Brigid Fong Yun

Hu Yin folded the letter. He decided to ignore it. The house was his, but he preferred to have it occupied by someone, no matter who.

*

The war with Japan continued. Meanwhile, the Communists were growing in power. Having failed to exterminate the Communists after five bandit-suppression campaigns, the Generalissimo was planning another massive attack. In the northwest, Mao Tse-tung had been building a Chinese Soviet Republic. The peasants supported his contradiction policy, struggling against rich landlords and sharing their property.

Hu Yin had learned a great deal about Mao, a scholar-soldier, a middle-class Hunanese. Like Chiang Kai-shek, he spoke with a thick native accent. Both men had strong leadership qualities and charisma. Both were true patriots, but they had totally different prescriptions for China's ills. Hu Yin believed that if these two men had shouldered Heaven together, Heaven would not have fallen. Because they were so different in their ideologies, Heaven had crumbled.

Chiang was handsome in his Nationalist uniform, lean and fit, his bearing straight, his face stern, his eyes deep, clear and sharp. His oratory was forceful, his language elegant—sometimes overly dramatic. His gestures were studied; his diction perfect. Only his heavy accent dampened his effectiveness, often raising bewildered eyebrows.

To Hu Yin, Mao Tse-tung was almost the opposite. He was a bit pudgy and wore sloppy, wrinkled uniforms of his own design, sometimes with patches on his knees. His hair was always windblown, he talked in an easy and folksy manner, punctuated by little chuckles. He loved to quote others, sometimes inaccurately to make it more colorful. His thick Hunan accent was a little easier to understand than Chiang's, but to many northerners it was still a little like "playing the guitar to the cows."

Hu Yin found that both men had one thing in common: a weakness for beautiful women. But it fitted nature's design, he decided. All the legendary heroes had had the same weakness. "Hero and beauty" were always spoken in one breath, as though a hero could not be a hero without a beautiful woman beside him. They were inseparable, like lips and teeth.

When Hu Yin thought of the Generalissimo, he wondered if Chiang was even more stubborn than Mao. He seemed determined to annihilate the Communists. Now he was mobilizing almost half a million men to do the job. Hu Yin had heard a rumor that Nanking had hired two generals from Germany, General Hans von Seeckt and Lieutenant General George Wetzel, who were Hitler's best strategists. They had presented a new plan to the Generalissimo to help him wipe out the Reds in China.

Back home that afternoon, Hu Yin sent his report to the Young Marshal in Wuhan. Two weeks later he heard from the Young Marshal, who requested that he hurry to Wuhan for an emergency meeting.

Hu Yin was reluctant to go, but it was an order. He spent all night thinking about the trip. Would he or would he not visit his home? Why was he so reluctant? Was he still hurt? Why couldn't he be indifferent? Indifference would make the trip much easier.

He laid out a piece of paper and started writing:

> Miss Fong Yun:
> Your letter was duly received several months ago. I may have a chance to come to Hankow for a brief visit in the next two weeks. This is to notify you . . .

He crumpled several versions and finally wrote this simple note:

> Miss Fong Yun:
>   May I advise you that I shall come to Hankow for a brief visit in the near future. I may drop in to take a look at my house.
>   Sincerely,
>   Hu Yin
>   January 2, 1936

47

The Young Marshal had established his Wuhan headquarters in Wuchang. When Hu Yin arrived, Chang Hsueh-ling was swimming somewhere with his new girlfriend, Miss Fourth Chow, two of his close aides and several bodyguards. The rest of the staff gave Hu Yin a roaring welcome. They had been friends and colleagues for more than ten years then and had shared many ups and downs.

While having tea in the spacious living room of the two-story Western building, Hu Yin learned that the Young Marshal had taken up swimming and weight-lifting to build his strength and stamina. His new title had been changed to Deputy Commander-in-Chief of the Bandit-Suppression Army of Hupei, Honan and Anhwei provinces. His headquarters was one of the few Western mansions built by European engineers during the construction of the Hunan–Hupei Railroad some twenty years earlier. This house, the largest and most luxurious, had been built by an Austrian. The Chinese had discarded its difficult name and simply called it Foreign Garden. The Nanking government had acquired it expressly for the Young Marshal, whom they still believed to be luxury-loving.

Hu Yin suspected that the Young Marshal had purposely given the government the impression that he was incorrigible, still indulging himself in golf, dancing, champagne parties, poker games and all the other European pleasures that made a man soft. He also suspected that it was the government's wish to keep him soft and corrupt. Obviously, a game was being played by both sides.

When the Young Marshal returned from swimming in Wuchang's East Lake, he was delighted to see Hu Yin. He needed Hu Yin to oversee his Wuhan office, for he might soon take a long trip somewhere. He looked surprisingly healthy, tanned, muscular and handsome. Miss Fourth Chow was a beautiful woman in her mid-twenties, charming and vivacious in her one-piece swimming suit. She took off her red swimming cap as soon as she entered the room, seductively shaking her long black hair loose in front of everybody. The Young Marshal gave her an affectionate pat on her round behind and sent her off to their living quarters.

"Hero and beauty," Hu Yin thought. "An inseparable combination."

Without changing, the Young Marshal sat down on a rosewood chair with a silk robe over his swimsuit. "Someone threw a stinking shoe at me when we were driving home this afternoon," he said with a laugh. "The guard caught the culprit—a fifteen-year-old street urchin. Now, why would a fifteen-year-old boy do a thing like that? Why?" He looked from one face to another. Nobody answered.

"Just a naughty boy who got spanked last night," one aide ventured. "He was probably trying to get even, and chose the Young Marshal as his target. I don't think it means anything."

The Young Marshal shook his head. "I think it has political implications. Hu Yin, can you offer an explanation?"

Hu Yin thought for a moment. "He probably knew who you are, Young Marshal. He is probably a Communist sympathizer."

"Exactly. I'm the Deputy Commander-in-Chief of the Bandit-Suppression Army. From this stinking shoe I've learned the mood of the nation. It's a message."

"What happened to the boy?" Hu Yin asked.

"I let him go. I even gave him a dollar for delivering a valuable message. He almost hit me in the face with that old smelly shoe; I should have boxed his ears instead."

Still laughing, the Young Marshal announced his plan to go to Sian again. Hu Yin did not have to ask why. A united front to fight the Japanese had become the man's obsession. All his appearances of soft living were just a cover-up. Probably the choice of the sexy Miss Fourth Chow as his mistress was part of it, too.

✳

The next afternoon Hu Yin went to see his house in Hankow. Crossing the river on a ferry, he told himself to remain poised and cool. But the moment he stepped into a ricksha in Hankow, he felt a vague anxiety that was disturbing enough to make him swallow hard. His hands were wet. He hated himself for being so vulnerable. Where was his strength? he asked himself. As the ricksha puller trotted toward his home, he told himself that no woman was going to make him nervous. It was simply a friendly call, brief and businesslike. His sole purpose was to inspect his house and to see how those two orange trees were doing which he had planted in the backyard. Nothing more.

The street was the same—a little dirtier, perhaps. A few yards away, he saw a schoolgirl about seven or eight standing in the doorway of his house, looking intently at the approaching ricksha, shading her eyes with a hand.

As Hu Yin was discharging the ricksha puller, the little girl, wearing a blue cotton school uniform, rushed to meet him. "Are you my papa?" she demanded excitedly.

She stopped a few feet away from him, her big round eyes staring at him, waiting anxiously for his answer.

"I guess you are Mabel," Hu Yin said.

With a little shriek, the little girl flew to him. "I knew you were my papa! I knew it, I knew it!" She threw her arms around him and hugged him repeatedly. "Papa, I've been standing at the door looking for you every day! Every day after school I'm here waiting for you. Mama's not home. Let's go in. Where is your luggage, Papa?"

"I didn't bring any luggage," Hu Yin said, feeling somewhat uneasy. He had not been prepared for such a welcome.

"Don't worry, we have everything," Mabel assured him. She took his hand and guided him into the house. "I have a brand-new toothbrush you can use. You have plenty of your old clothes here."

"Yes, I suppose I have."

The courtyard was neat and clean. Laundry hung on a clothesline, flapping in the gentle breeze. "Please watch your head, Papa," Mabel said. Hu Yin ducked under the clothesline and allowed himself to be led into the middle hall. Mabel made him sit down in a comfortable chair and she perched on its arm, still holding his hand. She called Woo Mah to serve tea.

While Mabel was chatting about how she had helped decorate the house, Hu Yin looked around. The old Chinese furniture had been re-placed with sofas and padded Victorian chairs. There was a large coffee table and a rug. The walls were decorated with Western paintings. An electric lamp with an elaborate shade stood on each lampstand. Hu Yin was pleased to see how cozy and warm the room had become.

Woo Mah came in with a tray containing a teapot and several cups. She was older and even plumper, with graying hair. She put the tea tray down, sank to her knees and started kowtowing to Hu Yin.

"No more kowtows, Woo Mah," Hu Yin said hastily. But Woo Mah gave him three anyway. Hu Yin accepted them, knowing that old habits died hard in China.

While he and Woo Mah were exchanging pleasantries, Mabel was busy pouring tea. "Oops, I forgot to ask," she said. "Cream and sugar, Papa?"

"Yes, please," he said, watching her busily playing the hostess. She was a lovely little girl with big round sparkling eyes and a bright smile. As he watched her, his heart began to melt. "Where do you go to school, Mabel?"

"A missionary school, Papa. Next year I'll finish grammar school. Mama wants me to learn English and French. She says we might have to move to a foreign country if China is conquered by Japan."

"China will never be conquered by Japan! I want you to know that, Mabel!"

"Are you a big officer, Papa?"

"What do you mean, *big?*"

"Are you a general?"

"No, I'm a colonel."

"Is a colonel bigger than a general?"

"Nobody is bigger than a general, except a field marshal or the President."

"Who are you working for, Papa?"

"I am working for China. All Chinese military men are working for China."

"Who is your boss?"

"Marshal Chang Hsueh-liang."

Mabel made a face. "I know who he is. He's a coward. He escaped from Manchuria without a fight. He only fights the Communists. Why do you work for him?"

"I work for China."

"How much does he pay you?"

"Enough."

"I don't like him. You should ask him for more money, Papa."

"You are a sharp little girl, aren't you?" Hu Yin said, amused.

"Our teacher says everybody should fight the Japanese. Who do you fight, Papa?"

Hu Yin decided to change the subject. "How is your mama?"

"She's fine. She's busy entertaining the troops."

"Oh?"

"She's an actress, don't you know? Papa, when did you leave home? Where have you been? Will you stay home now?"

Hu Yin laughed. "You ask me three questions in one breath. Which one do you want me to answer first?"

"Are you going to stay home from now on?"

"I am a busy working man, Mabel. I must leave tomorrow."

Woo Mah came back with small dishes of refreshments—watermelon seeds, sugared ginger, litchi nuts and sesame teacakes. Hu Yin was glad of the interruption. He picked up a few watermelon seeds and handed them to Mabel. "Teach me how to crack these."

Mabel dexterously cracked the seeds with her teeth. Her face was solemn. "Why are you so busy?" she asked.

"Because there is a lot of work to do."

"But you're not busy fighting the Japanese."

"All right," Hu Yin said with a smile, "I'll ask my boss for more money."

"I know he's rich. You ought to ask for a lot—unless he fights the Japanese."

"How much should I ask for?"

Mabel calculated for a moment, her big eyes screwed up to the ceiling. "I don't know," she finally said. "Twenty dollars?"

Hu Yin laughed. "I'll tell you what: if he decides to fight the Japanese, I won't ask for anything."

"If he decides to fight the Japanese, I'll even donate my allowance to him. We have donated money to Madame Chiang Kai-shek's New Life Movement. Madame Chiang told us not to drink, not to smoke, not to spit. We all donated our allowances last week. I donated fifty cents, my friend Fong Fong donated one dollar."

"One dollar! That's a lot of money."

"We donate work, too," Mabel said proudly.

"What do you do?"

"We go out in our Girl Scout uniforms; we try to catch those who smoke, drink and spit. If someone doesn't dress nicely, we scold him."

"That's interesting work. How do you catch these people?"

"Each of us brings a little stool. We stand on street corners. When a smoking man comes by, we stop him. One of us stands on the stool, takes the cigarette out of his mouth and tosses it away. If his hat is not worn correctly, we put it right and tell him not to wear his hat like a gangster."

"Do you do this every day?"

"We do it every Sunday."

"How many did you catch last Sunday?"

"I caught five."

"Were they angry?"

"Only one was angry."

"What did he do?"

"He said I was a naughty little she-devil. Then he picked up his cigarette from the street and walked away. After that, I caught a man whose clothes were dirty and wrinkled. He looked awful!"

"What did you do, offer to wash his clothes?"

"No." Mabel laughed. "We don't do that. We only give dirty people a scolding."

"That's not very polite."

"We are very polite. After we have scolded a man, we always give him a Girl Scout salute."

✱

That night, after Mabel had gone to bed, Hu Yin went to his room. His old mattress was gone. In its place was a double bed with fresh new bedding. Beside the bed was a nightstand and a lamp. A chair and an area rug were placed nearby. It looked like a hotel room, but it was much warmer than his old lonely mattress on the floor.

He went to bed wondering about Brigid. He had not seen her for more than eight years. How did she make a living? Obviously she had been doing all right, having redecorated the house and furnished it with rather expensive furniture. When Mabel had said that her mother was entertaining the troops, she had almost given him a jolt. As an actress, naturally she worked late. But how late? He looked at his watch. It was a few minutes before midnight. Turning in his bed trying to be more comfortable, he decided not to speculate about where she was or what she was doing. He was not really concerned—just curious.

He was awakened by a warm body stirring beside him.

"Papa, are you awake?" Mabel said.

"Y–yes. What are you doing here?"

"I couldn't sleep. So I came here. May I sleep with you?"

"Well, well . . . All right. . . ."

She hugged his arm. "Papa, do you like me?"

"Of course!"

"I was so happy to see you, Papa! I don't want to leave you, ever. May I go with you tomorrow?"

"We'll see. Let's talk about it tomorrow, all right?"

"All right."

"Go to sleep."

"Yes, Papa. Good night." She nestled closer to him and went to sleep.

*

It was a bright moonlit night when Brigid returned home from the Press Club, where she had been with Madame Sun. Inside, the house was quiet except for the singing of a lone cricket.

She went to Mabel's room. When she saw the empty bed, she became alarmed. It was well after midnight. She rushed to her own room. The girl was not there, either. She wakened Woo Mah, who sleepily told her that the Colonel had returned. Mabel might have gone to the Colonel's room.

Relieved, Brigid tiptoed into Hu Yin's room. The window was open. Bright moonlight was shining on his bed. He was sleeping on his back; Mabel was sleeping on her side beside him, her arm linking his tightly, like a child clinging to a big teddy bear. Both of them were sleeping soundly and peacefully. With a smile, Brigid left the room.

Next morning she got up early. She went to the kitchen and made a special breakfast: ham and eggs, French toast and French-fried potatoes. She had taught Woo Mah how to prepare Western food, but it always came out looking and smelling peculiar. This morning she did not want anything to go wrong.

She set the table herself. She wanted everything in its right place—fresh daisies in the middle, napkins neatly folded, hot tea in the padded tea warmer.

When everything was ready, she sent Woo Mah to announce breakfast. Presently she heard voices and Mabel's laughter. Hu Yin came in carrying Mabel piggyback.

"Mama, surprise!" she cried, flinging her arms in the air.

Brigid stood up. She and Hu Yin stared at each other, both tongue-tied.

Eight years of living in a big house with a fatherless daughter had frightened her occasionally; now, the sight of a man carrying her daughter on his shoulders suddenly changed a cold, lonely house into a warm home. She was grateful that Hu Yin had accepted Mabel so readily. In order not to breed insecurity in the child, she had built Hu Yin up as her father. But it was not until Mabel was almost six that she had begun to be curious about him. By talking about him often, Mabel had built an image of him and had actually missed him.

For a while Brigid had feared that Hu Yin's hostility would persist, theorizing that the more a man loved a woman, the more he would hate her after a betrayal. She understood Hu Yin's bitterness perfectly. If he had loved and respected her less, he would have been indifferent, and there would have been less hostility. The long silence had hurt her too, but it was not an agony of a shredded romance, only the pain of losing someone close and trusted. Now that he was back, it was time for her to pick up the broken pieces and carefully put them together again. A good man was so hard to come by. . . .

"Mama," Mabel said, "why don't you say hello to each other? This is Papa! Don't you recognize him? He came home last night!"

"Hello, Hu Yin," Brigid said softly.

"How are you, Fong Yun?" Hu Yin said, coming to the table and setting Mabel down. "You look good."

"So do you, Hu Yin." When Brigid finally came out of her stupor, she felt a little nervous. "Sit down, please. I've made a Western breakfast. I hope you don't mind. . . ."

"I love Western breakfasts," Hu Yin said, sitting down at the table.

Mabel leaped out of her chair. She had often pouted in the morning, refusing to say what bothered her. Now she was bubbly. "Mama, can I help?" she asked eagerly.

"Certainly," Brigid told her.

Mabel unfolded Hu Yin's napkin and tucked it under his chin, then poured a cup of tea for him. "Cream and sugar?"

"Yes, please," Hu Yin said, amused by the busy little girl trying to play hostess again.

When she picked up Hu Yin's fork and knife, Brigid said, "Mabel, I think Papa knows how to cut his own ham."

"But he eats with chopsticks all the time!"

"That's what you think," Hu Yin said. "I work for the Young Marshal, remember? He eats Western food all the time. I'll show you."

Mabel watched Hu Yin critically, but couldn't find fault with his table manners. They ate quietly for a moment. Mabel kept glancing at Hu Yin as though she were afraid he might sneak away when she wasn't looking.

"How nice it is to see you again, Hu Yin!" Brigid said. "For a long time I thought you had disappeared forever. I never heard from you, until I got your last letter. It came as such a pleasant surprise. Every day, Mabel has been standing at the front door waiting for you to arrive."

"Fong Yun," Hu Yin said hesitantly, "since we're so Westernized, I think I should call you Brigid from now on."

"I thought you would never change," Brigid said with a smile.

"B–Brigid," Hu Yin said with more difficulty, "I–I think we should make it legal. Will you marry me?"

As Brigid looked at him, tears began to well in her eyes. She nodded eagerly without saying anything, knowing that her voice would choke. The proposal came as such a surprise that she was overwhelmed.

"Papa," Mabel said, looking between them, "aren't you two married?"

"Not yet, Mabel," Hu Yin said.

"Where did I come from then?"

Brigid pulled herself together. She was sorry that in China girls were so ignorant. In France, a girl of seven would never have asked such a silly question. She herself had had plenty of sex education in her *lycée* in Paris. But it was no time for it now.

"Mabel," she said, "did you learn the story about the stork—the big white bird that flies over people's houses and drops babies along the way?"

"Yes, I even know how to draw a stork."

"Well, one night it just flew over our house and dropped you on the roof. And here you are."

Mabel, looking puzzled, turned to Hu Yin. "Didn't you do anything, Papa?"

"Well . . ." he said uncomfortably, "I climbed onto the roof and brought you down."

"That's not much of a job. Will I always be your daughter, Papa?"

"Always, Mabel, always!"

"Mama, why are you crying?"

"I'm so happy, Mabel, so happy!" Brigid sobbed. Unable to hold back her tears, she left the table and hurried to the bathroom.

"Why is she crying?" Mabel asked.

"She said she's happy," Hu Yin said, finishing his breakfast. "When people are happy, they laugh, they cry . . . they do all kinds of crazy things."

He squared his shoulders. He hadn't realized what a wonderful feeling it was to be a father. Pointing at Mabel's plate, he said, "Eat!"

48

The marriage ceremony was simple. The Reverend Contento, a Baptist minister in Hankow, officiated. The guests included Ding Fei, Sam Cohen and some of Brigid's theatrical friends. Woo Mah cooked a sumptuous dinner, which they ate immediately after the ceremony, eliminating the wedding cake. In all of Wuhan nobody knew how to make a wedding cake—except for a few in the foreign concession. Since it was Brigid's desire not to publicize the wedding, she had purposely avoided the concession, where she had been popular and the target of flirtatious males, single and otherwise.

Hu Yin was satisfied with the arrangements. His mind had been liberalized by the Young Marshal, whose unconventional life-style often shocked people, but many of his deeds had earned Hu Yin's admiration. Hu Yin requested only that a short notice be published in the classified section of a major newspaper, announcing their marriage in the past tense. This type of announcement was popular, along with all kinds of ads, some seeking missing persons, others selling houses, praising someone's admirable actions or scolding a wayward wife.

Wuhan was full of rumors and activities. The Nationalist government had stepped up its exterminate-bandits campaigns; secret agents fanned out in all directions, harassing and arresting Communist suspects. It was rumored that executions and mass burials were carried out every day in unknown locations.

Brigid had been working for the entertainment branch of the China League for Civil Rights, making a film of a variety show that had been commissioned by the Defense Ministry. To dampen criticism, the government had done its best to cooperate with Madame Sun, making a big show of being democratic.

The Russians had left Wuhan, unable to tolerate the Nationalists' persecutions. Mao Tse-tung had been consolidating his party and armies, cleverly increasing his anti-Japanese propaganda and clamoring for a united front. Meanwhile, his guerrillas infiltrated both the Japanese lines and the Nationalist positions, winning the peasants in the countryside and the students in the big cities.

Hu Yin was busier than ever, overseeing the work at the Young Marshal's Wuhan headquarters. The Young Marshal had been secretly coming and going, flying his private plane or driving one of his luxury cars. He would disappear for a few days at a time. Sometimes nobody knew where he had gone, not even Hu Yin or Miss Fourth Chow. Hu Yin had an idea what his commander was up to, but he kept quiet, knowing that the Young Marshal wanted to maintain his playboy image.

Hu Yin's domestic life was not as happy as he had hoped, for he soon realized that he had not really won Brigid's heart. He was bothered by a vague, unsatisfying feeling that the marriage was only one of convenience. But, happily, Mabel was a source of comfort to him. Every day, when he returned home from his office, he would find the girl standing at the doorway waiting for him. He would pick her up and carry her in, and Mabel would play hostess, serving him tea and watermelon seeds. It had become a daily routine and Hu Yin enjoyed it; it made him forget the problems in the office and his concern for the Young Marshal's security.

*

A leg was rubbing Brigid's. Without a word, she removed her pajama pants and lay on her back passively. It was routine. There was no pleasure, no excitement. The movement was automatic, mechanical. When Hu Yin's pumping increased in tempo, she knew it was time to react. She clutched him more tightly, breathed harder, faking a moan. She hated it—not the sexual act, but her falsehood. She always felt guilty afterward. Did he know that she felt nothing?

As always, Hu Yin said nothing. A few moments after the act, he would get up, go to the bathroom and presently she would hear water splashing. When he returned to bed, he remained silent, lying beside her motionless. She wished she knew what was going on in his mind. Why didn't he turn to her and say, "Look, Brigid, stop faking. It really doesn't make a damn bit of difference to me. You're just a machine."

She would have felt better if he had said that, for at least she wouldn't have felt so guilty. She could have treated the act as a wifely duty, like serving him breakfast or washing his clothes.

Several times she had attempted to ask him honestly how he felt, but she always changed her mind when the question reached the tip of her tongue. She had once been told by a gossipy woman that if a woman was frigid, a bottle of good champagne would remove her mental block. Perhaps she should try champagne next time. She would try anything. How she wished she could respond and enjoy it; she was wasting her prime of life. In a few years her "wolf age" would merge into her "tiger age" and then it would be gone. Nobody talked about the post-tiger age of a woman, as though there would be no more sex life left then. . . .

She heard Hu Yin snore, deep and even, not loud enough to be annoying. Once or twice she wished it were Bo Ho, but she quickly switched that thought off. She had successfully gotten Bo Ho out of her mind— permanently. Even Mabel's resemblance to him no longer disturbed her.

Thinking of Mabel, she felt lucky and grateful. Mabel had fulfilled a tremendous need in her—the need for motherhood. She had also brought her a husband, a man who was honest and dependable, kind and generous, and above all, who loved their daughter. But why this curse? Why this sexual unresponsiveness? Why this lack of chemistry? She must do something about it. She must try champagne!

*

When she woke up in the morning, Hu Yin was gone. For the last week or two she had hardly seen him except late at night. She too had been busy, having late rehearsals. But was Hu Yin really busy? she often wondered. Or was he trying to keep himself busy? Was he troubled by her unresponsiveness? Was the country in even deeper trouble?

She had been following the national and international news closely. By visiting the Press Club with Michael Steward once in a while, she had heard reports ahead of the newspapers; and what she heard was usually uncensored.

The latest news disturbed her deeply. The central government had been devoting all its military power to another attempt to wipe out the Communists. One million troops had been mobilized, and two generals from Nazi Germany had committed a massacre that horrified most of the foreign correspondents.

According to the report, General von Seeckt had started a scorched-earth campaign. He had ordered hundreds of miles of roads built into the Red sanctuary and thousands of concrete fortifications built in strategic areas. As soon as these were completed, the Nazi generals had sent waves of tanks and armored cars into the Communist-occupied areas and blanketed them with constant heavy artillery bombardment. As the troops moved forward to encircle the Communists, this massive exterminating-bandits campaign, as it was called, had brought dreadful suffering to the people. Famine had followed. For miles, thousands of dead babies, soldiers and civilians were left unburied. One of the leftist foreign correspondents claimed that he had recently returned from the battlefield. He estimated that the Communists had suffered at least sixty thousand casualties, and that a million people had been killed or had starved to death. Since the reporter was a leftist, Brigid hoped that he had exaggerated. Nevertheless, this had shocked the foreign concession so much that the visitors at the Press Club were mournfully quiet that day.

Brigid was having lunch with Michael at the club when she asked, "Why don't you write something about this, Michael?"

"What's the use?" he said with a shrug, his eyes bloodshot and his hair unkempt, as though he hadn't slept for days.

"Why do you say that, Michael?" She was surprised that Steward had changed from a fiery reporter to a despondent complainer.

"The editors are under the thumb of the publishers, the publishers take orders from the politicians, who in turn kowtow to industrial and commercial princes. The editors' mighty blue pencils knock all the teeth out of the biting dogs. We are all toothless dogs. Who needs us?"

"What happened to Madame Sun's interview?"

"They killed the dog. It never had a chance even to bark. I asked my colleagues. All their articles about Madame Sun have been killed. I guess the world is scared to death of the Reds. They would rather have the Nazis."

They finished lunch in silence.

*

That night, when Hu Yin came home, he looked disturbed. But when he saw Mabel he cheered up. They chatted and laughed and had their tea ceremony. After dinner he urged her to go to bed early, and he told her a long bedtime story that soon put her to sleep.

Brigid returned home late. She decided not to dampen Hu Yin's mood with the appalling news she had heard at the Press Club. She had bought two bottles of champagne and had them chilled in an icebox. Before bed, she poured two glasses and offered one to her husband.

He drank it with a slight frown. He had never cared much for champagne, but he finished it anyway. Brigid refilled her glass and drank it quickly, anxious for it to take effect, to knock down her cursed mental block. Tonight she was determined to prove to herself that she could do it, to show Hu Yin that she was not frigid.

After she had finished the first bottle, she thought she was ready. Her face flushed and her heart beating fast, she made the initial move. She started unbuttoning Hu Yin's shirt.

Looking surprised, he let her. She undressed him slowly, planting little kisses on his smooth, muscular body. On the bedstand, two glasses of champagne stood ready. She gulped down a mouthful and started undressing. Soon she began to feel a little dizzy. Before she climbed on him, she took another mouthful of champagne.

Hu Yin lay on his back, doing nothing and saying nothing. For the next twenty minutes she made love on top of him. So desperately did she want it to go well that every few moments she took a drink of champagne.

Yes, it was working, she kept telling herself. It was working. Her mental block was crumbling. She could feel pleasure. But it did not last long. Suddenly she felt nothing except the familiar dry contact.

She grabbed the glass and took yet another deep swallow. After a few moments of vigorous pumping, she refilled the glass. Her face wet with sweat, her heart beating violently and her expression desperate, she drank and pumped.

"Brigid," Hu Yin finally said, his voice sympathetic, "you look like a coolie woman slaving in a laundry."

She had begun to feel a little sensation again, but Hu Yin's remark killed it instantly. She climbed off and flopped down beside him, exhausted.

"Good night," Hu Yin said, turning away from her. Presently, she heard him snore. Feeling angry and frustrated, she tossed around, unable to fall asleep. Then she heard a heavy knock on the door. Hu Yin woke up. It was Woo Mah delivering an urgent message. Hu Yin opened the door. He tore the message open.

"What is it?" Brigid asked.

"A telegram from the Young Marshal."

"What does it say?"

"He wants me to go to Sian."

"Right now?"

"Yes, right now. A plane is waiting for me at headquarters."

Having stuffed a few changes of clothing into a suitcase, he kissed her on the forehead and left.

Brigid looked at her husband's pillow. It was so forlorn. She still could feel the warmth of his part of the bed, but that would soon disappear and his side of their bed would again be cold and empty. She felt a hot tear creep down her cheek. She looked at his pillow and whispered, "Hu Yin, am I ever going to see you again?"

49

It was a dark, cloudy night, with gusts of wind churning up thick dust in the northwest plains. The weather was so rough that the two-engined plane landed at the Sian airport only through the skill and luck of the pilot. Waiting on the tarmac was Captain Feng, the Young Marshal's adjutant, whom Hu Yin had known for many years.

Feng took Hu Yin to a waiting car, which sped through Sian's desolate suburbs and entered the ancient city gate, which was guarded by soldiers in heavy coats. Inside the city, the streets were dark and quiet, except for the noise of the wind and the Ford sedan.

From a secret two-finger signal, Hu Yin knew that Feng was not allowed to say anything in the car. Except for a quick greeting, they had remained silent. Riding in the front seat beside the driver was a guard holding a submachine gun. Even though Sian was General Yang's territory, it was no secret that the city was full of Kuomintang spies.

Hu Yin had surmised some time ago that the Young Marshal and Tiger Yang had been holding meetings off and on, planning a massive anti-Japanese and anti–civil war campaign, and promoting a united front that included the Communists.

Soon the car reached an iron gate guarded by more soldiers. A bare light overhead shone on a horizontal sign that read, THE HEADQUARTERS OF 17TH ROUTE ARMY. On the side was a perpendicular sign: SHENSI PACIFICATION HEADQUARTERS. Both organizations were headed by Yang. Seeing the car approaching, the guards quickly opened the double iron gates, and the car drove through almost without slowing down, bumping over holes and rocks on the dirt road.

Inside the gate was a tree-lined drive leading to a palatial building, also heavily guarded. The car stopped and an officer hurried over to open the door. When Hu Yin and Captain Feng stepped out, the officer saluted them. Hu Yin recognized him as one of the Young Marshal's bodyguards.

"Please follow me," Feng said, mounting the marble steps. "We are guests here tonight."

Hu Yin followed him. They returned the guard's salute as they entered the Western-style double doors. Inside the building, bare lights shone brightly in the foyer. Feng turned into a hallway on the right. The air was quiet but ominously tense; it reflected off the faces of the guards, especially Feng's.

Feng knocked on one of the doors and it was flung open instantly. Another guard saluted. The captain strode in, gesturing for Hu Yin to follow.

In the large meeting room, officers were sitting at a long conference table studying maps. At the head of the table was General Yang, a middle-aged man with a broad flat face, sharp slanting eyes and a pointed chin. The front part of his head was balding. He was a fairly good-looking man with a faintly friendly smile. Sitting on his right was the Young Marshal, casually dressed in a safari coat, his hair uncombed and his eyes tired. That was unusual, for he was ordinarily carefully groomed, except when he was playing tennis or riding horseback. Obviously he had been working without enough sleep.

Hu Yin stepped up and saluted. The officers rose to greet him, returning the salute. The Young Marshal pointed to an empty chair across the table from him and asked Hu Yin to sit down. There was no nonsense, no pleasantries exchanged. Among the two dozen men present were two civilians dressed as peasants. Hu Yin guessed they were the representatives of the Red Army in disguise.

The Young Marshal, who had been speaking, continued. "As early as last year, opposition to civil war, and a joint resistance to Japan, had already become the shared objectives of the three sides—the Communists, General Yang and myself. Tonight, we are here to discuss how such a common policy should be implemented. It is a most urgent task, for the Generalissimo has massed almost fifty divisions of his best troops to encircle Shensi Province in his effort to exterminate the Red Army. Civil war must be avoided by all means, to save men and matériel for our sacred duty—to resist the Japanese invasion. It must be done before it is too late!

"Why is fighting the Japanese our first priority? Some of you may have known Japan's effort to conquer China by every means she could possibly think of—terror, intrigue, military action and diplomatic threats; by manufacturing incidents, creating chaos and horror." Without consulting notes, the Young Marshal rattled off dates and places. It was an impressive display, a depressing litany of international military spending in preparation for an all-out invasion of aggression and provocation continued over many years.

The Young Marshal stopped as his voice began to choke and tears filled his eyes. Then, with an effort to control himself, he continued. "Brothers, are we living in an independent country? How much longer can we tolerate this? Brothers, an all-out Japanese invasion is imminent. We cannot ask Heaven to protect us.

"We must defend our country now! This is no time to kill each other. Every man, every gun, in all of China must be used to fight our common enemy! Now General Yang will tell you what we have planned to do."

General Yang, his face expressionless, glanced at the soldiers around the table. His voice quiet and without emotion, he said, "The Generalissimo has arrived in Sian. He is staying at the Lintong villa outside the eastern city gate. He is here to direct the most massive bandit-suppression campaign to date. As Marshal Chang has just said, facing an immediate Japanese invasion, we must save every man and every bullet for our national defense. Tomorrow Marshal Chang and I will present to the Generalissimo a petition urging him to change his suicidal policy. Today we must prepare for a possible bad turn of events. My chief of staff, General Tung, will brief you on what we have done in case of that possibility."

Tung took a sip of tea and stood up. He was a lean, small man with steel-rimmed glasses. He produced a piece of paper from his pocket and started speaking, occasionally consulting his notes.

"Both the Seventeenth Route Army and the Northeastern Army will announce a united front with the Red Army. We are ready to attack the Japanese in the northwest. We have no idea how the Generalissimo will react, but his power in Sian is awesome. However, we shall do everything to avoid a confrontation with the Central Government Army. After we have announced our plans for the united front, the whole nation, we hope, will support our patriotic effort. This in turn may change the policy of Chiang Kai-shek's clique. General Yang's instruction is *persuasion first.* We have drafted a declaration for a united front. The purpose of this meeting is for everybody present to study it and to make suggestions, and at the same time make the necessary military preparations for an emergency. First, the declaration . . ."

General Tung cleared his throat and read: "It is now five years since Japan occupied China. National sovereignty has been infringed upon and territories have been lost to the enemy. All of our fellow countrymen are greatly distressed.

"And yet Generalissimo Chiang Kai-shek, misled by his close advisers, had made our nation suffer greatly. We, Chang Hsueh-liang and Yang Fu-cheng, respectfully request the Central Government to: one: reorganize the Nanking government to admit representatives of all parties to jointly share the responsibility of saving our nation, two: end all civil wars, three: release all patriotic political prisoners, four: allow patriotic mass movement, five: safeguard political freedom, six: earnestly carry out the late Dr. Sun Yat-sen's will, seven: immediately organize a united front to defend our country against the foreign invasion."

The rest of the meeting was devoted to revising the declaration. Then important assignments were parceled out to the senior officers of both armies. Hu Yin had not slept for twenty-four hours, but the urgency of the meeting kept him awake. He was appointed coordinating officer of the united front. After the meeting adjourned, he almost sleepwalked to the car outside.

*

In the late afternoon, the wind cleared the sky and the bright sun lifted the winter chill. Two automobiles arrived at the Generalissimo's Lintong villa outside the eastern city gate. Both cars flew red and blue Nationalist flags.

Without waiting for the guards to open their car door, the Young Marshal and General Yang climbed out, followed by their aides. At the door of the villa two more guards saluted them. The two officers marched in, their faces grim. Each carried a briefcase. They hurried, their boots squeaking and clicking heavily on the shiny hardwood floor. At the door of an inner room, Hu Yin told a guard that Marshal Chang Hsueh-liang and General Yang Fu-cheng were there to see the Generalissimo.

When they were permitted into the room, Generalissimo Chiang, lean and in a neat uniform without decorations, was reading a document on his deep sofa, flanked by several other generals sitting in chairs. Hu Yin recognized one of them, the famous General Tai Li, Chief of the Secret Service. The generals rose, but they did not exchange salutes or greetings. They waited for Generalissimo Chiang to finish reading. He handed the document to Tai Li. "Take care of this and report back to me."

Then he turned his attention to the visitors, looking at the Young Marshal with a flicker of a smile. "Ah, Han Ching," he said affectionately. Obviously fond of the Young Marshal, he addressed him by his milk name. "I am glad you're here. I was about to summon you."

"I have come with General Yang Fu-cheng, Generalissimo," the Young Marshal said.

The Generalissimo stared at Yang with cold eyes. "Please take a seat, General Yang."

"We will not waste your time, Generalissimo," the Young Marshal said. Fishing out a document from a pocket, he handed it to the Generalissimo politely with both hands. "This is our petition for a united front."

As the Generalissimo read the petition, his face grew red with anger, his eyes hardened and his jawbones worked. He tossed the document on the coffee table and glowered at the Young Marshal. "Han Ching," he said, his voice harsh and his accent thicker—his accent always became heavier when he was excited—"I don't understand you. I thought you were loyal to my bandit-suppression policy. You know we will never fight the Japanese effectively without first eliminating the horrible disease within ourselves. The Communists must go! Why are you still so ignorant as to think of enlisting them as allies?"

"Generalissimo," the Young Marshal said, his voice polite and calm, "the Communists are a large force; they are all anxious to fight the common enemy . . ."

"A lie! They are China's poison! Fighting the Japanese is only their excuse for their own expansion. No, we must follow the present course— pacifying the country before resisting any foreign invasion,"

"Generalissimo," Tiger Yang spoke up, "I was ordered to fight the Communists, but today I must risk your anger and tell you that from now on I fight only foreign aggressors. I cannot compromise with my own conscience."

The Generalissimo cast him a murderous look. "I have been displeased with your troop-training programs. You have been ignoring my orders for years. That's why your troops are not well disciplined. Even the students in this city are rebellious."

"Sir, your methods only alienate the young; they further divide the country. That's why the Communists . . ."

"Are you working for me or for the Communists?"

"I am working for the welfare of the nation. It is most urgent that we . . ."

Chiang rose to his feet. "I am not going to listen to your lecture!" he shouted. He turned to the Young Marshal. "Han Ching, you either follow my orders or go play golf. Or go take an ocean trip!" Without another word he stalked into his bedroom.

All the others rose to their feet. General Tai Li grinned. Hu Yin had been told that Tai Li's grin usually sent chills down people's spines. He grinned back and followed the two generals out of the room. Nobody uttered a word. The rebuffed men strode from the room silently, their footsteps heavy and quick.

*

Back in General Yang's headquarters, an urgent meeting was called. Attending were the same senior officers of the two armies. His face ashen, Yang announced in a resigned, ominous voice, "We have urged the Generalissimo, in person and in writing, to reverse his dangerous policy, but our pleas have been rejected. It looks as though further efforts will be a waste of time. Any further pleas, no matter how sincere, will come to nothing. Therefore we have reached the end of the road. Marshal Chang and I have come to a painful conclusion: we must have Chiang Kai-shek arrested."

There was a loud intake of breath. To Hu Yin it was frightening, and yet it was like a shot in the arm, churning up his blood. He had never experienced such excitement before. Toughened by life, he had always regarded himself as cool in crises. He had massacred gangsters, robbed a grave and survived battles and skirmishes, but nothing seemed as terrifying, yet exhilarating, as the plan to arrest the Generalissimo. He found his hands sweating. But, as he saw it, the awesome job had to be done.

During the next two hours they discussed the plan and made detailed arrangements. Yang's 17th Route Army was to post guards within the city, blockade the Sian railway station and airport and seize any planes. A division would be dispatched to disarm the Central Gendarmerie and the Central Army units. A battalion would be sent to detain all the prominent members of the Central Government at the Sheking Guest House.

Soldiers from the Young Marshal's Northeastern Army would surround the Lintong villa and arrest Chiang Kai-shek. It was also his responsibility to post guards along the Sian–Lintong Highway.

With lightning speed, the troops took up their positions. It was midnight, December 11, 1936, a bright moonlit night, chilly and windless, when Hu Yin left General Yang's residence, a renovated ancient palace that had been built by a Ming prince. As coordinating officer of the two armies, he was practically in charge of the Generalissimo's arrest, under the direct command of the two generals. A crack regiment had been selected for the job.

Driving to join the officer of the regiment, Hu Yin wrote the date and time of this history-making task in his notebook. He studied the map and the description of the villa. He had already obtained pictures of the driveway, the garden and the interior of the villa, the number of rooms and which ones were occupied by the Generalissimo, his aides and the guards.

Before daybreak on December 12, Hu Yin and his men drove to Lintong and approached the villa under the well-planned cover of the regiment. Everything was quiet except for the crowing of a rooster in the distance. Just as they reached the gate, gunfire shattered the silence. Hu Yin dived for cover. Obviously Chiang's bodyguards had discovered the intruders.

Hu Yin's men returned the fire with their submachine guns and mowed down a few of the guards. Hu Yin fired his revolver from behind his cover of a bush and brought down two more. As he was getting up, he heard a noise behind him. He swung around with a flying kick. It landed on the man's cheek, knocking him down. As the attacker was about to throw a dagger at him, Hu Yin fired, hitting the man's leg. He yanked him up and found that it was one of Chiang's bodyguards who had just come out of an outhouse nearby, armed with nothing but a dagger.

Now Hu Yin's men poured into the building. A dozen soldiers, led by Hu Yin, burst into Chiang's quarters. In Chiang's bedroom, they found their quarry missing. His bed was still warm and his false teeth were still in a glass, soaking in a bluish solution.

"Search outside!" Hu Yin shouted at two soldiers, pointing to the open window. They leaped out the window and two more ran out the door in hot pursuit. Hu Yin quickly searched the room. Chiang's clothes were there, neatly hung in the closet. Losing no time, Hu Yin made direct telephone contact with the Young Marshal and General Yang, informing them of the successful occupation of the Lintong villa and its vicinity, and of the missing Generalissimo.

"One of the windows in his bedroom is open," Hu Yin reported. "Obviously he has escaped through that window."

"Who could have leaked our plan?" General Yang demanded angrily.

"I don't think anyone has betrayed us, sir," Hu Yin said. "His bed is still warm. He can't be too far away. I've sent out searchers."

"There is a big pond in the garden," General Yang said. "See if he has committed suicide . . ."

"That is very unlikely," the Young Marshal cut in. "He's not that kind of man. Check all the automobiles and report back to us."

Hu Yin ordered all the cars outside the villa checked. None were missing. He decided to join the search, and led a party into the rocky hills in back of the villa. They fanned out in all directions. Hu Yin and half a dozen men, weapons in hand, searched the barren hillside. Suddenly he heard a low moan. He made a quick gesture to his men to follow him.

Not far away he found an officer lying on a rock, his uniform soaked in blood. He was one of Chiang's aides, a Colonel Kwan, who confessed that he had carried the Generalissimo to this spot in spite of a bullet wound in his side. Unable to go farther, he had asked the Generalissimo to hide himself. "The Generalissimo has injured himself by jumping out the window," he said.

Hu Yin climbed a few rocks, knowing that the injured man could not have gone very far. Reaching a boulder a few yards up the slope, he saw a footprint. He circled the rock, his revolver ready. The Generalissimo was sitting in the dirt. Hu Yin fired three rounds into the air to signal that he had found him.

"Here I am," Generalissimo Chiang said, raising his hands. One of his shoes was missing.

"Please get up and follow us," Hu Yin said.

"Whose troops do you belong to?" the Generalissimo asked. "If you're with the Red Army, just shoot me."

"No, sir," Hu Yin said and told him what army he belonged to. The Generalissimo glared and attempted to rise, then grimaced and fell back again.

Hu Yin took off his coat and put it around the Generalissimo's shoulders. He ordered one of the soldiers to carry him. Without resisting, Chiang allowed himself to be carried down the hillside. Hu Yin immediately reported the capture to the Young Marshal by phone.

He heard a heavy sigh of relief on the other end of the line. "Take him to the Sian Pacification Headquarters. And see to it that he is comfortable."

A car was waiting on the road at the foot of the hill. When they reached it, the Generalissimo refused to get in. "You need medical attention, sir," Hu Yin urged. "We must take you to a place where you can rest and be comfortable."

But the Generalissimo stubbornly refused to be taken prisoner. "Call my own men," he persisted. "They will take me."

Unable to persuade him to comply, Hu Yin took hold of him and shoved him into the back seat of the car. Once inside, the Generalissimo demanded, "Where is Marshal Chang?"

"We are taking you to him right now, sir," Hu Yin said, getting into the car beside him.

✻

When Hu Yin arrived at the 17th Route Army headquarters, both the Young Marshal and General Yang were overjoyed. They immediately called an emergency meeting. When the senior officers arrived, the Young

Marshal declared, "General Yang and I have poked a hole in the sky! We have taken Chiang Kai-shek prisoner! The fate of the nation is now in our hands. All of us should take the responsibility on our shoulders. We must draft a message immediately and cable it to the Communist Party, asking them to send a delegation here to talk to us."

The senior officers plunged into a heated discussion. The message was drafted. A group of senior officers was organized to handle the possible military confrontation and a special committee was assigned to deal with the political turmoil that might follow the news of the arrest.

The message they drafted was the same as the public declaration they had prepared three days before, plus the announcement of the Generalissimo's detention.

While holding their breath for the nation's reaction, the Young Marshal and General Tiger Yang ordered several personnel changes. Hu Yin was charged with responsibility for carrying out the orders.

General Sun Wei-ru, one of the Northeastern Army commanders, was appointed Commander in Charge of Martial Law in Sian; General Chao Shou-shen became the Director of Sian's Public Security Bureau. All political prisoners must be released within three days, they decided. The local newspaper was to be renamed *The Liberation Daily*, with a new editor. All the other Kuomintang organizations in Sian were to be temporarily suspended and their heads replaced. Anti-Japanese education would be stepped up in the schools and in the armed forces.

In the next few days an official liaison office of the Red Army was set up in Sian, and the Northwest Bandit-Suppression Headquarters was replaced by the Provisional Northwest Military Commission of the Anti-Japanese United Front. The Shensi Provincial Government was reorganized. A circular telegram was issued to the nation announcing those changes.

Confined within the Sian Pacification Headquarters, Generalissimo Chiang was both depressed and defiant, refusing food and water. He asked for a piece of paper to prepare his will. This alarmed Hu Yin, who posted more guards to watch him day and night, and urged the Young Marshal to see the distraught and uncooperative man as soon as possible.

The Young Marshal went to see the prisoner that evening. The room was the best-furnished at the Pacification Headquarters. It had a private bath, and the bed and sofas were brand new, imported from France. It was what General Yang called "my foreign embassy," a special place to accommodate visiting foreign dignitaries.

Chiang was in bed when the Young Marshal and Hu Yin arrived. A tray of food was left on the bedside table, untouched. He was pale and gaunt, and his eyes were inflamed and hostile. After one quick glance at the Young Marshal, he refused to look at him again.

"Generalissimo, you must eat," the Young Marshal said. "If you don't like the food, let me know."

"Where is General Yang?"

"He is here, but he wants me to see you first."

"Send for him."

"Generalissimo, we still want you to study our petition," the Young Marshal insisted.

"I said, send for General Yang!"

The Young Marshal nodded at Hu Yin, who took the hint and hurried out. A moment later he returned with Tiger Yang, who saluted the Generalissimo smartly.

"Did you know of this beforehand?" the Generalissimo demanded.

"Yes," Yang answered, looking straight into the Generalissimo's eyes. The curt answer made Chiang tremble. He turned away from Yang, his chest heaving, his eyes closed as if trying to control his fury. Obviously the conspiracy of two subordinates was too much for him to bear.

The Young Marshal repeated the demand for a united front and a cessation of the civil war. There was no answer. His eyes tightly closed, Chiang lay on the bed, his head turned away, his chest heaving. Hu Yin watched him with a pain in his heart. Here was a man nobody had ever said no to. The whole nation had put him on a pedestal and worshiped him like a god—except the Communists. Twenty-four hours before, he had been the Commander-in-Chief of two million well-equipped troops, the most powerful man in China; now he was a prisoner trying to starve himself to death. It depressed Hu Yin to see this great leader so angry and yet so helpless.

He knew that the Young Marshal was equally troubled. Looking dejected, his eyes moist and his face white, the Young Marshal turned and walked out of the room. Tiger Yang looked at the Generalissimo contemptuously. He started to speak but changed his mind. He, too, walked out.

Hu Yin gestured at the two guards, who followed him out of the room. "Never take your eyes off him," he ordered. "Keep him as comfortable as possible." The guards acknowledged the order and returned to the room.

Catching up with the two generals, Hu Yin heard Yang tell the Young Marshal, "We will have to move him. If he dies, I don't want it at my headquarters."

"Why do you say that?" the Young Marshal asked. "Who says he's going to die?"

"He, himself," General Yang said. "He does not wish to live. I can tell all the signs." They walked to the car without another word.

✳

The next day Hu Yin was ordered to move the Generalissimo to the residence of General Gao, a division commander of the Northeastern Army. It was a comfortable mansion in another part of the city. Hu Yin went to the Generalissimo's detention room early, taking with him two junior officers and two soldiers carrying a stretcher. Outside, an ambulance was waiting.

The Generalissimo was lying on his back, staring at the ceiling. A glass of water, half full, was standing on his bedside table next to his false teeth. Knowing that the Generalissimo still refused to talk, Hu Yin asked the guards if he had eaten anything. They shook their heads.

"Generalissimo," Hu Yin said, "we have come to move you. Please get up."

The Generalissimo looked at him and then at the junior officers, who had pistols stuck in their belts and whose expressions on their dark faces looked ominous. He shuddered, thinking that he was going to be executed.

"I want to die right here," he said. "I won't move." He turned his face away, breathing hard.

Hu Yin hated to use force again. And, knowing Chiang's uncompromising nature, he withdrew without moving him.

✳

Back at the Sian Pacification Headquarters, General Yang was drumming on his desk with his fingers while the Young Marshal paced the floor. The tense atmosphere was oppressive. Hu Yin felt sorry for the Young Marshal, who was torn between his loyalty to the Generalissimo and his duty. As soon as they had heard Hu Yin's report on Chiang Kai-shek's unyielding attitude, General Yang rose from his desk and hit the table with his fist. "We'll have to shoot him," he said with an air of finality.

The remark so shocked the Young Marshal that he staggered. He swallowed hard, put both his hands out and said, stammering badly, "I— I'll talk to h-him. I'll talk to him right away. I've known him since I was a child. He's not an unreasonable man."

"All right," Tiger Yang said after a pause. "But there must be a limit to this. We've already waded into the water; we are wet up to our necks."

He started to say something else but stopped. Hu Yin was distressed. What was left unsaid was obvious. Tiger Yang had no choice but to shoot the prisoner.

That evening, nervous and without having eaten dinner, the Young Marshal and Hu Yin went to see the Generalissimo again. Hu Yin went with a heavy heart. Since his arrival in Sian, he had often identified his own problems with the Young Marshal's. He had won battles and minor skirmishes, but he could not win the heart of the woman he had loved all his life. He possessed her body but not her heart. The Young Marshal had the Generalissimo in custody; he had the power to release him or kill him, but he could not have the only thing he wanted—Chiang Kai-shek's consent to stop the civil war and fight the common enemy with a united front. Every time Hu Yin accompanied the Young Marshal into situations like this, he identified with him, agonizing over similar problems and lamenting their similar fates. Now the possibility of shooting the Generalissimo weighed heavily on his heart. But it was an act that nobody could prevent except the Generalissimo himself. If Tiger Yang insisted on taking such a drastic step, nobody could tell what China's future would be. Japan might cheer and escalate her military adventure, or she might meekly withdraw her troops and give up her campaign, knowing that a united China would be unconquerable.

The Generalissimo was taking a nap while the guards sat on two sofas, one watching the bed while the other dozed. When the Young Marshal and Hu Yin came in, they shot to their feet and saluted.

Without returning the salute, the Young Marshal approached the bed and stood there for a moment, staring down at the slumbering leader. "Generalissimo," he said quietly.

Chiang Kai-shek opened his eyes. Both Chang and Hu Yin saluted him. He closed his eyes again without saying anything. For the next several minutes he remained mute and unresponsive while the Young Marshal pleaded his cause. What he said was a repetition of what he had already said many times before, only this time his voice was shakier and more emotional.

Suddenly the Generalissimo opened his eyes wide, turned to him and interrupted. "Did you or did you not talk to Chou En-lai before you came here?"

The question stunned the Young Marshal. "Yes," he answered after a long pause. "But it was almost a month ago. I talked to many Communist leaders. They all agreed that if you would fight the Japanese, they would support you. They would even be willing to get rid of their Red Army insignia and become part of the Nationalist Army, and obey your orders."

"Are you so naive as to believe that?" Chiang said angrily in his high-pitched voice.

The Young Marshal was silent, looking hurt. Chiang went on. "After the Communists promised to fight the Japanese under the Nationalist flag, did you supply them with food, clothing and a large amount of your own private money? Well, did you or did you not?"

"Y–yes," the Young Marshal admitted.

"How stupid! How stupid!"

The Young Marshal's lips trembled. "Generalissimo," he said, his voice more desperate now, "to a military man there are only three choices: win, lose or surrender . . ."

"To a real military man, the word *surrender* is nonexistent. How can you represent two opposing sides? Where is your loyalty to your leader? Be off, be off!"

"My conscience compels me to say this, Generalissimo. My loyalty to you is not blind; there is something that is above loyalty—that is my patriotism . . ."

"There is nothing more to be said," Chiang interrupted. "If you are my subordinate, send me back to Nanking; if you are my enemy, shoot me!" With a wave of his hand, he turned away and refused to say another word.

The Young Marshal left the room, his eyes full of tears. Hu Yin followed him, secretly mourning the end of Chiang Kai-shek, an unyielding leader who believed only in himself and his own course, right or wrong. Hu Yin, too, was unable to hold back his tears.

50

A twin-engined plane circled the city of Sian against the cloudless blue early-morning sky, looking like a lost bird trying to find a hospitable place to land. The airport guards aimed their rifles at it, ready to shoot it down when it came within range. But something dropped from the plane. It was a sealed tube. A guard picked it up and found in it a letter addressed to the Young Marshal.

It was from W. H. Donald, an Australian reporter who had been the Young Marshal's friend for many years. Donald said that he had come on behalf of Madame Chiang, requesting a meeting with the Generalissimo.

When the Young Marshal read the letter, he heaved a long sigh of relief. If Mr. Donald had arrived a day later, it might have been too late. He immediately gave orders to the guard to signal the plane to land. In half an hour he and Hu Yin sped to the airport.

W. H. Donald, who had been working for a British paper, was a rumpled-looking, amiable man. Hu Yin learned that he at one time had been the Young Marshal's adviser. It was he who had accompanied him to Europe for the drug addiction cure. Now he was an adviser to Madame Chiang Kai-shek. When Donald and the Young Marshal greeted each other at the airport, Hu Yin knew that the friendship between them was warm and genuine.

Donald had brought two letters from Madame Chiang, one for the Generalissimo, the other for the Young Marshal, who read the letter in the car on their way to Sian. When he had finished, he folded it carefully —almost reverently—and pocketed it.

He said, "Madame hopes that in handling the Sian incident, I will take into consideration both my personal and official relationship with the Generalissimo, as well as the interest of the nation."

He stopped for a moment, trying to control his emotions, then went on. "W. H., you know that my affection for both the Generalissimo and Madame has never changed, and never will. But the officers and men of the Northeastern Army have been driven out of their homeland by the Japanese. It is natural that they demand resistance to Japan."

"I understand their feelings perfectly well," Donald said. "And I am sure Madame Chiang knows them, too."

"In order to secure the Generalissimo's release, we must resubmit the petition and seek his agreement. But before we do that, we must remove him to a more secure residence. General Gao, one of my division commanders, has agreed that we move the Generalissimo to his home. But so far the Generalissimo has refused to be moved."

"Is that very important?" Donald asked.

"For the Generalissimo's safety, it is," Hu Yin said, knowing that Tiger Yang was anxious to execute the prisoner and finish the whole affair.

"I'll see what I can do about that," Donald said.

That evening Donald reported that the Generalissimo had agreed to be moved. Next morning the Young Marshal went to see the Generalissimo again with the petition. When he came back, he looked dejected. The Generalissimo had again refused to discuss it.

Tiger Yang was getting more impatient. W. H. Donald had come and gone. The Central Government's punitive expedition was marching toward Sian. Warplanes thundered over the city every day in a show of airpower. Border counties south of Sian had already been bombed and thousands of civilians killed.

That afternoon Hu Yin heard Yang and the Young Marshal quarrel heatedly in Yang's office.

"There is no choice but to shoot him!" Tiger Yang shouted.

"The Japanese will be happy to hear that!" the Young Marshal shouted back.

"You are contradicting yourself. You always say he is pro-Japanese."

"I tell you I was wrong! After I read his diary, I knew he was *not* pro-Japanese. All he wants to do is delay the war with Japan."

"So he can use his men to destroy the Communists—and perhaps you and me!"

"That's not true!"

"Then tell me why he delays fighting the Japanese."

"Because we are not ready. We are not ready to fight a bandit nation as strong as Japan."

"Bunk!"

"We have seized his diary; do you want to read it?"

"No—I don't have time to read his diary. Besides, how do you know he's telling the truth?"

"This is very crucial, General Yang," the Young Marshal said, his voice pleading now. "Japan wants him dead. We must keep him alive. Or there will be a puppet government headed by Wang Chin-wei, the head of the pro-Japanese clique in Nanking."

"The Generalissimo is the head of that clique; don't you know that? Chiang Kai-shek must die!"

"Let's consult Chou En-lai. After all, this is supposed to be an alliance of three sides—you, me and the Communists."

"All right, we'll obey the majority," Yang said with an air of finality.

The Young Marshal came out of Yang's office, his eyes sad and his face ashen. He had lost a great deal of weight during the Sian incident. Without a word, he marched out of the building. Hu Yin followed him.

*

Chou En-lai and General Yeh Chien-yin of the Red Army arrived two days later on horseback during a storm. They had traveled two days with short stops for food and sleep. Both men looked exhausted; but, without delay, the Young Marshal escorted them to General Yang's headquarters for a closed-door meeting. Hu Yin sat in the outer office, waiting nervously for the final decision. Chiang's life was hanging on that decision; perhaps China's future was hanging on it. Sitting on a hard chair, he kept rubbing his sweating hands and making fists. Never in his life had he suffered such anxiety and suspense.

When the Young Marshal walked out, he was smiling. Hu Yin shot to his feet with a sigh of relief. The decision had been made. Chiang was to be detained, but his life was to be spared. Both Chou En-lai and Yeh Chien-yin believed that it would only benefit Japan if Chiang were killed. Besides, Stalin did not want Chiang to die, either—he would rather have Chiang than Japan ruling China.

But time was getting short. The Central Government's troops were marching closer. Their warplanes were overhead every morning. Anytime now a devastating civil war would explode. To prepare for that eventuality, General Yang moved part of his troops to Tungkwan to guard the main entrance to Sian. Meanwhile, the Red Army was sending troops to three border counties to face the first wave of government forces. Nobody wanted the war, but it would be a war for survival. The Sian troops would rather die than live under a Japanese puppet government.

Hu Yin kept a diary. Besides jotting down events, he also expressed his own feelings about the incident. He had now become a fatalist, thinking that he would probably die at Sian if no compromise were reached. When the government planes started bombing the city, he would at least try to save his diary. It would be his legacy, something for Mabel to keep. As possible disaster was looming in the immediate future, he began to miss Hankow and his home, particularly Mabel. When he thought about her, he lamented his fate. Perhaps he was destined not to have a happy and peaceful life—not to enjoy a family with four generations living under one roof and watching great-great-grandchildren play at his feet; not to have any of the pleasures a traditional Chinese dreamed of having in his old age.

The war seemed unavoidable. The students had started marching every day, urging a life and death battle against Chiang Kai-shek's Kuomintang. Troops were moving, trenches were being dug and fortifications built. On December 20, 1936, eight days after the Generalissimo's arrest, another lone plane appeared over Sian. It was the same one that had carried W. H. Donald there on Madame Chiang's behalf. Another tube was dropped in which a message was addressed to the Young Marshal and signed by Donald: "Madame Chiang and I have come to visit the Generalissimo. Please allow us to land."

The Young Marshal was elated. There was hope of peace if Madame Chiang had come personally. A flare was sent up to signal the plane to land.

Hu Yin accompanied the Young Marshal to the airport to meet the visitors.

Madame Chiang was wrapped in a heavy fur coat, her face white and her eyes red-rimmed. She was followed by her personal chef, a woman who knew what food to prepare in order to avoid aggravating Madame's skin allergy. W. H. Donald, also looking haggard, helped Madame step down from the plane. The Young Marshal stepped forward and greeted them warmly. Then he ushered them to the waiting automobiles. Accompanied by heavily armed guards, they drove directly to General Gao's residence, where the Generalissimo had been suffering severe pain from his injury and had become despondent.

Madame Chiang asked that she be allowed to see her husband alone for a few minutes. Knowing that it would be an emotional reunion, the Young Marshal and the others waited in the living room. When the Young Marshal was asked to go in a few minutes later, Hu Yin went in with him. W. H. Donald led the way.

The Generalissimo was sitting on a sofa. He was wearing the Young Marshal's silk robe over his pajamas. Madame Chiang was standing beside him, a smile on her face; but her eyes were still wet with tears. So were the Generalissimo's. The greeting was cordial, and the Generalissimo smiled for the first time. Obviously, he was glad to see his wife, even though he had previously objected to her visit.

"Mr. Donald," he said, "in her last letter, my wife threatened to come here. But you could have stopped her. It is foolish for her to risk her life like this."

"Generalissimo," the Young Marshal said, "there is no longer any danger. General Yang has softened his stand. But if the Central Government stops the punitive forces from marching toward Sian, I am sure we will have a peaceful solution."

"Generalissimo," Donald said, "you must realize there is a strong clique in your Nanking government that is obsessively pro-Japanese. At this moment they are determined to take advantage of the Sian incident to launch an all-out war against Sian. They are ready to attack the city with troops, artillery and bombs. It is most urgent that Your Excellency stop the massive attack plan before it is too late. If not, the consequences will be unthinkable. You would die in the attack and the pro-Japanese clique would seize power."

"Mr. Donald is right, darling," Madame Chiang agreed. "Before I left Nanking I had a quarrel with members of that clique. You must return to Nanking as soon as possible."

"How can I go?" Chiang said, spreading his hands. "I'm a prisoner here."

"You are free to go, Generalissimo," the Young Marshal said. "All you have to do is agree to the conditions of the petition."

Chiang turned to the Young Marshal sharply, his eyes hardening. "Are you still talking about that? Have I not already given you my answer?"

"Personally, I don't insist on your agreement, Generalissimo," the Young Marshal said, his voice desperate. "But General Yang will never release you if you refuse to accept the terms."

"Well, he can do whatever he wishes," Chiang said, glaring at the Young Marshal, "but tell him that I will not obey his orders!"

"Han Ching," Madame Chiang said to the Young Marshal, her voice sad, "is there any other way you can secure the Generalissimo's release?"

"General Yang has posted his troops on all the highways, and the airport is heavily guarded. The only way for the Generalissimo to get out of Sian is for him to disguise himself as a peasant. Then I'll find a way to smuggle him out of the city."

When Chiang heard the proposal, he flushed. "I will never leave this city in disguise!" he said heatedly. Then he turned to Madame Chiang. "Mei-ling, you and Mr. Donald should return to Nanking as soon as possible. It is so foolish for you to . . ."

"Darling," Madame Chiang interrupted firmly. "I have come here to live or die with you. I won't go unless you go. And that is final!"

The Generalissimo looked touched. But he still refused to compromise. The visitors withdrew unhappily. The Young Marshal was devastated. Hu Yin accompanied him to his modest residence. In the living room, Chang personally poured two glasses of whiskey. "Hu Yin, if I'd known I would get into this mess, I would never have committed such a blunder."

"Why do you call it a blunder, Young Marshal?" Hu Yin said sympathetically. "I still think it's an unusually brave attempt to save the country. It's our bad luck that the Generalissimo can't see clearly that the enemy is not us, but his own pro-Japanese clique."

They had nothing else to say, and started drinking to seek a moment's peace.

*

Next morning Chou En-lai arrived to see Chiang. The Young Marshal and Hu Yin escorted him to the residence immediately. When they reached General Gao's, Chiang was having his breakfast in bed. It was a good sign, Hu Yin thought. The Generalissimo had not only started eating, but seemed to enjoy his food. When he saw Chou, he attempted to get out of bed to greet him, but Chou stopped him. Chou still addressed him as Commandant, as he had worked for him at the Whampoo Military Academy in Canton many years ago. Chiang remembered him well and both exchanged pleasantries.

Charming and personable, Chou avoided mentioning the eight demands but talked about the sad affairs of the nation, especially the sufferings of the people. His voice calm and sincere, he was so persuasive that Chiang listened without interrupting. When Chou had finished, Chiang said, "I have never believed that socialism is the solution for China's problems. It simply does not fit China's conditions."

"Commandant," Chou said, "our country is about to be conquered by a foreign army. We are not even thinking about socialism or Communism. As Chairman Mao has declared, the defeat of Japan must take precedence over social revolution because it is absolutely necessary to win independence first. For that reason the Communist Party is willing to join forces with you against the Imperialist enemy. We cannot even discuss Communism if we are robbed of our freedom and of our country. Commandant, time is running out. Only you can save the country from total ruin."

Chiang was quiet. Everyone was nervously waiting for his response. Madame Chiang broke the silence. "Lissimo, I think Vice-Chairman Chou is right. Time is running out. You should immediately direct the Nanking government to cease hostilities for a few days so that we all can have a breathing spell to find a solution."

Under both Chou's and W. H. Donald's urging, the Generalissimo finally agreed to send a wire to Nanking to halt the bombing and the troop movements. A few hours later Nanking agreed to a five-day truce. Five days was a short time, but total war and the destruction of Sian were temporarily avoided.

*

Next morning the Young Marshal called Hu Yin to his office. He said that after haggling all night, General Yang had finally agreed to delete four of the eight conditions in the petition. He would like to take the shortened petition to the Generalissimo for another try, and he wanted moral support.

When the Young Marshal and Hu Yin arrived, a few more of Chiang's close associates were there, including Madame Chiang's brother, T. V. Soong, the Minister of Finance. After four hours of discussion, the Generalissimo grudgingly accepted the four conditions, but refused to sign anything. Once again disappointed, the Young Marshal offered to take a counterproposal to Yang.

It had been a grueling experience for both the Young Marshal and Hu Yin, who kept his diary brief, sensing that the end was near. The city had no air-raid shelters, houses were easy to burn and there was no adequate fire-fighting equipment. If the government air force started bombing Sian, the majority of the people in the city would perish. Hu Yin did not know why, but he was not afraid or worried. He wondered if it was a death wish that had turned him emotionless.

In his diary, he wrote:

Dec. 20. Madame Chiang told the Young Marshal that it would be a marvelous Christmas gift to her and to the nation if he could obtain the Generalissimo's release. The Young Marshal has exhausted every means except armed conflict with General Yang.

Dec. 21. The Young Marshal is more depressed than ever. Yang insists on a signed agreement with the Generalissimo before he can be released. The Young Marshal again suggested that both the Generalissimo and Madame Chiang escape in disguise. The Generalissimo absolutely refused. Madame Chiang said, "In no way will I be disguised to escape. I have come here to live or die with the Generalissimo."

Dec. 22. The young officers of both armies are clamoring to execute the Generalissimo before the Central Government warplanes start bombing Sian. The senior officers, especially those of the Northeastern Army, are trying to suppress the uproar. A rift is seen among the ranks. My heart goes out to the Young Marshal, who is running about like an ant on a hot stove.

Dec. 23. The Young Marshal is determined to get Madame out of Sian before it is too late. But she refuses to leave, saying that if she had been afraid, she would not have come. To save the lives of the Generalissimo and Madame, the Young Marshal is willing to risk an armed clash with Yang's 17th Route Army. It is a terrifying thought.

Dec. 24. No solutions. Yang's attitude has softened a little, but no decision. Tomorrow is the final day of the truce. Everybody's nerves are frayed. I am ready to end with Sian. Three times I have attempted to write to Mabel; three times I have discarded what I had written. It is better not to inform her of the tragedy. I begin to ask, "Why, why, why?" as the Young Marshal has so often asked. I cannot find an answer. In certain situations, man must face death, even though there are alternatives. Is it honor or is it a death wish? I don't know, I don't know!

Dec. 25. "Heaven has no dead-end street for man." An optimistic old saying. I never believed it until tonight. Tiger Yang has relented. The Young Marshal rushed to see the Generalissimo alone. A plane is ordered to take the Generalissimo and Madame out of Sian, departure immediate. For the first time, I knelt down and thanked the Buddha and the ancestors, and all the other kind gods, for this sudden turn of luck. I almost wept.

The Young Marshal and Hu Yin rode to the airport in the murky night. General Gao had been instructed to escort the Generalissimo and Madame Chiang to the waiting plane. The Young Marshal should have been euphoric, but he was quiet and held a suitcase tightly in his hands. Hu Yin wondered why he had brought it.

"I am going to Nanking with the Generalissimo," he said.

"Why?"

"Because I want to be responsible for the incident," the Young Marshal said. "Nobody is to blame for this but me."

"I think it is a mistake for you to go, Young Marshal. The Northeastern Army needs you here in Sian . . ."

"My mind is made up," the Young Marshal cut him short. "I have entrusted the affairs of the Northeastern Army to General Yang. He will be in temporary command while I am gone."

They arrived at the airport ahead of the Generalissimo. Soon a flicker of lights was seen in the distance. Army trucks were heard roaring. "They are here," the Young Marshal said. Now controlled excitement was evident in his voice. Hu Yin swallowed hard. He, too, felt an exhilaration that he had not experienced before. It was almost like witnessing a miracle, the light at the end of a long dark tunnel, a hope looming in hopelessness and despair. He felt like jumping up and cheering.

First arriving on the dirt road was a truckload of Manchurian troops in sheepskin caps, holding torches and with submarine guns slung over their shoulders. Following the truck were two Ford sedans. Bringing up the rear were two more truckloads of soldiers, rifles ready and and eyes roving.

Several aides got out of the first sedan. Two rushed to open the doors of the second one. General Gao, a stout, beefy man in a fur coat, stepped out of the front seat. From the back door, Madame emerged, followed by T. V. Soong and W. H. Donald. Finally, the Generalissimo came out, helped by General Gao personally. General Tai Li came out last. Under the torch lights, they all looked tired and disheveled, their faces white. Donald was hatless, his graying hair tossing in the wind. He was the only one who looked relaxed, a smile on his puffy face.

The Young Marshal, carrying his suitcase, stepped out from behind the soldiers and bowed to the Generalissimo and Madame. He asked for permission to go with the Generalissimo, who looked surprised. "Why must you go, Han Ching?" the Generalissimo asked.

"There is a great deal of explaining to be done about this unfortunate incident. And it is my responsibility to do it."

"If you're going to save my face," Chiang said, "forget it. You have no business going to Nanking with me."

"Darling," Madame said, "he speaks English. He can keep Mr. Donald company. Why not let him have a ride with us?"

The Generalissimo still objected, but the Young Marshal insisted on going with them.

When the plane took off, Hu Yin watched it soar into the dark night, its taillights blinking. He saluted smartly and did not bring his hand down until it had disappeared into ominous thick clouds.

✳

Hu Yin had not slept well. He could not grasp what was bothering him. Somehow the happy ending was overshadowed by many doubts.

Five days after the Generalissimo returned to Nanking, bad news came over the wire at the headquarters of the Northeastern Army: the Young Marshal, Chang Hsueh-liang, had been arrested and was awaiting a court-martial. The news did not surprise Hu Yin. He had had a premonition of disaster for five days, but he had not expected anything so dire.

The news caused an uproar among the younger officers of the North-eastern Army. Seventy regimental officers came to Hu Yin, asking him to take them to see General Yang. Still the coordinating officer, Hu Yin complied.

The young officers took a signed appeal to General Yang's office. One of them read it to the General, who listened intently, grim-faced. It said:

> When Marshal Chang Hsueh-liang left Sian, he ordered our Northeast-ern Army to follow your directions during his absence. Now the Central Government has detained him and our superiors remain indif-ferent, as if nothing has happened. We are, therefore, presenting to you our signed appeal and requesting that you lead us to fight Nanking. We demand the return of our leader, Marshal Chang, and nothing less. After he has returned to Sian, we will lay down our arms if we are ordered to do so.

While the young officer read, emphasizing each word, his throat be-came so tight with emotion that he was almost unable to finish. Most of the other officers broke into tears; a few even started to sob. But Tiger Yang could only express his sympathy.

"I fully understand your feelings," he said, "but it is inappropriate for me to make any such decision without consulting your senior officers. I am sorry."

Frustrated, the men returned to their units. Hu Yin had nothing to say to them. He thought that Yang had acted correctly. He fully understood the young officers' impulsiveness—they would have fought and died at the slightest provocation. He returned to his room, feeling as though his heart were weighed down by a ton of rocks. He too felt like fighting; but, being older, he knew how stupid such a move would be. He did not know what to do except pray for the Young Marshal's safety.

At night he was awakened by gunfire. He sat up and listened, then called his orderly, a young private who was clever and helpful. "What's going on?"

"Let me go find out, sir."

But he didn't have to. Captain Feng rushed in and asked Hu Yin to help settle a mutiny. A junior officer had shot a division commander, and another senior officer had demanded that the junior officer be arrested. The junior officer had refused to be arrested unless it was ordered by the Young Marshal. All the junior officers were now backing him up. They accused the dead senior officer of being a traitor, betraying their leader, the Young Marshal.

Hu Yin thought for a moment. He found himself surprisingly calm. Perhaps his emotions had already been shattered by the repeated bad news in the past two weeks, and even a revolt in his own army did not affect him. Besides, he had seen it coming—the disintegration of one of the best armies in China, well disciplined and well equipped, with an unquenchable desire to fight the Japanese, recapture Manchuria and return to their homeland in triumph. He could have cried for the demise of such a fine force. But his tears had dried; his heart was almost dead.

"Captain Feng," he said, "there is nothing I can do; even General Yang is unable to do anything. Leave them alone."

With a heavy sigh he returned to bed. Feng, looking shattered, withdrew without argument. He, too, seemed to have become a fatalist.

Hu Yin pushed the window open for some fresh air. A half-moon was shining in the dark clear sky. Silhouetted against it was a lone mountain, almost barren. Beyond the mountain, two hundred miles away, was the headquarters of Mao Tse-tung, Chou En-lai and the Red Army. He wondered how things were over there. Perhaps it was time to seek greener pastures. He could almost see himself—a lone rider trudging over the vast plain and over that barren mountain, with nothing but a small bundle, a gun and a heavy heart that was still seeking a bit of hope.

51

W hen Brigid came to breakfast, she was surprised to find Mabel still at the table. It was a late Sunday morning. The sun was shining on the table, which the girl had laid with fresh daisies and three dinner sets on a clean linen cloth.

"Good morning," Mabel said, her voice unhappy and her eyes downcast.

"Good morning," Brigid answered cheerfully, wondering why her daughter was getting more and more gloomy lately. She had always been high-spirited, especially in the morning. Even after her temper tantrums, she had always bounced back with smiles and giggles as soon as the storm had passed. She could switch a long face into a smiling one like a quick change of scenery on the stage.

Brigid looked at the extra plate and asked, "Why? Have you invited a guest to breakfast?"

"I laid it for Papa. It's time for him to come home."

"Did he write to you?"

"No, but he always comes home without telling anybody." She buttered her toast. "Mama, did you quarrel with him?"

"Of course not, darling," Brigid said with a smile. "What makes you think that?"

"He told me he would never leave home for more than a month. Now it has been two months."

"He had urgent business. Would you care for some coffee?"

"Papa said no girl should drink coffee or wine before she is eighteen."

Brigid poured herself a cup. She was disappointed that Mabel had stopped pouring coffee for her, for Mabel had loved to play hostess when Hu Yin was home. "Well, good," she thought. "In France girls start drinking coffee and wine before they are ten years old, and nobody is surprised."

"Mama," Mabel said, "where is Sian?"

"Sian is in the northwest. Why?"

"I thought so. Do you think Papa has been arrested by Chiang Kai-shek?"

"Mabel, please don't speculate like that. Your father has had nothing to do with the Sian incident."

"But he went to Sian with that Young Marshal who kidnapped Chiang Kai-shek!"

"I'm glad you have been reading the papers. It's a good habit."

"I didn't read the papers. Our teachers talk about it all the time. Mama, are you sure you didn't quarrel with him?"

"Please don't question me like that!" Brigid said sharply. "Of course I didn't quarrel with him!"

"He wouldn't have gone to Sian if he had been happy at home."

"Mabel, your father is a soldier. He goes wherever his duty calls him."

They ate quietly for a moment. Mabel was picking at her sausages without eating them. Before, she had had good table manners; now she was careless and sloppy, playing with her food like a spoiled brat. "Maybe I'll have a cup of coffee now, Mother."

"What did your father tell you? Didn't he say a girl should not drink coffee before she is eighteen?"

"I don't care."

Without arguing, Brigid poured a half cup for her. Mabel took a sip and made a terrible face. But she was determined to finish it. She blew her coffee, took several sips and blew it again, noisily.

"Mabel," Brigid said, staring at her with disapproval, "nobody blows hot coffee. It's bad manners."

The girl stopped, but kept sipping the coffee and making faces, as though it were bitter herb juice that she must force herself to drink.

Brigid kept quiet. She knew her daughter well. She was going through a phase. Before the next phase, she might grow out of this one.

"I think Papa will never come back," Mabel said, playing with her food again.

"What makes you say that?" Brigid asked, surprised.

"Because he went with that Young Marshal Chang Hsueh-liang. They say the Young Marshal is a playboy. He has many wives."

"That has nothing to do with your father."

"It has! The Young Marshal can teach him a lot of bad things. I hate him!"

Brigid put down her knife and fork and stared at her daughter. "Mabel, the Young Marshal has done a good deed!" she said quietly, her voice serious. "He stopped the civil war and united the Nationalists and Communists, so that we can all fight our common enemy. Didn't your teacher tell you that?"

"Yes, but I still hate the Young Marshal."

"Listen, young lady," Brigid said harshly, "you should never let your personal likes and dislikes dictate your opinion of a public figure. Personally, I don't like Chiang Kai-shek, but I still support him as a national leader and admire many of his qualities."

"The Young Marshal has many concubines."

"That's not true. The Young Marshal has only two women in his life, his wife and Miss Chow Number Four."

"See?" Mabel said triumphantly. "Besides his wife, he has four concubines. Number one, number two, number three and number four."

Brigid threw up her hands with a groan. "Mabel, Number Four doesn't mean number-four concubine! There are four girls in the family. She is the fourth daughter. I think it's about time you switched to a Chinese school. The missionary school has turned you into a foreign devil, ignorant of Chinese customs and traditions."

"I don't want to know Chinese customs and traditions. I hate concubines, bound feet, kowtows and pigtails."

"Be quiet, Mabel!" Brigid said, shocked that her daughter was still so ignorant. "After the revolution, concubines, bound feet, kowtows and pigtails were outlawed. Don't you know that? I'm going to take you out of that school next week. Just be quiet and eat your breakfast."

With a loud sob, Mabel threw her fork and knife down and ran out of the room.

Brigid finished her sausages and eggs without much appetite. She poured herself another cup of coffee, feeling angry and frustrated. Ever since Hu Yin had left home, she had been nervous and impatient. She had tried not to show her real mood in front of her daughter, often forcing herself to be cheerful; but now she found it increasingly difficult to hide her feelings. Her impatience with Mabel bothered her. She started to go to Mabel's room and apologize, but changed her mind. The girl had already been spoiled enough; more pampering would only make it worse.

She returned to her own room and changed her clothes. She had a luncheon engagement with Michael Steward in about three hours. Perhaps she should go meet him earlier instead of waiting for him to pick her up. Steward had two daughters and a son. Perhaps she should ask him about his experiences in raising three children.

She missed Hu Yin. In spite of their difficulties, she felt secure in his house. She did not know why; probably because Hu Yin was different from most other men. He was loyal and strong; he could also be murderous. She always had the gnawing feeling that Hu Yin was capable of doing anything; she even secretly believed that he was one of the conspirators who had kidnapped Chiang Kai-shek.

When she read about the Young Marshal's conviction for "organizing followers to coerce one's superior with brute force," she had begun to worry. The Young Marshal had been sentenced to ten years' imprisonment with deprivation of civil rights for another five years. Although the sentence had been suspended, he had been placed under close surveillance of the National Military Council. Had Hu Yin been detained? Was he waiting for trial? The suspense was wringing her heart.

*

Michael Steward was reading a magazine at the Press Club when she arrived. "I knew you would be here," she said as she walked into the large, empty reading room. "I wasn't sure if you were home or here. Eeny meeny miney mo; I counted on my fingers. And I picked the right one."

Her laughter was forced, but Steward did not detect it. He was the unsuspicious type; he was often too busy for trifling things, and Brigid liked that. "Too early for lunch," he said, looking at his watch. "Anyway, I'm glad you came early. It's such a beautiful morning. Let's not waste it. Where shall we go?"

"I feel like going to a Chinese teahouse, do you mind?"

"No, but I don't know any Chinese teahouses."

"We have two choices. Two of the best."

"Eeny meeny miney mo again?" Steward said, laughing. "I'll go for the one your fingers pick."

They went to Old Heavenly Pavilion in a back alley not far from the Press Club. Brigid said it was a typical old-fashioned teahouse serving typical Cantonese dim sum. "I'm on a Chinese cultural kick this morning," she said, walking briskly on the cobblestoned street in the warm sun, breathing the rare fresh air. Only on Sundays was the air breathable in Wuhan, since most of the factories stopped billowing black smoke into the air on that day.

"Why this sudden cultural kick?"

"This morning I scolded my daughter for being ignorant of Chinese customs. I threatened to pull her out of her missionary school. I even called her a foreign devil. Afterward I felt guilty. I myself had been a half–foreign devil all my life—eating foreign food, speaking foreign languages and seeing foreign-devil friends all the time. So I want to have something Chinese for a change."

The small teahouse was crowded. In a corner an old storyteller was telling tales of the Three Warring Kingdoms. Steward dropped a few coins into his collection cup before they sat down.

One of the waitresses was passing with a cart of small dishes of tidbits. Brigid ordered woolung tea and picked dishes of filled buns, braised ducks' feet, chicken livers, black bean spareribs and sticky ricecakes. She was not hungry, but the dim sum were light and appetizing. She poured tea and served Steward with her chopsticks, acting like a typical Chinese hostess. Steward watched her with a smile, loving the attention.

"Tell me what you read this morning," she said. "You almost buried your head in that magazine."

"I was reading an interview in a small literary magazine from Northern California. The citizens in Carmel are proud of their new neighbor, Colonel and Mrs. Joseph Stilwell. Stilwell has been appointed the military attaché to the American Embassy in China. He is supposed to be an Old China Hand, whatever that is."

"Any significance in that appointment?"

"Stilwell made a remark that might have gotten him the job," Steward said. "Everybody back home is scared to death of the Commies. But Stilwell had the guts to say, 'Don't be. The Chinese Communists might be just a *label.*' Well, I think Washington likes to hear what Stilwell has to say—to look at the other side of a coin, so to speak."

"What do you think?"

"I don't know. Perhaps he has a point. After all, Mao Tse-tung did say once, 'For people deprived of their freedom, the revolutionary task is not immediate socialism, but the struggle for independence.' You know the Communists played a strong hand in Chiang's kidnapping. It is also no secret that they were instrumental in his release. If the Communists' real interest is to grab power, Chiang wouldn't be back in Nanking. He might be up there flapping his wings right now." He turned his eyes heavenward with a little chuckle.

"You are a good analyst, Michael. What's going to happen now?"

"I'm not a prophet, but I think this Sian incident will change the course of history. I predict that Japan will step up her invasion of China before China becomes too strong. Without the civil war, and with a united front, China could be formidable. Mark my word, Brigid, we are going to see a lot of fireworks in the coming year. It might be the beginning of American involvement."

"It depresses me."

"That's an odd reaction from a Chinese." Steward looked at her with a frown. "It seems to excite the whole nation, making everybody rub his hands, ready to throw the first punch at the Japs."

"Any world war fought in China means greater destruction. The prospect depresses me. Let's talk about something else. By the way, you are an experienced parent . . ."

"Why do you say that?"

"Because you raised three children—a son and two daughters—did you not?"

"Yes, but I was never home long enough to raise any of them. After our separation, my wife had them; after our divorce, she maintained custody. Why?"

"Because I want to get some idea from a parent who knows how to raise daughters."

"Not from me. I don't know a damned thing about children—sons or daughters. I wish I were experienced. That's something I've missed terribly —a family life, with kids pulling at my legs or climbing my back, a dog fetching my paper and slippers and so forth. What do you want to know?"

"Never mind."

"Brigid, we're friends. If you have problems, tell me. As an old Chinese saying goes, 'Two stinking shoe repairmen are better than one wise man.' "

"My daughter gets moodier every day. I think she misses her father."

"Did she tell you that?"

"No, but her actions speak louder than words. Every day after school she stands at the front door, waiting for him to come back. When she was laying the table for breakfast this morning, she put out an extra place for him, as though she were sure he would show up. I shouldn't complain, but it makes me wonder if it's normal."

Steward swallowed a mouthful of food and wiped his lips with a hot towel that a waitress had left on a plate. Then he took his handkerchief and blew his nose. When he spoke, his eyes had become red and moist. "Brigid," he said with a sigh, "I have never been loved by a woman like that—wife or daughter. How I envy your husband! He doesn't know what he's missing. God, how I envy the guy!"

*

In Wuhan a new foreigner arrived, a square-jawed fellow in a Chinese Air Force uniform, ruggedly handsome. He was treated like a celebrity at the Press Club. Foreign correspondents and local newspaper reporters surrounded him the day he was brought in for an interview.

Brigid was at the club socializing when she was attracted by the hubbub. By listening to the interview she learned that he was an American named Claire Chennault. He had been hired by Madame Chiang Kai-shek to reorganize China's infant air force, which some foreign correspondents had ridiculed as a bird that couldn't fly.

Chennault promised to build the strongest air force in Asia. He had already named it the Flying Tigers. It was a name that sounded wonderful to Chinese ears—powerful, awesome and lucky, like a mythical animal in Chinese legends. For thousands of years, Chinese emperors had displayed imaginary beasts in their palaces, beasts with wings and horns, carved in jade or molded in bronze. They were supposed to repel evil spirits and bring good luck. Now the Chinese believed that Chennault's Flying Tigers would repel the Japanese invaders, and perhaps evil spirits as well.

When the Flying Tigers news broke, Wuhan was excited. Many of Brigid's neighbors asked her if she knew the foreigner. Brigid told them she had shaken his hand. That was enough. Quite a few people shook her hand so they could share a bit of luck with her.

When she told Michael about it at one of their regular luncheon meetings, he laughed. He knew something about Chennault. He was a soldier of fortune from the South—a hell raiser who had quit the U.S. Naval Academy because he hated its discipline. He would have loved to have flown and shot down enemy planes during World War I, but the U.S. government had said no—he was already too old to train. So he had spent the war years as a construction worker in Virginia and as a male nurse somewhere else—Steward wasn't sure where.

"I like him already," Brigid said, laughing. "His background says he's a down-to-earth, likable fellow. Most foreign military men are intimidating —like Bismarck. I think General Chennault will be different, even though his handshake almost broke my fingers."

Steward grimaced. "Another one of those guys who are lucky with ladies in China," he said enviously. "I understand that a girl reporter from a Chinese newspaper published a glowing article about him. The other day I saw her hovering over him like a hummingbird. My God, how I envy the guy!"

Brigid smiled and changed the subject.

*

Two days later Brigid found Chennault to be a lot more than Steward had described. He was a real combat pilot. That morning, when he demonstrated his flying skill, it was like a carnival. Thousands of people lined the streets to watch him do aerobatics. His single-engined plane dived and soared into the clear blue sky, doing somersaults and belly-ups. Every move was awe-inspiring, making the onlookers gape and catch their breath.

Soon the headquarters of the Flying Tigers was established in Wuhan. Five hundred planes arrived from various Chinese provinces, and a training program under Chennault's command was initiated. He scrapped all the previous Italian methods, declaring that the Italians had done all they could to sabotage China.

The united front resulted from the Sian incident, and the creation of the Flying Tigers alarmed the Japanese. As Steward had predicted, Japan's Kwuantung Army started a massive invasion of China.

One hot day in Wuhan, Brigid was about to cool herself in her Victorian bathtub when she caught sight of the headlines on her Chinese-language paper dated July 8, 1937.

She read it avidly, forgetting the heat and her cold-water bath:

JAPAN ATTACKS MARCO POLO BRIDGE OUTSIDE PEKING,
ALL-OUT WAR WITH JAPAN EXPECTED

On the night of July 7, several shots rang out, splitting the still midnight air outside Peking. The phone rang at the residence of Mayor Chu Teh-chuen. The mayor had just finished his bath. He picked up the phone with only a towel around his middle. The night was unbearably hot. The call was made by a member of the Political Council of Hopei and Charhar provinces. He reported excitedly, "The Japanese have demanded to search for a missing soldier in the suburban City of Wan Ping."

The mayor replied, "Tell them a search for the missing soldier will be allowed tomorrow morning." According to information from the Chinese Secret Service, the missing soldier had left his company to relieve himself in a bush and had returned twenty minutes later. But the Japanese used it as an excuse to fire on Chinese troops stationed nearby, accusing the Chinese of kidnapping.

In the morning, instead of searching the city, the Japanese moved hundreds of their crack troops, including artillery and machine-gun units, and attacked the Chinese garrison troops. Fierce fighting broke out. . . .

The paper went on to report that the Japanese had been holding manuevers in the Marco Polo Bridge area for weeks. The stone bridge, spanning the river on graceful arches, was eight hundred years old, decorated with stone lions on its parapets. It was a scenic beauty spot of North China, built to honor Marco Polo, the Ming Emperor's foreign visitor from Italy. Now it faced ruin along with the Chinese fortifications around the city of Wan Ping.

Brigid rushed to see Steward, hoping to get a more detailed report from the Press Club's wire service.

Steward was sending a report back to his employer in New York. When he had finished, he saw Brigid sitting on a sofa, shaking her crossed legs impatiently. "If you're worried about the war, relax," he said, coming over with a thick folder. "The two sides are holding a parley. The conflict has probably stopped already."

They had lunch at the club. No sooner had they finished coffee than fresh news came over the wire:

> 10,000 Japanese troops have crossed the Great Wall into Hopei Province; troop trains have passed through the border at half-hour intervals. The Chinese 29th Army has started retreating. Chiang Kai-shek declared from his summer resort in Kuling that China has reached the end of her patience. No further positions in North China would be surrendered. Armed resistance was absolutely necessary.

The Generalissimo's declaration appeared in all the Wuhan newspapers a few hours later. Firecrackers, drums and gongs were heard everywhere. People cheered and shouted patriotic slogans and paraded in the streets, demonstrating solidarity and all-out support of the government's decision to fight.

Almost immediately the schools held rallies, collected cash contributions and gifts to be distributed among the wounded heroes. Suddenly China was energized. People on the streets walked faster, their heads held higher, their voices louder and their eyes shining with hope and excitement. Mabel donned her Girl Scout uniform again and joined the other students to pass out anti-Japanese leaflets and to preach Madame Chiang's New Life Movement. She came home and reported that the war news had changed the people in the streets. Now they all wore their hats correctly; they had stopped spitting; many had given up smoking. Those who smoked looked timid and guilty, hiding their cigarettes behind their backs when the Girl Scouts approached them. If a Girl Scout threw a man's cigarette away, he did not curse or pick it up again, but walked away looking ashamed. For the first time since her last temper tantrum, Mabel looked cheerful and forgot about her father.

In Wuhan, the United Front became a reality after the Marco Polo Bridge incident. Political prisoners were released. The Red-hunting game in Wuhan stopped. The ban on anti-Japanese slogans was officially lifted. Mabel sang the new patriotic songs at the top of her voice every day, in school and at home. Luckily she had a good voice or Brigid would not have known where to hide.

By August, barely a month after the Marco Polo Bridge attack, many major warlords had offered their services to fight with the United Front. The Red Army happily submitted to the government's reorganization plan, changing their insignia for that of the 8th Route Army. Under

General Lin Piao, the new 8th Route Army, using mobile guerrilla tactics, promptly won a major battle in Shensi Province in the northwest. They attacked the Japanese at a pass of the Great Wall, killing or capturing an entire brigade of the best enemy troops.

Most of the foreign correspondents, heartened by the Chinese victory, went to the various fronts to cover the war. Steward was one of the last to leave Hankow. Brigid bought a large calendar and hung it near the dining table. While reading the Wuhan *Daily* and sipping coffee, she would jot down the brief war news on the calendar each day. Sometimes she would underline the important and positive items with a red pencil.

When Chiang Kai-shek announced that he had mobilized one hundred divisions, representing a total of more than a million men, to resist the enemy; that he had stockpiled enough ammunition for at least six months' intensive fighting; that he had acquired a hundred thousand horses to carry food and war supplies; Brigid cut the news out, pasted it beside her calendar and double-lined the numbers with her red pencil. She was jubilant, having caught the war fever like Mabel. Instead of waiting for her father at the door, Mabel wrote long letters to him, describing what she and her schoolmates had done to help win the war effort. The letters were returned by the post office for nondelivery, but Brigid did not have the heart to tell her. She hid the returned letters in her trunk, keeping them together with Mabel's childhood mementos—her doodlings and drawings, photos and scrapbooks.

Between August and November, most of the news was bad. After the seizure of Peking and Tientsin by the Japanese, Shanghai fell following a three-month siege. On November 20, Soochow, the key city in the Yangtze River Valley, was lost. Soon the Japanese started a merciless bombing of China's major cities. Wuhan suffered the first massive air raid. Most of Chennault's Flying Tiger planes were destroyed in spite of their heroic action against the enemy. Factories and government buildings were demolished. For a long time, Brigid did not use her red pencil, until one day she read about the enraged members of the League of Nations' bitter condemnation of Japan's action against China. She double-lined the item and pasted it on the wall.

The bad war news often depressed her, but not Mabel. The child was still rushing in and out, excitedly reporting what the students had been doing to help the war effort—collecting donations, making mittens for the wounded soldiers, drawing anti-Japanese cartoons, inventing slogans and writing fan letters to war heroes.

The air-raid alarm shrilled almost every day. The mournful blast lasted only a few minutes before waves of Japanese bombers arrived, dropping high explosives. Brigid and the servants invariably dashed for cover, usually hiding under sturdy tables and desks. When the government completed air-raid shelters, they ran for the nearest one as soon as they heard the wailing of the alarm, crowding into the dark tunnels with their few treasured possessions and sometimes a bite of food grabbed at the last minute.

Brigid seldom saw Mabel during an air raid; the schools had their own shelters and the students treated raids as a lark, running to the shelters, giggling and singing patriotic songs. Brigid was a nervous wreck. She demanded that Mabel stop going to school, but Mabel refused.

"Mama," she said cheerfully, "in the sky they look like birds dropping eggs. We're not afraid."

She was not afraid until one day several bombs dropped near her school. Coming out of the shelter, she stumbled over some dead bodies and saw that a few of them had no heads, arms or legs. One had been literally blown to pieces, with charred flesh scattered around. A dead man stared at her with his eyes wide open, looking angry and grotesque.

That night Mabel could not stop trembling. When she finally fell asleep, she abruptly woke up screaming. Brigid sat beside her most of the night, wiping sweat from her white face and soothing her with gentle words and lullabies. For two days Mabel was delirious, asking for her father. When she was able to eat, she kept asking, "Is there enough food for Papa?"

Many times Brigid could not control her emotions. She had to turn her head away and hold her breath to muffle her sobs. At night, when she was alone in her bed, she wondered if Hu Yin would ever come home. Why was there no news? Was he dead? "Hu Yin, Hu Yin!" she moaned, sobbing into her pillow. "Mabel needs you. Come home, please come home!"

✳

One morning Ding Fei paid her a visit. She said that the Nanking government was planning to move to Chungking. Both Nanking and Wuhan would be evacuated. Madame Sun Yat-sen had been offered a plane from the government. She planned to move to Chungking as soon as possible. "She will take you as a yellow fish," Ding Fei said, "a nonpaying passenger. I think you should move to a safer place."

"Are you going?"

"No, not yet."

"Why not?"

"Because I have no young children. But I'll go if the Japanese come one step closer. From what I've heard, they're not very good neighbors."

"Ding Fei," Brigid said, serving her coffee and some French pastry, "if you can make Mabel go, I'm ready."

"Why won't she go?"

"Go ask her. I'll give you ten minutes."

Ding Fei went into Mabel's room. Brigid poured a shot of whiskey into her coffee and started sipping it slowly. Every day she needed whiskey to calm her nerves.

In fifteen minutes Ding Fei came back, looking grim. "You're right. Five horses couldn't drag her out of this house. She still believes her father will come back at any moment."

"Want a shot of whiskey?"

"No . . . Come to think of it, why not?" Ding Fei laughed. "Who knows if we are going to live through tomorrow?"

Brigid poured a double shot into Ding Fei's coffee and added another to her own. "Ding Fei," she said, "I hate to discuss private problems with friends, but since liquor has loosened my lips, I am going to ask you a private question."

"Shoot. What is it?"

"Have you ever been frigid?"

Ding Fei stared at her, wide-eyed. "Hey, that's *too* private!"

"All right, forget it."

"Why do you ask?"

"I was frigid with Hu Yin. Do you think that's why he hasn't come home?"

Ding Fei thought for a long time, nursing her cup of coffee. "Brigid, men like to be loved, body and soul. If he knows that you only love his body or his soul, or fifty percent of this or that, he feels cheated; his big ego is hurt. Many men can take it; quite a few can't."

"Hu Yin is an attractive man. Why am I frigid with him?"

Ding Fei took another sip of her coffee, put the cup down and pointed a finger at her friend. "Brigid, listen. From now on don't ever say, 'I love this man only like a brother.' If you say that too often, you convince yourself that all men are brothers. When that day comes, you will *really* be in trouble. You might as well spend the rest of your life in a nunnery."

"Did I tell you I loved him only as a brother?"

"Too many times. You've convinced yourself you're his sister. What do you expect? Every time you sleep with him you think you're committing incest. Brigid, treat a man like a sex object once in a while. For five thousand years we women have been men's sex objects; it's about time we turned the tables. Pinch their flesh and tell them they're a nice mouthful.

Let them squirm or fall flat at our feet, we'll take our pick. If we pick them right, keep them; if we pick them wrong, toss them out like yesterday's newspaper!"

Brigid forced a smile. "Ding Fei, you sure have changed. I'm surprised at you!"

"Life changes a person; years change a person. A person should never stop changing, because the world is changing constantly. You change to fit your circumstances and surroundings, which never stand still."

"Take your pick! Toss out the wrong ones like yesterday's newspaper!" Brigid laughed. "Ding Fei, do you really believe that? Are you joking?"

"I'm serious, Brigid."

"What *is* the world coming to?"

"Nothing. But it will wipe out your ailment—frigidity."

✻

For a few days Japan relaxed its air raids on Wuhan. Brigid kept marking her calendar. Most of the news was good. Chinese troops were winning more battles, yet cities continued to fall. She suspected that the Chinese-language papers printed only the good news.

Mabel had returned to school. Early one afternoon Mrs. Shiao, a neighbor woman, came to see Brigid. She was distraught, her plump face washed by tears and her gray hair uncombed. Obviously she hadn't slept much. "Mrs. Hu," she wailed, "you must help me!"

"What's your problem, Mrs. Shiao?" Brigid asked, her heart thumping as she dreaded bad news.

"You know my son, my only son. He has joined a group of students who volunteered to help dig trenches for our soldiers at the front. He is only a student, Mrs. Hu; his duty is to study. I argued with him all night. Mrs. Hu, we have a million soldiers. I am sure they don't need students with thick glasses and weak arms to dig trenches. Your husband is a general; I'm sure he is the only one who can stop such foolishness. I shall be most grateful if you would please ask him to talk to my son . . ."

"Mrs. Shiao," Brigid interrupted, "I wish I could help. But my husband is not in Wuhan and he's not a general."

"But your daughter . . ."

"Don't believe my daughter. She promotes him all the time. She probably told people that her father was a three-star general with nine arms capable of performing all kinds of miracles. Let your son go, Mrs. Shiao. In a few weeks he'll come back with sore feet and a blistered hand, begging to go back to school."

"Amen!" Brigid heard a loud male voice behind her.

She turned and found two unexpected visitors—Sam Cohen and Ding Fei. They had brought some news from a foreign-language paper.

"Brigid," Ding Fei said seriously, "this is urgent. Read this report!"

Brigid grabbed the paper and read:

MASSACRE IN NANKING, the headline said. In the text it reported that the Japanese had begun burning, looting and raping in the capital city. At Ching Ling University, seven thousand women refugees were raped, then mowed down by machine guns. Japanese officers had made a contest of killing Chinese civilians with their Samurai swords. One of them had won by slaughtering 150. Another had won second place with a score of 135. They had invented slow tortures in Nanking as sports. Chinese victims were buried in the ground up to their chests, then army dogs were set on them. Cheering soldiers watched the frenzied dogs tear the victims' heads apart. . . .

Brigid stopped reading, her face ashen and her hands shaking. Mrs. Shiao asked what the paper had said. Brigid put a hand over her mouth, shook her head and rushed off to the bathroom to vomit.

Ding Fei picked up the paper and translated for Mrs. Shiao, who listened to the story grim-faced. Her eyes furious and her bosom heaving, she left without a word. When Brigid emerged from the bathroom, Ding Fei said, "Sam and I are going to Chungking. We want you to go with us."

"How?"

"Sam, tell her."

"I know a drunken pilot," Sam said. "He has a rattling cargo plane for hire. A rich family hired him to move the family to Chungking, and the pilot agreed to take a few yellow fish along. I think you ought to go. Chances of the plane making it are not good, but it's still better than entertaining the Japanese in the near future."

"Brigid, Nanking has fallen," Ding Fei said. "The next city to fall will be Wuhan. Think about it."

"When are you leaving?" Brigid said without hesitation this time.

"Tonight."

"We are your yellow fish, Sam," Brigid said. "A mother fish and a girl fish."

Next morning before dawn a dilapidated cargo plane took off from the Hankow airport, and soon it was swallowed by the thick morning fog. Its destination was Chungking, its future unknown.

VI

52

After four years, Brigid still could not get accustomed to the wartime capital, Chungking, a remote, ancient city built on cliffs by a muddy river. The open sewers, the streets with steep steps and the constant fog and rain were depressing; but everything in the temporary capital seemed to fit the mood of the war-torn country. Five years of tragic conflict with Japan had brought such untold misery to the Chinese people that a beautiful bright day often made the constant bad news even harder to accept. Since early 1942, Japan had spread the war to Southeast Asia after having occupied most of China. First Manila fell, then Malaya, Singapore and Rangoon followed.

Brigid wondered if the war was the reason she didn't really mind the bad weather. When she was lonely, she dreaded weekends, holidays and festivities. When she was bombarded with bad news, she wanted to hear rain and storm and water dripping into a washbasin from a leaking roof.

The morning was foggy; the news was as appalling as usual. But she had become more optimistic since Japan had attacked Pearl Harbor the year before. With America's involvement in the war, she knew that Japan would eventually be defeated.

She heard the water running in the bathroom. Mabel was taking a shower by pulling the spout of a watering can that was hanging from the ceiling. Brigid smiled as she visualized the funny picture. Fortunately, both of them had become accustomed to the inconveniences of their shabby living conditions. Still, compared to some of her colleagues, Brigid felt lucky. She had a two-room apartment with some semimodern facilities— a kitchen with gas, cold running water and a part-time amah who washed and cooked for them in the evening.

This morning Brigid had personally prepared Mabel's favorite breakfast —rice porridge, preserved vegetables and a dish of hard-boiled salted eggs sliced into bite sizes. As she sipped coffee and waited for Mabel, she glanced at the good news in the Chinese-language paper and the uncensored bad news in the English-language newsletter that was issued through diplomatic channels. As an interpreter for the International Relief Committee, for which she had worked for three years, she received all kinds of reading material. The good news reported victories at various fronts and the glorious deeds of the heroes killed in combat. The bad news told of

Japanese atrocities and their scorched-earth policy of "Kill all, burn all and destroy all" which had left many more Chinese towns in ruins and many more people massacred. The newsletter described how the Japanese in Burma had locked people in bamboo houses, then set them on fire, and how they had stripped others and tied them to trees for bayonet practice.

There was an article about the plight of the average Chinese soldier. He marched in straw sandals, slept under one blanket for every five men. He carried two grenades at his belt and wore a long black stocking around his neck with uncooked rice stuffed into it: his three-day field ration. In his pocket he carried a bit of red pepper and some salt to go with his rice. His pay was fifteen yuan of the new currency per month, ten of which were deducted for food. Dysentery and smallpox were rampant. Most of the soldiers were sick and starving; some of them died at the roadside before they even reached the front.

Such articles depressed Brigid terribly, but as they were a daily occurrence, she had gradually become immune to them. Besides, she read them with a grain of salt.

She missed Michael Steward's reporting and wondered where he was. She had not heard from him since she left Wuhan.

She also missed Hu Yin. For three years now, Mabel had not talked about her father. She, too, had almost given up hope of seeing him again. The last time they had discussed him, both had concluded that he was dead. But, in the back of her mind, Brigid still preserved a tiny seed of hope. When the war was over, it might germinate, sprout and suddenly bloom. Hu Yin would be back; everything would be all right. It would be like reliving her life all over again.

She heard the bathroom door bang shut. Mabel had come out with a white towel wrapped around her head. She was beautiful. At fifteen, she looked grown up, with a fully developed body. Her breasts were too large for her age, and she was wearing a bra. Her menstrual cycle had started a year earlier, and Brigid had given her sufficient sex education to avoid possible disaster. She trusted her daughter, and the two of them were loving and relaxed in each other's company. Brigid's friends often sighed and commented on how nice Mabel was, especially when they compared her to their own rebellious teenage children.

"Good morning, Mother," Mabel said cheerfully, kissing Brigid on the cheek. Then she plunged into her food. "How nice of you to buy salted eggs! When I die, I'll stuff myself with nothing but salted eggs, my first love . . . after you, of course, Mother."

"Please don't talk about death early in the morning," Brigid chided. "It's bad luck."

"All right, Mother."

"How pretty you are this morning," Brigid said, disapproving of her crimson lipstick. "You have already put makeup on. Are you going somewhere?"

"I promised to study at Ginger's house this morning. A big test next week."

Brigid wondered why she should wear makeup to study at a friend's house. "You always study at Ginger's house. I've never met her. Sometime I wish you would invite her here to study for a change."

"She has a sick mother," Mabel said, eating her breakfast ravenously. "She must keep an eye on her."

Brigid grimaced. Mabel's table manners still left much to be desired. But she had no complaints about her daughter's schoolwork. After Mabel had switched to a missionary school from the Chinese public school in Chungking, she had done well. She liked it. She had complained that the students in the Chinese school were not very lively. Besides, the English teacher in her Chinese school spoke English with such an awful accent that she could not stop giggling in class.

"By the way," Brigid said, "you haven't forgotten the party tonight, have you?"

"Of course not. Who invited us?"

"Ding Fei," Brigid said. With a laugh, she added, "She always wants to be your godmother, but she said the way you grew and conducted yourself, she thought she should really adopt you as her godsister. How you've grown, Mabel! If I hadn't lived under the same roof with you, I wouldn't recognize you after a week!"

"Thanks."

"I don't know what we've done, but we sure have done something right. You have grown into a marvelous young lady in every way."

"Thank you, Mother. I've got to go."

At the kitchen door, she turned. "Mother, leave the dirty dishes for me to wash, will you? It's my turn now. Don't you dare touch them!" Blowing her a kiss, Mabel went to her room.

Brigid shook her head with a smile and sighed. After all the terrible experiences in Wuhan, Mabel had grown up almost unscathed, except for minor blemishes such as eating her meals like a coolie. It was a miracle. . . .

*

The dungeonlike nightclub was crowded with smiling faces, the kind of hungry smiling faces that sex-starved servicemen usually wore when they were watching a dirty show. They were sitting below a raised stage the size of a boxing ring. Mabel Hu smiled and winked at them as she repeated the simple routine, prancing and peeling off her clothes seductively and slowly, piece by piece. She had learned it from an American burlesque dancer only a week before. Now she was the biggest draw at the Kitty Cat Club, an underground dive in Chungking. She hated it, but the money was good and she was doing it for Raymond Bowlesky, her Eurasian lover.

There were about two hundred Americans in the room, which was designed for one hundred customers. They were laughing and shouting encouragement. "Take it off, take it *all* off!" A few of them tossed dollar bills onto the stage.

Wriggling and shaking her midriff, Mabel began removing her remaining garments. When she unhooked her bra, she pouted and hissed and peeled it off slowly, feeling her young breasts with her fingertips, prancing to the beat of loud music that blared through a loudspeaker.

The bare light overhead felt like a heater, and she was sweating. She began to worry about her heavy makeup of rouge, mascara and crimson lipstick. She wished the one-hour performance were shorter so that she could bathe leisurely and go home. She had promised her mother to go to Ding Fei's party.

Some of the soldiers who were sitting in front tried to touch her, but she eluded their hands nimbly, pouting and winking. A few GIs waved five- and ten-dollar bills, urging her to come closer.

One soldier held out a twenty-dollar bill and told her to pick it up between her teeth. As she tried to do so, he grabbed her and tried to kiss her. She smelled his heavy beer-and-cigarette breath and struggled. Another soldier interceded, trying to pull him away. The first soldier punched him. Bedlam broke out and soon it became a free-for-all, fists and beer cans flying and bodies crashing onto tables and chairs.

Mabel had seen this happen before. She was glad that the fight had cut the show short by at least half an hour. She quickly picked up her clothes and the money from the floor and fled, ducking beer cans and leaping over fallen bodies. She reached the office door, flung it open and went in, slamming the door shut behind her.

Sitting behind a cluttered desk was Mr. Benson, the club's owner, a beefy man with a large beard, an intimidating-looking person with gentle manners. Raymond called him the Smiling Cobra and warned her never to cross him.

Mr. Benson was working on his books. He wore a dark blue eyeshade to protect his small, deep-set eyes from the single bare light overhead.

Sitting on a worn couch on his right were three other dancers, two white and one Asian. They were much older, all wearing scanty costumes and all smoking heavily, flicking cigarette ashes onto the cement floor.

Raymond Bowlesky, sitting on an old sofa across the small room from them, rose to his feet. As a Eurasian, he had slightly slanted eyes but fair skin and brownish hair. He was rather good-looking. He looked at his watch. "Finished?"

The music was so loud that it drowned out the noise of the brawl. "Yes," Mabel said. She approached Benson's desk with a charming smile. "I'm signing off, Mr. Benson."

Benson looked up from his books. "How come it's such a quickie?"

"Just pay me halftime, Mr. Benson. I've got to go to my mother's birthday party."

Benson counted out some money and pushed it to her with a grin. "Here's fifty, full five hours' pay. Make it up tomorrow."

"Thank you very much, Mr. Benson." Mabel stuffed the money into her stocking. "Oh, Mr. Benson—can I borrow another fifty? I have found a nice birthday present for my mom. I'll make it up tomorrow night."

Benson peeled several more bills off his big bundle of money and pushed them toward her. "Anything you say, sweetheart," he said with a grin. "Say happy birthday to your mom for me."

Outside the club, Raymond grabbed her arm and rushed her to his Plymouth, which was parked across the street.

"You're hurting me, Raymond."

Ignoring her, he opened the car door and pushed her into the passenger side. When he got in behind the wheel, he started cursing. "Goddamn it! Goddamn it!"

"What did I do wrong, Raymond?" she asked, looking puzzled.

"You know damn well you can't come here tomorrow night! You've been scheduled to perform at Jimmy's Saloon. What's the matter with you?"

"Relax! We'll go to Jimmy's, that's all."

Bowlesky pounded the steering wheel with both hands in frustration. "Mabel," he said, "you just promised Smiling Cobra to make it up to him tomorrow night. At fifteen, are you tired of living already?"

"Raymond, relax!" Mabel said impatiently. "We'll just go to Jimmy's. I've quit the job at the Kitty Cat."

Bowlesky snapped his fingers. "Just like that?"

"Yes. I did my last performance there tonight. Goodbye, Mr. Benson." She blew a kiss at the run-down building.

Raymond turned to her sharply, his face whitened with fright. "Look! You have just borrowed money from him, too! Do you want your body to turn up in that stinking river?"

Mabel was now busy wiping her lipstick off, using her little hand mirror. "How is he going to find me?" she said indifferently. "Chungking is a big city."

"Forget it," Raymond sighed, starting the car after throwing his hands up in despair. Mabel shrugged.

*

Bowlesky lived in a two-room apartment, unfurnished except for a bed, a table and four chairs. He used the table and chairs only when he had company for a game of poker or mahjong. None of his business associates knew where he lived.

Mabel cleaned her face in front of a broken hall mirror in his bedroom while he watched her from the bed. He came close and put his arms around her. "You always excite me when you do that," he whispered into her ear.

Mabel wriggled out of his embrace and pushed him away. "I have no time for that, Raymond. I have to go."

"Where? Meeting another lover?"

"Raymond, please! I'll make it up when I come back tomorrow."

"Are you using the same line on me?" He laughed. "Never mind." He flopped on his squeaky bed, put his hands behind his head and crossed his legs. "I can wait. You know I'm addicted to you, don't you?"

"Raymond, what about Kunming? Let's move to Kunming. Big rackets there. Selling lend-lease goods. Big money."

"Big money in Kunming?" He snorted. "Forget it! I like what I'm doing here."

"In Kunming we are talking about tens of thousands of dollars. What are you making here? Chicken feed."

Bowlesky laughed. He was amused by Mabel's capacity—calling three thousand dollars a shot chicken feed. The racket he was running was perfectly safe and easy. And his two associates demanded only ten percent of the profit each. One was a good printer who could fake college reports to perfection, the other had liaisons with American universities. All Bowlesky had to do was to apply for admission for fictitious students going to America for advanced study. With the admission papers he could go to the Department of Education and apply for foreign exchange at the official rate—twenty Chinese yuan to one U.S. dollar. On the black market the rate was two thousand yuan to a dollar. A perfect scheme to get U.S. money and resell it on the black market at about a two-thousand-percent profit. Each fictitious student could apply for a maximum of three thousand dollars. If he could come up with three fictitious students a week, he and his associates could be rich long before the war's end. He knew many other ways to profit from the war, but none was as good and safe as this one, and he had been doing it for more than five months with happy results.

"Mabel," he said, "if you do what I tell you, we'll make big money. Working at Jimmy's is part of the game . . ."

"Go get somebody else to play B-girl at Jimmy's," she interrupted. "I don't want to hustle colored water for your gangster friend Jimmy Katz for a percentage."

Raymond sat up and glared at her. "You didn't hear a word I said!" he said irritably. "You're going to work for Jimmy for tips only. And the tips are not nickels or dimes, either."

"If a customer tips only nickels and dimes, what do I do? Beat him on the head with a beer bottle?"

He threw up his hands with a moan. "Goddamn it, Mabel—you are either deaf or you don't listen! I want you to collect fountain pens, watches, rings or any trinkets the American servicemen have—anything but nickels and dimes. These things are better than gold on the black market. Let me just give you an idea. A three-dollar fountain pen is worth five hundred yuan. Apply that to the official rate. At twenty yuan to a dollar, that's twenty-five big smackers in U.S. money. Can't you pound that into your head, Mabel? And you don't have to screw somebody to get his fountain pen."

She ignored him. "Goodbye, Raymond," she said, giving him a wet kiss on the mouth. "Got to go."

Before she reached the door, he called, "Haven't you forgotten something?"

"What?"

Bowlesky fished a document from his breast pocket and tapped it with his fingers. "Your new school report."

With a little shriek, Mabel rushed back and grabbed it. "Sorry, Raymond. You are an angel." She looked at it and her eyes bugged with delight. "All straight A's!"

"Come here," Bowlesky said, wriggling the fingers of one hand and rubbing his groin with the other.

"I'll thank you tomorrow, Raymond. Promise." Blowing him a kiss, she was gone.

*

Mabel was only twenty minutes late. Brigid was at the door waiting, one hand clutching a purse and the other holding an umbrella.

"Sorry, Mother," Mabel said breathlessly. She paid the ricksha boy and gave him a handsome tip. "The ricksha man couldn't run. He has a hernia or something. Sorry I'm late."

"Sam Cohen has dispatched a jeep to pick us up," Brigid said, climbing into the back seat of the waiting vehicle. Mabel followed and plunked down beside her with a sigh. The driver was a young American in khaki fatigues. He kept glancing at Mabel in the mirror as he started the car, which roared and sped out of the narrow side street, bumping over the uneven pavement.

"Sorry to have kept you waiting, soldier," Brigid said.

The driver responded by raising a hand. "Don't mention it."

"Good thing Sam Cohen has access to everything," Brigid said. "If we had to go in a ricksha, it'd take hours."

"Who is Sam Cohen, Mother?" Mabel asked.

"You met him many times in Wuhan, when you were little. You'll recognize him. He's Ding Fei's boyfriend, or, rather, gentleman friend. I want you to call him Uncle Sam. Did you have a good study session at Ginger's?"

"Yes, Mother. Oh, I almost forgot. Here's something for you." Mabel took out her report card from her purse and handed it to her mother.

Brigid read it, her eyes glued on the report, her face breaking into a happy smile. "Mabel!" she said in a choking voice. "I just can't take my eyes off those beautiful A's! We've got to celebrate this! Do you mind if I show this to people at the party?"

"Please don't. They'll think we're show-offs."

"At least we must show it to Ding Fei and Sam Cohen . . ."

"No, Mother—I hate to be a show-off."

"You're so modest, Mabel. Anyway, you've made me very, very happy! And we must celebrate. We'll go to a good restaurant next Sunday. Just you and me."

"All right. Let's talk about it next week."

The jeep passed a high point in the city. In the distance they saw clusters of houses nestled on the bank of the muddy river. Across the river, terraced hills rose beyond the rice paddies and potato fields. Brigid looked at the fields and sighed.

"Mabel, I was never as good to my mother as you are to me. How I regret not having treated her better. She was born in Hunan. Those rice fields in the distance remind me of her home province. One of these days I'll take you there and sweep the graves of our ancestors."

"All right, Mother," Mabel said absentmindedly. She had formed a habit of agreeing with her mother automatically. Now she was busy thinking of Ding Fei's party. Would there be many young people? What would she do if it turned out to be a dull old fogies' gathering?

She remained silent as Brigid chatted and the jeep drove across the town, passing dilapidated tall buildings and abandoned shacks, most of them badly damaged by Japanese bombs. There were many burnt houses still inhabited. Dirty children were playing in the ruins while their mothers washed and cooked under gaping holes in the roofs. In the poorest section of the city, beggars lived in abandoned houses with rats and stray dogs. Many were too sick to stand up. Emaciated children lay beside them, waiting to die. Brigid had to turn her head away. Mabel just stared blankly, preoccupied with her private thoughts.

After more than half an hour of tortuous driving, they reached Sha Ping Pa, the other part of the town. It was a better area, with cleaner streets and nicer homes. Some of them were painted black, to be less visible to the bombers. Many of the windows were broken, but few people had replaced them, simply covering them with newspapers or cardboard. No one knew for sure if the Japanese would return the next day.

Driving through an even nicer part of the town, Brigid hated to look. The street, no matter how much better, was still depressingly crowded with coolies and ragged soldiers. There were vendors selling rotten fruit and vegetables and trucks loaded with refugees and their meager belongings, churning up dust or mud. On the main thoroughfare, shabby buses struggled amid handcars, rickshas and pedestrians. Gaunt passengers stared out dusty windows, looking gloomy. The whole city had an appearance of hopelessness and despair. Besides black smoke and fumes from buses and autos, there was a stench from uncollected corpses.

Ding Fei's apartment was not any nicer than Brigid's, but a lot bigger, being situated in the outer part of the city. When Brigid knocked, she heard music coming from the second-floor window. Mabel suddenly came alive.

"Ah, dancing!" she said excitedly. She did a few jitterbug steps on the street to the beat of the loud music.

Wang Mah, Ding Fei's maid, opened the door. Being from the north, she greeted the visitors with her customary salutation: "Have you eaten, Madame?"

"Hello, Wang Mah," Brigid said, laughing. "Of course I haven't. I expect your mistress to feed me."

Upstairs the party was in full swing. Two couples were dancing cheek to cheek; others were sitting around chatting and eating. Ding Fei was going from guest to guest, serving food and drinks. There were about twenty people in the living room, half of them Americans. Except for a colonel, the Americans wore baggy, unmatched civilian clothes. They were Bohemian intellectual types. The smartest dresser was Charlie Hong, the scrap-iron dealer, who did not look a day older than he had when Brigid had met him at the Wuhan Press Club many years before.

Ding Fei was delighted to see Brigid and her daughter. After hugging each of them, she took them around and introduced them to everybody.

Sam was in the kitchen preparing some Chinese specialty. Brigid dipped a finger in his sauce and licked it, making appreciative, throaty noises. For that, Sam gave her an extra kiss on the cheek.

"Is that Mabel?" he asked, raising his bushy eyebrows in surprise. Brigid looked through the kitchen door and saw her daughter already engaged in an animated conversation with Charles Hong.

"That's my girl," Brigid said proudly. "Isn't she a knockout?"

Sam did not respond at first. He looked a bit troubled. He had seen her somewhere in a bar, but he decided not to mention it. "Oh, yeah, yeah!" he said quickly, trying to change the subject.

"If I'm not senile," Brigid said, narrowing her eyes to get a better look, "that's Charles Hong."

"The same old Charlie. Still a bachelor, and still in the junk business."

"Obviously he is doing very well."

"Couldn't be better," Sam said. "He's one of the very few businessmen who is making a contribution to the war effort. Most of the others are busy making money on the black market. The thieves are making millions by stealing lend-lease material, from army boots to trucks."

Brigid knew what the war profiteers had been doing. Even goods from her organization had been found on Chungking's black market. It was too depressing to think about it. She dropped the subject. "Sam, who gave the party? You or Ding Fei?"

"It's Ding Fei's birthday. A surprise."

"How old is she?"

"I'm not supposed to tell. She was born in the Year of the Rat. Figure it out yourself."

"Women hate to figure that out. Let's say we all remain twenty-nine." Both laughed.

"How old is Mabel?" Sam asked.

"Fifteen. Isn't it surprising how much older she looks? I can't believe it."

Sam laughed. "Don't say that when she's eighteen. She'll hate you."

"By the way, how old is Charlie Hong?" Brigid asked.

Sam paused for a moment then returned to his cooking. "Let's say he's over thirty. A good-looking pair, aren't they?"

Brigid looked at her daughter again and smiled. She had never seen a girl of Mabel's age who could act so much like a charming grown-up woman, laughing and chatting, captivating her listener.

"Well," Brigid said with a chuckle, "if she knew how old Charlie is, she would declare she is twenty-five and he would believe her."

"Love is a game, Brigid," Sam said, concentrating on his cooking. "It's the only game in which both players win."

"Do they?" Brigid asked, turning back to Sam with an uncertain look.

"I certainly hope so."

More guests arrived. The apartment was now packed with people from all walks of life. The new arrivals were mostly American servicemen, Sam's friends. After the hors d'oeuvres, Sam finally carried out a large birthday cake with forty candles on it, singing "Happy Birthday." He placed it on the dining table.

Ding Fei made a wish and blew out all the candles with one breath. The guests applauded and demanded to know her wish. Ding Fei, an outgoing woman, did not mince words. "I wish it were a wedding cake," she said with a loud laugh.

"How about it, Sam?" one of his American pals asked.

Sam said nothing; he just chuckled.

"It's too late now," Ding Fei said.

"How many candles are there?" another guest asked.

"Just don't count them," Ding Fei said, laughing. "But I'll give you a hint: I've entered the tiger age."

"Sam, how old is that?" a third guest asked.

Sam shrugged. "No comment."

"That doesn't mean I was born in the Year of the Tiger," Ding Fei added. "Brigid, enlighten these people."

Brigid thought for a moment. "Well," she said with a solemn face, "that means she will be twenty-nine for a few more years."

There was laughter. "Miss Ding," an American soldier asked, "how many animal symbols are there in the Chinese horoscope?"

But before Ding Fei could answer, there was a disturbance at the other end of the living room. A drunken GI was chasing Mabel, waving a ten-dollar bill and asking her to do a striptease act. Sam got up quickly, took hold of the soldier and steered him away from Mabel.

"C'mon, George," he said, trying to placate him. "How can you ask a princess to take her clothes off? This is a birthday party. . . ."

"What's wrong with taking her clothes off at a birthday party? That's what she does at the Kitty Cat Club, isn't it? Hey, you must have hired her to do . . ."

Sam shut him up and steered him to the kitchen, talking to him in a lowered voice. Mabel picked up her purse and rushed to Brigid. "Mother," she said tearfully, "let's get out of here!"

Brigid wanted to ask Sam what had gone wrong, but decided to ask Mabel about it instead. She trusted her. "All right, Mabel," she said.

They left the apartment hurriedly, without saying goodbye to Sam or Ding Fei.

53

Raymond Bowlesky, twenty-two, alias Raymond Chen, Raymond Wilson or Ah Chen, depending on when or where his name was required, liked to use his Chinese name when dealing with Chinese. Only his pals knew where he lived, and he had never given his employers or his business associates his real address. As all his dealings were in cash; a pillowcase under his mattress was his bank.

As a Eurasian, he knew vaguely about his American father, mostly from what his mother had told him. His impression of his father was of a sailor in a white uniform and a cap hanging jauntily on the back of his head. His father was ruggedly good-looking; he had a bright smile and his mother had loved him. Raymond had not seen him since he was eight. Only recently his mother had learned that his father had disappeared during the attack on Pearl Harbor. It had been a blow to her, not because she had lost a long-absent lover, but because she considered him an honorable man who had kept sending money for their support.

Bowlesky's mother had had many lovers, but his father had always been Number One, and his photo occupied the most prominent place in their home and in her photo album.

Mabel had met Bowlesky at the missionary high school, but he had dropped out after a year and a half. During that time he and Mabel had liked each other and had often sneaked into the nearby air-raid shelter to experiment with sex.

When Bowlesky had appeared again suddenly, about nine months ago, they had renewed their affair and Mabel had started living a double life.

At home she was the well-behaved, studious daughter; with Bowlesky she became a wild teenager.

That rare sunny afternoon, Mabel got out of school two hours early, pretending she had a stomachache. By the time she arrived at Bowlesky's apartment, he was simmering with anger.

"Where have you been?" he yelled at her as she stepped into his untidy room, which was strewn with clothes, dirty dishes and empty food cans.

"My mother is sick."

"Again?"

"Yes, again."

"Your old lady is sick a lot. What's wrong with her?"

"Raymond, I've got news for you. You'd better listen to this sitting down."

"I'll take it with a grain of salt."

"You don't believe me?" Mabel whispered, starting to take off her clothes.

Bowlesky looked at her young breasts and swallowed. "Look, we have to go to Jimmy's . . ."

"Are you interested in the news or not?"

"News! What news?"

"I'm pregnant, Raymond."

Bowlesky was stunned for a moment. "Why tell me?" he said with a snort. "How do I know it's mine?"

"You're a son of a bitch!" She lunged at him with her fingernails flying. Bowlesky caught both her arms and pinned her down on the mattress. He stared at her full breasts and started kissing them. She struggled.

"Get off me, you turtle's egg!"

He tried to kiss her and she bit him. He let her go. "I ought to smash your face," he snarled. He licked the blood on his lips, then wiped his mouth with the back of his hand. "If you weren't pregnant, I'd knock your goddamned teeth out! Don't you ever bite me like that again!"

"So you believe me?" Mabel said with a smile.

"What are you going to do?"

"I want an abortion," she said.

"To kill my baby?"

"Yes! We can't afford it!"

Bowlesky grabbed two bottles of beer. "First, let's celebrate your pregnancy—the Chinese way. Kan pei, kan pei." He offered Mabel a beer; she pushed it away.

"I've already found a doctor," she said. "He'll do it for five hundred dollars."

"He'll have to collect it in Chinese ghost money."

They stared at each other for a brief moment, then he jabbed his finger at her. "Look—it's my flesh and blood. If anybody murders my baby, I'll kill him. That goes for you, too!"

Mabel gave him a passionate kiss on the mouth. "Raymond, that's exactly what I wanted you to say, you silly ass! I thought you'd never say it!" She flopped on the bed and said expansively, "Oh, boy! A baby of my own! Guess we still need that five hundred to buy a crib, diapers, bottles, toys, et cetera, et cetera." Suddenly she stopped and turned to Bowlesky with a snort, her eyes hardening. "Raymond, if you are thinking of selling the baby on the black market, I'll gouge your eyes out!"

Bowlesky laughed. "What makes you say a stupid thing like that? Why should I sell my own flesh and blood?"

"You'd sell anything, including your own mother."

He glanced at his watch. "Oh, my God! Four-thirty already! We've got to go to Jimmy's."

"Why Jimmy's? It's only afternoon. Who goes to Jimmy's at this hour?"

"A planeload of GIs landed in Chungking this morning," he said. "All fresh from the USA and all loaded with six months' pay. If half of them go to Jimmy's, you've got a gold mine there. You don't want the other girls to get ahead of us, do you? Besides their pens and watches, you might as well pick up some cash too, as a bonus." He stared at Mabel's half-nude body and swallowed. "Oh, what the hell!" he said and started throwing his clothes off.

*

Every day Brigid prayed for the war to end. But the fighting went on. More American volunteers and aid started pouring into Yunnan Province through the Burma Road. Cargo planes hopped over the Hump of the Himalayas day and night, ferrying lend-lease supplies into China. Kunming, the provincial capital of Yunnan, had become a metropolis buzzing with activity. Black markets were thriving; both Chinese and American profiteers found instant wealth by selling everything from medical equipment to jeeps and trucks.

Besides the World War, there were several miniwars being fought in China, verbally and on battlefields. The battle between the Kuomintang's Nationalists and Mao Tse-tung's Communists had never stopped; the conflict between Generalissimo Chiang Kai-shek and General Joseph Stilwell, Chiang's Chief of Staff, had stepped up, with mutual accusations being constantly flung at each other. Brigid had been following this private war closely, but was unable to decide who was right. Stilwell believed that all Chiang wanted was to wait for the foreign allies to defeat the Japanese so he could preserve his own strength and then get rid of the Communists. Chiang accused Stilwell of being arrogant and ignorant of Chinese conditions.

It was Sunday. Mabel had supposedly gone to study at Ginger Woo's house. Brigid was reading the Sunday paper over a cup of coffee when Ding Fei came to call. Brigid was happy to see her best friend. Whenever she and Ding Fei chatted at the kitchen table, fond memories of the past returned to her, making her forget her problems—temporarily, at least.

"I can't stay long," Ding Fei said as Brigid poured her a cup of coffee. "Sam wanted me to tell you something that may shock you. I want you to prepare yourself for the news."

"Believe me, Ding Fei, I've been so toughened by bad news that nothing can shock me anymore. Try me." After a short, bitter laugh, she became serious. "What's happened? Have we finally surrendered to Japan?"

"Where is Mabel?" Ding Fei asked, lowering her eyes as though this were a difficult mission.

"Studying at her schoolfriend's house. Why?"

"Brigid, this is serious," Ding Fei said, nursing her coffee cup. She stopped briefly, then went on with more difficulty. "Remember that soldier who caused the disturbance at my birthday party? Sam questioned him. He swore it was Mabel who performed at a place called the Kitty Cat Club. Sam knows that the dump is a front for some slave traders. They sell girls into prostitution." She looked up and stared straight into Brigid's eyes, her voice harsh. "Brigid, you'd better do something about Mabel before it's too late!"

Brigid closed her eyes. The information was so incredible that she didn't know what to say. "No!" she blurted out after a long pause, shaking her head vigorously. "I can't believe it! I simply can't! It has to be a case of mistaken identity. Anybody can make a mistake. That GI must be one of those Americans who believe all Chinese girls look alike."

"I just wish he were wrong, Brigid," Ding Fei said, looking distressed. "But you can't just ignore it. It's a matter of life and death. Girls often turn up in the Cha Lin River."

After she had pulled herself together, Brigid went to Mabel's room and searched for her address book. She had never met Ginger. Now she wanted to know where she lived. In Mabel's desk drawer she found a horrible mess.

This was Brigid's first shock. She had always had the impression that her daughter was clean and tidy. Mabel always made her bed, and her desk was always spotless and orderly, with books and notebooks piled neatly. On her dresser, the flowers were always fresh in the white ceramic long-necked vase. But inside the dresser, Brigid found a mess that was even more shocking—it was like a trash can full of cosmetics, dirty underwear, half-eaten apples, unfinished letters, coins, lipstick-smeared handkerchiefs, costume jewelry, watermelon seeds, tattered photos, biscuit crumbs, mildewed cheese—and condoms. That was enough. She slammed the drawer shut. There were two Gingers in Mabel's address book. One lived closer than the other. Brigid copied both addresses and left the house.

A maid answered the door at the first address. For a moment she did not know who Ginger was. When Brigid explained that she was the young miss who went to high school, the maid said with a smile, "I'll ask Miss Sung. You wait."

Miss Sung was a pretty girl, about Mabel's age. Yes, her English name was Ginger. Yes, she knew Mabel quite well, but Mabel had never been to her home and they had never studied together. Disappointed, Brigid thanked her and hurried back to the waiting ricksha.

The other Ginger lived in a better part of the city. She was a plain-looking young woman with thick glasses—the studious type. She told Brigid that she knew Mabel only casually; they played basketball together at school once in a while and exchanged Christmas and New Year cards every year; that was all.

Feeling faint, Brigid climbed into the ricksha and told the coolie to take her to the Kitty Cat Club. The ricksha puller had not heard of such a place. After many inquiries, they finally found a policeman who told her they were going in the wrong direction.

It was almost five o'clock when they arrived at the American-style nightclub. Outside, there were a few half-nude pictures of young girls posted on the brick wall of the converted warehouse.

The club was in a dingy alley off the main thoroughfare. A fat American wearing a brown suit, red bow tie, and sporting a fake rose was sitting in a cubicle selling tickets for five dollars each. Brigid did not have American money and paid ten thousand yuan for her ticket.

"One word of advice, lady," the fat man said, "if you try to ply your trade in there, the competition is tough."

Brigid forced a smile. "In my trade, the older the sweeter, don't you know?" She was really not in the mood to joke, but was trying to dispel a terrible sense of depression.

She went into the smoke-filled club with a sinking feeling, dreading what she was about to see, and praying that Mabel was not there. The dead air inside was heavy with the smell of stale beer, cigarette smoke, sweat and cheap perfume. On the right was a long bar with stools, most of them occupied by foreign customers, both civilians and servicemen. They were a noisy bunch, laughing and joking loudly; a few were hugging and feeling up the heavily made-up bar girls, who teased and screamed, speaking pidgin English with a singsong accent.

Brigid took a stool at the far end of the bar and ordered a double whiskey. On the other side she saw a small raised stage, surrounded by beer-drinking customers who applauded and shouted encouragement to a fat burlesque dancer with long, bright red hair tied in a bun.

"Lady, you want to talk to the manager?" the young white-jacketed Chinese bartender asked. He spoke perfect English and had a practiced smile.

"What for?" Brigid asked. "I'm here to look for my cousin."

"Well, we need all kinds here," the bartender said with a shrug. "Just a thought. No offense."

"That's okay, sonny," she said. "How many girls are working here?"

"It depends. There will be more at night. Those who can dance, dance; those who can talk, talk; those who . . . you know what I mean." He laughed. "Easy job, good pay. What does your cousin look like?"

"Do you have a girl named Mabel working here?"

"Names don't mean anything. Some girls change their names every day."

"She is young and pretty."

"They are all young and pretty." He glanced at the fat girl who was wriggling on the stage and shrugged. "Not all—but most of them."

By now the stripper had taken most of her clothes off. She was down to her G-string, doing bumps and grinds and swinging her bra in one hand. She had loosened her red hair, which she flipped and tossed clumsily, trying to be seductive. The audience yelled and urged her to take it all off. When she did, a few men tossed dollar bills onto the stage. She finished her number, picked up her money and clothes, and ran for a door in the back, blowing kisses all around.

Every time a new one came out, Brigid held her breath, praying it wouldn't be Mabel. After four girls had performed, she felt better. She had been so tense that she felt as though she were playing Russian roulette. Each time a girl came out, it was like the click of an empty revolver chamber, and she sighed with relief. To fortify herself, she ordered another double whiskey.

"Haven't you seen your cousin yet?" the bartender asked as he served her.

"How many more to go?" she asked after gulping down a large mouthful of her drink.

"Hard to tell, lady. They come and go. More at night. Stay for dinner if you wish. We serve American hot dogs and hamburgers. If you want a ham sandwich, order a little ahead of time. Ham's frozen, see? Everything's clean and safe. Care for a ham sandwich?"

"No, thanks."

A few men tried to pick her up. She discouraged them the best way she knew, saying, "I'm waiting for my husband." But some persisted. One of them had to be sent away by the bartender.

"Take my advice, lady," the bartender said. "Next time come with a beefy guy with a broken nose, husband or no husband. That's the only way to fend off these scavengers." Then he lowered his voice and added, "From one Chinese to another, if you're looking for something, this is the wrong place. You can wind up in the river."

Brigid was getting dizzy. She lost count of how many girls she had watched. Now she felt relieved. The chance that Mabel was not there was getting better. The whiskeys had begun to take effect. She felt high and courageous. It was silly for her to worry, she told herself. Mabel would never come to such a place to earn those dirty dollar bills. Besides, she didn't know how to do the bumps and grinds. She probably was home already and was waiting impatiently for dinner.

Brigid paid for the drinks. But just as she was searching for some change for a tip, she saw another girl bounce onto the stage nimbly and gracefully. She froze, then blinked twice to make sure it was Mabel. It was. The same hair, same build, same smile. She was the prettiest and the best dancer of them all. The audience went wild, applauding, yelling and tossing money onto the stage even before she started taking her clothes off.

Brigid felt a sudden pain in her chest. She clutched her heart and held her breath. "Lady, are you all right?" the bartender asked, alarmed.

"No, I am not," she said, choking. "Please get me a ricksha."

When she arrived home, it was almost dark. The maid had dinner ready. "Go ahead and eat," she said, and went directly to her bedroom. She closed the door and flopped onto her bed. All that time she had been dry-eyed, feeling only the pain. Now she felt the tears bursting out, washing down her cheeks. She turned on her pillow and cried, shaking the bed with uncontrollable sobs.

*

It was almost midnight when Brigid heard the front door slam. It was Mabel. Brigid could tell the way Mabel slammed the front door; she acted as though she were always in a hurry. Brigid began to realize that Mabel had a double personality. When she was with people, she was polite and considerate; when alone, she could be selfish and forgetful. Everything was crystal clear now. Mabel had been deceitful, playing the virgin daughter at home and leading the life of a whore elsewhere.

"Oh, my God!" Brigid moaned into her pillow, banging her bed with her fist. She had never known such crushing disappointment, such agony. It was even worse than the moment when Bo Ho had deserted her. Unable to bear the pain, she climbed out of bed, took out the feather duster from its holder, flung her door open and marched to Mabel's room. Wild-eyed and breathing hard, she rapped on the door.

"I want to talk to you, Mabel!"

Her angry voice surprised Mabel. There was a moment of silence. When Brigid rapped on the door again, Mabel shouted, "Can we talk tomorrow, Mother?"

"No. Right now! Open the door!"

As soon as the door opened a crack, Brigid pushed her way in and without another word began to whip Mabel with the long bamboo handle of the duster, grunting as she beat her. Mabel backed away from her, screaming.

"You whore! You dirty whore!" Brigid screamed as she continued to beat her daughter mercilessly. The maid rushed in and tried to shield Mabel from the whistling bamboo.

"Please stop! Please stop!" the maid cried. "Aiyoo, aiyoo!"

But Brigid could not stop. She whipped both of them until she was exhausted, then collapsed in the middle of the room.

The next morning she woke up in her own bed, feeling weak and dizzy. She managed to get up and stagger to the bathroom. After she had cleared her head with cold water and brushed her teeth, she felt better. She hoped she hadn't injured Mabel physically. She would go to her room and make up with her. Somehow she had vented all her anger. She would forgive her and they would start a new life. A girl Mabel's age needed love, not punishment.

She knocked on Mabel's door gently three times. "Mabel? Mabel?" she called.

There was no answer. She called a few more times. Still no answer. She pushed the door open. The room was empty; on the floor were heaps of discarded clothes and papers. The bed was unmade. Mabel's closet was open and empty and her suitcases gone.

On her desk was a note. Brigid grabbed it and read it with a sick heart, her hands shaking.

"Mother," it said, "I'm leaving you. We may not see each other again. Thank you for all the care and love. Mabel."

54

The baby was three months old. Mabel liked to breast-feed him but Bowlesky objected, saying that breast-feeding wrecked a woman's best asset. When he saw Mabel doing it that afternoon, cooing and enjoying it, he raked out a can of powdered milk from under the bed, tossed it in front of her and said, "He's ruining your figure. If cow's milk was good enough for me, it's good enough for him!"

"Well, it's not good enough for him," Mabel scoffed. "See what it did to you."

Bowlesky watched the baby suckling contentedly with little grunting gulps. He snatched him from her arms and held him beside his own face and demanded, "Tell me who's better looking, me or this little monkey?"

Mabel was always frightened when Bowlesky touched the baby. She tried to reach for the howling infant, but he lifted him hazardously high to get him away from her.

"Raymond!" she cried. "You're going to drop him!"

Bowlesky made several mocking attempts to drop the baby. "Please, Raymond!" Mabel begged. "Give him back to me! Don't hurt him—please!"

"From now on he isn't going to suck your boobs, understand?"

"All right, Raymond, all right!" she pleaded, her arms outstretched to receive her son. "Give him back to me, please!"

"Promise?"

"Promise!"

"Cover yourself up!"

Mabel buttoned her blouse and Bowlesky handed the baby back to her. She cradled it, rocked it and stuck her finger into his mouth. The baby stopped howling and started to suck the finger with little grunts. Mabel sat down on the bed, cooing and looking relieved.

"Raymond," she said without looking up, "will you please prepare a bottle for Junior?"

Bowlesky grimaced. He hated the name Junior. Without a word, he opened the can of powdered milk, shook some lumpy contents into a cheap soup bowl, filled it with faucet water and stirred it with a finger.

Mabel saw what he was doing and scowled. "That's not the way to prepare Junior's formula!"

"That's the way my old man prepared my feed," he snapped. "If it was good enough for me, it's good enough for him!"

"How do you know?" Mabel retorted. "Did you still suck a bottle when you were old enough to remember?"

"My old lady told me," he said with a gleeful grin, handing the bottle to her. "Do me a favor: don't call him Junior. He looks more like a monkey than a human."

The baby was about to cry. Mabel quickly stuck the bottle into his mouth and he sucked it hungrily with a sigh, grunting and gulping. "Will you give him a name, Raymond?" she asked.

Bowlesky kicked the can of powdered milk back under the bed. "Ask my mother. She'll give him a name and take care of him."

"What?" Mabel looked up, surprised. "What do you mean, she is going to take care of him? Nobody is going to take care of my baby but me!"

"Look," Bowlesky said. "You and I have a career to think of."

They had quarreled only occasionally before the baby was born. Now they bickered often and violently. To avoid another shouting match, Mabel decided to ignore him. She wasn't really keen about raising a baby, but losing an argument galled her. "You're just jealous," she said with a snort.

"Jealous?" He laughed. "Me jealous of this little monkey?"

"You're jealous because he sucked my breasts more often than you did."

"Look," he said, pointing a finger at his own head. "Since you haven't got much up here, you'd better take good care of your only asset there." He jabbed a finger at her breasts. "There is your capital. I want you to keep them firm and grapefruit sized, you hear?"

He had always been obsessed with her breasts, and she had begun to hate it. Besides, he was talking and acting more like a gangster, emulating his American film idols. A few months ago there had been pictures only of Jeanette MacDonald and Nelson Eddy; now the blackened walls were covered with enlarged photos of Humphrey Bogart and Edward G. Robinson.

She hated it all. She fell silent so he would drop the subject. She also hated his finger-jabbing and his calling her *baby* and *sweetheart*. His gangster-worship was getting so sickening that she had often thought of leaving him. When the baby got older, she would get a job and hire a nurse.

The war news was getting better every day. Japan had begun to lose ground on most fronts. She could hardly wait to see the war end so that she could start a new life on her own.

She turned on their battered radio. Again the news was encouraging. American B-29s had started raiding Japan proper for the first time.

Bowlesky was opening the folding table and the four folding chairs. She knew that he was setting up for a poker game with his gambling pals— three unsavory characters she hated to associate with, especially a narrow-faced man named Ah Sing. He owned a butcher business and always brought some choice pork loin for her to make dumplings. They expected to eat them as a sort of poker snack during the game.

"Poker again?" she asked with a grimace.

"Yes, poker again," Bowlesky said, tossing the cards on the table. "This time we're going to get 'em!"

"What do you mean, we? I hate poker; I'm not playing."

"Baby, you're not going to play, but you can assist. Listen, I have it all worked out. I want you to run back and forth to the kitchen and get things for the baby. While doing so, I want you to glance at their cards. Then give the baby some babytalk, which will be our code words . . ."

"Forget it!" she interrupted with disgust. "I'm not going to do it."

"What?" He glared at her. "This is the time for the baby to do us a good turn. To pay us for all this love and care we've . . ."

"I said forget it," Mabel retorted, her voice firm. "If you want to cheat, do it alone."

He shot her a dirty look and dropped the subject. He did not want to touch off a row that might bring more bad luck to his game.

Mabel knew that he had been losing steadily and owed gambling debts to most of his pals, especially Ah Sing, the Butcher, who had threatened to collect.

"Raymond," she said, her voice low but serious; "you'd better stop gambling before you lose another bundle. We can't afford it. Besides, the Butcher has threatened to collect. One day you might lose an eye or a limb. You heard his threat last time, didn't you?"

Bowlesky sniggered. "If he touches me, he's going to lose both his eyes and all of his five legs. Honey, stop worrying. It's my turn to have a winning streak. You just wait and see, regardless of whether you want to help or not." He wagged a finger at her and added, "When I win, don't expect me to buy you a diamond or a mink. So don't ask."

"Let's not count our eggs before they're hatched," Mabel said with a sneer.

Bowlesky's pals started arriving. Ah Sing was the first. He brought with

him the usual chunk of pork. Mabel got the impression that the pork was
meant not as a gift but as a warning, or a reminder that he was a butcher,
capable of cutting throats.

They started the game as soon as the third man had arrived. Ah Sing
was the oldest, about forty. He wore a loose blue cotton gown that had
a bulge under his right arm—obviously a weapon. He never smiled; his
narrow face was so out of proportion that it looked as though it had been
squashed by a car. His small eyes glistened under the bare light over the
card table. They gave Mabel the shivers.

The other two players, Chang and Mah, both about thirty, wore ill-
fitting Western suits. Their dark and blemished skins were marked with
pimples and scars, their faces expressionless. They looked almost like twin
brothers. All three were sharp players, quiet and calculating, and they won
most of the time.

Ever since she had walked out on her mother, Mabel had seen a storm
looming on the horizon. Raymond looked like a leaking boat about to sink.
As she prepared the pork in the kitchen, she glanced at the group at the
card table; they all resembled broken boats; they would all go down soon,
perhaps bringing her down with them. Considering her past, she thought
it was a marvel that she was still here. Her survival was probably a piece
of pure luck; it must have been an oversight of God's.

At the end of the three-hour game, Bowlesky had again lost all his cash
and a lot more on credit. Ah Sing pocketed his winnings and finished his
tea. Mabel was surprised that he did not mention Raymond's debt. But
Bowlesky volunteered.

"Ah Sing," he said in an ingratiating tone, "don't worry about what I
owe you. I'm working on a big deal. As soon as it goes through you'll get
every penny. Besides, we are friends. Friendship is more important than
money."

"Nothing is more important than money," Ah Sing said, lighting his
pipe with an enormous lighter that made a loud clicking sound. He sucked
on the old discolored pipe heavily, making his cheeks hollow and his face
even narrower.

"Look," Bowlesky said, "I'm a Christian and you can trust me. I
worship God. I really do!"

Ah Sing blew out some smoke heavily. "I worship nothing, just money;
and I trust nobody but myself."

His beady eyes glistened like an animal's under the bare electric bulb.
Bowlesky looked at him and seemed worried. He said with a little nervous
laugh, "Well, that's not a bad philosophy. In these days you've got to look
after yourself. But a little help from others won't hurt. You scratch my

back and I scratch yours. I know a lot of people who want to have their hogs and chickens butchered and cleaned by professionals. I can spread the word around."

"Just show me what you can do," Ah Sing said. Puffing on his pipe, he brought out a few cards and passed them to everyone, including Mabel.

Mabel glanced at the card.

AH SING, President
FIVE BLESSINGS BUTCHER SERVICE
Special service on request.

Telephone: 59872

"Special service?" Mabel asked. "What is that?"

"My services are not limited to butchering hogs and chickens," Ah Sing said ominously, casting a cold glance at Bowlesky.

"Are you passing out cards now?" Bowlesky asked with a nervous laugh.

"Why not? It's a trade, like carpentry . . . or grave digging."

As soon as the poker players had left, Mabel was ready for a storm. Every time Bowlesky lost, he had a temper tantrum. To Mabel's surprise, he did not say anything this time. Looking glum and noncommunicative, he quietly put the table and chairs away and left the apartment. Nothing unusual, she thought. Whenever he was moody, he acted like that. It was much better than shouting and making a scene.

Before she had moved in with him, there had been moments of tenderness, fun, even a bit of happiness. Now everything was dreary; even sex had become drudgery. All she did was climb in and out of bed to fulfill his needs; no feeling, no pleasure on her part. Hard work without pay. She wondered why she stayed. Sometimes she regretted that she had left her mother. But she would never have thought of going back and begging Brigid to take her back. And she wasn't sure that her mother would want to see her again.

She bathed the baby, talked and cooed at him and tried to give him a name. She asked the baby's opinion each time she called out an American name. The baby did not respond until she came up with a Chinese name, Pang Sin. It had no meaning. She just found it easy to pronounce and easy to remember. As soon as she asked the baby if he liked it, he gurgled and kicked.

"That's it!" she said excitedly, giving him a noisy kiss on the forehead. "Pang Sin! You like it, eh? All right, from now on you are Pang Sin Hu. It's better than Pang Sin Bowlesky. You don't look like a half-breed, not even a one-fourth breed, Pang Sin Hu! You have my eyes, my nose and my mouth. There is not a bit of foreign devil in you."

She breast-fed him until he stopped sucking, his little fists opened and eyes closed. Breathing evenly, he was sound asleep. After she had put him back in the crib, she reheated the leftover pork, ate a few pieces, took a shower and went to bed early.

When she woke up in the morning, she stretched and yawned, feeling good after a night's sound and dreamless sleep. When she glanced at the crib she bolted up. "Where's my baby?"

Bowlesky was in the bathroom washing himself. She heard the water splashing. "Raymond," she yelled, rushing to the bathroom. "Where is my baby?"

Bowlesky rubbed himself vigorously with a towel. "Don't look so damned scared," he said casually. "I took him to my mother last night. She'll take good care of him."

"You stole my baby!" Mabel screamed, hitting him with her fists. He caught her arms and tried to calm her.

"Listen, honey, I've got big plans for you today. I've booked you with both Mr. Benson and Jimmy Katz. From now on no more changing dirty diapers. You and I are going back to work. We've got to make some money!"

"Who says I'm going to make money for you? Go make your own money to pay your own goddamned gambling debts!"

He glared at her. "My debt is your debt, get that! You're going to work at the Kitty Cat Club four hours every afternoon, and four hours at Jimmy's every night. Easy job." Then he softened his voice and smiled. "Listen, baby, a whole bunch of American volunteers hit town yesterday. Six months in the Burmese jungle without a woman. They are all sex-starved bastards. Give them a good time, for patriotic reasons, huh? They're loaded."

Mabel spat at him. Stunned, Bowlesky slapped her. She stared at him. She was so furious that she found herself tongue-tied.

"No hard feelings, huh?" he said with a grin, wiping his face with the back of his hand.

She spat at him again and he slapped her harder, knocking her down.

"You stinking son of a bitch!" she shouted, a trickle of blood running down from the corner of her mouth. "You return my baby or I'll kill you!"

"You just try, sweetheart," he said with a mocking laugh, emulating the tough guys in the Hollywood movies.

Mabel struggled to her feet. "You're a sinking boat," she snarled. "I'm leaving before it's too late."

"Don't bother. I'm kicking you out!"

"Give me my baby back!"

"My mother has him. Go get him and get out of my life!"

He gathered up her clothes, stuffed them into her battered suitcase and tossed it out the door. She tried to grab a soup bowl to throw at him, but he spun her around and shoved her out too.

"Get lost, you two-bit whore!" he shouted and slammed the door shut.

55

Charles Hong switched off his radio in his spacious penthouse office on Tu Yu Road. Japan had surrendered. The victory news came so suddenly that he felt his throat tighten and tears well out of his eyes. He closed his eyes tightly, trying to control his emotions. It had been a long war. China had gone through eight years of untold suffering. Millions had died. Since Pearl Harbor, his scrap-iron business had been bad, for American aid had poured into China, and Chinese arsenals had been working at half capacity.

He had no regrets. His father, Henry Hong, had always said, "Do this for the motherland. Profit is secondary." His father, having made a fortune in clothing and food in Honolulu, always talked about the motherland, dreaming of retirement in China. He had wanted to build a house in his native village and enjoy his old age with great-grandchildren playing at his feet. He had donated a fortune to Dr. Sun's revolution.

Hong poured himself a drink and toasted the motherland, his father and himself, then smashed the glass against the wall for good luck. The sound of shattering glass brought his secretary, Miss Teng, rushing into his office, looking alarmed.

"That's all right, Miss Teng," he said with a smile. "I just smashed a glass in celebration."

Miss Teng, a studious college graduate who wore thick glasses, looked a bit puzzled.

"It's a Western custom," Charlie explained. "I have no idea how it originated, but it makes you feel good. Do it sometime."

Outside, noises of celebration had started. Charlie went to the window and looked down on Tu Yu Road, four stories below. He saw people pouring into the main thoroughfare, cheering and setting off firecrackers. In the distance, music of drums and gongs was approaching. Presently, a group of lion dancers appeared. They leaped and pranced in the middle of the street, bringing more celebrants out of their houses.

"Miss Teng," he said to his secretary, "you may go home today. This is a holiday."

"Thank you, Mr. Hong," Miss Teng said, dumping the broken glass into a wastebasket.

After Miss Teng had left, Charlie sat down at his desk and wrote several business letters and a long letter to his parents, telling them that he was winding up the scrap-iron business in China. He also told them his future plans, which included going back to college for a master's degree in business administration. He was not really iterested in business, but since he had not found any other profession that interested him, he decided to take his time to make the biggest decision of his life.

He sealed his letters carefully and put stamps on them properly on the upper right corner. He liked all his correspondence to look clean and neat, with names and addresses clearly written and evenly spaced. It was August 14, 1945, a memorable day. He made a large red circle around this date on his calendar.

It was a hot morning. Outside, the fog seemed to have been burned off by the summer sun. He turned off the electric fan, picked up his briefcase and left with a light heart, whistling "Oh, Susannah," one of the few songs he liked.

The crowd on the street was growing bigger, waving, singing and watching the lion dancers. The dancers made the lion stand on its hind legs and nod its head, its red eyes rolling, provoking cheers and laughter. The firecrackers and music were deafening. People were sweating, fanning themselves and shading their eyes against the sun with newspapers and folding fans. As he joined the celebrants, he heard a sob. He turned and looked. Sitting beside a battered suitcase near the office building entrance was a young woman. She had covered her face with both her hands; her shoulders were shaking with sobs. Charlie fished out a five-hundred-yuan note and tossed it in her lap. Since her eyes were still buried in her hands, she did not see it. He picked it up and said, "Here is some money to tide you over. Here, take it."

The woman wiped her eyes and looked up. Charlie stared at her, dumbfounded. He had seen this young woman before. He quickly squatted down to take a closer look.

"Aren't you Mabel Hu? What are you doing here?"

The bit of pepper she had placed in the corners of her eyes had worked: they were red and watery. She wiped them once more, blinked a few times and stared back at him, faking a surprised look. "Mr. Hong!" she cried tearfully. "Oh, Mr. Hong!"

She had rehearsed this little act at home. Everything had worked out according to plan. Now she must be careful not to spoil it. She covered her face with her hands and started sobbing again.

Charlie put a hand on her shoulder to comfort her. "What's wrong, Mabel? Why are you here weeping?"

She started to cry loudly, shaking her body with heartbroken sobs. Charlie took out his handkerchief and handed it to her.

"Stop crying and tell me what happened. Here, here, wipe your tears."

Mabel took the handkerchief and wiped her tears once more, swallowing hard. Then she tried to pull herself together. A small crowd had gathered around them to watch. Charlie took her arm and pulled her up. "All right—let's go somewhere and talk. Are you hungry?"

Mabel blew her nose and shook her head. Charlie picked up her suitcase. "Let's go back to my place," he said and hailed a ricksha coolie. His Dodge was being serviced and he was glad. He would have hated to fight traffic on such a day.

He tried to hire two rickshas but could not find another. Since Chungking rickshas were too narrow to carry two passengers side by side, he made her sit on his lap. She was wearing a light blue Western blouse and a white short skirt that barely covered her thighs. She leaned against him and stretched her legs slightly to expose more of their shapely length. He felt the warmth of her body and smelled a pleasant fragrance from her long black hair. When the ricksha bumped over a rough spot on the street, he held her tighter to keep her from rocking. It had been more than a year ago since he had met and chatted with her at Ding Fei's party. He had enjoyed the conversation and found her very attractive. But he had had a business appointment and had had to leave early. Before he had left, he had given her his business card. Later he had been sorry that he had not asked for her address. Next day he had attempted to call Ding Fei for it, but had felt awkward and given up. He had always been shy about asking for a woman's phone number or address, especially indirectly. What a miracle, he thought. On the day of the victory celebration he had walked right into her life. Was this fate?

Smelling her hair, he held her tight. From the bare legs that showed from under her short skirt, he could almost visualize her entire body, round and shapely. Her weeping on the street bothered him a little, but he would find out her problem soon enough. He had met her mother twice and had liked her. A cheerful, friendly lady, very attractive. Now the daughter was almost a replica of the mother, except younger and even prettier.

He lived alone in a spacious apartment, which he kept extremely tidy and clean. The landlady, who lived upstairs, came down to clean it for him almost every day, using it as an excuse to get to know him better. He might be a good catch for her own daughter, who at thirty was on her way to spinsterhood.

Mabel leaned against him comfortably and enjoyed the ricksha ride. She was determined to turn a new page in her life. The past several years had been a disaster. She was glad that she had left that cheap little hotel and the dull hotel-clerk's job. She was seventeen now, and it was about time to better her life. She needed a home and fresh start. It was such a relief that she had finally gotten away from Raymond and his shabby life of a not very successful con-artist.

The ricksha stopped at a two-story building on a fairly clean street. Most of the Western-style houses in the neighborhood still bore marks of the Japanese bombing, but, unlike other areas, the owners of the homes had spent time and money making repairs. Broken glass had been replaced, bomb craters filled and damaged roofs retiled.

Charlie tipped the coolie generously. He took Mabel inside, offered her whatever he had in the refrigerator—fresh fruit, chunks of cheddar cheese and bread.

"You may take a bath if you wish," he said. "Later, we'll go out to dinner."

Mabel was a little disappointed by the apartment. She had expected a beautiful home with servants and expensive furniture. She had thought that Charlie, being the owner of an American company, must be rich. But she was not going to show her disappointment.

"What a nice place you have, Mr. Hong," she said, walking around admiring the functional rattan chairs and the traditional couplet scrolls of Chinese watercolors and calligraphy on the walls.

"Please sit down," Charlie urged. "Do you feel better now?"

"Yes, Mr. Hong—and I thank you for that."

"Now tell me what went wrong. Why were you crying on the street? If you wish, you may tell me later, maybe after a bath and dinner."

"Am I going to inconvenience you?"

"Of course not! Make yourself at home. We have all day. After dinner I'll take you home."

"I can't go home," she said hastily, her voice sad and her smile disappearing.

"All right. Tell me what your problem is. Maybe I can help."

"My mother has a boyfriend," she lied. "He doesn't like me. I've had to move out."

"Does your mother know you've moved out?"

"She doesn't care what I do."

"Of course your mother cares! She might be looking for you everywhere. She may have gone to the police."

"She's glad to be rid of me," Mabel said, covering her face with both hands as though she were about to burst into tears again.

"All right, all right," Charlie said. "We'll not talk about it. You may stay here for a few days if you wish." He sat beside her on the rattan couch and put an arm around her, trying to comfort her. "Hungry?"

She nodded, sniffling. He handed her his handkerchief again and she dried her eyes with it. Then she wolfed down some cheese and ate an apple.

After a leisurely bath, she felt better and was hungry again. He took her to an expensive Szechuan restaurant for a spicy dinner.

Charlie suspected that Mabel had more problems than just her mother's boyfriend. Brigid had not struck him as man-crazy—someone who would kick her daughter out because of a masculine whim. But he decided not to pry into Mabel's private affairs; not yet. A little warning bell had rung in his mind when he had picked her up; but she was so attractive, even when she looked pitiful, he simply could not walk away. Besides, both mother and daughter were Ding Fei's friends.

He ate sparingly. She would now and then lift her head with a sweet smile and cast him a fleeting glance, a little mischievous, a little sexy. Those glances provoked in him a strong animal lust that he despised. He warned himself to be more respectful, and reminded himself that she was the daughter of a friend, half his age and probably a virgin. As he watched her sympathetically, he took several deep breaths to suppress his shameful thoughts. She was so innocent and yet so exciting and forbidding. . . .

It was still early in the evening when they finished dinner. In the distance he heard Western drum and bugle music. "A marching band!" Mabel said excitedly. "Let's go watch the parade."

"Parade? What parade?"

"The victory parade, don't you know?" she said, wiping her mouth with the hot towel which the waiter had just passed to her.

Fortified with food, she became more alive and talkative. "Mr. Hong, we have won the war, haven't you heard?"

"Of course I have heard. Didn't you see the lion dancers? We've been celebrating since early morning."

"We have beaten Japan! From now on, China is a world power. We are going to get Manchuria back. Oh, how much I want to go there! They say Manchuria is so rich that each time you pick up a rock, it's a piece of jade."

"That's what they said about California a hundred years ago. 'Each time you pick up a rock, it's a gold nugget.'"

"Mr. Hong . . ."

"Call me Charlie, please."

"May I? Oh, I'm so excited! I wish I could go to Manchuria! What are your plans, Charlie?"

"I will probably return to America after I have wound up my business in China."

Mabel watched him, her big brown eyes soft and dreaming. She had almost blurted out, "May I go with you, Charlie?" Her desire to go to America was stronger than her desire to go to Manchuria, but she had already learned how to play games with men. Never jump into a man's lap too soon. Play hard to get—that was one of the tricks—but not so hard as to lose him.

"How wonderful that you have a family to go back to, Charlie. I wish you the best of luck."

Now the band was getting closer. "Let's go watch the parade," he said, leaving money on the table.

They rushed out of the restaurant with many other customers who were also eager to join the official celebration. Whenever people heard a Western marching band, they knew it was official, for only the government could afford these bugles and drums.

Charlie Hong wished he had brought his camera. He would have loved to take pictures of the victory parade and send them to his father, who would show them proudly to everybody and say, "Who says China is weak?" China had been on the verge of collapse many times; Charlie had seen soldiers dying of starvation in Chungking. But still China had won the war.

With moistened eyes he saluted the flag and all those whose knees had not buckled during the past eight horrible years.

*

Back in his apartment, Charlie asked Mabel how old she was. "Twenty-one," she lied with a little chuckle. "Why?"

He poured two drinks, the best Irish whiskey, a gift from a business associate. "You are old enough to have this," he said, offering her a drink. "To victory—to us!"

After Mabel had downed her drink in three large gulps, she kissed him on the cheek—a long, affectionate kiss. "Thank you, Charlie," she said softly, with sincerity. "I don't know where I would be without you."

He liked a girl who was appreciative. "It's fate, Mabel," he said. "Even if you hadn't seen me outside my office building, fate would still have directed you to me. So there!"

While Mabel excused herself, Charlie sat in his favorite rattan chair and analyzed this bizarre encounter. He still wasn't too sure what he was going to do with her. Perhaps the best thing to do would be to pay her mother a visit in the morning and find out if she wanted her daughter back. If she wanted her, he should return her, whether Mabel wanted to go or not. It would be the only decent thing to do. After all, she was a responsibility. If Brigid rejected her, then he would think of the next step.

When Mabel came out of the bathroom, she was wearing his blue silk bathrobe, which hung loosely on her shapely body, showing part of her breasts and a lot of her legs. Charlie suggested that she sleep in his bed. He would use the living room couch.

"No, Charlie," she said. "You sleep in your bed; I'll sleep on the couch. I insist!"

"If you insist, okay," he said with a laugh. "I happen to like my bed." He went to the closet and brought out some extra bedding. When she bent over the couch to make the bed, he could see her breasts hanging out almost in full view.

Determined to act like a gentleman, he kissed Mabel on the cheek and said goodnight. Thereafter, tossing in his bed, he meditated, counted sheep and poured cold water on his sexual feelings with various noble thoughts. Still, it took him quite a while to fall asleep.

Suddenly he was wakened from his restless sleep by a warm body wriggling beside him and a soft thigh rubbing against his. For a moment he thought it was a dream. Then he felt somebody's warm breath tickling his face. When he realized what was happening, he heard a voice whispering into his ear, "Do you love me, Charlie?"

56

On his way to meet Sam Cohen, Charlie Hong thought of Mabel and her sexual expertise. She had taught him a lot in two weeks. He had always treasured virgins: he had vowed to marry a virgin. Now he had doubts about such virtuous thoughts.

He was surprised that Mabel knew so many varieties of lovemaking, from different kinds of kissing to various fancy positions. They had tried them all. On the whole it had been a marvelous experience. And Mabel seemed to enjoy it tremendously herself. That in itself was terribly exciting. Her heavy breathing and soft groans, her hungry expression, her impatient movements, her fingernails digging painfully deep into his sides, reminded him of a book about a nymphomaniac that he had read avidly in secret during his senior high school days in Honolulu.

Still, Mabel's rich experience bothered him. Where had she learned all that? How many people had she slept with? Would she be unfaithful? He would like to have somebody's expert opinion and advice. That was why he had called Sam Cohen and asked to meet him.

He arrived at the Chungking Café almost twenty minutes late. Sam was waiting and reading an English-language paper at a corner table in the crowded Western-style coffee shop. He was smartly dressed in a dark brown business suit and smelled of expensive cologne; his beard, with streaks of gray, was nicely trimmed. Sam had always been a ladies' man. Charlie Hong often wished he had Sam's charisma and his indescribable air of elegance—and perhaps a bit of his arrogance. Those qualities seemed attractive to many women.

"Sorry I'm a bit late," Charlie said as they shook hands over the little round table. He felt bad because Sam was always punctual.

"That's all right, Charlie," Sam said, folding his paper and putting it into his coat pocket. The young waiter in short white shirt and loose trousers came over with a soiled menu, which Sam waved away. "Just coffee, please." After the waiter had left, he said in a lowered voice, "You don't want to eat anything here. They serve Wartime Pastry only. No idea what's in them."

"I know," Charlie said. He would go along with Sam, whatever he said.

Sam lighted a cigar and blew out the blue smoke noisily. "Now, tell me what's on your mind."

Sam sounded a little patronizing, but Charlie did not mind; in fact, the superior air only enhanced a student's trust, creating a certain aura of confidence around the teacher. Charlie regarded himself as Sam's equal in business, but with women and sex, he needed Sam's coaching and direction. His problem was that he still could not separate sex from marriage.

"Well," he said, trying not to stammer. "I–I met a girl. I would like to have a bit of advice."

"Ah—a girl!" Sam said, his face brightening. "It's about time, Charlie. I've been wondering if you were a eunuch or what. Never showed much interest in the fair sex. What about this girl? Describe her a bit first. Like a doctor, I won't be able to write the right prescription unless I know something about the subject."

"Well, she is young and pretty," Charlie said hesitantly, not too sure how to describe her without revealing her identity. "And she is kind of . . . experienced."

"All desirable qualities in a woman, Charlie. Without them, a man has no business fooling around with her. So you have slept with her already."

"Y–yes, many times. That's my problem, Sam. I can't fool around with a woman unless I marry her."

"That's ridiculous!"

The waiter came with two cups of coffee. Sam poured some evaporated milk into his and added two teaspoonfuls of sugar. He stirred his coffee deliberately until after the waiter had left, then looked up and went on. "Listen, Charlie: sleeping with a woman is no different from dancing with a girl these days. You don't think of marriage when you dance with a woman, do you?"

"Well, sometimes I do."

"Then don't! Marriage is a serious business. Think about it only when you are in love. Are you in love?"

"Well, she is kind of experienced."

"Is that what bothers you?"

"Y–yes."

"What's wrong with experience?"

"I always thought a man should marry a virgin. Don't you?"

Sam took a sip of coffee, gave his cigar several puffs and said, "Marriage is like a business partnership, Charlie. If I want a business partner, I'd rather have someone who is experienced. If you are in love, never let that bother you. Never!"

Charlie's eyes sparkled instantly as though it was what he had hoped to hear. He asked anxiously, "Would you marry an experienced girl yourself, Sam?"

"Of course I would. Like dancing, it's a lot more enjoyable to dance with someone who knows how and doesn't have two stiff legs."

"That's exactly what I thought, Sam," Charlie said with controlled excitement. "Like my dance teacher in Honolulu. She was so good that I learned how to waltz in half an hour. After two lessons, I could do the intricate spiral turn and develop without tripping over my own feet. I know a lot of others who did, because they had mediocre teachers."

"Now tell me," Sam said seriously. "Think about it twice before you answer this very important question: are you or are you not really in love with this woman?"

"Well," Charlie said after a moment of soul searching. "Well, I am, Sam. Very much so."

"That's it, Charlie!" Sam said, putting out a hand for him to shake. "Let's set a date to tie the knot. I'll give her away if she needs a father. Does she have a father?"

Charlie shook Sam's hand limply. "Tie the knot? So soon?"

"I'll bet your parents have been badgering you to give them a plump little boy so that they can rock him on their knee. I know all Chinese parents do. For God's sake, Charlie, what are you waiting for? I want to meet her. Does she have a father or not?"

"Well, I guess she has. She doesn't talk too much about her family. Thank you for your advice, Sam. Guess I'm sort of enlightened now. If you think virginity isn't that important, then it isn't. I can sleep on that. Thanks a lot, Sam."

"Good!" Sam said, rising to go. "If you need any more advice, let me know. Since she is experienced, I don't suppose you need any pointers in the sex department—or do you?"

"If I do, I'll call," Charlie said, blushing a little. He was tempted to tell Sam who she was, but changed his mind. He left some money on the table and walked out with his mentor, who put a fatherly arm around him and hugged him affectionately.

"Charlie," he said, "one last piece of advice. Love is like a plant; it dies easily from neglect. Keep it fertilized."

"Fertilized? With what?" he asked, looking puzzled.

"Say 'I love you' once in a while. It's the cheapest fertilizer there is, and a woman loves it."

*

Charlie Hong got into his Dodge. "Who needs a virgin?" he told himself with a smile as he started the car. He was humming "Oh, Susannah." The next stop was to pay Brigid a visit. He had learned the address from Mabel in a roundabout way, for Mabel still did not want him to see her mother.

Having made sure it was the right place, he checked the address once more. He looked at the wood frame shack with a bit of apprehension. The neighborhood had probably seen better days. The front door was open. He walked in and was shocked by the shabbiness inside.

He knocked on the inside door, which had been red lacquered once but was now cracked and peeling. A toothless old woman with stringy and unkempt graying hair opened it. Looking like a witch, she peered at him suspiciously and asked curtly what he wanted. He wasn't too surprised. The war had made a lot of people rude and cranky, treating all strangers as enemies. Not taking offense, he decided to spread a little cheer in this angry society.

"Long live victory!" Charlie said with a big smile, giving the woman Churchill's victory sign. "How do you do, madame?"

"What do you want?" the woman repeated, ignoring his greeting.

"May I see Mrs. Hu? Her foreign name is Brigid Hu."

"No Mrs. Hu!" With an impatient wave of her hand, she slammed the door shut so hard that a piece of plaster fell off the wall.

Charlie smiled. He was thinking of his father's proverb: "Only the stupid annoys himself with unnecessary anger." Why was he not annoyed? he wondered. It must have had something to do with his sexual contentment. If so, this woman must have been terribly frustrated. Well, he thought, the way she looked, she should be.

*

Driving across town to see Ding Fei, Charlie found the traffic heavy, but was not at all impatient. He was savoring a soothing feeling of warmth and goodwill toward his fellow men.

He passed several sedan chairs carried by coolies. Riding in some of the chairs were flashily dressed women, most of them very pretty, peering out the openings boldly with their slightly puffy eyes. He had learned that these girls were returning home from marathon mahjong parties hosted by rich merchants or high government officials. He had attended a few of such deal-making and goodwill-buying functions. The girls were hired to serve drinks, crack watermelon seeds, light water pipes, play Chinese moon guitars or flutes and sometimes sing a song or two. They were high-class sing-song girls; they looked down on the "jeep girls" who entertained only foreigners and had no skills except speaking pidgin English with a fake accent.

As he was driving past one of the sedan chairs, he caught a glimpse of the young woman at close range. She smiled at him, her heavily made-up face half hidden behind her tiny folding fan. He wondered how many pretty young women had gone into the singsong profession. It chilled him as he thought of Mabel. Where had she learned all her man-pleasing skills? Had she been a singsong girl or a jeep girl?

He switched off the suspicion quickly, remembering one of his father's proverbs: "Without seeing or hearing, everything is clean."

When he reached a high point in the street, he could see the river in the distance. Heads were bobbing over its yellowish surface, which gleamed in the late afternoon sun. He had seen them before. Nationalist soldiers were swimming the river, holding their rifles over their heads to test their endurance. After victory, the army, navy and air force had been maneuvering almost every day in a show of China's military prowess. It was almost like flexing one's muscles after a fight. His father would have loved to watch this. His father was undoubtedly still celebrating the victory, boasting of the Chinese people's perseverance and a hundred other virtues.

That was Henry Hong—never forgetting that he was Chinese. In one of his latest letters, his father had wanted him to sell the remaining scrap iron and use the money to build a Confucian temple. "If the scrap-iron business is dead," he had said, "then try to revive the motherland's demoralized spiritual life. It is time to rebuild China by preserving the old sage's sacred teachings."

*

"Hello, Charlie," Ding Fei said cheerfully as she answered his knock. "What wind has blown you to this neck of no-man's land? If you've come to see Sam, he isn't here."

"I've come to see you and ask some advice," Charlie replied politely.

"Oh? I thought you were the genius. What about? If it's about business, I have a ready answer for you: go to Nanking. Ever since the victory, all kinds of doors have opened in Nanking for wheeler-dealers like you and Sam."

They went into the kitchen and sat at the kitchen table. Ding Fei poured two glasses of shao hsing wine.

"What are your plans?" Charlie asked. "Moving to Nanking?"

"It depends on Sam's business. He is thinking of importing lumber to China from Oregon. The Japanese did a good job destroying China. It will take ten years to rebuild. How about you?"

"I'll have to get rid of my scrap iron first."

"By the way, it's flattering for you to seek advice from me. If it's not about business, what is it?"

"First, where has Brigid moved to?"

The smile on Ding Fei's face disappeared instantly. The question hit her like an unexpected blow. For almost a year she had been brooding over this question. Ever since her disappearance, Ding Fei had blamed herself for the mystery. Both Brigid and Mabel had disappeared without a trace.

"Charlie," she said, her voice sad and pained, "that's a question I almost asked you. I've spent sleepless nights wondering where she has gone. When did you last see her?"

"The last time I saw her was here, at your birthday party. Before I came here, I went to see her at this address." He showed Ding Fei the address.

Ding Fei looked at it and frowned. "This is not where she used to live. Who told you she lived there?"

Charlie wondered if he should tell her the truth. He was disappointed that Mabel had given him a false address. "Forget it, Ding Fei," he said, trying to look casual and unconcerned.

"Is that all you want to know, Charlie?" Ding Fei asked with a deep frown.

"Well, there's something else. I'm thinking about getting married."

"Really?" Ding Fei asked, her smile returning. "Congratulations! Let's have a toast."

They drank and Ding Fei refilled their glasses. "Who is the lucky girl?" she asked.

Charlie hesitated.

"All right, surprise us," Ding Fei said with a laugh. She rubbed her hands together eagerly and said, "What kind of advice do you need from me?"

"I've had some advice from Sam, but I need a second opinion. What do you think of a woman who has had a lot of experience?"

"In what?"

"W—well," he started to stammer. He found it more difficult to discuss the subject with a woman. "Well . . . in sex."

Ding Fei stopped laughing and wagged an accusing finger at him. "Charlie," she said, her voice serious, "have you been playing around?"

"I played around only a little with this one. But she is awfully experienced."

"Charlie, you shock me. How can you think of marrying a loose woman like that? How can a single woman gain so much experience unless she is promiscuous? She must have been sleeping with every Chang San and Li Su. Toss her out! You deserve something much better."

"B—but I can't just toss her out."

"Why not? Did you get her pregnant?"

"No. But she has no place to go."

"Where did you meet her?"

"I picked her up on the street," he said uncomfortably.

"Oh, my God! A streetwalker!" Ding Fei cried, this time looking genuinely horrified. "Charlie, I want you to rush to the nearest doctor for a checkup, right this minute! Good thing you came to me for advice before you made the greatest blunder of your life!"

"Ding Fei, she is Mabel—Brigid's daughter."

Ding Fei stared at him, dumbfounded. Slowly she broke into a happy smile. "Charlie, why didn't you tell me in the first place?" She leaned forward and gave him a resounding kiss on the forehead, then she heaved a long sigh of relief. "Charlie, you have done a good deed! Where did you find her?"

"On Tu Yu Road, two weeks ago."

"I take back everything I just said about her. She is an awfully nice girl. That's why Sam and I introduced her to you in the first place. We always prayed that one of cupid's arrows would hit both of you right in the heart. So it finally did, eh? That calls for another drink."

She refilled the glasses. "Now tell me everything."

Charlie did not know how to respond to such a sudden about-face. Ding Fei laughed and went on. "Charlie, don't look so confused. A moment ago I was talking about a total stranger, a woman I knew nothing about; now I'm talking about the daughter of my best friend. I've known both of them all my life."

"So you knew Mabel was experienced."

"I didn't say that. Listen, Charlie, Brigid was raised in France, a country where everyone is liberated. They publish a lot of sex books. Anyone can learn all there is to know about sex without being loose or promiscuous."

"It figures," Charlie said, somewhat comforted by Ding Fei's explanation. "No wonder she knows a lot about the French style."

"She is a nice girl, Charlie. I'll vouch for her."

"So you approve of her?"

"I not only approve," Ding Fei said enthusiastically, "I want to host your wedding party. How is she?"

"Who? Mabel?"

"Yes. Is she all right?"

"She is . . . I guess," he said, looking a bit uncertain.

"I'm awfully glad you found her, Charlie," Ding Fei said, her enthusiasm mounting. "You two will make a wonderful couple. It's not easy to find a girl today who is both innocent and experienced. Oh, you lucky dog!"

"I guess I am," he said, becoming more assured. "Thank you, Ding Fei."

"I want you to be kind to her," she said, feeling a bit motherly. "Love is fragile, Charlie. You have to fertilize it once in a while to keep it healthy. You understand, don't you?"

"How?" he asked. "What fertilizer?"

"Bring her flowers and ask no questions. A woman loves flowers and hates any invasion of her privacy. Always remember that."

Having finished three glasses of wine, Charlie began to feel dizzy. "Of course, Ding Fei," he said happily. "With both Sam's fertilizer and yours, I can't go wrong—can I?"

57

M abel ate her breakfast alone. She missed her mother's salted eggs, sausages and French toast, but her maid, Han Mah, made a millet-porridge breakfast that Charlie Hong liked: a yellowish gruel to be eaten with side dishes such as preserved turnips and braised chicken livers with aniseed. Charlie could enjoy the same breakfast for the rest of his life, but Mabel could eat it only with an indifferent appetite.

For six months now she had forced herself to like whatever Charlie loved. She was determined to make the marriage work. The wedding had been the highlight of her life. Although small, it had given her a tremendous sense of security; it had driven away all her fears and feelings of uncertainty. Charlie, a solid man with a conservative life-style, had made some adjustment, but it was she who had made the most changes, to suit him. Indeed, sometimes she had felt like a wild horse being reined in too tightly, but she knew it was for her own good.

The only thing that still bothered her was her illegitimate child, Pang Sin. How long was she going to keep him a secret? If she told Charlie about it, how would he respond? Would it damage the marriage? Every time she thought about it her heart sank, and yet the little boy always returned to her mind, giving her moments of longing and an unquenchable desire to hold him and rock him.

She had plenty of pocket money besides a bank account of her own, with a large amount deposited that she never had any reason to touch. Charlie was more than she had expected, except for one thing—excitement. He was not dull, but somehow life with him was predictable; she could almost tell what their life would be like for the next ten years—same dishes, same routine, same kind of lovemaking. Charlie had eliminated many of her variations in bed, claiming that they made him squirm. He enjoyed only the conventional style, which to her was as insipid as the millet-porridge breakfast.

In conjugal love, Charlie was easily satisfied. But she was still longing for the ultimate elusive moment—the tremendous climax with rainbows and fireworks that so many women talked about. So far she had only imagined it.

Charlie had taken a business trip to Chungtu, the second-largest city in Szechuan Province. He had invited her to go but she had declined. She did not like his business trips. She had taken a few and most of the time she had had nothing to do but cut her toenails in a gloomy hotel room while waiting for him to return from long meetings.

He had been gone for two days now, and she had begun to miss him. One good thing about Charlie was that he could be trusted; she never had to worry about where he was or what he was doing. His rigid moral standards would keep him from visiting brothels or flirting with somebody's secretary.

She ate half a bowl of the millet porridge and asked Han Mah to take the breakfast away. She had just finished redecorating their apartment. This morning she was going to have a long soak in her new bathtub and read the classic romance *Dream of the Red Chamber*. After a month of shopping and redecorating the apartment, there was not much to do except soak, read and cut her toenails. Restlessness had begun to seep in, and she wished her mother were there.

Ever since Mabel had learned that her mother had disappeared, she had begun to think of her more often. She even missed that fateful night her mother had whipped her. She was sure that the maid, trying to shield her, had been hit more than she had. Thinking about it now, she wished she had received all the blows.

Mabel counted her blessings and thought about how lucky she was. She could see a comfortable future looming on the horizon—if she could find her mother and share the good fortune with her. How she missed Brigid! Her mother had always been a protector, a comforter, a counselor, someone who always came to her rescue no matter what, when or where; whose love was always true and genuine, never conditional or selfish. Suddenly she became very sentimental. She felt her throat tighten, and tears began to fill her eyes.

Han Mah rapped on the bathroom door and announced that a foreign devil gentleman was here to see her. Like most of the common people, Han Mah still called all non-Chinese foreign devils, which had become a merely a term without bad connotations.

"All right, Han Mah. Ask him to wait in the living room."

She did not even try to ask Han Mah to get the visitor's name, for the maid would not be able to pronounce it anyway. Mabel had known quite a few foreigners, mostly her mother's friends. Perhaps this one had some news about Brigid.

She dressed quickly, went to her bedroom and put on a bit of makeup. Charlie had bought her a large collection of cosmetics and beauty aids, from clear-eye potions to unnecessary-hair pluckers. Her perfume bottles stood like a jungle on her dresser.

She took a last look at herself in the mirror—light-green Western suit with matching stockings and high-heeled shoes, long black hair swept up into a bun that rested on top of her head. It made her look tall and elegant. She prayed that this stranger would bring her good news about her mother, and for good luck she pinned a red silk rose on her lapel.

Thinking positively, she walked into the living room. The red-haired young man with a red beard did not get up to greet her. He was sitting on her favorite sofa, grinning at her, his legs crossed, his arms folded over his ill-fitting dark brown suit.

"Hello, Mabel," he said familiarly, as though he had known her for years.

Mabel stared at him, her heart sinking. She recognized his voice; she could tell that those hard, slanting eyes were Asian. The red hair and red beard did a good job hiding his identity—an excellent disguise. It had almost fooled her.

"How did you find me, Raymond?" Her voice was tense with fear.

Bowlesky broadened his grin. "It was easy. But let's not waste time talking about that. Did you miss me, honey?"

"Raymond, I'm married now. Please leave me alone . . . please!"

"I know. I've changed, too. By the way, I'm Raymond Carnahan now. A good Irish name. How about my new hair and beard? Like 'em? Permanent dye."

"Please, Raymond," she pleaded. "I can't stand here talking to you like this. My husband might come home any minute."

"Hey, is this how you greet an old flame? No kiss, no hug?"

"What do you want, Raymond?" she blurted out, trying not to sound angry.

"What do I want?" He laughed. "You sound like a lady talking to a beggar. C'mon, sweetheart—I'm your lover and mentor. I taught you everything. I bet you hooked your husband because of all the tricks you learned from me."

"Please go! Please!"

"Go? Just like that?"

"All right. How much do you want?"

"I don't want your money, honey. Do you think I'm a gold digger? If I was, I never would have taken you in . . ."

"I said, what do you want, Raymond?" she interrupted him, her voice desperate.

"I want you! I want you to come back. I've got our future all planned. Look, this time we are going to make it—and make it big!"

"All right, Raymond," she said, knowing that arguing with him would not accomplish anything. She must get away from him; the way he talked nauseated her. "Let's discuss that another time. I have to go. Let me have your address. I'll come and talk."

Bowlesky shook his head slowly with a frozen grin. "You can't get rid of me so easily, honey. Let's talk now."

"I can't! I must go!"

"Go where? Oh, I know—to meet your husband." He chuckled. "Your husband will have to wait." Suddenly he stopped grinning, leaned forward and said seriously, "Mabel, your husband is out of town. Don't treat me like an idiot. Don't make me angry, huh?"

She stared at him, a bit frightened. She had never seen him look like this before. Years ago, when he had been angry, he had looked more funny than intimidating; now his glaring eyes alone gave her a chill. He leaned back, recrossed his legs and grinned again.

"Remember Mr. Benson? He used to like you. Still does. He's my business partner now." He put a placating hand out and added quickly, "Don't jump to conclusions yet. You are not going to do anything you don't like. In fact, I won't allow it. You are mine and I have a duty to protect you."

Mabel couldn't bear to hear any more. She went to the door and opened it. The maid came in with a tray of tea and watermelon seeds. She served tea automatically as a routine whenever there was a visitor.

"Han Mah, the foreign gentleman is leaving," Mabel announced.

Bowlesky folded his arms and made no sign of leaving. "Ah—tea!" he said. "I'll go as soon as I've had my tea."

Han Mah served the tea and withdrew. Mabel was disappointed that the maid had not sensed anything wrong. Knowing that it was impossible to get rid of him now, she decided to change tactics. She closed the door and came to him, saying softly, "All right, let's talk."

He took several more sips of tea and sighed. "Mabel, you abandoned me to marry someone else; that's not very nice. But I still have a soft spot in my heart for you. I'll make a deal. You come to work for me. I'll even let you live here with your husband. Just come to work for me every day, as though you were going to an office. I'll treat you as my partner and let you share the profits. Or . . ." He stopped. Nursing the teacup, he stared at her with the same frozen grin.

"Or what?" she asked fearfully.

He put the teacup down, grabbed her by the arm and flashed a photo in her face. "Take a look at this. Recognize it?"

It was a photo of both of them, taken two years earlier. Both were nude. Bowlesky was sitting in a chair and Mabel was kneeling on the floor, kissing his large erect penis. She vaguely remembered that both of them had been drunk. He had had pictures taken with a camera with an automatic device.

She was so disgusted that she turned her head away sharply. A moment later she felt fury surging in her and tried to snatch the photo. He jerked it beyond her reach and chuckled. "Nobody is going to see this picture if you cooperate. I am a friendly man. You should appreciate the fact that I loathe violence. But if I'm crossed, I have ways to persuade people. I'll personally deliver a few of these pictures to your husband."

*

Bowlesky lived in a small wooden house in a back alley a few blocks away. The house was newly whitewashed, with glass windows and a tiled roof. Obviously he was doing better in his new enterprise. Freshly pasted on the door was a lucky saying, OPEN DOOR TO GREAT TREASURE, written on a strip of red paper.

Inside, the rooms were sparsely furnished. The middle room, which served as a living room, had a square dining table in the center with four straight-backed chairs around it. In the back was a black-lacquered *kang*, the old-fashioned daybed designed for opium smoking.

There was a Chinese canopied double bed in each of the two bedrooms. One was neatly made and the other looked slept-in. The walls were also newly whitewashed. The small kitchen was almost bare, except for a gas stove, a cutting board and a large built-in basin under a leaking faucet. "I just moved in," he said, as he showed Mabel the rooms. "You'll have to help me decorate the place. We'll conduct a training program here for Mr. Benson. Remember him?"

Mabel was so demoralized now that she simply obeyed. It seemed there was no way out but to do Raymond's bidding until she and Charlie moved away from Chungking. Right now the foremost thing in her mind was to protect her marriage.

"Raymond," she said agreeably, "as long as we are making money, I'll think about it."

"Now you're talking sense, Mabel. Both of us love money!" He planted a kiss on her lips and looked at her hard. "What's the matter? You don't look very happy."

She smiled. "All right, Raymond—tell me about our new enterprise. What's in it for me? What do I get out of it? I won't work for nothing, you know."

Bowlesky took her in his arms and whispered, "Can't talk business until I've had my dinner. I miss the old days; you know that. . . ."

Mabel wriggled out of his arms and started for the living room. "I have no appetite until I learn the nature of our partnership. I may not like it, you know."

Bowlesky followed her. "The same old Mabel," he said, laughing. "Slippery and difficult. Reminds me of the good old times. All right, let's talk. When I'm more hungry, I'll enjoy my dinner a lot more."

"Cut the crap!" she said, sitting down at the dining table and trying to act like the old Mabel of those wild and uninhibited days. She put her hands on the table and looked around. "I like the joint. Much better than the old dump. Is this going to be a whorehouse or a murder syndicate?"

"Nothing of that kind, Mabel. You know I'm not going to do anything illegal. This is going to be a training school. We train high-class singsong girls for Mr. Benson. Remember him?"

"Who could forget him?"

"He likes you. As long as we don't cross him, we'll have this place forever. Steady income, fun . . ."

"Let's talk about money," Mabel said, acting as though the subject of money had cheered her up. "After all, we have a baby to raise. By the way, how is Pang Sin?"

"Growing like a pig."

"I want to see him."

"Anytime. He's being pampered by my old lady. Don't change the subject, honey. Let's talk about money, as you said. How about paying Mr. Benson, our money tree, a visit tonight? I want you to renew your friendship with him."

"If the money is good, I'll even sleep with him. But not tonight." With a wave of the hand and a grimace she dismissed the subject.

Bowlesky watched her with a smile. The old Mabel was indeed coming back. He liked it. Her expression, her wave of disgust and the arrogance had all returned, reminding him of those difficult days of fun and danger. "Mabel," he said, sounding knowledgeable and confident, "Nanking is where the money is these days."

"That was what you said about Manchuria," she said, dismissing his remark with another wave of her hand.

"Manchuria is being taken over by the Communists. They don't gamble or whore, and they object to being rich. That's not my life-style. You always learn from experience. This time we can't miss. Besides, we have Mr. Benson as our partner, a man with experience and money . . ."

"Tell me the deal before I lose interest," Mabel interrupted, her voice impatient.

"Good! You're getting eager. I like that," he said, knowing that delaying tactics always worked, just like her way of playing coy when he wanted sex. "Here's the deal. We recruit Szechuan girls, train them as first-class ladies of joy. Mr. Benson will ship them to Nanking to entertain the rich and powerful. An easy job. And tons of money to be made. Meanwhile, you and I will continue to experiment and invent new techniques to enhance the pleasures of love. We'll combine fun with business, enjoy what we are doing and make tons of money. It's the greatest blessing in life!" He stopped smiling and seized her hand. "But if you cross me, Mabel, you know what will happen, don't you? I have a whole collection of those photos we took two years ago. If you don't do what I tell you, your husband will receive a few of them, delivered by my special messenger." He tightened the grip on her hand and smiled again. "Shall we start our experimenting now? I have a few new ideas. You'll like them. Let's go, huh?"

Nauseated, Mabel allowed herself to be guided into one of the bedrooms.

58

C harlie Hong returned from Chungtu in the morning. He looked relaxed and happy, a new dark suit on his slightly overweight body, which, according to fortune tellers, befitted any successful businessman. Even in Szechuan, the richest province in the south, the common greeting was still "Congratulations—you have grown fat."

Charlie winced when both Mabel and Han Mah welcomed him back with this peculiar greeting. Immediately, Mabel felt tight inside. Not to show her nervousness, she forced herself to be cheerful and chatty. She ate the millet breakfast with short little sighs, a way of showing she was enjoying it. She even tapped her rice bowl appreciatively with her chopsticks between bites as Charlie did. But she could hardly bear to look at the food—Raymond Bowlesky and his new enterprises had ruined her appetite. Now and then she had to take a deep breath to relieve her tension. Luckily, Charlie was unobservant; a suspicious husband would easily have detected her troubled mind.

"What fun did you have in Chungtu, Charlie?" she asked, pretending to be intensely interested. "Did you play mahjong with friends?"

"You know I loathe mahjong. Besides, I didn't have time."

"Of course you don't like mahjong. But it's a shame!" she said. "Because the glow on your face indicates luck. You'll win on a mahjong table regardless of whether you like it or not."

"I had great luck in business in Chungtu," Charlie said after he had swallowed a large mouthful of food. He tapped his bowl and reached for some more.

"I'm sure you had a very profitable two weeks there. I missed you, Charlie."

"Not just profitable," he replied, with a piece of chicken liver poised in front of his mouth, "also lucky in other things. Something unusual happened." He tossed the food into his mouth and chewed with a closed-mouthed smile.

"Tell me about it."

"It's a surprise. Don't eat too much. We're going out to lunch."

Her heart leaped. At two in the afternoon she was supposed to be at Raymond's for their daily meeting. She forced herself to eat another mouthful of the thick yellowish porridge. "Can we do it another time, Charlie?" she asked, trying to keep her voice calm and casual.

Charlie looked up from his rice bowl. "Why? Do you have another engagement?"

"I have to see a doctor." Her unconvincing smile made her uncomfortable.

Charlie noticed it. "Are you sick? You look worried."

"No, Charlie, just a checkup. An ounce of prevention is better than a pound of cure, so they say." She giggled.

"Change it. You can't miss this lunch, Mabel."

Charlie's voice was so firm that she didn't argue. A checkup was no emergency, and she didn't want to arouse his suspicions by inventing another excuse. Perhaps the lunch wouldn't last more than an hour. She still had enough time to make the appointment. When she thought of Raymond, she shuddered. The double life was going to be so nerve-racking that she wished Raymond were dead.

"Charlie," she said, trying to sound cheerful, "when are you going to wind up your business in Szechuan?"

"Not for a while. I've just signed a new contract with a tung oil producer. I'm in this oil business in a big way now. Why? Don't you like Szechuan?"

"I hate it!" she blurted out. Mabel was no longer acting. She was telling the truth. "I wish we could move away. I'm dying to visit Honolulu."

"It's not going to be easy for you, Mabel. First we'll have to get you the necessary immigration papers. It may take time." After swallowing another piece of chicken liver, he added hastily, pointing his chopsticks at her, "But we'll get them, don't worry. Anyway, you can go there as a visitor for Christmas."

Mabel's heart sank. Christmas was still more than eight months away. She said with a wince, "I don't think I can last that long."

Charlie laughed. "You can't last eight months? What are you, something perishable?"

"I'm just sick and tired of Chungking."

"So am I," Charlie said cheerfully. "But we can't simply say that about any place until we are retired, can we?"

"I'm sure you can buy and sell tung oil anywhere. I know that Yunnan is a big tung-oil-producing province . . ."

"Mabel," he interrupted, "I know what's bothering you. After today's lunch, you'll change. You'll feel better. Just wait and see."

"Why do you say that?"

"Because that's in your horoscope."

She tensed. Did he know what was bothering her? Could he read her mind?

"Why is this luncheon so important, Charlie?" she asked, trying her best to hide her anxiety.

"I told you—it's a surprise." After swallowing his last mouthful of food, he laid down his rice bowl and chopsticks and rubbed his hands. "Well, well, no more questions. This is all I can tell you now."

✻

Charlie had left for a business meeting. Mabel kept looking at her watch in their bedroom. The midday sun had backed out of the window an hour ago. She sat at her dressing table, thinking positively to keep her mind occupied. Charlie must have made a marvelous business deal in Chungtu. Perhaps the luncheon was planned for her to meet somebody who was involved in his successful tung oil transactions.

But the anticipation of the luncheon was overshadowed by her meeting with Raymond. The short hand of her diamond-studded wristwatch was fast approaching noon. The luncheon gave her an ominous feeling; it loomed like the last meal served to a prisoner before the execution. The anxiety had become almost unbearable.

In an effort to divert her mind from Raymond, she thought about her mother; of Charlie and their future. She recalled her pleasant days in Wuhan, her school and the Girl Scout activities. Only when she remembered her father did she feel a jolt. For years she had forced herself to hate him; she wanted to detest him for having abandoned her and her mother. But it was a torturous effort . . . like someone trying to put a curse on a loved one. She even imagined herself sticking pins in a voodoo doll. She sank the pins into it fiercely but felt the pain herself. It was an odd sensation, both painful and enjoyable, sadistic and masochistic, a mixture of love and hate. The more she loved him and missed him, the more she wanted to hurt him and to bear the pain herself. For many years she had learned to forget him, to wipe his image out of her mind like erasing a picture from a blackboard with a few angry strokes.

She heard the door open and close. Charlie had returned to pick her up. As she quickly mended her makeup, she looked in the mirror and saw him come in.

"I'm ready, Charlie," she said, rising from her dressing table.

Charlie stood at the door, looking at her admiringly. "What a beautiful dress!" She glanced in the mirror at her shimmering green cheongsam and smoothed out a minuscule wrinkle. The dress clung to her shapely body.

"You like it?" she asked with a smile.

"I never saw anything more beautiful," he said, still staring at her. "Where did you get it?"

"You bought it for me, remember?" She laughed. "Charlie, your memory is getting so short that one day you'll ask who I am."

He remembered. Last Christmas he had wanted to buy a dress made in a color he liked, but Mabel had insisted on another color. She had won. He walked around her, eyed her like an art connoisseur and added with a sigh, "I must say your taste is better than mine, Mabel. I love it!"

She appreciated his admiration. For a brief moment she almost forgot her problems, but as she picked up her purse, her hand was shaking and her fear returned.

"Let's go," she said, walking out of the bedroom ahead of him. She did not want him to look at her too closely, for her forced smile could hardly hide the anxiety in her eyes or the haggard look under her makeup. It was not easy to pretend. She found it hard to act cheerful while feeling depressed.

Charlie was a careful driver, always courteous to pedestrians; he always gave other vehicles the right of way, and his constant stop and go increased her anxiety. She kept swallowing hard to ease the tight feeling in her chest.

The streets were as crowded as ever since the victory. More people had moved back to the city. Rickshas carrying women and children followed wheelbarrows and pushcarts loaded with luggage and furniture, cluttering the street and causing bottlenecks. Buses, and old trucks overloaded with lumber and building material, roared past and exuded black smoke, their drivers honking impatiently. People had started to repair their houses, and the din of hammering was heard everywhere, like firecrackers on a New Year's Day. But the victory had also brought worse times to many. The Americans were gone and many businesses catering to them were closed. Beggars roamed all over the city, running after rickshas, singing their memorized phrases, "Spare a coin, masters and mistresses! Do a good deed! Plant a blessing for your next life!"

At every stop, Charlie would hand a few coins to gnarled or bony begging hands. The slow trip made Mabel a nervous wreck, secretly wringing her wet hands, thinking how she could have enjoyed the outing if she had not had Raymond in her life. What a curse! Why was life so complicated? Was this her fate? Was God teasing her with both fortune and misfortune? It would have been a lot easier to bear if she had simply been a beggar with nothing to worry about but getting hold of a few coins.

The Dodge stopped in front of the Szechuan Palace Hotel, one of the high-class Western-style hotels in Chungking. Charlie leaped out. He was practically the only automobile owner who did not hire a chauffeur. He enjoyed driving, opening doors and helping people in and out. If he had driven strangers, they certainly would have tipped him.

The doorman in a Western military uniform opened the glass door quickly as Mabel and Charlie approached the hotel. A wide smile on his face, Charlie guided her to the thickly carpeted staircase in the spacious lobby. There were chandeliers and heavy velvet drapes. The shiny marble floor was meticulously clean, with large pots of palms and brass spittoons placed beside Western sofas and chairs. Two uniformed bellboys rushed over, eager to carry their luggage.

"No luggage," Charlie said, tipping both of them generously.

A year ago Mabel would have thought that such extravagance was simply a way of being nouveau riche, but now she believed that Charlie was only being philanthropic. It was his way of spreading the wealth, like robbing himself to feed the poor. She had always thought such persons existed only in romantic novels; now she was walking into a luxury hotel with one. She felt like a princess entering a mysterious castle with a prince, her hand on his arm, the world at her feet, pursuing new excitement and new surprises, with unknown fortunes awaiting them in one of the rooms.

He stopped at a door and smiled at her with a wink, like a magician ready to produce a miracle. "Knock," he whispered.

With a forced smile and a heavy heart, Mabel knocked three times gently.

"Your hand is shaking," he said with a little laugh.

"Yes," she said, trying to cover her nervousness with a giggle.

"You should be. Just wait and see. It's my birthday gift to you, Mabel."

The door opened. Mabel stared at her smiling mother, framed in the doorway. She was dumbfounded. Was this a dream?

"Mabel!" Brigid said, extending her arms to her a bit hesitantly, as though unsure of her daughter's response.

Mabel was still staring at her mother in astonishment. It was such a total surprise that she could not believe it was real. When she saw that it was not a dream, she felt tears rushing into her eyes. "Mother," she said, flinging her arms around her. "Mother, mother . . ." Her voice started to choke. She held Brigid tightly and cried unashamedly, letting her emotions pour out like water breaking over a dam.

✳

Raymond Bowlesky poured another gin and took a deep drink from the tall glass. He paced the living room floor and kept looking at his watch, getting increasingly irritated. Mabel was more than three hours late. It was an insult, as if she were saying, "Go ahead and mail those pictures—see if I care!"

He imagined himself bringing out all the porno photos, selecting the best two, stuffing them into an envelope, licking the envelope and sealing it.

"I'll show you, you bitch!" he mumbled. He sat down and gulped his gin.

He looked at his watch again. He would wait ten more minutes, no more. If she did not show up in ten minutes, he would deliver the photos personally.

As he was about to pour himself another drink, the door opened. Mabel came in and greeted him cheerfully. Tossing her purse on the table, she walked to him mincingly and sat down on his lap.

"Darling," she said in a sexy voice, "miss me?"

"Where have you been?" he snapped.

She cupped his face in both her hands and planted a kiss on his mouth. "My husband has come home, Raymond. Can I move in with you?"

"Sure, baby," he said, smiling, surprised but pleased. "But why? What's wrong?"

"He's suspicious," she said with a snarl. "He locked me up for three hours. I had to break a window to get away."

"Well, well." He laughed. "Lucky you have a man to come to! You don't belong to him, sweetheart; you belong to me. Look, I have a great future planned for us. I even got a name for our company—Raymond and Mabel Enterprises, Inc. Like it?"

"What's Inc.?"

"It means everything's legal. We can also call it Limited, like many big British enterprises. Take your pick."

"Why Limited? It's not very impressive."

"All right—Inc., then."

"Are you sure it's legal?"

"It's impressive and legal, what more do you want? Listen, just like I told you—we supply entertainment to fellows like Mr. Benson. Thieves can steal a clock and get caught, but the law can't touch the clockmaker. Got the picture?"

"Raymond, can we have some calling cards printed?"

Bowlesky was getting a bit tipsy. "What? What cards?"

"Business cards. I want to go into this in a big way. I'm your partner, am I not? If so, I want to be vice president and have the title printed on my business card. Even your friend Ah Sing, the Butcher, has a business card—President of Five Blessings Butcher Service. We should have a brochure, too, with pictures. We supply singsong girls, barmaids, belly dancers, the lot. We can also have a special service on special request. Know what I mean, Raymond?" She licked her lips and touched her breasts with sexy sighs and moans.

Bowlesky laughed. "Why not? We've got our specialty, too, haven't we? Inventing new techniques and new varieties is our specialty."

"Raymond, it's like money in the bank. In our brochure, we'll have illustrations. We won't use our own pictures; we'll use models and duplicate the good ones. Let's study the pictures we have and see if we can improve on the poses. Where are our pictures, honey?"

"They're all under the mattress . . ." He stopped, grabbed her arm and looked at her suspiciously. "Is this a trick? Are you trying to steal those pictures?"

She jerked her arm free. Pretending that she was hurt by his suspicion, she snarled and tried to hit him. He blocked her blows and placated her. "Okay, okay. I was just kidding . . ."

"You are disgusting!" she said, plunking down on another chair. "I don't see how we can work together if you're so damned suspicious!"

He went over to her and tried to kiss her, but she turned her head away. "Baby," he said apologetically, "I'm sorry. I apologize."

"Give me my purse," she said, sniffing. Her imitation of a gun moll amused her but also gave her goose pimples.

Bowlesky picked up her purse from the table and brought it to her. She fished out a handkerchief and blew her nose, then she dabbed her eyes. He sat beside her and kissed her again lingeringly. She did not respond, as though she were still mad at him. As he continued to kiss her and feel her all over, she began to groan and wriggle, arching her body, moving it up and down as though she were aroused.

There was a knock on the door. Bowlesky ignored it. The knock was repeated. With a low curse, he turned to the door. "Who is it?"

"A message from Mr. Benson," a high-pitched voice said.

"I'll wait in your bedroom, Raymond," Mabel whispered, disappearing into the next room.

Bowlesky unbolted the door and opened it. Ah Sing, the Butcher, grinned at him. Bowlesky glared at him in surprise. "What do you want?"

"I'm delivering this," Ah Sing said, plunging a six-inch knife into his chest. With a low moan, Bowlesky sank to the floor.

Mabel heard the moan in the next room. She waited a minute or two, taking a deep breath to calm her nerves. The plan had worked, but now a new source of fear seized her. She went into the living room, her heart thumping violently. Ah Sing had left. Raymond was lying on the floor, just inside the door, in a pool of blood, his eyes staring at the ceiling, his mouth open and the blade still in his heart. She shuddered. The sight of him made her feel faint, but the new anxiety prodded her to take quick action. She lifted the mattress. The photos were all there, lying amid scattered bank-notes and silver dollars. She stuffed the photos into her purse and slipped out, closing the door gently.

Outside, the alley was quiet and dark. She hurried to the main thoroughfare, where streetlights were ablaze, traffic heavy and noises deafening. Ah Sing was waiting for her in the doorway of a closed pawnshop. He was picking his teeth under the red signboard with golden characters, his narrow gaunt face expressionless.

Mabel took a bulging envelope from her purse and handed it to him. Without looking at her, he grabbed it and slipped it into his black cotton tunic. After glancing to his right and left, he sauntered away casually and melted into the crowd.

Walking in the opposite direction, Mabel could not get rid of the memory of Raymond's staring eyes. She told herself repeatedly, "Relax! Relax! People die like ants every day. He was just like another dead ant."

59

Charlie had rented a spacious room for Brigid on the second floor. She had a view of the river and the terraced land beyond, with mountains as a backdrop. With the constant haze, the view looked like a Chinese watercolor. She had never tired of gazing at it. She was glad that Charlie was doing so well. The past four years, on the whole, had been good to them in spite of the war between the Nationalists and the Communists. But the first year had been rough because of Mabel's bouts with depression and nightmares. A psychiatrist had diagnosed her problem as a neurosis caused by a repressed anxiety. The psychiatrist had offered to dig it out of her subconscious, but Mabel had declined, saying that she had found a Chinese cure—acupuncture. After a few months of treatment by an old herb doctor, Mabel's nightmares had gradually stopped. Brigid was greatly relieved, for she couldn't bear to see Mabel look like a porcupine, with needles sticking out all over her body.

Mabel had enjoyed her mother's attention, but she had also detected a change in Brigid that bothered her. She sometimes found her mother's forced laughter very disturbing. A few times she had questioned her about her sudden disappearance a few years ago, but her mother had always given the same answer: "I got married for six months in Chungtu. That's a page of my life I must forget." The last time she answered the same question, she had added, "Please don't ask me again."

Mabel was grateful that her mother had reappeared. It was lucky that Charlie's business deals had been widely publicized in Chungtu; otherwise her mother never would have contacted him. Mabel was thankful.

The happy surprise still amused her. Like a magician, Charlie had produced her mother out of his hat. Hating to lose her mother again, she had preached the pleasures of Four Generations Living Under One Roof.

Brigid enjoyed her age of fifty-six. She often chuckled at a Chinese woman's notions about age. At fifty, a Chinese woman considered herself already old and was anxious to reach sixty; at sixty, she could hardly wait to reach seventy; at seventy, she would add a few years to her life to make herself more venerable and respected. Four generations living under one roof seemed to be a Chinese woman's ultimate goal in life, with great-great-grandchildren's little feet padding around her, chasing each other and wetting their pants.

It amused Brigid that her daughter should advocate such a silly idea.

The civil war between the Communists and the Nationalists had not abated since the end of World War II. American mediators had been running back and forth, tearing their hair in exasperation. Once they had almost patched up the quarrel.

Brigid had followed the peace conference closely in 1945. Before the peace talks Mao Tse-tung had publicly declared that Chiang Kai-shek was a treacherous butcher. But as soon as he had spat out such venom, General Patrick Hurley, the American Ambassador, had escorted Mao to Chungking for a peace talk with Chiang Kai-shek. Hurley had obtained a guarantee from the Generalissimo that Mao and his party would be returned to Yenan unharmed.

Mao and his deputy, Chou En-lai, had stayed in Chungking for forty-one days and had had a total of nine meetings with Chiang, plus numerous minor meetings with other Kuomintang members. Most of the Kuomintang leaders had reservations about Mao's sincerity. They would have liked nothing better than to butcher him when such a chance presented itself.

Now it seemed that it had, and a few of them had started plotting to do it. Chu Chen, the head of the Justice Department, had told the Nationalist leaders, "As soon as these bandit chiefs have finished their talks, we should haul them into jail and then execute them publicly. Should the American mediators protest, we'll just have to tell them that this is China's internal affair and that they have no right to meddle."

Chu Chen had even drawn the famous Hung Men Banquet as a lesson. He said that during that historic event, the King of Wu had invited his enemy, Liu Pang, to a peace conference. During a banquet, the King should have had his enemy killed. But since he had not, he had been obliged to cut his own throat years later when Liu Pang had besieged the King's capital.

The Hung Men Banquet's example had impressed many Kuomintang members, but the Generalissimo had objected to the murder plan. Mao must have heard about it, for during his stay in Chungking he had been amiable and cooperative; he had even joined the Nationalists in shouting slogans, such as "Long live the Three Principles!" "Long live the Republic of China!" "Long live President Chiang!"

Publicly he had also announced, "We should all get together under the leadership of President Chiang and put Dr. Sun Yat-sen's Three Principles into practice." He had repeatedly asked to see Chu Chen, the most prominent Communist-hater, but Chu Chen had steadfastly refused to see the "bandit chief."

In the meantime, General Tai Li, the head of Chiang's Secret Service, had prepared another murder plan. He had secretly ordered Mao's airplane tampered with. A mechanic had assured him that loosening a screw in the engine would cause their plane to crash, and that the incident would end the bandit chief's life without offending America, the peacemaker. When Chiang Kai-shek heard about it, he immediately called Tai Li to his office and sternly lectured him. Ding Fei had said that Chiang had probably saved Mao's life twice.

All the government intrigues had been reported by Ding Fei, Brigid's only source of confidential information in those days. Brigid missed Ding Fei and Sam Cohen, both of whom had finally left China and presumably gone to New York.

She also missed Hu Yin, often wondering if he was dead. But nobody could be sure of anything until the dust had settled in China. One year it almost did. Chiang's army had captured Yenan, the Communist capital. The first place they raided was Mao Tse-tung's personal cave. They found that Mao had escaped, but his cigarette was still burning in an ashtray.

They searched every cave and bush in the surrounding area but there was no Mao to be found. He was very close and yet invisible. Nobody knew where he was hiding.

Mao did not mind a long dragged-out war with the Nationalists. He had advocated a "talk talk, fight fight" strategy that irritated the Americans, who had finally thrown up their hands in disgust and declared, "To hell with them. Let's go home."

In early 1949 the civil war returned to Chungking. The Red armies swept southward like a tide, isolating Chiang's armies in the southwest. Chiang had ordered his remaining forces to withdraw to Szechuan Province. Bombing and shelling once again sent refugees running in all directions. The city was in turmoil. Students marched and countermarched. Political prisoners were made to kneel in the streets; two shots were fired at their heads. Nobody collected corpses anymore. Wild dogs and rats feasted on the dead.

Brigid had long since become a fatalist, but she was surprised to find that now many others had also changed. Restaurants and theaters were doing a roaring business. People spent all they had enjoying themselves, as though it were their last fling.

By the fall of 1949 the war was about over. The Communists had taken most of the northern provinces. Chiang Kai-shek and the Nationalists, badly mauled but still fighting, were ready to retreat to Taiwan. On October 1 the Communists officially declared the founding of the People's Republic of China in Peking, with Mao Tse-tung as the Chairman and Chou En-lai the Premier.

It was an early morning. Brigid read in the morning paper that the Communists had reorganized the provincial government of Hunan and had appointed General Hu Yin as Hunan's new Governor. She brought the paper to the breakfast table, trembling with excitement. "I must go to Hunan," she announced.

Both Charlie and Mabel read the news. Mabel was equally excited. "If it is Papa, I'll go with you," she said. "Do you think it's Papa?"

"You can't go," Charlie insisted. "I've already made plans for you to go to Hong Kong. You too, Brigid. I'll try to get you the necessary papers to emigrate to America later."

"Going to America?" Mabel said, clapping her hands like a little girl. "Mother, aren't you excited? Charlie, where are we going?"

"To Hong Kong first."

"You two must go," Brigid said, looking troubled. "But I have a husband."

"How do you know it is the same Hu Yin?" Charlie asked. "Hu is a popular name in China."

"I'll take my chances."

"Charlie," Mabel said, "can we wait? I haven't seen my father for so many years. I wonder how he looks in a general's uniform."

Charlie sighed. Mabel still sounded like a child. "Communists all wear the same baggy uniform, soldiers or generals," he said patiently. "Wrinkled and dirty, with bulging pockets. Probably filled with dry rice and preserved vegetables. Mabel, we must get out before it is too late."

"Charlie, why are you so afraid of the Communists?" Brigid asked. "They are not monsters with three heads and six arms, you know."

"I am an American citizen and a capitalist. The Communists have started attacking America in their newspapers. I don't know how I am going to be treated, and I'd hate to stay and find out. Mabel, we are getting out!"

Charlie was direct and firm, different from his usual self. He had always been flexible; he had never given orders. His requests had always been polite, made in the form of a question. Ordinarily it would have been more in his nature to say, "Mabel, will you ask your mother and see if she cares to go with us?" Now he gave orders.

But Brigid had made up her mind. "You two must go," she repeated. "But I'm going to Hunan."

Mabel looked at Charlie, then at Brigid, unable to make up her mind whether to go to America or to Hunan with her mother. Her desire to go to Hong Kong was strong, but her fear of losing her mother again was so overwhelming that she finally said, "Charlie, give us one week. Mother and I will go to Hunan first. We'll let you know if the new Governor there is my father. Then we'll decide what to do. Is that all right, Charlie? Please?"

Charlie was quiet. He looked pensive as he toyed with his food.

"That settles it, Mother," Mabel said with a wink.

*

Mabel and Brigid talked about the trip with increasing enthusiasm, casting side glances at Charlie as they discussed Hunan's special attractions, all for Charlie's benefit. It was the rice bowl of China; it had produced hot-tempered heroes and passionate beauties. It was a province where people claimed that they had seen walking corpses and chi kung experts who could spin on their stomachs on the point of a spear.

Charlie listened without comment. He finished his breakfast in silence.

The next day, Charlie came home with two theater tickets. He told

Mabel that Mei Lan-fang was going to give his last performance in Chungking and he had purchased two tickets for them. But he could not make it because of an important business meeting.

Brigid and Mabel were delighted, for Mei Lan-fang was so famous that his name was like "thunder in everybody's ear." His performance would be the most coveted theatrical event in China.

As if going to a European opera house, Brigid and Mabel dressed in their Sunday best that evening and went to the Chungking Pavilion Theater in a horse carriage. The show had already started when they were escorted to their reserved seats. The house was packed. The audience had started socializing, and nobody paid much attention to the stage. They applauded automatically to give the actors face while they made business deals, cracked watermelon seeds and sipped tea. Waiters tossed hot towels above people's heads; peddlers hawked tidbits and candy.

Mei Lan-fang, the star, was the last to appear on the four-hour program. The excited spectators applauded and shouted "Hao hao hao" at his every note and gesture. During his performance, all activities stopped. Nobody discussed business, sipped tea or cracked watermelon seeds.

After the theater, Brigid and Mabel went to a restaurant for an evening snack. In the distance, cannon roared and machine guns rattled. Sometimes the night sky was lit with flashes of explosions. Few of the pleasure-seekers paid the war much attention. They had stopped thinking of tomorrow; all they wanted was to live today to the fullest before it was too late.

Brigid had often heard people quote an old maxim: "Pluck the flowers while they are still in bloom; don't wait until there is nothing there but bare branches." Or, simply: "Have wine, get drunk."

Brigid repeated these sayings as they took a small corner table in the packed restaurant. Most of the rich had left the province and the country. The not-so-rich did not have enough money to flee, so they sought pleasure, tossing their futures with a flourish into the unknown. Their excited conversation and loud laughter sometimes drowned out the distant guns.

The two women ordered a jar of wine and dishes of tidbits. When the warm rice wine arrived, they proposed toasts to each other, to fate, to Charlie and to Hu Yin, the Military Governor of Hunan.

They were slightly drunk when they left the restaurant. They walked along Tu Yu Road, the main thoroughfare, where the streetlights were blazing as though the city were also defying death.

They talked and laughed, ignoring the approaching gunfire. The boulevard had been only partially repaired after the Japanese bombing several years earlier. Some of the collapsed buildings were still there, squatting in the semidarkness like giant ghosts. Most of the property owners had delayed their rebuilding projects, knowing that war would return and destroy the city once more.

Brigid and Mabel reached a section where most of the buildings were in ruins. As they walked arm in arm, singing, Brigid stopped abruptly. She recognized the area; she had seen photos of it in a recent newspaper article, which had told the story of a policeman patrolling the area one night and having a vision. He had seen cheerful pedestrians strolling on the clean boulevard, bargaining with shopowners, selecting articles from stalls and buying food from street hawkers; lanterns were swaying gently in the breeze, and music was in the air, mingled with laughter, peddlers' bells and rickshas' beeping horns. People were smiling and greeting each other merrily. The prewar scene was so real that the policeman could even smell the food.

As he approached a stall to buy two steaming buns, suddenly the scene changed. There was nothing but broken bodies half buried in the debris of destruction. Wild bony dogs bared their yellow fangs at him, snarling. Rats scurried through the area, gnawing at rotting corpses. The policeman had fainted and been revived in a hospital.

Brigid caught her breath and shuddered.

"What's the matter, Mother?" Mabel asked.

"Nothing, Mabel, nothing. I was just reliving the experience of a policeman I read about. Let's go home now. Charlie might become worried."

Charlie was not home when they returned by ricksha, but the lights were on. Brigid was tired and said goodnight. As she was about to go to her room upstairs, Mabel called her. It was the same frightened voice that Brigid had heard so many times before. With a sinking feeling, she rushed into the living room.

On the coffee table were several stacks of silver dollars and a pile of small gold bars. Mabel, her face white and lips trembling, handed her a note. "Read this, Mother," she said, and turned away. She sank into a chair and started to cry.

Brigid read the note twice.

> Dears,
> I have gone to Hong Kong on the last plane, arranged by the American Consulate General. I must leave before it is too late. I hope I have left enough money for you to live on for a while. Farewell, dears. I will always love both of you.
>
> Charlie

VII

60

When the steamer docked, the sun had burned off the heavy fog. The River Hsiang was now bathed by the warm sun, buzzing with life and activity. Small steamers, barges, fishing junks and sampans plowed on undulating yellowish water in both directions. The wharf was crowded with people—coolies, passengers, hawkers and beggars, all looking busy and energetic. "It must be because of the hot peppers," Brigid thought.

The skyline was not too different from that of Chungking, with a few five- or six-story Western-style buildings rising amid squalor and rickety wooden houses. The city was ugly but colorful, full of bright signboards.

They hired a pedicab, which was wider than a ricksha and was pedaled by a coolie on a bicycle. They settled at Tai Hu Inn, a fleabag located in a narrow three-story brick commercial building. Their double room was on the second floor, with a glass window facing the street.

The hotel supplied three meals, and they had a marvelous lunch in the crowded dining room, eating heavily spiced pork and vegetable dishes and using extra-long chopsticks, the specialty of Hunan.

"Well, Mabel," Brigid said as she laid down her rice bowl and chopsticks on the greasy tablecloth. "This isn't all that bad. I haven't had such a good meal in a long time now. I'm ready and eager to pay your father a visit."

Mabel suddenly looked nervous and worried. Brigid thought she was missing Charlie.

"Mother," Mabel said, "I ought to tell you something. I think I'm pregnant."

Brigid was stunned. "You mean I'm going to be a grandmother?" she finally asked.

Tears burst out of Mabel's eyes. "I wish I had told Charlie. Maybe he wouldn't have left us."

"Mabel, let it be a happy surprise for him. I'm sure we'll see him again. Let's refresh ourselves and go see the new grandfather. I can hardly wait to see his face when we bring him the good news." As soon as she had said that, her heart sank. She hadn't seen him for so long; she didn't know what to expect. Perhaps she had been too optimistic and presumptuous.

They arrived at the large marble provincial government building by ricksha. Four soldiers of the People's Liberation Army were guarding the

Western-style gate. When Brigid told one of them that she wished to see the Governor, the soldier saluted and told them to follow him. The Governor was waiting for them. Then Brigid knew it was the right Hu Yin, for she had dropped him a note informing him of their visit before they had left Chungking.

They were escorted to the main building. Its marble steps led to an impressive double door. Inside, employees rushed in and out of rooms, carrying papers and files. Through the open doors, Brigid could see others with their heads buried in papers at their desks, working. The place was quiet but busy, full of energy and high working spirit, something Brigid had never seen before.

They followed the soldier to the Governor's office at the back of the building. Hu Yin rose from his large desk as they entered. He looked much older. His graying hair was combed straight back. He wore a dark blue Mao suit, baggy and wrinkled. They stared at each other for a brief moment, as though trying to refresh their memories of the old days. Brigid broke the silence.

"Hu Yin . . . how are you?"

Hu Yin came out from behind his desk and shook hands with both of them. "This is Mabel, I suppose," he said, looking at her with a smile.

"Papa!"

Mabel's voice hit him. It was the same sweet voice, but lower and grown-up. Holding back his tears, he opened his arms. Mabel fell into them and held him tightly.

"Papa! Oh, Papa!" she said, choking. "It's been such a long time!"

His eyes red and moist, Hu Yin held her at arm's length and looked at her tenderly. He swallowed hard. "You haven't changed much, Mabel. A lot taller and much prettier. You thought I was dead, did you?"

"As a matter of fact, yes," Mabel said. She was his little girl again, talking with a naughty voice, resenting his tardiness. "You must have thought we were dead, too."

"When I was in Yenan, I heard about the Japanese scorched-earth tactics. They flattened Wuhan with bombing and burning. Everything was destroyed and there were very few survivors."

"Papa, that was your own Communist propaganda," Mabel said with a laugh. "Are you a Communist now?"

"Yes, Mabel," Hu Yin said with a nod, casting Brigid a quick glance, as if trying to seek her approval.

Mabel laughed. "You are the first Communist I have met. Charlie should see you, Papa. He thinks Communists are scary. Mother told him that a Communist doesn't have three heads and six arms. But he still wouldn't come."

"Who is Charlie?"

"That's my husband." She paused for a moment, then added in a lowered voice, "He went back to America."

Hu Yin stopped smiling. He seemed to have a great deal to say about America and Americans, and he showed his resentment in his hardened eyes. But he refrained from making any comment.

Brigid sensed the change in Hu Yin's mood. "You are going to be a grandfather, Hu Yin," she said, knowing that such good tidings were always a cure-all medicine in China—like Tiger Balm Ointment or Eight Diagram Pills.

The good news indeed brought a smile back to Hu Yin's face. "Well, well," he said. "You'll have to tell me more about your marriage, Mabel. Let's go home and be more comfortable. Where is your luggage?"

"In a little fleabag downtown," Mabel said.

"Why go to a hotel?"

"Because Mama wasn't sure you wanted us back. Just in case you didn't we still have a fleabag to go back to." She took Hu Yin's arm and teased, "You still have time to change your mind, Papa."

"Well," Hu Yin said with a laugh, "if you still serve a good cup of tea with cream and sugar, as you did in Wuhan, I think I'll keep you. Besides, we don't want you to feed fleas, do we? Hunan fleas have an enormous appetite."

Both laughing, they walked out of the office arm in arm. Brigid followed them. She felt a little uncomfortable about being neglected, but she was happy that Mabel was still Hu Yin's little girl and that the happy Wuhan days had returned to them.

The living quarters were in the back of the Governor's offices, across a large yard and garden. The brick buildings were darkened with age, but the grounds were neat and clean and the Oriental garden well cared for. During the short walk, Mabel and Hu Yin talked and laughed as though they had never left Wuhan. Whenever the subject touched on the past, Hu Yin would cast a quick glance at Brigid, who listened and smiled, happy for Mabel.

She did not mind remaining in the background. After all, she and Hu Yin had plenty of time to talk at night and to fill in the gaps in their lives. She knew politically she and Hu Yin had no argument. She did not hate Communism, as so many people in Chungking did, even though she knew very little about it. She doubted whether Hu Yin knew much about it, either. It had been a trend in Wuhan once, and she remembered that some of the fashionable people had talked about Marx as though they were discussing the latest fashion.

His living quarters were large; the once whitewashed walls were darkened with age and the European furniture looked clumsy and worn. The Persian carpet in the living room smelled of mildew, but everything else seemed tidy and clean.

"We have five bedrooms upstairs," Hu Yin said as he led them to a group of sofas in the living room. "This house was built by a warlord. Somehow all warlords in China liked Western-style living."

"Don't you have any servants, Papa?" Mabel asked, as she looked around, admiring the spacious room with large windows and high ceilings.

"No," Hu Yin said. "Nobody has servants. We all do some manual labor."

A young woman in a baggy Mao suit came in from another room, wiping her hands on her white apron. She was slightly plump and had short hair, rosy cheeks and a pleasant smile that showed her sparkling white teeth.

"Oh, let me introduce you," Hu Yin said hastily. "This is my wife, Comrade Lan Mei."

Lan Mei gave her hands some extra wiping. "You are Fong Yun and you are May Po," she said, shaking hands warmly with both of them. "My lover has already told me about you."

"*Lover* means husband or wife," Hu Yin said, somewhat embarrassed. "A Communist term. It shows we are equal. By the way, I've changed your foreign name, Mabel, to Chinese. May Po means 'Beautiful Wave.' Do you like it?"

Both Mabel and Brigid looked crushed. The word "wife" was such an unexpected blow that there was a moment of stunned silence. But Lan Mei covered it up quickly. "I'm so happy to meet both of you. Hu Yin showed me your letter. We've been expecting you day and night!"

"I'm happy to meet you, too, Lan Mei," Brigid said with a forced smile. She was doing her best to sound happy and casual. Now her dream had turned into a nightmare; her happiness crumbled like a fresh flower being ground under a cruel foot. She tried to convince herself it was only fate; it was the cursed war, which had played even worse tricks on millions of others. Compared to those who had been maimed or killed, she should feel grateful. . . .

Suddenly she felt a dull pain in her chest and an onrush of depression. To suppress it, she kept telling herself how lucky she was; it was a miracle that they were both still alive and seeing each other again after so many years of forced separation. It was unfair to hate anyone, especially Hu Yin. She had owed him a great deal and he had owed her nothing. She had no claim on him except perhaps his name; and even that had been changed by the Communists. Hadn't he said that the words "husband" and "wife" had been banished from the language and replaced with "lovers"? Choking back her tears, she told herself, "It's Heaven's will; what can you do?"

Sensing an awkward moment, Hu Yin bade everybody sit down. As they sat in the enormous living room, Lan Mei ran back and forth from the kitchen, serving jasmine tea, watermelon seeds, egg rolls and sesame candy.

"Papa, tell us what rabbit holes you hid in all these years," Mabel said.

"I hid in foxholes more often than in rabbit holes," Hu Yin said. "By the way, the caves where I lived in Yenan were not much bigger than rabbit holes."

"What did you do besides give landlords a hard time?"

"I fought the Japanese more often than I liquidated landlords."

"I knew you would," Mabel said, laughing. "You were a landlord yourself. What are you going to do with your big house in Wuhan, Papa?"

Hu Yin did not comment. He just laughed. Mabel couldn't stop asking him questions. Hu Yin told her his experiences in the Red Army, his years of fighting the Japanese as a guerrilla behind enemy lines in the northwest.

"Papa," Mabel said like a bubbling little girl, "thank God you are still alive and kicking! I think all those Japanese soldiers who took shots at you were poor marksmen."

Without a word, Hu Yin lifted his Mao uniform and revealed his torso. He pointed out his bullet wounds, one on his left side, two on his stomach and one on his right arm.

"And a couple more on my thighs," he said. "Yes, they were bad shots. No one hit me in a vital part. All the bullets missed my heart . . ."

"Papa, Papa, please!" Mabel stopped him, squeezing her eyes shut tightly to avoid looking at the scars. "I don't want to hear about it!"

"But I'm proud to say I have no wounds on my back," Hu Yin said with a laugh, pulling his clothes down.

While Hu Yin and Mabel chatted, Lan Mei served a Shantung chiao tze dinner. It was delicious, filled with ground pork and spiced black mushrooms and ginger. They all ate ravenously, sucking the juice out of the chiao tze and smacking their lips. They all enjoyed the simple peasant meal without bothering with cultivated table manners.

Afterward, Hu Yin and Mabel continued to chat and laugh as though there were nobody else at the table. They had a lot to talk about, teasing and reminiscing about the old days.

Brigid offered to help with the dishes, but Lan Mei would not allow guests to wash dishes. The word *guest* hit Brigid hard. It was like a knife twisting in her already painful wound. But she tried to be philosophical. How could she compete with a young woman like Lan Mei?

She watched Lan Mei disappear into the kitchen with the dishes. Lan Mei had a somewhat mannish walk, her posture straight and her head held high without looking proud or arrogant. Under her loose Mao uniform Brigid could tell that she had a voluptuous body. She was perhaps in her early thirties, and had a dimpled smile. Her hands were red and roughened; obviously she had worked hard all her life. As Brigid watched her coming in and out of the kitchen, serving food and drinks, she kept telling herself she was foolish to be jealous, even though the pain was still gnawing at her heart.

She decided to take a walk; she wanted to look over the city and visit the places she had known so many years ago.

First she headed for the rice store that had housed the revolutionary headquarters. The street had been widened on one side and paved with rock slabs. She still recognized some of the stores on the old side. The buildings on the new side were bigger and taller; a few of them had Western façades, with glass windows and balconies. Progress was obvious. Electric wires tangled on the widened side like cobwebs, and pedicabs had replaced many of the rickshas. There was an occasional automobile or motorcycle roaring through the streets, honking and puffing smoke.

She walked on the old side, trying to find the rice store. When she located the right block, she tried to remember the exact location. It was a corner store. When she found the alley, she noticed that the rice store was gone. It was now a tobacco shop with the storefront newly painted red, a large black-lacquered wooden signboard hanging over the entrance horizontally. It read, FUKIEN TOBACCO CO.

She went into the store and asked what had happened to the Forever Prosperous Rice Company. The middle-aged man sitting behind a desk in the back peered at her over his steel-rimmed glasses and shook his head. "Never heard of it," he said and went back to his bookkeeping, flicking an abacus with one hand and wetting his writing brush with the other. Two apprentices were busy weighing brownish water pipe tobacco on hand scales and wrapping it with yellow paper into little triangular parcels. Then they collected the coins from the counter and tossed them into a money chest in the middle of the store, purposely missing it and spilling coins onto the floor for good luck.

"Proprietor," Brigid asked again, "the rice store was at one time the front for the revolutionary headquarters. You must have heard about it.

"My father bought the store thirty years ago," the storeowner said. "But he never told me who sold it to him. Sorry, madam."

"Could I talk to him?" Brigid asked. "I'm sure he . . ."

"He passed away twenty years ago, madam," the proprietor said, forcing a smile.

Brigid decided not to ask any more questions. She knew that Old Liu, her old servant, could no longer be alive. People had come and gone in her life, swept away in the ocean of Chinese history.

It was getting dark. She headed back to the Governor's mansion, but after walking two blocks, she changed her mind. She decided to return to the hotel. Suddenly she felt alone in the world. Old Liu was gone. Ding Fei and Sam Cohen had left China. Bo Ho had abandoned her years ago. Hu Yin belonged to somebody else. Even Mabel had cut her ties, like a little bird that had learned to fly on its own.

Now Brigid had nobody, and was approaching sixty, suffering from the inevitable signs of age—wrinkles under her chin and streaks of gray in her thinning black hair. And she had just discovered that when she looked for signs in the distance, she had to narrow her eyes to focus: a sure sign of old age.

The evening traffic was heavy and the streets were buzzing with activity. Ignoring the fortune tellers, letter writers, peddlers, beggars, traveling barbers and cobblers soliciting business on the street, she walked listlessly toward the hotel. Most of the old Changsha streets had been burned during the big fire, but the new ones still smelled of the same food, the same joss sticks and the familiar whiffs of night soil from the nearby vegetable patches. The pigtails were now gone; clothes were different. Gowns were more shapely and coolie blouses shorter. All the changes made her feel more like an alien from a different era.

Forlorn and dejected with the consciousness of the onslaught of age, she walked into the dingy hotel.

*

"Where is Mama?" Mabel asked.

"She might be in the kitchen helping Lan Mei with the dishes," Hu Yin said.

They had talked for a long time. Mabel was sorry that she had neglected both her mother and Lan Mei, but the reunion had revitalized her and given her a sense of security. Once again her father had proved a rock, solid and dependable. After Wuhan, she had always had a feeling of living on shifting sand or being tossed in a rough sea, haunted by fear and nightmares. Now she felt safe, as though she were anchored in a storm shelter, her father's protective arm always within reach.

Now it pained her to think of her mother, whose forced laughter and gaiety had indicated her wounded emotions.

"Where is my mother, Lan Mei?" she asked in the kitchen.

Lan Mei had put the clean dishes away and was sweeping the floor. "She has gone to take a walk. She said her mother was born in Changsha and she wanted to reacquaint herself with the city."

Hu Yin came into the kitchen and told Mabel that he had sent for a soldier, who would go to the hotel to collect their luggage. "You'd better go with him," he said.

The jeep stopped at the Tai Hu Inn. The soldier followed her in to help with the luggage. Brigid was not there. As Mabel started to pack, she discovered that her mother's luggage was gone. On one of the beds was a note written on the hotel stationery:

> Dear Mabel:
> I have decided not to move into your father's house. It would be too painful. I am sure you understand. Right now I don't know where I will go, but please don't worry about me. I have drifted before and I know how to take care of myself. I don't know what to tell your father, so I'll leave that to you. I am sure you will be very happy living with him. He was a good father, and I am sure he still is. Please take good care of him.
> Love, Mother.
> P.S. As I write this note, I know how Charlie felt when he left a note for us and went away.

Mabel stared at her mother's slanting handwriting and tried to blink back her tears. For a brief moment she felt the old anxieties returning. Once again she had lost her mother's helping hand. She was frightened, visualizing herself struggling again in a sea of emotional turmoil. She sat on the bed, swallowing hard, trying to suppress the fear that was rising in her.

"What's the matter?" the young soldier asked. "Are you sick?"

"I'm all right," she said after a deep breath. "Please take the large suitcase down. I'll bring the rest."

After the soldier had gone, she sat quietly for another moment, thinking hard of her father and calling for his help. In her mind's eye she saw him rushing to her rescue, reaching out his protective hand. She gripped it and clung to it. Gradually, the fear subsided.

61

Like Chungking, Changsha was dirty, sloppy and built haphazardly; but the old signboards were colorful, and the daily washing that flapped in the breeze on sunny days made the whole city appear gay and festive. The laundry was like creative decorations that had been designed by a mad artist to celebrate a holiday.

Mabel hated the weather because it was too damp and wet for her liking; but the lush vegetation was eye-catching. Everything grew vigorously, giving Hunan the name of China's rice bowl. She loved to sit in her upstairs room and watch the Hsiang and its islands from a distance. Yu Lou Chou, the largest, looked like an artistically potted planter. The landscape was always beautiful, regardless of the weather, soothing and restful to the eyes.

She also discovered that the rainy days were not too depressing. On a winter day, sitting near a stove with a cat on her lap, listening to the raindrops, she could relax and forget her troubles. Hu Yin, her father, had told her that only in Hunan could one enjoy such peaceful moments alone. It was almost like meditation. He did not know why—probably because Heaven created little corners here and there on earth for man to have some peace. She knew that in Hunan one needed such a sanctuary, for outside everything was tense and fiery, like the Hunanese.

The Hunanese she found both likable and hateful, but never dull. They were temperamental and warm, often going to extremes. China would not have had rebellions or revolutions without the Hunanese. In other provinces, when men quarreled, they rolled up their sleeves, shouted and spat for a long time, but nothing would happen; when people in Hunan quarreled, they came to blows first and talked later. On the whole, Mabel liked them more than she detested them. They were down-to-earth; and in associating with them, she always knew where she stood. You either liked them or hated them; therefore no time was wasted in guessing or beating around the bush.

During the past five years, living with her father and raising Jimmy Hong, she had been fairly happy, even though she still missed her mother. Hu Yin had been more anxious to find Mabel's first-born child, Pang Sin, the son of Raymond Bowlesky, than he had been to locate Brigid. Mabel believed that Hu Yin still loved her mother, but in New China no one was allowed two wives; and she knew that the present young wife would never give him up. Besides, there was no reason for her father to divorce Lan Mei. She was a Hunan woman, energetic and hardworking, probably passionate behind closed doors.

Under Communist rule, the country seemed to be in better shape now. The five-year plan had just been completed. Most of the landlords and beggars had been eliminated. The campaigns against this and that were almost over, except for two major ones: one against insects and the other against America.

The campaign against America had started when China became involved in the Korean War in 1950. Five years later, the hate-America campaign was still going on. Hu Yin said that it was because there had been a similar hate-Communists campaign going on in America. An American senator named Joseph McCarthy had stirred up a lot of "hate Commies" sentiment among the American people. And the American 7th Fleet had been patrolling the China Sea to prevent China from seizing the island of Taiwan, which the Nationalists had settled. In a way, Hu Yin said, America was still meddling in China's internal affairs.

It was a drizzling morning. Mabel had a quick breakfast with Jimmy. Hu Yin and his wife had already gone to their separate jobs. In New China everybody rose and went to work early. Mabel was the only one who had a hard time following such rigid schedules. Jimmy had started nursery school. Hu Yin had objected to the boy's English name, but Mabel had argued that the name *Jimmy* sounded like *Lucky Rice* in Chinese. Never winning an argument with Mabel, Hu Yin had finally accepted it.

On her way to Professor Chang's lecture at the nearby Changsha Normal College, Mabel first went to the East Is Red Nursery School. Carrying the five-year-old boy on one arm and holding an umbrella with the other, she hurried along the wet street, dodging pushcarts, pedicabs and workingmen carrying water from the river. River water was the main source of water in the city, and water carriers, swinging their buckets balanced on bamboo poles, were quite a sight to watch every morning. Their grunts and powerful trotting always gave Mabel a boost, like a dose of miracle energizer. Sometimes she would imitate the coolies, bouncing Jimmy on her arm, grunting and trotting as she approached the nursery school, making Jimmy laugh.

Jimmy was a happy little boy. He looked a little like his father. Both she and Hu Yin had been indulging him. Yet, instead of being spoiled, he seemed polite and obedient. As she arrived at the school, she put him down and pretended she was out of breath.

"I'm exhausted, Jimmy," she said. "Now you can trot into the school yourself."

Laughing and bouncing, Jimmy hopped toward the door. He tripped over a rock and fell flat on his face. Mabel quickly picked him up and wiped his muddy nose. Jimmy made a few attempts to cry, his eyes red and his little mouth twisting. Mabel wiped the mud away from his trousers with her handkerchief and then made a mock attempt to wipe his nose with the dirty cloth. Giggling, Jimmy pushed it away and cried, "Wipe your own nose!" That ended the tragedy. Both laughing, they stopped at the two-story brick building that had been confiscated from a liquidated land-lord.

There were posters on the wall, mostly exhorting people to wage an all-out war against insects. The largest one urged an especially vicious attack on flies. A swarm of horseflies had clustered on it, feasting on a bit of paste. A passerby picked up a rock and flung it at the dark heap. A bull's-eye. He had killed at least a dozen. Smiling triumphantly, he dusted his hands and said, "Death to Imperialists and horseflies!"

Mabel smiled back and hurried through the gate in spite of Jimmy's protests. The boy also wanted to pick up a rock and hit some flies. But she firmly hustled him into the yard. She did not want to be too late for Professor Chang's lecture.

Comrade Feng, the nursery school teacher, was conducting her morning yango dance class in the large courtyard. She was a thin, middle-aged woman with high cheekbones and downcast, slanting eyes. When she talked, she often stared at the floor peevishly, as though she held a grudge against the world. Mabel did not care much for this peculiar woman, and she was sorry that Jimmy had to be exposed to such a grouchy character. But in New China everything was controlled and regimented by the government. Living quarters and schools were assigned. There was no choice and everybody had to make the best of it.

When Comrade Feng saw them come in, she interrupted the class to announce in her high-pitched voice, "Being tardy is an old habit of bureaucracy. Is it allowed in the New Order? Children, answer me!"

The class shouted in unison, "No!"

Mabel apologized and tried to explain why she was late, but Feng cut her short. "No excuse is necessary. Gee Mee Hong, fall in!"

Jimmy looked at his mother and joined the group a bit hesitantly. He seemed to be intimidated by the teacher, like the other two dozen children. Mabel held her temper. One of these days she would give Comrade Feng a piece of her mind and then make a dramatic exit with Jimmy in tow. After all, her father was the Governor of Hunan.

Feng clapped her hands twice and ordered the class to resume. The pupils pranced in a circle, twisting their hips and singing revolutionary songs. Mabel heard those songs every day, broadcast on loudspeakers everywhere, praising Chairman Mao and the New Order. The music was rather pleasant.

Jimmy warmed up easily. He was already prancing and singing with gusto, having shed his shyness and timidity. The unsmiling Comrade Feng kept clapping her hands to beat time, her almond eyes moving around to see who was out of step. If she found anything wrong, she shouted in her shrill voice to correct it. She was such a disciplinarian that whenever she glared, even Mabel shuddered. Mabel often wondered if Feng was an Old Tree Trunk who had joined Chairman Mao's famous Long March in 1934. Most of those who had were called Old Tree Trunks, a term for a high-ranking cadre. She would like to know Feng better and make sure that she would not turn Jimmy into a Communist robot.

After the planting-dance class, Comrade Feng lined the students up and started her routine question and answer period. She stood in front of the line and looked from one end to the other, her eyes roving like searchlights. The pupils stood upright, chests out and chins raised. They looked as if they were afraid even to blink.

Satisfied, Comrade Feng shouted, "Is proletarian dictatorship good or bad?"

"Good!" the children shouted in unison.

"Is freedom of thought good or bad?"

"Bad!"

"Is Confucius good or bad?"

"His thoughts are feudal poison!"

"What has New China done to landlords, capitalists and Confucius?"

"We have liquidated them!"

"What else must we get rid of?"

"Insects and rats!"

"Who else must we struggle against besides landlords, capitalists and Confucius?"

"Buddhist monks and nuns!"

"Why must we struggle against them?"

"Because they are unproductive!"

"What must we make them do?"

"We must make them give up their religion!"

"What else?"

"We must make them engage in productive activities!"

"Such as what?"

"Such as getting married!"

"Oh, my God!" Mabel thought. "They are robots already."

*

She was half an hour late when she arrived at Professor Chang's political initiation class, which was sponsored by the city as a public service. The students came from all walks of life. Most were ignorant of Marx and Lenin, but too old to go back to school. Mabel, anxious to be useful in the New Order, considered herself ignorant and had been going to the lectures for more than two months now. She did not really get much out of the class, but found Chang an interesting character. Sometimes, after the class, she would linger and talk to him. She often wondered if his lectures had double meanings. He occasionally praised some of the new policies with ambiguity or sugar-coated irony. Because of that, his messages often fell on the average ear like water falling on a rock. Mabel had seen people stare blankly; a few had even dozed and snored. "It's a case of playing the guitar to a cow," she had told her father, quoting the old saying. Hu Yin had warned her not to criticize anyone so openly.

"If you must criticize," he added, "sugar-coat your message; make it ambiguous."

She discovered that the only things one could attack safely were American Imperialism, landlords, capitalists, insects and rats. China had fought a major war in Korea and still felt the postwar pains. Her father had said that her connection with America and Americans could easily lead her to trouble if she were not careful.

The classroom was half full when she entered. Professor Chang stopped his lecture and waited for her to take her usual seat in the front row, peering at her over his horn-rimmed glasses. He was a small man in his fifties and wore an ill-fitting Lenin uniform. His glasses rested precariously on the tip of his button nose. He had to push them up once in a while to keep them from slipping off. Mabel always expected him to sneeze; she waited to see his glasses fly.

After she was seated, the professor cleared his throat and finished his sentence praising Chairman Mao. Saying a few nice things about Mao was the opening at all his lectures. It was like warming up one's automobile to protect the life of the engine.

The topic of today's lecture was logic, an offbeat subject. Mabel liked offbeat subjects, for they often turned out to be sugar-coated criticisms of the New Order, which could not be safely delivered otherwise. But this morning the professor did not elaborate on the subject. He simply said that today, logic had been discarded like an old newspaper.

"Let me give you an example," he said, peering at his students as though he were trying to see how many were doodling or taking catnaps. "Six years after the Liberation, some people are still hoarding American money; but if anyone says he loves American money, he goes to jail. See what I mean?"

He grinned at the students and paused, waiting for those who were listening to draw their own conclusions. "I just received a copy of *Ta Kung Pao*, the Communist paper published in the British colony of Hong Kong," he went on. "An article in the paper said that America is a country of no culture, that American literature is shallow and its movies are trash . . . so on and so on. And yet, right under the article is a large movie advertisement. One says, *The Happy Year*, MGM's great picture of humor and human interest. Another says, *Best of the Badmen*, a most delightful Technicolor picture, Columbia's unsurpassed production. A third says, *I Walk Alone*, a great Paramount Super Picture with a profound story of social significance, an undying masterpiece, so on and so on. See what I mean?"

Mabel heard someone snore in the back. The professor stopped his lecture briefly, peering over his glasses to see who the offender was. Having spotted the culprit, he said with a grin, "Another nocturnal animal. Will the person next to him give the tired one a gentle nudge?"

Someone did and the sleeper woke up with a start, grunting and smacking his lips.

"Thank you," the professor said, still grinning. He resumed his talk. "Logic, therefore, is dead. As Chairman Mao has well said, 'Contradiction is the key in elimination. We must contradict all the old arguments, bring down all the old habits. . . .' " He went on to discuss the essence of contradiction and the proletarian dictatorship, until someone else in the back started to snore. Once again the professor stopped the lecture and urged someone to give the tired one a nudge.

Mabel had learned that the majority of the students were Nationalist turncoats and reformed capitalists, landlords and prostitutes. There were a few ex-merchants who wanted to devote their lives to the New Order and become Tree Trunks. Mabel suspected that most of Professor Chang's lectures were similar to guitar-playing in front of a cow. Even she had often found his messages too ambiguous to grasp. His message about logic was confusing enough. Was he really for logic or against it? He did not say and nobody seemed to care.

When Mabel left the class, she was more convinced than ever that Professor Chang was in fact a satirist attacking the New Order. As the old saying went, he was "hanging out a goat head but actually selling dog meat."

During the past five years, she had watched the country change. The first five-year plan had been a success. For the first time, modern China was totally united; the warlords were gone; programs of reconstruction and deflation had brought economic improvement, and land reform had lifted the poor out of slavery. If Professor Chang was still bitter, using the classroom as his stage to air his complaints and let off steam, he was treading on dangerous ground.

*

It was 10:00 A.M. Mabel took a bus to her office in the eastern part of the city, a half hour's ride through Changsha's teeming business district. For almost a year now she had been working for Comrade Wang, the leader of the Hunan People's Cultural Working Group. Wang was a bulky man in his early forties. He had an oily moon face with heavy eyebrows that hung over his small, beady eyes like window awnings. He had a booming voice and a hearty laugh. When he laughed, he threw his head back and crowed. Mabel called it "a rooster heralding the daybreak." She found him amusing, but wished he were better looking and that his wrinkled Lenin uniform were a little less baggy. After all, she had to spend from six to eight hours a day with him working as his assistant. She suspected that he had given her the job for ulterior motives.

The Hunan People's Cultural Working Group had liquidated Confucius two years earlier and had turned the large Confucian temple into its headquarters. The sage's statue on the altar had been destroyed. In its place were portraits of Marx, Lenin and Chairman Mao. Some neighborhood citizens, in order to show their devotion to the New Order, still came to the former temple to make offerings of food and incense at the Communist altar. Comrade Wang, who had lectured against superstition, allowed such foolishness to go on, because the food was good for evening snacks and the incense drove away insects and mosquitoes.

The group had forty-five members, divided into three sections that worked on various projects in their separate wings. The Drama Group was the busiest and most popular. The Propaganda Group had the easiest job, writing worn-out, hackneyed slogans on strips of paper and pasting them on every available wall in the city. The nursery school's anti-insect posters were this group's product, and the paste seemed to be horseflies' favorite diet. The work of the Teaching Group was the most tedious. When Comrade Wang promoted Mabel from art teacher to his special assistant, she was happy to get out of the Teaching Group. The disadvantage of her new job was that she had to work longer hours and spend more time alone with Wang in his private office. Most of the time there was not much to do but listen to Wang's talk about sexual liberation and the *cup-of-water movement.*

She did not mind being alone with him as long as he kept his distance. But if he ever progressed from talk to funny business, she was ready to report him to his superior, the city's Party Secretary.

When she arrived, Wang had begun his daily harangue to the members in the courtyard. The temple was old and gloomy, with cobwebs still hanging in its corners. Only the courtyard was pleasant, with gnarled old pines growing twisted in bonsai fashion. The potted azaleas and gardenias, nourished by the constant rain, kept blooming almost all year round.

The members were sitting in a circle on the ground, listening with rapt attention as Comrade Wang stood in the center and spoke in his booming voice. His eloquent and rapid words came out like those of a medicine salesman in an open-air market. Mabel wondered if he had been some kind of salesman before the Liberation. She had often purposely arrived late so that she did not have to sit in the front row, as Comrade Wang had a habit of spraying saliva when he got excited.

"We are experiencing a new tide and a new culture!" he was saying, gesticulating wildly. "The worst enemies of New China are family ties and nationalism. Therefore, the duty of the Cultural Working Group is to help disband families and build an international kingdom of happiness through Communism. We are carrying out these duties in villages and army camps by setting ourselves as living examples of the advanced people in New China! Therefore, I want you, before you start the day's work, to examine your own mind and your own convictions. Are you or are you not firm believers in what we are preaching? Now I want you to close your eyes and lower your heads and give yourselves a five-minute self-examination."

Comrade Wang repeated these remarks every morning, and the self-examination had become a ritual. After that, there would be another lecture. In New China, leaders loved to lecture, as Mabel had found out. They did it to show their loyalty to the New Order and to Chairman Mao, and the listeners showed their loyalty by listening to them with unflinching attention and adoring eyes, as most of the members of the group were doing now.

His next topic was female chastity. That made everybody sit up and listen eagerly.

"Chastity was one of Confucius's virtues," he said, looking at the young female members, moving from face to face as if the lecture were aimed only at them. "Untold Chinese women have been ruined by it. Why? Because young widows were not allowed to remarry before the Liberation; many were even requested to commit suicide. Why? Because Confucius said a woman must remain loyal to her husband, dead or alive. Confucius's filial piety was another so-called virtue. We in the New Order cannot tolerate it! Why?"

He stopped and looked at his listeners, turning from face to face for more emphasis. "Because it is a rope that ties members of a family together like hogs. Hogs are clumsy enough, but after being tied, they are no better than dead. Loyalty, to give you another example, is also poison. It is like a halter around everybody's neck. It made servants obey their masters, wives obey their husbands, workingmen obey their employers. It has laid a four-thousand-year-old foundation of feudalism in China!"

The listeners showed obvious disappointment when he switched the topic from sexual behavior to such dull and worn-out virtues. But most of the members still pretended to listen with interest. Mabel prayed for Comrade Wang to end his discourse so they could get down to work.

Work didn't start until after lunch—rehearsing plays, writing propaganda strips and preparing children's textbooks. In the late afternoon, after a day's routine work, almost everyone left. But Comrade Wang wanted Mabel to help him make preparations for a giant public meeting to struggle against Mrs. Leigh, an American missionary who had remained in China after the Liberation. This meeting was to be staged in the public ground in about a week. Wang asked Mabel to come to his office, a small dark room with no other decoration but the portrait of Chairman Mao and some cobwebs.

Comrade Wang poured two cups of tea from a thermos bottle and offered her a cup. She sipped her tea and waited for him to discuss the meeting to struggle against Mrs. Leigh. But, to her chagrin, he kept talking about the cup-of-water-movement. "Sex," he said, his round face squeezed into a big smile, "as discovered by the most advanced scientific research in the great Soviet Union, is in fact a twin brother of thirst. When a person is thirsty, he simply goes to a water fountain to take a drink, or orders a glass of beer or a cup of water. Because sex is scientifically no different from thirst, why should it be treated differently? This is the fundamental trouble with the Chinese tradition."

Mabel was sure he had invented all this high-sounding rhetoric to fool the ignorant, so he could impress them and take advantage of their admiration. Unable to stand it any longer, she interrupted him and reminded him that she was fundamentally troubled by a Chinese tradition—she had a son to pick up at the nursery school. Comrade Wang ignored her and went on.

"The Chinese have always treated sex with the most secretive and ashamed attitude, as though quenching the most natural desire were like committing a heinous crime."

After gulping down his tea he poured another. "Don't worry about picking up your son," he said after a chuckle. "I personally recommended Comrade Feng to head the nursery school. She will be happy to take care of him for an extra hour or two. More tea?"

"No, thank you," Mabel said, secretly amused by Wang's maneuvering. Obviously he was using the struggle meeting to keep her there so that he could seduce her with his sex lecture.

"In the old days," he went on, "when a bride was carried to the bridegroom's home in a sedan chair, she was taught to express her shame and sorrow by weeping loudly or she would have been regarded as a licentious woman. Before a man said 'I love you' to his sweetheart, he had first to look to his right and left to make sure that nobody was around to hear him, lest he be regarded as frivolous and indecent. When a woman said 'I love you' to a man . . . Ah! That was an outrage! Women were not supposed to make such a shameful remark to any man."

He stopped to take another gulp of tea and swallowed it noisily. "So!" he continued triumphantly. "The cup-of-water movement, introduced by the world's most advanced country, Soviet Russia, is the only cure for that deep-rooted, rotten tradition. It will tear down the four-thousand-year-old barrier that has frustrated millions of men and women in China and turned us into the most sexually starved race on earth. We, the progressive members of the Cultural Working Group, must set a living example and encourage others to be more progressive and daring . . ."

"Comrade Wang," Mabel interrupted him again, "I have borne two sons, one out of wedlock. I tricked another man into marrying me and I bore him the other. Before that, I danced in the nude in front of hundreds of men and fucked every one of them. Am I progressive and daring enough? If you want to seduce me with all that talk about a cup-of-water movement, my answer is, forget it—I'm not thirsty!"

She picked up her handbag and stalked out of the room, leaving the stunned Comrade staring after her, gasping for air like a beached fish.

62

I t was a fine Sunday, the first day of Hate America Week. A parade and an accusation meeting were scheduled in the afternoon to struggle against Mrs. Leigh. Mabel decided to attend the meeting to see what crimes the missionary had committed. She had met Mrs. Leigh and her husband a few times before the Korean War, and the news of the meeting had come as a shock.

That morning she had been asked to pick up Jimmy early. All the city schools had been requested to participate in the Hate America campaign in the afternoon. When she arrived at the school, the children were having their early lunch in the dark, stuffy dining hall. She went to Comrade Feng's office, which also served as the nursery school director's living quarters—a large room furnished with a rickety table for eating, a small desk and several plastic chairs. In the back was her bed—two benches and a wooden board. The room was scrupulously clean and orderly, as befitted the character of a cold disciplinarian.

When Mabel walked in, she was surprised to find Comrade Feng bouncing a little boy about one year old on her knee. There was another woman in the room, carrying a tiny baby bundled in an old brown blanket. The little boy was dressed in a bright red jacket, matching pants and tiger-head shoes. The embroidered tiger heads on the shoes were supposed to have the magic power to drive away evil spirits. Mabel noticed that most of the Chinese children still wore them on important occasions.

Comrade Feng bounced and tickled the giggling boy and laughed. It was the first time Mabel had heard her laugh: she had always considered Feng incapable of even smiling. It was quite a discovery. For a moment she couldn't believe her eyes.

"Oh, it's you," Comrade Feng said, setting the boy on her lap. He immediately started climbing on her shoulder to play with her duck-tongue cap. She introduced the young woman as her niece from Hsiangtan, a nearby county. The niece had made a special trip to Changsha to see the parade.

A bell sounded outside. "Lunch is over," Comrade Feng said. "Come and watch."

The young woman put the sleeping baby on the bed. Comrade Feng handed the little boy to his mother and they all stepped into the courtyard. The moment Feng saw the pupils, she was the same old martinet again, unsmiling, her voice chilly and stern.

The pupils were dressed in blue uniforms. They had red armbands on their right arms that bore the words LITTLE SOLDIERS. The custodian, an old man with a limp, was putting up two large pictures on the short wall inside the entrance. It was a wall built in every large mansion to block evil spirits. Since evil spirits could not make turns, these walls served the purpose of warding them off. Now the *devil-go-away wall* in the nursery school had become the poster wall. The custodian brushed gobs of thick paste over other pictures and slogans and posted the new ones side by side, almost covering the wall. One displayed a monster, its fangs dripping blood, one of its hairy hands holding a skinny little man whose eyes bulged and whose tongue hung out painfully. A legend said, CHIANG KAI-SHEK AND THE TAIWAN PEOPLE.

The other poster was a painted tiger, baring its fangs, with blood dripping from its mouth. On the upper right corner, a huge clenched fist was raised over the tiger's head like a hammer. The legend said, DOWN WITH THE AMERICAN PAPER TIGER.

After the custodian had smoothed out both posters, he brought two buckets of mud balls to the middle of the yard, grinned at Comrade Feng and limped away.

"Little soldiers!" Feng said to the two dozen pupils, "this afternoon you are going to join the parade and take part in the Hate America ceremony. I want you to practice hitting the paper tiger and its running dog, Chiang Kai-shek, so that you may win some prizes for the school at the ceremony. Now pick two mud balls and hit the targets. First Chiang Kai-shek and then the paper tiger!"

The children, shouting, "Down with the American Paper Tiger! Down with Chiang Kai-shek!" marched to the buckets. Each picked up two mud balls and started pelting the pictures with them. For a brief moment, the balls flew wildly, splashing all over the wall. The custodian observed the mess with a grimace.

"What's wrong with you?" Comrade Feng said, marching to Jimmy Hong and grabbing him by the arm. "Why don't you throw your second mud ball?"

Jimmy stared at her without answering.

"Answer me!" she yelled at him. "Why don't you hit the American paper tiger?"

"I can't," the little boy said timidly, his round brown eyes looking frightened.

"Why can't you? Answer me! Why can't you?" Comrade Feng shook his arm, demanding an answer.

Jimmy, still holding the mud ball in one of his hands, was fighting back tears.

"Everybody hit the paper tiger; why can't you? Hit it! Hit!" Comrade Feng screamed.

But Jimmy stubbornly refused. He stared at Comrade Feng, his mouth twisting. Mabel hurried to him and removed the mud ball from his hand.

"All right, all right," she said. "You don't have to hit the paper tiger if you don't want to."

"How dare you!" Comrade Feng said, glaring at her. "Who is running this school, you or I?"

"Sorry, Comrade Feng," Mabel said, dropping the mud ball into the bucket. "I told him his father is an American citizen. Maybe that's why he refuses to hit the American paper tiger."

"This is not the way I run my school!" Feng said with a snort. "Everybody must do what he or she is told to do! Don't think that because he is the grandson of the Governor, he has special privileges."

"Sorry—I never thought of that," Mabel said coldly, taking her son's hand. "Come, Jimmy. Let's go home."

As she dragged her son out of the school, she heard Comrade Feng shout to the other pupils, "All right, children, go wash your hands and take a short nap. I don't want to see anyone yawn at the parade."

✳

Hu Yin was home tending his miniature gardens in the middle hall. On Sundays he loved to cultivate bonsai and build artificial lakes, bridges and hills with pine trees and pavilions on them. He displayed his creations along the walls amid tanks of goldfish. It was his hobby in his old age, and he spent all his available spare time tending them. When Mabel and Jimmy returned, the boy made a beeline for one of the fish tanks.

"Wash your hands first," Mabel said.

"My hands are clean," Jimmy protested, wiping them on his trousers.

"Not on your trousers!" Mabel cried, steering him toward the kitchen. Jimmy reluctantly went to clean his muddy hands. Hu Yin smiled. He knew how much his grandson enjoyed feeding the fish. The boy took the job seriously. He would measure the feed carefully with a spoon, sprinkle it on the water slowly, then, with great fascination watch the fish gulp it down, swimming, twisting happily and flapping their colorful fins and tails.

"What happened to his hands?" Hu Yin asked.

"He was told to hit Chiang Kai-shek and then the American paper tiger with mud balls," Mabel said, making a face.

"Ah, that again," Hu Yin said with a shrug. "I thought they would have invented something new for the children to do. Did he make a bull's-eye?"

"Nobody could tell who hit what," Mabel said, starting to water some of the plants with a long-nosed can. "But they made an awful mess of that devil-go-away wall. Then Jimmy got in trouble with Comrade Feng. He refused to hit the American tiger."

Hu Yin looked up, surprised. "He refused, eh?" he said, laughing. "What did Comrade Feng say?"

"She told both of us off," Mabel said. She mimicked Comrade Feng in a trilling voice. "Don't you think that because he is the Governor's grandson he has special privileges."

"Did she say that?" Hu Yin asked, raising his graying eyebrows in surprise.

"Yes. That woman is a strange creature!"

"Well," Hu Yin said, amused, "perhaps she is one of a dying species."

"What do you mean, Father?"

"She is not afraid of speaking her mind. We used to call that kind of person 'a little pebble in the gutter, smelly but hard.' "

"But this morning I caught her bouncing a little boy on her knee, tickling him and laughing. I never thought she could laugh. It was like seeing one of the goldfish jump out of its tank and dance on its tail."

Hu Yin smiled. "She is one of those rare ugly oysters with a little pearl in it, Mabel."

"Pearl or no pearl, I'm going to take Jimmy out of that school!" Mabel said with a snort.

"Mabel," Hu Yin said, resuming his bridge building, "the Communist Party is splitting like the old Kuomintang: The left consists of some very powerful Old Tree Trunks. The radicals want to kill human emotions and incentive. They want everybody to follow their Party line blindly. Sometimes you just don't know what is going on in people's minds."

Jimmy entered from the kitchen, his hands washed. He was drying them on his trousers.

"Not on your trousers!" Mabel threw up her hands in despair.

"Come here, Gee Mee," Hu Yin said, sitting down in a chair and patting his knee. "Tell me what you did in school today."

Jimmy climbed onto his grandfather's knee and demanded, "I want you to tell me a story first."

"Again?"

"I feed your goldfish and you tell me stories; that's our agreement, Grandpa."

"A sharp little bargainer," Hu Yin said with a laugh. "Just like your mother." He turned to Mabel and added, "He will make a sharp little businessman one of these days. Always bargaining."

"Show Grandpa what pictures you drew this morning," Mabel said.

"Ah, pictures," Hu Yin said. "I'll buy them if I like them."

Jimmy leaped off his knees and dashed to his room. Hu Yin chuckled.

"See how a little incentive works on him? The radicals never understand human nature."

"Father," Mabel said, "aren't you going against the new Party line?"

"Well, the rascals can't be in power forever."

Jimmy came back with his drawings. He gave them to his grandfather.

"Ah, pictures," Hu Yin said, studying one of them upside down. Jimmy turned it around for him. "What is it?"

"He started it as a horse," Mabel said, "and finished it as a battleship. Isn't he clever?"

"Oh, yes, indeed! It looks like a horse this way, and a battleship that way." Hu Yin turned the picture right and left, studying it.

Jimmy squirmed in his lap. "Grandpa, are you going to tell a story or not?"

"Oh, a story. I forgot. You want a story, eh? Let me see—I have told all my stories."

"Tell that story again," Jimmy insisted. "The one about the Ugly One and the wicked landlord."

"Oh, that one. Well, once upon a time . . ."

Mabel withdrew from the room quickly. She had heard the tale a million times. It was Jimmy's favorite and he never seemed to get tired of it.

*

The parade started at Nan Chung Street and proceeded to Su Men Kao, both busy streets in the southern part of the city. It was not a long parade; it consisted of two huge flags; one, the red five-star flag of the People's Republic of China and the other the hammer and sickle of the Big Brother Country, the Soviet Union. Following the flags were a dozen portraits the size of average windows, carried by sturdy comrades in Lenin uniforms. Besides the portraits of Chairman Mao and Commander-in-Chief Chu Teh, the rest were foreigners with big mustaches, whom most of the Chinese could not identify.

Behind the portraits marched a twenty-four-man band, playing new patriotic songs praising Chairman Mao and the New Order. After the band came the yango dance group—a dozen young girls dressed in bright red farmer's blouses and trousers and red cotton shoes with white soles. They pranced, twisted their hips and smiled at the onlookers who packed the street three deep, craning their heads to watch.

Following them came the automobiles and jeeps, all Russian-made, carrying Old Tree Trunks and Russian Big Brothers. Marching behind the cars were the students, the Liberation comrades and the free participants, all waving little red flags.

The free participants had been organized by the Cultural Working Group under the direction of Comrade Wang, who was racing up and down giving them directions. "Smile, smile!" he shouted in his booming voice. "Look happy! And don't spit!"

"When do we shout the slogans?" one of the free participants asked.

"Very soon," Comrade Wang assured him. "Don't march stiffly. Relax, everybody! Relax! Remember, you are the representatives of the proletariat, the masters of New China." He pointed at a cripple and shouted, "Wei, you! Are you dancing or suffering from piles?"

"I am lame," the man said.

"Well, bend your good leg a little and walk as if you were not lame. This is not a parade of the disabled." He raced off, shouting, "Relax, everybody, and smile! Look happy! Now the slogans! Shout as loud as you can and shout together! I don't want to hear anybody break wind after everybody else has stopped, do you hear? Now shout! One and two . . ."

The free participants consulted a piece of paper and started shouting:

"Long live Chairman Mao!"

"Long live the Proletarian Dictatorship!"

"Down with the Imperialists!"

"Down with the American paper tiger and its running dog, Chiang Kai-shek!"

"Long live the Friendship and Mutual Assistance Movement between China and the Big Brother Country, the Soviet Union!"

"We, the people of New China, must stand up like giants!"

They shouted the slogans repeatedly as they marched stiffly, until they reached Pa Go Ting, a busy section of the city. The accusation meeting had already started. Hundreds of onlookers had gathered below the hastily built platform in the middle of the street. The stage was gaily decorated with flags and banners and pictures of Chairman Mao and Big Brother Stalin. Mabel pushed into the crowd behind the paraders and watched the proceedings from a spot with a fairly good view of the stage.

Conducting the meeting was an Old Tree Trunk in a Lenin uniform a size too large for him. He was a small man with sharp eyes and a high-pitched voice. He held a little stick, which he waved and pointed at people as he talked.

When the band from the parade had stopped playing, the Old Tree Trunk planted himself in the middle of the platform, his legs wide apart and his hands outstretched to quiet the crowd.

"I am Comrade Liu," he shouted. "I am the District Political Director. Today we are holding this accusation meeting to struggle against an American missionary woman who murdered twelve Chinese orphans seven years ago. Only recently have we discovered evidence."

The crowd roared and shouted, "Down with the American paper tiger! Down with the Imperialists! Long Live Chairman Mao!"

Then the Political Director gave a speech citing atrocities the Western

Imperialists had committed against China, from the Opium War to the Korean War. After the speech, he waved a hand to the group of soldiers below the platform and shouted, "Bring the American woman up."

Four Liberation comrades brought a tall, thin American woman to the center of the stage. She was attired in an old dark dress, her gray hair was disheveled and one shoe was missing. Following them were six men in farmer's blouses and trousers of coarse blue cotton. The woman was wrinkled and pale. Mabel had never seen a white woman look so pitiful. Before the Korean War, she had met this missionary woman and her husband, Dr. Leigh, who had lived in China for more than thirty years. Twice she had attended their Sunday services and one of their tea parties in their little Presbyterian church.

Now Mrs. Leigh was the subject of a public struggle meeting, accused of a horrible crime—multiple murder. Standing behind her in a semicircle were the official accusers. Mabel felt sad as she watched the widow, who stood erect and grim-faced, staring blankly into space. Comrade Liu turned to the crowd, shook his stick at Mrs. Leigh and shouted, "Brethren and comrades, here is a living example of all that's most vicious, most greedy and most cruel in American Imperialism. Under the direction of Wall Street, she and her dead husband murdered twelve innocent Chinese children." At this moment, a group of young people below the platform echoed the indictment with angry slogans. "Down with American Imperialism!" they roared. "Long live Chairman Mao! Long live Comrade Stalin!"

After the slogan-shouting, the six official accusers, introduced by Comrade Liu as relatives of the slain orphans, stepped forward one by one and accused Mrs. Leigh of killing their beloved ones on behalf of Wall Street. The young people below the platform responded to each accusation with more slogan-shouting.

When the last accuser had finished, Comrade Liu once more stepped forward and said, his voice shaking with emotion, "Patriotic comrades, you have heard with your own ears the inhuman atrocities committed by this American woman and her husband. Now I shall let you be the judges. You, the common people, the new masters of China, should know what to do to an enemy like this American."

A man in the audience raised his hand and shouted, "Yes! We should punish any crime committed by foreigners in China; but nobody told us how this woman and her husband did it. Why did they do it? What is Wall Street? Is it a street that sells children's flesh, or what?"

"Patriotic comrades!" Comrade Liu stopped the man by raising both his hands. "We will be just! We are going to answer all these questions. We will not wrong an innocent person. Before we reach our verdict, I will let you meet the person who eight years ago worked for this American woman and her husband. This person will bear eyewitness to the murder, for she saw with her very own eyes how those twelve poor innocent children were tortured and slain. She will tell you her horrible experiences, which have haunted her for eight long years." He turned around and called, "Comrade Feng—the key witness."

From behind the Liberation soldiers, Comrade Feng, the East Is Red Nursery School teacher, emerged. She was dressed in a new Lenin uniform; her hair was combed and carefully oiled. A soldier carrying a large platter filled with white bones stepped out with her and stood beside her stiffly.

Mabel looked at Comrade Feng and shuddered. Like a bean pole, Feng stood silently on the platform, her small, puffy eyes glaring, her thin lips tightly pursed. "A horrible woman," Mabel thought. "A robot molded by the extremists." Whatever she was going to say had probably been ordered by the Party Secretary, word for word. Mabel controlled a strong desire to throw a rock at this narrow-faced fanatic.

After some more slogan-shouting by the young people, Comrade Liu raised his hands and quieted them. Everybody seemed to hold his breath, waiting for Comrade Feng to begin. Mabel wondered why it took so long for her to speak. Comrade Liu was smiling at her expectantly. The soldier with the platter of bones stood motionless, casting impatient glances at her without moving his head.

"Brethren and comrades." Comrade Feng finally broke the silence, her voice quiet but firm. "We must hate America, but it is not necessary to hate all Americans. I was ordered to be the witness to the murder because I worked for this American woman eight years ago. The Upper Level wanted me to tell all the details, so that I can earn many merits. Yes, I like to earn merits, but how can I tell anything? These children died of cholera. This American woman and her husband tried to save them. This American woman is innocent, I tell you. She and her husband did not kill the children. I know because I nursed them."

She picked up two bones from the platter. "Yes, these bones were dug up in the backyard of the orphanage," she went on. "But are they human bones? Are they children's bones? Any pigheaded turtle's egg can tell you they are not!" She raised a bone above her head and shouted, "You can all see this is not a human bone; it is the bone of a dog's hind leg!"

There was a rumbling murmur below the platform. Comrade Liu stepped in front of Comrade Feng, raised his hand and shouted, "Brethren and comrades, there is some mistake in this case. Some slight mistake. The meeting is over. You will hear from us. The meeting is over!"

While the people were dispersing, laughing and talking, Mabel watched Comrade Feng being hustled away by Comrade Liu and the Liberation soldiers. She was amazed by the sudden turn of events.

That evening, after Professor Chang's class, she told Chang about Mrs. Leigh's accusation meeting. The professor said he knew the Leighs and used to attend their Sunday afternoon tea in their home. "That Feng woman was loyal to them," he said. "If she didn't rebut the false accusation publicly, somebody else would be forced to testify, and that would be the end of the missionary woman. She risked her own life to protect . . ."

He stopped and turned his head away, his shoulders shaking with emotion. Mabel was taken aback, since she had never seen the professor act in this manner. Feeling uncomfortable, she bade the professor goodnight and left.

On her way home she kept thinking of Comrade Feng. She regretted that she had wronged her and called her "a pebble in the gutter"; the woman turned out to be a real oyster with a pearl, just as her father had said.

63

Comrade Wang had exciting news to report. He would speak about it at the regular morning meeting.

Whenever Wang had exciting news, Mabel took a back seat to avoid his saliva.

But the next morning Wang used a new technique, reporting the news with restraint. He was serious and talked quietly, pausing frequently for emphasis and, more surprising, he rarely gestured to make a point. This somehow made everybody very alert, including Mabel. For the first time she listened with concentration, wishing he would speak a little louder and a little faster.

Comrade Wang told them about a new assignment. The Changsha Cultural Working Group had been ordered by the Provincial Party Secretary to participate in a worthy project: going to Honan Province to help tame the Chingho, a turbulent river known as the curse of Honan. It flooded the province annually, causing famine and disease, washing out crops and homes. Every spring, thousands died and tens of thousands fled, begging and selling their children in the hope of giving them a better life.

The grand plan to eliminate the curse was to cut a canal along Tai-hang Mountain to direct the water to a reservoir which would irrigate the land in drought areas. Everybody was eager for the trip.

"Some say it's God's will that the people of Honan must suffer," Comrade Wang concluded in a quiet tone and with an earnest expression on his face, emphasizing every word by punching a finger down like a one-finger typist. "Others say it is impossible to cut through hundreds of miles of rock mountain to build a trench canal, claiming it is a hopeless task that nobody can accomplish. But Chairman Mao says that those chickenhearted defeatists should learn from the Foolish Old Man who moved a mountain. As a matter of fact, the Foolish Old Man inspired the people of Honan a year ago, and thousands have already started the project."

*

This was the last regular meeting before the trip. As soon as it was over, Mabel left the former Confucian temple to pay Professor Chang a visit. Then she would go home and pack. The next morning a bus would take the group to Honan, a north-central province south of the Yellow River.

For two years, 1955 and 1956, China had been going through marked changes. The friendship with the Big Brother Country, the Soviet Union, was gradually cooling off; Chairman Mao's Big Leap Forward had failed, causing widespread crop failures and production snafus. The backyard furnaces encouraged by Mao to boost iron production had produced nothing but unusable scrap; some people had even melted their kitchen utensils to meet the production quota and to earn useless merits. The biggest change was that the Lenin uniform had been renamed the Mao uniform.

Mabel arrived at Professor Chang's college on her bicycle, eager to hear some more of the professor's paradoxes. She had no idea when she would return from Honan—perhaps in several years—and no one was sure if she would attend his class again. The professor had said the previous week, "In the New Order, one must have a flexible mind. Why? Because a person who hates dog meat must eat dog meat or else. So one must be able to imagine that dog meat is tender beef and eat it with pleasure." It was double-talk that a casual listener could not make much sense of, but if someone chewed it over a little, Mabel thought, the message would land the professor in jail.

Professor Chang was having lunch when she arrived. He was living in a bungalow behind the school buildings. The small middle room, a combination of living and dining room, was littered with peanut shells and cigarette butts, and the dining table was piled high with books. Only a small space was cleared for him to eat a bowl of noodles. On the wall, facing the entrance, was the inevitable picture of Chairman Mao, looking benevolent.

"I'm eating my coolie lunch," the professor said. "Care for a bowl of noodles with red-cooked ox veins? Hot and spicy . . ."

"No, thanks," Mabel said. She took a seat on the rattan couch, which was shiny from overuse and had one short leg.

"Don't mind the peanut shells and the cigarette butts. I know—a terrible habit. But circumstances form a man's bad habits. The school attendant sweeps the floor only once a week. He refuses to empty ashtrays or wastebaskets, saying it is beneath the dignity of a proletarian. So, when he is due to sweep the floor, I dump everything on it. He is due any minute now."

Mabel laughed and asked the professor why sweeping the floor was not beneath the dignity of a proletarian. The professor said that sweeping was a service rendered to a school, which was serving the public, whereas emptying ashtrays or wastebaskets was servitude to a master. "So!"

Mabel told him that she was leaving for Honan with the Changsha Cultural Working Group the next morning and that she was going to miss his lectures.

"You are going to miss nothing," he said, "just a lot of hot air that goes over the heads of everybody but you. I wish you would discard everything I have said as 'Mrs. Wang's foot-binding cloth—long and stinking,' as the saying goes."

"You gave me the impression that you were holding grudges against something," Mabel said with a smile. "A little bitter, aren't you?"

The professor picked up some noodles with his chopsticks and studied them for a moment. Then he shoved them into his mouth and swallowed them without much chewing.

"Mabel," he said with a sigh, "I hope this is obvious only to you, not to the others. By the way, are you a Tree Trunk?"

"No," Mabel said with a chuckle. "Do I look that old?"

"There are many young Tree Trunks around," the professor said. "Especially Female Tree Trunks."

"Well, I'm not one of them. I'm just curious. Tell me, what do you think of the on-again-off-again Hate America campaign?"

"Why do you ask?"

"Because my husband is an American citizen. I haven't made up my mind what to do if I am required to participate in such a campaign in

Honan. Your remark about dog meat last week seems relevant in my case."

"Ah!" he said, pretending to recite Shakespeare with a British accent. "To hate or not to hate, that is the question." After a short laugh, he went on seriously. "Mabel, hatred is a human emotion; it cannot be ordered. You either hate something or you don't. Yes, propaganda can sway your emotions, but usually it is not personal; it is public frenzy. Do you have a personal reason to hate America? Such as a stinker for a husband?"

"No. I happen to love my husband, and he happens to love America. That is my dilemma. How about you, professor?"

"I spent four happy years in California. I had an interesting affair at Stanford. The young woman taught me how to dance the jitterbug and sing 'Doggie in the Window.' That is enough to make me feel good about those four years. Today, in this anti-American atmosphere, I feel like a chicken in a duck coop. I must pretend to be a duck and yet try to ridicule a duck's waddle. So I let out my steam by double-talking and this . . ."

He went to the window, threw it open and shouted at the top of his lungs, "Damn you, you poisonous scorpion and cobra, you vermin of a dog! Oh, I curse you! You rotten turtle's egg! May the heavenly thunderbolts strike you to ashes! Oh, damn you! You son of a disease-ridden pig! You bloodsucking monster! Let five galloping wild horses tear your carcass to pieces! Let vultures devour your rotten remains!"

He finished, returned to the table and laughed. Mabel, flabbergasted, laughed with him. "Who was the target of that verbal barrage?"

The professor pointed at himself. "Partly me, partly a few others. I don't have to name names, do I?"

"Why you?"

He sighed. "Talk is therapy, so I'll tell you."

Professor Chang told of his bitter experiences during the exterminate-one's-kin-in-the-name-of-righteousness movement a few years earlier. Everyone had been encouraged to accuse his or her relatives who were landlords, capitalists, counterrevolutionaries or Kuomintang running dogs. His father had been a landlord, and in the name of righteousness, Chang had been forced to denounce and exterminate his father. During the accusation meeting, his father had been so heartbroken that he had died of a stroke. Even in death, the old man had looked at him accusingly, as though he would never forgive the son who had betrayed him.

"After that day, I've been nursing a deep hatred for myself," he said, covering his face with both hands. His shoulders shook with remorse.

Feeling uncomfortable, Mabel waited. She did not know what to say.

Now she understood why the professor had cried when discussing Comrade Feng's behavior. Finally the professor pulled himself together, blinked his moist eyes and grinned. "So you see, without my secret formula, I could have killed myself or wrung somebody's neck."

"What do people say when they hear all those curses?"

"Simple. I just tell them that I am cursing whatever is fashionable to curse at the time. Currently, the fashionable targets are cats and dogs, insects and rats."

64

The great Tai-hang Mountain rose thousands of feet into the blue autumn sky. For three months hundreds of working brigades had been constructing the trench canal along the mountain's rocky side—thousands of laborers stretching miles along the cliffs like ants, digging, chiseling and carrying supplies and tools. Both men and women had been mobilized in the nearby counties to tame the Tai-hang Mountain and the Chingho River, the curse of Honan.

When the Changsha Cultural Working Group arrived by bus, Mabel stared at the magnificent mountain in awe. She had never expected that such a beautiful sight could be so merciless. Along with the tumultuous Chingho, water from the Tai-hang Mountain ravished the poor province annually, spreading its wrath hundreds of miles to the lowlands, demolishing everything in sight.

Mabel had read about the floods and the droughts and the famines. Her throat tightened when she remembered the poignant "Song of Feng Yang," depicting families that had fled the famine country. She had seen an old man and his granddaughter begging in Changsha not too long ago. With the young girl beating a broken drum and the old man a cracked gong, they had gone around the coolie markets singing and begging for a few coins or some leftovers.

> Say Feng Yang, sing Feng Yang,
> Feng Yang was once a wealthy town.
> But cursed by the birth
> of our emperor Chu Yuan-chang.
> Rich men took to lowly trades,
> Poor men's sons were sold out of town.

I have no more children to sell,
With my flower drum I beg around.

As she recalled the singing refugees from a famine country, a heavy hand clapped on her shoulder. "What are you staring at? Let's get to work!"

She knew it was Comrade Wang. Every time he put his hand on her shoulder, he gave her a meaningful little squeeze.

They had just disembarked from the bus at the temporary village of wooden sheds and tents. Carrying their luggage—bundles and plastic bags —the members of the Working Group started along the dusty road to their assigned tents a short distance away.

There were hundreds of yellow canvas tents pitched in groups along the Chingho and at the foot of the Taihang. They were tents left behind by the Russians, who had finally withdrawn from China, taking their aid, equipment and grievances. The best of friends had now become enemies, and nobody in China mentioned the Big Brother Country anymore.

The nearest twenty tents were pitched in a circle, with the largest in the middle serving as the dining and meeting hall. This was the Number 15 Working Brigade. Comrade Wang's Working Group was to teach the illiterate workers how to read and write. The group would organize entertainment and propagate Communist ideology. Every member was enthusiastic about the assignment, especially Comrade Wang.

It was dusk; the setting sun had slipped behind a peak, which was silhouetted against the flaming sky like a massive tent towering over the little tents. In the distance the laborers were winding up the day's work. Down in the valley, cooking smoke curled up everywhere. Many of the workers, carrying tools and lunch baskets, had already returned, looking tired and dusty. They were soaked with sweat, but happy and laughing. Dogs barked, leaping and wagging their tails to welcome their masters.

The Working Group members had been ordered to live among the native workers. Mabel was assigned to Tent 5, sharing it with eighteen single women. Wang had told the group that he had done his homework and knew that No. 15 Working Brigade had the most advanced members.

"It means that this brigade has more girls," one of the cultural workers had whispered to Mabel, nudging her and winking.

Mabel smiled. She knew. Wang had developed new mannerisms that he supposed were attractive to women. Besides the hearty laugh that resembled a rooster's crow, he squared his shoulders frequently to indicate his manliness. He joked to put the women at ease and coughed to show a bit of authority. He also loved to do little favors for pretty women, especially Mabel. Once he had whispered to her, "If you want me to, I'll stand on my head and do the yango dance for you." Then he had thrown his head back and chortled like a rooster heralding daybreak.

The Cultural Working Group members settled down happily in their assigned tents. The next day being free, they washed and relaxed. Thereafter in the daytime the village was quiet. At night, after the workers returned, there was laughter and music as they sang and played the fu chin and the harmonica. Some sat in front of their sheds or tents chatting, sipping tea and cracking watermelon seeds. But it was not all relaxation after dinner. Soon after the kitchen work group had finished cleaning the utensils and the dining hall, the bell sounded and the workers rushed to the hall for a cultural meeting.

Mabel came to the first of these meetings with the eighteen occupants of Tent 5. They were robust peasant women in their late teens and early twenties. None of them were very pretty and Mabel wondered if that was the reason they were not married. Mabel liked all of them. Moreover, she was determined to turn them into the kind of female workers she had visualized—literate, assertive and attractive. Her secret desire was to make them all so desirable that male workers would flirt with them. Life shouldn't be all drudgery at a camp; there should be fun and romance; there should be competition. If she could marry a few of them off and help them earn more working points, she would consider her efforts a success.

Soon after Mabel and her charges had taken their seats, Comrade Wang, accompanied by another man, entered. For a brief moment there was no sound except for some coughing. Mabel knew that the other man was the brigade leader, Comrade Kung, a small, weather-beaten man with a leathery face and graying hair. He wore a new Mao uniform and a duck-tongue cap, both neat and tidy. He scanned his audience with a flicker of a smile, cleared his throat and said in a high-pitched, cracked voice, "Today we are fortunate to have Comrade Wang and his Changsha Cultural Working Group here to participate in our work. Let's welcome our new friends and comrades!"

He clapped and all the others followed enthusiastically. Smiling broadly, Wang returned the applause. The brigade leader cleared his throat once more and continued. "As we all know, our task, building the canal and the dams in Honan, was inspired by Chairman Mao's quotation, 'Learn from the Foolish Old Man who moved the mountain.' If the Foolish Old Man could move a mountain, there is no reason why the people of Honan cannot tame a river. Chairman Mao wants us to repeat the legend of the Foolish Old Man to remind us that nothing is impossible. The Chinese people are God! If we stand up and dig together, we can move any obstacle in the world. So you see, it is Chairman Mao who inspired us to remove the cursed famine from Honan. And we will remove it! Now, Comrade Wang will take over the meeting."

Clapping his hands, Comrade Kung stepped back, while Comrade Wang, smiling broadly and pushing back his shoulders, stepped forward. Wang raised his hands to acknowledge the applause, then waved for quiet. In his booming voice, he said, "As Comrade Kung just said, 'We will move the mountain! We will win because Chairman Mao is behind us!' Let us sing 'The Song of the Helmsman.'"

He raised his hands, gesturing for them to stand up. "One and two . . . ," and they all joined him in the song:

> Sailing the ocean depends on our helmsman,
> All living things depend on the sun.
> Moistened by rain and dew, young plants grow.
> Making revolution depends on the thought of Mao Tse-tung.
> Fish will not live without water.
> Melons will not thrive without vines.
> The revolutionary masses cannot do without the Party.
> Mao Tse-tung's thought is the never-setting sun!

When the song was over, Comrade Wang gestured for everybody to sit down. "Brethren and sisters," he said, "I have asked the Party Secretary to supply ten thousand copies of Chairman Mao's little red book to be distributed. In a few days everyone will have a copy of this treasure!"

He raised his copy over his head and patted it fondly. "This little book contains all of Chairman Mao's important quotations. By reciting them every day, you will gain courage and energy; you will never again go to a fortune teller for your future because you will know that it will be bright. Here, let me read a few of the Chairman's famous sayings."

He opened the book at random and started reading:

" 'Be resolute, fear no sacrifice and surmount every difficulty to win victory!

" 'Fear neither difficulties nor death!

" 'Be prepared against war, be prepared against natural disasters, and do everything for the people!

" 'Let rural villagers encircle the cities!

" 'Political power grows out of the barrel of a gun!

" 'Support whatever is opposed by your enemy!

" 'Combine theory with practice!

" 'The masses are the real heroes!' "

He stopped for a moment, pausing to emphasize his next quotation. "Brethren and sisters, Chairman Mao also told us to criticize the wrong and the incorrect because criticism can clear the air, just as a heroic effort can clear away difficulties. During the Great Leap Forward, he said, and I quote, 'Comrades, you should analyze your responsibilities, and your stomachs will feel more comfortable if you move your bowels and break wind.' "

There was some giggling in the audience. Wang gestured for quiet. "This is no joke, brethren and sisters," he said, his voice stern. "Always treat your task with dead seriousness! We are talking about moving a mountain—not about goats' beards or donkeys' tails!"

✳

For the next few weeks, Comrade Wang conducted the evening meetings religiously, with singing and quoting from Chairman Mao's little red book. Mabel was glad that the rest of each meeting was devoted to teaching the illiterate workers to read and write. To her, Comrade Wang's routine was only wasted time, while the cultural workers' other programs were constructive and useful.

Mabel's eighteen women had become so enthusiastic that their tent was no longer merely a dormitory, but an active little club. The docile peasant girls had been fired up. Now they could stand up at meetings and deliver little speeches and quote Chairman Mao. They had learned to do the yango, wriggling their hips seductively and challenging men to arm-wrestling matches.

Mabel had abandoned her romantic idea of marrying off some of the girls, for she regarded her eighteen girls as superior in every way to any of the males of Brigade 15. They were cheerful and lively. She had helped them redesign their baggy clothes, and when they changed into their altered garments, their shapely young bodies showed to their best advantage, never failing to turn male heads. Comrade Wang would visit Tent 5 at every opportunity, ogling the girls and swallowing hard. Which was why Mabel had second thoughts about romance. In her opinion, romance without proper matching was like throwing flowers on a heap of cow dung.

The whole brigade was seized by move-the-mountain fever, toiling from dawn to dusk. The women carried water and debris and sang inspiring songs that could be heard miles away.

Every morning, the brigade's loudspeaker woke everybody up with the song "East Is Red." When the workers heard it, they became energized, eager for the day's work. Mabel also felt her blood churning, her heart beating fast and her adrenaline flowing. She had joined the girls in their physical labor a few times and had discovered that they were doing the lowest types of chores in the brigade. This bothered her. She was determined to do something about it.

One day, on the girls' day off, she and they were sitting on the floor mattresses in the tent, relaxing and chatting. Outside, the loudspeaker kept talking: the same monotonous, pompous male voice, droning on like a phonograph record. Without a word, Mabel sat down on her mattress and wrote what she had learned from the loudspeaker, then condensed its message and embellished it with one of her own. When she had finished, she read it to the girls for their response.

"Sisters and brethren, before the Liberation, Honan Province was known as the place of *four poors*—poor mountains, poor water, poor fields and poor people. There was always famine caused by floods and drought. Every year thousands of the people died. How could we let this go on? That is why we are now trying to change nature to save the people. Sisters and brethren, since the work has started, all of us have labored with one heart. Our bodies have been washed in sweat, our hands badly cut and scratched, our feet blistered, our clothes torn. But we edge on, never tiring, never complaining. Men and women work equally hard, but alas, are women equal? Are women allowed to do better jobs than carrying burdens like donkeys and buffalo? Are women paid equally? Why are women making only half as much as men do? Why is there no female voice on the loudspeaker? We demand that a woman do the talking on the loud-speaker for a change. We demand an equal voice, equal opportunity and equal pay."

The girls all liked what she had written. "Tomorrow we'll demand equal time and deliver this message on the loudspeaker. Who volunteers to deliver it?"

Half the girls shot up their hands. Mabel selected Little Aster, a big, robust peasant with rosy cheeks, to be their spokesman. Little Aster re-hearsed the speech a few times and Mabel was amazed how much better she sounded than the male voice. She had a clear and expressive voice that reminded her of a bell. All the girls agreed.

"So you see?" Mabel said, her enthusiasm mounting. "We can do anything as well as a man can do it, if not better."

"And men cannot do everything we can!" one of the girls shouted, waving a fist dramatically. "Can they bear children?"

"Listen, sisters," Mabel said, "we've been complaining about women's unequal treatment. It is time we stopped talking and did something about it. Tomorrow, besides demanding that this message be read on the loud-speaker by Little Aster, we will ask the brigade leader why only women carry debris. Can't we do anything better? Now tell me, what is the best job in the brigade?"

"Spike-hammering," Blue Orchid said. "My brother does it. He has better pay and more prestige than all of us."

"Can you do it?" Mabel asked.

"I–I think so," Blue Orchid stammered.

"Of course you can! And we will show them! Ask your brother to teach you, Blue Orchid. After you've learned it, we will demand that you be allowed to drive spikes. We will demand equal opportunity and equal pay."

Several girls raised their fists and shouted, "We will all learn spike-hammering. We will show them we can do everything a man can do!"

Suddenly they all were shouting, demanding to become spike-hammer-ers.

Soon the shouting and singing had fired every girl in the valley. Within a week, Little Aster's bell-like, clear voice was heard on the loudspeaker every morning, championing women's rights and giving the men indiges-tion.

65

Now the occupants of Tent 5 were even prouder and more high-spirited than before. They were the first to rise, carrying food and equipment to their worksite. They sang the loudest and walked about with bounce and élan, like soldiers marching to war. When Mabel observed the change in her charges she secretly—and a bit sadly—declared the demise of romance. No men would marry such intimidating females, now or in the future. But the girls did not seem to be concerned. In two months they had learned how to hammer spikes.

One morning Mabel and the girls marched to the brigade leader's shed. Comrade Kung was brushing his teeth outside his little wooden cubicle. He looked flustered when he saw them striding toward him with deter-mined expression. He quickly rinsed his mouth and stood his ground, staring at the approaching women with a heavy frown. "Comrade Kung," Mabel began, "the working members of Tent Five have some complaints to make."

"Of course, of course," Kung replied nervously. "Chairman Mao has said, 'Let a hundred flowers bloom.' The Party encourages you to speak up. What is it?"

"We are not treated equally," Purple Orchid said in her tight, tense voice.

"Of course not," Comrade Kung said. "You have aired that on the loudspeaker. Fine rhetoric. But the salary is paid according to work. Some types of work are more difficult and more important than others. Naturally the pay scale is different . . ."

"That's why they are here, Comrade Kung," Mabel interrupted. "They demand equal opportunity to do a man's work."

"Of course, of course—but which job do you think you can do?"

"Tell him, Purple Orchid."

"We could hammer spikes," Purple Orchid blurted out.

Kung's jaw dropped and he staggered. When he steadied himself, he stammered, "S–spike-hammering?"

"Yes—we can do it!" a few girls exclaimed simultaneously.

Comrade Kung threw his head back and laughed.

The girls looked at each other, not knowing what to say next. Suddenly Purple Orchid piped up with a new surge of courage. "If the Foolish Old Man could move a mountain, women certainly can hammer spikes."

Comrade Kung was stunned again by this unexpected reply, delivered with such force and daring. He coughed a few times to delay his answer. Unable to find anything appropriate to say, he croaked, "Of course, of course. . . ."

✳

The road to spike-hammering proved bumpier than the girls had expected. After they had received Comrade Kung's permission to try, no spike-hammering crew would accept the eighteen women from Tent 5. So, for a while, the girls continued to cart debris.

Meanwhile, more workers were recruited. The additional workforce presented more housing problems. Some put up sheds in available spaces, others dug caves to live in, many simply bedded down in nooks and crannies in the rocky cliffs. Every day the workers, stretching for miles along the Tai-hang cliffs, carried water, sand, stone blocks and building materials. Women did the carrying while the men hammered spikes, spread mortar and built embankments. None of the skilled jobs were done by women. Angered, Mabel decided to recruit Chairman Mao's help.

Early one morning, singing "East Is Red" and shouting slogans, the girls from Tent 5 once again marched toward the brigade leader's shed. Over the loudspeaker, Little Aster's voice was heard.

"Sisters, brethren and comrades, the battle to split the mountain is going on by leaps and bounds. Do you hear the noise? Watch the heroic workers! Some of them holding spikes and others swinging massive sledge-hammers and striking the spikes in steady rhythm. Many are loading the holes with explosives and blasting the mountainsides, cutting, blasting and cutting again. The work goes on. But the heroes of labor are all men. Where are the women? They are nothing but men's beasts of burden."

By this time Mabel and her girls were arriving at Kung's shed. When he saw them coming, he rolled his eyes heavenward in despair, feeling like a debtor seeing a mob of collectors bearing down on him with murder in their eyes. Before they stopped, he raised both his hands placatingly. "All right—stop right there!"

"Comrade Kung," Mabel said, "the workers of Tent Five have some complaints."

He made a face. The words *Tent 5* began to sting him like a bee. "Of course, of course," he said soothingly. "Let's . . ."

"You have heard the message on the loudspeaker," Purple Orchid interrupted him. "But have you read Chairman Mao's little red book?"

Kung flushed with anger at a peasant woman's daring to challenge him with such a question. Before he could reply, Purple Orchid went on. "If you have, you are only paying lip service to Chairman Mao's important quotations. He said, 'Women hold up half the sky.' If you agree with Chairman Mao, then we demand equal opportunity. We want to hammer spikes!"

"Of course, of course," Comrade Kung said hastily. "But the crew refuses to accept you; what can I do?"

"We don't need their permission," Purple Orchid retorted, her voice loud and firm. "We have organized our own crew. We have named ourselves the Iron Women Squad. We demand spikes and sledgehammers and other necessary equipment. We will go split apart the mountain on our own."

"Wait a minute, wait a minute, sisters," Kung pleaded with a note of scorn in his voice. "We can't do that!"

Purple Orchid produced the little red book and waved it in front of Kung's nose. "Women hold up half the sky, Comrade Kung. Did Chairman Mao or did he not say that?"

Comrade Kung's face whitened. With a false laugh he said, "Of course, of course. . . ."

✱

Two hours later the Iron Women Squad was on its way to its worksite, carrying lunch and new equipment. It was a cold day; chilly winds whipped the mountainside. In spite of the wind, they were sweating. Divided into teams, they assaulted the mountain with such gusto that Mabel felt exuberant whenever she heard the din—bugles blowing, barrows and tipcarts squeaking, the sounds of metal striking rock, of explosions and the howling wind. They all blended into a symphony of furious battle against nature. The worksite loudspeakers kept urging them on, with Little Aster's bell-like voice ringing through the valley and echoing in the mountains.

The members of the squad were dressed differently this morning, their hair tied into knots, their trouser legs rolled up to their knees and their sleeves to their elbows, sashes tied around their waists. Today was the test day, which would prove their equality: they were going to hammer spikes.

In the distance, explosions rent the air and clouds of acrid smoke billowed over many of the worksites. The girls, their faces beaming, broke into "East Is Red" and shouted slogans. They wanted everybody to be as aware of them as they were of the deafening explosions and the smoke. Their next goal was to join the shock brigade. They wanted to work side by side with the daredevils who hung on ropes down the face of the cliffs, swinging out, then pivoting inward like flying eagles as they tried to dislodge rocks with steel picks.

Arriving at the new worksite, they shouted, "Split the granite! Drive the steel spike in! Display the spirit of the Foolish Old Man! Women hold up half the sky!"

The male workers looked at them askance. Some laughed. A few even taunted them. "Go back and get pregnant, sisters; that's what you can do best! Don't smash your pretty hands, sisters! If you hurt your hands, who is going to wash our clothes?"

A couple of the bolder girls fought back and challenged a man to hold the spike while she hammered it.

"What? Hold the spike while you females swing the hammer? I want to live a few more years, sister." He laughed loudly and turned away.

"C'mon, you big heroes!" Purple Orchid shouted, spitting into her hands, ready to swing. "If you have gall as big as your mouth, hold the spike! If you are cowards, keep your mouths shut and watch us!"

"Let that bookworm hold it," a man said angrily, pointing at Mabel. "She's the one who put the devil into all of you. She's the one who's turned the world upside down."

"C'mon, I challenge you heroes of labor with big mouths," Purple Orchid sneered. "Any volunteers? No volunteers? What a pack of sissies!"

"We'll show you!" Autumn Moon shouted. She snatched up a steel spike and held its point against a rock. "Hit it, Purple Orchid . . ."

CHINA SAGA * 493

"Let me do it," Mabel interrupted. "We'll show them that even a woman bookworm can do it." She held the spike with one hand, motioned to the astonished Purple Orchid and ordered her to swing.

Holding their breath, they watched Purple Orchid, who hesitated.

"Swing it!" Mabel demanded, her voice firm and loud.

Spitting into her hands once more, Purple Orchid gripped the handle of her sledgehammer tightly. Taking a deep breath, she grunted and swung it with all her strength. The hammer fell heavily on the head of the spike, sending sparks out like a firecracker. The spike jumped under the impact. Mabel grimaced.

Resetting it on the white mark made by the first blow, she closed her eyes and shouted, "Swing!"

Everybody watched tensely. Purple Orchid swung again. The spike jumped and Mabel grimaced. The tremendous blow had blunted the point. She heard a few men catch their breath. Enduring the pain in her hand, Mabel felt her blood churning and her heart beating violently. Changing to a second spike, she held it with the other hand. "Swing!" she shouted.

Purple Orchid swung again, blow after blow, until she had finally drilled a blast hole in the enormous chunk of granite.

Many of the male workers cheered; others just stared at them admiringly, dumbfounded. A few put out their thumbs and commented, "Chairman Mao is right; you women can sure hold up half the sky!"

*

Some of the girls were lounging on their mattresses while their comrades sat at the long, crude table in the middle of the tent, sipping tea and cracking watermelon seeds. This was their day off. They were still elated over their triumph at the worksite, where they had impressed their male co-workers with their newly acquired skill. They had noticed that the men had stopped looking at them askance, making snide comments about their rough hands and big feet. But the girls had started gossiping about the men, comparing them to cuts of pork at a butcher shop, commenting on which cuts they preferred, how to cook pork livers and intestines and what to do with pigs' ears and tails. As they discussed the men in these terms, they giggled or screamed with laughter, but not without serious moments when they became a bit dreamy: romance was not totally dead in their hearts. All of them had an imaginary lover, tall and strong, with bright eyes and white even teeth, and who rode a shiny bicycle—the best cut of pork. He would bring them the most coveted gifts—a few yards of Japanese polyester, a new radio with a clock in it, a fragrant ham from Yunnan, or even a few bars of scented soap. The girls had not yet decided exactly which movie star he would look like, but believed that he was somewhere waiting and dreaming the same kind of dream. At such moments some of them would turn their eyes heavenward, cup their chins in their hands and let out long sighs. Others would turn on their mattresses languidly, hugging a pillow with their eyes half-closed, a faint dreamy smile on their faces.

Mabel welcomed such moments, happy that tenderness and sentiment were still alive and kicking in these toughened hearts. As she watched them, she herself became tender and loving, hungry for a man. Humming a little love song, she waltzed around the tent.

Suddenly her moment of romance was broken by the intrusion of Comrade Wang, who walked in and announced, "Members of the Iron Women Squad, I take my hat off to you."

He removed his duck-tongue cap and bowed to nobody in particular. "You have proven Chairman Mao's words: 'Women hold up half the sky.' Sisters, you have won the men's love and respect."

"How about equal pay?" someone squeaked. "That's what we're interested in, you know."

"Let's discuss that. Am I invited to sit down?"

Two girls at the table made room for him. Squaring his shoulders, he took the seat while the others got up from their mattresses and joined him at the table.

"Sisters," he said, scanning their faces with erotic little chuckles, "that's what I've come here for—to tell you what I've planned to do. The first thing I'm going to do tomorrow morning is to visit Kung, the brigade leader . . ."

"Forget Kung," Purple Orchid interrupted. "All you get from him is 'Of course, of course!' "

She mimicked the brigade leader and everybody laughed. Comrade Wang threw his head back and crowed like a rooster, drowning out the hilarity.

"You are right, sisters; no use going to him. He is full of wind. You know what I'm going to do? I'm going to demand your equal pay."

"And equal opportunities," Autumn Moon chimed in. "We want to join the shock squad next!"

Comrade Wang was stunned for a moment, but soon recovered.

"That's right," another girl said. "We want to be the daredevils and earn the highest pay."

Comrade Wang's bushy eyebrows jumped excitedly. "Ah, daredevils! I know you sisters have great gall. I know you sisters are going to liberate all the women in China and demand your equal rights for them, too."

He fished out a little pamphlet from his pocket and patted it lovingly. "Sisters, I have here a little forgotten movement that was so popular a few short years ago. I suppose you all have heard of the cup-of-water movement, have you not?"

He scanned their faces again. Some shook their heads, a few made faces, but most of them stared at him blankly. Mabel knew what he was driving at. She smiled. Comrade Wang was now acting like a billy goat, pawing the dirt in front of a herd of sheep.

"Sisters," he was saying, rubbing his hands eagerly, "the cup-of-water movement was first discovered by the most advanced scientific researchers in the Big Brother Country, the Soviet . . . uh . . . in Eastern Europe. The scientists there told us that when a person is thirsty, he or she simply goes to the kitchen and drinks a cup of water. Do you drink of cup of water with embarrassment? Of course not! Since the great scientists in the Soviet . . . uh, Eastern Europe discovered that sex is no different from thirst, why should it be treated differently? Sisters, women are not free; women have been pressured by tradition to act shy and secretive about sex. You have been made to believe that quenching the most natural of all desires is shameful, like committing a terrible crime. . . ."

He stopped, closed the pamphlet reverently and patted it a few times. "Sisters, that is why the cup-of-water movement is so important. It is the only cure for that deep-rooted silly tradition that has been weighing heavily on Chinese women for thousands of years. This movement will tear down the ancient barrier that has prevented the free expression of love; it will destroy the inhibitions that have frustrated millions of Chinese women . . ."

"And turned the Chinese into the most sex-starved race on earth!" Mabel broke in, finishing the sentence for him. She had heard Comrade Wang's talk about the cup-of-water movement many times before.

"Well, Comrade Wang," Mabel said, "the members of the Iron Women Squad are certainly the most progressive women in China. They will join you in promoting this great movement. Come back tonight and we shall all give it a try."

✳

Comrade Wang arrived almost half an hour early. It was a moonlit night. He chuckled apologetically for being early, but said that the moon and the singing crickets made him impatient.

"No problem," Mabel said, inviting him to sit down at the long table. The tent had been tidied, the benches arranged in such a way that the girls were sitting in a semicircle around him.

They all looked cheerful, muffling a giggle or two. Comrade Wang scanned them one by one, chuckling and swallowing hard. He rubbed his hand eagerly, like a hungry man waiting for the biggest meal of his life.

"We have studied what you read to us, Comrade Wang," Mabel said. "The members of the Iron Women Squad all agreed to participate in your cup-of-water movement. Is that right, sisters?"

"Yes!" the girls called out in unison, loud and clear.

Comrade Wang beamed. "Wonderful, wonderful! I congratulate you for your progressive spirit. You won't regret it, I promise you. Shall we move to more comfortable quarters and proceed?"

He looked at the nearest mattress and started unbuttoning his Mao coat, chuckling with anticipation.

"We are going to offer you a cup of water, Comrade Wang," Purple Orchid announced with a giggle. "Are we not, sisters?"

"Yes, we are!" they shouted.

"Yes, yes," Comrade Wang said happily. "I suggest one at a time, eh, sisters? But if you insist, sharing a cup is not objectionable, either. All drinking at the same time can be fun, too."

"We want to drink all at once, Comrade Wang," Purple Orchid said. Suddenly she dashed a cup of cold water into Comrade Wang's broad, smiling face. "This is my cup of water!"

And all the others brought their cups of water from under the table and dashed them into Wang's face, giggling loudly. With a cry, Wang covered his face and leaped up, upsetting the bench. Groaning and cursing, he fled into the darkness.

Outside, the loudspeaker started the routine bedtime speech.

Little Aster's cheerful voice drowned out the chorus of giggling. "Sisters, brethren and comrades, another happy day! Another victory! We have defied calamities and conquered many more precipices. Soon the man-made river will be suspended on the side of the great Tai-hang Mountain and wind through its undulating ranges. This magnificent sight, this man-made marvel, will be our Great Wall, which will change our fate. Soon we shall see women in their best clothing shopping at leisure, rosy-cheeked children riding in baby carriages pushed by their fathers, musicians beating drums and gongs celebrating weddings and birthdays. In our countryside, goats will be grazing amid spring flowers, drinking beside brooks. People will be fishing in ponds, girls doing their laundry at our new canal side, happy farmers harvesting their rich crops, and the elderly tending their lush vegetable gardens. Everywhere bees will be buzzing and birds will be singing. . . ."

66

Lying beside Lan Mei, Hu Yin thought of Brigid, wondering where she was and what she was doing. Human beings were funny, he thought; when God created them He might have been mischievous and stuck a bit of flypaper in their hearts, making them sticky. Somehow he felt that his concern for Brigid was like a fly that got stuck.

"What are you thinking about?" Lan Mei asked, nestling closer to him.

"Something not too interesting," he said. If he had been twenty years younger, he would have turned over, taken her in his arms and done what would have come naturally. But at his age, he found that supply and demand were becoming more and more unbalanced. With Brigid it would have been different; both of them would have grown old together and found other things more interesting than exercises in bed. He decided to change the subject and divert Lan Mei's mind to something that had been everybody's concern—the direction of the Party's policies.

Being Party members, both had been following the line faithfully; but things had been happening in the Forbidden City in Peking that were disheartening and worrisome. The Party was splitting wider. The radicals —the left-wing extremists—were accelerating their campaign against the right-wing moderates—the pragmatists. It was a seesaw battle. Hu Yin knew that the power behind the left wing was Chiang Ching and General Lin Piao. They were the two most formidable foes of the moderates, Chou En-lai, Liu Shao-chi and Teng Hsiao-ping, who wanted China to be modern, more open, to catch up economically with the rest of the world.

"Lan Mei," Hu Yin said, "what I read every day is official reports. At your office it is easy to learn unofficial things. What is the latest news from your hygienic grapevine?"

Lan Mei worked for the Bureau of Hygiene as a supervisor. She said with a coquettish smile, jabbing a finger at his shoulder, "Chairman Mao swam nine miles in the Yangtze. That's pretty good at his age. Chiang Ching must be very happy. She is half his age, you know."

The strong hint made Hu Yin a little uncomfortable: it brought the subject back to the problem of supply and demand. He wished he could make Lan Mei happy, but he wasn't sure of himself.

"It was in the paper," he said. "What else have you heard? Anything about the radicals?"

"The inside information is that they want to turn the Chinese people into docile tools, silent cogs and obedient sheep. Can you think of any additional descriptions?"

"No, I can't."

The troublesome left wing had been successful in diverting Lan Mei's mind from sex. She turned, lay flat on her back and stared at the ceiling. "I wonder who is directing the trend," she said pensively. "Must be somebody powerful and influential. In history, the most influential force has always been pillow talk, those words whispered into the Emperor's ear by his favorite concubine."

Hu Yin knew that she meant Chiang Ching, Mao's wife. He kept quiet. He did not want the conversation to lead back to the old subject—he was sure that Chairman Mao had the same problem as he.

"By the way," he said, again changing the subject, "I received a letter this morning. Mabel is coming home."

"Is she?" Lan Mei said, turning toward him excitedly. "When?"

"She did not say. In a few days, I suppose."

"Does she know that her first son is here?"

"Pang Sin? No."

"Let's surprise her," Lan Mei said. "I want to see her face when Pang Sin walks into the room to greet her."

"She may not recognize him," he said with a laugh. "She may offer him her hand and say, 'Pleased to meet you; how do you do?' " Suddenly he became serious. "Pang Sin is a gloomy boy; he must have had a rough life. Since his arrival two days ago, he has not smiled once."

"How old is he?"

"Gee Mee is twelve; Pang Sin must be eighteen."

"He looks much older."

"That's because he's big. He is one-fourth Caucasian, you know."

"I can tell from his eyes and nose, which are two sizes bigger than yours and mine. Who is his father?"

Hu Yin shrugged. "Somebody half and half. Mabel was reluctant to discuss him. Most of the Eurasians in China are the results of wild oats sown by American servicemen."

"It's amazing that you found this boy," Lan Mei said. "Your daughter will be grateful."

"It was not easy to find him. It took me two years. I had only his grandmother's name to go by. If she had moved out of Chungking, Pang

Sin would have been lost forever, like a grain of sand in the ocean."

"I hope that he and Jimmy get along."

Hu Yin sighed. "They have hardly spoken to each other." He was quiet for a moment, looking worried. "They are like the tropics and the North Pole. But the ice will melt and they will get along."

*

The wire said that Mabel would arrive by bus on a Sunday afternoon, summer of 1962. She had been away for four years, and Hu Yin wanted her homecoming to be a significant event. The entire house had been cleaned and scrubbed; Stalin's picture had been taken down. During the past four years Hu Yin had missed Mabel's jokes and laughter; she had been the life of the Governor's mansion. Luckily he had had his goldfish and miniature gardens. The country had also made tremendous progress in spite of the Russians' withdrawal, the failure of the Great Leap Forward and the so-so results of the collective program that had forced the peasants to turn their private plots into communes.

Hu Yin was particularly proud of China's ability to develop nuclear weapons and space rockets without foreign help. Those giant scientific steps had made the West sit up and blink their eyes. China was no longer a sleeping dragon; she had become a world power. She had defied super-power Soviet Russia and refused to be one of her *silent cogs*.

Whenever he thought of all those accomplishments, he felt a glow of pride and satisfaction. From now on he would find more time to enjoy his family—his wife, daughter and two grandsons.

Mabel arrived an hour later than scheduled. It was expected. Buses and trains had never been on time; being late was still a tolerated habit. Civilian life had always been relaxed in China, and still was.

Mabel was thinner and darker. In her self-designed Mao uniform, she even looked fashionable, with her duck-tongue cap sitting on her short, frizzy hair at a jaunty angle. She first hugged Hu Yin, then Jimmy and finally Lan Mei, who felt a bit embarrassed by this Western way of greeting.

"We have a surprise for you, Mabel," Hu Yin said, indicating a chair. "You'd better sit down first."

Laughing and exuberant, Mabel plunked down on the chair. "All right, Father, surprise me. But I have an idea what it is."

Hu Yin clapped his hands three times and a boy of about eighteen entered from the kitchen, a tall, good-looking lad with longish hair and fair skin. But he had a drooping mouth that made him look a little cynical, as though he were sneering at something. He walked with a slight swagger and a devil-may-care sort of air. Stopping beside Hu Yin, he cast Mabel a quick glance, then turned to Hu Yin for instructions.

"Well, you know what to do, Pang Sin," Hu Yin said with a little chuckle.

Pang Sin looked at Mabel again. With a flicker of a smile, he said in a casual voice, "Hello, Mother."

"Mabel, this is the surprise," Lan Mei said, eagerly waiting for a tearful reunion.

For a fleeting moment, Mabel looked disappointed; she had expected to see her mother. But she quickly recovered and rushed to her first-born with open arms. "Oh, Pang Sin, Pang Sin!" She hugged the boy repeatedly. Pang Sin was stiff and uncomfortable. Mabel held him at arm's length and laughed. "What a big tall handsome man!" She rushed to her father and gave him a kiss on the cheek. "Father, what a wonderful surprise! Thank you! How did you find him?"

"It's a long story. But tell Pang Sin your great accomplishment in Honan Province first."

"We built a trunk canal, complete with solid stone embankment," she said enthusiastically, looking first at her son, then at her father. "It's like a suspended snake in the middle of the Tai-hang Mountain. It's a marvel, Father! It's China's new Great Wall. We call it Red Flag Canal. It has three branch canals, aqueducts, tunnels and dams. From now on there will be no more droughts or floods in Honan. We have tamed nature. Like the Foolish Old Man, we have moved the mountain. Stop me, Papa. Every time I talk about it I'm so worked up that I never stop."

"You can stop now," Hu Yin said with a laugh. "We've read all about it in the newspapers. What about some interesting tidbits, some human-interest stories that you don't read about in the papers?"

"I have a lot of those to tell, too," Mabel said, laughing with him. "We've created the Iron Women Squad and tamed Comrade Wang. You won't recognize him now."

"I imagine you've cowed him quite a bit," Hu Yin said.

"We have shrunk him from a rooster into a little mouse."

Hu Yin laughed. "Just don't create any Iron Women Squads in Hunan! By the way, what surprise did you have in mind?"

Mabel almost said that she had expected to see her mother. Instead, she took Pang Sin's hand and raised it. "This is it, Papa. You have 'hit the spike right on the head,' as we used to say in Honan." She turned to Pang Sin and asked, "Where have you been all these years?"

"Chungking—where else? We were too poor to move."

"Of course," Mabel said. "Chungking was war-ravaged. Everyone was poor. Did you go to high school, Pang Sin?"

"Here and there," he said with a twist of his mouth. "I was an oil bottle."

"What's an oil bottle?"

"That's someone who is dragged by his mother or grandmother from one lover to another," Pang Sin said with another twist of his mouth.

Mabel felt hurt, as though her son had purposely twisted a knife in her heart. She said nothing. It was Hu Yin who mended the fence and suggested that they all go out for dinner. Lan Mei was glad, for she was disappointed in the reunion and did not feel like cooking.

*

After a week of rest Mabel went back to work. Comrade Wang had indeed changed. He looked subdued and had stopped laughing like a crowing rooster heralding daybreak. Mabel had visited Professor Chang several times. The professor had also changed; he had stopped cursing. He was quiet and had grown a stomach.

In 1962, anti-American feeling was still running high. Ho Chi Minh praised China as a staunch ally and China was sending Hanoi ammunition, supplies and advisers.

Hu Yin was enthusiastic. The pragmatists within the Party were gaining power. His position in the government seemed secure. At home, he had two grandsons to do his little errands. He still favored some of the old traditions and old values, such as filial piety and respect for the elders. He liked Jimmy a little more than he did Pang Sin, but he hid his feelings, always trying to treat both of them as equals. At twelve, Jimmy knew how to please his grandfather. He was always eager to serve him his ginseng soup and tap his shoulders to relax him.

It was one of the rare evenings when Hu Yin relaxed in the middle room with his grandsons, enjoying his ginseng soup and the flowery rhythm of Jimmy's shoulder massage. Pang Sin couldn't sit still.

"Are you restless, Pang Sin?" Hu Yin asked.

"N–no," Pang Sin said, wriggling in his chair.

"Don't lie," Hu Yin said with a smile. "When a boy keeps shifting his weight in a chair, he either has a flea biting his bottom or he is bored. At my age, I know something about human behavior. It isn't a sin to be bored, but lying is."

Pang Sin threw his legs out, stretched and put his hands behind his head, striking his devil-may-care pose. Hu Yin frowned.

"Pang Sin," he said quietly, "at your age I got bored easily, too. But a young man should adopt some good hobbies to keep his mind occupied."

Pang Sin shrugged.

"What hobbies did you adopt when you were young, Grandpa?" Jimmy asked.

"I practiced martial arts. That is an excellent one. It strengthens your body and cleanses your soul."

"I want to learn it," Jimmy said.

"How about you, Pang Sin?" Hu Yin asked.

Pang Sin merely shrugged again. He did not need any soul-cleansing. As for strength, he preferred weight-lifting, and he still had his dumbbells and fifty-pound weights.

"Pang Sin," Jimmy said, "if you don't learn martial arts, a smaller man can beat you up easily."

Pang Sin pointed two fingers at Jimmy and made popping sounds with his lips. "I can kill any martial artist with one finger—like this. Can you fight a gun with your bare hands?"

"We are talking about exercise, not killing," Hu Yin said. "I'll buy a Ping-Pong table tomorrow. We'll have family matches every week." Then he changed the subject. "Well, well, let's talk about ambition. Jimmy, you first. What do you want to be when you grow up?"

"I want to be a farmer."

"A good choice," Hu Yin said. "I was a farmboy, too, until a famine drove us off our land. Today we have no more famines. The Communist Party has gotten rid of all of China's curses—flood, drought, famine, diseases, insects and rats. What do you want to be, Pang Sin?"

"A scientist, I guess," Pang Sin said indifferently.

"Ah, a scientist," Hu Yin exclaimed. "How can a country progress without scientists?"

The conversation was interrupted by Lan Mei, who poked her head in from the kitchen. "Hu Yin, will you come here for a moment?"

Hu Yin nodded. He rose, somewhat worried by Lan Mei's anxious expression. She usually looked cheerful.

Sitting at the kitchen table was a middle-aged farmer, gaunt and dried up, with a heavily wrinkled, weather-beaten face. He was Woo, Lan Mei's brother. It took Hu Yin a moment to recognize him. They greeted each other warmly.

"Hu Yin," Lan Mei said, pouring a cup of tea for him, "my brother says our father was arrested in Hsiangtan. They put a dunce cap on him and paraded him in the village. They taunted him, tortured him and poured manure over his head."

"Why?" Hu Yin asked, feeling his anger rising. He hated cruel and humiliating treatment of anyone, and had campaigned to stop it.

"The crops failed in our village this year," Woo said. "People have been eating grass roots and tree bark. When they found that father still had rice to eat, they accused him of hoarding food."

"He saved a little rice during better times," Lan Mei said. "But that is not a crime."

"Crop failures?" Hu Yin asked. "All I have read were glowing reports on Hunan's bumper harvests."

"You know that all those glowing reports are lies to glorify Chairman Mao's communes," Lan Mei said with controlled anger. "They want collective farming to look good. Nobody said a word about the famine in Hunan."

"I am going to order a car," Hu Yin said, rising. "We'll go there immediately and see what is going on."

*

Ya Li Middle School was not far from the Governor's mansion. Pang Sin, a second-year student at the middle school, was four years ahead of Jimmy. He was smart, and made a point of enjoying his seniority. Walking home from school, he always walked a few steps ahead of Jimmy. He talked loudly, his voice commanding and patronizing, often ending a sentence with, "Do you understand?"

Jimmy didn't seem to mind his half brother's haughty attitude. When he followed him, he often admired Pang Sin's broad shoulders and muscular legs. He thought Pang Sin was a lot more knowledgeable about the world than most of their fellow students. He also believed that Pang Sin could beat anybody up, including Tao, the captain of the soccer team, who was the student leader and a "girl killer." He often wondered why the girls at the school worshiped Tao, not Pang Sin.

Following a few steps behind Pang Sin, Jimmy listened to his half brother discuss the state of the nation. Pang Sin was eloquent and talkative when he was alone with Jimmy. Every time they walked home from school, the half hour became Pang Sin's political platform. He lectured like a professor.

"Now," Pang Sin was saying, "I don't care what order it is, old or new; men like you and me must fend for ourselves. Have you heard about the *dogtail weed* philosophy? When there is a gale that topples trees and blows down houses, a dogtail weed always bends with the wind. After everything has been demolished by the wind, only the dogtail survives. Do you understand?"

"What are you driving at, Pang Sin?" Jimmy asked, trying to keep up with him.

"Follow the trend! I want you to carry Mao's little red book and memorize most of his sayings. Whatever you do, always quote the Chairman. Right or wrong, you will survive."

"I know—every pig farmer thanks Chairman Mao whenever he has a good litter. Everybody credits his success to Mao's quotations. I think it's superstition."

"Don't be stupid. It's following the trend, understand?"

"What trend?" Jimmy asked after a moment, unsure of what Pang Sin was talking about.

"Number one: be bold enough to criticize the Russians," Pang Sin said. "Number two: attack *capitalist roaders*—call Liu Shao-chi the *Chinese Khrushchev.*"

Jimmy did not quite understand him, but he was impressed. "How do you know all this, Pang Sin?"

"The rising power in Peking is Chiang Ching. You know who she is, don't you?"

"Chairman Mao's wife?"

"That's her. She has Lin Piao behind her. You know Lin Piao, don't you?"

"The head of the military," Jimmy said. "I don't know his title."

"Never bother with titles. They change like a woman's underwear. Always test the wind; see which way it blows. Right now, Chiang Ching is about to churn up a big gale, and behind her is the man with the gun. Tell me, what did Chairman Mao say about power?"

"Well, well . . ." Jimmy said, trying to remember.

Pang Sin snapped his fingers. "C'mon, c'mon!"

"Power . . . power grows out of the barrel of a gun?" Jimmy said hesitantly.

"That's right! And when you say it, say it loud and clear—understand?"

*

When they arrived home, their grandfather had returned from a two-day trip to Hsiangtan County. Hu Yin was talking to two visitors in the middle room. Jimmy had never seen his grandfather look so agitated; he was pounding the table and talking about what he had seen in Hsiangtan.

Jimmy and Pang Sin stopped at the door to listen. Jimmy recognized one of the visitors as Hu Yin's aide, Comrade Ting; the other was an older man wearing a neat Mao uniform with a large Mao button pinned on his chest. Jimmy guessed he was a high-ranking provincial Party member. The Mao button was his badge. He had heard that his grandfather was not the number-one man in Hunan; the Party Secretary at the provincial Party headquarters was. This man might be the Second or Third Party Secretary.

"It is a shame that we should lie about the real conditions in the province," Hu Yin was saying. "The famine is the worst I have ever seen, and yet we are painting a false picture to glorify a mistaken policy!"

"I wouldn't call it mistaken, Comrade Hu," the older man said. "Collective farming is still in an experimental stage. There are some shining examples in Hopei Province . . ."

"I am not interested in Hopei Province! I am the Governor of Hunan, and people here have been dying of starvation. I have seen men drink their own urine to save water for their children. I have tasted roots and tree bark with my relatives, and I still have a stomachache. I don't want that to happen in Hunan. I called President Liu last night. The President authorized me to right the wrong!" He turned to his aide, his voice firm and angry, and ordered, "I want all taxation eliminated for a whole year in the affected areas. I want the collective farms redistributed to the peasants. Let them farm the little plots that they owned before. Give them some incentive so they will work harder and enjoy some personal gain. Nobody can . . ."

"Governor Hu," the older man interrupted, "this is against Chairman Mao's collective farming policy. Chairman Mao said . . ."

"I don't care what Chairman Mao said!" Hu Yin cut him short. "Please go back and tell the Party Secretary that it is my decision to have this ghastly situation alleviated." Then he turned to his aide and added, "Call an urgent meeting first thing in the morning. We'll work on an immediate program to aid the disaster area." He rose and curtly adjourned the meeting.

Outside, Pang Sin pulled Jimmy away from the door and whispered, "He is going against the wind. That's stupid!"

"He is carrying out the wish of the President," Jimmy protested.

"Liu Shao-chi? He has defied the Chairman long enough. He's finished! You'll see!"

✳

Mabel was returning from a visit to Professor Chang, who had invited her to have a cup of mao tai and a dish of peanuts. She had found the professor mellowed, his bitterness gone. She had begun to enjoy her visits, chatting, relaxing and laughing at nonpolitical jokes. Ever since the Communist Liberation, everyone had been awash in politics. They were bombarded with propaganda; the air was filled with political songs and the walls covered with inflammatory slogans. Mabel discovered that the two hours she spent with Professor Chang were refreshing; she could relax and breathe freely without hearing or saying anything about politics.

Walking along Nan Chung Kai, the main thoroughfare, on her way back to the Governor's mansion, she was shocked to see beggars pouring into the city. She had heard about Anhwei beggars in the past. They crowded into the railway stations after their communes had failed in Anhwei Province. Some of them had become professional beggars, roaming from one city to another in bands. When they were fed, they would shout, "Long live Chairman Mao!" When they had nothing to eat, they would insult anyone in power to invite arrest. After all, there was always a bowl of cold porridge served in jail.

Mabel wondered if they were from Anhwei. She stopped and listened to their conversation. Apparently they were natives of Hunan. Had Hunan, China's rice bowl, now become a beggars' breeding ground? The thought hit her like a blow. With a heavy heart, she hurried home.

Arriving home, a second shock greeted her. The Governor's mansion was surrounded by soldiers with fixed bayonets. At the gate, two of them stopped her.

"I live here!"

"So the Governor has a maid now," one of the soldiers jeered.

"I am his daughter. Let me in!"

"Let her in," a third soldier said. "He deserves to see his daughter."

Inside, Mabel immediately knew that something was seriously wrong. The middle room was full of people. Loud, angry voices were heard. She rushed in and was confronted by yet more soldiers, who also demanded to know who she was. Hu Yin was arguing with two men in uniform, obviously high-ranking officers, even though they wore baggy green uniforms without special belts or insignias.

"I am staying right here, comrades," Hu Yin shouted. "I will not go!"

"You are under arrest," one of the officers said, his voice polite but firm. "I have orders. Please do not make it necessary for us to use force."

In the back of the room, Lan Mei was arguing with another group of soldiers, demanding that they stop searching the house and withdraw immediately. "If this is official business," she shouted, "go to his office tomorrow! Get out! Get out!"

Pang Sin and Jimmy stood nearby, watching quietly. A soldier pointed his revolver at Hu Yin and two others started to put handcuffs on him. Hu Yin resisted and the soldier with the revolver struck him across the face, breaking the skin on Hu Yin's cheekbone and drawing blood. When Jimmy saw his grandfather hurt, he leaped forward and shouted, "Let him go, let him go!" As he tried to push the soldiers away from Hu Yin, one of them slapped him hard and knocked him down.

Mabel felt a blinding fury surge through her. She hit the nearest soldier and tore through the others to get to her son. They tried to stop her, but she struggled, kicking and screaming. She was finally subdued. Two men pinned her arms behind her while she continued to resist. It was Hu Yin who finally quieted her.

"Mabel, Mabel," he said, his voice strangely calm now. "It's all right. I'll go with them. Whatever it is, I will solve it and be back."

"Why are you arresting him? What has he done?" Mabel screamed at them.

They ignored her and marched Hu Yin out of the room. Jimmy had struggled to his feet, wiping the blood from his mouth, his eyes furious. Pang Sin had watched the whole episode without saying a word, expressionless except for his drooping mouth.

The family kept vigil that night, waiting for news, but there was none. At dawn, Lan Mei washed her face, brushed her teeth and changed her clothes. She was going to find out what had happened to Hu Yin. Mabel offered to go with her but she declined.

"I am a Party member and an official of a government agency," she said. "I have access to the inner circle for information. I believe your father will be back."

It was not until noon that she returned. She walked in like a zombie, her face ashen and her lips trembling. She was accompanied by Comrade Ting. He had an agonized expression on his thin young face, which suddenly looked older. Mabel leaped up from her chair.

"What happened?" she demanded, her heart thumping with fear. She felt the old tightness in her chest that was almost suffocating her.

Lan Mei did not answer, nor did she look at anyone. She walked straight into her room, her hair disheveled and her feet dragging. Mabel turned to Ting sharply. "You tell me," she ordered, her voice almost hysterical. "What's happened to my father? When is he coming back?"

Ting sank into a chair. "They've convicted him," he said tonelessly.

"Convicted him of what?" Mabel said angrily—as if Ting were the judge. "What has he done?"

"They convicted him of being a counterrevolutionary. . . ."

"That's dog fart! What specific crime did he commit? I can refute any accusation they can think of. I am his daughter—I know there is absolutely nothing those tin heads can find fault with! What counterrevolution? Let them count on their dog's paws . . ."

"Comrade Hu," Ting interrupted her wearily. "They planned a public meeting to struggle against the Governor tomorrow. They were going to put a dunce cap on him, parade him and let the people decide what to do with him. A proud man, he could not stand the humiliation." Ting squeezed his eyes shut and held his breath for a moment, then went on in a choked voice. "A proud man, he was not able to face the humiliation. He hanged himself this morning."

Mabel felt a stabbing pain in her heart. She sank to the floor with a moan, and everything went black.

67

For the first time on a regular schoolday at Ya Li Middle School, all classes had been dismissed, classrooms vacated and blackboards covered with "big-letter posters" accusing the teachers of assorted crimes against the revolution. The school had been seized by the student Red Guards.

Jimmy Hong, wearing his ill-fitting Red Guard green uniform, his five-cornered cap and sneakers, entered the dean's office. The empty room was littered with papers, drawers were open, files rifled, wall maps torn and flowerpots smashed. The wall clock, its glass broken, was still ticking, showing 1:30 P.M.; the calendar on the dean's desk had been flipped to February 12, 1966. Only half an hour ago the dean had been dragged out of his office to join the other accused staff of the school.

Jimmy had been ordered by Pang Sin to search the dean's office for important documents that could be used against the official in the scheduled public struggle meeting. Pang Sin was now a Hunan University Red Guard leader, commanding the middle school Red Guards in Changsha.

Jimmy's heart wasn't in the job. He picked up a few documents from the floor, glanced at them and then tossed them on the desk. Someone had already searched the room, and it was stupid for him to go through the papers again. Besides, he resented Pang Sin's patronizing air. Since his half brother had taken a trip to Peking and been received by Chairman Mao, he had not only become the Chairman of the Changsha Red Guard Revolutionary Committee; he had become a pain. Because of Pang Sin's connections, Jimmy had been elected as a backbone member of the Great Proletarian Cultural Revolution. He liked the title but didn't care for the work.

He came out of the school building empty-handed, ready to face his demanding half brother. The accusation parade had already started, heading for the public ground, where executions used to take place. He had seen criminals shot there many times. Before the Liberation, hundreds of the condemned had been decapitated, and headless ghosts had been reported by a number of townspeople. He was glad this was only an accusation meeting. Nevertheless, the thought of it made him shudder. His own grandfather, Hu Yin, had killed himself to avoid the humiliation. . . .

He heard the familiar sounds. Besides slogan-shouting, some Red Guards were beating drums and gongs to attract a bigger crowd. "Down with the reactionary academic authorities!" they shouted. "Down with cow ghosts and snake demons!"

Jimmy caught up with the parade. More than three hundred Red Guards were marching the thirty-odd accused teachers and administrators to the struggle meeting. The accused wore dunce caps and carried dirty brooms, broken shoes and smelly mops on their backs. Hanging from their necks were buckets of rocks to bend them down in humiliation. Jimmy could see the wire cutting deeply into their necks. They staggered under the weight, grimacing in pain.

As soon as they arrived at the public ground, the "struggling" began. The members of the backbone Red Guards ordered the accused to stand in a row. Calling them the Black Gang, the backbone members started pouring black ink over the heads of the accused.

Dripping ink, some of the teachers glared defiantly; others bowed their heads, but nobody talked back or resisted. Having exhausted the ink, the backbone members consulted a list and hung on each of the accused a placard that described his crimes. Most were accused of being reactionaries; some were named *class enemies* and a few were called *capitalist roaders* and *corrupt ringleaders*.

Pang Sin looked in high spirits as he waved a long stick and ran back and forth shouting orders. He forced some of the accused to say, "I am a black gangster! When this is over I am going to beg Chairman Mao to forgive my crime!" A few improvised on the chanting, adding a line or two. One of them said, "I am going to kneel down in front of Chairman Mao, burn incense and beg . . ."

Before he had finished, Pang Sin slashed him with his stick. "Burn incense?" he sneered. "Do you wish Chairman Mao dead? Say it again! And say it correctly!"

More beatings followed. A few women in the crowd fainted. But the accusation meeting went on.

＊

Since Hu Yin's death, the family had moved into a modest two-bedroom apartment. Jimmy and Pang Sin shared the larger room.

Jimmy tidied his bed. He was reluctant to pick up Pang Sin's clothes from the floor, but on second thought, he did. He folded them and laid them on Pang Sin's messy bed. Finally, with a surge of brotherly love, he tidied up his brother's bed. After all, Pang Sin had taken care of him at school, protected him from being attacked by other Red Guard factions. Pang Sin had even invited him to go to Peking to struggle against capitalist roader Wang Kwang-mei, the First Lady, wife of President Liu Shao-chi. It was a glorious assignment; it had Chairman Mao's blessing and General Lin Piao's promise of noninterference from the military. It was rumored that President Liu had already been arrested.

There were twelve members in the delegation, all hand-picked by Pang Sin. For a week the members had learned how to walk like Pang Sin. Those who wore glasses had removed them to look more manly. Each member had been issued a special armband and a green canvas bag which contained a copy of *The Selected Works of Mao Tse-tung.* Wearing the armband and carrying the green bag, strutting with a haughty expression, a Red Guard would be an enviable sight, admired by his peers and by all the pretty girls.

Jimmy put on his new green uniform, the five-cornered cap and the armband, slung the bag across his shoulder and studied himself in the mirror. He was happy with what he saw: a truly manly looking trooper. If he could only develop the right air and the right walk, he would be quite a sight. He was glad that he did not need glasses. A few of the nearsighted backbone members could hardly see without them. Every time they looked at something they had to narrow their eyes, and that did not help their appearance of virility any.

Having brushed a few wrinkles out of his uniform, he worked on his gait. He took a few steps toward the mirror, remembering his half brother's jaunty swagger. Pang Sin had told him how to swing his arms. His hands should not go higher than the upper pocket of his uniform; his steps should be measured, not more than two feet. He should look dignified, relaxed, casual, with a devil-may-care sort of air.

Jimmy could hear Pang Sin's voice in the kitchen talking to his girl-friend, Do Do, a member of the backbone delegation. She was the best-looking girl in Ya Li Middle School. She was too good-natured to be a Red Guard, but Pang Sin had wanted her to be a member, and she was delighted to have the opportunity to visit Peking. Jimmy envied Pang Sin all the more because of Do Do. He wished there were another girl like her at Ya Li.

Giggling and sighing came from the kitchen. Whenever there was silence, Jimmy felt a pang in his heart: he knew they were kissing. The longer the silence, the more he suffered. He made a few attempts to peek, but stopped every time he reached the door. It would only make him more jealous.

He practiced his walk some more and wondered when his mother would come home. Since Hu Yin's suicide, Mabel had changed completely. She had started drinking heavily; she had become careless about her looks and health. Sometimes she would bring a lover home and keep drinking in her room until the man sneaked out furtively. And she would remain in a stupor for days, refusing to eat or dress properly. Sometimes Jimmy sus-pected that his mother was trying to kill herself. Pang Sin scoffed at this.

Jimmy worried about Do Do. At sixteen she shouldn't have stayed out so late. He wondered if he should go in the kitchen and remind Pang Sin that it was after midnight. Just as he was about to change his clothes, he heard the giggling and happy voices stop, followed by Do Do's scream. Jimmy quickly opened the door a crack and listened. Obviously Pang Sin wanted sex, trying to force Do Do into his mother's room.

"Don't touch me!" Do Do was shouting. "Leave me alone!"

"C'mon, don't be stubborn. Go in there!"

"I don't want to go into your mother's bedroom!"

"I said go in there!" Pang Sin said angrily.

"Let me go, let me go!"

There was scuffling. Jimmy had decided to intervene when he heard his mother's voice. From her hysterical laughter, he knew she was drunk again.

"Come in, come in!" she said, dragging a man into the kitchen, which also served as their living room and dining room.

Jimmy recognized him immediately. It was Professor Chang. The pro-fessor greeted everybody amiably, but Pang Sin glared at him. Do Do, a few of her buttons torn off, left quietly.

"What's the matter?" Mabel looked between the door and Pang Sin with raised eyebrows. "Lovers' quarrel?"

Pang Sin shrugged.

"I must go," Professor Chang said. "Goodbye, everybody."

"Wait, wait!" Mabel screamed after him, staggering toward the door. Before she reached it, she started to fall. Jimmy caught her.

"All right, Mother," he said soothingly. "Time to go to bed."

"Him again?" Pang Sin said with a sneer.

"Are you talking about me, Pang Sin?" Mabel asked as Jimmy helped her toward her bedroom door.

"Yes. Why must you waste your time with that bookworm? You know he is one of the Four Olds we're trying to eliminate!"

"Uh, uh, politics again," Mabel said unsteadily, wagging a finger at Pang Sin. "No political talk. . . . Professor Chang and I have taken an oath. From now on we talk about anything but politics. You want to argue? I'll argue. I'll tell you why . . ."

"Mother, Mother, please!" Jimmy firmly guided her into her room. "Go to bed, Mother. We love you. Please take care of yourself."

Pang Sin ignored them. He poured himself a glass of water, rinsed his mouth noisily and spat the water into the sink. Then he drank the rest of the water in noisy gulps. Inside Mabel's room, Mabel was talking to Jimmy.

"You know what subject the professor and I have agreed to talk about?" she said in a slurred voice. "Bees and flowers. Anything that is far, far away from politics. Today we talked about women's bound little feet, and how men loved them before the revolution. We even wrote a song about them."

When Jimmy came out of Mabel's room after having persuaded her to stop singing and go to bed, Pang Sin mimicked, " 'We love you! Please take care of yourself.' Do you still say that sort of thing to her?"

"What's wrong with that?" Jimmy demanded.

"It's against the trend," Pang Sin said with a snort. "It's stupid!"

68

The country had been stirred up by Chairman Mao's personal poster, BOMBARD THE HEADQUARTERS, urging people to sack President Liu Shao-chi and Wang Kwang-mei, his wife. Liu had already been arrested.

The twelve backbone members arrived in Peking by train, waving red flags with white characters that read CHANGSHA RED GUARDS. Before the trip, they had gone through the necessary exercises: "raiding, looting, dragging out and beating people up." They had all proven their young *tiger spirit* and had sworn to smash the old world of gods and ghosts. Many even had had their courage tested by sleeping in graveyards and visiting morgues alone at night.

Jimmy had avoided "dragging out" people and beating them up, for he freely admitted that he lacked tiger spirit. But he participated in raiding temples and smashing old religious signs and idols. He had also avoided destroying antiques and art objects such as scroll paintings and calligraphy, claiming that those things had never adversely affected his revolutionary spirit. This sort of claim would have disqualified him as a backbone member of the Red Guards, but because he was Pang Sin's half brother, he had again been spared his peers' ridicule and *bitterness speaking.*

During the train ride, he and the other members had met Red Guard delegates from other cities. They had compared notes on their accomplishments. The Wuhan members had built a bonfire of all the Chinese classics collected in Hupeh Province by thousands of Red Guards. The bonfire had burned for three days, with flames leaping three stories high.

Such tales turned Jimmy's stomach. He had to keep reminding himself that he was a Red Guard and must not show any sign of weakness, such as frowning or squirming. There was another female member in the Changsha delegation besides Do Do. Both girls had shown a lot of *tiger spirit* and *big gall.* During the entire trip, Do Do had made a face only once. It was when one of the Wuhan delegates had boasted about his clever method for locating a counterrevolutionary.

"The first thing you do is examine his bookcase," he said. "You see how much dust is on the cover of his *Selected Works of Mao Tse-tung.* If it is thick, you can safely drag him out to struggle against him for being a hypocrite."

It was late at night when they arrived at the train station. The welcoming party of two men and a woman met them and took them to Tsing Hwa University, in Peking's suburbs. The one-hour bus ride was festive, with the loudspeaker blaring out spirit-lifting songs. The members of the welcoming party were university students. For the first time, Pang Sin showed some respect and had eliminated "Listen," "Understand?," "That's stupid!" and other patronizing terms from his speech.

The struggle meeting against Wang Kwang-mei, wife of President Liu Shao-chi, had been scheduled for 10:00 A.M. the next morning at Tsing Hwa University, the birthplace of the Great Proletarian Cultural Revolution.

"Comrade Chiang Ching has a special message for you brave little soldiers from China's middle schools," one of the university students who greeted them announced. "She fondly calls all of you 'my little patriotic devils.' After you have successfully struggled against the capitalist roader Wang Kwang-mei, she wants you to go back and search for the rest of the demons and hobgoblins, drag them out of their lairs and wipe them all out!"

"General Lin Piao has also sent his words," the woman member of the welcoming party said. "He wants you to continue to make rebellion under the leadership of our great helmsman, Chairman Mao, our great, great leader and the red, red sun!"

"What did Premier Chou En-lai say?" Jimmy asked eagerly. He had always admired Chou.

"The Premier was rather quiet this afternoon," one of the male students said. "I think his stomach ulcer has kicked up again. But he smiled a lot and sent his warm greetings."

"Now let's shout some slogans," the other student suggested. And they all shouted slogans as the bus bumped its way toward the beautiful Tsing Hwa campus in the bright moonlight.

During the trip, Jimmy learned how the Peking Red Guards had tricked Wang Kwang-mei out of hiding. They had called her personal doctor, claiming that her daughter, Ping Ping, was hospitalized at Peking Medical College Hospital after an accident. When Wang Kwang-mei called back, they forced Ping Ping to tell her mother that she had been seriously injured and that she wanted to see her. Half an hour later, Wang Kwang-mei sped to the hospital and was immediately pounced on by the waiting Red Guards.

For the first time, Jimmy wondered if he was going to enjoy the trip; but the prospect of seeing Peking in all its glory gave him a boost in spirit.

He had seen Wang Kwang-mei's pictures many times. She was an attractive woman, always wearing a cheongsam. He had always wanted to see a woman in a cheongsam; it was so much more eye-pleasing than the shapeless, baggy Mao uniform. His sympathy had already gone to the accused. . . .

*

All the classrooms at Tsing Hwa University had been turned into temporary dormitories for the visiting Red Guards. The Changsha delegation was put in a spacious room partitioned with blankets hung on wires. The two girls slept behind the blankets on cots, while the rest slept on thin straw mattresses on the floor.

Jimmy tossed on his mattress for a long time, unable to sleep. The moonlight flooding into the room and the constant singing of the crickets outside kept him awake. His eager anticipation at seeing Peking was now almost ruined by his mixed feelings about the accusation meeting.

He woke up with a slight headache early next morning and immediately resented the high spirits of his fellow Red Guards. They reminded him of a pirate band that could hardly wait to lay its hands on a captured treasure chest.

After a quick breakfast of cold buns and lukewarm bean curd juice provided by the welcoming committee, they arrived at the meeting ground. The *stage of struggle* had been constructed on a large open lawn in front of the science building. Over the stage hung a huge banner, bearing the words A STRUGGLE MEETING AGAINST CAPITALIST ROADER WANG KWANG-MEI. On each side of the platform was a smaller banner. One said, THE MONKEY KING SWINGS HIS POWERFUL CLUB. The other said, THE UNIVERSE IS CLEANSED OF ITS HEAVY DUST.

Shortly before 10:00 A.M., the Red Guard delegations, more than five thousand strong, arrived and settled on the ground. The meeting started as soon as the chairman, a Comrade Kai, appeared. Kai mounted the platform nimbly and gave a short introduction to the event. He was an agile little man in his early thirties, obviously a Tree Trunk from the Party's left wing. After the introduction, he called, "Drag out the capitalist roader Wang Kwang-mei to face the people!"

Now the Red Guards became very agitated. Many pointed and shouted, "There, there!," "There she is!," "She is being dragged out!" Some of them climbed to their feet to have a better look, but were shouted down by others sitting behind them. There was more slogan-shouting: "Down with Wang Kwang-mei!," "Down with the stinking wife of the Chinese Khrushchev!"

A number of Guards were busy aiming at the platform with their little Japanese cameras. When Wang Kwang-mei was pushed to the middle of the platform, there was a series of clicking sounds and flashbulbs went off.

Wang Kwang-mei was dressed in a blue Mao uniform a size too large for her slim body. She was forced to wear a string of Ping-Pong balls around her neck. Jimmy thought she was much better looking than most of the young women in the crowd, but not nearly as attractive as the pictures he had seen—especially the ones she had had taken in Indonesia not too long ago when she and her husband had paid Indonesian President Sukarno a state visit and she had worn a cheongsam.

Guarded by four girl Red Guards, she was forced to walk around on the

stage a few times so that the crowd below could get a better look at her
and jeer at her big pearl necklace, the Ping-Pong balls. Whenever she
lowered her head, one of the female Guards would jerk her hair sharply
to make her look up—rough treatment that made Jimmy squirm. It made
him think of his grandfather. For the first time he felt glad that his
grandfather had hanged himself to avoid similar humiliation.

Soon the struggle started. The chairman of the meeting shouted,
"Wang Kwang-mei, what do you think of this meeting struggling against
you?"

With a faint smile, Wang Kwang-mei thanked those who were attending the mass meeting and welcomed everyone who had come to criticize
her; but she requested that everything they said at the meeting not be
publicized, for she was still a national figure. Such a meeting might damage
China's national honor.

Many in the audience snickered. A few even shouted that they felt
insulted by her audacity in mentioning national honor. She was the one
who had damaged China's reputation by having her picture taken with
foreigners in her sexy clothes and painted face.

The chairman raised his hands for quiet, saying that precious time
should not be wasted in idle talk. He made the first serious accusation,
recounting how she had sent her supporters to squash the student movements during the first stage of the Great Cultural Revolution. "This
account must be settled," he concluded.

There was a roar in response. "Throw her in jail!" "Repay blood with
blood!"

"What do you say to that?" the chairman asked the harried and dispir-
ited woman.

"I apologize." Her voice was barely audible.

"Confess your crime, Wang Kwang-mei!" an angry voice from the
audience demanded.

"Yes, yes, confess, confess!" the others howled.

She lowered her head and apologized again, confessing in such a low
voice that Jimmy could hardly hear her. When she finished, she extended
her hand to the chairman, but he pushed it away disdainfully and shouted,
"We haven't finished with you yet!"

Then a stout Woman Tree Trunk mounted the platform and accused
Wang of antirevolutionary crimes: (1) talking peace with Imperialists,
reactionaries and revisionists, (2) encouraging individuals to compete for
profit, (3) encouraging individual ownership of small businesses and small
private plots.

Then a young Male Tree Trunk climbed onto the stage and accused her of avoiding the three togethers: she had never eaten together, lived together or worked together with a poor peasant; therefore she had acted like a "low-down stinking capitalist lady."

After some others had accused her of similar offenses, the chairman asked her if she pleaded guilty to all these crimes. Wang refused to admit to any of the errors, saying only that she did not have enough *awareness*. One of the accusers poked her sharply in the head with a stubby finger and commanded her to study Mao Tse-tung's *Selected Works* more diligently to heighten her awareness.

Although still smiling, Wang looked incensed at such a suggestion. She said that one of her neighbors in the Forbidden City had even sold her husband's personally autographed copy of Chairman Mao's *Selected Works* to a foreigner. There was immediate speculation in the audience that the neighbor was none other than Chiang Ching, Mao's wife. For it was no secret that the two women lived next door to each other at the South Central Lake and had been feuding and bickering.

Grabbing the opportunity to introduce himself, Pang Sin rose to his feet and shouted, "Mr. Chairman, my name is Pang Sin. I am the head delegate from Changsha. May I suggest that we order Wang Kwang-mei to recite the first quotation from Chairman Mao's little red book or other selected works? Let her prove her honesty."

"That's right!" some Red Guards responded: "Let her repeat the first sentence of Chairman Mao's book." "Show your knowledge, Wang Kwang-mei!" "What is the first sentence of Chairman Mao's *Selected Works?*" "Recite, you stinking capitalist dog!"

Beaming to his right and left, Pang Sin sat down, conscious of the girl Red Guards who were casting him admiring glances. Jimmy felt increasingly uncomfortable and depressed. Was this the way to treat a country's first lady? Why must they trample her dignity like this? For a while he could not bear to look at the stage.

The chairman raised a copy of Mao's book and waved it in front of Wang. "Wang Kwang-mei," he said, "the masses want you to recite the first sentence in this book. Do it to prove your honesty!"

Taking a deep breath, Wang started to recite in a halting voice, "The main force that provided guidance to the nation . . . is the Communist Party. The foundation of ideology is from Marxism . . ."

"Wrong, wrong!" someone shouted.

"She forgot Leninism!" another chimed in.

A third waved his fist. "How dare you change Chairman Mao's quotation?"

"Comrades, comrades," Wang Kwang-mei said placatingly. "I am sorry that I omitted Leninism in the quotation, but Comrade Lin Piao has said, 'We should study Chairman Mao's works creatively . . .' "

"Wang Kwang-mei," the chairman cut her short, "you have failed your test; now you have the audacity to argue. It proves that you have a poor attitude toward your critics."

"Strike her down!" some Red Guards in the audience started shouting again. "Throw her in jail!" "Labor camp for this stinking counterrevolutionary!"

"Wang Kwang-mei," a girl Red Guard rose to her feet and screamed, shaking a finger at her, "when you and Liu Shao-chi led a goodwill mission to the Southeastern Asian countries, you asked Comrade Chiang Ching if you should wear high-heeled shoes and jewelry at state dinners. Comrade Chiang Ching said you should not. She even advised you to wear something coarse to indicate that you are a proud proletarian Tree Trunk. You agreed, did you not?"

"Y–yes, I agreed," Wang said, trying to remember the conversation.

"But when pictures came out in the newspapers, you were dressed like a flower. You not only wore high heels and jewelry, you even shamelessly flirted with President Sukarno of Indonesia. Did you not?"

Wang smiled uncomfortably. With a note of disdain in her voice, she said, "I may have worn some jewelry, but I certainly would not call friendly conversation flirting . . ."

"Wherever you went," the girl interrupted her, "you always stood close to Sukarno, trying to share his limelight, did you not?"

"I was representing China, naturally . . ."

Her accuser ignored this and pressed on. "Why did the welcome crowd in that country wave portraits only of you and your husband? There was not a single portrait of Chairman Mao or Comrade Chiang Ching. Why? Why?"

"I had nothing to say about what a host country would do or would not do . . ."

"Answer me this question," the girl again interrupted her. "When you returned from the trip, you brought back many gifts. All you gave Comrade Chiang Ching was a photo. You did not even pay her a courtesy call. Is that true?"

"We are both government workers." Wang tried to justify her lack of neighborliness. "Very often we meet at official functions. There is no reason for us to . . ."

Now the girl Red Guard was addressing Wang but was looking to her right and left. "Wang Kwang-mei, is it true that Comrade Chiang Ching was not happy about your rudeness?" she screamed. "It is a known fact that she tore up the picture you gave her—a picture taken with Sukarno and your capitalist husband, surrounded by half-naked Indonesian dancing girls. Comrade Chiang Ching tore up that picture and rightfully said, 'How can such a shameless woman represent China? It is a great loss of dignity for all of us!' Did she say that?"

Jimmy was surprised that the audience response to this accusation was not very strong. There was some scattered applause and some chuckles. He looked at Do Do, who was sitting between him and Pang Sin.

She looked back and winked. "That's understood," she whispered. "Chiang Ching is known to be a jealous woman. She was once an actress; did you know that?"

"No," Jimmy said.

"I heard that her big success was playing the role of Nora in *A Doll's House.*" She lowered her voice and added confidentially, "Some say she was at one time a Shanghai broken shoe, too."

"What's a broken shoe?" Jimmy asked.

"A harlot," Do Do whispered.

"Sh—sh!" Pang Sin hushed them angrily.

They fell silent. But Jimmy felt a little comfort in the knowledge that Do Do was with him.

The next morning, with a heavy heart, Jimmy learned that Madam Wang had been thrown into jail.

69

The Great Proletarian Cultural Revolution rose like a tremendous flood, sweeping across the entire nation. No place was spared. Mao Tse-tung's Red Guards roamed the country, taking trains, boats, buses and trucks, armed with the little red book and carrying nothing but a bag with a few changes of clothes. Most of them did not have money. Their armbands were their transportation and meal tickets. They slept in the best places they could find—hotels, temples and private homes. Some compared them to a plague of locusts and fled before they arrived. Everywhere, intellectuals, artists and ex-capitalists were forced to sweep the streets and clean public latrines to expiate their incorrect thoughts, present or past. They were urged to expose others, especially their own relatives, to help redeem their own crimes.

Jimmy Hong was tired of searching homes and dragging people out for struggle meetings. When he mentioned that he missed school, Pang Sin laughed.

"School? What for? Didn't Chairman Mao say that we must learn from the poor peasants?"

"What can poor peasants teach me besides fertilizing their crops with their own manure?"

"What do you care?" Pang Sin said. "If Chairman Mao says so, how can you go wrong?"

Since their return from Peking, Jimmy saw Do Do more frequently. She often found excuses to come while Pang Sin was out making rebellion with his gang of Red Guards. She brought Mabel hot buns and meat dumplings she had made herself, chatting with them while Jimmy served tea.

Mabel was steadily deteriorating. She had lost weight and looked prematurely old, with sagging skin and bloodshot, cloudy eyes. It was one of the reasons Jimmy had refused to participate in any more rebellion-making.

One day Pang Sin said, "It seems strange that you have time to see a lot of Do Do, but no time to go making rebellion."

"I told you, I have to take care of Mother. She's sick—can't you see?"

"Listen, what did I tell you about emotional detachment?" Pang Sin spoke loudly so that Mabel could hear him in her room.

"What emotional detachment?"

"One must sever all family ties; one must show his emotional detachment from all his kin. That is the prerequisite for being a Red Guard; didn't I tell you that?"

"I don't care."

"You need to be brainwashed," Pang Sin said with a disdainful scowl. "If you weren't my brother, I would have dragged you out and struggled against you like all the other ghosts and hobgoblins."

"Aren't you contradicting yourself, brother? You don't drag me out and struggle against me because I'm your brother. Isn't that a family tie?"

Pang Sin stared at him as though he were a moron. "It is the trend," he said contemptuously. "Follow the trend!" Then he put a hand on Jimmy's shoulder and added in a softened voice, "I do everything for your protection. Now that Liu Shao-chi and his gang are down, we must bend with the wind, understand?"

"I don't care!"

"Now you sound like a spoiled brat." Pang Sin laughed indulgently, hugging his shoulder. "Listen—I want you to have a bright future! This is a golden opportunity for both of us to earn some merits and establish a good track record, understand? When the time comes, you and I will be like this: 'Swish!' " He shot his right arm up like an arrow to indicate the rise of their future careers. "Remember Little Lee?"

"The stinking little pebble in the gutter," Jimmy sneered. He was a classmate. "What about him?"

"He is going to struggle against his own father. I want you to help him and earn some merits."

"No!"

Pang Sin looked at him askance. "Ha!" he said derisively. "Do Do refused to go, too. Is that a coincidence?"

"What coincidence? You're a suspicious dog!"

Pang Sin raised his hand to strike him but changed his mind. "All right, Jimmy. Prove to me that you aren't stealing my girl. Go with me to the struggle meeting. If you refuse, then I know there is something going on between you two."

✱

The crowd was large in front of Little Lee's house in Ox Tail Lane, not too far away. Little Lee's father, a professor at Peking Normal University, had already been paraded in the street with a dunce cap. Now he was forced to kneel in front of his house to face the charges. The sole accuser was his son, Little Lee, a moody boy of seventeen who walked with a swagger and whose eyes were full of hate.

Under the direction of Pang Sin, the struggle meeting started with Little Lee reading a list of accusations. His tearful mother, a plump woman of about fifty, was being held back by two girl Red Guards. She had been trying to get to her husband, screaming and scolding her son, "Let your father go! He has a heart condition! Whatever you say is a lie! Oh, you heartless beast! God is punishing me for having raised you! Why has this happened to our family? Your father is an upright man! Is that a crime? What kind of son are you?"

Ignoring his mother's scolding, Little Lee read his accusations in a monotonous tone, his eyes cold and his expression emotionless.

"Lee Chao-ming is a reactionary teacher; he preaches hard work and competition. In teaching, he is only interested in a student's high marks. He objects to Chairman Mao's new saying that all intellectuals must learn from the poor peasants and reform their incorrect thoughts through hard labor. At home, he does not even wash rice bowls. He still keeps his foreign books and has hidden them where nobody can find them."

When he finished, he folded the paper and looked at Pang Sin for direction. Pang Sin stepped up, pointed a stick at the accused and asked, "Do you admit these crimes?"

"No, I do not!" Lee Chao-ming protested, his voice nervous and tense. "My teaching method is the only one that will make my students learn and achieve a goal. Otherwise, why go to school?"

"Listen, this man is not going to admit his crimes!" Pang Sin shouted. "He is not going to repent. What are we going to do with him?"

Some Red Guards waved their fists and shouted, "Strike him down!" "Beat him up!" "Wipe him out!"

"Little Lee," Pang Sin said, "it is up to you. Show your emotional detachment! Earn your merits and establish your record. Show your loyalty to the Party by severing your family ties. All of us here are your witnesses."

Little Lee swaggered up to his father, grabbed his graying hair and started banging the man's forehead on the ground, accusing him of a crime with each blow. His mother by now was hysterical, moaning and shrieking. Lee Chao-ming endured the punishment without a sound. Finally, when blood was pouring down his father's face, Little Lee began to falter; his accusing voice weakened and his actions became hesitant. Suddenly he stopped and turned away, unable to continue, with tears seeping from his tightly closed eyes.

Pang Sin pushed the boy aside, grabbed the older Lee and continued the torture, calling out an accusation with each thump: "This is for your first brother, who is a corrupt bureaucrat; this is for your second brother, who writes filthy songs; this is for your third brother, who is a greedy capitalist; this is for your fourth brother, who is an American running dog!"

By the time he had finished, there was a large pool of blood on the ground and both the accused and his wife had fainted.

Jimmy, unable to bear the sight, fled from the meeting, his face ashen and a hand over his mouth, trying to blank out the picture in his mind. The sickening sound of the victim's head striking the ground, the blood, the torn pieces of skin, and the professor's blood-washed face, his agonized expression and his upturned eyes showing only white, made him feel like vomiting.

Suddenly he felt a hand taking his from behind. It was Do Do.

"Are you all right?" she said, handing him a handkerchief.

He wiped his mouth and the beads of sweat from his forehead. "Thanks," he said with a smile. "I'm all right now."

They walked away quietly. Behind them the shouting of slogans could be heard again. The struggle meeting went on.

70

Jimmy Hong got off the train and decided to walk home. After four years of rebellion-making and six long years of the May Seventh School, working with the impoverished peasants in Hsiangtan County, walking had become a habit. Three or four miles of brisk walking would have been a hardship before he went to the May Seventh School, but now it was as easy as scratching an itch.

He thought of the six years and wondered if it had been worth it. He had been obliged to abandon his schooling, like everybody else. He had learned very little about modern farming, and doubted whether he had contributed anything to China's agriculture progress except his physical labor. What he had gained was a lot of muscles. For that he thanked Chairman Mao, who had established the May Seventh School when he declared on that day in 1970 that all Red Guards must work in the countryside.

Now that he had finished May Seventh School, it was time for him to catch up on his education. He had applied for a university custodian's job and a position as school librarian. Both jobs would give him easy access to books and lectures.

During the long walk home, he thought about the school and why Chairman Mao had created it. Through years of whispered communication with his fellow inmates, he had come to the following conclusion:

Chairman Mao had finally realized that the Red Guards had gotten out of hand, doing more damage than good. They had destroyed most of what China had built, disrupted communications and transportation, uprooted a culture that Mao himself had cultivated. When the Chairman heard that some Red Guards had misused his little red book, declaring that it could miraculously do all and cure all, he knew that they were creating a new superstition to replace the old ones. Women had laid his book on an altar, kowtowed to it and prayed to it for an extra son. A worker in Changsha had burned a copy and sprinkled its ashes around the house to drive away evil spirits.

But Chairman Mao had become really angry when he heard that Red Guards had smashed the hands of musicians, artists and surgeons to show the world that New China did not need them. At that point he decided to stop the "crazy little devils" before it was too late. The Red Guard fanatics had rampaged across China for too long, alienating the masses and doing just the opposite of what he had intended them to do in the first place—serve the people.

He was tempted to throw the lot of them in jail; but where would he find a jail big enough to house ten million little red devils?

Chairman Mao had always had a sixth sense. He may have been getting senile in his old age, but nonetheless his antennae had told him that some of the Red Guards had been manipulated to try to undermine his rule. He had sensed that Lin Piao was plotting to overthrow him, and that his own wife, Chiang Ching, had a secret desire to become China's next Empress Dowager.

Besides his sixth sense, Chairman Mao always had a solution for every problem, even if the solution happened to be a bit like mending the fence after the goat has escaped. In this case it was to disperse the Red Guards to rural areas to learn from the poor peasants. It would be their punishment . . . a sentence of four to six years at hard labor.

Jimmy Hong felt that he had served his time in full and that six years had been taken out of his life. He resented it, but he felt luckier than the musicians, artists and surgeons whose hands had been crippled, and the countless others who had committed suicide—like his own grandfather.

He found his apartment tidy and empty. There was a thin coat of dust over everything in his mother's room. The room that he and Pang Sin had occupied had an appearance of being slept in, and he wondered if his half brother had returned from his May Seventh School in another part of China. Then he discovered some women's clothes in the closet. They were not his mother's. Where was Mabel? He hadn't heard from her for almost six months, and he had started to worry. He felt uneasy as he examined them. They seemed to belong to someone young, and there were two white gowns that looked like nurses' uniforms.

He went to the kitchen, which was clean and tidy except for a few unwashed rice bowls and a pair of chopsticks in the sink. Perhaps someone had eaten a quick bowl of noodles and then rushed back to work. He looked around and saw a note standing against the wall on the kitchen table. It said:

> Jimmy,
>   Your mother had a cancer operation and is recuperating at Hsiang Yah Hospital. I am working there as a nurse and staying here at her request. She has received your letter and knows that you are coming

home, but she insists that you not visit her until she is ready to receive relatives and friends.

Do Do, Dec. 4, 1976

Without unpacking, Jimmy immediately rode to the hospital on his old bicycle. It was almost half an hour's ride to the Western-style hospital across town. He hurried to the desk and found the number of his mother's room.

"How is she?" he asked anxiously.

"She is still asleep," the desk nurse said.

He inquired about Do Do and was told that she had gone to lunch. He decided to see his mother. Without permission, he went to her room. When he saw her, he was shocked. She was nothing more than skin and bones, and was ghastly pale. She was almost bald, her sunken eyes tightly closed and her thin eyebrows knitted, as though she were still in pain, even in her sleep. Unable to bear the sight, he quickly backed out and almost bumped into a nurse.

"What are you doing here?" she demanded.

Without answering, he hurried out of the hospital, his throat tight with emotion. Riding home, he could not get rid of the horrible image.

It was late at night when Do Do returned. She was thinner and prettier, and did not look much older. Six years had given her poise and an air of confidence. There was an aura of sensuality about her, almost like a flower blooming in its full glory.

They greeted each other politely, both feeling tongue-tied. Finally, her laughter and eager questions relaxed him, making him inquisitive about her—as much as she was about him. Neither of them had anything new or exciting to tell, but every word was devoured hungrily by the other. Jimmy's life on the farm had been dull compared to her years of service as a barefoot doctor in Kwei Chow, another poor province that had never spun free of chronic poverty. The only fame that province had was its excellent mao tai, which an American President had enjoyed in the People's Great Hall in Peking in 1972, where millions of TV watchers all over the world had observed him toasting Chinese dignitaries like a Chinese.

They turned their conversation from personal experiences to the fate of New China. After the death of Mao Tse-tung, Chou En-lai and the mysterious plane crash that killed General Lin Piao, China had been changing. The life and death struggle between the right and the left was still going on, but the pragmatists, headed by Teng Hsiao-ping, had been gaining power. Jimmy and Do Do discussed the new trend with excitement, oblivious to the passage of time. It was not until Mabel's wall clock struck midnight that Jimmy felt a jolt. It reminded him of his sick mother, and his heart sank. He stopped talking and his smile disappeared.

"What's the matter?" Do Do asked, looking worried.

"What are the chances of my mother pulling through?"

"Dr. Shung is a pessimist, but he gave her a seventy-five-percent chance of recovery. If he said that, the chances are one hundred thirty percent —like the best mao tai!"

Her crisp laughter brought a smile back to his face.

"Oh, I almost forgot," she said, bringing out a letter from her uniform pocket. "This is for you. I've carried it for days, waiting for you to come back."

It was from his mother, written in a shaky hand. He tore it open anxiously.

> Dear Jimmy:
>
> Tomorrow morning I am going into surgery. If I don't survive, please remember that everybody goes sooner or later. If God allows me to live a few more years, I will accept the bonus with gratitude but without excitement, for my life has already passed by and the remaining trip will be a slow dance, dull if not torturous. The only attraction is that we will be together again for a while.
>
> May I make a request, Jimmy? If you intend to find your father after China has opened up, please don't bring him to see me until I am ready. That goes for you, too, my son. I don't want anybody to see me in this condition. The new hope in China has made me vain again. If I survive this illness, I will get up, put on my best dress and kiss my loved ones. But not until then.
>
> Love, Mother.

As he read the letter, he felt warm tears welling out of his eyes. Embarrassed, he wiped them quickly and put the letter in his pocket. Do Do gathered more tidbits from the kitchen and refilled his teacup. When she sat down again, it was close to him.

Suddenly he felt an overwhelming desire to grab her and kiss her. Fighting her scent and the warmth of her body, he rose and moved to another chair, squeezing his eyes tightly shut and holding his breath.

Do Do stared at him, looking alarmed. "What's the matter, Jimmy?"

He had to tell her the truth. Painfully, he confessed. He had always loved her but he did not know where to find the strength to resist her. It was getting even harder; it was an agony.

"Please don't seduce me, Do Do," he said, his voice uneven. "It's already hard enough. Sometimes even looking at you is torture."

Do Do laughed; it sounded to him like a bitter laugh. "Don't worry," she said. "I've always treated you like a brother—sometimes like my girlfriend. Seducing you has never entered my mind." She got up, picked up her clothes and left.

Surprised, Jimmy stared after her. "A girlfriend?" he thought. "Is that how she thinks of me? Am I feminine to her?" Stung by her remark, he found his loyalty to Pang Sin crumbling. "I should have done it," he told himself.

Lying on his bed, he couldn't stop thinking about Do Do. He imagined that he was kissing her passionately and that she was responding hungrily. Groaning with passion, she clutched him tightly, her fingernails cutting deeply into his flesh.

He quickly switched off his thoughts of Do Do; after all, she was still Pang Sin's girl.

*

To Jimmy's pleasant surprise, Do Do came to see him that Sunday and brought food for lunch. She acted cheerful, as though nothing had happened. Neither of them mentioned the incident of three nights earlier.

Pang Sin returned that afternoon. He was dark and lean, his face weather-beaten, his eyes red with infection. The May Seventh School had made him bitter and cynical. He was surprised to see Do Do, who looked fresh and spirited as she wrapped chiao tsu in the kitchen.

"Hello, Pang Sin," she greeted him cheerfully.

For a brief moment Pang Sin could not believe his eyes. He looked at her suspiciously. "Hello," he said gruffly, dropping his travel bag. "Where is my mother?"

"Don't you know?" she asked, surprised. "Didn't she write to you?"

"We never wrote. What happened?"

"She's in the hospital."

"Oh. Where is my brother?"

"I heard him singing a sexy song in his room," she said. "He's probably still there." She was disappointed by Pang Sin's indifference to Mabel's illness. "Pang Sin—your mother is in the hospital!"

"What do you expect," he said, "the way she abused herself."

"She just had an operation," Do Do replied sharply. Her words sounded like an accusation rather than information.

"How long has Jimmy been home?" he said, looking around the room.

"Three days," she replied coldly. "Would you like a cup of tea?"

"You sound like a hostess. Are you two married?"

Do Do laughed. "Of course not. What makes you say a thing like that?"

Pang Sin smiled. Believing that she was still his girl, he pulled out a chair and sat beside her. "Yes—I would love a cup of tea. But let's have a proper greeting first." He tried to kiss her, but she rose quickly to pour tea for him.

Jimmy came out of his room singing, wearing only shorts and an athletic shirt. Pang Sin looked at him suspiciously.

"Isn't this my loving brother?" Jimmy said with a note of sarcasm in his voice. "Welcome home, Pang Sin!"

Pang Sin decided to be casual. He greeted and hugged Jimmy warmly. "You're taller, Jimmy," he said. "Are you still growing?"

"Not physically. How was your May Seventh School?"

Pang Sin made a face. "Probably the same as yours. Ask yourself. What do you mean, 'not physically'?"

"I hope I've grown mentally," Jimmy told him, putting on some fresh clothes that Do Do had washed for him. Pang Sin glanced at Do Do and then at Jimmy, wondering if they were living together.

Jimmy was uneasy; he did not know why. This man was not the Pang Sin he remembered. He was accustomed to Pang Sin's old patronizing air: the warm greeting and the embrace almost made him cringe.

"Has the May Seventh School done you some good?" he asked, sitting down at the table.

Pang Sin sensed his brother's coolness. He made a face again without saying anything negative. The political wind had changed so much that almost anything he said could be used against him. "Well, the school didn't change *you* much, Jimmy, did it?"

Do Do came over with two cups of tea. Pang Sin put an arm around her waist and squeezed her affectionately. "I hope you've been taking good care of my girlfriend, Jimmy."

"I just came home three days ago," Jimmy said. "She has been taking good care of me."

"Really?" Pang Sin said, raising his eyebrows in surprise. "Does she wash and cook?"

"Let me cook the chiao tsu," she said, wriggling out of Pang Sin's arms. She picked up the chiao tsu that she had wrapped and carried them to the stove.

"Sure," Pang Sin said, following her eagerly with his eyes. Then he turned to Jimmy and asked, "She's a good cook, isn't she?"

"Why ask me?" Jimmy said, sipping the hot tea. "You enjoyed her cooking before."

"I always enjoyed her cooking. How about you?"

Jimmy knew that his brother was trying to fathom their relationship.

"Why don't you save time and ask me a direct question, Pang Sin?" he said with a grin.

"Don't talk about me, you two!" Do Do said from next to the stove. Bending low, she poked at the fire, her blue cotton tunic and trousers taut over her body, revealing a shapely figure with small round hips.

Pang Sin swallowed. "Tell me, Jimmy," he said, trying to sound casual, "did she wash your clothes?"

"Pang Sin," Jimmy said, "why don't you come to the point and ask me if she lives here?"

"You think I'm jealous, don't you?" Pang Sin said with a forced laugh. "Why should I be? Haven't I always trusted you, Jimmy? By the way, I have applied for the officers' training school in Paoting. They may come to check on my background. I want you and Mother to give the right answers . . ."

"You haven't even asked where Mother is," Jimmy cut in. "Aren't you concerned?"

"Of course I'm concerned! She's in the hospital."

"I told him, Jimmy," Do Do said, putting a pot of water over the fire and covering it.

"You can't be too careful these days," Pang Sin said. "Sometimes a wrong answer can ruin a person's life."

"What do you want me to say if they check on you?" Jimmy inquired.

"Forget all my activities during my Red Guard days. I don't want any of my past record revealed to them."

"Why? You always wanted to build a glorious record . . ."

"Jimmy, Jimmy," Pang Sin interrupted him impatiently. "The political winds have changed! I protected you once; now it's your turn to protect me."

"Why should I?"

Pang Sin glared at him. "Aren't we brothers? Aren't we family?"

"You destroyed all family ties years ago, didn't you? Isn't it too late to revive them now?"

Pang Sin shook his head with a heavy sigh. "Listen, Jimmy—follow the trend! Swing with the wind. Didn't I pound that into your head years ago?"

"Yes, you did. But no matter how hard you pounded, I didn't listen— and I'm glad I didn't."

"You're an ingrate!" Pang Sin said contemptuously. "Just wait till the wind blows the other way again; you'll come to me on your knees begging for my help. Just wait and see!"

"Pang Sin," Jimmy said, "I may as well tell you now: I still care for you as my brother, but I am not going to lie about your past. No matter which way the wind blows, you will be you and I will be me!"

"You mean you won't swing with the wind?"

"I will swing only in the right direction. So will Mother, when she gets well."

"I don't give a damn about Mother. She's like a discarded empty bag, absolutely useless in the New Society . . ."

"Watch what you say!" Jimmy said angrily.

"I'll say more! She slept with every Chang San and Li Su in this neighborhood! She's a whore!"

Jimmy spat at him. When he turned to walk out, Pang Sin grabbed him and slapped him. "Nobody spits on me—remember that!"

Jimmy spat at him again. Pang Sin kept slapping him, each blow harder than the last. Jimmy, furious beyond control now, swung back wildly and knocked his half brother against the wall. Knowing that he was not Pang Sin's match in a fight, he began to back away. When Pang Sin advanced toward him menacingly, ready to pounce on him, Jimmy picked up a chair and smashed it over his head, knocking him down. Then he grabbed Pang Sin by the hair and started banging his forehead on the floor.

"This is for Chiang Ching, the leader of the Gang of Four; this is for Gangster Number One; this is for Gangster Number Two; this is for Gangster Number Three . . ."

"Stop it, Jimmy! Stop it!" Do Do screamed. But Jimmy didn't hear her. He kept banging his half brother's head on the floor, pouring out his pent-up fury. When the repeated blows tore open the skin on Pang Sin's forehead and blood started pouring out, Do Do rushed over and pushed Jimmy away. "That's enough! Stop it!"

With blood covering his face, Pang Sin staggered to his feet, dazed. Jimmy cast him a contemptuous glance and walked out of the room. Do Do made Pang Sin sit down, brought out a medicine kit from her purse and started dressing his wound while Pang Sin mumbled and cursed.

Soon Jimmy came out of his room, carrying his battered suitcase. "Do Do," he said, "please tell my mother I'm going to Peking. She'll hear from me."

"Go to hell!" Pang Sin yelled at him. "You'll hear from me, too, you son of an American dog!"

Ignoring him, Jimmy walked out.

*

The short bus ride to the train station was slow, but Jimmy didn't mind. He had plenty of time. The streets were crowded with people; they seemed excited about China's change of direction and the government's modernization program. At the crossroads at Pa Kuo Ting, a mass meeting was in progress. A group of students were burning effigies of Chiang Ching and three of her supporters. They were shouting, "Down with the counterrevolutionary Chiang Ching!" "Down with the Gang of Four!"

The loudspeaker in the bus station was reporting the arrest of the Gang of Four. The news brought a shockwave to the passengers on the bus. After a moment of stunned silence, wild cheers broke out, followed by singing and more slogan-shouting. Soon everyone joined in.

> Arise, arise!
> Those who don't want to be slaves!
> Continue the struggle!
> Fight for freedom!
> Arise, arise!

According to the report, the three male members had been arrested in their offices in the Forbidden City by order of Marshal Yeh Chien-yin, the head of the military, and Hwa Kuo-feng, the head of state—both members of the moderates. When the soldiers went to the Fishing Terrace in Peking's suburb, where Chiang Ching, Mao's wife, was living in luxury, they arrested her over her fierce protests.

As the head of the gang, she had wrecked countless careers and almost destroyed Chinese civilization. Now the downtrodden people, the loudspeaker proclaimed rhetorically, could rise again like ghosts rising from the dead. The voice described with relish how this tiger lady, who had dreamed of becoming the next Empress Dowager, had kicked and screamed as she was being hauled away to jail.

To Jimmy, the arrest of the Gang of Four seemed to open a thick cloud and allow the sun to shine through.

Arriving at the train station, he saw people celebrating the good news. Laughter was heard everywhere; smiles appeared on every face. For the first time in years, he heard firecrackers exploding amid the music of drums and gongs; it was almost like a New Year's celebration.

He climbed into the train and took a window seat. He thought of Pang Sin and Do Do, feeling guilty about his love for his brother's girlfriend. It was an exciting time; yet he was lonely, and vague about his immediate future. Soon the Chinese people would be free to choose where to live and where to work. Soon there would be pretty women walking around in colorful clothes instead of drab Mao uniforms that made male and female look alike. Soon there would be competition; opportunities would knock on doors and incentives would fire people up. Doctors and artists no longer had to sweep streets and clean latrines; ignorant Tree Trunks could no longer rise above the educated to become university presidents or factory managers. But all those bright possibilities could not resolve his personal difficulties.

He would like to find out how to get in touch with his father through the newly established U.S. and China Liaison Office. He would also like to find out in Peking how to participate in the four modernization programs that the pragmatists had so enthusiastically endorsed. He could visualize Mabel getting well, becoming young and vigorous again. He could see her, dressed in a colorful choengsam, rushing to meet his father.

Jimmy was astonished to find that the train was almost empty—probably because this was an extraordinary day. Everyone was busy celebrating the downfall of an unpopular regime that had shackled the Chinese nation for years. Yes, it was almost like a second revolution. He stretched, trying to relax and enjoy the anticipation of a new era, but the lingering loneliness made him tense.

Suddenly he felt a gentle tap on his shoulder. He looked up. Do Do, carrying a suitcase and a few bags, was looking at him, breathless, her face flushed from running. The sight was like a fresh breeze that swept away his depression.

She smiled. "Is this seat taken?"

"No!" he blurted out. He rose quickly and helped her put her belongings in the luggage compartment overhead. "Are you going to Peking, too?" he asked, fearing that she was going somewhere else.

"Isn't that where you're going?" she asked, making herself comfortable beside him. She sat so close to him that their thighs touched and the scent from her hair filled his nose.

The train was gathering speed. They listened to the whistle and the clicking of the wheels, quietly savoring the warmth between them. Both sensed the new beginning they would share. Neither felt words were necessary.

ABOUT THE AUTHOR

C. Y. LEE, born in Hunan Province, is a graduate of Southwest Associated University in China and received an M.F.A. degree from Yale Drama School in 1947. When he finished college in China, prior to his American education, he served as a secretary to a Chinese sawbwa, and his experience working for this potentate on the China-Burma border resulted a few years later in his writing a series of articles for The New Yorker.

In 1957 Mr. Lee published his first novel, Flower Drum Song, which was an instant best-seller. A year later it became a Rodgers & Hammerstein Broadway musical, and two years later a Universal film. Subsequently he worked as scriptwriter with David Brown at Twentieth Century–Fox.

After returning to full-time fiction writing, Mr. Lee settled in Southern California with his wife, a daughter and a son. He is a member of The Dramatists' Guild and Authors League of America.